SCOTICHRONICON

SCOTICHRONICON
by
WALTER BOWER

New edition in Latin and English
with notes and indexes

General Editor: D E R WATT

King Malcolm Canmore and the thane of Fife.
Corpus Christi College, Cambridge MS 171, fo. 88

SCOTICHRONICON

by

WALTER BOWER

in
Latin and English

General Editor
D E R WATT

Volume 3

Books V and VI

Edited by
JOHN and WINIFRED MACQUEEN
and D E R WATT

ABERDEEN UNIVERSITY PRESS

First published 1995
The *Scotichronicon* series, originally published by
Aberdeen University Press, is now published by
The Mercat Press at James Thin
53–59 South Bridge, Edinburgh EH1 1YS

© University of St Andrews 1995

British Library Cataloguing in Publication Data

**A catalogue record for this book is available from
the British Library**

ISBN 1873644 493

Typeset from author generated discs by Servis Filmsetting Ltd., Manchester
and printed and bound in Great Britain by Antony Rowe Ltd.,
Chippenham, Wiltshire

Contents

Book VI

Preface

Responsibility for this volume has been simply divided. The text, translation and notes on Book V are the work of Winifred and John MacQueen, whilst the similar work on Book VI is by Donald Watt. All three editors have criticised each other's drafts, and the general introduction and index are their joint work. They gratefully acknowledge help given by Professor E.K.Borthwick and Professor H.L.MacQueen of the University of Edinburgh and Professor R.J.Bartlett of the University of St Andrews.

Julian Crowe of the Computing Laboratory of the University of St Andrews has been giving assistance that is much appreciated as computer technology moves forward and techniques pioneered when this enterprise was first undertaken in the mid 1980s have had to be changed. Mercat Press continue as understanding publishers, using still (by permission of the University of Aberdeen) the imprint of Aberdeen University Press with which the whole series began.

Thanks are due to the Master and Fellows of Corpus Christi College in Cambridge for giving us continuing access to their MS 171 as the main basis of this edition, and for a further contribution towards the financial cost of its publication. Other generous donors are the British Academy and the University of St Andrews (both of whom have been staunch in their support of this enterprise over many years now), the TSB Foundation for Scotland, the Keepers of the Quaich, William Grant and Sons, and Fife Regional Council. All these donations are gratefully acknowledged, for without this continuing assistance the completion of this edition would not be possible.

Donald Watt

Introduction to Books V and VI

The Manuscripts

As with the other books in the central section of the Cambridge, Corpus Christi College MS 171 which is the principal source of this edition, the folios used for this volume (fos. 87v-130) are generally entire and legible. Only exceptionally are marginal additions cut off by a binder at the edge of a page or partially deleted as a result of the ink becoming rubbed on the fragile paper. When this does happen the Donibristle MS can as usual be relied on to fill the gap. There is one illustration of King Malcolm Canmore and the thane of Fife in the half-page at the foot of fo.88 following the list of rubrics for Book V and before the start of c.1 overleaf (see frontispiece).

Book V ends at the foot of fo.109, with the list of rubrics for Book VI starting immediately overleaf and running on for nine lines at the top of fo.110. The rest of that folio with the top half of fo.110v has been used for two quite lengthy additional items for Book V, which presumably came to hand too late to be inserted in their proper places. They have been written here in different inks, and so presumably at different times. The first is marked by a special symbol for insertion between c.36 and c.37, where on fo.101v a marginal note explains that it has been placed at the end of Book V. It has been printed here as a separate chapter numbered c.36a to avoid disturbing the original numbering of the chapters that follow. The second extra item added on fos. 110-110v is a version of the Coronation Charter of King Henry I of England, which is mentioned in a marginal addition to c.39 as being placed eight folios further on (p.117, ll.49-50). This item also has been printed here as a separate chapter numbered 39a.

There is a marked break at the end of Book VI c.23 (fo.117v of the Corpus MS). About half-way down the page the chapter finishes raggedly with an incomplete date. The blank space underneath has at some later date been filled with a statement in a large bookhand regarding the respective responsibilities of Fordun and Bower for what has gone before and what follows after. Its content does not correspond exactly with the statement at the end of Book XVI c.39 below, which is in a similar bold hand, and it is likely to have been added after Bower's death (see p.461). Then follows a section (cc.24-47) on the lives of the bishops of St Andrews, ending with a brief account of the arrival of Bishop James Kennedy in 1442 (fo.126). This was the time when Bower was composing his chronicle

xiii

(cf. above Vol.1, p.25, and below Vol.8, p.xv), and he must have anticipated adding further details about this and possible future bishops, for he then left the rest of fo.126 and all of fo.126v blank. And when he resumed on fo.127 with his section on the priors of St Andrews, he numbered the chapters cc.49-57, thus leaving no.48 available for extra material on the blank pages. Only in the two MSS copied in the 1480s (the Brechin and Harleian MSS) was the opportunity taken by the scribe to insert brief variant details about Bishop Kennedy's activities and death in 1465 (see p.492). The account of Prior James Haldenston in c.57 is complete with mention of his death in July 1443 (p.437); but no attempt was made at the end of this chapter in any of the MSS to add anything about his successor, though William Bonar was appointed prior by the pope as early as September 1443 (*CPL*, ix, 354-5; cf. 350).

There is an anomaly in the numbering of the chapters of Book V in the Corpus MS. in which on fo.107 two successive chapters are given the same number 54, and the error is continued with the numbering of the remaining chapters to the end of the Book. But in the Donibristle MS this simple error is corrected, and it is its revised numbering that is followed here.

The more substantial additions to the basic text of the Corpus MS occur as follows in the margins:

> Book V cc.9 (fo.91), 13 (fos.93-95), 14 (fo.92v), 18 (fo.95), 21 (fo.96v), 22 (fos.96v-97), 32 (fo.100), 34 (fos.100v-101), 35 (fo.101), 36 (fos.100v-101), 36a (fo.110), 39 (fos.102-101v [sic]), 39a (fos.110-110v), 40 (fo.102v), 42 (fos.103-103v), 43 (fos.103v-104), 48 (fo.105), 60 (fo.108v).

> Book VI cc.14 (fo.115), 16 (fo.115), 19 (fo.116), 21 (fo.116v), 22 (fo.117), 24 (fo.118), 26 (fo.118v), 40 (fo.124), 43 (fo.124v), 45 (fo.125v), 46 (fo.125v), 52 (fo.127v).

As usual these additions are all written in the main text-hand, so that they must have been added before Bower's death in 1449 or very soon afterwards, and certainly before 1455 (which is the latest date for the Royal MS, which includes these additions within its main text). Most of them contain extra information which had presumably come to hand after the main text had been copied out in its present form, and wherever possible the editorial notes identify the sources from which they have been culled. These additions are particularly numerous (and inconveniently lengthy around fos.100-104) in Book V cc.32-43, where Bower (or someone after his death) was more and more adding materials from a variety of sources to the basic story that he was taking from Fordun. Sometimes it appears that he was including a series of short items likely to have been found together in an earlier chronicle now lost (see p.186). This seems to have borne a close, probably generic, relationship to the *Chronicle of Melrose* and the

Chronicle of Lanercost, and may have belonged to the cathedral priory library at St Andrews (see Vol.5, p.xvii). And it is not surprising that for Book VI (especially cc.40-46) Bower found additional information about bishops of St Andrews that he decided to add in the margins.

A few alterations to the main text which perhaps point to authorial rather than scribal corrections may be found at V c.19, text l.8; VI c.37a, l.54; c47, l.1; c.54, rubric and ll.2-3.

Bower provided his revised text for Book V here in the Coupar Angus MS as far as c.54, l.18 ('eius'), when he breaks off with a reference to the 'Magnus Liber' (i.e. the Corpus MS) for the remaining chapters of the book. But the Coupar Angus MS today has lost its pp.131-4 (i.e. the equivalent of V c.31, l.9 ['inexplicabili'] to c.35, l.1 ['Edgarus']). A shorter version of this missing material survives in the Perth MS fos.122-124v. One long extra passage was composed for the Coupar Angus MS in association with V c.9 here, and is included in the editorial introduction to that chapter. For Book VI the Coupar Angus MS follows the Corpus MS with the usual minor changes for cc.1-23 (note two rather longer additions to c.22 in its textual notes). Then the equivalent of cc.24-57 on the bishops and priors of St Andrews is moved to form a separate section near the end of the MS (pp.433-40 and 449). Four more leaves (i.e. pp.441-8) are now missing, covering the equivalent of VI c.51, l.2 ('providencia') to c.56, l.22 ('successive in') in the Corpus MS, and this time there is no back-up in the Perth MS. This section in the Coupar Angus MS is entitled 'Liber Alius', or alternatively described as 'primus liber extravagans' (c.24, ll.1-2 note; cf. Bower's description of his Book VII as 'liber extravagancium'). There is one long addition to c.42 here, and two more to c.45 (see editorial notes).

Besides the edition by Goodall, a version of Book VI had earlier in 1722 been printed by Thomas Hearne (see Vol. 8, p.xiii). Though Hearne was primarily interested in editing the work of Fordun, it happens that the principal MS which he used (Cambridge, Trinity College MS 0.9.9. [cited here as FC]) had been written as late as 1480 × 1496, and included the full list of rubrics from Bower's Book VI, together with texts of cc.1-23 (and also the extra items included here as V cc. 36a, 39a). These materials are printed in Hearne, iii, 495-549. Hearne also included (ibid., 550-637) a version of VI cc.24-57 here, derived apparently from the Royal MS (MS R), collated with the Harleian MS (MS H). But none of Hearne's text corresponding with Book VI has been collated for this edition.

Content and Sources

Bower continues in Book V as in the previous books to base his story on the work of John of Fordun in his *Chronica Gentis Scotorum* (though this title goes back no further than the Skene edition of 1871 [*Fordun*, p.xxxii]). And the same is generally true of the first twenty-three chapters of Book VI, as is rather ambiguously explained at the end of c.23. Up to this point he has in following Fordun's work been careful (he says) to identify any passages which he himelf has introduced into the story. In fact all of cc.1-8 of Book VI had been added by Bower, and the whole of the rest of the book (cc.24-57) forms a digression by him on the lives of the bishops and priors of St Andrews that has no counterpart in Fordun's book.

It happens that the fifteen chapters printed by Skene as his Appendix I (*Fordun*, 387-401) appear in only three of the seven surviving Fordun MSS (FG, FA, FC in order of writing); Bower did not use any of these MSS, but the lost MS which he did use must similarly have indicated that these chapters had been composed by Fordun as part of a Book VI of his *Chronica* that was never completed. They have a preface of their own (which Bower took over as his VI c.9 here) which explains why at this stage of his story (i.e. after reaching the death of King David I in 1153 at the end of his Book V) Fordun decided to go back to the time of the coming of the Anglo-Saxons to England to match his earlier account of the achievements of David's ancestors in Scotland with a shorter account of the deeds of his ancestors through his mother St Margaret in England. These fifteen chapters formed for Fordun a separate and complete unit, much of it drawn specifically from the *Genealogia Regum Anglorum* of Ailred of Rievaulx, which had been composed 1153-4 to inform the young Henry II of England about his ancestors as he prepared to ascend the throne of that country. Here for convenience in their original version they are cited simply as *Fordun* Book VI.

But the *Chronica* is not the only work relating to the period before 1153 found in the Fordun MSS. We need to refer also to the forty-one chapters printed by Skene as his Appendix III (*Fordun*, 406-37). Skene correctly describes them as 'capitula ad *Gesta Annalia* prefixa'. *Gesta Annalia* is the title given by him (ibid., p.xxxi) to the series of 190 short and often disparate annals covering the period 1153-1385 which he prints ibid., pp.254-383. Bower was to make regular use of them from his Book VIII onwards (see Vol.4, p.xix). Skene's policy of attaching the first annal of this series (which he calls no.1) to the end of Fordun's Book V makes chronological sense, and implies that these *Gesta Annalia* are a continuation of the *Chronica* in a less-developed form. This is indeed how these annals appear in two of the Fordun MSS (FD and FB). But in three other Fordun MSS (FG, FA, FC) these annals appear in a different part of the MS unconnected with Book V. Instead they start with the forty-one chapters put by Skene into his Appendix III, and run on chronologically without any break or special heading into the chapters which he calls *Gesta Annalia*. The forty-one chapters are clearly not 'attached' at the beginning of the *Gesta Annalia* (i.e. 'praefixa'), but form an ordinary part of them. It follows that since these complete *Gesta* start from the reign of Alfred in England rather than from 1153, they have a substantial overlap with Fordun's *Chronica*, where Alfred is dealt with as early as Book IV c.18. The *Gesta Annalia* as a whole therefore were not designed by Fordun as a continuation of his *Chronica*, even if the late fifteenth-century scribes of MSS FD and FB (and Skene) selected the post-1153 chapters to serve this purpose. Instead they were intended to stand alone separately as a work in a different style. From textual comparisons (see detailed discussions below) it is clear that many of the early chapters were composed before Fordun developed more elaborate parallel passages for his *Chronica* down to 1153, though the collection of annals for 1153-1385 may well have continued over an extended period. The lost exemplar of the two MSS FD and FB ends with an annal for 1363; but it must have been written in or after 1389, for there is a reference to Archibald de Douglas as earl of Douglas in annal 177 (*Fordun*, 377, n.3); and it has been suggested that the text of MS FD at any rate appears to have been altered on a matter of substance in relation to political circumstances in Scotland sometime between 1388 and ca 1405 (*SHR*, lxxiii [1974], 135). Fordun may have been still alive and working then; but there is no need to assume that he must have been, for a mention in the *Chronica* (V c.50) of Walter de Wardlaw with the title of cardinal (which implies a date in 1384 or later) may also be a piece of scribal up-dating. And if these MSS which end at 1363 could thus be adjusted later, the same may have happened to the lost exemplar of the three mid- to late- fifteenth-century MSS FG, FA and FC in which the collection of annals has been extended from 1363 to 1385 by the addition of just five extra items. These are open questions which allow us to be uncertain about Skene's supposition that Fordun himself produced two editions of the *Gesta Annalia* (*Fordun*, pp.xxxii-xxxiii). For the present purpose it is enough to call attention to the fact that Bower's text in his Books V and VI for the period before 1153 can be traced back not only to its immediate source in Fordun's *Chronica*, but also to Fordun's earlier composition, which is here cited as his *Early Gesta*. There are occasions (e.g. V c.42, ll.3-5) when he preferred to follow the latter text rather than the former.

It has recently become clear that the content of the texts in both of Fordun's works can be traced further back to a source which was known to Bower also. This bears a close relation to the unpublished Madrid, Royal Palace Library MS II. 2097. This neat MS was copied by a single scribe sometime between 1460 and 1488 for Dunfermline

Abbey in West Fife (hence its siglum here 'DMS'), and therefore in its present form was not a source that Bower ever saw. But it seems likely that the monks of Dunfermline commissioned the writing (and up-dating in some cases) of this miscellaneous collection of items to replace older copies of each of them that were already in their library. There are five sections at the beginning of this MS (which has been in Spain since the early seventeenth century) comprising texts which in some form must have been known to Fordun and/or Bower. (1) fos.1-17v, a version of Turgot's *Life of St Margaret* containing extensive passages not found in the standard text of this work hitherto known in the *Acta Sanctorum* and other editions. Fordun quotes passages which are found only in this MS. (2) fos.17v-20, historical notes 1093-1107 compiled in continuation of Turgot's *Life*, and wrongly thought by Fordun and Bower to have been part of that Life. Here the unknown author is cited as the Dunfermline Continuator. (3) fos. 21v-26, a family history of St Margaret's kingly predecessors and successors down to James III of Scotland, which duplicates material in other sections of the MS. It must have been known to Fordun and Bower in a form that had not followed the royal line to so late a date. Its unknown author is here cited as the Dunfermline Chronicler (cf. V c.21, l.61n). (4) fos. 26-41v, a collection of forty-two stories of miracles performed through the agency of St Margaret. One of these relating to the battle of Largs in 1263 is copied by Bower (X c.15). (5) fos. 41v-68, the Life and Miracles of St Waltheof by Jocelin of Furness. This was certainly the text used by Bower (VI cc.1-8, 25, 28-34). Bower may also have used exemplars of two other sections of this MS: first, fos. 106v-107v, containing stories about St Augustine of Canterbury (III cc.33-35); and second, fos. 108v-110v which contain the account by Josephus of the destruction of Jerusalem (II cc.31-32). In the editorial notes for each chapter here details are given of how passages similar to various sections of this Dunfermline MS in Madrid were incorporated successively in Ailred's *Genealogia* or Fordun's *Early Gesta*, then Fordun's *Chronica* Books V and VI, and Bower Books V and VI. Exceptionally there are passages (e.g. V c.35, ll.21-41) where Bower himself clearly has direct knowledge of some of the texts later copied into this Dunfermline MS.

In Book V Bower follows Fordun in deploying his material around three main themes: the antecedents of Malcolm III's accession involving the downfall of Macbeth (cc.1-8); the reign of Malcolm and his marriage to Queen Margaret (cc.9-26); and the reign of David I (cc.41-62). In the first Bower adds little to Fordun. In the second he makes free use of Fordun's material, which he rearranges with extended references to events in England and on the continent. He includes some Scottish material not in Fordun, for instance in c.9, the privileges granted to Macduff, and in c.17, the alternative account of the meeting of Malcolm and Margaret, probably derived from the chronicle, now lost, mentioned above (pp.xiv-xv). He extends Fordun's use of Turgot's *Life of Margaret*, but maintains his predecessor's approach to the text in which the emphasis is laid on the queen's works of corporal charity somewhat at the expense of her more intellectual and reforming qualities. Turgot gives Malcolm only a subsidiary role: Bower and Fordun both tend to present him as the queen's equal in the good works which they jointly performed – Malcolm is even (c.23, rubric) called 'saint'.

Bower (cc.39-40) accepts Fordun's interest (derived from DMS and shared by the author of the Poppleton MS) in the daughters of Margaret and Malcolm, Matilda, first wife of Henry I of England, and Mary, wife of Eustace III count of Boulogne. Bower uniquely makes Queen Matilda play the leading part in the drama usually associated with Lady Godiva of Coventry.

Bower follows Fordun in his peculiar treatment of the long reign of David I, covering, as it does, the entire period in only four chapters (c.41-44), to which is appended (cc.45-59) a lament for his death, made up of a series of extracts, first (c.45) apparently from the *Genealogia regum Anglorum* of Ailred of Rievaulx, second (cc.46-59) from the *Eulogium Davidis Regis Scotorum* of the same author. The *Genealogia* is also the apparent source of cc.61-62, which deal with David's ancestry on his mother's (i.e. Queen Margaret's) side as far back as the Anglo-Saxon divinity Woden. David's paternal descent from Noah by way of a series of Irish kings and heroes is set out (c.60) in a genealogy given to Fordun 'long ago' by Cardinal Wardlaw (ca 1320-87) perhaps in the mid-1360s when the latter was royal secretary with full access to official archives. The main purpose of the genealogy is to validate the authority of the monarch with whom it concludes (David I) and inspire him to follow the good example of his predecessors. In cc.41-44 Bower makes occasional small additions to the text provided by Fordun. In cc.45-49 the only additions made by Fordun or Bower to the text of Ailred is the list (c.48) of religious houses founded by David. Most of the items were supplied by Fordun, but Bower gives some supplementary information. Both Fordun and Bower, it is clear, regarded the *Genealogia* and *Eulogium* as forming a single text, which does not correspond to anything now surviving. The form is that of a commemorative sermon rather than a chronicle or history. Ailred's reputation as saint, churchman and personal friend of David may explain the surprising prominence given to his work.

In Book V Bower (sometimes following Fordun, sometimes not) makes use of narrative material associated with the position and rights of individual Scottish families of distinction – providing, as it were, charter-myths of these families. The dialogue between the exiled King Malcolm and Macduff (cc.1-6), together with (or perhaps despite) Macduff's subsequent actions against the usurper Macbeth (c.7), leads to the grant (c.9) of certain privileges to Macduff and his descendants, the earls of Fife. In a marginal addition to c.36 (ll.2-27) Bower explains how the head of the Carron or Scrimgeour family gained the hereditary right to be royal standard-bearer and constable of the Castle of Dundee. In both these cases hypothetical source-documents validated family claims and may have been preserved in royal or family archives. A similar source may underlie the story of the establishment in Lothian of the descendants of Godwine and his son Robert (cc.27, 28, 30, 34).

For c.36a Bower used an unidentified 'ancient little book', probably originating in Scone. The foundation legend of Inchcolm (c.37) is probably based on documents preserved on the island.

Outwith Scotland Bower in Book V concentrated on two main events, the Norman Conquest of England and the First Crusade. He greatly expanded Fordun's account of the former, often by way of marginal additions in MS C, basing himself on familiar sources such as William of Malmesbury and Henry of Huntingdon, as well as DMS and the now lost chronicle referred to above (pp.xiv-xv). Occasionally he worked from less familiar material; thus he took c.13, ll.129-56, from the anonymous continental *Brevis Relatio de Origine Willelmi Conquestoris*; c.14, ll.64-69 he took from the commentary *Super sapientiam Salamonis* of the English Dominican Robert Holkot (d. 1349). He appears to have based an enigmatical passage in c.21 (ll.43-45) on a corrupt version of an early-fifteenth-century English document, a less corrupt version of which was incorporated in the *St Albans Chronicle* now generally attributed to Thomas Walsingham (d. ca 1422).

In c.31 Bower's account of the First Crusade is ultimately based on the anonymous *Gesta Francorum et Aliorum Hierosolymitanorum*, completed probably in 1099. There may have been some intermediate source which we have not identified. The further information given in c.32 is mainly taken from Martin of Troppau. In c.33 Bower makes use of the *Liber prophetiarum seu visionum* of St Bridget of Sweden (ca 1303-73).

Bower's more general concern with the history of the Empire and Papacy leads him mostly to the use of Martin of Troppau. He also depends (cc.19, 20) on the *Legenda Aurea* of James de Voragine (ca 1230-ca 1298) and (c.32) on the *Epistles* of Peter of Blois (ca 1135-ca 1205). It should also perhaps be mentioned that Bower (c.7) quotes a single line from the influential *De planctu Naturae* (which he calls *De Conquestione Nature*) of the poet and philosopher Alan of Lille (ca 1128-1203).

The kernel of the first part of Book VI is the material which Fordun had prepared for a book to follow his Book V. Bower used it in amended form (cc.9-23), reproducing Fordun's original preface to this section, in which the kings of the Scots are rhetorically addressed.

They have been able to read about certain actions and virtues of their Scottish royal ancestors; but now they are to learn about some of the charitable works and warlike activities of their English royal ancestors, so that they may rejoice that two such glorious roots have been joined together (c.9). The reference is to the marriage of King Malcolm Canmore and Queen Margaret, so that the English side of the story ends with Edward the Confessor, with King Harold son of Godwine condemned as a traitor (c.23). It is not specified which kings of the Scots are being addressed, but the chance is taken to urge on them in general not to become degenerate. It is their duty 'to maintain the traditions of the brilliant fighting force of a victorious fighting island, that is of the Scots and the English'. This approving approach to the activities of the Anglo-Saxon kings contrasts markedly with Bower's normal hostile criticism of the kings of England since the usurpation by the Normans in 1066. The emphasis is on illustrating the extent to which the English kings had respect for their clergy; the Danes are regarded as instruments of Satan (c.12); and any serious challenges to royal authority are condemned as treachery. Both Fordun and Bower after him judge kings of bygone eras in the light of standards which they wanted to see maintained in their own day.

Bower was not content, however, just to follow Fordun's lead for Book VI. Rather awkwardly in his c.1 (ll.5-7) he assumes knowledge of what is to follow in cc.9-23 about King David's mother's ancestors, and widens his appreciative study of David's whole family by bringing in his wife's father and elder son by her first marriage, the two Waltheofs, the one an Anglo-Saxon earl who martyr-like was executed by William the Conqueror, the other the saintly abbot of Melrose in Scotland in David's own day. This is his excuse for bringing into his story (cc.1-8) a series of chapters selected from the *Life* of the saint by Jocelin of Furness, which had been written probably ca 1207 for the edification of King William, together with his young son Alexander and his brother Earl David. Bower later has an equally thin excuse for inserting a further series of chapters from this *Life* when describing the lives of the bishops of St Andrews (cc.25, 28-34), with the negative justification that when Waltheof was elected to this see, he refused office! We can conclude that Bower was determined to find opportunities to spread knowledge of a saint whom he regarded not only as an honour to the kingdom of Scotland, but as himself a Scot (c.2). Besides hagiographical anecdotes we can learn much from this *Life* about the characteristics of both the Augustinian and Cistercian religious orders in the twelfth century, about the subtleties of the relationships of kings and the lay aristocracy with the monastic movement in its heyday, and about the ideals which Bower himself as an Augustinian abbot thought important. 'Just as a deer longs for springs of water, so did [Waltheof's] soul long for God as a living spring' (c.30). Bower's extracts from this *Life* are disjointed and offer only part of the story of St Waltheof's career and influence; but buried as they have been only in Latin for too long, they form a major source for Scottish history that offers important opportunities for further study.

Bower's explanations (cc.24, 49) of his decision to devote more than half of Book VI to an account of the bishops and then the priors of the Augustinian cathedral monastery of St Andrews are again tenuous in relation to the broader focus of his chronicle. He was in no position to do the same for any others of the Scottish dioceses. But as a former member of the cathedral community he must have had access to records kept there, even if the information he found for bishops before the twelfth century was unhelpfully sketchy. His biographies of these bishops were to be followed in the early sixteenth century by similar compilations for the bishops of Dunkeld and Aberdeen, but Bower's lives of the priors is unique. Historians of St Andrews and of its buildings are therefore very well served with detailed information such as is not available for other cathedral sites, and now that Bower's account has been translated here for the first time, this information should acquire wider currency. Though the earlier notices of both bishops and priors are essentially factual, presumably reflecting the scanty nature of his sources, those nearer to Bower's own day contain elements of praise and criticism that indicate his own attitudes. Such items should be read in the light of his lengthy appreciative accounts of Bishop Walter Trayl (1385-1401) and Prior James Bisct (1394-1416), the two men who were in office when Bower was a young canon at St Andrews. His own ideas and standards were moulded by them, and he was grateful for it.

He had long experience himself as a religious superior at Inchcolm before he composed his book. He also had a training in canon law in the new university at St Andrews, so that he had a lawyer's knowledge of how things should be (cc.37a, 39, 54). He therefore, for example, felt entitled to emphasize the rights of the St Andrews cathedral community in episcopal elections against intrusive royal or papal authority (cc.42, 44). And he was not above sniping at bishops whom he regarded as having behaved badly (c.41), whilst admiring any who were modest in their material ambitions (cc.39-40). Such judgments by a holy abbot reflect his partisan view of the leaders of the secular clergy in the Scotland of his own day. He allocates seemingly disproportionate space to the career of John Scot, who failed to secure the see of St Andrews after election by the canons in 1178, but later became bishop of Dunkeld (cc.35-40), because he had available a *Life* of this bishop that is now lost. He does not quote the text of this *Life* as he does that of Waltheof, but rather makes use of it to develop a reflective account of his own. In fact the disputed episcopal election of 1178 at St Andrews was the one major dispute of this kind ultimately between papal and royal authority in the whole history of the church in medieval Scotland. Bower is aware of its unusual character. Coming as it did so soon after the famous dispute in England over Thomas Becket, he tries to suggest parallels, some of which are valid and others faulty because of his lack of exact knowledge of the dating of events. But more fundamentally he demonstrates in his discussion sympathetic understanding of the problems raised by this case for both pope and king – a consequence no doubt of his long experience as a churchman on the royal council. The whole story (which is unusually well documented) is not to be found here; but Bower is a good guide to the complexity of it all.

Since part of King William's difficulties in this case arose over an oath which he made that John Scot was never to be bishop of St Andrews, Bower offers a canonist's discussion of when an oath must be kept and when it may be disregarded (c.37).This leads to an excursus (c.38) on the evils of perjury in general – 'for I see every day something that grieves me, that very many people both when serving on juries and when bearing witness take little or no care over making their oaths void'. This is matched earlier (cc. 26-29) by a discussion of when it is right and necessary for someone elected to high office in the church (such as a bishopric or an abbacy) to accept the responsibility even if it is against his wishes, and when it is legitimate to shun the promotion. The context is St Waltheof's refusal to accept election as bishop of St Andrews, which had to be explained away since normally it was a man's duty to accept office, especially if so instructed by a religious superior. In this case Bower introduced several exempla to illustrate various solutions to the problem (including at least three from Thomas of Cantimpré [below Vol.5, pp.xviii-xix]), before coming to the conclusion that the saint must have received an instruction from the Holy Spirit to the effect that in his case it was preferable for him to continue the life of contemplation as abbot of Melrose rather than accept the bishopric. It was mainly in the course of these discussions that Bower had the opportunity to insert some literary allusions e.g. to Horace, Lucan, Juvenal, Augustine, Bede and Hildebert of Lavardin. Otherwise his quotations are from chroniclers such as Florence of Worcester, William of Malmesbury, Henry of Huntingdon and Martin of Troppau.

Methods of Editing

See Volume 8, pp.xx-xxiv for a general description of the methods followed in this edition. Unlike Volumes 1 and 2 it is possible in much of this volume to introduce editorial dates in the right-hand margin of the translation where they are thought to be sufficiently accurate to be helpful. Where these are partly or wholly within square brackets, the explanation of the dating is to be found in the notes.

Lists of Abbreviations

I. Sigla

AS:	*Acta Sanctorum*
B:	Scottish Record Office, GD.45/26/48 (Brechin MS)
C:	Cambridge, Corpus Christi College, MS 171 (Corpus MS)
CA:	National Library of Scotland, Adv.MS 35.1.7 (Coupar Angus MS)
D:	Darnaway Castle, Forres, Donibristle MS
DMS:	Madrid, Royal Palace Library, MS II.2097 (Dunfermline MS)
E:	Edinburgh University Library, MS 186
FA:	Wolfenbüttel, Germany, Cod-Guelf.538 Helmst.
FB:	British Library, Cotton MS Vitellius E.XI
FC:	Cambridge, Trinity College, MS 0.9.9.
FD:	Dublin, Trinity College, MS 498
FE:	British Library, Harleian MS 4764
FF:	Edinburgh, Scottish Catholic Archives, MM2/1 (Scots College MS)
FG:	British Library, Add.MS 37,223
G:	Goodall's printed edition of Bower
H:	British Library, Harleian MS 712
P:	National Library of Scotland, Adv.MS 35.6.7 (Perth MS)
R:	British Library, Royal MS 13.E.X
S:	Skene's printed edition of Fordun

II. Words

app. appendix
art.cit. (article cited)
bk. book
c century (e.g.12c)
c./cc. chapter/chapters
ca circa (about)
cf. (compare)
col./cols. column/columns
d. died
dau. daughter
del. deleted
dép. département
ed. edited
edn edition
ff. and following (pages etc.)
fo./fos. folio/folios
ibid. (in the same place)

interlin. interlineated
l/ll line/lines
lac. lacuna
MS/MSS manuscript/manuscripts
n. note
no./nos. (number/numbers)
om. omitted
p./pp. page/pages
para. paragraph
pt. part
s.a. (under the year)
sect. section
s.v. (under that head)
trans. translated
ut cit. (as cited)
vol./vols. volume/volumes
+ add after word signalled

III. Names of Counties

In the notes places in English, Welsh and Scottish counties (as defined between the 1890s and the 1970s) are identified by the following abbreviations for these counties.

ABD	Aberdeenshire	KNT	Kent
ANG	Angus	LIN	Lincolnshire
AYR	Ayrshire	MDX	Middlesex
BDF	Bedfordshire	MLO	Midlothian
BWK	Berwickshire	MOR	Morayshire
CAM	Cambridgeshire	NTB	Northumberland
CLA	Clackmannanshire	PER	Perthshire
CMB	Cumberland	ROX	Roxburghshire
DNB	Dunbartonshire	SFK	Suffolk
DOR	Dorset	SLK	Selkirkshire
DRH	Durham	SOM	Somerset
ELO	East Lothian	STL	Stirlingshire
FIF	Fife	WLT	Wiltshire
GLO	Gloucestershire	YOE	Yorkshire (East Riding)
HMP	Hampshire	YON	Yorkshire (North Riding)
HNT	Huntingdonshire	YOW	Yorkshire (West Riding)
KNR	Kinross-shire		

IV. Publications

Aberdeen Registrum   *Registrum Episcopatus Aberdonensis* (Spalding and Maitland Clubs, 1845).

Ailred, *Eulogium*   Ailred of Rievaulx, *Eulogium Davidis Regis Scotorum*, in Pinkerton, *Saints*, ii, 270-85.

Ailred, *Genealogia*   Ailred of Rievaulx, *Genealogia Regum Anglorum* (PL, 195, cols. 711-38).

Alfred the Great   *Alfred the Great. Asser's Life of King Alfred and other contemporary sources*, trans. S.Keynes and M.Lapidge (Harmondsworth, 1983).

AMW   *Annals of the Reigns of Malcolm and William, Kings of Scotland*, ed. A.C.Lawrie (Glasgow, 1910).

APS   *The Acts of the Parliaments of Scotland*, ed. T.Thomson and C.Innes (Edinburgh, 1814-75).

Arbroath Liber   *Liber S.Thome de Aberbrothoc*, i.e. Arbroath (Bannatyne Club, 1848-56).

ASC   *The Anglo-Saxon Chronicle*, trans. and ed. D.Whitelock and others (London, 1961).

ASC (Plummer)   *Two of the Saxon Chronicles Parallel*, ed. C.Plummer (Oxford, 1892-9).

ASE   Sir Frank Stenton, *Anglo-Saxon England*, 3rd edn (Oxford, 1971).

AU Annals of Ulster, ed. W.M.Hennessy, 4 vols. (Dublin, 1887-1901).

Baker, 'Legend' D.Baker, 'Legend and reality: the case of Waldef of Melrose', in *Church, Society and Politics*, ed. D.Baker *Studies in Church History*, xii (1975), 59-82.

Barlow, *Rufus* F.Barlow, *William Rufus* (London, 1983).

Barrow, *Kingdom* G.W.S.Barrow, *The Kingdom of the Scots* (London, 1973).

Barrow, *Unity* G.W.S.Barrow, *Kingship and Unity. Scotland 1000-1306* (London, 1981).

Bede Bede's Ecclesiastical History of the English People, ed. B.Colgrave and R.A.B.Mynors (Oxford, 1969).

Black, *Surnames* G.F.Black, *The Surnames of Scotland* (New York, 1946).

Boece, *Scottorum Historiae The Chronicles of Scotland compiled by Hector Boece. Translated into Scots by John Bellenden, 1531*, ed. R.W.Chambers and others, 2 vols. (STS, 1938-41).

Brut y Tywysogyon Brut y Tywysogyon or The Chronicle of the Princes, ed. T.Jones (Cardiff, 1955).

Byrne, *Kings* F.J.Byrne, *Irish Kings and High-Kings* (London, 1973).

Cameron, *Apostolic Camera* A.I.Cameron, *The Apostolic Camera and Scottish Benefices 1418-88* (Oxford, 1934).

Cantimpré, *De Apibus* Thomas de Cantimpré, *Liber Apum aut de Apibus mysticis sive de Proprietatibus Apum* (Paris, 1516).

CDS Calendar of Documents relating to Scotland, ed. J.Bain and others (Edinburgh, 1881-1986).

Chron.Holyrood A Scottish Chronicle known as the Chronicle of Holyrood (SHS, 1938).

Chron.Picts.-Scots Chronicles of the Picts: Chronicles of the Scots, ed. W.F.Skene (Edinburgh, 1867).

Chronicon Elegiacum 'The Metrical Chronicle commonly called The Chronicon Elegiacum MCCLXX', in *Chron.Picts-Scots*, 177-82.

CMH Cambridge Medieval History, ed. H.M.Gwatkin and others, 8 vols. (Cambridge, 1911-36).

Coupar Angus Chrs. Charters of the Abbey of Coupar Angus (SHS, 1947).

Cowan, *Parishes* I.B.Cowan, *The Parishes of Medieval Scotland* (Scottish Record Society, 1967).

CP G.E.Cokayne, *The Complete Peerage*, ed. V.Gibbs and others (London, 1910-59).

CPL Calendar of Entries in the Papal Registers relating to Great Britain and Ireland: Papal Letters (London, 1893-).

CPL Benedict XIII Calendar of Papal Letters to Scotland of Benedict XIII of Avignon 1394-1418 (SHS, 1977).

CPNS W.J.Watson, *The History of the Celtic Place-Names of Scotland* (Edinburgh, 1926).

CPP *Calendar of Entries in the Papal Registers relating to Great Britain and Ireland*: *Petitions to the Pope* (London, 1896).

Crawford, *Scandinavian Scotland* B.E.Crawford, *Scandinavian Scotland* (Leicester, 1987).

CSEL *Corpus Scriptorum Ecclesiasticorum Latinorum* (Vienna, 1866-).

CSSR *Calendar of Scottish Supplications to Rome*, vols.i-iii (SHS, 1934-70), vol.iv (Glasgow, 1983).

Curtius, *Latin Middle Ages* E.R.Curtius, *European Literature and the Latin Middle Ages*, trans. Willard R. Trask (London, 1953).

DDC *Dictionnaire de droit canonique* (Paris, 1935-65).

DHGE *Dictionnaire d'histoire et géographie ecclésiastiques* (Paris, 1912-).

Dictionary of the Irish Language *Dictionary of the Irish Language based mainly on Old and Middle Irish Materials* (Dublin, 1990).

Diss *Radulfi de Diceto* [*Diss*] ... *Opera Historica* (RS, 68, 1876).

DML *Dictionary of Medieval Latin from British Sources* (Oxford, 1975-).

DNB *Dictionary of National Biography* (London, 1885-1900).

DOST *A Dictionary of the Older Scottish Tongue* (1937-).

Douglas, *William the Conqueror* D.C.Douglas, *William the Conqueror* (London, 1974).

Dowden, *Bishops* J.Dowden, *The Bishops of Scotland* (Glasgow, 1912).

Du Cange Du Cange, *Glossarium Mediae et Infimae Latinitatis*, new edn (Niort, 1883-7).

Duncan, *Kingdom* A.A.M.Duncan, *Scotland: The Making of the Kingdom* (Edinburgh, 1975).

Dunfermline Registrum *Registrum de Dunfermelyn* (Bannatyne Club, 1842).

EHR *English Historical Review*.

ES *Early Sources of Scottish History*, ed. A.O.Anderson (Edinburgh, 1922; republished Stamford, 1990).

ESC *Early Scottish Charters*, ed. A.C.Lawrie (Glasgow, 1905).

Eubel, *Hierarchia* C.Eubel, *Hierarchia Catholica Medii Aevi*, 2nd edn (Munster, 1913-23).

Extracta *Extracta e Variis Cronicis Scocie* (Abbotsford Club, 1842).

Florence, *Chronicon* *Florenti Wigorniensis* [*Florence of Worcester*] *Monachi Chronicon ex Chronicis* (English Historical Society, 1848-9).

Forbes, *Lives* *Lives of S. Ninian and S. Kentigern*, ed. A.P.Forbes (Edinburgh 1874).

Fordun *Johannis de Fordun, Chronica Gentis Scotorum*, ed. W.F.Skene (Edinburgh, 1871-2) [all references to vol.1 unless otherwise stated].

Fox, *Henryson* Denton Fox, *The Poems of Robert Henryson* (Oxford, 1981).

Freeman, *William Rufus* E.A.Freeman, *The Reign of William Rufus and the Accession of Henry I* (Oxford, 1882).

Friedberg *Corpus Juris Canonici*, ed. E.Friedberg (Leipzig, 1879-81).

Haddan & Stubbs, *Councils* *Councils and Ecclesiastical Documents relating to Great Britain and Ireland*, ed. A.W.Haddan and W.Stubbs (Oxford, 1869-71).

Hasegawa, 'Catalogue' I.Hasegawa, 'Catalogue of ancient and naked eye comets', *Vistas in Astronomy*, xxiv (1980), 59.

Hastings, *Dictionary* *Dictionary of the Bible*, ed. J.Hastings (Edinburgh, 1929).

HBC *Handbook of British Chronology*, 3rd edn, ed. E.B.Fryde and others (London, 1986).

Hearne *Johannis de Fordun Scotichronicon cum Supplementis et Continuatione Walteri Boweri*, ed. T. Hearne (Oxford, 1722).

Historical Atlas *An Historical Atlas of Scotland c.400-c.1600*, ed. P.McNeill and R.Nicholson (St Andrews, 1975).

History of Northumberland *A History of Northumberland* (The Northumberland County History Committee, Newcastle-upon-Tyne and London, 1893-1940).

Hogan, *Onomasticon* Edmund Hogan, *Onomasticon Goedelicum* (Dublin and London, 1910).

Hudson, *Kings* B.T.Hudson, *Kings of Celtic Scotland* (Westport, Connecticut and London, 1994).

Huntingdon *Henrici archidiaconi Huntendunensis Historia Anglorum* (RS, 74, 1879).

Kelso Liber *Liber S. Marie de Calchou* i.e. Kelso (Bannatyne Club, 1846).

KKES M.O.Anderson, *Kings and Kingship in Early Scotland*, revised edn (Edinburgh and London, 1980).

Knowles and others, *Heads* *The Heads of Religious Houses, England and Wales, 940-1216*, ed. D.Knowles and others (Cambridge, 1972).

Lanercost *Chronicon de Lanercost* (Maitland Club, 1839).

Lebor Gabála *Lebor Gabála Érenn. The Book of the Taking of Ireland*, ed. R.A.Stewart Macalister, 5 vols. (Dublin, 1938-56). [*Reim Riograide* or *Roll of the Kings* occupies vol.v, 137-565.]

Le Neve, *Fasti 1066-1300* *John le Neve, Fasti Ecclesiae Anglicanae 1066-1300* (London, 1968-).

Life of Ailred Walter Daniel, *The Life of Ailred of Rievaulx*, ed. F.M.Powicke *London, 1950)*.

McFadden, 'Edition' G.J.McFadden, 'An Edition and Translation of the Life of Waldef, Abbot of Melrose, by Jocelin of Furness', Columbia University thesis, 1952 (University Microfilms edn).

MacQueen, *Allegory* J.MacQueen, *Allegory* (London, 1970).

MacQueen, *Numerology* J.MacQueen, *Numerology* (Edinburgh, 1985).

McRoberts, *St Andrews* *The Medieval Church of St Andrews*, ed. D.McRoberts (Glasgow, 1976).

Mâle, *Religious Art*   Emile Mâle, *Religious Art in France. The Thirteenth Century*, trans. M.Mathews (Princeton, 1984).

Malmesbury   William of Malmesbury, *Gesta Regum Anglorum* (RS, 90, 1887-9).

Martin   *Martini Oppaviensis Chronicon Pontificum et Imperatorum* (MGH, *Scriptores* [folio], xxii [Hanover, 1872], 377-475).

Mas Latrie, *Trésor*   J.M.J.L.Mas Latrie, *Trésor de Chronologie* (Paris, 1889).

Melrose   The Chronicle of Melrose, ed. A.O.Anderson and others, facsimile edn (London, 1936).

Memoriale ... B.Brigidae   Memoriale effigiatum librorum prophetiarum seu visionum B.Brigidae alias Birgittae, ed. O.Magnus (Rome, 1556).

MGH   Monumenta Germaniae Historica (1826-   ).

MRHEW   *Medieval Religious Houses England and Wales*, ed. D.Knowles and R.N.Hadcock (London, 1953).

MRHS   *Medieval Religious Houses Scotland*, 2nd edn, ed. I.B.Cowan and D.E.Easson (London, 1976).

Myres, *Settlements*   J.N.L.Myres, *The English Settlements* (Oxford, 1986).

NCE   New Catholic Encyclopaedia (Washington, D.C., 1967-   ).

NEB   The New English Bible (Oxford and Cambridge, 1970).

Nennius   Nennius. *British History and Welsh Annals*, ed. John Morris (London and Chichester, 1980).

Nicholson, *Later Middle Ages*   R.G.Nicholson, *Scotland: The Later Middle Ages* (Edinburgh, 1974).

OBMLV   The Oxford Book of Medieval Latin Verse, ed. F.J.E.Raby (Oxford, 1959).

O'Brien, *Corpus*   Corpus Genealogiarum Hiberniae, vol.i, ed. M.A.O'Brien (Dublin, 1976).

OBSV   The Oxford Book of Scottish Verse (Oxford, 1966).

OCD   The Oxford Classical Dictionary, 2nd edn (Oxford, 1970).

OCL   The Oxford Companion to Law (Oxford, 1980).

ODCC   The Oxford Dictionary of the Christian Church, 2nd edn with corrections (Oxford, 1983).

ODEPN   The Concise Oxford Dictionary of English Place-Names, 4th edn (Oxford, 1960).

ODP   The Oxford Dictionary of Popes (Oxford, 1986).

ODS   The Oxford Dictionary of Saints, 2nd edn (Oxford, 1987).

OED   A New English Dictionary on Historical Principles [later *Oxford English Dictionary*] (Oxford, 1888-   ).

O'Rahilly, *History and Mythology*   Thomas F.O'Rahilly, *Early Irish History and Mythology* (Dublin, 1946).

Origines Parochiales   Origines Parochiales Scotiae (Bannatyne Club, 1851-5).

Pinkerton, *Saints* *Pinkerton's Lives of the Scottish Saints*, ed. W.M.Metcalfe (Paisley, 1889).

PL Patrologiae Cursus Completus Series Latina, ed. J.P.Migne (Paris, 1857-66).

Pluscarden *Liber Pluscardensis*, ed. F.H.J.Skene, 2 vols. (Edinburgh, 1877-80) [all references to vol. i unless otherwise stated].

Poole, *From Domesday* A.L.Poole, *From Domesday Book to Magna Carta 1087-1216* (Oxford, 1951).

Pryde, *Burghs* G.S.Pryde, *The Burghs of Scotland* (Oxford, 1965).

Raine, *North Durham* Appendix to J.Raine, *The History and Antiquities of North Durham* (London, 1852).

RCAHM *Reports of the Royal Commission on the Ancient and Historical Monuments and Constructions of Scotland* (Edinburgh, 1909-).

Reim Riograide See *Lebor Gabála.*

Rivet and Smith, *Place-Names* A.L.F.Rivet and Colin Smith, *The Place-Names of Roman Britain* (London, 1979).

Robertson, *Concilia* *Concilia Scotiae: Statuta Ecclesiae Scoticanae*, ed. J.Robertson (Bannatyne Club, 1866).

RS Rolls Series (London, 1858-96).

Runciman, *Crusades* S.Runciman, *A History of the Crusades* (Cambridge, 1951-4).

SAEC *Scottish Annals from English Chroniclers 500 to 1286*, ed. A.O.Anderson (London, 1908; Stamford, 1991).

St Andrews Liber *Liber Cartarum Prioratus Sancti Andree in Scotia*, i.e. St Andrews (Bannatyne Club, 1841).

Scot.Pont. R.Somerville, *Scotia Pontificia* (Oxford, 1982).

SEHI James F.Kenney, *The Sources for the Early History of Ireland: Ecclesiastical* (New York, 1929); revised edn by Ludwig Bieler (Dublin, 1979).

Series Episcoporum *Series Episcoporum Ecclesiae Catholicae Occidentalis ab Initio usque ad Annum MCXCVIII*, ed. O.Engels and S.Weinfurter (Stuttgart, 1982-).

Setton, *Crusades* K.M.Setton, *A History of the Crusades*, vols. i-ii, 2nd edn (Madison, Wisconsin, 1969).

SHF Société de l'histoire de France

SHR Scottish Historical Review

SHS Scottish History Society

Simeon, *Durham* Simeon of Durham, 'Historia Dunelmensis Ecclesiae', in *Opera Omnia* (RS, 75, 1882-5), i, 1-169.

Simeon, *Kings* Simeon of Durham, 'Historia Regum', in *Opera Omnia*, ut cit., ii, 1-283.

Sjoestedt, *Gods and Heroes* M.L.Sjoestedt, *Gods and Heroes of the Celts*, trans. M.Dillon (London, 1949).

SP   The Scots Peerage, ed. Sir J. Balfour Paul (Edinburgh, 1904-14).

STS   Scottish Text Society.

Stubbs, *Charters*   W.Stubbs, *Select Charters*, 9th edn (Oxford, 1913).

TDGAS   Transactions of the Dumfriesshire and Galloway Natural History and Antiquarian Society (1862-   ).

Theiner, *Monumenta   Vetera Monumenta Hibernorum et Scotorum Historiam Illustrantia*, ed. A.Theiner (Rome, 1864).

Thompson, *Motif-Index*   Stith Thompson, *Motif-Index of Folk-Literature*, 2nd edn, 6 vols. (Copenhagen, 1955-8).

TRHS   Transactions of the Royal Historical Society (1872-   ).

Turgot, *Margaret   Life of St Margaret by Turgot*, in Pinkerton, *Saints*, ii, 135-96.

VCH   The Victoria History of the Counties of England (London and Oxford, 1900-   ).

Vincent   Vincentius Bellovacensis [*Vincent of Beauvais*] *Speculum Historiale* (Douai, 1624; reprinted Graz, 1965).

Walther, *Initia*   H.Walther, *Initia Carminum ac Versuum Medii Aevi Posterioris Latinorum* (Göttingen, 1959).

Walther, *Proverbia*   H.Walther, *Proverbia Sententiaeque Latinitatis Medii Aevi* (Göttingen, 1963-7, 1982-6).

Watt, *Fasti   Fasti Ecclesiae Scoticanae Medii Aevi ad Annum 1638*, 2nd draft, ed. D.E.R.Watt (Scottish Record Society, 1969).

Watt, *Graduates*   D.E.R.Watt, *A Biographical Dictionary of Scottish Graduates to A.D.1410* (Oxford, 1977).

Word-List   Revised Medieval Latin Word-List from British and Irish Sources, ed. R.Latham (London, 1965).

Wyntoun   The Original Chronicle of Andrew of Wyntoun, ed. F.J.Amours (STS, 1903-14).

Book V

Book V

1

De Macduff c'

*ᵃ*Postquam igitur Macduff applicuisset apud Ravynsor in Anglia, Malcolmum festinus adiens, captato collacionis apto tempore, reditum illi suasit, et quod ad regni se transferat regimen, diu nimis sua tantum nec alterius desidia*ᵇ* tardatum, ardenter adortatur. 'Nec quicquam', inquid, 'de mea fidelitate diffidas. Nam me pater tuus 5 semper fidelem habuit, eciam et tibi multa sustinens incomoda fui fidelis, sum et ero vita comite. Regni quoque principes pro parte majori*ᶜ* tuo nomine michi sub sacramento fidem dantes firmam, et illis similiter hoc idem ego faciens, non in dolo, firmiter credas quia corde sumus et animo tuum fideliter ad obsequium conjurati. Omnis itaque 10 vulgi scio veraciter corda possides; tuo sub explicato vexillo pro te sanguinem gaudenter effundere concurret, tibi domino legio placidum reddendo famulatum.' Auditis enim huiusmodi sermonibus, corde multum gavisus est. Sed an fideliter vera suaserat, an prodiciose*ᵈ* ficta, vacillanti sepius animo revolvens, quodammodo 15 timuit. Nam hoc idem antea reditus sui per quosdam partis adverse callide suasum est, ut deciperent. Et igitur hoc illum prudenter modo cautus, ut sequitur, attemptavit. 'Amice', inquit, 'karissime, tibi tuisque consodalibus quantum valeo regracior, vobis vicem sed tibi precipue rependam pro meritis posse tenus, Deo dante. De tua 20 presertim amodo fidelitate securus, archana quedam cordi meo*ᵉ* naturaliter infixa, quod ea celaveris, non ambigens tibi, karissime, revelabo. Sunt quedam*ᶠ* immania que mecum ab inicio creverunt flagicia, quamvis id me facturum quod exigis adducere prevales, ymmo si michi coronam, omni remota difficultate, tribuas, hec in vos 25 me diu regnare | non permittent. Quorum utique primum est detestande libidinis miranda carne radicata voluptas, incredibilem me virginum corruptorem ac mulierum efficiens. Unde veraciter scio, quod dominandi potestate suscepta, nobilium violando thoros,*ᵍ* virginum raptus non vitarem. Igitur scelus huiusmodi nequam in 30 populo frequentantem, a regni principibus, verum eciam a ruralibus,

---

a	*large decorated initial capital* P *C; similar but different letter* D
b	dissidia *CA*
c	*S;* majores *C*

d	prodicione *CA*
e	non *CA*
f	*CA;* quidam *C*
g	*CA;* thorum *C*

Book V

1

Concerning Macduff etc.

So after Macduff had landed at Spurn Head in England, he lost no
time in going to Malcolm, and after watching for a suitable time for a
meeting, he advocated his return [to Scotland], and earnestly
exhorted him to undertake the government of the kingdom. This had
5 been too long delayed by his own inactivity only, not that of anyone
else. 'And have no misgivings', he said, 'about my loyalty. For your
father always considered me to be loyal, and I have always been loyal
to you also, in spite of the many hardships this has caused me. I am,
and always will be, loyal as long as I live. The magnates of the
10 kingdom also for the most part have given their firm assurance on
oath to me in your name, and I likewise have done the same to them in
good faith. You may undoubtedly believe that we have together with
heart and mind faithfully sworn allegiance to you. I know for certain
that you possess the hearts of all the people; they will rush joyfully to
15 pour out their blood for you under your banner, once it has been
unfurled, rendering ungrudging service to you their liege lord.'
Malcolm was secretly very pleased at hearing remarks like these; but
he was somewhat afraid as he went over and over it in his mind, in
doubt as to whether Macduff's advice was genuine and given in good
20 faith, or whether it was treacherously false, for this same advice about
his return had been craftily given to him by certain men of the
opposing side. And so as a precaution he put Macduff to the test in the
following manner. 'My very dear friend', he said, 'I return what
thanks I can to you and your associates. I shall repay all of you, but
25 you especially, for your services as far as possible, if God grants it.
Since from now on I am confident of your loyalty, I shall, without
beating about the bush, reveal to you, dearest friend, certain secret
traits implanted in my heart by nature, because you will keep quiet
about them. There are certain monstrous vices which have grown
30 with me from the beginning. Even if you are able to induce me to do
what you demand, even if every obstacle is removed, and you bestow
the crown upon me, these vices will not permit me to reign over you
for very long. The first of these vices is the amazing pleasure I take in
abominable lust that is rooted in my flesh, and that turns me into a
35 seducer beyond belief of young girls and women, so that I know
beyond a doubt that if I gained the supreme power, I would inevitably
violate the beds of my nobles, and rape young girls. Therefore I am

3

[quorum]*h* uxoribus abutar et filiabus, de regno me penitus expellendum non ignoro. [Idcirco]*h* michi melius videtur alieno regno privatus degere, quam a regia dignitate sus-[cepta],*h* culpis exigentibus, per insurgentes subditos ignobiliter degradari.'   35

h   D; lac.C

2

De variis exemplis per Malcolmum positis quod multi reges amiserunt regna

'Nunc autem inducam exempla tibi quid et quanta mala potentibus et variis regibus, propter immoderate libidinis usum, transactis temporibus contigerunt. Tarquinius vero Superbus olim Romanorum rex potens cum triginta quatuor annis regnasset, eo quod filius eius eciam Tarquinius uxorem Colatini Lucreciam stupro violasset, regnum 5 (quod non ignoras) perdidit. Nam cum ea patri maritoque ceteris eciam amicis, ex hac injuria questa fuerat, in omnium conspectu sese pugione percuciens occidit. Exinde vero tanta sunt in ira cives concitati, quod postquam exclusum regem abicerent, numquam passi sunt aliquem qui nomen haberet Tarquinii nec umquam insuper 10 super se regem habere consenserunt. Novissimus itaque sui generis, rex Assiriorum Sardanapallus, vir muliere corrupcior, ut sue voluptatis expleret libidinem, inter scortorum greges habitu feminio colo purpuram tractavit. Unde tante fuit execracioni cunctis habitus, ut regnum simul et vitam amitteret, ita quod in eo sue generacionis linea 15 regnare desierat. Rex vero Francorum filius Merovei*a* Chilpericus, pater Magni Clodovei, cum esset nimium luxurie deditus, suorum filias subditorum | et uxores stupro violasset, ipsum a regno dejecerunt, nec usque post annos octo transactos, et tunc nisi casu fortuito, promittentem ad minus sub caucione continenciam, iterum 20 in regem susceperunt. Edwius eciam rex nuper Anglorum nimis petulans, in tantum luxuriosis usus est lasciviis quod eo die quo sacratus est in regem, cum [inter]*b* proceres de regni seriosis rebus ageretur, ex eorum surgens medio prorupit in cameram, in complexum meretricis devolutus. Quem Sanctus Dunstanus abstrahens a 25 cubiculo, perpetuum sibi fecit inimicum. Propter enim talia vicia, seu illis majora, regni proceres ipsum semper in odium et quasi non regem habuerunt. Et quidem regni nostri Scocie rex dudum Culenius, nonne

fo.89

a   Merovei filius for filius Merovei CA   b   P

aware that if I practise this kind of wicked crime amongst my people, I
should be utterly driven out of the kingdom, not only by the magnates
40 of the kingdom but also by the peasants whose wives and daughters I
shall abuse. Therefore it seems better for me to live as a private citizen
in someone else's kingdom than to be ignobly deposed by my
rebellious subjects from the royal office that I had undertaken,
through the compulsion of my sins.'

2

*Various examples cited by Malcolm [to show] that many kings
have lost their kingdoms*

'Now I shall give you some examples of what happened to various
powerful kings, and of what great misfortunes they suffered in past
times because of their uncontrollable lust. Tarquin the Proud, at one
time a powerful king of the Romans, lost his kingdom (as you are
5 aware) after a reign of thirty-four years, because his son, also called
Tarquin, raped Lucretia the wife of Collatinus. For after she had
complained about this injury to her father, her husband and the rest
of her friends, she stabbed herself to death with a dagger before the
eyes of all. Then the citizens were so infuriated that after they had
10 deposed and expelled the king, they never allowed anyone to go by the
name Tarquin, and refused ever afterwards to have a king ruling over
them. The last of his line Sardanapalus king of the Assyrians, a man
more depraved than a woman, used to weave purple cloth with the
distaff dressed in woman's attire in the midst of droves of harlots to
15 satisfy his desire for sensual pleasure. This caused him to be so
abominated by everyone that he lost both his kingdom and his life,
and with him the lineage of his family ceased to reign. Since Childeric
king of the Franks, son of Merovech and father of Clovis the Great
was inordinately given over to lechery, and had raped the daughters
20 and wives of his subjects, they deposed him, and did not take him
back again until eight years later, and even then only by a fluke, when
he promised at least some restraint under guarantee. Also Eadwig a
recent king of the English who was exceedingly lascivious was so far
gone in excesses of lechery that on the day on which he had been
25 consecrated king, while the magnates were discussing important state
business, he rose up from among them, rushed into his chamber, and
fell into the arms of a whore. St Dunstan made for himself an enemy
for life by dragging him out of his bedroom. Because of such vices or
even worse ones the magnates of the kingdom regarded him with
30 hatred, and did not look upon him as their king. And indeed was not
Culen the former king of our kingdom of Scotland killed by one of his

propter luxuriam a suo subdito, videlicet raptum filie sue virginis,
occisus est? Hibernie vero regnum finem habuit in Roderico rege   30
libidinoso, de nostri quippe generis stirpe progenito, qui sex simul

uxores, non ut | rex Christianus, habere, nec eas propter amissionem
regni dimittere voluit, licet ab ecclesia tota tam archiepiscopis quam
episcopis sepe monitus, et ab omnibus indigenis tam principibus
quam privatis, terribiliter minando correptus fuerat; ab eis igitur   35
omnibus contemptus est, nec sibi de cetero, vel regi cuiquam,
dignantur actenus obedire. Propterea regnum illud, avorum nostrorum temporibus dudum insigne, nunc, ut vides, in xxx^{ta} vel amplius
regnis miserabiliter est divisum. Quid moror in talibus? Centum enim
tibi regum et principum exempla proferre valeo, quos hoc solum   40
incontinencie vicio protinus obruere non ignoro.'

3

De responsis Makduff ponentis exemplum Octaviani

Cui Makduff, quasi dedignando surridens, ait: 'Numquid hoc tibi
placens videtur aut competens responsum michi reddere? Nec michi
solo, sed tuis benevolis, quorum nuncii fungor officio? Nobis videlicet
omnibus, qui pro te regnum et predia deseruimus, filios et uxores ac
nostri generis nacionem? Insuper et vitam nostram mortis periculo   5
nuper posuimus, ut decuit; eciam si quod tuum est audacter feceris,
ponemus peramplius in futurum. Sed quid hec tua significare velit
inanis excusacio, multum admiror. Vereris, ut estimo, regni culmen
ascendere, propter immoderatam tue voluptatis cupidinem, sperans
te feminei generis in regno copiam habere non posse, filiabus   10
nobilium exceptis et uxoribus. Nonne talis racione caret excusacio?
Numquid et tu rex existens ad tuam explendam^a libidinis luxuriam,
pulcherrimas regni virgines ad libitum^b ac placidissimas habere poteris
mulieres? Audacter dicam, vere poteris. Licet regum quorum
incontinencie ponis exempla, tam Sardanapalli quam Chilperici seu   15
Roderici luxum dupliciter exsuperes, vel insuper imperatoris Octo-
viani, qui libidini serviebat usque ad probrum vulgaris fame. Nam, ut
historie referunt, inter duodecim virgines et totidem corruptas solitus
est accubare.^{c} Nec tamen ob id "imperatoris felicissimi" nomen

---

a G; explende C c +Quod quia valde penituit nato in carne
b +quamvis non ad licitum CA Dei Filio de intemerata virgine ut
                                                cognovit CA

subjects because of his lechery, that is to say the rape of his young
daughter? The kingdom of Ireland ended with the lecherous king
Roderick, descended from a branch of our own stock, who most
35 improperly for a Christian king wished to have six wives at the same
time, nor did he wish to give them up even if it meant losing his
kingdom, although he was often warned by the whole church both by
archbishops and bishops, and reprimanded with terrible threats by all
the inhabitants both magnates and private individuals. So he was
40 despised by them all. They refused to obey him in future, and to this
day they decline to obey any king at all. Therefore that kingdom for
long distinguished in the days of our ancestors is now, as you see,
miserably divided into thirty or more kingdoms. Why should I waste
time on such matters? I can produce you a hundred examples of kings
45 and emperors who, I know, owe their utter downfall to this vice of
intemperance alone.'

3

Macduff in reply produces the example of Octavian

Macduff said to him with a scornful smile: 'Surely you do not consider
this to be an acceptable or adequate answer to make to me, and not
just to me but to your supporters also, for whom I now perform the
office of messenger, that is to say all of us who for your sake have
5 deserted our kingdom and our estates, our sons and wives and the
people of our nation. Moreover we have recently placed our lives in
danger of death, as we were bound to do, and we will place them in
even greater danger in future, if you will play your part courageously.
I am completely baffled however as to the meaning of this useless way
10 of excusing yourself. In my opinion you are afraid to ascend the
supreme height of the kingdom because of your unbridled desire for
sensual pleasure, not realising that you could have an abundance of
the female sex in the kingdom apart from the wives and daughters of
the nobles. Surely such an excuse is unreasonable? When you are
15 king, will you not be able to have at will the most beautiful young girls
in the kingdom and the most complaisant women to satisfy your
lecherous lust? I shall speak boldly. You will indeed be able to do so
although you outdo twice over the lechery of the kings whose
intemperance you give as examples, Sardanapalus, Childeric and
20 Roderick, or in addition the emperor Octavian, who was a slave to
lust to the point of notoriety in common report. For, as the histories
record, it was his custom to lie down between twelve virgins and the
same number of women whom he had seduced. Yet he did not forfeit
the title of "most felicitous emperor", nor his popularity with the

amisit, seu populi favorem, qui morientem planxit dicens: "Utinam 20
non nasceretur, aut non moreretur." Vir, qui certe numquam aut
tantam reipublice potenciam ad se traxisset, aut tamdiu potiretur, nisi
magnis studiorum et nature bonis habundasset. Imperium namque
Romanum mirifice firmavit, rexit et auxit; urbem variis et invisis
antea decoravit edificiis, hoc dicto glorians: "Urbem latereciam 25
reperii, relinquo marmoream." Similiter et tu, si regni tui fines
decenter ampliaveris, pace rexeris, et legibus edificiis illud [et]^d novis
ornaveris, nomen boni regis aut favorem gentis tanto scelere non
amittes. Et quod olim ipse de sua Roma gloriando cecinit, hoc de tuo
regno canere possis: "Scociam inveni dudum legibus egentem, 30
frugibus et armentorum gregibus sterilem, modo bonis omnibus et
pace relinquo fecundatam.'"

d   CA

4

De secunda temptacione Malcolmi se furem asserentis, et responsis M[acduff]

'Vera sunt hec', inquit Malcolmus, 'que loqueris, sed adeo pronus
meus semper est animus et preceps ad hoc vicium, quod vix aliquando
racione poterit refrenari. Sed adhuc hoc vicio multo vilius obstat
flagicium, pre pudore vero tacendum; nec tibi tamen amico celan-
dum, ymmo in secreto recitandum. Fur quoque sum et latro nequam; 5
nam omne pulcrum aut delectabile seu visu placens, ut ferrum magnes
ex natura, meum cor miserum illud attrahens, vehementer | appetit,
ac cetera corporis membra necessitate quadam alliciens, incessanter
dirigit ad furandum. Hoc firmum teneas, me non^a furari videtur michi
penitus impossibile. Ergo multum tolerabilius est atque jocundius, 10
ostiatim egere mendicus, aut mori finaliter, quam per me regni
locatum in apice majestas regia tam infami scelere violetur. Excellen-
cioris persone semper casus in vicium minoris lapsum, comparacione
scandali, multo longius antecedit.' Cui Makduff: 'Hoc utique verum
est, quia quanto gradus alcior, tanto casus gravior. Quanto nempe 15
quisquis honoris gradibus sit exaltatus alcior, tanto debet esse
virtutibus eximior; et quanto virtutum in arce scandit sublimior,
tanto sibi viciorum est si cadat voragine, magis pudor. Dupliciter
quoque princeps, virtutum declinans a tramite delinquit, quia

fo.89v

a   interlin.C

25 people who mourned him, as he was dying, with the words: "Oh that
he had never been born or that he would never die." He was a man
who would certainly never have won for himself such great power in
the state, nor would have kept that power for so long, if he had not
been blessed with great gifts both natural and acquired. For he
30 strengthened, ruled and extended the Roman empire in an amazing
way; he adorned the city with a variety of buildings never seen before,
boasting of it in these words: "I found a city brick, I leave it marble."
Similarly you too, if you extend as you ought the territory of your
kingdom, rule it in peace, and adorn it with laws and new buildings,
35 you will not lose the name of good king or popularity with the people
in spite of such great wickedness. And you would be able to sing about
your kingdom what Octavian once sang boastfully about his Rome:
"Previously I found Scotland without laws, unproductive in grain
and herds of cattle, now I leave it abounding in all good things and at
40 peace."'

4

The second of Malcolm's tests where he declares that he is a
thief, and the reply of Macduff

'What you say', said Malcolm, 'is true, but my mind is always so
inclined to rush headlong into this failing that it can scarcely ever be
restrained by reasoning. But I am hampered by a much worse vice still
than this failing, which I should really keep quiet about for very
5 shame, but yet I must not hide it from you who are my friend, or
rather I must recount it in secret. I am also a thief and a wicked
robber; for anything that is beautiful or delightful or pleasing to the
eye attracts my wretched heart, as a magnet by its nature attracts iron,
and it has a violent craving for it, and enticing the other parts of my
10 body by a kind of irresistible pressure incessantly directs them to
steal. Be absolutely certain that it seems to me utterly impossible that
I should cease to steal. So it would be much more endurable and
pleasing that I should live in poverty as a beggar going from door to
door, or finally to die, rather than that I should injure the king's
15 majesty by such a wicked crime, if I was elevated to the supreme
position in the kingdom. The downfall of a distinguished person
always far, far exceeds the descent into vice of a more obscure person
in the degree of scandal involved.' Macduff answered him: 'This at
any rate is true that the higher the rank the more serious the fall.
20 Surely the higher anyone is elevated in the ranks of distinction, the
more he ought to excel in virtues; and the higher he climbs on the
pinnacle of virtues, the more disgrace there is for him if he falls into

seipsum et primo viciis involvit, et iterum humili populo prebet   20
exemplum delinquendi. Nam ut dicitur:

   Mobile mutatur semper cum principe vulgus.

Sed ut ad priora revertar. Hoc quod dicis, non furari, vel ut superius
dixeras non mechari, tibi videtur impossibile, cum lege divina quam
propria manu scripsit stare non potest. Scripsit vero: "Non mecha-   25
beris", "Non furtum facies", ergo credendum non est Deum nobis
impossibilia sub precepto pro*b* lege*c* servanda,*d* sed possibilia scrip-
sisse. Nam secundum apostolum: "Nemo temptatur supra id quod
potest sufferre," quia proculdubio vicia queque, sive virtutes, in
nostro libero constant arbitrio, sive spernenda sive fienda. Omnia   30
quippe divina precepta, sive bona faciendo, sive mala cavendo,
servare possumus, si competentem diligenciam ac voluntariam
adhibeamus. Ergo nec ista valens est, neque precedens excusacio,
quia furti facinus ex rerum provenit inopia, quis ignorat? At econtra
regia majestas semper habet esse locuplex, et omnimodis continue   35
diviciis, plena nichil*e* egens. Quis ergo sane mentis furari non desinet,
qui cunctis habundanter opibus gloriatur? Nichil umquam tibi rex
existens, non aurum, non argentum, non lapides preciosi, seu gemme,
deerunt, nec quicquid breviter cordi tuo placidum fuerit vel jocun-
G i,248   dum. Fortis igitur eris animo, regis | officium opulens arripere cures,   40
et execranda flagicia, fetentis luxurie videlicet et illud inops avaricie
crimen furtum inducens, procul abicere non recuses.'

b   *S*; sub *C*   *d*   *corrected from* servandata *C*
c   legeque *for* lege *CA,P*   *e*   + nigē *del.C*

5

Tercia temptacio Malcolmi

Malcolmus autem hac sequenti proposicione problematis intima
cordis amici sui Macduff nondum plene*a* probati rimari volens,
respondit: 'Grata quidem michi sunt et utilia que memoratis utrisque
tegendis viciis prebes antidota;*b* sed restat adhuc tercii facinoris
intactum vulnus, quod infidelitatis est, et doli latens in me nephas.   5
Fateor equidem occulte sum falsus, et dolose machinacionis commentor sive conjector*c* artifex, fidem paucis promissam servans, et

a   *CA*; pleni *C*   *c*   commentorum sive conjectorum *for*
b   *S,P*; antitoda *C*   commentor sive conjector *CA*

the abyss of vices. Likewise a prince who deviates from the path of
virtues does twofold wrong, because he first of all involves himself in
25 vices, and in the second place he affords an example of wrong-doing
to the lower classes. For, as it is said:

The fickle mob always changes with its leader.

But to return to our previous discussion. This statement of yours that
it seems impossible to you to avoid stealing or, as you said earlier, to
30 avoid committing adultery is a denial of the divine law, which [the
Divinity] wrote with his own hand. He wrote: "Thou shalt not
commit adultery. Thou shalt not steal." So we must not believe that
God wrote what was impossible for us in his commandment for
keeping his law, but what is possible. For according to the Apostle:
35 "No one is tempted beyond what he can endure", because undoubtedly all vices or virtues depend on our free will, whether we reject
them or practise them. We can indeed keep all the divine command-
ments whether for doing good or avoiding evil, if we apply sufficient,
whole-hearted diligence. So neither this nor your previous excuse is
40 valid. Who is not aware that the crime of theft arises from poverty?
But on the contrary the majesty of a king always involves being
wealthy and continually abounding in all kinds of riches, wanting for
nothing. Who therefore being of sound mind will not cease to steal,
when he glories abundantly in every kind of treasure? When you are
45 king, you will lack for nothing ever, not gold, not silver, not precious
stones nor jewels, nor in short whatever is pleasing or delightful to
your heart. So be brave-hearted, and see to it that you seize the rich
office of king, and make up your mind to throw far away the
abominable vices of stinking lechery and that contemptible sin of
50 avarice that leads to theft.'

5

Malcolm's third test

Malcolm felt that he had not yet fully proved his friend Macduff's
loyalty, and so, wishing to examine the very depths of his heart by
setting out the following difficulty, he replied: 'The antidotes that you
offer for concealing both types of vices that I have mentioned are
5 pleasing and useful to me, but there still remains untreated the wound
of a third vice which is that of faithlessness and the sin of fraudulence
which is lurking within me. I am, I confess, secretly false and a skilled
deviser or plotter of cunning machinations, keeping with few the
promises I have made, while falsely promising to all that I would
10 faithfully observe them. This is the unfailing wickedness innate in my

omnibus simulando promittens fideliter observandam. Mei quidem interioris animi continuum hoc inest scelus ut, si quandoque facultas suppetat, occulto pocius blande simulacionis officio quemquam 10 decipere mallem, quam in aperto dubiis fortune casibus causam committere terminandam. Et ideo sicut in precedentibus viciis, et in hoc eciam crimine michi subveniens, illud queso subtiliter aliquo tui sagacis ingenii velamine pallias; et quicquid tue proposicionis tenor exigerit, me totis offero viribus ad implendum.' Hoc vero cum 15 audisset Macduff supra modum attonitus est; et cum aliquanti temporis spacio tacuisset, suspirans ait: 'Ve nobis miseris, miserorum miserimis! Ve nobis, nobis, dico, qui^d saltem te sectari contendimus virum ineptum et inglorium, imbutum viciis, et omni virtute destitutum! Ve nobis, ut quid nati? Quam infelices dici possumus! 20 Quid infortunii nobis^e accidit! Nonne tricipiti sumus | adverso casu perplexi? Nam trium execrabilium malorum nos oportet admittere saltem unum. Aut videlicet, amissis liberis et uxoribus cunctisque temporalibus, perpetuum subire vagos exilium; aut regi servire tiranno, qui neque nobis neque reipublice jure principari^f debeat; cui 25 proprium et omni tiranno consuetum est, crudelem in populo dominacionem et insaciabilem avariciam exercere. Aut tibi de jure regi legio subdi, quod absit, cum proprie confessionis asserat tenor, indignum te regem esse vel principem aut primatem. Nam libidinosum et furem et, quod pejus est, ymmo facinorum omnium 30 vilissimum, fateris te falsum, subdolum et perfidum atque versutum deceptorem. Ecce quid aliud superesse videtur malicie genus quam nullatenus te proditorem appellas? Sed profecto sequitur, quia cuiuscumque cordis hec vicia condantur in intimis, non excidit, quin latens inibi prodicio socia reperiatur. Ergo quia tocius iniquitatis 35 succense faces^g in te conveniunt, et tuo siquidem adversario fervens inest et improba cupiditas, superbaque regnat et intolerabilis crudelitas, vestrum uter michi numquam dominabitur; exilium magis eligo sempiternum.' Et hiis dictis ulterius | se continere non valens, erumpentibus lacrimis genas ubertim rigabat; sed et pugnis immoder- 40 ato gemitu collisis, flens et ejulans, ac versus boream lamentando respiciens ait: 'Valeas, O Scocia, natale solum pro perpetuo!'

fo.90

G i,249

---

d   quia *CA*   f   *CA*; principare *C*
e   non *CA*   g   fata *CA*

innermost soul that, if the opportunity were to arise at any time, I
would rather deceive a person by the secret method of flattering
pretence than openly to commit my cause to be decided by the
doubtful chances of fortune. And on that account, just as in the
15 preceding vices, come to my aid in this fault also, and please delicately
draw over it some veil devised by your keen mind, and whatever the
purport of your proposal demands, I offer myself with all my
resources for its implementation.' When Macduff heard this, he was
thunderstruck beyond measure; and after remaining silent for some
20 time, he said with a sigh: 'Woe to us miserable creatures, most
miserable of the miserable! Woe to us, us I say, who strove at least to
follow you, a man worthless and inglorious, steeped in vices and
devoid of every virtue! Woe to us! Why were we born? How unhappy
can we be called! What misfortune has been our lot! Are we not
25 entangled in three-fold adversity? For of three abominable evils we
must accept at least one. Either we must lose our children and wives
and all our worldly possessions, and endure perpetual exile as
vagrants, or we must be subservient to a tyrant king who has no right
to rule over us or our country, whose special mark and custom, as
30 with all tyrants, is to exercise harsh domination and insatiable greed
over the people, or to be subject to you our lawful liege king, which
heaven forbid, since the purport of your own confession asserts that
you are unworthy to be king or prince or magnate. For you admit that
you are lecherous and a thief and, what is worse or rather the vilest of
35 all crimes, you admit that you are false, underhand and faithless, as
well as a cunning deceiver. Behold what other type of wickedness
remains except to call yourself an outright traitor? It assuredly
follows that when these vices lodge in the depths of a person's heart,
inevitably their ally treachery will be found lurking there also. So
40 since the kindled fires of total wickedness meet together in you, and
your adversary has consuming, monstrous greed innate within him,
while arrogant and intolerable cruelty reigns supreme, neither of you
will ever be my lord and master. I choose instead everlasting exile.'
And with these words he could not restrain himself any longer, and
45 his cheeks were drenched as his tears gushed out; but dashing his fists
together and groaning immensely, weeping and wailing and looking
sorrowfully towards the north, he said: 'Farewell, Scotland, my
native land, for ever!'

6

Quod Malcolmus de sua fidelitate confisus secum ad regnum redire promisit

Abiuntem[a] ilico Macduff, quoniam ipsum super omnia detestari
perfidiam ad plenum expertus, et effectus de fidelitate iam securus,
Malcolmus propere sequitur, et quod gressum Macduff sisteret,
secum habiturus colloquium rogat dicens: 'Amicorum omnium
gratissime, pre cunctis viventibus diligende, nichil actenus [certum 5
agnoscens][b] an fidus esses vel infidus, expavi ne tu, sicut aliquando
quidam perversi, quod non nescis, fictis ambagibus, sicut et illi quod
emulis traderer, michi reditum hortatus fueras. Idcirco te talibus
volui variis questionibus experiri. Et quia probatus odire nosceris doli
notam et prodicionis, superhabundancius habeo quam estimas, et 10
semper habebo, te fidelem. Non enim, laus Deo, luxuriosus sum aut
latro vel perfidus, sicut te probando talibus me finxi viciis deditum.
Absit hoc a me procul, ut michi validius quam ceteris hominum, hec
immunda vel hiis similia predominentur piacula, que viro sunt
cuilibet abhominanda. Eya! proinde, mi dilecte, ne formides. Non eris 15
a patria vel liberis exul, ymmo post regem primus in regno.
Confortare deinceps, sisque robustus. Tu me reduces in terram
meam, terram quam nobis dedit Dominus et patribus nostris
excolendam.' Hoc autem audiens, [Makduff][c] pronus in terra corruit,
et velut ante merendo lugubris singultibus pre angustia, pre nimio iam 20
exultans gaudio, totus in lacrimis suffusus, suos amplexando pedes
osculatus est, dicens: 'Si quidem hec vera sunt que loqueris, ad vitam
de morte me reducis. Festina, domine, festina, deprecor, ne tardaver-
is, et libera populum tuum te super omnia desiderantem.'

> Si servare velis insontes quosque fideles, 25
>   actenus expertes omnibus auxiliis,
> illis, quos pressit hostis iam per tria lustra,
>   subvenias[d] miseris mitis amore Dei.
> Non super hiis studeas segnis, sed impiger hostem
>   prosternas, populum alleviando pium. 30
> Ense tuum femur cingatur et arma capesce;
>   corporis omnis habes forcia membra, liquet.

---

a   G; Abeuntem S; Abinvicem C   c   CA
b   P   d   S; subveniens C

6

*Malcolm, reassured about Macduff's loyalty, promised to
return to the kingdom*

Instantly, as Macduff was going away, Malcolm hurried after him,
since he had proved to the full that Macduff loathed treachery above
all else, and he was now certain of his loyalty. He asked Macduff to
stop so that he could speak to him, saying: 'Dearest of all my friends,
5   deserving to be loved beyond all living creatures, since I was unsure
up to this point whether you were loyal or disloyal, I was afraid that
you, like certain evil men from time to time, as you are aware, had
urged my return with ambivalent lies as they did, in order that I might
be handed over to my enemies. Therefore I wished to examine you
10 with these various tests, and because you have passed the test, and are
known to hate the ignominy attached to deceit and treachery, I
consider, and always will consider more superabundantly than you
imagine, that you are loyal. I am not, praise be to God, loose-living or
a robber or treacherous. I only pretended that I was given over to such
15 vices in order to put you to the test. Far be it from me that these or
similar foul sins which are abominated by all men should hold a
greater sway over me than over the rest of humanity. Come then, my
dear friend, be no longer afraid. You will not be an exile from your
country or your children, but rather the first in the kingdom after the
20 king. From now on take courage, and be strong. You will take me
back to my own country, the country which the Lord has given to us
and our forefathers to inhabit.' On hearing this Macduff fell on his
face on the ground, and just as before in grieving and sobbing
mournfully from distress, now exultant with exceeding joy, he was
25 totally bathed in tears. He clasped and kissed Malcolm's feet, saying:
'If what you say is indeed true, you restore me from death to life.
Hurry, lord, hurry, I implore, do not delay and set free your people
that long for you above all else.'

         If you wish to save all the innocent and faithful,
30   hitherto lacking any assistance at all, for love of God
         kindly come to the aid of those wretched people,
         hard pressed by the enemy throughout fifteen years.
         Do not ponder this at leisure, but vigorously
         overthrow the enemy, and relieve your loyal people.
35   Gird your sword on your thigh, and take up arms.
         You have strong limbs in all your frame, it is clear.

Scotus et es genitus priscorum cespite regum;
prospere procedens regna patris subies.
Regni, promitto, pocieris jure corona;   35
omnia jura tibi, nulla debentur ei. |

Audax jure tuo sis semper bella parare,
non tamen incaute bella sumenda putes.
Nec preceps certes nisi sors dictaverit umquam;
ex improviso fallitur omnis homo.   40
Es pugnaturus, campum non preparet*e* hostis,
ad loca bellandi semper adesto prior.

e   *corrected from* preparat C

7

De regressu Malcolmi in Scociam et bello quo cecidit
Machabeda

Finitis enim talibus problematum examinacionibus, ac omni dubita-
cionis ambiguitate remota, nunciare clanculo suis amicis ipsum
MacDuff Malcolmus Scociam remisit, ut caute se preparent, suum*a*
absque dubio sperantes reditum infra breve. Ipse vero postquam
[Macduff]*b* recesserat, regis Eadwardi quantocius adiit presenciam, 5
ab eo humiliter postulans quosdam ex Anglie proceribus, qui gratis
secum in Scociam regnum recipere proficisci volebant, ex favore
permittere dignaretur. Cuius peticioni continuo rex mitis annuens,
liberam cuilibet volenti facultatem tribuit. Insuper et seipsum cum
exercitus potencia, si necesse fuerit, ferre presidium graciose com- 10
promisit. Unde sancto mitissimoque regi, qui cunctis misericors
consultus aut injuste tribulatis pronus adjutor extitit, immensas
referens gracias ab eo recessit; et quamprimum paratus, procerum
Anglie solo Siwardo Northumbrensium comite secum assumpto,
Scociam proficiscitur possessurus. Neque vero regni fines adhuc 15
attigerat, dum, sparso rumore per precedentem MacDuff, minus
caute negocii consilia servantem, totum audierat regni populum
dissencione commotum, ac in partes inter MacKabedam et Makduff
divisum. Quamobrem Malcolmus cum sua milicia celerius properans
non*c* quievit donec, hinc inde junctis agminibus, fortem exercitum 20

a   S.P; dubium C   c   +quivit *del.*C
b   P

You are a Scot, and are sprung from a line of ancient kings.
In triumphant progress you will approach your father's
    kingdom.
40   You will gain the crown of the kingdom by right, I promise.
All rights are due to you, not to him.
Be always ready to do battle, confident in your right.
Do not however suppose that battles are to be undertaken
    rashly.
45   Never rush into a fight, unless chance dictates it.
The unexpected is a snare for all.
When you are about to fight, do not let the enemy forestall
    you on the field.
Always arrive first at the site for the battle.

7

The return of Malcolm to Scotland and the battle in which Macbeth was slain

Once the investigations into these dilemmas were completed, and all
doubts and ambiguity removed, Malcolm sent Macduff back to
Scotland secretly to tell his friends to make their preparations
stealthily in expectation of Malcolm's definite return shortly. After
5 Macduff had departed, Malcolm went into the presence of King
Edward at the earliest opportunity, humbly petitioning him that he
would graciously deign to permit certain of the nobles of England,
who were willing of their own accord to set out with him for Scotland
to win back his kingdom. The king kindly gave his immediate assent
10 to his request and granted full licence to anyone who wished.
Moreover he graciously promised that he himself would come to his
aid with his military might, if it were necessary. Then Malcolm
withdrew from his presence, expressing his boundless gratitude to the
saintly and kind-hearted king who was merciful to all who consulted
15 him, and ready to help those who were unjustly afflicted. As soon as
he was ready, Malcolm set out to win Scotland for himself, taking [1054]
with him as his companion Siward earl of Northumbria alone of all
the English nobles. He had not yet crossed the border of the kingdom,
when he heard that the whole population of the kingdom was in
20 turmoil, and divided into factions between Macbeth and Macduff.
Macduff as he was going ahead had spread the news [of his coming],
rashly failing to keep to the agreed procedure. So Malcolm with his
soldiers increased his speed, and did not rest until he had assembled a
strong army with contingents joining in from all sides. Many of those

confecisset. Ex hiis autem multi qui Machabedam prius sequebantur
ab eo statim deficientes, Malcholmo totis viribus adheserunt. Cotidie
deinceps suum minui robur, eius quidem augeri cernens, partibus
subito relictis australibus, boreales peciit, ubi terrarum angustis
amfractibus et silvarum abditis tucius sperabat se tueri. Insperate 25
tamen festino gressu Malcolmus ipsum ultra montes et usque
Lunfanan insequitur, ac ibidem repente levi bello transceptum, cum
paucis resistentibus interfecit anno domini m° lvi^{to} mense decembri
die quinto. Omnis enim populus ab eo bellandum productus
Malcolmum non ignorabat verum sibi dominum; ideo resistere sibi 30
bello renuens, primo lituorum strepitu campum reliquid fugiendo.
Willelmus de predicto bello sic scribens ait: 'Siwardus Northumbrie
comes jussu regis Eadwardi cum Scotorum rege Machabeo congres-
sus, vita regnoque^{d} spoliavit. Ibidemque Malcolmum filium regis
Cumbrorum regem instituit.'^{e} Ecce quomodo Willelmus, nullam 35
Malcolmo victorie laudem ascribens, Siwardo totum attribuit, cum in

G i,251

veritate solus ille cum suis et | vexilligero, tocius victorie causa fuit.
Hoc utique sperandum est, quod populus Machebedicus, absente
Malcolmo, de bello non fugisset, eciam si cum Suardo rex Eadwardus
cum suis presens affuisset. 40

Scriptor

Ecce eciam^{f} quomodo, ymmo quodammodo, innatum est Anglicis
queque^{g} per Scotos laudabilius congesta parcissime cum oporteat
collaudare. Vereor ne admodum invidorum Anglorum historici
fataliter infatuentur, quibus aliena prosperitas adversa, aliena^{h}
adversitas, prospera judicatur. Hii in aliena gratulacione tristantur, in 45
aliena tristicia gratulantur. Constat ex hoc quod cum aliquid
discripturi sint de Scotorum fame serenitate, aut hanc eleganti stilo
obnubilare conantur, aut ipsorum gloriam sola taciturnitate furari.
Cum enim altercacio olim fiebat de observacione Pasche inter Sanctos
Columbanum (allegantem pro se magistrum suum Sanctum Colum- 50
bam) et Wilfridum, sic recitat Beda Wilfridum respondisse: 'Si
sanctus vester Columba, ymmo et noster si sanctus est, c'.' De
huiusmodi invehit Alanus, De Conquestione Nature, dicens: 'Probitatis gloriam degloriat livor inglorius.'

d	vita regnoque *P*; vitaque regno *C*	g	*C,CA*; quoque *D*
e	+Hec ille. *CA*	h	+adversa pros *del.C*
f	*interlin.C; om.P*		

25 who had previously followed Macbeth, immediately defected from
him, and went over to Malcolm with all their strength. Thereafter
Macbeth, perceiving that his might was diminishing daily, while
Malcolm's was increasing, suddenly left the southern regions and
made for the north, where he thought he could defend himself more
30 securely in the narrow defiles and hidden depths of the forests.
However Malcolm by a quick march unexpectedly pursued him over
the mountains and as far as Lumphanan, and there suddenly
intercepted him in a light skirmish, and killed him along with the few
who resisted on 5 December 1056. For all the people that Macbeth led   [1057:
35 out to battle knew full well that Malcolm was their true lord; therefore 15 Aug.]
they refused to fight a battle against him, and fled away and deserted
the field of battle at the first sound of trumpets. William [of
Malmesbury] writing as follows about the aforesaid battle says:
'Siward earl of Northumbria joined battle with Macbeth king of Scots
40 by order of King Edward, and deprived him of his life and his
kingdom. And he installed Malcolm son of the king of the Cumbrians
as king in that same place.' See how William ascribes everything to
Siward, depriving Malcolm of all glory in the victory, when in actual
fact Malcolm alone with his own men and standard-bearer was
45 responsible for the whole victory. This at any rate we must suppose,
that Macbeth's people would not have fled from the battle, if
Malcolm had not been there, even if King Edward had been present
with his forces along with Siward.
See also how, or rather, it is somehow instinctive with the English
50 to be very sparing with their praises, when they ought to praise
warmly some laudable achievements of the Scots. I am afraid that the
historians of the all-too envious English are fatally infatuated in
considering another nation's success as an adversity, and another's
adversity as a success. They are sad when others rejoice, they rejoice
55 when others are sad. It follows from this that when they are about to
give a description of some brilliant Scottish exploit, they either try to
obscure it with their exquisite style of writing or steal the Scots' glory
merely by passing over it in silence. For once when a dispute arose
about the observation of Easter between St Colman (referring to St
60 Columba as support for his views) and St Wilfrid, Bede relates that
Wilfrid replied as follows: 'If your St Columba or rather if our St
Columba etc.' Alan of Lille, *The Complaint of Nature*, inveighs
against this sort of thing saying: 'Inglorious envy robs honourable
glory of its glory.'

8

Excusatur populus cuiuscumque regni ab injusto rege bello
fugiens

Autor

fo.91

Populus enim iste fidelis excusari[a] de fuga poterit, qui, diu sub
tirannide pressus, surgere non valens aut non audens, assidue tamen
sui regis in corde crudelem animadvertit mortem, | heredis eciam
injustum tanti temporis exterminium; anxiam itaque sub viro
contribule propriam subjeccionem amplius subesse dedignans, occa-   5
sione sumpta locum illi fugiendo dedit regnum indubie recipiendi.
Videtur enim, et verum est, ut estimo, quod regni cuiuslibet populus
indigena fidelis, amoto vi capite suo videlicet rege, vel quodlibet
opprobrium paciente, cum eo nimirum compatitur, et quasi proprium gemendo suum improperium lamentatur; cum proverbio   10
dicatur: 'Cuius caput dolet, cetera membra languent.' Et hoc verum
est, membra[b] sana, que capitis compaciuntur dolori, non putrida sive
cancerosa, que capitis sui[c] dolentis langorem non senciunt. Talium
enim membrorum ex tactu sepe contigit, ut quedam membra morbum
incurabilem incidant, et adeo quandoque tali morbo caput ex eis   15
eciam inficitur, unde totum corpus effici poterit monstruosum.
Nonne corpus quodcumque merito monstrum dici poterit, cuius pes,
infimum dico membrum, igneo morbo corruptum, nec tempestive per
manus artificum[d] cauterio sedatum, digniora transgrediens membra,
veneno sui caput inficiens evellat, ac supra collum et humeros se loco   20
capitis contra naturam collocaverit? Eodem vero tempore belli de
Lunfanan et anno rex Wallie Griffinus comitem Herfordie Radulphum e bello fugavit, et occisis eiusdem urbis episcopo Levogaro[e]
necnon Egelnotho vicecomite cum multis aliis urbem totumque
comitatum ignibus cum episcopo pio concremavit. Hoc statim   25
Siwardus, postquam a suo rege per certum audierat nuncium,
confestim jussus domi rediit, nequaquam | ulterius Malcolmo ferre
presidium rediturus. Subito namque post mortem Machabede
convenerunt quidam ex eius parentela sceleris huiusmodi fautores,
suum consobrinum nomine Lulach cognomine[f] fatuum ad Sconam   30
ducentes, et impositum sede regali, regem constituunt. Sperabant
enim sibi quasi regi populum obedire libenter. Nullus tamen illi

G i,252

a	D,CA; exiusari C,R	d	CA; artificium C
b	+ videlicet CA	e	Levegaro D
c	corrected from sue C	f	ignomine CA

8

The people of any kingdom who flee from an unlawful king in battle are absolved from blame

That loyal people cannot be blamed for their flight, since they were oppressed under a tyrannous regime, neither able nor daring to rise in revolt, but always brooding over the cruel death of their king in their hearts and the unjust banishment of his heir over such a long period of
5 time. And so refusing to submit any longer to their distressful subjection under a man of no higher rank than themselves, they seized the opportunity, and by their flight gave [Malcolm] the chance of definitely recovering the kingdom. For it seems, and it is true in my opinion, that the loyal indigenous people of any kingdom, when its
10 head, that is its king, has been forcibly removed, or has suffered any kind of insult, certainly suffers along with him, and mourns for the taunt he has suffered, as if they were lamenting a reproach to themselves, since it says in the proverb: 'If the head aches, the rest of the body is sick.' And this is true of a healthy body which suffers along
15 with the headache, not of decayed or cancerous bodies which do not feel the sickness of their aching head. For it often happens from contact with such diseased parts of the body that certain parts fall into incurable diseases, and sometimes their head is also infected by them with this kind of disease to such an extent that the whole body can be
20 rendered monstrous. Surely any body whatsoever can rightly be called a monstrosity, whose foot, that is its lowest part, wasted away by a feverish illness that has not been assuaged in good time with cautery at the hands of physicians, invades worthier parts, and infecting its head with poison removes it, placing itself upon the neck
25 and shoulders in place of the head contrary to nature? At the same time and year of the battle of Lumphanan the Welsh king Gruffydd turned Radulf the earl of Hereford to flight in battle, killed Leofgar [1055-6] the bishop of the same city and the sheriff Ælfnoth along with many others, and burnt down the city and shire along with the holy bishop.
30 As soon as Siward heard about this from his king through a reliable messenger, he immediately hurried back home, as he was ordered, never again destined to come back to give aid to Malcolm. Immediately after the death of Macbeth certain members of his [1057: Aug.] family who were in favour of this kind of crime took his kinsman
35 Lulach by name, the Idiot by nickname, to Scone, placed him on the royal throne and made him king. For they expected that the people

parere volebat, aut aliquibus factis vel fiendis communicare. Audiens autem hoc Malcolmus suos comites ipsum huc illucque persequendum emisit; sed in irritum quatuor^g mensibus suos deducunt conatus, 35 donec in superioribus partibus scrutantes, inventum loco qui dicitur Essy provincie Strathbolgy cum suis sequacibus occidunt; vel, ut quidam tradunt, ibidem casu Malcolmus obvium habens interfecit, anno domini m^{mo} lvii° tercia die mensis aprilis ebdomada Pasche feria

Scriptor   quinta. | De hiis duobus intrusis regibus habentur hii versus: 40

Ter senis annis Scociam rexit Machabeda
in cuius regno fertile tempus erat.
Hunc in Lunfanan truncavit morte crudeli
Duncani natus nomine Malcolmus.

Mensibus infelix Lulach tribus extiterat rex,   45
armis eiusdem Malcolmi cecidit.
Fata viri fuerunt in Strathbolgin apud Esseg,
quo sic incaute rex miser occubuit.

Hos in pace viros tenet insula Iona sepultos
in tumulo regum Judicis usque Diem.   50

g   + vix *CA*

9

De successione Malcolmi in regnum et aliis incidentibus^a

Autor   Prostratis ubique cunctis hostibus vel ad suam deductis pacem, idem sepe dictus Malcolmus apud Sconam, presentibus regni majoribus, in trono regali positus est,^{b} et in omnium Scotorum gloriam et honorem eodem aprili mense die Sancti Marci coronatus, ac eodem videlicet anno domini m° lvii° et imperatoris Henrici iiii^{ti} (sive ut predixi tercii) 5

Scriptor   anno primo, qui Henricus imperavit annis ferme l. | ⟨Malcolmi igitur regno pacato, pro^c retribucione sua thanus de Fife tria peciit pro se et dominis sive thanis de Fife suis successoribus, videlicet quod regem locaret in sede tempore^d sue coronacionis; et quod in omni exercitu bellico regis, ubi oppansum foret eius vexillum, vangardiam guber- 10 naret; quod eciam ipse et omnes in posterum de sua cognacione, pro subitanea et improvisa occisione, gauderent privilegio legis Macduf, ubi generosus occidens solvendo xxiiii marcas ad kinbot, et vernaculus xii marcas remissionem plenariam exinde reportarent.^{e}⟩

a   aliis incidentibus *interlin.over* eius pugna
     cum quodam proditore *del.C*
b   regaliter coronatur *for* positus est *CA*
c   + fidelis servicii *CA*

d   sive cathedra regali die *for* tempore *CA*
e   plenariam exinde reportarent *CA*;
     consequentur *C*

would gladly obey him as their king. No one however wished to obey
him or to have any part in what they had done or were going to do.
When Malcolm heard this, he sent out his thanes in all directions to
40 track him down, but for four months their efforts were expended in
vain, until as they were searching in the higher regions, he was found
in a place which is called Essie in the district of Strathbogie, and they
killed him along with his followers, or as some report, Malcolm came
upon him by accident in the same place and killed him in 1057 on 3
45 April on Thursday in Easter Week. The following verses are about the   [1058:
two intruded kings: 17 Mar.]

> For eighteen years Macbeth ruled.
> In his reign it was a time of fertility.
> Duncan's son Malcolm by name
50 killed him at Lumphanan by a cruel death.

> The luckless Lulach was king for three months.
> He was slain by the sword of the same Malcolm.
> The man met his fate in Essie in Strathbogie
> where the unhappy king was thus rashly slain.

55 The island of Iona possesses these men buried in peace
> in the tomb of the kings till the day of the Judge.

9

The succession of Malcolm to the kingdom and other events

Having overthrown or brought into his peace all his enemies
everywhere, the oft mentioned Malcolm was set on the royal throne at
Scone in the presence of the magnates of the kingdom, and he was
crowned to the glory and honour of all Scots in the same month of
5 April on St Mark's day in the same year 1057, the first year of the reign   [1058]
of the emperor Henry IV (or as I said before of Henry III). This Henry   25 Apr.
reigned for almost fifty years. So now that the kingdom of Malcolm
was at peace, the thane of Fife made three requests as his reward for
himself and his successors as lords or thanes of Fife, namely that he
10 should place the king on his throne at the time of his coronation, and
that in all the king's campaigns when his banner was unfurled he
should command the vanguard, and also that he himself and all his
kinsmen in future should enjoy the privilege of the Macduff law in the
case of unpremeditated and involuntary killing, by which a nobleman
15 who killed would obtain full remission thereafter on payment of
twenty-four marks as 'kinbot', and in the case of a yeoman on
payment of twelve marks.
    At that time there was famine and plague in the whole earth. In the

G i, 253;
Scriptor

Tunc temporis fames et mortalitas fuerunt in universa terra. Huius 15
tempore quidam potens, dum sederet in convivio, repente a muribus
circumvallatus est; et cum esset innumerabilis multitudo murium, et
multi convive, de nullo captabant nisi de illo; sed cum a suis in pelago
maris deductus esset, nil ei profuit, quia mures navim sequentes ipsam
usque ad aque introitum corrodebant. In terram igitur positus, a 20
muribus totus dilaceratus est et comestus. Idem dicitur cuidam
principi Appollonie contigisse. Et hoc minus mirum judicatur, quia
pro certo dicitur quod in quibusdam terris, si leopardus aliquem
momorderit, confestim murium copiam advenire, ut vulneratum
commingant; immundum urine diluvium hominis exitium^f comitari. 25
Tempore namque Machabede magna fertilitas erat in Scocia, qui

fo.91v

anno domini m° l Rome argentum spargendo | pauperibus distribuit.

Anno domini m^mo xxvi^to obiit Richardus secundus dux Normannorum, cui successit Richardus iii eodem anno defunctus. Cui
successit Robertus frater eius,^g pater Willelmi Bastard. Ut sciatis quot 30
fuerunt duces ante Willelmum, et a quo originem habuerunt, patet
per metra:

Hic Normannorum sequitur generacio, quorum
Rollo dux primus genitus de stirpe Dacorum,
ex Dacia sumpsit nomina Rollodanus.   35
Rollo Willelmum, Wil. Richard, Rique Richardum,
Richard Robertum, Robertus Wil. genuit Bast.^h

Et quia fuerunt nisi tres reges de stirpe Danica (Cnutus scilicet
Hardknutus et Haraldus) paulisper hic de eis loquendum est; sed
postea in loco suo de eisdem immorandum. Anno m° xvii Knutus 40
filius Suani tocius Anglie suscepit imperium, et duxit in uxorem
Emmam filiam Richardi ducis Normannorum, que prius erat uxor
Ethelredi regis; ex qua Hardeknutum postea Danorum et Anglorum
regem et Guinildam filiam genuit, que nupsit postea Henrico
Romanorum imperatori.^i Anno m° xxviii° rex Knutus^j Noreganos, 45
Olavum regem suum propter eius sanctitatem spernentes, multa auri
et argenti copia cecatos corrupit, et l magnis navibus Norwegiam
devectus, Olavum de illa expulit, sibique eam subjugavit; et anno
sequenti idem Knutus Anglorum Danorum et Noreganorum rex
Angliam rediit. Anno quoque sequenti Sanctus iste Olavus rex et 50
martyr, Haroldi regis Noriganorum filius, quem Knutus expulerat, in
Noraga perimitur a suis. Et anno sequenti Knutus magno cum
honore Romam profectus, ingencia munera Sancto Petro in auro et
argento optulit, et ut scola Anglorum libera esset a Johanne papa
impetravit.   55

f   CA; excitium C
g   +ut sci del.C
h   +Tres juxta cronicas fuerunt
    Normannorum Richardi, sed quia tercius
    modicum dux supervixit ideo metrista de

                                    eo reticuit del.C
i   +Anno sequenti in Nativitate Domini
    rex Knutus perfidum Edericum del.C;
    om.R; in text and underlined D
j   +Or del.C

time of Malcolm a certain potentate while sitting at dinner was
20 suddenly surrounded by mice, and although there was a vast crowd of
mice and many diners, they went after no one but him. And when he
was taken out to the open sea by his servants, it did him no good,
because the mice followed the ship, and gnawed away at it until the
water began to come in. So he was put ashore, and was completely
25 torn apart and eaten up by the mice. The same thing is said to have
happened to the prince of Apollonia. This is considered to be less
amazing because we have it on good authority that in certain lands if a
leopard has got its teeth into anyone, a large number of mice hurry to
the spot in order to urinate on the wounded man; a foul flood of urine
30 accompanies the man's death. In the time of Macbeth there was great
fertility in Scotland. In 1050 he distributed money which he scattered   1050
among the poor in Rome.

In 1026 Richard II duke of the Normans died, and he was   1026
succeeded by Richard III who died in the same year. He was   [1028]
35 succeeded by his brother Robert the father of William the Bastard. So
that you may know how many dukes there were before William, and
from whom they took their origin, it is revealed in verse:

Here follows the generation of the Normans, of whom
Rollo was the first duke, sprung from Danish stock.
40   From Denmark he took the name Rollodane.
Rollo was the father of William, William of Richard,
Richard of Richard.
Richard was the father of Robert, Robert was the
father of William the Bastard.

45 And because there were only three kings of Danish stock, that is Cnut,
Harthacnut and Harold, we must mention them only briefly at this
point, but we will devote more time to them later at the appropriate
place. In 1017 Cnut the son of Swein established his rule over the   1017
whole of England, and married Emma the daughter of Richard duke
50 of Normandy, who was previously the wife of King Æthelred. They
were the parents of Harthacnut, later king of the Danes and the
English, and a daughter Gunhild, who later married Henry the
emperor of the Romans. In 1028 Cnut dazzled and bribed with a great   [1028-9]
abundance of gold and silver the Norwegians who spurned their own
55 king Olaf because of his saintliness. Cnut sailed to Norway with fifty
war galleys, expelled Olaf from that country and made it subject to
himself; and in the following year the same Cnut returned to England
king of the English, the Danes and Norwegians. In the following year   [1030]
also that St Olaf king and martyr the son of Harold king of the
60 Norwegians, who had been expelled by Cnut, was killed in Norway by
his own people. And in the following year Cnut set out for Rome with   [1027]
great honour, and made huge offerings in gold and silver to St Peter,
and obtained his request from Pope John that the English school
should be exempt from taxation.

10

De eodem Knuto et aliis incidentibus

Parcat scribe et scriptori lector, quod usquequaque secundum seriem
annorum non*a* omnia intitulantur, quia propter intricabiles digres-
siones et variarum historiarum prolixitates, et earum sparsim |

G i,254   collectiones et memorie labilitates, ⟨omnia non occurrunt ordine
situanda;⟩ nam ut ait Seneca: 'Omnia fluunt, et in assidua diminu- 5
cione labitur humana memoria, ad congerendum varia quorum
subjecta fluida sunt et caduca.' Hec ille. Anno domini m° xxxii ecclesia
Sancti Eadmundi regis et martyris dedicata est, in qua rex Knutus,
communi consilio presulum et optimatum suorum, ejectis presbyteris
secularibus, monachos imposuit. Ignis pene inextinguibilis multa per 10
Angliam loca concremavit. Anno m° xxxv Knutus rex ante obitum
suum super Noreganos Suanum filium suum instituit regem, super
Danos Hardeknutum et Emme filium Haroldum*b* super Anglos
locavit. Postea ii idus novembris apud Scateberiam vita decessit, et
Wintonie in veteri monasterio tumulatur. Non multo post tamen 15
regnum Anglie inter Haraldum et Hardknutum dividitur. Robertus
dux Normannorum obiit; cui successit filius eius Willelmus Bastard
puer. Anno m° 36 innocentes clitones Alveredus et Eadwardus regis
Ethelredi filii, ad colloquium matris sue a Richardo avunculo suo
venerunt. Quorum socios comes Godwinus quosdam cathenavit et 20
postea cecavit; nonnullos, cute capitis abstracta, cruciavit et manibus
et pedibus amputatis mulctavit; multos eciam venundari fecit, et
mortibus variis ac*c* miserabilibus apud Geldifordiam sexcentos viros
occidit. Alveredi vero oculos insidiis intercepti jussit erui apud Hely,
ibique non multo post mortuus est. Eadwardus vero rediit in 25
Normannia cum festinacione. Anno sequenti Haroldus rex Merciorum et Northumbrorum, ut per totam Angliam regnaret, a
principibus et populo, spreto fratre suo Hardeknuto, quia nimium in
Denemarchia morabatur, eligitur. Emma quondam regina immiseri-
corditer ab Anglia expulsa, ab Aldwino Flandrensium comite 30

fo.92   honorifice suscipitur. Anno m° xxxix° iemps extitit asperima, | et
Hardeknutus rex Danorum Flandriam devectus, ad matrem suam
Emmam venit. Anno m° xl° obiit Haroldus rex Londoniis et in
Westmonasterio sepelitur; et Hardeknutus in regem elevatur. Quem

---

a   *interlin.C*   *c*   + ms [?] *del.C*
b   *del., with* Eadwardum *in margin C*

10

More about Cnut and other events

The reader must show indulgence to the author and writer for the fact
that all events are not always recorded year by year, since not
everything that happens can be arranged in chronological order
because of complicated digressions, the great length of various
5 histories, having to gather them together from scattered sources and
the waywardness of memory, for as Seneca says: 'Everything is in a
state of flux, and human memory fails and becomes ever feebler for
gathering together a variety of items whose foundations are unstable
and liable to fall.' In 1032 the church of St Edmund king and martyr   1032
10 was dedicated. By the common counsel of his prelates and nobles
King Cnut placed monks in it, after expelling the secular priests.
Many places in England were burnt down in a fire that was almost
impossible to put out. Before his death in 1035 King Cnut appointed   1035
his son Swein as king over the Norwegians, placed Harthacnut over
15 the Danes and Emma's son Harold over the English. Later in the year
on 12 November he died at Shaftesbury, and was buried at the Old   12 Nov.
Minster in Winchester. However not long afterwards the kingdom of
England was divided between Harold and Harthacnut. Robert duke
of Normandy died, and his son William the Bastard succeeded him
20 while still a boy. In 1036 the innocent Æthelings Alfred and Edward   1036
sons of King Æthelred came from their Uncle Richard to converse
with their mother. Certain of their companions were thrown into
chains by Earl Godwine, and later had their eyes put out; some he
scalped and crucified, and [some] he punished by amputating their
25 hands and feet; he also caused many of them to be sold [as slaves], and
he killed six hundred men at Guildford by various wretched deaths.
He ordered Alfred's eyes to be gouged out at Ely, after he had been
caught in an ambush, and he died there soon afterwards. Edward
hastily returned to Normandy. In the following year Harold king of
30 the Mercians and Northumbrians was chosen to rule over the whole
of England by the nobles and people, since his brother Harthacnut
had fallen out of favour because he was spending too much time in
Denmark. Ex-Queen Emma who had been mercilessly expelled from
England was honourably received by Baldwin count of Flanders. In   [1037]
35 1039 there was a very severe winter, and Harthacnut king of the
Danes travelled to Flanders, and came to his mother Emma. In 1040   1040
King Harold died in London, and was buried at Westminster; and

Godwinus multis donariis, et per jusjurandum sui et multorum 35
aliorum nobilium, regem sibi pacificavit. Anno sequenti Eadwardus
Ethelredi^d quondam regis Anglorum filius de Normannia, ubi multis
exulaverat annis, venit Angliam; et a fratre suo Hardeknuto rege
honorifice susceptus, in curia eius mansit.

Anno m° xliii° mortuo Hardeknuto, Eadwardus in regem sublima- 40
tur. Anno m° xlvii Magnus Noreganorum rex Sancti Olavi filius,
fugato Swano, Danemarchiam sibi subegit, et in illa regnavit; at non
multo post obiit, et anno sequenti Swanus Danemarchiam recepit, et
Haroldus Harfahger Siwardi regis Noreganorum filius, et ex parte
matris frater Sancti Olavi, patruus scilicet Magni regis, Noregiam 45
repeciit, et per suos nuncios pacem cum rege Anglorum fecit. Anno
m° l tempore regis Scocie Makbede, rex Eadwardus absolvit Anglos a
gravi vectigali xxx^m librarum, xxx° et viii° anno ex quo pater suus rex
Ethelredus primitus Danicis id solidariis solvi mandarat. Quo in
tempore orta est magna sedicio inter regem et comitem Godwinum, 50
pro eo quod tradere noluit morti sororium suum comitem Bononien-
sem, cuius milites, stolide hospicia querentes apud Dover ubi
applicaverat plures e civibus peremerunt. Qui et ipse ad castrum |

G i,255 Dover cum suis confugerat. Tandem Godwinum cum rege^e placitare
volentem, postquam bis super regem exercitum duxerat, et secundo 55
dilapsus fuerat ab eo, super fugientem diem constitutum cum quinque
filiis rex exlegavit. Rex Eadwardus Willelmum Bastard comitem
Normannie, ad se in Anglia venientem, magno cum honore suscepit,
et multis donatum muneribus ad propria remisit. Hec breviter
perstrinximus, ut sciat lector quanti et quot annis, non solum 60
Normanni usque Willelmum Bastard, sed et eciam Dani, regnum
Anglie tenuerunt. De quibus datis habentur hec metra:

> Quomodo nunc cura, Dacorum fit genitura.
> Non fuerant nisi tres Anglorum regna tenentes;
> Knowt Harald Harphaw genuit de pelice; sed Knwt 65
> ex Emma Knwt Hard. cui frater tercius Edward.
> Natus Godwini comitis fuit ultimus Harald.

d D; Etheredi C   *e* +cum rege del.C

Harthacnut was made king. Godwine made his peace with him by
means of many gifts and by oaths sworn by himself and many of the
40 other nobles. In the following year Edward son of Æthelred a former
king of the English came to England from Normandy where he had
lived in exile for many years; and he was honourably received by his
brother Harthacnut, and remained at his court.

Harthacnut died in 1043, and Edward was raised to the kingship. In   [1042]
45 1047 Magnus king of the Norwegians and the son of St Olaf put Swein   1047
to flight, imposed his rule on Denmark, and reigned there; but he died
soon after, and in the following year Swein recovered Denmark, and
Harold Hardrada the son of Sigurd king of the Norwegians and a
stepbrother of St Olaf on their mother's side and so an uncle of King
50 Magnus regained Norway, and made peace with the king of the
English through his envoys. In 1050 at the time when Macbeth was   [1051]
king of Scotland King Edward ceased to exact the heavy tax of thirty
thousand pounds from the English in the thirty-eighth year after his
father King Æthelred had first ordered it to be paid to the Danish
55 soldiers. At this time there arose a great conflict between the king and
Earl Godwine, because [the king] refused to hand over for execution
his brother-in-law the count of Boulogne, whose soldiers had killed a
number of citizens, as they were rudely demanding quarters in Dover,
where the count had landed.The count himself had taken refuge in
60 Dover castle along with his men. At last after Godwine had twice led
an army against the king, and for the second time had slipped through
the king's hands, the king set a time limit for the fugitive, and then
outlawed Godwine along with his five sons, although Godwine
wished to plead before the king. King Edward received William the   [1051-2]
65 Bastard count of Normandy with great honour when he came to him
in England. He presented him with many gifts and sent him back
home. We have given a brief summary of these events so that the
reader may know how many and for how long not only Normans up
to the time of William the Bastard, but also Danes held the kingdom
70 of England. The following lines of verse are concerned with these
matters:

The generation of Danes was as follows.
There were only three who held the kingdom of England.
Cnut was the father of Harold Harefoot by a prostitute,
75   but the father of Harthacnut by Emma; his brother Edward
was the third.
Harold son of Godwine was the last.

11

Autor

De quadam pugna regis Malcolmi
cum quodam milite proditore

Erat enim rex Malcolmus satis humilis, corde fortis et animo, corporis
viribus prepotens et audax, non temerarius sed maturus, ac multis
aliis dotatus virtutibus, ut in sequentibus apparebit. Primis regni sui
novem annis, Eadwardo rege vivente, firmam pacem Anglis et
communionem et usque adventum Willelmi Bastard observabat. 5
Anno dicti regis Eadwardi xiii° fratris sui filius regis quondam
Eadmundi Irneside, cui nomen Eadwardus, ex Hungaria venit in
Angliam uxorem secum ducens Agathen, Eadgarum filium*a* et duas
filias Margaritam postea Scotorum reginam et Christianam sanctimonialem, quem rex patruus et tocius Anglie populus exultantes 10
receperunt, de quibus prolixior sermo fiet postmodum suo loco.
Turgotus:*b* 'De rege Scotorum Malcolmo Canmore magnanimo
dignum aliquid dicendum duximus, ut cuius fuerit cordis, quanti vel
animi, unum eius opus hic exaratum legentibus declarabit. Relatum
est aliquando sibi*c* quendam de suis summis proceribus illum 15
occidendum cum suis hostibus convenisse. Imperat rex hec nuncianti
silencium, siluit et ipse, proditoris qui forte tunc aberat, expectans
adventum. Qui cum ad curiam cum apparatu magno regi venisset
insidiaturus, rex ei*d* suisque vultum solitum atque jocundum pretendens, finxit se nichil audisse vel scivisse que mente recolebat. Quid 20
plura? Ipse*e* rex omnes venatores suos summo mane cum canibus
⟨fecit⟩ convenire. Et iam noctem Aurora abegerat, cum rex vocatis
ad se cunctis proceribus et militibus in venando spaciatum ire festinat.
Venit interim ad quandam planiciem latam, quam in modum corone
densissima silva cingebat. In cuius medio colliculus unus quasi 25
turgescere videbatur, qui diversorum colorum floribus, pulcra

quadam varietate depictus, fatigatis quandoque militibus ex | venatu
gratum prebebat accubitum. In quo cum rex ceteris superior*f*

constetisset, secundum legem venandi | quam "Tristram" vulgus
vocat, singulis cum canibus et sociis singula loca delegat, ut obsessa 30
undique bestia, ubicumque eligeret exitum, mortis exicium inveniret.
Ipse vero rex seorsum ab aliis solus abcessit cum solo suum secum
retinens proditorem.'

a	Etheline *CA*	*d*	eis *CA*
b	*underlined C*	*e*	+ipse *del.C*
c	ipsi regi *for* sibi *CA*	*f*	superius *CA*

11

A duel between King Malcolm
and a treacherous knight

King Malcolm was quite unassuming, brave-hearted and spirited,
very powerful in bodily strength and daring, not rash but dependable,
endowed with many other good qualities, as will appear in what
follows. In the first nine years of his reign while King Edward was   1057-66
5 alive, he observed unbroken peace and close contact with the English
up to the arrival of William the Bastard. In the thirteenth year of the
said King Edward the son of his brother the late King Edmund
Ironside, whose name was Edward, came from Hungary to England   [1057]
with his wife Agatha, his son Edgar and two daughters, Margaret
10 who was afterwards queen of Scots, and the nun Christina. His uncle
the king and the people of the whole of England welcomed them
joyfully. They will be dealt with at greater length later on at the
appropriate place.
    Turgot says: 'We thought that something fitting should be said
15 about Malcolm Canmore the great-spirited king of Scots to show our
readers what his disposition was and how great his spirit by setting
down here just one of his deeds. It was reported to him one day that a
certain one of his chief nobles had arranged with his enemies to kill
him. The king ordered the bearer of this information to keep quiet
20 about it, and he himself said nothing, but waited for the arrival of the
traitor, who happened to be away at the time. When he came to the
court with a great retinue to lay a trap for the king, the king exhibited
towards him and his followers his usual cheerful expression,
pretending that he had heard or knew nothing of what he was plotting
25 in his mind. To cut a long story short, the king himself caused all his
huntsmen to meet together early next morning with their hounds.
And Aurora had already driven night away, when the king
summoned all his nobles and knights to his presence, and quickly
proceeded to go out hunting. He came meanwhile to a certain broad
30 plain, which was surrounded by a very dense wood shaped like a
coronet. In the middle of the wood there was seen to swell up as it were
a small hill which was embroidered with flowers of various colours, a
beautiful patchwork. At times it offered a welcome couch for knights
weary after hunting. When the king had taken his stance there higher
35 up than the others, he allotted separate positions to each of his
companions with his hound according to the law of hunting, which is

12

De confusibili exsuperacione proditoris

'Ab omnium autem aspectu et auditu remoti, rex subsistit, et vultu torvo volvente pugnam in hec verba prorupit: "Ecce," inquit, "ego et tu mecum, solus cum solo, similibus armis protecti. Non est qui michi, licet regi, assistat, nec tibi subveniat; nec est qui videat aut audiat, nisi arbiter Deus. Nunc ergo si vales, si audeas, si cor habeas, imple 5 quidem opere quod corde concepisti, et redde hostibus meis quod promisisti. Si me occidendum putas, quando melius, quando securius, quando liberius, quando tandem virilius? An venenum parasti, sed hoc muliercularum esse quis nesciat? An insidiaris lectulo? Hoc possunt et adultere.ᵃ An ferrum, ut occulte ferias, occultasti? Hoc 10 sicarii non militis esse, nemo qui dubitet. Age pocius quod militis est, et non proditoris. Age quod est viri, et non mulieris. Atque solus cum solo congredere, ut saltem prodicio tua turpitudine videatur carere, que numquam infidelitate carere potest." Actenus vir ille nequissimus hec vix sustinuit, et mox verbis eius quasi gravi fulmine percussus, de 15 equo cui insidebat citissime descendit, projectisque armis ad pedes regis corruit cum lacrimis atque tremore cordis ita dixit: "Domine mi rex, ignoscat michi ad presens hoc meum velle iniqum tua regia potestas. Et si usque modo aliquid super huiuscemodi tradicione tui corporis cor meum malignum conceperit, amodo delebitur, et in 20 futurum contra omnes me tibi fidelissimum, Deo cum sua genitrice teste, promitto." Cui rex ait: "Noli, amice, timere, noli pavere a me, nichil nec per me mali pro re ista sustinebis. Obsides tamen in pignore jubeo quod michi nomines, atque adducas." Quibus nominatis et statim postmodum adductis, rex inquit: "In regis verbo tibi dico, res 25 ante promissa stabit." Ille vero proditor regis voluntati, in hiis que premisimus oportuno tempore satisfaciens, sic revertitur ad socios de

Scriptor hiis que fecerant vel dixerant nemini loquentes.' | Circa idem tempus anno scilicet domini mᵒ liiᵒ Emma (que et Elguina) quondam Anglorum regina obiit Wintonie. Rex Eadwardus et comes Godwi- 30 nus ac filii sui ad invicem reconsiliati sunt, receptis pristinis dignitatibus suis, et Normanni fere omnes ax Anglia exlegantur.

---

a adulteri *CA*

commonly called "Tristram", so that their prey would be beset on all
sides, and wherever it chose a way out, it would find destruction and
death. The king himself went away alone apart from the others,
40 keeping only his traitor with him.'

12

The traitor is overcome by shame

'When they were well away from being seen or heard by anyone, the
king stopped, and with a grim countenance that foreboded a fight
said: "Look, I am alone, and you are alone with me, with equal arms
to protect us. There is no one to help me, although I am the king, and
5   no one to assist you, nor is there anyone to see or to hear except for
God our witness. So now if you are able, if you dare, if you have the
heart for it, put into practice the plan that you have conceived in your
heart, and render to my enemies what you promised. If you think that
I deserve to be killed, when would you have a better opportunity?
10 When could you do it more safely? When more freely, when finally in
a manner more befitting a man? Or have you prepared poison? But
who does not know that this is the method of feeble women? Or will
you lay siege to my bed? Even adultresses can do this. Or have you a
sword concealed, so that you may strike in secret? All agree that this is
15 the way of an assassin not a knight. Come, [choose] rather the part of
a knight, and not that of a traitor. Come, [choose] the man's part, and
not the woman's, and meet me in single combat, so that at any rate
your treachery may seem to have no taint of cowardice, although it
can never be free from the taint of faithlessness." At this point that
20 very wicked man could hardly endure it, and soon, as if thunderstruck by his words, he very quickly got down from the horse on
which he was sitting, and throwing down his weapons, he collapsed at
the king's feet in tears, and with trembling heart spoke as follows:
"My lord king, may I be forgiven now by your royal power for this my
25 evil intention. And if up to now my wicked heart has conceived any
plot of betraying your person in this way, from now on it will be
eradicated, and I promise that in future I will be most faithful to you
against all comers, as God and His mother are my witnesses." The
king said to him: "Do not be afraid, my friend. Do not fear anything
30 from me. You will suffer no harm as far as I am concerned from this
incident. I command you however to give me the names of hostages as
a pledge, and bring them to me." When the hostages had been named,
and immediately brought to him, the king said: "I give you the king's
word for it; the promise I have given you will be honoured." That
35 traitor having promptly satisfied the king's wishes in these matters

Anno sequenti caput Reys fratris Griffini regis Walensium ad regem
Eadwardum in vigilia Epiphanie apud Glawornam allatum est.
Godwinus comes ac proditor, cuius filiam rex duxerat in uxorem,   35
feria ii^a Pasche ad mensam juxta regem consedens buccella gutturi
adherente semisuffocatus, a filiis ad cameram exportatus, quinta post
hec feria decessit; modum autem huiusmodi vindicte lacius suo loco
inferius recitabimus. Cui successit Haroldus filius eius in comitatum,
et Haroldi comitatus datus est Algaro Leofrici comitis filio. Anno m°   40

G i,257   lv^to Siwardus | dux Northimbrorum, fidus amicus Malcolmi regis,
Eboraci obiit. Cuius ducatus Tostio fratri Haroldi ducis datus est.
Non multo post Algarus predictus, sine culpa a rege Eadwardo
exlegatus, Hiberniam mox peciit, et xviii navibus piraticis acquisitis,
et auxilio regis Walensium Griffini maxime fretus, tandem suum   45
recuperavit comitatum, combusta prius civitate Herefordensi et
monasterio Sancti Alberti regis et martyris; et in eo quibusdam
canonicis et cccc occisis c'.

13

De morte regis Anglorum Eadwardi et de quadam visione c'

Dominice Incarnacionis anno m° lxvi obiit pie memorie Eadwardus
rex, honor et gloria Anglorum dum vixit, eorum ruina dum moritur.
Scriba   Willelmus:

Rex Eadwardus pronus in senium, eo quod ipse non susceperat filios, et
Godwini videret invalescere natos, misit ad regem Hunorum (sed   5
Turgotus dicit ad imperatorem) ut filium sui fratris Eadmundi Irneside
Eadwardum cum omni familia sua mitteret, futurum ut aut ille aut filii
fo.93   sui succedant hereditario jure regno Anglie, | orbitatem suam
cognatorum suffragio debere sustentari. Igitur continuo postquam
advenerat, apud Sanctum Paulum Londonie fato defunctus est,   10
Eadgaro filio superstite cum sororibus prenominatis, quem pro genere
regno proximum rex proceribus commendavit. Rex demum, postquam
exactis in regno non plene xxiiii^or annis, obiit vigilia Epiphanie. In

which we mentioned before, returned thus to his companions, telling
no one what they had done or said concerning these matters.'
   About the same time, that is in 1052, Emma (who was also called   1052:
Elguina) formerly queen of the English died at Winchester. King   [14 Mar.]
40 Edward and Earl Godwine and his sons were reconciled to each other;
they recovered their former dignities, and almost all the Normans
were banished from England.
   In the following year the head of Rhys the brother of Gruffydd king   1053: 5 Jan.
of the Welsh was brought to King Edward at Gloucester on the eve of
45 Epiphany. Godwine the earl and traitor, whose daughter the king had
married, while sitting at table next to the king on Monday in Easter
week, half-choked on a morsel of food which stuck to his throat. He   12 Apr.
was carried to his room by his sons, and died thereafter on Thursday
in Easter week. We will deal with the manner of this kind of
50 punishment more fully further on at the appropriate place. He was
succeeded in his earldom by his son Harold, and Harold's earldom
was given to Ælfgar son of Earl Leofric.
   In 1055 Siward duke of the Northumbrians and a loyal friend of   1055
King Malcolm died at York. His dukedom was given to Tostig
55 brother of Duke Harold. Not long afterwards the aforesaid Ælfgar
was banished by King Edward although he had done no wrong. He
presently went to Ireland, acquired eighteen galleys, and, relying
heavily on help from the king of the Welsh, Gruffydd, he at length
recovered his earldom, having first of all burnt down the city of
60 Hereford and the monastery of St Æthelbert king and martyr, and in
it certain canons and four hundred others were killed etc.

13

The death of Edward king of the English and a certain vision

In the one thousand and sixty-sixth year of our Lord's Incarnation
there passed away King Edward of pious memory, the honour and
glory of the English while he lived, and their downfall when he died.
William [of Malmesbury] says:

5   When King Edward was declining into old age, since he had had no
         sons of his own, and since he saw that the sons of Godwine were
         becoming more powerful, he sent to the king of the Hungarians (but
         Turgot says to the emperor) asking him to send Edward the son of his
         brother Edmund Ironside with all his family, [saying] that either he or
10   his sons would succeed to the kingdom of England by hereditary right,
         and that the support of his kinsmen should come to the aid of his
         childlessness. Then no sooner had Edward son of Edmund Ironside
         arrived than he died at St Paul's in London, leaving his son Edgar and   [1057]

crastino quidem, adhuc recenti luctu regalis funeris, Haraldus Godwini filius, a majoribus extorta fide, secundum alios consencientibus, 15
arripuit diadema regni, quod vix per novem menses tenuit, nam a
Willelmo Bastard bello peremptus est. ⟨Rex Noricorum Haroldus
cognomento [Harfagar, frater]ᵃ beati Olavi regis et martyris, et Tostius
frater Haroldi [regis]ᵃ Anglie, venientes cum exercitu apud Standford-
brig, [occiduntur]ᵃ ab Haroldo Anglie invasore.⟩ ⟨Post mortem 20
Haroldi Godwini filium⟩ᵇ proceres Eadgarum in regem eligerent, et a
quibusdam electus est, ut a rege mandatum fuerat, sed episcopos non
habebant assertores.ᶜ

Hec ille. Verum in hoc eos errasse michi videtur, et apud Deum et
populum. Apud Deum, quia quem ipseᵈ genitura tantorum regum 25
progenitorum, justa generacionis procreatum linia, regnandum
pretulit, eis respuere non licuit, nec insontem linguis omni gladio
preacutis, injuste justoᵉ privare patrimonio, scientes quod etas regia,
vel puerilis, vel senilis, vel eciam simplicitas in fidelitate constat, et
regimine subditorum. Apud populum vero, cum in suam propriam 30
confusionem atque regni cunctorum indigenarum scandalum et
obprobriumᶠ sempiternum non secundum justiciam legis, sed cordis
affectum sequentes, supra se virum erigunt,ᵍ tocius juris regnandi
inexpertem, Haroldum filium Godwini traditoris filii Edrici proditoris, quorum non fama sed infamia variis notatur in scripturis, ineptum 35
tale membrum in regem sibi loco recti capitis statuentes. Ex quo brevi

G i,258   postmodum | contigit, quod misere per aliena regna vagi dolentes, a
propriis expulsi sunt edibus, nec habentes ubi reclinarent capita,
dicente propheta: 'Quoniam qui malignantur exterminabuntur,
sustinentes autem Dominum hereditabunt terram.' Igitur ipse Domi- 40
nus illam sanctam regalem liniam, se sustinentem, ab eis sed non ab eo
derelictam, hereditare terram simul et regnare volens, felici Scotis
omine, cum sua regaliʰ linia gratis conjunxit. Ex quibus, eo
providente, deinceps et actenus regio sedentes in solio pululant reges,
et usquequo sibi placuerit pululabunt. Per visionem sequentem 45
ostensam Sancto Eadwardo in extremis laboranti patet, quod in
premissis clerus errabat. Willelmus:

Postquam rex elinguis sopore biduo jacuisset, expedita loquela,
'Duos', inquit, 'michi monachos assistere vidi, quos Normannia
religiose vivere, et mori feliciter noveram. Se Dei nuncios esse prefati, 50
dixerunt: "Quoniam primores Anglie, duces, episcopi et abbates non
sunt ministri Dei, sed Diaboli, tradidit Deus hoc regnum post obitum
tuum, anno uno et uno die in manus inimici. Pervagabuntur demones
totam hanc terram."' Cumque se rex hoc ostensurum populo diceret,

a   D; lac.C
b   Post ... filium in margin replacing Post
    quem in text, with only quem del.C
c   assentatores CA
d   ipsa CA

e   +principe del.C
f   D; obpprobrium C
g   eligunt CA
h   +Iñā [?] del.C

his sisters named above. The king commended Edgar to the nobles as
15   nearest by birth to the kingship. Finally the king died on the vigil of the
Epiphany after completing not quite twenty-four years on the throne.   [1066:]
On the following day while the grief for the king's death was still fresh,   5 Jan.
Harold son of Godwine obtained fealty from the magnates by force, or
with their consent according to others, and seized the diadem of the
20   kingdom which he held for scarcely nine months, for he was killed in
battle by William the Bastard. The king of the Norwegians Harold
surnamed Hardrada the brother of the blessed Olaf king and martyr
and Tostig brother of Harold king of England came with an army to
Stamfordbridge, and were killed by Harold the usurper of England.
25   After the death of Harold son of Godwine the nobles would have   [14 Oct.]
chosen Edgar as king, and he was actually chosen by certain of them, as
had been instructed by the king, but they did not have the support of
the bishops.

But it seems to me that the nobles were wrong to do this, both in the
30   sight of God and of the people. In the sight of God because they ought
not to have rejected the man whom He himself had chosen to reign by
his descent from such great kings his ancestors, since he was born of
the legitimate line of succession, nor should they have unjustly
deprived an innocent man of his rightful inheritance by tongues
35   sharper than any sword, knowing that the age of a king, whether
young or old, or even feeble-mindedness does not deprive him of the
loyalty of his subjects or his rule over them. In the sight of the people
since to their own undoing and the everlasting shame and reproach of
all the indigenous inhabitants of the kingdom, not according to legal
40   rights but following the emotions of their hearts, the nobles raised a
man to rule over them who had no right whatsoever to reign, Harold
son of the traitor Godwine who was the son of the treacherous Eadric,
whose infamy rather than fame is recorded in various writings, setting
up such a worthless limb as king over themselves in place of their
45   rightful head. As a result shortly afterwards it happened that grieving
as they wandered wretchedly through foreign kingdoms, the nobles
were driven from their own homes with nowhere to lay their heads, as
the prophet says: 'For evildoers will be destroyed, but they who hope
in the Lord shall possess the land.' So the Lord himself, wishing that
50   saintly royal line, that was standing firm, abandoned by the nobles
but not by Him, to possess the land and reign over it as well, with a
happy omen for the Scots, graciously united it with the Scottish royal
line. From them under God's providence kings sitting on the royal
throne in succession and to this day have flourished, and will flourish
55   as long as God wills it. It is clear from the following vision shown to St
Edward in the final stages of his illness that the clergy were wrong in
their actions described above.
William [of Malmesbury] says:

After the king had lain in a coma for two days without the power of
50   speech, when he regained his speech, he said: 'I saw standing beside me

ut olim Ninivite peniterent, 'Neutrum', aiunt, 'erit, quia nec penite- 55
bunt, nec Deus eis miserebitur' c'.

Item Willelmus:

Ita Angli, qui in unam coeuntes sentenciam regni potuissent reformare
ruinam, dum nullum ex suis volunt, alienum induxerunt.

⟨Willelmum silicet Bastard, cuius magnitudinem futuram mater 60
sompnio previdit, que intestina sua per totam Normanniam et
Angliam extendi vidit et dilatari.*i* Ipso quoque tempore quo idem puer
natus humum primo attigit, ambas manus*j* pulvere pavimenti implevit,
stricte manus complodens. Quo facto, astantes multum ammirantes de
vivaci tenacitate pulveris, obstetrix fausto omine acclamavit, eum 65
duorum regnorum quasi regem futurum, Normannie scilicet et Anglie.
Unde pacatus in Normannia, cum Angliam peteret ut Haroldum
regem impeteret, in egressu navis pede lapsus, audivit acclamari sibi a

proximo milite: 'Tenes Angliam, comes, rex | futurus!' Aroldus*k*
revertens a bello quo regem Noricorum vicerat, misit exploratores qui 70
intra castra deprehensi [jussi]*l* sunt a Willelmo circumduci per tentoria,
et mox large pasci et renumerari, ac ad dominum suum incolumes
remitti. Redeuntes nunciaverunt ducis magnificenciam. Et addunt,
pene omnes in exercitu illo presbyteros videri, quia scilicet tamquam
totam faciem cum utroque labio rasam haberent; Angli enim superius 75
labium, pilis incessanter fructificantibus, intonsum dimittunt. Willelmus monachum legatum misit [tria]*l* ferentem, ut scilicet Haroldus vel
regno secundum condiciones discederet, vel sub eo regnaret, vel [certe,
spec-]tante*l* utroque exercitu, gladio rem ventilaret. Haroldus legatum,
nec responso dignatus, turbide abegit. Illam [noctem]*l* Angli totam in 80
cantibus et potibus insompnem duxerunt, Normanni autem tota nocte
confessioni peccatorum vacantes, [m]ane*l* Dominico corp-[ore commu-
nic-]arunt.*l* Comes arma poposcit, et casu loricam inversam induit

ministris tumultuantibus. | Quem*m* casum risu corrigens, 'Vertetur',
inquit, 'comitatus meus in regnum.' Tunc cantilena de Rolando a 85
haroldicis*n* inchoata, | prelium commissum est. Pugnatum est utrimque
acriter. Fossatum quoddam preruptum Angli fugientes noto sibi
compendio invaserunt, ubi tot Normannos conculcavere, ut tumilo
cadaverum planiciem*o* campi equarent. Haroldus a longe ictu sagitte in
cerebro percussus occubuit. Jacentis femur unus militum gladio 90
proscindens,*p* ignominie notatus est a Willelmo, et milicia pulsus. Idem
Willelmus eadem die discurrendo, [pugnando,]*q* hortando, tres equos
fortissimos sub se fessos amisit. Susurrabant ei custodes corporis, ut a
[periculo se]*q* subtraheret, sed persistitur usque noctem. Nichil sanguinis ex eius corpore tractatum est, quamvis jaculis multis [impetere- 95

tur.]*qr* | Corpus Haroldi matri repetenti sine precio remisit, licet illa
multa per legatos optulit. Die Natalis Domini coronatus est ab

---

i	*corrected from* dilatatam C	*n*	+inchoata *del.*C
j	+ambas manus *del.*C	*o*	+campium *del.*C
k	+rex futurus *del.*C	*p*	+ignomine *del.*C
l	D; *lac.*C	*q*	D; *lac.*C
m	+causam *del.*C	*r*	+*extra word or words at end of folio* C

two monks who, I knew, lived according to the monastic rule in
Normandy, and died happily. Declaring that they were messengers of
God, they said: "Since the magnates of England, dukes, bishops and
abbots are the servants not of God but of the Devil, God has handed
65   over this kingdom after your death into the hands of your enemy for a
year and a day. Demons will range over the whole land."' When the
king said that he would reveal this to the people, so that they might
repent, as did the people of Nineveh in time past, they said: 'Neither
will happen, because they will not repent, nor will God pity them' etc.

70   Again William [of Malmesbury] says:

Thus the English who could have rebuilt the ruin of their kingdom if
they had been of one mind, since they would have none of their own
countrymen, allowed a foreigner to come in, that is to say William the
Bastard whose mother foresaw his future greatness in a dream. She saw
75   her womb extending and spreading over the whole of Normandy and
England. Also at the very time when this same child was born and
touched the ground for the first time, he filled both hands with the dust
on the floor, clapping his hands tightly together. Then the bystanders
were much amazed at his vigorous grasp of the dust and the midwife
80   exclaimed at the happy omen that he would be king as it were of two
kingdoms, that is Normandy and England. Then having imposed
peace in Normandy he set out for England to attack King Harold. His
foot slipped as he was getting out of his ship, and he heard a soldier who
was standing next to him exclaim: 'England is in your grasp, count and
85   king to be!' As Harold was returning from the battle in which he had
defeated the king of the Norwegians, he sent out scouts. They were
arrested inside the camp, and were ordered by William to be escorted
around the tents, and presently to be lavishly fed, presented with gifts,
and sent back to their lord unharmed. When they returned, they
90   reported the magnificence of the duke, and they added that almost
everyone in that army seemed to be priests because they had their
whole face and both lips shaven; for the English allow their upper lip to
go unshaven, with the hairs constantly sprouting. William sent a monk
as envoy with three conditions, that Harold should either leave the
95   kingdom according to the conditions, or should reign under William,
or at any rate should decide the issue with the sword with both armies
looking on. Harold drove the envoy roughly away disdaining any
response. The English spent that whole sleepless night in singing and
drinking, while the Normans occupied the whole night in confessing
100   their sins, and in the morning they took communion. The count
demanded his armour, and inadvertently put on his hauberk the wrong
way round, as his attendants bustled about him. As he put this mistake
right with a smile, he said: 'My county will be turned into a kingdom.'
Then after the heralds struck up the Song of Roland, the battle was
105   joined. Both sides fought fiercely. The English as they fled entered a
certain steep ravine by a shortcut known to them, where they trampled
to death so many Normans that they made the ravine level with the
plain by the mound of corpses. Harold was struck on the skull with an
arrow shot from the distance, and he fell dead. One of the soldiers

Aldredo episcopo Eboracensi, nolens hoc munus suscipere a Stigando
Cantuariensi, quia nec legitime factus erat archiepiscopus. Vexillum
regium Haroldi Romam misit Willelmus ad papam, quod erat in 100
hominis pugnantis figura, auro et lapidibus arte sumptuosa contex-
tum. Nam et antequam Angliam intrarat, audita causa eius transitus,
et quam injuste Haroldus occupaverat, Alexander papa vexillum ei in
omne regnum Anglie cum sua misit benediccione. Cuius virtute affisus,
licencius sibi regnum conquestioni subjacere putabat.   105

Hec Willelmus. Dum iste Haraldus navigare^s vellet in Normanniam,
contrariante sibi vento, applicuit in Pontevim. Quem Wido comes
eiusdem arrestavit, et in custodia tenuit donec Willelmus B[astard]
eum liberavit. Cui data sorore ipsius Willelmi in conjuge, homagium
et fidelitatem fecit. Tria sacramenta super philacterium quod 110
vocabant Oculum Bovis fecit, quodque ei fidem et promissionem,
quam ei faciebat, bene custodiret. Libertati igitur donatus et Angliam
reversus, invenit regem Eadwardum in extremis laborantem. Qui
quasi oblitus sacramentorum que Willelmo in Normannia fecerat,
persuasit regi infirmanti, ut sibi coro- | nam Anglie concederet. Quo 115
audito, rex E[adwardus] non immemor quod Willelmo comiti
Normannie cognato suo regnum Anglie iam [dudum sub]^t certa
forma concessisset, respondit Heraldo hoc nullomodo se posse
facere, quia inde W[illelmum] comitem Normannie heredem fecerat.
[Eadwardo igitur]^t rege mortuo, Haraldus quasi insanus, postponens^u 120
quicquid Willelmo B[astard] de regno Anglie juraverat, [videlicet
quod illi illud]^t post mortem regis E[adwardi] servaret, regnum
invasit, et vitam propterea amisit. Eidem Willelmo ad bellum
accessuro, [quidam loricam inversam]^t sibi imposuit. Quod ille
animadvertens fideliter dixit: 'Si ego in sortem crederem, hodie 125
amplius in bellum [non procederem. Sed ego numquam]^t sortibus
credidi, neque sortilogos amavi. Sed in omni negocio Creatori meo
me semper commendavi. [Et in hac fide persistens,]^t et justiciam partis
mei recognoscens, contra perjurum adire bello non pertimescens,
[belli certamen aggredior, et letus, si]^t contingat, morior.' Interfectus 130
est in [illa pugna Haraldus et duo fratres c'.]^t⟩

fo.95

---

s　　D; navigaret C　　　　　　　　u　　+ quicquid $del.C$
t　　D; lac.C

110 hacked his thigh with his sword as he lay on the ground, and was reprimanded for cowardice by William, and discharged from the service. William on the same day also lost three very strong horses worn out under him, as he rushed around fighting and exhorting [his men]. His bodyguards kept whispering to him that he should withdraw
115 from danger, but the fighting went on till nightfall. No blood was shed from his body, although he was the target for many javelins. He sent back Harold's body to his mother at her request without ransom, although she offered large sums of money through envoys. He was crowned on Christmas Day by Ealdred the bishop of York, since he   25 Dec.
120 refused to accept this service at the hands of Stigand of Canterbury, because he had been made archbishop illegally. William sent to the pope in Rome the royal banner of Harold, which was in the form of a warrior, sumptuously woven with gold and precious stones. For before William had set foot in England, Pope Alexander had sent a banner to
125 him for the whole of England with his blessing, when he had heard the reason for his invasion, and how unjustly Harold had usurped the throne. Trusting in the power of this banner, he considered that it legitimised the subjection of the kingdom to his conquest.

When Harold was intending to sail to Normandy, and the wind was
130 against him, he put in at Ponthieu. He was arrested by Guy the local count, and was held in custody until William the Bastard set him free. He was given William's sister in matrimony, and did homage and swore fealty to him. He swore three oaths on a phylactery which they call the Bull's-Eye, and which would keep good watch over his fealty
135 and the promise which he made to William. So when he had been given his freedom and returned to England he found King Edward in the last throes. As if unmindful of the oaths which he had sworn to William in Normandy, he tried to persuade the king in his weakness to grant him the crown of England. When he heard this, King Edward
140 had not forgotten that long ago he had formally granted the kingdom of England to William count of Normandy his kinsman, and he said in answer to Harold that he could by no means do this, because he had made William count of Normandy his heir. So when King Edward was dead, Harold like a madman disregarded the oath he had sworn
145 to William the Bastard concerning the kingdom of England, namely that after the death of King Edward he would keep the kingdom for him, and usurped the throne, losing his life as a consequence. As William was about to go to battle, someone put his hauberk on the wrong way round. Noticing this he said firmly; 'If I believed in chance,
150 I would not proceed any further into battle today. I have never believed in fortunes or fortune-tellers, but in all matters I have always entrusted myself to my Creator. And steadfast in this faith, recognising the justice of my cause, and not afraid to join battle against one who has broken his oath, I approach the clash of battle,
155 and will gladly die, if this should occur.' Harold and his two brothers were killed in that battle etc.

14

De quibus causis Willelmus Bastard venit in Angliam

[Autor] Audiens autem Willelmus Bastard comes Normannie quod Haroldus*ᵃ* Eadwardi consobrini sui regnum usurpasset, ⟨et quod proceres
regni erant inter se divisi,⟩ variis causis stimulatus, in Angliam venit:
primo pro rupto federe quod simul pepigerant juramento, quod ei
tunc castrum Dorobernie, et post mortem Eadwardi regnum Anglie 5
sibi daturum firmavit Haroldus.*ᵇ*

ii° quod filiam suam adhuc impuberem ducere*ᶜ* uxorem promisit,
quam, ut quidam ferunt, exoculatam ab eo et crinibus*ᵈ* detruncatam,
sic eam a se repudiatam et ad patrem cum dedecore remisit
deturpatam. 10

iii quia pater suus Godwinus cognatum suum Ethelredum cum
pluribus Anglis et Normannis apud Hely proditorie peremerat,
omnibus eius comitibus preter decem decapitatis.

iiii*ᵗᵒ* quia in despectum sui ipse Robertum archiepiscopum et
Odonem consulem cum omnibus Francis exterminasset de Anglia. 15

fo.92v ⟨Ut plenius pateat quare Haraldus prestitit juramentum Willelmo
Bastard, sic repperi scriptum in cronica Anglorum:

Haraldus transiens in Flandream tempestate compulsus est in Ponti-
cam provinciam applicare. Quem captum*ᵉ* consul Ponticus Willelmo
duci Normannie reddidit. Haraldus autem juravit Willelmo super 20
reliquias sanctorum, se filiam eius ducturam, et Angliam post mortem
Eadwardi regis ad opus eius servaturum. Summo igitur honore
susceptus, et muneribus amplis ditatus, cum reversus est in Angliam
perjurii crimen incurrit.

In cronica sequenti ponit Willelmum Bastard sororem suam dedisse 25
Haraldo in conjugem.⟩

fo.93v ⟨[De quo habentur hii versus:

Dux non intravit regnum racione regendi,
sed magis Haroldum petitur modus]*ᶠ* interemendi.
Hic [qui germanam dicti ducis]*ᶠ* ac uterinam 30
iam sibi sponsatam transmisit vile relictam,
namque suos crines [fecit mu-]tilare*ᶠ* per aures.
Quem dux despectum judicat esse suum.

---

a   *corrected from* Haraldus *C*
b   *interlin.C*
c   duceret *CA*
d   +deturne *del.C*
e   +W *del.C*
f   D; *lac.C*

14

The reasons for the coming of William the Bastard to England

When William the Bastard count of Normandy heard that Harold
had usurped the kingdom of Edward his kinsman, and that the
magnates of the kingdom were divided among themselves, various
reasons induced him to come to England. Firstly because the
5 agreement that they had sealed with an oath together had been   [1064]
broken, in that Harold had asserted that he would at that time give
him Dover castle, and after the death of Edward the kingdom of
England.

Secondly that Harold promised to marry William's daughter who
10 was then under-age, but, as some say, he blinded her and cut off her
hair, and sent her back to her father in disgrace, having rejected and
dishonoured her in this way.

Thirdly that his father Godwine had treacherously killed William's
kinsman Alfred together with many English and Normans at Ely,
15 with all his companions save ten having been beheaded.

Fourthly that to spite him Harold had banished from England the
archbishop Robert and Count Odo with all the French.

To make it clearer why Harold swore an oath to William the
Bastard, I found the following passage in the Chronicle of the
English:

20   As Harold was crossing to Flanders, he was driven by a storm to put
        into land in the province of Ponthieu. He was captured by the count of
        Ponthieu, and handed over to William count of Normandy. Now
        Harold swore to William on the relics of the saints that he would marry
        his daughter, and would keep England for his benefit after the death of
25   King Edward. So having been received with the greatest honour, and
        enriched with generous gifts, he returned to England, and brought on
        himself the charge of perjury.

In the following chronicle it states that William the Bastard gave his
sister to Harold as his wife.
30   These lines of verse are about this:

        The duke did not enter the kingdom in order to rule,
        but rather seeking a way to kill Harold.
        He sent back the said count's very own sister,
        who had been betrothed to him, meanly abandoned.
35   For he caused her hair to be cropt above her ears.
        The count judged this as an insult to him.

Hinc trux intravit dux regnum, quo [spol-]iavit
Haroldum timide regnantem, nam sine lege.⟩   35

Hiis igitur et aliis causis Willelmus irritatus, undecumque collectis
viribus transfretavit in Angliam, et ⟨ut premittitur⟩ eundem Haroldum levi bello et facili ii idus octobris apud Hastyngis regno simul et
[Scrip-]tor^f vita privavit. | Deinde pacifice ab Anglis tamquam princeps proprius
susceptus, et^g Londonias pacifice apud Westmonasterium ab Aldredo 40
Eboracensi archiepiscopo in regem coronatus est. Et sic facta est
mutacio Excelsi dextra, quam ingens cometa in exordio eiusdem anni
designaverat. Unde versus:

Anno milleno sexageno quoque seno |
G i,261   ⟨a genito Verbo, duce regnante superbo,⟩   45
Anglorum mete flammas sensere comete.

Anno sequenti idem rex Willelmus Normanniam rediit, ducens secum
Dorobernensem archiepiscopum Stigandum, clitonem Eadgarum,
comites Edwinum, Morkarum et Walteum et multos alios de
nobilioribus Anglie secum obsides, et thesauros innumerabiles. 50
Rediens vero Anglorum terram militibus suis divisit, et Anglis
importabile tributum imposuit, et sic debacando, dominus de gente
Anglorum, quod diu cogitaverat, perfecit. Quam terram sevicie
Normannorum aspere et callide tradidit ad exterminandum. Quod ita
factum est, ut vix aliquis princeps de progenie Anglorum esset in 55
Anglia, sed omnes ad servitutem et merorem redacti fuissent, ita
eciam ut Anglicum^h vocari esset obprobrium. Propter quod^i delibera-
vit quomodo linguam Saxonicam posset destruere, et Angliam et
Normanniam in idiomate concordare. Et ideo ordinavit quod nullus
in curia regis placitaret nisi in Gallico; et iterum quod quilibet puer 60
ponendus ad scolas addisceret Gallicum, et per Gallicum Latinum,
que duo usque hodie observantur in Anglia.
Autor   Anno domini quo supra imperatoris Henrici iiii^ti ii^o, regisque
Malcolmi x^o, Padbrunna Germanie civitas cum ecclesia majore
combusta est. In monasterio autem monachorum eiusdem civitatis 65
quidam Scotus erat, Paternus nomine, multo tempore reclusus, qui
sepius hoc incendium predixit. Petrus Damianus:

In quadam urbe Theutonica erat quidam servus Dei nomine Paternus
juxta monasterium in cella reclusus. Cui revelatum est quod, nisi
populus per penitenciam cicius Deum placaret, infra xxx dies tota 70
civitas incendio periret. Promulgata est visio, sed noluerunt converti.
Ille quidem preciosa queque monasterii auferri jussit, ut essent salva.
Tandem a vii urbis regionibus subito ignis exoritur, et totam urbem

g   interlin.C   i   + ordinavit quomodo del.C
h   + loqui vel CA

Hence the grim count entered the kingdom, which he pillaged
from Harold, who reigned fearfully because illegally.

So roused to anger by these and other causes, William gathered his
40 forces together from all sides, and crossed over to England, and, as
before described, he robbed Harold of both his kingdom and his life in
a light and easy battle at Hastings on 14 October. Then he was   [1066:]
peacefully received by the English as if he were their proper prince,   14 Oct.
and was crowned in Westminster abbey in London by Ealdred   [25 Dec.]
45 archbishop of York. And thus a revolution was effected by the right
hand of the Exalted, which had been prophesied by a huge comet in
the beginning of the same year. Whence the lines:

> In the ten hundred and sixty-sixth year
> From the Word made flesh, in the reign of the proud count
50 > the bounds of the English felt the flames of a comet.

In the following year King William returned to Normandy, taking   1067: [Feb.]
with him as hostages the archbishop of Canterbury Stigand, Edgar
the Ætheling, the earls Edwin, Morcar, Waltheof and many others of
the nobles of England, and countless treasures. When he returned he   [Dec.]
55 divided up the land of the English amongst his knights, and imposed
an insupportable tax on the English, and raging furiously in this way
as lord and master of the English people, he accomplished what he
had planned for a long time. He harshly and cunningly handed over
this land to the savagery of the Normans for its destruction. This was
60 so successful that there was scarcely any magnate of English descent
in England, but all had been reduced to slavery and grief to such an
extent that it was a reproach to be called English. So he reflected on
how he could destroy the Saxon tongue, and unite England and
Normandy in language. And so he decreed that no one should plead
65 in the king's court except in French, and again that any boy to be
placed in the schools should learn French and Latin through French,
and these two rules are observed in England to this day.

In the year of our Lord given above and the second year of the   1067
emperor Henry IV and the tenth year of King Malcolm Paderborn a
70 city in Germany was burnt down along with its cathedral. In a
monastery of monks in the same city there was a certain Scot Paternus
by name, a recluse of long-standing, who frequently predicted this
fire. Peter Damian says:

> In a certain German city there was a servant of God by name Paternus
75 > shut away in a cell near the monastery. It was revealed to him that if the
> people did not appease God very quickly by repentance, the whole city
> would be destroyed by fire within thirty days. His vision was made
> public, but they refused to be converted. He ordered all valuables
> belonging to the monastery to be carried away for safe-keeping. At last
80 > a fire suddenly arose in seven regions of the city, and burnt down the

cum monasterio in cineres combussit. Cumque ad cellulam viri Dei ignis pervenisset et rogaretur exire, noluit, sed omnia judicio Dei 75 committens cum sua cellula combustus est.

15

De misera et proditoria vita qua vivebant Angli

Huius miserande cladis belli de Hastyngis quo regnum suum et ob quam causam Angli perdiderant, Willelmus gemens, suis inscripsit cronicis, quam hac eciam inscribi cronica placuit, ut illius exemplo nostri cavere discant principes, ne quando talibus aut tantis onerati, quod absit, flagiciis, quod hostibus ut ipsi resistere bello nequiant. 5 Willelmus:[a]

Illa fuit dies fatalis Anglie, funestum excidium dulcis patrie, pro novorum dominorum commutacione. Iam pridem enim moribus Anglorum insueverat, qui varii admodum pro temporibus fuerunt. Nam primis adventus sui annis, vultu et gestu barbarico, usu bellico, 10 ritu phanatico vivebant. Sed postmodum, Christi | fide suscepta, paulatim et per incrementa temporis pro ocio quod actitabant exercicium armorum in sccundis ponentes, omnem in religionem operam insumpsere. Taceo de pauperibus; de regibus dico, qui pro amplitudine potestatis licenter indulgere voluptatibus possent. 15 Quorum quidam in patria, quidam Rome, mutato habitu, celeste lucrati sunt regnum, beatum nacti commercium. Quid dicam de tot episcopis, heremitis, abbatibus? Nonne tota insula tantis reliquiis indigenarum fulgurat, ut vix aliquem[b] vicum insignem pretereas, ubi novi sancti nomen non audias? Postea tamen, aliquibus transactis 20 temporibus, non paucis ante Normannorum adventum annis, opti-mates, gule et veneri dediti, ecclesiam more Christiano mane non adibant, sed in cubiculis et inter uxorios amplexus matutinarum solempnia et missarum a festinante presbytero auribus tantum libabant. Vulgus in medio expositum preda potencioribus erat, ut vel 25 eorum exhaustis substanciis, vel corporibus | in longinquas terras distractis, acervos thesaurorum congererent. Illud erat abhorrens a natura, quod multi ancillas suas ex se gravidas, ubi libidini satisfecis-sent, aut ad publicum prostibulum, aut ad externum obsequium venditabant.[c] Clerici literatura tumultuaria contenti vix sacramen- 30 torum verba balbuciebant.[d] Stupori erat et miraculo ceteris, qui grammaticam nosset. Monachi subtilibus indumentis et indifferenti genere ciborum regulam ludificabant. Potabatur in convivio ab

G i,262

fo.94

---

a *underlined C*
b S,CA; aliquod C
c S; venditerabant C
d -l- *interlin.*C

whole city with its monastery. And when the fire arrived at the little cell of the man of God, and he was asked to come out, he refused, but entrusting everything to the judgment of God, he was burnt to ashes along with his little cell.

15

The wretched and treacherous life which the English lived

As William [of Malmesbury] groaned over this pitiful defeat in the battle of Hastings by which the English lost their kingdom, and the reason for the defeat, he included it in his chronicles, and we have decided that it should be included in this chronicle also, so that our
5 princes may learn caution from its example, lest at any time they are burdened with sins of such a kind or so great, which Heaven forbid, that like the English they are unable to withstand the enemy in battle. William [of Malmesbury] says:

That was a fateful day for England, the deadly destruction of a sweet
10 native land in the change-over to new masters. For long ago the land had grown accustomed to the ways of the English, who were very adaptable to circumstances. For in the first years of their coming they were barbarians in expression and bearing, warlike in occupation and heathen in ritual. But later they adopted the Christian faith, and
15 gradually with the passage of time, in keeping with the leisure which they enjoyed, they put the practice of arms in second place, and devoted their efforts to religion. I say nothing of poor people, I am speaking about kings who could freely indulge in pleasures proportionate to the extent of their power. Some of them at home, some in Rome,
20 by changing their style of dress gained a heavenly kingdom in a shrewd business transaction. What shall I say about so many bishops, hermits, abbots? Does not the whole island blaze with such great relics of the native inhabitants that you can scarcely pass a village of any significance where you would not hear the name of some new saint?
25 Later however after some time had passed, many years before the coming of the Normans, the nobles given over to gluttony and lust did not go to church in the morning in the manner of Christians, but lying in their beds clasped in the arms of their wives, they only half-heard the offices of Mattins and the Mass, as a priest gabbled through them. The
30 ordinary people left unprotected were a prey to the more powerful, who were enabled to amass heaps of treasure, either by draining their resources or by selling them as slaves to distant lands. It was the unnatural practice of many men to sell their maidservants after they had made them pregnant, either to a common brothel or to service
35 abroad, when they had satisfied their lust. The clerics, content with superficial learning, could scarcely stutter the words of the sacraments.

omnibus in hoc studio noctes perinde ut dies perpetuantibus. In cibis
enim urgentes crapulam, in potibus irritantes*e* vomitum. Unde 35
sequebantur vicia ebrietatis socia, que virorum animos effeminant.
Hinc factum est, ut magis temeritate et furore precipiti, quam sciencia
militari ⟨Willelmo⟩ congressi, uno prelio et ipso perfacili servituti se
patriamque pesumdederint. Nichil enim temeritate levius, sed quicquid cum impetu inchoat, cito desinit vel compescitur. Verum sicut in 40
tranquillitate malos cum bonis fovet plerumque Dei serenitas, ita in
captivitate bonos cum malis nonnumquam eiusdem constringit
severitas.

Scriptor

Anno m*of*lxix° comes Rodbertus Cumyn cum septingentis fere viris
a Northumbris occiditur. Quo in tempore Alexander ii*us* cum esset 45
Lucanus episcopus concorditer a cardinalibus in papam est electus.
Contra hunc fuit Cadulus, qui fuit Parmensis episcopus, et fere ab
omnibus Lumbardie episcopis in papam electus, asserentes papam
non debere eligi nisi de paradiso Italie. Qui Cadulus cum magno
exercitu bis Romam veniens, violenter voluit papatum optinere, sed 50
non potuit. Deinde Alexander papa ad rogatum Henrici imperatoris
descendit in Longobardiam, et in Mantua solempniter celebrato
consilio, pacificatis omnibus, ad urbem est reversus. Eodem tempore
Normanni, qui in prejudicium domini pape regnum Appulie occupa-
verant, fines Campanie devastabant, quos dux Godefridus et 55

G i,263

comitissa devota filia Sancti Petri Matildis expulerunt. Hec | Matildis
fuit adeo potentissima, quod eciam cum imperatore bello durissimo
congressum habuit. Que cum amplissimis possessionibus habun-
daret, totum patrimonium suum super altare Sancti Petri optulit, et
hucusque dicitur Patrimonium Sancti Petri. 60

e   S; irritantibus C   *f*   interlin.C

16

De applicacione felici Eadgari Ethlyn et sororis sue Sancte Margarite in Scociam

Scriba

Turgotus:

Cernens autem Eadgarus Ethling res Anglorum undique perturbari,
ascensa nave cum matre et sororibus in patriam reverti, qua natus
fuerat, conabatur. Sed Summus Imperator, qui ventis imperat et mari,
mare commovit, et in spiritu procellarum exaltati sunt fluctus eius. 5

Anyone who knew any grammar was a source of amazement and
wonder to the rest. The monks made a mockery of their rule with fine
clothes and indiscriminate eating of food. Drinking at dinner parties
40   was universal, as they turned night into day in this pursuit. For in
eating they practised gluttony, and they drank until they were sick.
This led to the vices that go hand in hand with drunkenness and that
emasculate the minds of men. The result of this was that when they
fought against William with recklessness and headlong fury rather
45   than military expertise, by one battle and a very easy one at that they
condemned themselves and their country to slavery. For there is
nothing more unreliable than recklessness, and whatever begins
impetuously soon stops or is suppressed. But just as the serenity of God
usually cherishes the bad along with the good in peaceful days, so in
50   conditions of slavery His severity sometimes fetters the good along
with the bad.

In 1069 Earl Robert de Comines with about seven hundred men   1069:
was killed by the Northumbrians. At this time Alexander II was   [29 Jan.]
elected pope unanimously by the cardinals when he was bishop of   [1061]
55   Lucca. Opposed to him was Cadalus who was bishop of Parma, and
was elected pope by nearly all the bishops of Lombardy, asserting that
a pope should only be chosen from the parvis of Italy. This Cadalus
came twice to Rome with a large army, wishing to obtain the papacy   [1062-3]
by violence, but he did not succeed. The pope Alexander at the
60   request of the emperor Henry went down into Lombardy, and
solemnly celebrated a council in Mantua, pacified everyone and   [1064]
returned to the city. At the same time the Normans, who had seized
the kingdom of Apulia against the interests of the lord pope,
devastated the territory of Campania. They were driven out by Duke   [1066
65   Godfrey and Countess Matilda, the devout daughter of St Peter. This   × 1069]
Matilda was so powerful that she even clashed with the emperor in a
very hard-fought battle. Since she had an abundance of great riches,
she made an offering of her whole patrimony on the altar of St Peter,
and to this day it is called the Patrimony of St Peter.

16

The felicitous landing of Edgar the Ætheling and his sister St Margaret in Scotland

Turgot says:

When Edgar the Ætheling perceived that the affairs of the English were
everywhere in turmoil, he took ship and attempted to return to the land
in which he was born along with his mother and sisters. But the
5   Supreme Ruler who rules the winds and the sea stirred up the sea, and

Seviente vero tempestate, omnes in desperacione vite positi, sese Deo
commendant et puppim pelago committunt. Igitur post plurima
pericula et immanes labores misertus est Dominus desolate familie sue,
quia ubi humanum deesse videtur auxilium, ad Dominum necesse est
recurrendum. Innumeris tandem quassati pelago periculis, coacti sunt 10
in Scociam applicare. Applicuit igitur illa sancta familia quodam loco
qui Sinus Sancte Margarete deinceps ab incolis appellatur. Nec hoc
casu contigisse, sed eam Summi Dei providencia credimus ibidem
advenisse. Igitur in dicto sinu pref-[ata]*a* commorante familia, cunctisque rei finem cum timore expectantibus, nunciatum est regi Malcolmo 15
suum adventum, qui tunc ab eodem loco haut procul cum suis
manebat, et ad navem nuncios dirigens, rem inde veram sciscitabatur.
Nuncii autem illuc venientes, et magnitudinem navis preter solitum
admirantes, regi que viderant festinant quantocius indicare. Quibus
auditis, rex plures et prudenciores prioribus de summis suis proceribus 20
illac direxit. At illi sicut nuncii regie*b* majestatis suscepti, virorum
proceritatem, mulierum venustatem, ac familie tocius industriam non
sine admiracione*c* diligencius considerantes, gratum apud semetipsos
inde colloquium conferunt. Quid plura? Eventum rei, et rerum seriem,
ac causam nuncii ad hoc destinati dulci alloquio*d* et eloquenti dulcedine 25
investigant. Illi autem, ut novi hospites et advene, causam et modum
suorum applicatuum verbis plica carentibus eis humiliter exponunt et
eloquenter. Reversi autem nuncii cum seniorum reverenciam, juvenum

fo.94v

vero prudenciam, matronarum | maturitatem, et juvencularum venus-
tatem suo regi nunciassent, quidam subintulit dicens: 'Vidimus ibi 30
quandam dominam, quam ob forme incomparatam speciem, et
eloquencie jocunde facunditatem, cum ob ceterarum fecunditatem
virtutum, illius familie judicio meo dominam, suspicans tibi, rex,
annuncio, de cuius mirabili venustate et moralitate mirandum magis
censeo quam narrandum.' Nec mirum si illam dominam crediderint, 35
quam dominam non solum illius familie, sed eciam post fratrem Anglie
tocius heredem, ymmo regni sui participem futuramque reginam

G i,264

divina predestinaverit providencia. | Rex autem audiens illos Anglos et
ibidem adesse, propria persona illos visitat et alloquitur, et unde
venerunt, aut quo vadant plenius explorat. Anglicam enim linguam 40
simul et Romanam eque ut propriam plene didicerat, cum post patris
sui mortem xiiii annis in Anglia mansisset, ubi forte de cognicione
huius sancte familie aliquid audierat, quare cum eis micius ageret et
benignius se haberet.

a   D; lac.C
b   S,CA; regii C

c   corrected from admistracione C; ad
      admiracionem D
d   eloqueo CA

its waves rose high with the blast of the winds. As the storm raged, all
were put in despair of their lives, they commended themselves to God,
and entrusted their ship to the sea. So after very many dangers and
immense hardships the Lord took pity on His desolate family, since
10   when human aid is seen to fail, one inevitably turns to the Lord. At last
battered by countless perils on the sea, they were forced to land in
Scotland. So that saintly family landed at a certain place which since
that time has been called St Margaret's Bay by the local inhabitants.
And we believe that this did not happen accidentally, but that she came
15   to that place by the providence of the most high God. So while the
aforesaid family lingered on the said beach, and were all fearfully
awaiting the outcome of the affair, their arrival was reported to King
Malcolm, who was at that time staying with his people not far from
that place. He dispatched messengers to the ship to find out the true
20   state of affairs there. The messengers went to that place, were amazed
at the unusual size of the ship, and hurried as quickly as possible to tell
the king what they had seen. When he heard this, the king dispatched a
larger number of envoys to that place, more intelligent than the
previous ones and drawn from the ranks of his greatest nobles. They
25   were made welcome as envoys of the king's majesty, and having
carefully assessed with no small admiration the nobility of the men, the
beauty of the women and the earnestness of the whole family, they held
a pleasant conversation with each other thereafter. To cut a long story
short, the envoys appointed for this purpose inquired into the final
30   outcome, the sequence of events and the reason [for their coming], with
sweet eloquence and eloquent sweetness. They for their part, as being
strangers and incomers newly arrived, explained to them humbly and
eloquently the cause and manner of their landing in words with ut
guile. The envoys went back and reported to their king the cour   y
35   shown by the older men, the good sense of the younger men, the
wisdom of the matrons and the loveliness of the young girls, and one of
them added the words: 'We saw there a certain lady, who, I tell you,
Your Majesty, I suspect and judge is the mistress of the family on
account of her incomparable beauty of person and wealth of pleasing
40   eloquence as well as abundance of other good qualities. Her wonderful
charm and character I consider easier to admire than to describe.' And
no wonder they believed her to be the mistress, who was the mistress
not only of that family but also heiress to the whole of England after
her brother, and indeed predestined by providence to be the consort
45   and future queen of Malcolm's kingdom. Now the king when he heard
that they were English and were at that place, visited them and spoke to
them in his own person, and inquired more fully where they came from
and where they were going. For he was as fluent in the English and also
the French language as in his own, since after the death of his father he
50   had stayed in England for fourteen years, where, as it happened, he had
heard something to acquaint him with this saintly family, so that for
this reason he dealt with them more gently and behaved more kindly
towards them.

17

De conjugio Malcolmi regis et Margarite

Rex igitur utcumque Margaritam viderat, eamque de regio semine
simul et imperiali genitam esse didicerat, ut eam in uxorem duceret
peciit et optinuit,[a] tradente eam Eadgaro Ethling fratre suo, magis
suorum quam sua voluntate, ymmo Dei ordinacione. Nam sicut olim
Hester Assuero regi pro suorum salute concivium divina providencia, 5
ita et hec illustrissimo regi Malcolmo copulata fuit in conjugium, nec
tamen quasi captiva, ymmo multis habundans diviciis, quas patri suo
Eadwardo tamquam heredi, rex Anglie suus patruus prius dederat.
Quem[b] eciam ipse Romanus imperator Henricus (sicut ante paulo
prediximus) non minimis honoratum muneribus in Angliam misit. 10
Quarum partem permaximam hec sancta regina secum in Scociam
transtulit. Attulit eciam plurimas sanctorum reliquias omni lapide vel
auro preciosiores. Inter quas fuit illa sancta crux quam nigram[c]
vocant, omni genti Scotorum non minus terribilem quam amabilem
pro sue reverencia sanctitatis. Nupcie quidem facte sunt non procul a 15
sinu maris quo applicuit, et magnifice celebrate anno domini m° lxx[od]
loco qui dicitur Dunfermelyne, quem tunc temporis rex habebat pro
opido. Erat enim locus ille naturaliter in se munitissimus, densissima
silva circumdatus, preruptis rupibus premunitus. In cuius medio erat
venusta planicies eciam rupibus et rivulis munita ita[e] quod de ea 20
dictum esse putaretur:

Non homini facilis vix adeunda feris.

Willelmus:

Omnes Anglorum profugos Malcolmus libenter recipiebat, tutamen-
tum singulis quantum poterat impendens, Eadgarum cum Stigando 25
Cantuariensi et Aldredo Eboracensi archiepiscopis, sed Eadgarum
precipue, cuius sororem pro antiqua memoria nobilitatis jugalem sibi
fecerat. Eius causa conterminas Anglie provincias rapinis et incendiis
infestabat. Eboracum unicum rebellionum suffugium ipse Malcolmus
rex cum suis, et Eadgarus, Marcherius et Weldeofus cum Anglis et 30
Danis nidum tirannidis sepe fovebant, sepe duces illius trucidabant,

a +xiiii regnacionis sue anno *CA*
b *G*; Quas *S,C*
c +crucem *in later hand D*

d lxvii *in margin, apparently as a correction for* lxx° *D*
e *P; om.S,C*

17

The marriage of King Malcolm and Margaret

As soon as the king saw Margaret, and learned that she was of royal
and also imperial descent, he sought to have her as his wife, and
succeeded, with Edgar the Ætheling her brother giving her away,
more in accordance with the wishes of her people than her own desire,
5 or rather at God's command. For just as Esther was married to King
Ahasuerus by divine providence for the salvation of her fellow
countrymen, so Margaret was united in wedlock with the most
illustrious King Malcolm, not however as a captive but rather having
abundance of great riches, which had previously been given to her
10 father Edward by his uncle the king of England as his heir. The
Roman emperor himself (as we mentioned a little before) sent him to
England, and presented him with generous gifts. This saintly queen
brought over to Scotland a very large part of this wealth. She also
brought very many relics of the saints more precious than any gem or
15 gold. Amongst these relics there was that holy cross which they call
the Black Cross, inspiring awe as well as love in the whole people of
the Scots out of reverence for its sanctity. The wedding took place not
far from the bay of the sea where she landed, and was celebrated with
great magnificence in 1070 in the place which is called Dunfermline, [1070 ?]
20 which the king had as his capital at that time. For that place was
naturally very well fortified in itself, being surrounded by a very dense
forest and protected by sheer cliffs. In the middle of the forest there
was a charming plain also protected by rocks and streams, so that one
might think that this place was being referred to in the line:

25   Not easy of access to man, scarcely approachable by wild
             beasts.

William [of Malmesbury] says:

          Malcolm freely received all the English fugitives, affording protection
          for each one as far as he could, Edgar along with Stigand archbishop of
30   Canterbury and Ealdred archbishop of York, but Edgar especially
          whose sister he had married because of her long line of noble descent.
          For Edgar's sake he harried the neighbouring provinces of England   [1070]
          with plundering and arson. King Malcolm himself with his men and
          Edgar, Morcar and Waltheof with the English and Danes often
35   breached the defences of York, which had been the only refuge for

quorum singillatim exitus si commemoravero, fortasse superfluus^f ero.
Hii duo Stigandus et Aldredus cleri principes Londoniis fuerant cum
Eadgarus iste filius Eadwardi filii Eadmundi Irneside post regis

G i,265 Eadwardi mortem, post itaque Willelmi Bastard | victoriam, ab 35
omnibus aliis promotus fuisset in regem, si non ipsi nequiter
restitissent.

Illis autem et omnibus dictum esse puto per prophetam: 'Juste
judicate filii hominum.' Sed quoniam injuste judicabant, reddidit
Deus juste judicium idem in caput suum, adeo quod a possessionibus 40
cunctis statim expulsi, sub alas^g eius quem injuste respuerant refugii
locum querentes, latenter Scociam advenerunt.

Scriptor In vetusta cronica sic repperi scriptum:

Anno m^o lxx rex Malcolmus Angliam usque Diveland sive Cliveland^h
vastavit, et tunc clitoni Eadgaro et sororibus Margarite et Christine 45
sive Christiane, ubi eas invenit regem Anglie fugientes,ⁱ ut in Scociam
irent in reditu pacem suam donavit, et Margaritam postea sibi in
matrimonium junxit. Stigandus ab archiepiscopatu deponitur a legatis
Alexandri pape, et multe alie persone, quia Eadgarum ne regnaret spre-

fo.95 | verunt. Et mortuo Aldredo archiepiscopo, Thomas et Lanfrancus 50
archiepiscopi consecrantur, Lanfrancus a suffraganeis, Thomas a
Lanfranco. ⟨Lanfrancus et Thomas Romam profecti pallia ab
Alexandro papa susceperunt.⟩

---

f   + non S   h   sive Cliveland *interlin.C*
g   alis *CA*   i   fugientibus *CA*

18

De filiacione Malcolmi et Margarite

^aAnno ^b ⟨m^o lxx^c [incepit ordo Grandimontensis sub patre Stephano
regule canonicorum Sancti Augustini.^d] ^e In alio loco repperi
scriptum. 'Anno domini m^o lxvii Sancta Margarita co-[pulata fuit]^f
matrimonialiter regi Malcolmo anno regni sui^g xiii.^h Hic Angliam
usque Cly-[veland]^f vastavit, et rediens per Wirwidam, que dicitur 5
Ostium Weri fluminis, intravit Scociam, et invenit [ante]^f se Eadgarum Ethling et sorores suas Margaritam et Cristinam in nave

---

a   + Autor *in margin, relating to original*   d   Augustimi *D*
     text before insertions C   e   *D; lac.probably after del.C*
b   + quo supra *del. when following additions*   f   *D; lac.C*
     were made in margin C   g   *D; suo C*
c   m^o lxxvi *D*   h   xii *in margin as a correction D*

rebels and was now a nest of tyranny, and often slew its leaders.
Perhaps I should be over-zealous if I were to record their deaths
individually. These two Stigand and Ealdred had been the leading
clerics in London when this Edgar son of Edward son of Edmund
40   Ironside after the death of King Edward and likewise after the victory
of William the Bastard would have been promoted to the kingship by
all the others, if the clerics had not wickedly opposed it.

I think that it should be said to them and to all men in the words of the
prophet: 'Judge justly, sons of men.' But since they judged unjustly,
45 God justly brought the same judgment on their heads, so that they
were immediately driven out of all their properties, and came secretly
to Scotland, seeking a place of refuge under the wings of the man
whom they had unjustly rejected.
I have found the following account in an old chronicle:

50   In 1070 King Malcolm laid England waste as far as Develand or   1070
Cleveland, and at that time he extended his protection to Edgar the
Ætheling and his sisters Margaret and Christina or Christiana, when
he found them fleeing from the king of England, in order that they
might return to Scotland, and he later married Margaret. Stigand was
55   deposed from his office of archbishop by legates of Pope Alexander,   [1070]
and many other clerics were similarly deposed because they had
prevented Edgar from becoming king. And after the death of
Archbishop Ealdred, Thomas and Lanfranc were consecrated as
archbishops, Lanfranc by his suffragans, Thomas by Lanfranc.
60   Lanfranc and Thomas set out for Rome to receive the pallium from   [1071]
Pope Alexander.

18

The children of Malcolm and Margaret

In 1070 the Grandmontine Order of the rule of the Canons of St   1070
Augustine began under Father Stephen. In another place I found
written: 'In 1067 St Margaret was united in matrimony with King   [1070 ?]
Malcolm in the thirteenth year of his reign. He laid waste England as
5   far as Cleveland, and returning by Wirwida which is called
Wearmouth, he entered Scotland, and found before him Edgar the
Ætheling and his sisters Margaret and Christina hiding in a ship near
Culross; and he married Margaret.' King Malcolm and Margaret had
six illustrious sons, Edward, Edmund, Æthelred, Edgar, Alexander
10 and the most energetic of all kings David, and two daughters Matilda,
afterwards queen of England, nicknamed 'the Good', and Mary
countess of Boulogne. Later on at the appropriate place they will be
dealt with individually. The king often invaded the northern

[Autor]

latitantem [prope]^f Culros; et Margaritam matrimo-[nio copula-
vit.']^j⟩ | De qua^i Malcolmus rex genuit ex Margarita sex inclitos filios,
scilicet Eadwardum, Eadmundum, Ethelredum, Eadgarum, Alexan- 10
drum et omnium regum strenuissimum David, et duas filias,
Matildem scilicet postea reginam Anglie cognomento Bonam, et
Mariam comitissam Bononie, de quibus singulis postea suo loco
dicetur. Sepissime autem rex boreales Anglie provincias a primo
regnacionis tempore Willelmi Bastard usque post eciam eius obitum, 15
valida manu ingressus, omnia vastando circumquaque destruxit;
animancia queque predis et rapina hostiliter abstulit, cunctaque visui
humano que non abstulit, flammis et ferro de superficie terre
crudeliter^j consumpsit. Innumerabilium itaque catervas hominum
abduxit, ita quod in regno suo domus ferme vel casa nequaquam 20
extiterat, que virilis sexus aut feminei^k captivos non tenebat. Quorum

G i,266

autem enumerando, quis | explicare poterit quot et quantos benedicta
regina regis conjux, dato precio, libertati restituerit, quos de gentibus
Anglorum abducens captivos hostilis violencia redigerat in servos?
Continuis autem excidiis et depredacionibus rex Angliam intrans, 25
Northumbriam ultra flumen These vastavit. Tandem cum nobilibus
tocius Northumbrie concordatus, omnem patriam, episcopo Wal-
therio Dunelmensi cum aliis pluribus apud Gatishede occisis, preter
castra quedam in dedicionem accepit; omnesque comprovinciales ad
pacem suam et fidem redegit. Et licet Malcolmus pro xii villis in 30
Anglia existentibus homo Willelmi Bastard devenerit, provocatus
tamen per quosdam Norhumros,^{l} hominium illud abjecit. Et tales
irrupciones pessimas et strages eis importabiles non immerito
cumulavit. Vincencius: 'Circa annum Henrici iiii^{ti} xiiii hinc Scotis,
hinc Francis Angliam incursantibus, Angli tanta fame consumuntur 35
ut quidam humanam carnem et multi carnibus equinis vescuntur.' |

Scriptor

Anno m^o lxxii Willelmus Scociam intravit, cui occurrens rex
Malcolmus, in loco qui dicitur Abernethy homo suus devenit pro
terris in Anglia. Rex Willelmus in reditu de Scocia, temere per suos
capellanos de Sancto Cuthberto explorare volens, territus a Dunelmo 40
et sub velocitate recessit. Anno sequenti clito Eadgarus cum rege
Willelmo pacificatus est. Anno eciam sequenti illum Hildebrandus in
papam electus est, et G[regorius] vii^{us} dictus. Hunc Cencius prefecti
filius in nocte Natalis Domini, cum primam missam in Sancta Maria
Majore ad presepe Domini celebraret, cepit et in turre sua posuit. Sed 45
Romani eadem nocte turrim destruxerunt, papam liberando, et
predictum Cencium extra urbem ejecerunt. Hic Gregorius totus
contra Henricum, quia discidium procurabat, et Romane ecclesie
unitatem scindere voluit, invehitur. Imperator vero Wormane consilio xxiii episcoporum et multorum nobilium congregato, jubet omnia 50

---

i   De qua *interlin.*C   *k*   *corrected from* femenei C
j   + abstulit *del.*C   *l*   Norhumberos D

provinces of England with main force from the early days of the reign
15 of William the Bastard until after his death, devastating and
destroying everything all around. With hostile intent he removed
every living thing as booty and pillage, and everything that he did not
remove from human view, he savagely did away with by fire and
sword from the face of the earth. He abducted droves of people
20 without number so that in his kingdom there was hardly to be found
any house or hut at all which did not contain prisoners of male or
female sex. In the account of these prisoners who will be able to
expound how many and how great they were whom the blessed queen
and consort of the king restored to liberty by paying ransom, after
25 they had been abducted from the peoples of England by enemy
violence, and reduced to slavery? Now the king as he invaded England
with continual devastation and plundering laid waste Northumbria
beyond the river Tees. Finally he came to an agreement with the
nobles of the whole of Northumbria, and after Walcher bishop of
30 Durham along with many others had been killed at Gateshead, he   [1080]
accepted the surrender of the whole country except for certain castles;
and he compelled all the Northumbrians to submit to his peace and
fealty. And although Malcolm did homage to William the Bastard for
twelve vills in England, nevertheless after he had been challenged by
35 certain Northumbrians, he gave up his allegiance. And he quite
rightly gave them full measure of such destructive raids and massacres
that were insupportable to them. Vincent says: 'Around about the
fourteenth year of Henry IV, while the Scots were invading England
from one direction and the French from another, the English were
40 consumed with such a great famine that some of them ate human
flesh, and many of them horse-flesh.' In 1072 William invaded   1072
Scotland, and King Malcolm came to meet him at a place which is
called Abernethy, and did homage to him for his lands in England.
King William on his return from Scotland, rashly wishing to find out
45 about St Cuthbert from his chaplains, was chased out of Durham and
speedily withdrew. In the following year Edgar the Ætheling made   1073
peace with King William. Also in the year following that Hildebrand
was elected pope and was called Gregory VII. He was captured and
put in his tower by Cenci the son of the prefect [of Rome] on
50 Christmas night when he was celebrating the first mass in Santa Maria   25 Dec.
Maggiore at the Lord's crib. But the Romans demolished the tower
on the same night when they set the pope free, and banished the
aforesaid Cenci beyond the city bounds. This Gregory was wholly
opposed to [the emperor] Henry, and inveighed against him because
55 he caused dissension, and wished to split the unity of the church of
Rome. The emperor convened a council of twenty-three bishops and   [1076: Jan.]
many nobles at Worms, and ordered all the decrees of Pope Gregory
to be annulled; in response to this the pope held a council of nine
hundred bishops, excommunicated the emperor, and released all his

decreta G[regorii] pape cassari; propter quod imperatorem, consilio
nongentorum episcoporum habito, excommunicavit et a fidelitate et
juramento omnes sibi adherentes absolvit. Imperator vero Maguncie
ipsum a papatu, quantum in ipso erat, deposuit et Wibertum
Ravennensem episcopum pro eo fecit antipapam. Et anno m° lxxxi°   55
Henricus hostiliter Romam adversus papam adiit, et continuavit
obsidionem usque ad noctem Palmarum, ubi fit magna congressio
parcium et quamplures occisi.

19

*De eisdem G[regorio] et Henrico et censura simili Ambrosii
contra Theodosium imperatorem*

fo.95v

Post hec Henricus ad papam Gregorium in Longobardiam veniens,
nudis pedibus super nivem et glaciem pluribus diebus stans, vix
absolucionem impetravit. Interim vero Henrico imperatore in Italia
existente, principes Alemannie in Porchein convenientes, quendam
Radulphum ducem Saxonie in regem sibi elegerunt. Quem, quia papa   5
G[regorius] ad peticionem imperatoris Henrici non conventum,

G i,267

convictum vel confessum excommunicare noluit, imperator, | cruento
bello victoria contra ipsum habita,[a] dictum Wibertum instinctu dicti
Henrici, excommunicati plurimi episcopi sediciosi apud Brixiam
convenientes reintruserunt, Clementem[b] vocantes. Quem rex Henri-   10
cus primus in terram corruens, cum omnibus aliis mox adoravit, et
cum [ipso][c] Romam veniens sine cardinalibus a Bononia, in die
Pasche ab eo coronam imperii sumpsit. Propter quod a Gregorio
papa cum denuo excommunicatus fuisset cum suo antipapa ipsum et
cardinales cum multa hostilitate in urbe obsedit. Sed post depopula-   15
cionem agrorum et vinearum, cum imperator sibi populi Romani
favorem attraxerat, destructo Capitolio et Urbe Leonine, papa
G[regorio] cum cardinalibus in castro Sancti Angeli concluso, quod
obsesserat. Quem Christianus princeps Robertus Guiscardi rex
Apulie cum magno exercitu veniens, et Romam uno die capiens,   20
imperatore cum suo antipapa usque Senas fugiente, de castro cum
cardinalibus educens, in palacio Lateranensi reposuit, in hoc imperatori consencientes exilio et aliis penis graviter affligendo. Qui
Gregorius post in Apuliam descendens, Salerni mortuus est, miraculis coruscando. Similem isti prelato G[regorio] Ambrosium Mediola-   25
nensem fuisse cognoscimus, de quo in Historia Tripartita dicitur,
quod cum apud Thesolonicam orta sedicione, quidam judices fuissent

---

a +convocata curia in Brixina *del.*C   *c*   G
b *corrected from* clementes C

60 adherents from their oath of allegiance. The emperor deposed him   [1080: June]
    from the papacy at Mainz as far as lay in his power, and created as
    antipope in his place Guibert bishop of Ravenna. And in 1081 Henry   [1083: early]
    came to Rome with hostile intent against the pope, and kept up the
    siege right until Palm Sunday when there was a great clash of factions,   [1084:
65 and very many men were killed.   24 Mar.]

19

More about Gregory and Henry, and a similar rebuke from
Ambrose to the emperor Theodosius

After this Henry came to Pope Gregory in Lombardy, standing with   [1077: Jan.]
bare feet in snow and ice for many days, and only just obtained
absolution. Meanwhile the princes of Germany met in Forchheim   [Mar.]
and chose a certain Rudolph duke of Saxony as their king, while the
5 emperor Henry was in Italy. Because Pope Gregory refused the
request of the emperor Henry to excommunicate Rudolph, when he
had not been summoned, convicted or confessed, the emperor
defeated him in a fierce battle. A large number of dissident bishops
who had been excommunicated met at Brixen, and again intruded the   [1080: June]
10 said Guibert at the instigation of the said Henry, calling him Clement.
King Henry first of all fell to the ground, then did obeisance to him
with all the rest, and coming to Rome with him from Bologna without
the cardinals, he received the imperial crown from him on Easter day.   [1084:
Because of this he was again excommunicated by Pope Gregory, and   31 Mar.]
15 along with his antipope he laid siege to him and the cardinals in Rome
with much hostility. But after laying waste the fields and vineyards,
the emperor won over the favour of the Roman people to himself,
destroyed the Capitol and the Leonine City, while Pope Gregory was
shut up with the cardinals in the castle of S. Angelo which Henry had
20 besieged. The Christian prince Robert Guiscard king of Apulia came
with a great army and captured Rome in one day. The emperor fled
with his antipope to Siena, and Robert brought the pope out of the
castle along with the cardinals, and restored him to the Lateran
palace. There he harshly inflicted exile and other punishments on the
25 emperor's supporters. Gregory later went down into Apulia, and died   [1085:
at Salerno in a blaze of miracles.   25 May]
    We know that Ambrose of Milan (an account of him is given in the
Tripartite History) resembled Gregory, because when revolt arose in
Thessalonica, certain judges had been stoned by the populace, and the
30 emperor Theodosius indignant at this ordered all of them to be killed,

a populo lapidati, Theodosius imperator indignatus jussit omnes
interimi, nocentes ab innocentibus non secernens, ubi fere quinque
milia hominum sunt occisi. Cum igitur imperator Mediolanum 30
venisset, et ecclesiam intrare vellet, occurrit ei Ambrosius ad januam
eique aditum prohibuit dicens: 'Cur, imperator, post causam tanti
funeris non agnoscis molem tue presumpcionis? Sed forte recognicio-
nem peccati prohibet potestas imperii. Decet te, ut vincat racio
potestatem. Princeps es, O imperator, sed conservorum. Quibus ergo 35
oculis aspicies communis Domini templum? Quibus calcabis pedibus
sanctum pavimentum? Quomodo manus extendes, de quibus sanguis
adhuc stillat innocentum?[d] Qua presumpcione ore tuo poculum
sanguinis eius percipies, dum furore sermonum tuorum tantus injuste
sit sanguis effusus? Recede ergo, recede, ne secundo peccato priorem 40
nequiciam augere contendas. Suscipe nunc vinculum quo te Dominus
nunc ligavit. Est enim medicina maxime sanitatis.' Hiis sermonibus
imperator obediens gemens et flens ad regalia remeavit.

d   CA; injustus C

20

De eodem

Cum ergo diu in fletu mansisset, Rufinus magister militum causam
tante tristicie requisivit. Cui ille: 'Tu', inquit, 'mea mala non sentis,
quia servis et mendicantibus aperta sunt templa, michi vero ad ea
ingressus non est.' Et hec dicens, singula verba singultibus interrum-
pebat. Cui Rufinus: 'Curro', inquit, 'si vis ad Ambrosium, ut tibi 5
excommunicacionis solvat vinculum quo te ligavit.' Et ille: 'Unde
poteris suadere Ambrosio quia non verebitur imperialem potenciam,
ut lege possit privari divina?' Sed cum promitteret quod eum flecteret,
imperator ire precepit, et ipse post paululum est secutus. Mox autem
G i,268   ut | Ambrosius Rufinum vidit, et causam aggressionis eius cognovis- 10
set, ait: 'Impudenciam canum imitatus es, O Rufine, tante videlicet
necis autor existens, et nunc pudorem ex fronte detergens, non
erubescis supra majestatem latrare divinam.' Cumque Rufinus pro
imperatore supplicasset, et diceret eum sequi, superno zelo accensus
fo.96   Ambrosius | ait: 'Ego tibi predico quoniam ingredi eum sacra limina 15
prohibebo. Si vero potestatem in tirannidem mutaverit, necem
libenter suscipio.' Quod cum Rufinus imperatori nunciasset: 'Per-
gam', inquit,[a] 'ad eum, ut justas in faciem contumelias percipiam.'

a   G; inquam C,D

making no distinction between the guilty and the innocent. Almost
five thousand people were killed. So when the emperor came to Milan,
and wished to enter the church, Ambrose met him at the door, and
forbade him to enter saying: 'Why, your majesty, after causing so
35 many deaths, do you not recognise the magnitude of your presumption? But perhaps imperial power precludes acknowledgement of sin.
You ought to allow reason to rise superior to power. You are the
ruler, your majesty, but ruler of your fellow-servants. With what eyes
then will you look upon the temple of the Lord, who is the lord of all?
40 With what feet will you tread the holy pavement? How will you reach
out your hands from which the blood of the innocent is still dripping?
With what boldness will you receive the cup of His blood with your
lips, when by the mad fury of your pronouncements so much blood
has been unjustly shed? Withdraw therefore, withdraw lest you
45 contrive to compound your former wickedness with a second sin.
Take up now the chain with which the Lord has now bound you. For
it is the medicine that brings the greatest salvation.' The emperor
obeyed these words, and went back to his palace groaning and
weeping.

20

The same

So when he had continued weeping for a long while, Rufinus the
Master of the Soldiers inquired the reason for such great grief. The
emperor said to him: 'You are not affected by my misfortunes,
because the temples are open to slaves and beggars, but for me there is
5 no admission to them.' And as he said this, he groaned with every
word he uttered. Rufinus said to him: 'I will run, if you wish, to
Ambrose, so that he may release you from the chains of excommunication, with which he bound you.' And the emperor said: 'What
means have you to persuade Ambrose to give up divine law, since he
10 has no fear of imperial power?' But when Rufinus promised that he
would persuade Ambrose, the emperor ordered him to go, and he
himself followed a little later. Now as soon as Ambrose saw Rufinus,
and learned the reason for his coming, he said: 'You have the
impudence of a dog, Rufinus, responsible as you are for such a
15 massacre, and now you have wiped shame from your face and do not
blush to bark at the majesty of God.' And when Rufinus had pleaded
for the emperor, and said that he was following behind, Ambrose was
incensed with the wrath of Heaven, and said: 'I give you notice that I
shall forbid him to cross the sacred threshold. If he transmutes his
20 power into tyranny, I accept death gladly.' When Rufinus reported

Cum ergo venisset, et sua solvi vincula postulasset, occurrens
Ambrosius et ingressum prohibens ait: 'Quam penitenciam ostendisti   20
post tantas iniquitates?' Et ille: 'Tuum est, pater, imponere et meum[b]
obtemperare.' Unde cum[c] imperator allegaret ut[d] David adulterium
et homicidium perpetrasset, ait Ambrosius: 'Qui secutus es errantem,
sequere corrigentem.' Quod ita gratanter imperator suscepit, ut
publicam penitenciam agere non recusavit. Cum itaque reconsiliatus   25
ecclesiam intrasset, et intra cancellos staret, requirit Ambrosius quid
ibi expectaret. Cui cum diceret se percepcionem sacrorum misteri-
orum expectare, ait Ambrosius: 'O imperator, interiora loca tantum
sacerdotibus sunt collata. Egredere igitur, et hanc expectacionem
cum ceteris communem habe.' Cui imperator mox obedivit. Cum   30
ergo Constantinopolim reversus, extra cancellos staret, mandavit
eidem episcopus ut intraret. Et ille ait: 'Vix discernere potui que
differencia sit imperatoris et pontificis.[e] Vix enim veritatis inveni
magistrum Ambrosium, namque solum novi vocari pontificem.'[f]

 [g]Anno m⁰ lxxv^to Philippus rex Francorum ab obsidione[h] Doll   35
fugavit regem Willelmum. Anno m⁰ lxxvii Robertus Curthose
guerram contra patrem suum regem Willelmum movit, auxilio
Philippi regis Francorum, eo quod Normanniam sibi coram eodem
rege promiserat, et non dederat.

 Anno m⁰ lxxix rex Malcolmus Angliam usque ad Tynam vastavit. 40
Eodem anno rex Wilelmus a filio suo Roberto, et eciam Willelmus
Red frater eius, ante castellum Gerboreth vulnerati sunt et in fugam
conversi.[i]

b + op *del.C*	episcopus missus a rege Willelmo
c + pr *del.C*	Northumbriam vastavit. Et in continenti
d et C	rex Willelmus filium suum Robertum
e CA; sacerdotis C	contra Malcolmum in Scociam usque ad
f + Hec ibi. CA	Eaglesbret misit, qui nullo perfecto
g *perhaps* Autor *in margin and del.C*	negocio reversus Novum Castellum
h + castrum de *in margin* D	condidit *del.C; included in text R;*
i + Anno sequenti Odo Bajocensis	*om.*D,CA

21

*Quod Northumbrenses regi Malcolmo datis obsidibus
adheserunt*

Autor

Anno m⁰ lxxx rex Willelmus postquam regnum omnibus ad velle
dispositis optinuisset, in transmarinis partibus cum filio suo Roberto
concordatus est. Cumque eidem in Normannia adhuc existenti
nunciatum fuerat, quod quidam finium suorum incole habitatores
scilicet Northumbrie ad regem Malcolmum ab eo divertissent,   5
adversus eos Odonem fratrem suum Bajocensem episcopum, quem

this to the emperor, he said: 'I shall go to him myself, in order that I
may receive his just rebukes face to face.' So when he came, and had
asked for his chains to be removed, Ambrose came to meet him, and
forbade his entry, saying: 'What penitence have you shown after
25 committing such great crimes?' And he said: 'That is for you, father,
to impose, and for me to obey.' Then when the emperor alleged that
David had committed adultery and murder, Ambrose said: 'Do you
who have followed him in his wrong-doing, follow him in his
amendment.' This the emperor accepted so thankfully that he
30 consented to perform public penance. When he entered the church
after his reconciliation, and was standing inside the chancel, Ambrose
asked him what he was waiting for there. When he told him that he
was waiting to receive the sacred mysteries, Ambrose said: 'Your
majesty, the inner places are reserved for priests only. So go out, and
35 wait to receive in common with all the others.' The emperor soon
obeyed him. Then when he returned to Constantinople and stood
outside the chancel, the bishop told him to go inside. And the emperor
said: 'I was scarcely able to distinguish what the difference was
between an emperor and a pontifex. For I only just found Ambrose
40 master of the truth, and I know that only he is to be called pontifex.'
  In 1075 Philip king of the French turned King William to flight [1076]
from the siege of Dol. In 1077 Robert Curthose declared war on his [1077-8]
father King William with the help of Philip king of the French,
because William had promised Normandy to him in the presence of
45 the king, and had not given it to him.
  In 1079 King Malcolm devastated England as far as the Tyne. In 1079
the same year King William was wounded in front of the castle of
Gerberoy and turned to flight by his son Robert, as was William
Rufus brother of Robert.

21

*The Northumbrians gave hostages and sided with King
Malcolm*

In 1080 after King William had secured the kingdom, and arranged
everything to his own satisfaction, he was reconciled with his son 1080:
Robert in the lands overseas. And when it had been reported to him [12 Apr.]
while he was still in Normandy that certain people living on his
5 borders, that is the inhabitants of Northumbria, had gone over from
him to King Malcolm, he sent against them his brother Odo the [spring]

comitem Cancie fecerat, cum magna milicia recipiendos misit. Atque
Northumbri, datis regi Malcolmo prius obsidibus, Scotis firmiter
adheserunt, et Odo, patria vastata, rediit partes ad australes.
Recedentem igitur Odonem Malcolmus persecutus est, copiis suis | 10

aliqualem stragem dedit et circa Humbri fluminis litora, exercitu fuso,
Normannorum et Anglorum terras incredibili cede circumquaque
destruens, cum predis ac spoliis infinitis in patriam reversus est. Cuius
assiduas sediciones irrupciones rex Willelmus ferre non valens,
Robertum filium suum, ut regi Malcolmo bellum inferret, Scociam 15
misit. At ille nullo parto negocio revertens, Novum Castrum condidit
super Tynam. Diu namque postquam Willelmus Angliam invaserat,
Northumbrorum proceres et australium multi civitatem Eboracensem cum tota patria Scotorum fulti presidio multis annis tenuerunt,
crebras irrupciones atque crudelissimas cediciones trans Humbri 20
flumen facientes in Normannos. Woldeofum comitem Siwardi filium,
quem rex Malcolmus fidelissimum semper habebat amicum, quem
eciam rex Willelmus supra ceteros Anglorum sibi resistencium magis
metuerat, conjugio sue neptis Judith deceptum callide cepit, ac diu
detentum in vinculis postmodum jussit decapitari. Funus autem eius 25
apud Croland delatum est et sepultum. Cuius mortem injustam, et

opinionem esse veram, manifeste Deus | ibidem ostendens, innumera
pro eo miracula misericorditer operatur. Willelmus: 'Waldeofus alias
Waldevus in Eboracensi pugna plures Normannorum solus obtrun-
caverat, ut eius utar verbis, "unos et unos per portam egredientes 30
decapitans." Nervosus lacertis, thorosus pectore, robustus et procerus toto corpore, quem *Digera* Danico vocabulo (id est "Fortem")
cognominabant.' Willelmus rex anno regni xv^{to} de transmarinis
expedicionibus rediens, totam Northumbriam vastavit.

Anno m^o lxxxiiii^{to}. ⟨Hoc anno fundatur Cartusia regule Benedicti 35
sub patre Brunone Theutonico.⟩ De unaquaque hyda per Angliam
sex solidos accepit. Et anno m^o lxxxvi fecit describi totam Angliam, in
qua reperiuntur ecclesie parochiales quadraginta quinque milia et
xvii; comitatus xxxvi milia; item feoda militum sexaginta milia ccxv,
de quibus religiosi habent xxviii, milites xv.^{a} Quo anno clito Eadgarus 40
Ethlin frater Sancte Margarite cum ducentis militibus mare transiens,
Apuliam adiit. Cuius soror Christiana monasterium Rumeseia
intravit et sanctimonialem habitum suscepit. ⟨Repperi autem sic
scriptum [quod]^b Agatha mater Sancte Margarite et Cristina so-[ror]^b
eius apud Novum [Castrum]^b super Tyne sponse Christi [conse-]crate^b 45
sunt.⟩ Anno m^o lxxxvi reliquie Sancti Nicholai de Mirreia usque ad
Barensem transferuntur.

---

a   + *line left blank C*   *b*   *D; lac.C*

bishop of Bayeux, whom he had made earl of Kent, with a large force
to win them back. The Northumbrians having previously given
hostages to King Malcolm clung firmly to the Scots, and Odo
10 returned to the southern regions, after laying waste the country. So
Malcolm pursued Odo as he withdrew, and inflicted a certain amount
of damage with his forces. Deploying his army, he destroyed the lands
of the Normans and the English on the banks of the river Humber
with incredible slaughter all around, and returned to his own country
15 with countless booty and spoils. King William could not endure his
constant dissensions and incursions, so sent his son Robert to [autumn]
Scotland to wage war on King Malcolm, but he returned without
achieving any success. He founded Newcastle-upon-Tyne. For a long
time after William's invasion of England, many nobles of the
20 Northumbrians and southerners had held the city of York and the
whole of the countryside for many years with the support of the Scots,
making frequent raids across the river Humber against the Normans
and causing savage slaughter. Earl Waltheof son of Siward, whom
King Malcolm always regarded as a most faithful friend, and whom
25 King William feared more than all the rest of the English who held out
against him, was captured after he had been cunningly tricked by
marriage with William's niece Judith. Later, after he had been held
prisoner for a long time, William ordered him to be beheaded. His [1076]
body was brought to Croyland, and buried there. It has been clearly
30 shown that the view that his death was unjust is correct by the
countless miracles performed by God in his mercy in that same place
on his behalf. William [of Malmesbury] says: 'Waltheof, also known
as Waldevus, slew many of the Normans by himself in the battle of
York, to use his own words "beheading them one by one as they came
35 out through the gates." He had sinewy arms, a brawny chest, and was
big and strong over all his frame. He was called *Digera* (that is
"strong") in the Danish language.' King William, returning from his
overseas expeditions in the fifteenth year of his reign, laid waste the 1081
whole of Northumbria.
40 1084. In this year the Carthusian order of the rule of Benedict was 1084
founded under Father Bruno the Teuton. William received six
shillings from each and every hide throughout England, and in 1086 1086
he caused the whole of England to be surveyed. In it are found 45,017
parish churches, 36 earldoms, likewise 60,215 knights' fiefs, of which
45 the religious have 28,000, the knights 15,000. In this year Edgar the
Ætheling brother of St Margaret crossed the sea with two hundred
knights, and landed in Apulia. His sister Christina entered a
monastery at Romsey, and put on the nun's habit. I have found it
recorded that Agatha the mother of St Margaret and Christina her
50 sister were consecrated as brides of Christ at Newcastle-upon-Tyne.
In 1086 the relics of St Nicholas were transferred from Myra to Bari. [1087]

22

De obitu Willelmi Bastard et de successione
Willelmi Rufi filii

Anno Malcolmi regis xxxi rex Anglie Willelmus Bastard Conquestor
obiit Rothomago anno quo supra.[a] Nam cum ipse Franciam cum
grandi exercitu invaserat, et opidum quod Mathunton nuncupatur
obsesserat et omnes ecclesias in ipso opido sitas, duosque reclusos
igne succenderat, inde Normanniam rediit. Sed isto reditu dirus 5
viscerum dolor illum apprehendit, et magis ac magis de die in diem
gravabat. Cum autem ingravescente egritudine diem sibi mortis
iminere sensisset, fratrem suum Odonem Bajocensem | episcopum, et
comites Morkarum, Rogerum, et Siwardum cognomento Barn, et
Ulnotum regis Haroldi germanum quem a puericia in custodia, et 10
omnes quos vel in Anglia vel in Normannia custodie manciparat,
relaxavit. Deinde filio suo Willelmo regnum tradidit Anglie, et
Roberto primogenito suo qui tunc in Francia exulabat comitatum
Normannie concessit, ⟨et Henrico juniori filio thesaurum;⟩ et sic
celesti viatico munitus, postquam xx[ti] annis mensibus xi genti 15
Anglorum prefuit, v° iduum septembrium die regnum cum vita
perdidit, et Cadomi in ecclesia Sancti Stephani sepultus est, et quam
ipse a fundamentis construxerat bonisque ditaverat. ⟨Anno domini
m° lxxxvii epitaphium eius:

[C]esariem,[b] Cesar, tibi [s]i[b] natura nega-[vit][b]   20
hanc, Willelme, tibi [s]tella[b] cometa dedit.⟩

Autor
Cuius corpus per Secanam Cadamum delatum est. Willelmus:
'Varietatis humane tunc fuit videre miseriam, quod homo ille, tocius
olim Europe honor, antecessorum suorum omnium potencior, sedem
eterne requiecionis sine calumpnia impetrare non potuit. Namque 25
miles quidam, ad cuius patrimonium locus ille pertinuit, clara
contestans voce rapinam, sepulturam inhibuit dicens avito jure solum
suum esse, nec illum in locum quem violenter invaserat pausare
debere. Quocirca volente Henrico filio, qui solus ex liberis aderat,
centum libre argenti litigatori persolute audacem calumpniam 30
compescuerunt.'

G i,270

---

a   vir singularis severitatis et censura. Alia   b   D; lac.C
    cronica dicit eum obisse anno m° xcii° for
    anno quo supra CA

22

The death of William the Bastard and the succession of William Rufus his son

In the thirty-first year of King Malcolm William the Bastard the
Conqueror king of England died at Rouen in the year given above. 1087:
When he had invaded France with a large army, and had besieged the 9 Sept.
town which is called Mantes, and had burnt down all the churches
5 and two recluses in that town, he returned to Normandy. But while he
was on the return journey, he was seized by a dire internal complaint,
and he became worse and worse by the day. As his condition
deteriorated, and he felt that the day of his death was at hand, he
released his brother Odo the bishop of Bayeux and the earls Morcar,
10 Roger and Siward surnamed Barn, and Wulfnoth the brother of King
Harold, whom he had kept in prison since his childhood, and all those
whom he had kept under guard either in England or in Normandy.
Then he handed over the kingdom of England to his son William and
the county of Normandy to Robert his eldest son, who was then in
15 exile in France, and he granted treasure to Henry his youngest son.
And so fortified by the last rites of the church, after he had ruled over
the English people for twenty-one years and eleven months, he lost his
kingdom along with his life on 9 September 1087, and was buried in
the church of St Stephen in Caen, which he himself had built from the
20 foundations, and had enriched with gifts. His epitaph is as follows:

Nature denied you majestic tresses, Your Majesty
but you were given them, William, by a starry comet.

His body was taken along the Seine to Caen. William [of
Malmesbury] says: 'Then one could see the wretchedness that arises
25 from the fickleness of human fortune, in that that man once the glory
of the whole of Europe, more powerful than all his predecessors, was
not able to obtain a place for his eternal repose without dispute. For a
certain knight, to whose patrimony that place belonged, claiming in a
loud voice that it was theft, forbade the burial, saying that the ground
30 was his by ancestral right, and William ought not to repose in that
place which he had violently invaded. So by the wishes of his son
Henry, who alone of his children was present, the payment of a
hundred pounds of silver to the disputant put a stop to his rash
accusation.'
35 His son William quickly made for England, taking with him

Scriptor

Willelmus autem filius eius Angliam festinato adiit, ducens secum
Morkarum et Wlnotum; sed mox ut Wintoniam venit, illos ut prius
fuerant custodie mancipavit. Post hec anno scilicet domini m^{mo}
lxxxvii vi^{to} kal. octobris die dominico in Westmonasterio a Lanfranco   35
archiepiscopo in regem consecratus est, et regnavit annis xiii.
Thesaurum patris sui, ut ipse jusserat, ecclesiis et pauperibus
⟨erogavit⟩ per Angliam.^{c} Ulnotum Haroldi quondam regis Anglie et
Duncanum Malcolmi regis Scocie filios a custodia laxatos, et armis
militaribus honoratos, abire permisit.^{d} ⟨De ipso infra libro vii   40
capitulo xxxi cum sequentibus.⟩ ⟨Anno domini m° lxxxviii omnes
fere comites et proceres Anglie machinati sunt regem prodere, sed
nichil profecerunt. Anno domini m° xcvi rex Willelmus fratri suo
Roberto Curthose ad expedicionem passagii Terre Sancte vi^m vi^c lxvi
librarum prestitit, et Normanniam in vadimoniam ab eo accepit.   45
Anno domini m° ci° concordati sunt Henricus Bewclerk rex Anglie
cum dicto Roberto fratre suo, ut rex annuatim persolveret sibi iii^m
marcarum, et comes sibi Normanniam quietam clamaret; quod et
factum est. Anno m° cv rex Henricus mare transivit et receptus est a
[Normannis pacifice. Anno sequenti petit]^e comes Robertus restitu-   50
cionem Normannie, sed nichil profecit; propter quod iratus Bajocas
incendit. Quo comperto, rex H[enricus] cum exercitu mare transiens,
Tenerchebrai^f Robertum fratrem suum seniorem, et Robertum de
Stutevil, et Willelmum comitem de Morton devicit, cepit et
incarceravit.   55

fo.97

Cronica que Margarita vocatur | dicit sic quod Willelmus Bastard
genuit iii filios, videlicet Robertum Curtose primogenitum, cui dedit |

G ,271

Normanniam scilicet hereditatem suam, Willelmum Ruffum, cui
dedit Angliam conquestum suum, et Henricum Bewclerk, cui dedit
thesaurum suum et terram nullam. Robertus vero in Terram Sanctam   60
profecturus partem Normannie Henrico fratri suo vendidit, quam
habita pecunia eidem abstulit, quod Altissimo valde displicuit. Sed
qui dixit 'Michi vindictam et ego retribuam', vindictam in tempora
distulit et vicem ei reddidit. Quia cum eum in actibus Jerosolomitanis
cum Godefrido Bollone gloriosum reddidisset, et regnum Jerosolim   65
sibi oblatum renuisset, flagellavit eum Dominus desidia perenni, et
Henrico fratri suo cui regnum Anglie auferre volebat, carcere
perpetuo tradidit dampnandum. In quo finem presentis vite^g accepit.⟩

c   + ut ipse jusserat *del.C*   f   +castrum obsedit, *G*
d   + imperante adhuc Henrico quarto *CA*   g   +finivit *del.C*
e   *D; lac.C*

Morcar and Wulfnoth; but as soon as he came to Winchester, he put
them in prison as they had been before. After this in the year 1087 on
Sunday 26 September in Westminster Abbey he was consecrated king   26 Sept.
by Archbishop Lanfranc, and he reigned for thirteen years. He spent
40 his father's treasure, as he himself had ordered, on churches and the
poor throughout England. He released Wulfnoth son of Harold,
formerly king of England, and Duncan son of Malcolm king of
Scotland from custody, bestowed knightly arms upon them, and
allowed them to depart. For more about William see below Book 7,
45 Chapter 31 and following.

In 1088 almost all the earls and nobles of England plotted together   1088
to betray the king, but they were unsuccessful. In 1096 King William   1096
paid six thousand, six hundred and sixty-six pounds to his brother
Robert Curthose for a crusade to the Holy Land, and received
50 Normandy as surety from him. In 1101 Henry Beauclerk king of   1101
England came to an agreement with the said Robert his brother that
the king would pay him the sum of three thousand marks annually,
and that the count would quit-claim Normandy to him. And this was
done. In 1105 King Henry crossed the Channel, and was received   1105
55 peacefully by the Normans. In the following year Count Robert asked   1106
for the restitution of Normandy, but he was unsuccessful in this.
Angered by this rebuff, he burnt down Bayeux. When Henry heard
this, he crossed the channel with an army, and defeated, captured and [28 Sept.]
imprisoned his elder brother Robert and Robert de Stuteville and
60 William count of Mortain at Tinchebray.

The chronicle which is called 'Margaret' says that William the
Bastard had three sons, namely Robert Curthose the eldest, to whom
he gave Normandy, that is his own inheritance, William Rufus to
whom he gave his conquest, England, and Henry Beauclerk to whom
65 he gave his treasure, but no territory. When Robert was about to set
out for the Holy Land, he sold a part of Normandy to his brother
Henry, but took it from him once he had the money. This greatly
displeased the Most High, but He who said 'Vengeance is mine. I shall
repay' delayed vengeance for some time, and exacted payment from
70 him. Because although the Lord had made him glorious in his exploits
in Jerusalem along with Godfrey de Bouillon, and he had refused the
kingdom of Jerusalem which was offered to him, the Lord punished
him with perpetual inactivity, and handed him over to his brother
Henry, from whom he had wished to take away the kingdom of
75 England, to be condemned to everlasting imprisonment, in which he
reached the end of this present life.

23

De Sanctorum Malcolmi et Margarite virtuosis operibus

fo.97;
Autor

Scriptor

Scriba

Scriptor

G i,272

De illius^a magnifici regis Malcolmi et regine^b virtutum operibus et elemosinarum largicione, sicut in Legenda vite beate regine Turgotus^c testatur, hic aliqua breviter^d recitabo. Sicut enim David propheta in Psalmo cecinit: 'Cum sancto sanctus eris', sic et ipse rex a sancta regina sanctis operibus frui, et animum ab iniquis, eius hortatu, ut verificetur quod dixerat Paulus: 'Per mulierem fidelem sanctificabitur vir infidelis', didicit refrenare. Nimirum ipsam tam venerabilis vite reginam, quoniam in eius corde Christum inhabitare prospexerat, ille quodammodo formidabat offendere, sed pocius votis eius et prudentibus consiliis per omnia celerius properabat obedire. Que eciam ipsa respuerat, eadem et ipse respuere; et que amabat, amore amoris illius amare.

Unde et libros in quibus ipsa vel orare consueverat vel legere, ille licet ignarus literarum sepe manuversare solebat et inspicere. Et dum ab ea quis eorum esset carior audisset, hunc et ipse cariorem habere cepit, et sepius deosculari et contrectare. Quandoque eciam advocato aurifice, ipsum codicem auro gemmisque perornari precepit, atque perornatum ipse rex ad reginam quasi sue devocionis indicium referre consuevit.

Didicit et eius exemplo vigilias noctis frequenter orando producere, et cum gemitu cordis et lacrimis devotissime Deum orare. 'Fateor,' inquit Turgotus, 'fateor magnum misericordie Dei miraculum mirabar, cum viderem interdum tantam orandi regis instanciam, tantam inter orandum in pectore viri secularis compunccionem. In Quadragesimali tempore et diebus Adventus ante Dominicum Natale, nisi major secularis occupacio impediret, peracto matutinali officio, et aurore missarum solempniis celebratis, rediens in cameram rex pedes sex pauperum cum regina lavare, et aliquid quo paupertas consolaretur solebat erogare.^e | Summa quippe cura fuit camerario, ut ante introitum regine per singulas noctes pauperes introduceret, qualiter ad serviendum eis, ymmo Christo in eis, ingrediens ipsa paratos inveniret. Hiis peractis, quieti se ac sopori contulit. Cum vero, mane facto, de lecto surrexit, precibus et psalmis diu insistebat | et

5

10

15

20

25

30

---

a illorum *CA*	*d* +et pauca inter multa abinde extracta
b et regine *interlin.C*	*CA*
c +Sanctiandr' olim episcopus *CA*	*e* +Inter hec trecentos *del.C*

23

The virtuous works of the Saints Malcolm and Margaret

I shall at this point deal briefly with some of the virtuous works and
almsgiving of that magnificent king Malcolm and his queen, as
Turgot testifies in the Legend of the life of the blessed queen. For just
as the prophet David sang in the Psalm: 'In the company of the holy,
5 you will be holy,' so the king himself learned from the saintly queen to
enjoy saintly works, and with her encouragement to refrain from
wickedness, to confirm the truth of what St Paul said: 'Through his
Christian wife a heathen man is sanctified.' Not surprisingly he was
afraid to offend in any way the queen herself, whose manner of life
10 was so much to be revered, since he had observed that Christ dwelt in
her heart, or rather he was eager to obey her requests and wise
counsels promptly in all respects. What she rejected, he also rejected;
and what she loved, he loved from love of her love.
   So although he was illiterate, he often used to handle and examine
15 the books from which she was accustomed to pray or read. And when
he heard from her which of them was particularly dear to her, he also
began to regard it as particularly dear, and to kiss and caress it often.
Sometimes also he would summon a goldsmith and give orders that
the book was to be embellished with gold and precious gems, and
20 when it had been embellished, the king himself would take it to the
queen as a mark of his devotion.
   And he learned from her example frequently to prolong the
watches of the night in praying, and to pray to God devoutly with
heart-felt groans and tears. 'I confess,' says Turgot, 'I confess that I
25 marvelled at the great miracle of God's mercy, when at times I saw
such great earnestness in prayer on the part of the king, such great
remorse in the heart of a layman at prayer. During the period of Lent
and the days of Advent before Christmas, unless he was prevented by
important temporal business, after the completion of Mattins, and
30 when the solemnities of the early morning Mass had been celebrated,
the king would return to his chamber, and along with the queen would
wash the feet of six poor people, and bestow on them something to
alleviate their poverty. It was the chief duty of the chamberlain to
bring in poor people every night before the entrance of the queen, so
35 that on entering she would find them ready for her to serve, or rather
for her to serve Christ in them. After this was done, she went off to rest
and sleep. When it was morning she arose from her bed, and devoted

inter psallendum misericordie opus peragebat. Novem enim infantulos orphanos omni auxilio destitutos prima diei hora ad se fecit 35
introduci reficiendos. Jusserat namque cibos molliores, quibus
infantilis etas delectatur, illis cotidie preparari, quos allatos ipsamet,
flexis genibus,^{f} illis apposuit, sorbiciunculas eis fecit, et cocliaribus
cibos in ora illorum mittere dignabatur. Ita regina, que ab omnibus
populis honorabatur, pro Christo et ministre officio sollicite, et matris 40
dulcissime fungebatur pietate. Potuit satis congrue illud beati Job
dicere: "Ab infancia mea crevit mecum miseracio, et utero matris mee
egressa est mecum.'"

f + ilel *del.C*

24

Adhuc de eodem

Autor   'Inter hec trescentos pauperes in regiam aulam consuetudo erat
introduci, quibus per ordinem circumsedentibus, cum rex et regina
ingrederentur, a ministris ostia claudebantur. Exceptis enim capellanis, quibusdam religiosis et aliquibus ministris, illorum elemosine
operibus interesse nulli licuerat. Rex ex una, regina vero ex altera 5
parte, Christo in pauperibus servierunt, magnaque cum devocione
cibos et potum specialiter ad hoc preparatos^a optulerunt. Fuerunt
autem rex et regina caritatis operibus ambo pares, ambo cultu pietatis
insignes. Quo facto, rex pro temporalibus et regni sui negociis sese
sollicitus occupare, regina solebat ecclesiam intrare, ibique prolixis 10
precibus et lacrimarum singultibus seipsam Deo sacrificium corditer
immolare.

Scriptor   Exceptis enim horis de Sancta Trinitate, de Sancta Cruce, et de
Sancta Maria, intra diei et noctis spacium duo vel tria hiis sanctis
diebus psalteria complevit; atque ante publice celebracionem misse 15
quinque vel sex privatim sibi missas decantari fecit. Hiis expletis, cum
reficiendi tempus instaret, xxiiii^{or} pauperes ante refeccionem suam
fo.97v   ipsa humiliter | ministrando refecit.' Hec Turgotus.

Scriba   Anno m^o lxxxviii^o fere omnes comites et proceres Anglie paraverunt regem suum Willelmum Red prodere, sed nichil profecerunt. 20
Anno sequenti terremotus extitit per Angliam permaximus. Et anno
sequenti idem Willelmus regem Francorum Philippum per pecuniam
occulte transmissam ab obsidione sui castri in Normanniam abire
fecit. Quo in tempore ventus vehemens percussit Londonias. Anno

a *D*; preperatos *C*

much time to prayers and psalms, and while reciting the psalms she
performed the work of mercy. For in the first hour of day she had nine
40 orphan babies who had no means of support brought in to her to be
fed. For she had ordered that mild food which is pleasing to infancy
should be prepared for them daily. When it was brought in, she herself
knelt to serve them, made little drinks for them, and was not too
proud to spoon food into their mouths. So the queen, who was
45 revered by all peoples, for Christ's sake performed the duty of a
careful servant and the devotion of a very sweet mother. She could
fittingly have employed that saying of blessed Job: "From my infancy
my compassion has grown with me, and it emerged with me from my
mother's womb."'

24

The same continued

'Meanwhile the custom was for three hundred poor people to be
brought into the royal court, and when they were seated all round in
order, the king and queen entered, and the doors were shut by
attendants. For except for the chaplains, some religious, and some
5 attendants, no one was permitted to be present at their works of
almsgiving. The king on one side and the queen on the other served
Christ in the persons of the poor people, and offered food and drink
specially prepared for this purpose with great devotion. For the king
and queen were both equal in works of charity, both outstanding in
10 the pursuit of holiness. After this the king would devote careful
attention to temporal matters and the business of his kingdom, while
the queen would go into the church, and there offer herself
wholeheartedly as a sacrifice to God with prolonged prayers and
tearful sobs.
15 Apart from the Hours of Holy Trinity, Holy Cross and St Mary she
read through the psalter within the space of a day and a night two or
three times on these holy days; and before the celebration of the Mass
in public she had five or six Masses sung privately for herself. After
she completed these devotions, when the time for taking a meal was at
20 hand, before her own meal she fed twenty-four poor people, humbly
ministering to them herself.' Thus Turgot.
In 1088 almost all the earls and nobles of England were prepared to 1088
betray their king William Rufus, but they did not succeed. In the
following year there was a huge earthquake throughout England. 1089:
25 And in the following year William persuaded Philip king of the [11 Aug.]
French to depart from the siege of his castle in Normandy by the 1090
secret transfer of money. At this time London was shaken by a violent

insuper sequenti reconsiliati sunt rex Willelmus et frater suus 25
Robertus; quo in tempore Henricus Bewclerk frater eorum Montem
Sancti Michaelis occupavit, et regis terram vastavit; quem rex et
comes per totam Quadragesimam obsederunt, sed nichil profecerunt.
Tandem inter eos inita pace, Angliam rediens cum duobus fratribus
cum grandi exercitu occurrit regi Malcolmo iam Northumbriam 30
vastanti in provincia Loidis. Quos comes Robertus ea condicione
pacificavit, ut rex Scocie Malcolmus regi Willelmo obediret, et rex
Willelmus regi Malcolmo duodecim villas quas sub patre suo
habuerat redderet, et xii marcas auri singulis annis daret. Willelmus:

35
Idem rex Willelmus, cum in Normannia contra fratrem pugnaturus
fuisset, resolvit prelium, infectaque re quam intenderat, eo quod eum
G i,273   Scotorum et Wallensium | tumultus vocabant, in regnum cum
ambobus fratribus se recepit. Statimque primo contra Walenses, post
in Scotos, expedicionem movens, nichil magnificencia sua dignum
exhibuit, militibus multis desideratis, peremptis et interceptis. At vero 40
tunc satagente Roberto comite, qui familiarem iam dudum apud
Scotos locaverat graciam, inita est concordia inter Malcolmum et
Willelmum; verumptamen multis controversiis utrobique, fluctuante
justicia propter utrorumque animositatem. Idemque Malcolmus anno
secundo postmodum ab hominibus Roberti Mwbray comitis North- 45
umbrensium magis fraude quam viribus occubuit.[b]

Hec ille.

b   occupavit CA

25

De fundacione Dunelmensis ecclesie per regem Malcolmum, et obsidione castri Murealden, et interfeccione eiusdem Malcolmi

Anno m° nonagesimo tercio rex Willelmus dedit archiepiscopatum
Cantuar' Sanctissimo Ancelmo abbati Beccensi, et episcopatum
Lincolnie cancellario suo Roberto Bloeth. Quo in anno iii° idus
augusti rex Malcolmus novam Dunelmensem ecclesiam fundare
cepit, et edificare, ponentibus eodem rege Malcolmo, Willelmo 5
eiusdem ecclesie episcopo, et Turgoto priore primos lapides in
fundamento. Fundavit itaque ecclesiam Sancti Trinitatis de Dunfermelyne ante diu, quam multis ditavit donariis et redditibus. Cumque
maximam predam ex Anglia, more solito, ultra flumen These de
Clefeland, Richemond et alibi sepius abduceret,[a] castrumque de 10

a   adduceret D,CA

gale. And in the following year King William and his brother Robert 1091
were reconciled; at this time their brother Henry Beauclerk seized
30 Mont St Michel, and devastated the king's land. The king and count
laid siege to him throughout the whole of Lent, but achieved nothing.
At last peace was established amongst them, and [William] on his
return to England with his two brothers and a large army met King
Malcolm in battle, as he was laying waste Northumbria in the district
35 of Leeds. Count Robert made peace on condition that Malcolm king
of Scotland would swear allegiance to King William, and King
William would return to King Malcolm the twelve vills which he had
held under [William's] father, and would give him twelve gold marks
every year.
40   William [of Malmesbury] says:

When King William had been about to fight against his brother in
Normandy, he broke off the battle, and without accomplishing what he
had intended, because he was called away by uprisings of Scots and
Welsh, he returned to the kingdom with his two brothers. He
45   immediately mounted an expedition first of all against the Welsh, and
later against the Scots. His performance did not match his splendour,
with many knights lost, killed and cut off. But then through the efforts
of Count Robert, who had long ago invested in friendly relations with
the Scots, peace was established between Malcolm and William; but
50   with many points of dispute on one side or the other, justice wavered
because of the animosity on both sides. Malcolm was slain two years 1093:
later by the men of Robert de Mowbray earl of Northumberland more [13 Nov.]
through trickery than from strength.

25

The foundation of the church of Durham by King Malcolm,
and the siege of the castle of Murealden, and the assassination
of Malcolm

In 1093 'King William gave the archbishopric of Canterbury to the 1093
most saintly Anselm abbot of Bec, and the bishopric of Lincoln to his
chancellor Robert Bloet. In this year on 11 August King Malcolm 11 Aug.
began the foundation and building of the new church at Durham,
5   with King Malcolm, William the bishop of the church and Turgot the
prior laying the first stones of the foundation. He had likewise long
before founded the church of the Holy Trinity at Dunfermline, and
endowed it with many gifts and revenues.
When, as was his custom, he often used to carry off much booty
10 from England beyond the river Tees, from Cleveland, Richmond and
other places, and when he was besieging the castle of Alnwick (or

Alnewik (sive Murealden, quod idem est) obsideret obsessosque sibi
rebellantes opido affligeret, hii qui inclusi fuerant ab omni humano
excludebantur auxilio. Et cum tam forti et impetuoso exercitui vires
deesse cognoscerent, inito consilio, novo prodicionis ingenio usi sunt
in hunc modum: unus autem pre ceteris pericior, fortis robore, et 15
audax in opere, se discrimini mortis optulit, ut vel se morti traderet,
aut socios a morte liberaret. Nam regis prudenter adiit exercitum, ubi
nam esset rex et quis benigne interrogans, querentibus causam
inquisicionis dixit se castrum regi traditurum, et in argumentum fidei
claves eiusdem in hasta sua coram omnibus portavit oblaturus. Quo 20
audito, rex doli nescius incaute a tentorio inermis exiliens et minus
provide occurrit traditori. At ille quesita oportunitate, inermem
regem armatus transfixit, et latibula silve vicine festinanter est
ingressus. Sicque rex ille strenuus obiit die Sancti Bricii. Turbato
igitur exercitu, dolor dolorem accumulat, nam Eadwardus regis 25
primogenitus a Northumbris letaliter | vulneratur. Qui xvii kal.
decembris anno prenotato tercia die post patrem apud Eadwardisle
forestam de Jedwod fatis cessit, et sepultus est in ecclesia Sancte
Trinitatis de Dunf' juxta patrem ante altare Sancte Crucis. Willelmus:
'Rex Malcolmus, postquam cesus fuerat, apud Tynmoth' multis 30
annis humatus est, et postmodum ab Alexandro filio suo Scociam ad
Dunf' deportatus.'*b*

G i,274

---

b   reportatus *CA*

26

De morte Sancte Margarite et obsidione Castri Puellarum per Donaldum Ban

fo.98

Quod ut audivit regina, multis ante infirmitatibus ad mortem pene
cruciata, ymmo quod verius est, Spiritu Sancto prescivit, confessione
facta, et in ecclesia communione devote percepta, Deo se precibus
commendans, animam sanctam celo reddidit, xvi kal. decembris, die
iiii*to* post mortem regis anno quo supra in Castro Puellarum. Itaque 5
cum adhuc corpus regine esset in castro ubi illius felix anima ad ipsum
quem semper dilexerat migravit, Donaldus *Bane* frater regis, cuius
audita morte, ⟨auxilio regis Norwegie⟩ regnum multorum manu
vallatus invasit, et predictum castrum, ubi regis justos et legales
sciebat heredes, hostiliter obsedit. Sed quia locus ille natura sui in se 10
valde munitus est, portas solummodo credidit custodiendas, eo quod

Murealden which is the same thing), and was causing great suffering
to the besieged who were rebelling against him, those who had been
trapped inside were shut out from all human aid. When they realised
15 that their strength was insufficient to oppose such a strong and
aggressive army, they took counsel, and adopted a novel device of
treachery in the following manner: one man who was cleverer than the
rest, physically strong and daring in action, offered himself to risk
death so that he would either bring death on himself or free his
20 comrades from the threat of death. He cautiously approached the
king's army, asking politely where and which one was the king. To
those who asked him the reason for his enquiry he said that he would
surrender the castle to the king, and as proof of his good faith he
carried for all to see on his spear the keys of the castle to hand over to
25 them. When the king heard this, unaware of any trick, he rashly
rushed out of his tent, and unarmed and unthinking ran towards the
traitor. This was the opportunity the traitor had looked for, and being
armed himself, he stabbed the defenceless king, and quickly found a
hiding-place in a nearby wood. And thus that vigorous king died on St
30 Brice's day. The army was thrown into confusion, and grief was piled   13 Nov.
on grief, for Edward the king's eldest son was fatally wounded by the
Northumbrians. He died on 15 November in the year previously   15 Nov.
noted at Edwardisle in Jedforest two days after his father, and was
buried in the church of the Holy Trinity in Dunfermline beside his
35 father in front of the altar of the Holy Cross. William [of
Malmesbury] says: 'After King Malcolm was killed, he lay buried for
many years at Tynemouth, and afterwards he was conveyed to
Dunfermline in Scotland by his son Alexander.'

26

The death of St Margaret and the siege of Edinburgh castle by Donald Ban

When the queen heard this, she was already almost tortured to death
with many infirmities or, as is nearer the truth, she had foreknowledge
by the Holy Spirit. She made her confession, received communion
devoutly in church, and commending herself to God in her prayers,
5 she gave back her saintly soul to heaven on 16 November three days   1093:
after the death of her husband in the year given above in Edinburgh   16 Nov.
castle. While the queen's body was still in the castle where her blessed
soul passed over to Him whom she had always loved, Donald *Ban* the
king's brother, having heard of his death, invaded the kingdom with
10 the help of the king of Norway and, supported by a large military
force, laid siege with hostile intent to the aforesaid castle where he

introitus aut exitus aliunde non de facili pateat. Quod intelligentes qui intus erant, docti a Deo, meritis ut credimus sancte regine, per[a] posticum ex occidentali plaga sanctum corpus deferebant. Ferunt autem quidam in toto itinere illo nebulam subnubilam omnem 15 familiam illam[b] circumdedisse,[c] et ab aspectibus hostium miraculose protexisse, ut itinerantibus in terra vel mari nichil obfuit, sed ad optatum prospere locum, ecclesiam scilicet de Dunf', ubi nunc in Christo requiescit, sicut ipsa prius jusserat, pervenientes, deportarunt. Sic quidem Donaldus regnum optinuit, veris heredibus effugatis. 20

Scriptor | De inclito rege Malcolmo habentur hec metra:

> Ter deca quinque valens annis et mensibus octo
> Malcolmus sanctus rex erat in Scocia.
> Anglorum gladiis in bello sternitur heros;
> hic rex in Scociam primus humatus erat.   25

Autor   Interea Eadgarus ethling frater iam dicte regine, timens illud quod generaliter dictum est, suis evenire posse nepotibus,[d] 'Nulla fides in regno[e] sociis', ideo tucius eos ad tempus esse credidit subtrahere, quam avunculo secum regnaturos committere. Omnis enim in errore consortem sibi querit, in regno nullus. Quamobrem filios et filias regis 30 et regine sororis sue congregatos, in Angliam secum secrecius transduxit, et eos per cognatos et cognitos, non manifeste sed quasi in

G i,275 | occulto, nutriendos destinavit. Timuit enim ne Normanni, qui tunc temporis Angliam invaserant, sibi vel suis malum molirentur, eo quod Anglie regnum eis hereditario jure debebatur. Et licet ibidem, 35 quasi secreto, tempore parvo mansisset, tamen divulgatum est apud regem quod eius assisteret tradicioni. Sicque, quod verebatur, accidit in hunc modum:

a	interlin.C	d	Lucani *for* quod ... nepotibus CA
b	+cum del.C	e	regni *for* in regno CA
c	-de- interlin.C		

27

De Orgaro calumpniante Eadgarum

Eodem tempore regnante Willelmo secundo miles quidam degener Anglicus, Orgarus nomine, gratum se exhibere regi volens, convenit calumpnians eundem clitonem Eadgarum (videlicet genere gloriosum

knew the king's rightful and lawful heirs were. But because that place
is by its very nature strongly fortified in itself, he believed that only the
gates had to be watched, because entry or exit at any other point is
15 plainly not easy. Those who were inside realised this, and on the
instructions of God through the merits of the saintly queen, as we
believe, carried the saintly body out through a postern gate on the
west side. Some say that during the whole of that journey a cloudy
mist surrounded that whole family, and miraculously protected them
20 from being seen by the enemy, so that as they travelled no obstacle
came in their way either by land or sea, but they arrived safely with her
body at the longed-for place, that is the church of Dunfermline, where
now she rests in Christ, just as she herself had previously commanded.
Thus Donald *Ban* obtained the kingdom, having put the true heirs to
25 flight. These verses are about the famous King Malcolm:

> For thrice ten and five years, eight months,
> the saintly King Malcolm was mighty in Scotland.
> The hero was laid low in battle by the swords of the
>   English;
30 he was the first king to be buried in Scotland.

Meanwhile Edgar the Ætheling brother of the aforesaid queen,
fearing that the common saying 'There is no good faith among
partners in kingship' could apply to his nephews, on that account
believed that it would be safer to remove them for the time being
35 rather than to entrust them to their uncle to reign along with him. For
in wrong-doing everyone searches for an accomplice for himself, but
no one does so in the case of kingship. So he gathered together the
sons and daughters of the king and the queen his sister, and took them
secretly into England with him, and arranged for them to be looked
40 after by kinsmen and acquaintances, not openly but in secret. For he
was afraid that the Normans who had taken over England at that
time, would devise some harm for him or his family, since the
kingdom of England was due to him by hereditary right. And
although he had stayed there in hiding so to speak for only a short
45 time, nevertheless it was reported to the king that he was involved in
treason against him. And so what he feared happened as follows.

27

The false accusation of Orgar against Edgar

At the same time during the reign of William II a certain degenerate
English knight Orgar by name, wishing to ingratiate himself with the
king, brought an action falsely accusing this Edgar the Ætheling (that

nam sic ipsum nominabant) de regis Willelmi predicti tradicione. Causa autem coram rege super hoc prolata, quia Eadgarus de regia 5 stirpe fuerat progenitus, et regno jure Anglico proximus; rex causam esse veram, ut sibi precaveret, autumans, actorem vi et proteccione regia tuebatur. Nec incerta iam de Eadgaro poterat esse sentencia, si crimen impositum probari potuisset. Hinc anxius effectus Eadgarus cepit diligencius inquirere, si quis vel verbo vel consilio cause partis 10 sue auderet favere. Verum timor regis eum premia pollicentem prevenerat, quia se non impune optimates illi favere posse credebant, qui pro eius defensione regis odium incurrissent. Fluctuanti igitur et nimia anxietate dejecto, miles de Wintonia, Anglicus*a* nacione, genere non ignobilis, nomine Godwinus, veteris parentele ipsius non 15 immemor, opem se prestaturum in hac re tam difficili compromisit. Instabat iam dies huius cause diffinicioni prefixus. Affuit continuo actoris superciliosa persona. Qui quoniam corporis viribus prestare videbatur, et propter periciam bellandi, quam satis noverat, nullum sibi certamine | parem estimabat; sed et huic estimacioni favor regis 20 accessit. Quibus elatus, facile probaturum se credebat quicquid alteri imposuisset. Eo igitur sic calumpniante, compellitur Eadgarus se duello defendere, vel alterum pro se bello subrogare. Sic enim lata sentencia rei veritatem expectabat. Godwinus igitur, Eadgari causam in se capiens, interposito ut moris est utrimque juramento, Eadgarum 25 se defensurum exponit. Fit mox hinc inde magnus armorum apparatus. Pugnaturi conveniunt; Orgarus favore regis elatus, regiis satellitibus hinc inde vallatus, insignibus eciam armorum ornamentis splendidus procedit. Godwinus econtra, licet non equali ducum favore regi favencium, non minori tamen confidencia animi, locum 30 certaminis est ingressus. Qui etsi regis iram pro partis adverse tuicione formidaret, jure tamen hanc nature vicem rependendam arbitrabatur, ut illius causam ageret, quem justius sibi ceterisque auctorem*b* natura dominari debuisse cognoverat. Hinc eciam calumpniatorem cum justa animadversione increpat, qui Anglicus genere existens, 35 nature videretur impugnator. Quem enim ut dominum venerari debuerat, utpote de jure generis existens, cui se et omnia sua debuisset. Silencio | namque per preconem omnibus imposito, et vadiis utrorumque a judice in certaminis locum projectis, ut Deus secretorum cognitor huius cause veritatem ostenderet, proclamante, 40 postremo res armis, et causa Superno Judici committitur.

fo.98v

G i,276

---

a + natura *del.*C   *b* S; actorem C,CA

is 'glorious by birth', for this was the title given to him) of treason
5 against the aforesaid King William. The case on this charge was
brought before the king's presence, because Edgar was descended
from royal stock, and was next in line to the kingship by English law.
The king to safeguard himself declared the charge to be valid, and
supported the plaintiff with his royal power of protection. And there
10 could no longer be any doubt about the condemnation of Edgar, if the
charge brought against him could have been proved. Edgar was
troubled about this, and began to make careful enquiries as to
whether anyone would dare to support his side of the case either by
speaking or giving advice. But fear of the king frustrated his offers of
15 rewards, because the magnates believed that they could not support
him with impunity, since they would have incurred the hatred of the
king if they defended him. So as he was at a loss and weighed down
with excessive anxiety, a knight from Winchester, English by birth
and nobly born, by name Godwine, mindful of Edgar's ancient
20 lineage, promised that he would lend his aid in this difficult case. Now
the day was at hand that had been arranged for the determination of
this case. The supercilious person of the plaintiff promptly appeared.
Since he was seen to excel in physical strength, and because of his skill
in fighting at which he was adept, he considered that he had no equal
25 in combat; and in addition to this estimation he had the support of the
king. Puffed up by these considerations he believed that he could
easily prove any accusation that he had brought against his opponent.
So because of this man's false accusation Edgar was compelled to
defend himself in a duel, or to substitute another man for himself in
30 the fight. For by getting a decision in this way he hoped to establish
the truth of the matter. So Godwine took Edgar's cause upon himself,
and after the customary exchange of oaths on both sides he publicly
declared that he would champion Edgar. Immediately there was a
great preparation of arms on both sides. They came together to do
35 battle. Orgar stepped forward elated by the support of the king,
protected by the king's henchmen on both sides, and resplendent in
his richly ornamented armour. Godwine on the other hand, although
he did not have the same support from the nobles who supported the
king, yet with no less self-confidence, entered the place for the contest.
40 Although he feared the king's anger because of his championing of
the opposing side, he still considered that he ought by rights to repay
this natural debt to further the cause of him whom he knew ought
with more justice to hold sway over himself and all the rest as their
natural overlord. Hence also he rebuked the false accuser with just
45 reproach, on the grounds that being English by birth he appeared as
an opponent of the natural order. For he ought to have venerated
Edgar as his lord, since he was by right of birth the man to whom he
owed himself and all that he had. When silence had been imposed on
all by the herald, and the pledges from both sides had been thrown

28

De eodem duello

Nec mora, insurgit alter in alterum, actor in defensorem. Mox ictus
hinc geminantur et inde. Orgarus, impetu facto, dum alter scuto
ictum excipit,*a* partem scuti non modicam amputat. Nec segnius
Godwinus, ictu gravissimo accensis animis, in ictum consurgit, et
dum alter flectit scutum incaucius, inter capud et humerum ictu   5
vibrato, os illud cum lorice nodis prorumpit, quod cervici humerum
conjungit sinistrum. Sed hoc ictu capulus solvitur et manum ferientis
fefellit; et gladius de manu tenentis*b* labitur. Hoc hostis comperto,
licet vulnere graviter affectus, manuque leva debilitatus, gravius
tamen in adversarium consurgit, eumque tanto facilius debilitaturum   10
esse se existimans, quod eo caruisset adjumento quo precipue
pugnare debuisset. Spes tamen ipsa dominum suum fefellit. Nam
Godwinus, licet adversario pro posse toto obsistente, scuto protenso,
inter immanes ferientis ictus gladium iamdiu elapsum sustulit de
terra. Quem cum firmiter ob capuli diminucionem tenere nequivisset, 15
duobus digitis anterioribus aciem gladii complexus, et si absque
lesione adversarium suum ledere feriendo non posset, impugnando
tamen, et ictus funestos jaciendo, non adversario suo videbatur esse
inferior. Non enim aut incursioni hostis cessit, aut ab ictibus ille
cessavit. Uno quidem ictu cum capitis diminucione adversarii sui   20
oculum eruens, ictu iterato partem reliquam hostis fraudulenti
corporis adeo inutilem vulnerando effecit, quod pedes habere*c* non
ultra subsistere Orgarus visus*d* est, sed*e* pene mortuus terre prosternitur. Iamque cum magno fragore armorum hosti prostrato ille non
piger pedem imposuit, et subito fraus et calliditas hostis iam evacuata 25
detegitur, ac reus perjurii palam arguitur. Abstracto namque cultro,
qui caliga latebat, ipsum perfodere conatur, cum ante initum
congressum juraverit*f* se nichil nisi arma decencia militem in hoc
duello gestaturum. Mox tamen perjurii penas persolvit. Cultro
siquidem erepto, cum spes reum desereret, crimen protinus confite- 30
tur. Attamen hec confessio nichil ad vitam illi profuit elongandam.
Undeque vero vulnere succedente vulneri, perfodebatur, donec

a   accepit *CA*   *d*   *CA*; nisus *C*
b   ferientis *CA*   *e*   + penu *del.C*
c   *interlin.C*   *f*   juraverat *CA*

50 into the place for the contest by the judge, who proclaimed that God
    who knows what is hidden would show the truth of this case, the affair
    was finally committed to arms and the cause to the Celestial Judge.

28

The duel continued

They lost no time, as the one rose up against the other, the plaintiff
against the defendant. Soon strokes came thick and fast on this side
and on that. Orgar made an attack, and while his opponent took the
blow on his shield, he cut off a large part of the shield. Godwine was
5 no less active: his temper roused by the heavy stroke, he rose up to
strike, and while his opponent was rashly lowering his shield, with a
forceful stroke between the head and the shoulder he broke that bone
which joins the left shoulder to the neck together with the knots of his
cuirass. But the hilt of his sword was loosened by this stroke and
10 cheated the hand of the striker; his sword slipped from his grasp. His
opponent noticed this, and although seriously wounded, and with his
left hand damaged, nevertheless he rose up more violently against his
adversary, thinking that he would all the more easily disable him,
because he was deprived of the assistance of that with which he should
15 particularly have fought. However this hope deceived its master. For
although his adversary was opposing him with all his might and main,
Godwine held out his shield, and amid the mighty blows of the striker
raised from the ground the sword which had just fallen from his grasp.
Since he was unable to hold it firmly because of the loss of the hilt, he
20 grasped the edge of the sword with his first two fingers, and even
though he could not do any harm to his adversary by striking without
injury to himself, nevertheless by attacking and aiming deadly
strokes, he appeared to be a match for his adversary. For he neither
gave ground before the attack of the enemy, nor did he cease from
25 strokes. With one stroke indeed he gouged out the eye of his adversary
with damage to his head, and with repeated strokes he wounded and
rendered the rest of his treacherous enemy's body so useless that
Orgar no longer seemed able to keep his feet, but collapsed on the
ground more dead than alive. And now as the enemy fell with a great
30 clatter of arms, his opponent was not slow to place his foot upon him,
and immediately the deceit and cunning of his enemy was now openly
revealed, and he was publicly proved guilty of perjury. For he drew
out a knife which lay hidden in his boot, and tried to stab his
opponent, although he had sworn before the beginning of the conflict
35 that he would bear nothing in this duel but knightly weapons. Soon
however he paid the price for his perjury. When the knife was

animam impiam vis doloris et magnitudo vulnerum expelleret. His itaque peractis, huius duelli casus omnes mirantur, et justum Dei judicium sunt laudantes, eo quod, calumpniatore expugnato, is qui 35 veritatis fuerat et innocencie defensor, nec unum quidem wlnus ab impetente fuerit[g] perpessus. Nam exinde tam regi quam ducibus, ob insigne virtutis indicium, acceptissimus extitit adeo quod superati | hostis terras et possessiones hereditario jure rex ei concederet possidendas.   40

fo.99

---

g   fuerat *D, CA*

29

G i,277   *De Duncano filio Malcolmi notho regnum a Donaldo patruo*
optinente et eius morte

Invaso siquidem regno Scocie per Donaldum, legitimis itaque regis Malcolmi heredibus, Eadgaro scilicet Alexandro et David (qui licet minor fuerit etate, majori[a] tamen preditus virtute) propter metum illius in Anglia commorantibus. Nam alii tres filii regis majores non fuerunt tunc superstites. Eadwardus namque, ut dictum est, occiditur 5 cum patre. De Ethelredo nichil certum scriptis invenio ubi sit mortuus;[b] sepultus vero creditur in antiqua ecclesia Sancti Andr' in Kilrimonth.[c] Eadmundus vir strenuus, et in Dei servicio devotus, apud Montem Acutum in Anglia post mortem humatus requiescit. Sed aliter Eadmundum obisse Willelmus scripsit, ut in sequentibus 10 apparebit. Interea Duncanus Malcolmi regis filius nothus, cum obses erat in Anglia cum rege Willelmo Rufo, armis militaribus ab eo insignitus, et eius auxilio suffultus, in Scociam superveniens, patruum suum Donaldum[d] fugavit, et in regem susceptus est. Qui cum per unum annum et sex menses regnasset, avunculi sui[e] Donaldi dolo, 15 quem sepius bello vicerat, per comitem[f] de[g] Merenez nomine Malpetri, Scotice Malpeder, apud Mothechyn cesus interiit, et in insula Iona sepultus.[h] Quo mortuo, Donaldus iterum regnum invasit, ac tribus annis tenuit, cum ante Duncanum per sex menses regnasset, |

---

a	*CA,S*; major' *C*; major *D*
b	+ vel *del.C*
c	+ sub arculari testudine australis lateris chori sicut adhuc apparet manifeste *CA*
d	+ ban *CA*
e	*CA; corrected from* suo *D*; suo *C*
f	amminiculum cuiusdam comitis *for* comitem *CA*
g	+ le *CA*
h	+ De qua dicitur *del.C*

snatched from him, and hope deserted the guilty man, he immediately
confessed his crime. However this confession did nothing to prolong
his life. As wound succeeded wound, he was pierced all over, until the
40   violence of the pain and the extent of his wounds expelled his wicked
soul. When this was concluded, everyone marvelled at the outcome of
this duel, and praised the just judgment of God, because the false
accuser had been beaten in the fight, and the man who was the
champion of truth and innocence had not suffered even one wound
45   from his attacker. Thereafter he found great favour with the king and
the nobles because of this outstanding proof of his prowess, to such an
extent that the king granted him the lands and possessions of his
vanquished foe to be held with hereditary rights.

29

*Duncan bastard son of Malcolm obtained the kingdom from
his uncle Donald; his death*

Donald usurped the kingdom of Scotland while the lawful heirs of
King Malcolm, that is Edgar, Alexander and David (who, although
he was the least in age, was yet endowed with the greatest virtue)
remained in England for fear of Donald. For the other three older
5   sons of the king were no longer alive at that time. Edward, as has been
stated, died along with his father. I have found nothing definite in the
records concerning where Æthelred died; he is believed to have been
buried in the ancient church of St Andrew in Kilrymont [beneath the
arched vault of the roof on the southern side of the choir, as is still
10   clearly visible]. Edmund a vigorous man, devout in the service of
God, rests in England, having been buried after his death at
Montacute. But William [of Malmesbury] gives a different account of
Edmund's death, as will appear in what follows. Meanwhile Duncan
the bastard son of King Malcolm, when he was a hostage in England
15   with King William Rufus, was invested by him with the arms of
knighthood, and supported by assistance from him, he came into
Scotland, and put to flight his uncle Donald, and was adopted as king.   [1094: May]
When he had reigned for one year and six months, through the
trickery of his uncle Donald, whom he had often defeated in battle, he
20   died, slain at Mondynes by a mormaer of the Mearns, Malpetri by   [12 Nov.]
name, in Scots Malpeder, and he was buried on the island of Iona.
After his death Donald again usurped the kingdom, and held it for
three years, in addition to the six months he had reigned before
Duncan. He was humbled even unto death by Edgar, as will appear in
25   what follows. The following verses are about these unhappy kings:

Scriptor   et per Eadgarum usque ad mortem humiliatus, ut in sequentibus 20
           patebit. De quibus infaustis regibus dicitur:

> Mensibus in regno sex regnavit Donaldus,
> Malcolmi regis frater, in Albania.
>
> Abstulit huic regnum Duncanus Malcolomides.
> Mensibus tot anno rex erat in Scocia.   25
> Hic fuit occisus per Merenez in Monathechne
> Malpeder comitem; plebs premit omnis eum.
> ⁱRursus Donaldus, Duncano rege perempto,
> ternis rex annis regia sceptra^j tenet.
> Captus ab Edgaro visu privatur, at ille   30
> Rescolbyne obiit, ossaque Iona tenet.

Scriba   Itaque post funestam mortem regis Malcolmi, illi duo Donaldus
           scilicet et Duncanus annis quinque qualitercumque regnaverunt. |
G i,278   Willelmus de predicto Eadmundo scribens ait: 'Solus fuit Eadmundus 35
           filiorum regis et Margarite filius, a bono degener,^k qui Donaldi patrui
           nequicie particeps, fraterne^l non inscius cedis Duncani, fuerit pactus
           sibi regni dimidium. Sed captus et perpetuis compedibus detentus
           ingenue penituit, et ad mortem veniens cum ipsis vinculis se timulari^m
           mandavit, professus se plexum merito pro fratricidii delicto.' Hiis 40
           igitur in hunc modum, Donaldo scilicet et Duncano ac eciam
           Eadgaro pro regno certantibus, Magnusⁿ Noricorum rex, filius regis
           Olavi filii regis Haroldi cognomento Harfagar, exercitu navali
           marinos vortices peragrans, Orchades insulas et Mevanias Scocie
           regno suo subegit, que antiquo jure regno Scocie pertinere solebant. 45
           Nam a tempore Ethdaci Rothai pronepotis^o Simonis Brek, qui
           primus omnium Scotorum insulas incoluit, hucusque per spacium
           ferme duorum milium annorum, et antequam rex Scotorum Fergus
           filius Feredach solum Albionis intravit, per annos circiter quingentos
           easdem insulas continue Scoti sine aliqua interrupcione possidebant. 50

---

i   + Rex *del.C*   m   tumulari *CA*
j   *CA*; dona *C*   n   *corrected from* Magnorum *C*
k   degenere *CA*   o   *P*; pronepote *C,S*
l   fraterni *CA*

30

De reditu filiorum Malcolmi ex Anglia
et fuga Donaldi e bello

Eadgarus interim clito videns Donaldum regnum Scocie, quod suis ex
jure debebatur nepotibus, nequiter invasisse, nec illud, licet per
internuncios sepius amicabili mediante concordia requisitum, volentem reddere, commotus in ira, collectis undeque ingentibus amicorum
copiis, auxilioque Willelmi regis supradicti vallatus, adversus Donal- 5

Donald brother of King Malcolm reigned
for six months in the kingdom of Albany.
Duncan son of Malcolm took the kingdom from him.
He was king in Scotland for the same number of months.
30   He was killed by Malpeder a mormaer of the Mearns
in Mondynes; the whole people rose against him.
After King Duncan was killed, Donald again
held the royal sceptre for three years.
He was captured and blinded by Edgar, but he
35   died at Rescobie, and Iona holds his bones.

So after the mournful death of King Malcolm, those two Donald
and Duncan reigned for five years in a manner of speaking. William
[of Malmesbury] writing about the aforesaid Edmund says: 'Edmund
alone of the sons of the king, and he a son of Margaret as well, fell
40 away from virtue, in that he was an accomplice in the wickedness of
his uncle Donald, and guilty of the fratricide of Duncan, in return for
half the kingdom for himself. But after he was captured and kept in
perpetual chains, he showed nobility in repentance, and, as he
approached death, he gave instructions that he should be buried with
45 his chains, asserting that he was deservedly punished for the crime of
fratricide.'
So while they, that is Donald, Duncan and also Edgar were
competing for the kingdom, Magnus king of the Norwegians son of
King Olaf, the son of King Harold surnamed Harfagar, traversing the
50 waves of the sea with an army of seafarers, subdued to his rule the   [1098]
Orkney and Mevanian islands of Scotland, which had previously
belonged to Scotland by ancient right. For from the time of Eochaid
Rothay the great-grandson of Simon Brecc, who was the first of all
the Scots to settle the islands, right up to this day throughout the
55 period of nearly two thousand years, and for about five hundred years
before the king of Scots Fergus son of Feradach set foot on the soil of
Albion, the Scots possessed these islands continuously without
interruption.

30

The return of the sons of Malcolm from England and the flight of Donald from battle

Meanwhile Edgar the Ætheling, seeing that Donald had wickedly
usurped the kingdom of Scotland which was rightly due to his
nephews, and was unwilling to hand it over, although this had
frequently been requested through go-betweens in peaceful overtures
5 of friendship, was roused to anger. Gathering together from all sides

dum profectus est, ut, eo expulso, nepotem suum Eadgarum juvenem, Malcolmi regis ex sorore Margarita filium, regem Scocie constitueret. Cui erga natale solum properanti, et hostium sedicionem timenti, astitit in visu noctis silencio beatus Cuthbertus dicens: 'Fili, noli timere, quia placuit Deo dare tibi regnum; et hoc tibi signum. Cum 10 vexillum meum tecum de monasterio Dunelmi tuleris, et contra adversarios illud erexeris, tibi exurgam in auxilium, et dissipabuntur inimici tui, et qui oderunt te fugient a facie tua.' Expergefactus itaque adolescens, avunculo suo Eadgaro rem retulit, et ille Deo se et omnes suos et patrocinio Sancti Cuthberti committens, quod sanctus 15 hortando jusserat, animosius adimplevit. Postea facto congressu, |

et Sancti Cuthberti vexillo*a* levato, quidam miles Anglicus genere Robertus nomine, filius antedicti Godwini, paterne probitatis imitator et heres, duobus tantum militibus comitatus in hostes irruit; et fortissimis qui ante aciem quasi defensores stabant peremptis, 20 antequam insimul appropinquarent exercitus, Donaldus cum suis in fugam versus est, et sic incruentam victoriam, Deo propicio, meritis Sancti Cuthberti feliciter optinuit. Ecce quomodo populus indigena fidelis veretur resistere contra verum et liegium*b* dominum, ut supra de rege Machabeda. Caveant igitur et abhorreant regnorum inva- 25

sores injusti, | ne fidelem populum adversus legittimum et liegium*b* dominum vel heredem bellandum magis ducant, quam bonum filium contra patrem. Eadgarus itaque animosior effectus, suis omnibus etsi non opus esset animos viriles reparat, paternum regnum sibi de jure debitum ingreditur, et ingredienti ab indigenis absque contradiccionis 30 obstaculo gaudenter offertur. Sed et ab illo susceptum deinceps honorifice gubernatur.

---

a   *corrected from* vexillato C   *b*   *first* -i- *interlin.*C

31

Transitus Christianorum maxime Francorum ad Terram Sanctam et capcio Jerosolim

Anno domini m° nonagesimo viii*a* fundata est abbacia Cistercii*b* ⟨in diocesi Cabilonensi,⟩ unde:

a   xcix *for* nonagesimo viii *CA*   *b*   +et ordo *CA*

the huge forces of his friends, and supported by the help of the
aforesaid King William, he set out against Donald, in order to expel   [1097: Oct.]
him, and establish his nephew the young Edgar son of King Malcolm
and his [the Ætheling's] sister Margaret as king of Scotland. As the
10   young Edgar was hurrying towards his native land, and was in fear of
an uprising of his enemies, blessed Cuthbert appeared before him in a
vision in the silence of the night saying: 'My son, be not afraid,
because God has decided to give you the kingdom; and this will be the
sign for you. When you take my banner with you from the monastery
15   of Durham, and raise it against your adversaries, I shall arise to help
you, and your enemies will be scattered, and those who hate you will
flee from your face.' So the young man awoke, and reported the
matter to his uncle Edgar, and he, entrusting himself and all his
people to the protection of God and of St Cuthbert, enthusiastically
20   carried out what the saint had commanded in his exhortation. Later
when battle was joined and the banner of St Cuthbert was raised, a
certain knight English by birth, Robert by name, the son of the
aforesaid Godwine, and imitator and heir to his father's valour,
rushed against the enemy accompanied by only two knights. They
25   killed the bravest fighters who stood in front of the battle array as
champions. Before the armies clashed with each other, Donald was
turned to flight along with his men, and in this way Edgar successfully
obtained a bloodless victory by God's favour and by the merits of St
Cuthbert. See how a loyal indigenous people scruples to fight against
30   their true liege lord, as we noted above in the case of King Macbeth.
Therefore let unlawful usurpers of kingdoms beware, and shrink from
leading a loyal people to fight against their lawful and liege lord or his
heir, any more than they would lead a good son against his father. So
Edgar's spirits rose, and he restored the spirit of manliness to all his
35   people, even though there was no need for it. He entered upon his
father's kingdom that was owed to him by right, and as he entered it
was joyfully offered to him by the native people without let or
hindrance. And after he had taken over the kingdom, it was thereafter
honourably governed.

31

The passage of Christians especially the French to the Holy Land and the capture of Jerusalem

In 1098 the abbey of Cîteaux in the diocese of Châlons was founded.   1098
Hence:

In the year eleven hundred minus one
the Cistercian order began under Father Robert.

Anno milleno centeno quo minus uno
sub patre Roberto cepit Cistercius ordo.

Quo in anno papa Urbanus ii^{us}, consilio Turonensi celebrato, pene 5
totum occidentem provocat in Terre Sancte subsidium, maxime in
regno Francie. Igitur Henrico imperatore existente^c innumerabilis
multitudo Gallicorum cruce signata in Terre Sancte subsidium,
inexplicabili labore per terram, et tandem per Constantinopolitanam
urbem transeuntes, Antiochiam pervenerunt, dividentes se ad passa- 10
gium in tres partes. Unius partis Francorum prefuerunt exercitui
nobilis Godefridus de Bolon dux Lothoringie, Petrus Heremita, et
Baldwinus comes de Monte ⟨frater Godefridi.⟩ Ex eleccione preficitur ⟨Raynaldus⟩^{d} Lombardis, Longobardis et Alemannis; et ista pars
intravit et peragravit Ungarie regionem. Secunda pars intravit in 15
Sclavinie partes, scilicet comes de Sancto Egidio Reymondus et
Podiensis episcopus. Tercia pars per antiquam Rome viam ad
passagium fecit transitum, videlicet dux Boemundus sapientissimus,
Richardus de Principatu, Robertus Curtose Normannorum comes,
Robertus comes Flandrensis, Hugo Magnus, Eurardus de Puisacio, 20
Achardus de Monte Merlay, Usuardus de Musione, Tancredus
Marcisi filius, Richardus princeps et Ranulphus frater eius, Robertus
de Surdavalle, Robertus filius Turstani, Humfredus filius Radulphi et
Richardus filius comitis Ranulphi, comes de Rustignolo cum
fratribus suis, et Boello^e Carnotensi, Alredus de Cognato^f et 25
Humfredus de Monte Scabioso. Sed precipui capitanei huius
exercitus fuerunt Godefridus, Boemundus, comites Blesensis, Flan-
drie et Sancti Egidii. Prima civitas^g quam ceperunt fuit Nicea, que est
caput tocius Romanie, quam ex condicto diliberaverunt tradi^h
imperatori Romanorum,^{i} qui et Constantinopolis perfido tunc 30
Christiano.

ii Erachia, quam obtinuit Boymundus^j cum suis. iii Tharsum, quam
optinuit Tancredus cum suis, quam tradidit Balduino fratri Godo-
fridi. iiii^a Cesarea Cappadocie, quam optinuit Reymondus et comes

G i,280   Sancti | Egidii. Quinta Rusa, quam optinuit Petrus de Roasa. vi^a 35
regalis civitas Antiochia, que fuit quasi inexpugnabilis, sed tandem
diliberata per quendam ammiratum de genere Turcorum, cui nomen
Pirrus, domino Boemundo et suis. vii castrum magnum et opidum cui
nomen Thalamania, quod^k optinuit quidam miles comitis Sancti
Egidii, cui nomen Reymondus Piletus.   40

viii urbs in Siria, que vocatur Abbara, quam invasit Reymondus de
Sancto Egidio. Nona civitas permaxima in Siria Marra nomine, quam

c	anno ... xlii, et Eadgari regnacionis primo	g	Primam civitatem C,D
	CA	h	G; terci C,D
d	*in margin replacing* Reymondus *in text* C	i	Romamorum C,D
e	*corrected from* Boella [?] C	j	*corrected from* Baymundus C
f	+ Alredus [?] filius Marc [?] filius primi	k	+ oper del.C
	Walteri *in margin, probably del.*C		

5 In this year Pope Urban II, while holding a council at Turin, incited [1095]
almost the whole of the West especially in the kingdom of France to
go to the aid of the Holy Land. So in the time of the emperor Henry a
countless host of Frenchmen took the cross to go to the aid of the
Holy Land, enduring indescribable hardship on land, and, finally
10 crossing over by way of the city of Constantinople, they reached
Antioch, dividing themselves into three contingents for the expedition. The army of one contingent of the French was commanded by
the noble Godfrey de Bouillon duke of Lower Lorraine, Peter the
Hermit and Baldwin count of Hainault brother of Godfrey. Rainald
15 was chosen to command the Lombards, Longobards and Alemanns;
and that contingent entered and passed through the region of
Hungary. The second contingent entered the territory of the Slavs,
that is to say Raymond count of Saint-Gilles and the bishop of Le
Puy. The third contingent made their passage for the expedition along
20 the Via Egnatia, that is Duke Bohemond the Wise, Richard of the
Principate, Robert Curthose count of the Normans, Robert count of
Flanders, Hugh the Great, Everard of Le Puits, Achard of Mount
Merlay, Isoard of Musio, Tancred son of the Marquis, Prince
Richard and Rainulf his brother, Robert of Sourdeval, Robert son of
25 Turstan, Humphrey son of Radulph and Richard son of Count
Rainulf, the count of Rossignuolo with his brothers, and Boel of
Chartres, Albered of Cagnano and Humphrey of Monte Scabioso.
But the chief captains of this army were Godfrey, Bohemond and the
counts of Blois, Flanders and Saint-Gilles. The first city which they
30 took was Nicaea, which is the capital of all Rūm, which they liberated [1097:
and handed over by agreement to the Roman emperor who is also 19 June]
called emperor of Constantinople, at that time a faithful Christian.
The second city was Heraclea which Bohemond took with his
forces. The third was Tarsus which Tancred took with his men, and
35 which he handed over to Baldwin brother of Godfrey. The fourth city
was Caesarea of Cappadocia which Raymond and the count of Saint-
Gilles took. The fifth was Rusia which Peter of Roaix took. The sixth
was the royal city of Antioch, which was practically impregnable, but
was at last handed over by a certain emir of Turkish nationality whose [1098:
40 name was Firouz, to Lord Bohemond and his men. The seventh was 3 June]
the great fort and town whose name is Tel-mannas, which was taken
by a certain knight of the count of Saint-Gilles, whose name was
Raymond Pilet.
The eighth was a city in Syria which is called Albara, which
45 Raymond of Saint-Gilles seized. The ninth was a very large city in
Syria Marra by name, which was taken by the said count of Saint-
Gilles. The tenth was the very beautiful city Kephalia by name taken
by the same count. And likewise the eleventh, Ibelin, was taken by the [1099:
same count. The twelfth was Jerusalem which was taken by all the 15 July]
50 nobles, that is Bohemond, Godfrey, the count of Saint-Gilles etc.

dictus comes Sancti Egidii optinuit. Decima est civitas pulcherima
nomine Kephalina, optenta per eundem. Sic eciam xi Gibellum per
eundem. xii Jerosolim, quam optinuerunt omnes nobiles, videlicet 45
Boemundus, Godefridus, comes Sancti Egidii c'.

    xiii civitas Neopolitana, quam conquisiverunt Tancredus et comes

fo.100   Eusta- | chius. xiiii civitas magna Ascalonia, quam optinuerunt
omnes nobiles; et non tantum istas, sed et plura munitissima castella
et opida.*l*   50

---

l   +Quo *del.C*

32

De eodem

Quo in tempore antequam Antiochia caperetur, et de qua capienda
quasi fuit desperatum, Sanctus Andreas apostolus apparuit cuidam
rustico simplici peregrino ⟨nomine Petro⟩ Provinciali genere dicens:
'Veni, ostendam tibi lanceam qua perforatus fuit Christus, postquam
capta fuerit civitas.' Qui eius animacione, capta civitate,*a* presente R. 5
comite et capellano suo, in ecclesia Sancti Petri fodiens terram, in loco
de quo revelacionem habuerat lanceam invenit. Dubitantibus autem
plerisque utrum esset lancca Christi, quidam Bartholomeus nomine,
cui eciam Christus apparens de lancea significavit. Qui cum ipsa
lancea per ignem xiii pedum, quem fieri jusserat, illesus transivit. Et 10
sic exercitus fiduciam in Christo et in ipsius lancea habentes, intrepidi
processerunt per Achon, que tunc Ptholomeida dicebatur. Venerunt
Cesaream, ubi cum essent, columbam desuper volantem anciperiter
unus graviter plagatam dejecit, circa quam reperte sunt litere quas
deferebat talis sentencie: 'Rex Acharon duci Cesaree salutem. 15
Generacio canina venit, gens contenciosa, contra quas per te et per
alios legem tuam defendas. Idem annuncia aliis civitatibus.' Post hec,
ut prediximus, venientes Franci ceperunt Jerosolim. Est autem
Jerosolim civitas in montanis sita, rivis, fontibus et silvis carens,
excepto fonte Siloe, ubi quandoque sufficiens aqua reperitur. Fuerat 20
autem post Titi et Vespasiani destruccionem per Helyum Adrianum
mirifice reparata, sed non in eodem loco ubi prius. Ibi Godefridus, qui
factus fuerat*b* rex, secundo anno mortuus sepelitur. ⟨Scriptum reperi
quod cum rogaretur Deus ut per ignis visionem in vigilia Pasche
ostenderet, quem regem [Jerosolim]*c* prefici vellet, et apparuisset 25

---

a   *D;* citate *C*   *c*   *D; lac.C*
b   +ibi *del.C*

The thirteenth was the city of Nablus which was conquered by Tancred and Count Eustace. The fourteenth was the great city of Ascalon which was taken by all the nobles; and not only these cities, but many more well-fortified castles and towns.

32

The same

At this time before the capture of Antioch, and when there was little hope that it would be captured, the apostle St Andrew appeared to a certain simple peasant pilgrim Peter by name, a native of Provence, saying: 'Come, after the city has been captured, I will show you the
5   lance with which Christ was pierced.' Inspired by this vision, after the city had been captured, and in the presence of Count Raymond and his chaplain, he dug down into the earthen floor in the church of St Peter, in the place that had been revealed to him, and found the lance. While most people were not convinced that it was the lance of Christ,
10 a certain man called Bartholomew to whom Christ had also appeared and given signs concerning the lance, passed unharmed with the lance through a fire thirteen feet long, which he had ordered to be made. So the armies trusting in Christ and in His lance, advanced confidently through Acre, which was then called Ptolemais. They came to
15 Caesarea, and when they were there a dove flying over them was badly hurt and thrown down by a hawk. Around it was found a letter which it was carrying, which read as follows: 'The king of Accaron sends greetings to the emir of Caesarea. A generation of dogs has come, and a quarrelsome people, against whom see that you defend your law by
20 your own efforts and those of others. Report this to the other cities.' After this, as we said before, the French came and captured Jerusalem. Now Jerusalem is a city situated in hilly country without streams, springs or woods, except for the spring of Siloam, where water is never found to fail. After its destruction by Titus and
25 Vespasian it had been wonderfully rebuilt by Aelius Hadrian, but not on the same site as before. Godfrey who had been made king of Jerusalem died and was buried there in the following year. I have found it recorded that when God was asked to show by a vision of fire on the vigil of Easter whom He wished to be made king of Jerusalem,

super lanceam Roberti Curthose filii Willelmi Bastard, | magna demencia respuit illud regnum, spe regni Anglorum. Unde justo Dei judicio utroque frustratus, caniciem peregit in vinculis fraternis. Anno domini m° cii ordo Tironensis incepit per abbatem B[ernardum] apud vetus Tiron' in nemore, sed postea in planicie vallis.⟩　30 Creduntur autem tunc transfretasse plus quam ducenta milia Francorum*d* in subsidium Terre Sancte. O quantum distant moderni principes et commilitones*e* ab illis qui tunc fuerunt, qui Sancto Spiritu afflati in unaquaque quasi provincia centeni et milleni ad huiusmodi transitus expedicionem se cruce signarent! Sed nostri nunc satellites et　35 satrape solum delectantur in cedibus et rapinis, in extorsionibus subditorum et bellis intestinis. Propter quod dicit Blesensis in epistola:

> Hodie militaris disciplina, quam Vegecius Renatus et plerique alii docuerunt, prorsus evanuit. Olim enim se vinculo juramenti milites　40 obligabant, quod starent pro rei publice statu, quod in acie non fugerent, et quod vite proprie utilitatem publicam prehaberent. Sed et hodie enses suos recipiunt de altare, ut profiteantur se filios ecclesie, atque ad honorem sacerdocii, ad subsidium Terre Sancte, ad tuicionem pauperum, ad vindictam malefactorum et patrie liberacionem se　45 gladium accepisse. Porro in contrarium res versa est. Nam ex quo hodie militari cingulo decorantur, statim insurgunt in christos Domini, et deseviunt in patrimonium Crucifixi, spoliant et predantur subjectos sibi pauperes, et miserabiliter atque immisericorditer affligunt miseros, ut in doloribus alienis illicitos appetitus et extraordinarias impleant　50 voluptates.

d　interlin.over Christianorum *del.C*　　　　*e*　+qui f *del.C*

33

De virtute quinque locorum in Jerosolim

Deus pater loquitur domine Brigitte, ut capitulo ultimo libri sexti Revelacionum, informans eam de virtute illorum quinque locorum que sunt Jerosolim et Bethleem, et de gracia quam recipient peregrini visitantes illa loca cum humilitate devota et vera caritate.

> Primus locus est ubi Maria nata et educata fuit; ergo qui ad illum locum　5 devote venerit, non solum mundabitur, sed et erit vas in honorem meum. Secundus locus est Bethleem; tercius Calvarie; quartus Ortus Sepulcri; quintus Mons Oliveti. Qui ad ista loca venerit mundus, cum

30 and the fire had appeared above the spear of Robert Curthose the son
    of William the Bastard, in a fit of great madness he rejected that
    kingship, since he hoped to become king of the English. So having
    failed to obtain either kingdom, he spent his old age imprisoned by his
    brother.
35   In 1102 the Tironensian order was instituted by the abbot Bernard
    at old Thiron in a grove, but later on level ground in a valley.
        It is believed that at that time more than two hundred thousand
    French crossed over to give help to the Holy Land. What a difference
    there is between present day princes and their knights and those who
40 were alive then, who, inspired by the Holy Spirit, in their hundreds
    and thousands in practically every province took the cross for this
    kind of expedition! But our present day leaders and their henchmen
    take delight in nothing but slaughter and pillage, in extortions from
    their subjects and civil wars. On this subject [Peter] of Blois says in a
45 letter:

        Today the military discipline which Vegetius Renatus and most other
        authorities taught has utterly vanished. For formerly knights pledged
        themselves with a binding oath that they would stand firm for the good
        of the state, that they would not run away on the field of battle, and that
50   they would regard the common good as more important than their own
        lives. But today they receive their swords from the altar in order to
        profess themselves sons of the church, and that they have received their
        sword for the honour of the priesthood, for the relief of the Holy Land,
        for the protection of the poor, for the punishment of wrong-doers and
55   the liberation of their country. But the opposite to this is what actually
        happens. For nowadays as soon as they are adorned with the military
        sword-belt, they immediately rise up against the Lord's anointed,
        plunder the church's temporalities, and despoil and rob the poor
        people who are subject to them, and miserably and mercilessly afflict
60   the wretched, so that they may satisfy their unlawful appetites and
        abnormal desires in making others suffer.

33

The virtue of five places in Jerusalem

God the Father spoke to the Lady Bridget, as in the last chapter of
Book 6 of the *Revelations*, informing her of the virtue of those five
places which are in Jerusalem and Bethlehem, and about the grace
which pilgrims, who visit those places with devout humility and true
5 love, will receive.

        The first place is where Mary was born and brought up; so anyone who
        comes with devotion to that place will not only be cleansed, but will
        also be a vessel for my glory. The second place is Bethlehem; the third is

bona et perfecta voluntate,*a* habebit videre et gustare quam dulcis et
suavis sum ego Deus.   10

Item Nostra Domina per revelacionem ostendit domine Brigitte, ut
habetur libro vii, capitulo xiiii, indulgenciam et graciam quam boni
peregrini habent visitantes sepulcrum Domini cum recta intencione et

fo.100v   sancto proposito. | Ubi eciam pulcre informat Brigittam de salva-
cione domini Karoli militis filii sui mortui, quem, ut ego Scriptor 15
audivi, dominus Willelmus de Lyndesey de Birys*b* ad Sanctum
Sepulcrum in militem cinxit. Post multas altercaciones hinc inde inter
Mariam et Diabolum coram judice Christo pro anima dicti Karoli
concertatas, sicut revelavit domina Brigitta,*c* inter cetera talia de filio
suo*d* dicebat.   20

G i,282   Et ecce Deus sic diu rogatus in ipsius cor suum benedictum spiritum
infudit. Virgo*e* Mater Dei dedit illi ex virtute sua | quicquid sibi defecit
in armis spiritualibus et indumentis que pertinent ad milites qui debent
intrare in regnum celi ad Summum Imperatorem. Sancti eciam in
celesti regno collocati, quos iste miles in mundo vivens dilexit, de suis 25
meritis ipsi sibi*f* consolacionem addiderunt.*g* Ipse namque thesaurum
congregavit, sicut illi peregrini qui cotidie caduca bona commutant in
eternales divicias; et quia ipse sic fecit, ideo gaudium et honorem
perpetuum optinebit,*h* et specialiter pro illo ardenti desiderio quod
habuit peregrinando ad sanctam civitatem Jerosolim, et pro eo quod   30
desideravit frequenter vitam suam libenter bellando exponere, ut Terra
Sancta reduceretur ad dominium Christianorum. Ad hoc, ut gloriosum
Dei sepulcrum in debita haberetur reverencia, si ad tantum opus
sufficiens extitisset.

Et post pauca finaliter: 35

Filius*i* loquebatur: 'Quando intrastis templum meum dedicatum
sanguine meo, sic mundati estis ab omnibus peccatis vestris, sicut tunc
levati essetis de fonte baptismatis. Et propter labores et devocionem
vestram alique anime consanguineorum vestrorum, que erant in
Purgatorio, hodie liberate sunt, et intraverunt celum in gloria mea. 40
Nam omnes qui veniunt ad locum istum cum voluntate perfecta se
emendandi, juxta meliorem conscienciam suam, nec volentes recidi-
vare in priora peccata, hiis omnia priora peccata totaliter dimittuntur,
et augetur eis gracia proficiendi.'

Hec ibi. Ista propterea hic intromittimus*j* ut lectores avidius aspirent 45
ad tam salubrem expedicionem subeundam. Quam certe*k* impediunt
Anglici, commoventes in tantum omnia regna sibi contigua, ut quasi
ad nil aliud valeant vacare, quam se contra ipsorum machinamenta et

---

a	+mundus ... voluntate *repeated and del.C*	*g*	a- *interlin.C*
b	+miles *P*	*h*	possidebit *P*
c	D; Brigitte *C*	*i*	Christus *P*
d	+Karolo *P*	*j*	inservimus *P*
e	+virgo *del.C*	*k*	multum *P*
f	*interlin.over* ipsi *del.C*		

10 Calvary; the fourth the garden of the Sepulchre; the fifth the Mount of Olives. Anyone who comes to those places in purity and with good and perfect volition will be able to see and taste how sweet and pleasant I God am.

Likewise Our Lady showed the Lady Bridget through a revelation, as recorded in Book 7, Chapter 14, the indulgence and grace which good
15 pilgrims obtain from visiting the Sepulchre of the Lord with right intention and holy purpose. Where also she beautifully informs Bridget about the salvation of the knight Sir Charles her dead son, whom, as I Scriptor have heard, was knighted by Sir William Lindsay of the Byres at the Holy Sepulchre. After many arguments on both
20 sides between Mary and the Devil who were competing for the soul of the said Charles before Christ as judge, as revealed by Lady Bridget, she said the following among other things about her son.

And behold after God had been pleaded with for a long time in this way, He poured his blessed spirit into Charles' heart. The Virgin
25 Mother of God gave him from her own virtue what he lacked in spiritual arms and accoutrements which pertain to knights who are due to be enrolled in the kingdom of Heaven under the Supreme Commander. The saints also who were established in the heavenly kingdom, and whom that knight had loved while he lived in the world
30 added consolation to him from their own merits. He gathered up treasure, just as those pilgrims do who daily exchange fleeting possessions for eternal riches; and because he did so, he will obtain everlasting joy and glory, and especially because of that burning desire which he had for going on pilgrimage to the Holy City of Jerusalem,
35 and because he had frequently desired to endanger his own life, while fighting gladly so that the Holy Land might be brought back under Christian rule, to the end that the glorious sepulchre of God might be held in due reverence, if only he could have been good enough for such a great task.

40 And finally after a short passage:

The Son was speaking: 'When you entered my temple dedicated by my blood, you were cleansed from all your sins, just as you would have been relieved of them at that time from the baptismal font. And because of your labours and devotion some souls of your kinsmen
45 which were in Purgatory have today been set free, and have entered Heaven in my glory. For all who come to that place with the perfect intention of amending their ways according to the better promptings of their conscience, and are unwilling to relapse into their former sins, have all their previous sins totally forgiven, and the grace of making
50 progress is increased in them.'

We insert these matters here so that our readers may more eagerly aspire to undertake such a salutary expedition. The English certainly interfere with this by disturbing all the kingdoms on their borders to such an extent that their neighbours have no leisure for anything else

insultus[l] defensare. Per ⟨Christianos, et principaliter⟩ Francos,[m] ut premisimus, capte erant premisse civitates Turcorum, et non sine 50 maxima difficultate et divino miraculo illa nobilis civitas Antiochena adhuc remanens sub fidelitate Christiana anno quo supra; et de quo sic dicitur:

> Dum fuit urbs capta tam nobilis Antiochena,
> undecies centum si subtrahis inde bis unum, 55
> tunc tot erant anni Domini de Virgine nati.

[n]Eciam anno sequenti Jerosolim capta est feria vi, idus julii.

l   +subdolos *P*   n   +Quo *D; del.C*
m   +igitur *del.C*

34

Autor

De successione regis Eadgari et de Beruico c'

[a]Igitur ab incarnacionis dominice anno m° nonagesimo viii°, imperatoris Henrici xlii, Eadgarus regis Malcolmi et Margarite filius Donaldo patruo successit, et ix annis cum tribus mensibus regnavit. Ab ipso quidem ipse Donaldus captus est in Rescolpyne, et cecatus, ac perpetuis carceribus dampnatus, et in Iona humatus. Alii tamen[b] 5 quod in Dunkelden', alii in Dunfermelyn. In regnum vero pacifice cum Eadgarus[c] sublimatus fuerat, et cuncta pro sua voluntate |

disponenda susceperat, illud Salomonicum[d] reminiscens: 'In diebus bonorum non immemor sis malorum.' Sancti Cuthberti ducis sui non immemor, monachis Dunelmensibus terram suam de Coldynghame 10 cum omnibus illius appendiciis imperpetuum dedit, concessit et confirmavit. Addidit eciam vir magnificus, sed et rex munificus, munus muneri, hoc est villam nobilem de Berwik cum appendiciis, episcopo et suis successoribus Dunelmensibus dedit, et possidendam confirmavit. Quantum et quale donum regis episcopatus totus 15 gratanter accipiens, in pace bona possedit, donec Ranulphus episcopus illud non immerito hoc modo demeruit. Eadgaro rege ad regem Anglie Willelmum tendente, Robertus ille filius Godwini, de quo superius fit mencio, de licencia regis ad terram a rege sibi datam in Laudonia moratus est, et dum ibidem castellum edificare niteretur, a 20 provincialibus subito et baronibus tandem Dunelmensibus circumventus, eodem Ranulpho episcopo agente, captus est. In qua tamen

a   Anno domini m° ciii° incepit ordo   b   *G;* tunc *C*
     Cluniacensis sub Bernone et Odone   c   *D;* Eadwardus *C*
     successive abbatibus *in margin C*   d   +remiss *del.C*

55   except to defend themselves against their machinations and attacks.
The aforesaid cities of the Turks were captured by the Christians, and
principally by the French, as we said before, and it was not without
the greatest difficulty and a divine miracle that the noble city of
Antioch still remained under the Christian faith in the year mentioned   [1098]
60   above; The following lines illustrate this:

If you subtract from eleven hundred twice one,
then that was the year of the Lord born of the Virgin
in which the noble city of Antioch was captured.

In the following year Jerusalem also was captured on Friday 15 July.   [1099:]
15 July

34

The succession of King Edgar; and Berwick etc.

So in 1098, the forty-second year of the emperor Henry's reign, Edgar   [1097]
son of King Malcolm and Margaret succeeded his uncle Donald, and
reigned for nine years and three months. He captured Donald at
Rescobie, put out his eyes and condemned him to perpetual
5   imprisonment. He was buried on Iona. Some say however that he was
buried in Dunkeld and others in Dunfermline. When Edgar had been
raised to the throne without opposition, and had arranged everything
according to his own wishes, mindful of that saying of Solomon: 'In
the days of prosperity, do not forget the bad times', he did not forget
10   his guide St Cuthbert, and gave, granted and confirmed in perpetuity
to the monks of Durham his lands of Coldingham with all their
appurtenances. And as a generous man and bountiful king he added
gift upon gift, that is to say he gave and confirmed possession of the
noble town of Berwick with appurtenances to the bishop of Durham
15   and his successors. The whole bishopric gratefully received the king's
great and magnificent gift, and possessed it in good peace until Bishop
Ranulf deservedly lost it in this way. While King Edgar was on his
way to visit William king of England, Robert the son of Godwine,
who was mentioned above, took up residence with the king's leave on
20   the land that the king gave him in Lothian. While he was engaged in
building a castle there, he was suddenly surrounded and made captive
by the local inhabitants and finally by the barons of Durham at the
instigation of that bishop Ranulf. In this captivity he left behind with
the inhabitants of the whole region a great memory of his courage.
25   When King Edgar heard about this on his return, he brought him
back with him to Scotland with honour, after he had been set free on

capcione magnam sue virtutis memoriam apud tocius regionis incolas dereliquit. Quod rex Eadgarus rediens ut audivit, illum ex precepto regis Anglie liberatum secum in Scociam reduxit cum honore. Et 25 quicquid ante episcopo donaverat, omnino sano con- | silio sibimet reservabat. | Robertus vero Scoticatus et a bonus Scotus effectus, non multo post regi et domino suo Eadgaro valedicens,^e Jerosolimam peregre profectus est, ubi quamplurima^f sue virtutis indicia dereliquit. Hoc anno iii nonas novembris mare litus egreditur, et villas ac 30 homines quamplures, boves et oves innumeras demersit.

Anno xi secundi Willelmi regis supramemoratus Noricorum rex Magnus Orchadas^g insulas et Mevanias, et si que alie jacent in Occeano, armis subegit; et dum obstinatus Angliam per Anglesiam petebat, occurrerunt ei comites Hugo Cestrensis et Hugo Scroboriensis 35 et ipsum armis expulerunt. Cecidit ibi Hugo Scroboriensis.

⟨Anno domini m° c° ix rex Henricus Heliensem ecclesiam abbacialem mutavit in episcopatum; et [ecclesia Tironensis fundata est.]^h Anno | sequenti Godricus heremita intravit in locum silvestrem qui dicitur Finkall prope Dunelm', et ibi militavit Deo [annis circiter 40 lx]^h ubi multa per eum operatur miracula Deus.

Anno precedenti venerunt monachi de Tironio ad Selkirk in Scocia, [quorum unus nomine]^h Radulphus factus est primus abbas de Selkirk, et anno domini m° cxv obiit B[ernardus] primus abbas Tironii. Cui successit [Radulphus]^h primus abbas de Selkirk. Et paulo 45 post obiit Radulphus abbas de Tironio, cui successit [Willelmus]^h abbas de Selkirk [et]^h Herbertus factus est tercius abbas de Selkirk et primus de Kalco, quia monasterium illuc translatum est per regem David anno m° cxxvi; et post duos annos post translacionem conventus fundavit ecclesiam de Kalco.⟩ 50

fo.101
Scriptor

Autor;
Willelmus

G i,285

G i,286

e   + in illa magna expedicione Godefridi de   *g*   + et *CA*
     Bolone *CA*   *h*   *D; lac.C*
f   + cum ceteris suis Scotis *CA*

35

De conjugio sororum suarum Matildis cum rege Henrico et Marie comiti Bononie

G i,283

Erat autem iste rex Eadgarus homo dulcis et amabilis, cognato suo regi Sancto Eadwardo^a per omnia similis; nichil durum, nichil tirannicum aut amarum in suos exercens subditos, sed eos cum

a   Eadgwino *for* Sancto Eadwardo *CA*

the order of the king of England. And all that Edgar had previously
given to the bishop, he sensibly kept completely to himself. Robert
was Scotified and turned into a good Scot, and not long afterwards he
30 bade farewell to his king and lord Edgar, and set off on pilgrimage to
Jerusalem, where he left behind him very many proofs of his valour.
On 3 November of this year the sea invaded the shore, and drowned   [1099:]
very many villages and people and innumerable oxen and sheep.   3 Nov.]
William [of Malmesbury] says:

35   In the eleventh year of King William II the aforementioned king of the
        Norwegians Magnus subdued by force of arms the Orkney and
        Mevanian islands and whatever other islands lie in Ocean, and while he
        was resolutely making for England by way of Anglesey, he was met by
        the earls Hugh of Chester and Hugh of Shrewsbury, and they drove
40   him out by force of arms. Hugh of Shrewsbury was killed there.

In 1109 King Henry changed the status of the abbey church of Ely   [1108]
to a bishopric; and the church of Thiron was founded. In the
following year the hermit Godric went into a wooded place which is   [ca 1110]
called Finchale near Durham, and he served God there for about sixty
45 years, during which time God performed many miracles through his
agency.
In the preceding year monks came from Thiron to Selkirk in   [ca 1113]
Scotland, one of whom Radulph by name became the first abbot of
Selkirk, and in 1115 Bernard the first abbot of Thiron died. He was   [1116]
50 succeeded by Radulph the first abbot of Selkirk. And a little later
Radulph the abbot of Thiron died, and was succeeded by William   [1118]
abbot of Selkirk, and Herbert became the third abbot of Selkirk and
the first of Kelso, because the monastery was transferred there by
King David in 1126; and two years after the transfer of the monastery   [1127]
55 he founded the church of Kelso.

35

The marriage of his sisters Matilda to King Henry and Mary to the count of Boulogne

King Edgar was a sweet and lovable man, resembling his kinsman the
saintly King Edward in all respects; there was nothing harsh or
tyrannical or severe in his treatment of his subjects, but he ruled and
guided them with the greatest affection, goodness and kindness. In the
5 fourth year of his reign on 2 August the king of England William   1100:
Rufus went out hunting in the New Forest, and was killed by Walter   2 Aug.

maxima caritate, bonitate et benevolencia rexit et correxit. Eius
autem anno iiii^{to}, iiii^{to} nonas augusti, rex Anglie Willelmus Rufus, 5
cum in Nova Foresta iret venatum, a Waltero Treil quodam milite
transmarino, inscio et immeditato,^{b} feram aliquam volente sagittare
[occiditur]^c, multa flagicia luens una horula, nec postea verbum
edidit; de quo amplius infra dicetur. Ab omnibus suis statim relictus,
et in carro a rusticis devectus, sub turre Wintonie sepelitur. Successit 10
autem in regno sibi frater suus junior Henricus cognomine Bewclerk.

Cui rex | idem Eadgarus sororem suam Matildem eodem anno dedit
uxorem, quam Sanctus Ancelmus Cantuarie archiepiscopus die
Sancti Martini proximo reginam consecravit et inunxit. Mariam vero
sororem suam juniorem Eustachio juniori comiti Bononie nuptui 15
tradidit. ⟨Hic Eustachius frater fuit Godefridi de Bonone et Baldwini
regum Jerosolim.⟩ De quarum moribus et earum bonis actibus
aliquid scire cupienti in hoc postea libello erit utcumque declaratum.
Genuit autem Anglie idem rex Henricus ex regina Matilde filium
nomine Willelmum. Qui cum etatis esset xvii annorum, ex Norman- 20
nia cum patre rediens in Angliam, et Richardus frater eius nothus,
soror eius cum nepte, atque Richardus comes de Cestria, et multi
nobiles tam viri quam femine, cum centum quadraginta militibus et
quinquaginta nautis, omnes in mari submersi sunt apud Barbiflech;
rex cum paucis vix evasit. ⟨De quibus sic scriptum est: 25

　　Dum Normannigene, Gallis clare superatis,
　　　Anglica regna petunt, obstitit ipse Deus.
　　Nam fragili rate dum percurrit mare cimba,
　　　intulit excito nubila densa mari.
　　Dum vagi ceco rapiuntur tramite naute, 30
　　　ruperunt imas abdita saxa rates.
　　Sic mare dum superans [tabulata per ultima serpit,]^d
　　　mersit rege satos, occidit orbis honos.⟩

Itaque rex genuit ex Matilde filiam nomine Matildem, que, prudencia
forma diviciis imperio digna, nupsit Henrico iiii^{toe} imperatori 35
Romano. Huic Matildi fecit Henricus rex Anglie pater eius omnes
proceres Anglie fidelitatem jurare, priusquam mare secundo transiret, quia preter ipsam heredem regni non habebat. Genuit autem
predictus Bononie comes Eustachius ex predicta Maria sorore
Matildis regine filiam nomine Matildem, que virum strenuum 40
Stephanum comitem Mauritanie, regis Henrici nepotem, postea
regem Anglie, sponsum accepit, de regali simul et consulari stirpe
progenitum. Omitto filias, propono matres exemplum viventibus, que
cum seculi pompa, quod raro reperitur, divites sanctis extitere
virtutibus. Pauperes utriusque sexus, cuiuscumque condicionis 45
essent, ac si Christi membra fuissent, coluerunt. Religiosos, clericos,

b　immediato D
c　*Skene*

d　D; *lac*.C
e　+alias quinto CA

Tirel a knight from overseas, unintentionally, without premeditation, as he was aiming to shoot some wild beast. William, atoning for his many sins in one short hour, did not utter a single word thereafter;

10 more will be said about him later on. He was immediately abandoned by all his men, and was carried off in a cart by country people, and buried under Winchester tower. He was succeeded in the kingdom by his younger brother Henry surnamed Beauclerk. In the same year King Edgar gave him his sister Matilda in marriage, and St Anselm

15 the archbishop of Canterbury consecrated and anointed her as queen on the next St Martin's Day. He gave his younger sister Mary to be   11 Nov. married to Eustace the younger count of Boulogne. This Eustace was the brother of Godfrey de Bouillon and Baldwin the kings of Jerusalem. To anyone wishing to know something about the

20 characters and good deeds of these women, some information will be given later in this little book. Now Henry king of England and Queen Matilda had a son William by name. When he was seventeen years old, as he was returning from Normandy to England with his father, he and Richard his bastard brother and his sister together with the

25 king's niece and Richard earl of Chester and many nobles both men and women together with one hundred and forty soldiers and fifty sailors were all drowned in the sea at Barfleur; the king only just   [1120: managed to escape along with a few survivors. The following lines   25 Nov.] give an account of this:

30   While the Normans after a famous victory over the French
       were making for the kingdom of England, God himself
          opposed them.
       For while their bark with fragile hull was traversing the sea,
       he stirred up the sea and plunged it in dense cloud.
35   While the sailors were snatched away as they wandered along
          a path they could not see,
       hidden rocks burst the bottom of the boat.
       So while the sea gaining the mastery crept along the furthest
          decks,
40   it drowned the king's sons, and the glory of the world
          perished.

So the king had by Matilda a daughter called Matilda who, deserving as she was of imperial rank by reason of her wisdom, beauty and wealth, married the Roman emperor Henry IV. Her father Henry

45 king of England made all the nobles of England swear fealty to this Matilda before he crossed the sea for a second time, because he had no heir to the kingdom apart from her. Now the aforesaid Eustace count of Boulogne had a daughter called Matilda by the aforesaid Mary sister of Queen Matilda, who took a vigorous man Stephen count of

50 Mortain nephew of King Henry and afterwards king of England as her husband, born as he was of royal and also consular stock. I make no mention of the daughters. I bring forward as an example to the

sacerdotes et monachos amore sincero^f velut patronos et suos futuros
cum Christo judices, tenerime dilexerunt. Postquam Eadgarus in pace
bona ix, ut supradictum est, annis et iii mensibus regnum gloriose
rexisset, apud Dunde, sive ut alii ferunt apud Edinburgh, vi idus   50
januarii vitam finiens, in ecclesia Dunf' ante magnum altare juxta

Scriptor   patrem tumilatur. | De quo dicitur:

> Trimensis Edgarus regnavit ter tribus annis;
> rex Edinburgo fertur obisse probus.

f D; cincero C

36

G i,285   *De rege Alexandro i^o*

Autor   Illi successit frater eius Alexander cognomine Fers.
fo.100v;   ⟨Dicitur autem *le Fers*, pro eo quod patruus suus comes de Gowri
[Scriptor]   dedit sibi ad donum^a in baptismo terras de Lyff et Invergowri, unde
quando factus fuit rex, apud Lyff^b regale palacium cepit edificare,
cum ecce quidam satellites de le Mernez ⟨et Murrey,^{c}⟩ de nocte regem   5
infra ambitum palacii capere assilierunt, et^d cum postes^e effringere
conarentur,^{f} quidam cubicularius eius, Alexander Caron nomine,
regem callide per latrinam eduxit, et apud Invergowri^g liburna
ascensa, partes austrinas Scocie peciit,^{h} et collecto grandi exercitu,
contra rebelles properavit. Et quia Deus sibi in periculo affuit, volens   10
sibi^i gracias referre, apud Sconam ecclesiam monasterialem fundavit,^{j}
datis sibi in dotem et glebam^k terris de Lyff et Invergowri, cum suis
confestim expedicionem continuavit. Et cum perventum fuerat ad
aquam de Spey, inimicis in magno exercitu^l trans ripam conglobatis,
et aqua nimium succrescente, dissuasum est regi aquam, donec   15
minueretur, transvadare. Qui quasi ira succensus, visis inimicis suis
conspiracionem minitantibus, et se non prevalens continere, vexillum

a	+ut moris est *CA*	h	expeciit *CA*
b	+apud Lyff *del.C*	i	+tanquam gratus *CA*
c	le Murrave *for* Murrey *CA*	j	in illa sua expedicione fundare manucepit
d	+ecce *CA*		*for* ecclesiam ... fundavit *CA*
e	pestes *CA*	k	et glebam *om.CA*
f	conabantur *C*	l	magna multitudine rebellum *for* in magno
g	+per *CA*		exercitu *CA*

living the mothers, who showed themselves rich in saintly virtues
while involved in secular magnificence, a combination that is seldom
55   found. They looked after the poor of both sexes, no matter what their
condition, as being members of Christ. They tenderly loved religious,
clerics, priests and monks with sincere affection as their advocates
and future judges along with Christ. After Edgar had gloriously ruled
the kingdom in good peace for nine years and three months, as stated
60   above, he reached the end of his life at Dundee, or as others maintain   [1107:
at Edinburgh, on 8 January, and was buried in the church of   ? 8 Jan.]
Dunfermline before the high altar next to his father. These lines are
about him:

Edgar reigned for nine years and three months;
65   the worthy king is said to have died at Edinburgh.

36

King Alexander I

He was succeeded by his brother Alexander nicknamed 'the Fierce'.
He is called 'the Fierce' because his uncle the earl of Gowrie gave him
as a baptismal gift the lands of Liff and Invergowrie. When he became
king, he began to build a royal palace at Liff, when behold certain
5   ruffians of the Mearns and Moray made an attempt to capture the
king by night within the precincts of the palace, and when they were
trying to break down the doorposts, one of the king's chamberlains
called Alexander Carron cunningly led the king out through a latrine.
He went aboard a galley at Invergowrie, and made for the southern
10   regions of Scotland, gathered together a large army, and hurried
against the rebels. Because God had supported him in time of danger,
he wished to show his gratitude to Him. So he founded a monastic
church at Scone, and after he had given them the lands of Liff and
Invergowrie as endowment and glebe, he quickly resumed his
15   expedition along with his men. When they arrived at the Water of
Spey, his enemies were massed together in a great army on the
opposite bank; and as the water was rising excessively high, the king
was advised not to ford the Water until it subsided. He was blazing
with anger at the sight of his enemies threatening conspiracy, and not
20   being able to contain himself, he handed over his banner to his
chamberlain (the aforesaid Alexander) to carry; and these two were
the first to attempt the ford; the army followed, and the enemy was
turned to flight. From this time the said Alexander and his heirs were

suum suo cubiculario Alexandro premisso ferendum contulit;[m] et
prius hii duo vadum temptant;[n] exercitus sequitur, et inimici[o] in
fugam[p] convertuntur.[q] Et abhinc dicto Alexandro et suis heredibus 20
vexilliferis, propterea a rege terre[r] perpetue | conferuntur. Sed quia
isdem Alexander in gladiatorio ludo manum Anglico amputavit, illud
cognomen *le Scrimgeour* sibi et succedentibus hucusque reliquit.⟩
⟨De prodicione Moravien' habes supra libro iiii[to], capitulo xxvii
cum sequente.⟩   25
Anno domini m[o] c[mo] vii[o] et imperatoris Henrici v[tis] primo, cui nupsit
Matildis filia[s] Matildis bone regine Anglie, | et stetit cum imperatore
conjunx xx[ti] annis, prolem non suscipiens ex eo. Iste, suscepto
imperio, capiens patrem suum in vinculis mori fecit, et quia sic patrem
suum dehonestaverat, justo Dei judicio creditur eum sine herede 30
decessisse. Nam neque filium neque filiam habens defunctus est. Cui
successit Lotharius dux Saxonie. ⟨Imperatrix ista post mortem mariti
nupta est Gaufrido Plantgenet comiti Andigavie, qui genuit ex ea
Henricum Secundum Anglie regem.⟩ | Rex iste Alexander regnavit
annis xvii. Erat enim vir literatus et pius, clericis et religiosis satis 35
humilis et amabilis, ceteris subditorum ultra modum terribilis, homo
magni cordis, ultra vires suas in omnibus se extendens. Erat itaque in
construendis ecclesiis et reliquiis sanctorum perquirendis, in vestibus
sacerdotalibus librisque sacris conficiendis et ordinandis studiosissi-
mus; omnibus advenientibus eciam supra vires liberalissimus; circa 40
pauperes ita devotus, ut in nulla | re magis delectari quam in eis
suscipiendis, lavandis, alendis, et vestiendis videretur. Matris enim
vestigia sequens, eam in piis actibus adeo emulatus est, ut tot et tantis
donariis ditaverit tres ecclesias, ecclesiam videlicet Sanctiandr' de
Kilremonth, et ecclesias Dunfermelinensem et Sconensem, unam a 45
patre et matre fundatam, alteram a seipso in honorem[u] Sancte
Trinitatis et Sancti Michaelis archangeli, superiori sede regni Scona
fundatam et erectam. Ipse est qui Cursum Apri beato Andree
contulit, qui eciam monasterium canonicorum de Insula Emonia
juxta Inverkethin fundavit, qui tot et tanta privilegia prestitit ecclesie 50
predicte Sancte Trinitatis de Scona, quam fundatam edificavit loco
quo reges antiquitus tam Picti quam Scoti sedem regni primam
constituerunt; et illius temporis more, scemate lapideo constructam
dedicari fecit. Ad cuius dedicacionem ⟨factam per Turgotum Sancti
Andr' episcopum,⟩ precepto regis urgente, totum pene regnum 55
concurreret. Ipsam quidem ecclesiam, Deo disponente, cum pertinenciis omnibus canonicis regularibus ab ecclesia Sancti Oswaldi de
Nostell' vocatis, et ceteris post eos usque finem seculi Deo servituris,
libere tradidit gubernandam.

fo.101

Scriptor

Scriba;
G i,286

fo.101v

m	+ quia noverat enim viribus et audacia prevalere *CA*	*q*	dilabuntur *CA*
n	pretemptant *CA*	*r*	+ et redditus *CA*
o	+ viso regis vexillo displicato *CA*	*s*	+ anno *CA*
p	+ precipites *CA*	*t*	+ Sancte *del.C*
		u	honore *C*

standard-bearers, and because of this they had lands conferred on
25 them by the king in perpetuity. But because this Alexander cut off a
hand in an English tournament, he left the surname *Scrimgeour* for
himself and his successors right to this day.

You will find an account of the treason of the men of Moray above
in Book 4, Chapter 27 and following.
30 [Alexander began to reign] in 1107 the first year of the emperor 1107
Henry V, whom Matilda daughter of Matilda the Good queen of
England married. She was his wife for twenty years without having [1114]
any children by him. When he became emperor, he captured his father
and let him die in prison, and it is thought that he died without an heir
35 by the just judgment of God, since he had dishonoured his father in
this way. For he died without a son or daughter to his name. He was
succeeded by Lothair duke of Saxony. After the death of her husband [1125]
the empress married Geoffrey Plantagenet count of Anjou, and they [1128]
were the parents of Henry II king of England. King Alexander
40 reigned for seventeen years. He was a well-educated and devout man,
deferential and friendly to clerics and religious, but excessively
terrifying to the rest of his subjects; he was a great-hearted man,
extending himself in all directions beyond his strength. He was very
enthusiastic in constructing churches, searching for relics of the
45 saints, and in the manufacture and arrangement of priestly vestments
and sacred books; he was also very generous beyond his means to all
comers; so devout was he in respect of the poor that there was nothing
that seemed to give him greater pleasure than receiving, washing,
feeding and clothing them. Following in his mother's footsteps, he
50 rivalled her in holy deeds to such an extent that he endowed three
churches with many great gifts, that is to say the church of St Andrew
at Kilrymont and the churches of Dunfermline and Scone, the one
founded by his father and mother, the other founded by himself to the
glory of the Holy Trinity and St Michael the archangel, which was
55 founded and built at Scone the chief seat of the kingdom. It was he
who conferred the Boar's Chase on blessed Andrew, and who also
founded the monastery of canons of the island of Inchcolm near
Inverkeithing, and who conferred so many great privileges on the
aforesaid church of the Holy Trinity at Scone, which he founded and
60 built in the place where both the Pictish and the Scottish kings from
ancient times had established the chief seat of their kingdom; and he
had it dedicated after it had been built of stone construction in the
manner of that time. In response to the king's command almost the
whole of the kingdom flocked to its dedication, which was performed
65 by Turgot bishop of St Andrews. Under God's dispensation he
unreservedly handed over the church with all its pertinents to be
governed by canons regular who were summoned from the church of
St Oswald of Nostell, and to all the others who would serve God after
them until the end of the world.

36a

[De fundacione Scone]ᵃ

fo.110;
G i,316

Anno domini m° c° vii Eadgarus Scotorum rex filius Sancte Margarite iiiiᵗᵘˢ idus januarii obiit. Cui successit Alexander frater eius. Iste primus, matris vestigia sequens, eam in piis actibus adeo emulatus est, ut tot et tantis donariis ditaverit tres ecclesias, videlicet ecclesiam Sanctiandr' in Kilrymond, et ecclesias de Dunfermelyn et Sconensem 5 in honore Sancte Trinitatis, unam a matre fundatam, alteram a seipso in sede regni fundatam et erectam, ut posteri sui mirarentur animum regis, et plus ab ipsis avellicaverint, quam adjecerint, excepto quod illustris successor eius frater rex David eas in statu bonoᵇ tenuerit, precipue Dunf', ubi ipse in Domino repausat. Iste nobilis rex 10 Alexander evocavit ab ecclesia Sancti Oswaldi que est in Nostelis, de concessu tunc prioris eiusdem Adelwoldi, postea episcopi Karleolensis, sex religiosos, devotos et discretos canonicos, qui regulam beati Augustini, et in seipsis arctius servarent, et aliis sequendam verbo et exemplo proponerent, supplicans eidem ut ipsos sine dilacione liberos 15 et absolutos ad se transmitteret. Venerunt igitur, ut rex jusserat, sex numero canonici, graves moribus et religione maturi. Inter quos et Robertus, vir preclare prudencie, qui statim pre aliis electus est in priorem de Scona, et post paucis annis interpositis, prefato rege annuente, electus est in episcopum Sanctiandr', post obitum domini 20 Turgoti eiusdem episcopi, qui in Dunelmi, quo quondam erat prior, diem clausit extremum. Premissa reperi in antiquo libello post scripcionem libri, ubi eciam dicitur quod anno domini m° c° xxii obiit Sibilla regina Scocie, nupta dicti regis Alexandri, in Insula de Lochtey iii idus julii. Quam insulam cum omni dominio sibi adjacente donavit 25 rex Alexander canonicis de Scona pro anima regine jure perpetuo possidendam.

---

a   *side-note on fo.101v at start of c.37 draws attention to this misplaced passage* De fundacione Scone ulterius vide in fine

huius quinti libri *with an identifying mark leading to fo.110* C

b   + posuerit *del.*C

36a

The foundation of Scone

Edgar king of Scots son of St Margaret died on 10 January 1107. He
was succeeded by his brother Alexander. He was the first, following in
his mother's footsteps, to rival her in holy deeds to such an extent that
he endowed with many great gifts three churches, that is to say the
5 church of St Andrew at Kilrymont and the churches of Dunfermline
and Scone to the glory of the Holy Trinity, the one founded by his
mother, and the other founded and built by himself in the chief seat of
the kingdom, so that his descendants were amazed at the generosity of
the king, and subtracted more from the churches than they added,
10 with the exception that his illustrious successor his brother King
David kept them in good condition, especially Dunfermline where he
himself rests in the Lord. The noble king Alexander summoned from
the church of St Oswald, which is at Nostell, with the permission of its
prior who at that time was Æthelwulf, later bishop of Carlisle, six
15 religious, devout and prudent canons, who kept the rule of the blessed
Augustine very strictly in themselves, and offered it for others to
follow by word and example, beseeching the prior to send them to him
without delay, free and discharged from their obligations. So they
came, as the king had ordered, canons six in number, serious in
20 character and long-practised in religion. One of them was Robert, a
man of outstanding wisdom, who was immediately elected in
preference to the others as prior of Scone, and a few years later with
the consent of the aforesaid king he was elected as bishop of St
Andrews after the death of sir Turgot bishop of the same, who died in
25 Durham where he was formerly prior. I found the aforesaid in an
ancient little book after the writing of this book. It is also recorded
there that Sibylla queen of Scotland, wife of the said King Alexander
died on the island of Loch Tay on 13 July 1122. King Alexander gave
this island with all the domain adjacent to it to the canons of Scone to
30 be possessed in perpetuity for the soul of the queen.

1107:
[? 10 Jan.]

[ca 1120]

[1124: Jan.]

1122:
13 July

37

De fundacione Emonie

Scriptor

Anno domini m° c^{mo} xiiii fundatum est monasterium de Scona, ⟨et
dedicatur per Turgotum Sanctiandr' episcopum monachum Dunelmensem;⟩ et circa annum domini m^m centesimum vicesimum tercium,
non minus mirifice quam miraculose, fundatum est monasterium
G i,287   Sancti Columbe de Insula Emonia juxta Edenburgh.^a Nam | cum 5
nobilis et Christianissimus rex dominus Alexander primus hoc
nomine ob certa negocia regni passagium faceret trans Portum^b
Regine, subito exorta est tempestas valida, flante africo,^c et ratem
cum naucleris, vix vita comite, compulit applicare ad Insulam
Emoniam, ubi tunc degebat quidam heremita insulanus qui servicio 10
Sancti Columbe deditus ad quamdam inibi capellulam, tenui victu,
utpote lacte unius vacce et conchis ac pisciculis marinis collectis,
contentatus, sedule se dedit. De cuius quidem tali annona rex cum suis
commilitonibus admodum non paucis per tres dies continuos,
impellente vento, vitam gratulanter^d transigebat. Sed cum pridie in 15
maximo maris periculo et tempestatis rabie quassatus, de vita
desperaret, votum fecit sancto ut si eum cum suis ad insulam
incolumem perduceret, ad eius laudem in ipsa insula talem memoriam
relinqueret, quod navigantibus et naufragis ad asilum cederet et
solamen. Hac itaque occasione actum est, ut fundaret ibidem 20
monasterium canonicorum, sicut inpresenciarum cernitur. Tum
eciam quia Sanctum Columbam semper et a juventute speciali
venerabatur honore. Tum insuper quia parentes ipsius per aliquot
annos infecundi, sobolis solacio erant destituti, donec devocione
supplici^e Sanctum Columbam implorantes, gloriose consequti sunt 25
quod tam hanelo^f desiderio diu quesierunt. Unde versus:

M c, ter i, bis et x literis a tempore Christi,
Emon, tunc ab Alexandro fundata fuisti
Scotorum primo. Structorem canonicorum
transferat ex imo Deus hunc ad astra^g polorum.   30

Ante hoc, anno^h domini m° c°, Henricus Bewclerk a Mauricio
Londonensi episcopo in regem consecratur, qui Ancelmum Cantuar-

a	Inverkethine *CA*	e	simplici *CA*
b	Portam *CA*	f	h- *interlin.C*
c	*interlin.over* vulturno [?] *del.C*	g	altra *CA*
d	glorianter *CA*	h	+c' *del.C*

37

The foundation of Inchcolm

The monastery of Scone was founded in 1114, and dedicated by [ca 1120] Turgot bishop of St Andrews and monk of Durham; and about the year 1123 the monastery of St Columba on the island of Inchcolm [ca 1123] near Edinburgh was founded in a way that was as remarkable as it
5 was miraculous. For when the noble and most Christian lord king Alexander the first of this name was making the crossing at Queensferry in pursuit of some business of the kingdom, a violent storm suddenly arose as wind blew from the south-west, and compelled the ship with its crew scarcely clinging to life to put in at the
10 island of Inchcolm, where a certain island hermit lived at that time. He was dedicated to the service of St Columba, and earnestly devoted himself to it at a certain little chapel on the island, content with a meagre diet consisting of the milk of one cow, shells and little fish that he gathered from the sea. The king with his very large number of
15 fellow soldiers gratefully lived on this food of his for three days on end under compulsion from the wind. But on the previous day when he was giving up hope of surviving, as he was being buffeted by the very great danger of the sea and the madness of the storm, he made a vow to the saint that if he brought him safely to the island along with his
20 men, he would leave on the island such a memorial to his glory as would serve for asylum and solace to sailors and victims of shipwreck. This is how it came about that he founded a monastery of canons in that same place, just as it can be seen at the present day. There was also the fact that he had always even from his youth revered St
25 Columba with particular honour. There was moreover the fact that his parents had been infertile and deprived of the comfort of children for some years, until they implored St Columba with suppliant devotion, and gloriously achieved what they had long sought with eager desire. Hence the lines:

30   One thousand, one hundred and twenty-three digits from the
          time of Christ;
      then, Inchcolm, you were founded by Alexander
      the first, king of Scots. May God transfer
      this founder of canons from the depths to the stars of
35   Heaven.

Before this in 1100 Henry Beauclerk was consecrated king by Maurice 1100: bishop of London. He recalled Anselm archbishop of Canterbury, [5 Aug.]

iensem, a fratre suo rege Willelmo exulantem, revocavit. Ranulphum Dunelmensem episcopum in custodia London' posuit. Quo anno Robertus Normannie, Robertus Flandrensis et Eustachius Bono- 35 niensis comites de Terra Sancta repatriaverunt. Anno sequenti rex Jerosolimorum Baldwinus successor et frater*i* Godefridi Cesaream Palestinam cepit. Anno m° c iiii*to* corpus Sancti Cuthberti ostensum est et incorruptum inventum et flexibile, et translatum est apud Dunelmum in novam ecclesiam. Anno m° c vii° in consilio apud 40 London' statutum est ut nusquam ulterius*j* per dacionem baculi vel anuli de episcopatu vel | abbacia per regem vel quamlibet laicam manum aliquis investiretur.

fo.102

i et frater *interlin.*C *j* G; alterius C

38

De investitura prelatorum per seculares principes, et huiusmodi officii renunciacione, et beato B[ernardo]

Hiis temporibus Henricus iiii*to* Theutonicorum rex cum magno exercitu venit in Tusciam, ut Rome coronaretur in imperatorem, et ad papam Paschalem premissis nunciis, per literas refutabat omnem investituram episcoporum, abbatum et aliorum clericorum super quam alii imperatores predecessores sui questionem cum | Romanis 5 pontificibus habuerant, et juramento tam imperatoris quam suorum principum super hoc dominus papa accepto... Postquam tam clerus quam populus extra portas versus montem de mandato domini pape eidem obviassent, et eum usque ad summitatem graduum Sancti Petri conduxissent, et eum ibi summus pontifex cum cardinalibus et 10 episcopis expectasset, rex adveniens, post pedum oscula, se invicem osculati sunt; et se per manus tenentes, postquam ad portam argenteam pervenissent, et papa super investitura refutanda juramen- tum repetisset, rex cum suis consilio habito, papam et cardinales cum tota curia captivavit, et ideo non immerito, eadem mensura qua 15 mensus est patri suo spirituali, remensum est sibi per filium suum carnalem Henricum v*tum*, ut supra eodem libro, capitulo 36. Huius eciam temporibus, quidam ex clero Romano perversi contra ipsum Romanum pontificem surgentes, tres heremitas, videlicet Albertum, Arnulphum et Theodoricum, diversis temporibus erigere in papam 20 presumpserunt; qui licet in principio domino pape multas infesta- ciones fecissent, in fine tamen de ipso prostrati sunt. Eodem tempore rex Hungarie ad moniciones pape, per literas suas scribens eidem, renunciavit investituris episcoporum et aliorum prelatorum, quas usque ad illa tempora reges Ungarie facere consueverunt. Anno m° 25

G i,288

who had been exiled by his brother King William. He put Ranulf
bishop of Durham in prison in London. In this year Robert count of
40 Normandy, Robert count of Flanders and Eustace count of Boulogne
returned home from the Holy Land. In the following year the king of   1101:
Jerusalem, Baldwin, the successor and brother of Godfrey, captured   [spring]
Caesarea in Palestine. In 1104 the body of St Cuthbert was exhibited   1104: [Sept.]
and was found to be undecayed and pliant. It was transferred to the
45 new church in Durham. In 1107 it was decided in a council at London   1107: [Aug.]
that nowhere any longer should anyone be invested in the office of
bishop or abbot by the giving of a staff or ring by the king or any lay
hand whatsoever.

38

The investiture of prelates by secular princes and the
renunciation of this kind of service, and blessed Bernard

At this time Henry IV king of the Teutons came with a great army into   [1110]
Tuscany, in order to be crowned emperor at Rome. Sending envoys
on ahead to Pope Paschal, he renounced in a letter all investiture of
bishops, abbots and other clerics, concerning which other emperors
5 his predecessors had been in dispute with the Roman pontiffs; and
when the oath of both the emperor and his princes on this matter had
been accepted, the lord pope... After both clergy and people had gone   [1111:
to meet the king outside the gates towards the hill by order of the lord   12 Feb.]
pope, and had escorted him right to the top of the steps of St Peter's,
10 and the supreme pontiff awaited him there with his cardinals and
bishops, the king came, and after kissing [the pope's] feet, he and the
pope embraced each other; and holding each other's hands, they
arrived at the silver gate, and the pope again asked for an oath on the
renunciation of investiture. The king took counsel with his people,
15 and seized the pope and the cardinals together with the whole papal
Curia, and deservedly too with the same measure that he meted out to
his spiritual father, it was meted out to him again by his son in the
flesh Henry V, as recorded above in this same book, Chapter 36. Also
in this pope's reign certain wicked Roman clerics, rising in revolt
20 against the Roman pontiff, had the audacity to elevate at different
times as pope three hermits Albert, Arnulf and Theodoric. Although
to begin with they launched many attacks upon the lord pope, in the
end however they were overthrown by him. At the same time the king
of Hungary in response to warnings from the pope wrote to him, and
25 in his letter renounced investitures of bishops and other prelates,

cix Turgotus prior Dunelm' consecratus est in episcopum Sanctiandr'
iii kal. augusti. Et anno sequenti cometa apparuit; et fluvius Trenta
exsiccatus est a mane usque ad terciam, spacio unius miliarii. Anno
domini m° cxiiii flumen Themisii defecit, ita ut a puero transvadari
possit. Eodem tempore Bernardus, habens annos xxii, sub abbate   30
Stephano qui fuit tercius in Cistercio abbas, cum sociis xxx^{ta}
Cistercium ingreditur, quorum quinque erant fratres sui uterini, filii
strenuissimi militis Cecillini de Fontanis, anno scilicet domini m^{mo} c^{mo}
xiii ⟨a constitucione domus Cisterciensis xv^{to}.⟩ Cum autem Bernardus cum fratribus suis domum paternam egrederetur, Guido primo- 35
genitus videns Guinardum fratrem suum minimum puerum ludentem
ad pilam in platea cum sodalibus: 'Eia,' inquit, 'frater Guinarde, ad te
solum respicit omnis terra possessionis paterne.' Cui autem puer non^a
pueriliter respondit dicens: 'Vos ergo celum^b habebitis, et michi
terram solum relinquitis. Non^c ex equo facta est hec divisio.' Modico 40
igitur tempore cum patre remansit, sed relictis omnibus fratres
postmodum secutus est. Cui superfuit una virguncula heres, que post
fratres ordinem eundem sanctimonialium intravit. De isto Bernardo
dictum est:

Hic vir Bernardus floret in^d scriptis quasi nardus.   45

⟨Qui monasteria centum sexaginta fundavit, et die [transitus sui]^e
superfuerunt de filiis suis monachis vii^c.⟩

a	+ tamen CA	d	+ diu del.C
b	+ celum not del.C	e	D; lac.C
c	+ est del.C		

39

G i,289

De morte sororum regis Alexandri et de laudibus earum

Autor   Ipsius Alexandri regnacionis anno xi soror eius Matildis regina
Anglorum obiit cognomine, Bona kal. maii, sepultaque est honorifice
in ecclesia Sancti Petri London' apud Westmonasterium in oratorio
retro magnum altare. Cuius eleganter et curiose constructi in medio
tumili summitate sancti regis Eadwardi reliquie conduntur opere   5
sumptuoso, et circa tumilum undique reges honorifice sepeliuntur.
De cuius regine et^a virtutibus habentur huiusmodi metra:

a   interlin.C

which kings of Hungary had been in the habit of performing up to that time.

In 1109 Turgot prior of Durham was consecrated as bishop of St Andrews on 30 July. And in the following year a comet appeared; and the river Trent dried up from the morning right to the third hour for a distance of one mile. In 1114 the river Thames shrank to such an extent that it could be crossed on foot by a child.

1109:
[1 Aug.]
1110:
[29 May]
1114

At the same time Bernard entered the monastery at Cîteaux at the age of twenty-two under Abbot Stephen who was the third abbot at Cîteaux, along with thirty companions, five of whom were his own brothers, the sons of the vigorous knight Tescelin Sorrel of Fontaines, in 1113, the fifteenth year from the founding of the Cistercian Order. Now when Bernard was leaving his father's house along with his brothers, the eldest Guy, seeing his brother Nivard who was a very small boy playing at ball in the courtyard with his friends, said: 'Oh, brother Nivard, all the land that our father possesses falls to you alone.' To him the child unchildlike replied: 'So you will have Heaven, and to me you leave only Earth. This is not an equal division.' So he stayed behind with his father for a short time, but afterwards left everything, and followed his brothers. Their father had only one little girl left to be his heir, and she entered the corresponding order of nuns after her brothers. The following line is about Bernard:

[1112]

> This man Bernard blossoms in his writings like spikenard.

He founded one hundred and sixty monasteries, and on the day of his death seven hundred monks his sons [in God] were still living.

[1153]

39

The death of the sisters of King Alexander and their eulogies

In the eleventh year of Alexander's reign his sister Matilda queen of the English nicknamed 'the Good' died on 1 May, and was buried with great honour in the church of St Peter at Westminster in London in a chapel behind the high altar. In the middle of this elegantly and elaborately constructed chapel the remains of King Edward the Confessor are preserved on top of a tomb of ornate workmanship, and all around the tomb kings are buried with great honour. The following lines are about this queen's virtues:

1118:
1 May

> Prosperity did not bring her joy, nor adversity sorrow;
> she laughed at adversity, and feared prosperity.

Prospera non letam fecere, nec aspera tristem;
aspera risus ei, prospera terror erant.
Non decor effecit fragilem, non sceptra superbam;　　　　　10
sola potens, humilis; sola pudica, decens.
Mai prima dies, nostrarum nocte dierum
raptam, perpetuam fecit inire diem.

Cuius epitaphium sic literis aureis scriptum habetur:

Hic jacet Matildis regina Bona Anglie, uxor quondam regis Henrici 15
Primi, filia Malcolmi regis Scocie et uxoris sue Sancte Margarite, que
obiit anno domini m^{mo} c^{mo} xvii^o. De cuius bonitate et morum probitate
dicere omnia non sufficeret dies.

⟨Sponsus eius rex Henricus persuasione eius et consilio^b anno m^o cii
constituit canonicos regulares^c in Karleyl. Causa autem quare Bona　20
vocata est fuit hec. Inolevit tunc temporis in Anglia quedam
consuetudo pessima et servilis angaria communienses nimium
depressiva. Erat enim regina compaciens valde, et super pauperes
afflictos pia gestans viscera. Adiit propterea regem et obnixe sedule
importuneque peciit huiusmodi corruptelam e medio tolli. Rex^d tam 25
multiplicatis intercessionibus pulsus et devictus, tandem commotus
sic fertur respondisse: 'Dummodo tu, domina, unam rem quam
expostulo feceris, perficiam quod hortaris.' At illa jocundata,
improvise tamen, petendam rem concessit, credens dominum regem
nil velle petere preter quod decens licitumque foret et honestum. 30
Edixit ergo sibi rex ut pro eius amore nudata | omni veste meridic
quoquam^e Londoniarum mediam plateam a fine ad finem equitaret.
Cui ultro consenciens, ameniore die nacta, capitis sui capillis et aureis
cincinnis decenter scapulis et corpore oppansis, et usque genua
protensis, rege et populo spectantibus equitaturam perfecit. Propter 35
quod quamplurimum a rege condilecta, et ab omni populo commen-
data, Bona deinceps regina est vocata; et universa plebicula de domo
servitutis et | angaria perpetue liberata. Unde per literam regina
impetravit huiusmodi manumissionis libertatem. Cuius copiam vide
infra folio viii post titulos sequentis libri.⟩　　　　　　　　40
Willelmus:

fo.101v

G i,290

fo.102

Uxor Henrici regis ex antiqua regum et illustri stirpe descendit Matildis
filia Malcolmi regis Scotorum, a teneris annis sanctitudine egregia, |
materne pietatis emula, nichil sinistrum quantum ad se moribus
admittens. Preter regium cubile, pudoris integra, nulla eciam suspi- 45
cione lesa; cilicio sub regio cultu convoluta, nudipes diebus xl^e terebat
ecclesiarum limina. Nec horrebat pedes lavare morbidorum, ulcera
sanie distillancia contrectare^f manibus, longa postremo protelare

fo.102v

b　+ipsius regine CA　　　　　　　e　+equitaret del.C
c　+et fundavit nobile monasterium CA　f　D; cotrectare C
d　+tand del.C

Beauty did not weaken her, nor did royal rank make her
    proud;
she alone was powerful, and yet humble; she alone was
    chaste, and yet beautiful.
15   The first day of May snatched her away, bringing night on
    our days,
but giving her entry to eternal day.

Here is her epitaph engraved in letters of gold:

20   Here lies Matilda the Good queen of England, formerly wife of King
    Henry I, daughter of Malcolm king of Scotland and his wife St
    Margaret. She died in 1117. A day would not be long enough to
    describe fully her goodness and high moral character.

In 1102 her husband King Henry established canons regular in [1123]
Carlisle as a result of her persuasion and advice. The following
25 passage explains why she was called 'the Good'. At that time in
England there had grown up a very wicked custom and servile levy
that bore excessively heavily upon the commons. Now the queen was
very kind-hearted, and she felt a pious compassion for the afflictions
of the poor. So she approached the king, and begged resolutely,
30 earnestly, in season and out of season that this kind of malpractice
should be abolished. The king impelled and overcome by such
manifold pleadings was at last moved, and is said to have replied as
follows: 'Provided that you, madam, do one thing that I stipulate, I
shall carry out what you urge.' She joyfully albeit rashly agreed to
35 what would be asked of her, believing that the lord king would not be
willing to ask anything that was not seemly, lawful and honourable.
So the king decreed to her that for love of him she should ride stripped
of all clothing at midday along the middle street in London from end
to end. She willingly gave her consent to him, and choosing a
40 favourable day, with the hair of her head and her golden ringlets
decently spread over her shoulders and body, and reaching right to
her knees, she completed her ride under the eyes of the king and the
people. On account of this she was loved most dearly by the king and
praised by the whole people, and henceforth was called 'the good
45 queen'; and the whole of the common people was released in
perpetuity from the house of servitude and servile levy. Then the
queen obtained by a charter the privilege of release from servitude of
this kind. See a copy of this charter eight folios below after the chapter
headings of the following book.
50   William [of Malmesbury] says:

The wife of King Henry was descended from the ancient and illustrious
line of kings, Matilda daughter of Malcolm king of Scots, of
outstanding sanctity from her earliest years, rivalling her mother's
piety, admitting nothing evil to her character as far as lay in her power.
55 Except for the king's bed she was completely chaste, unsullied even by

oscula, et mensam apponere; sed et in servicio Dei audiendo wluptas
unica. Inter hec erepta est patrie magno provincialium dampno, suo   50
nullo. Nam et funus nobiliter curatum, apud Westmonasterium
quietem accepit, et spiritus se celum [incolere]*g* non frivolis signis
ostendit. Obiit regno post xvii annos et sex menses libenter relicto.

Hec ille.

Maria namque soror eius comitissa Bononie tercio ante suum   55
obitum anno de hac vita migravit, et apud Bermondisay ex altera
parte London' in monasterio Sancti Salvatoris in pace quiescit. Que
regina sorore non minor extitit probitate, licet regia caruerat
dignitate. Tumulus autem eius marmoreus, regum et reginarum
imagines habens impressas, genus quiescentis demonstrat. Et in   60
superficie eiusdem tumuli titulus literis aureis scriptus vitam et
originem breviter ita comprehendit:

> Nobilis hic tumulata jacet comitissa Maria;
>   actibus hec nituit, larga, benigna fuit.
> Regum sanguis erat; morum probitate vigebat,*h*   65
>   compaciens inopi. Vivat in arce poli.

Hee vero duo sorores, Matildis et Maria filie regis Malcolmi et
Margarite, sui generis celsitudinem conjugio, morum ingenuitate,
sciencie magnitudine, rerum temporalium larga in pauperes et
ecclesias dispensacione, decenter ornaverunt.   70

---

g   G   *h*   Regum ... vigebat *om.CA,P*

39a

[*Copia litere manumissionis populi Anglorum*]*a*

fo.110;
G i,316
Copia litere manumissionis populi Anglorum facta per Matildem
reginam Anglie filiam Sancte Margarite regine Scotorum, quam ad
eius instanciam concessit vir eius Henricus Bewclerk filius Willelmi
Bastard anno c' m° cc° x.

Henricus rex Anglie omnibus baronibus suis tam Francigenis quam   5

---

a   *in a marginal addition to c.39 above at*   *text, which was copied in full on the first*
     foot of fo.101v, reference is made to this   *available blank page C*

any suspicion. Wrapped in a hair-shirt under her royal robes, she wore
out the thresholds of churches barefooted during Lent. Nor did she
shrink from washing the feet of the diseased, or touching with her
hands ulcers dripping with pus, and finally giving them protracted
60   kisses, and setting their tables; but her particular pleasure was in
hearing divine service. In the midst of these activities she was snatched
away at great loss to the people of the country, but at no loss to herself.
For her body was nobly cared for, and received its rest at Westminster,
65   and her spirit showed by no slight signs that it was an inhabitant of
heaven. She died gladly relinquishing her royal rank after seventeen
years and six months.

Her sister Mary countess of Boulogne departed this life three years   [1116:
before Matilda's death, and rests in peace at Bermondsey on the other   31 May]
side of London in the monastery of St Saviour. She was not inferior to
70   her sister the queen in moral worth, although she was lacking in royal
rank. Her tomb of marble with the likenesses of kings and queens
engraved on it shows the lineage of her who rests there. And on the
surface of that tomb an inscription written in golden letters briefly
summarises her life and origin thus:

75   Here lies buried the noble countess Mary;
          she shone brightly in her deeds, she was generous and kind.
          She was of the blood of kings; her strength was in her upright
              character,
          and she was compassionate to the poor. May she live in the
80   heights of Heaven.

These two sisters indeed, Matilda and Mary, daughters of King
Malcolm and Margaret fittingly embellished their high birth by their
marriage, their nobility of character, the extent of their learning, the
generous distribution of their worldly goods to the poor and the
85 churches.

39a

Copy of a letter emancipating the people of the English

Copy of a letter emancipating the people of the English issued by
Matilda queen of England daughter of St Margaret queen of Scots,
which at her insistence her husband Henry Beauclerk son of William
the Bastard granted in 1210.   [1100:
                                  5 Aug.]
5   Henry king of England sends greetings to all his barons both French
         and English in origin. Know that I by the mercy of God and the
         common counsel of the barons of England have been crowned king of
         the same kingdom. And since the kingdom was oppressed with unjust

Angligenis salutem. Sciatis me Dei misericordia et communi consilio
baronum Anglie eiusdem regem regni coronatum esse. Et quoniam
regnum oppressum erat injustis exaccionibus, ego, respectu Dei et
amore quem erga vos omnes habeo, sanctam Dei ecclesiam imprimis
liberam facio, ita quod neque vendam nec ad firmam | ponam, nec 10
mortuo archiepiscopo vel episcopo sive abbate aliquid inde accipiam
scilicet de dominio ecclesie vel de hominibus eius donec successor in
eam ingrediatur. Et omnes malas consuetudines quibus regnum Anglie
injuste opprimebatur inde aufero. Si quis baronum vel comitum vel
aliorum qui de me tenent mortuus fuerit, heres suus non emet terram 15
sicut faciebant tempore patris mei, sed legittima et justa relevacione
eam relevabit. Similiter et homines baronum meorum legittima
relevacione relevabunt terras suas de dominis suis. Et si quis baronum
vel aliorum hominum meorum filiam suam vel sororem vel neptem vel
cognatam nuptui tradere voluerit, mecum inde loquatur; sed nec ego 20
aliquid de suo pro hac licencia*b* accipiam nec ei defendam quin eam*c*
det, excepto si eam velit jungere inimico meo. Et si mortuo barone vel
alio homine meo filia heres remanserit, ⟨illam dabo con-[silio ba-
]ronum*d* meorum [cum terra]*d* sua. Et si mortuo marito uxor remanserit
et⟩ sine liberis fuerit, dotem et maritacionem suam habebit, et eam non 25
dabo nisi secundum velle suum. Si vero uxor cum liberis remanserit,
dotem quidem et maritacionem habebit, dum corpus suum legittime
servaverit, et eam non dabo nisi secundum velle suum. Et terre [et]
liberorum custos erit sive uxor sive alius qui juste esse debebit. Et
precipio ut omnes barones mei ita se contineant erga filios vel filias vel 30
uxores hominum suorum. Et commune monetagium quod capiebatur
per civitates et comitatus, quod non fuit tempore regis Eadwardi, hoc
ne amodo sit omnino defendo. Si quis | monetarius captus fuerit vel
alius aliquis cum falsa moneta, recta justicia inde fiat. Omnia placita et
omnia debita que patri vel fratri meo debebantur condono, exceptis 35
rectis firmis et exceptis illis que pacta fuerant pro aliorum hereditatibus
vel pro hiis rebus que justius aliis*e* contingebant. Et si quis pro
hereditate sua aliquid pepigerit [illud condono,] et omnes relevaciones
que pro rectis hereditatibus pacte erant. Si quis baronum vel aliorum
hominum meorum ⟨infirmabitur,⟩*f* sicut ipse disposuerit dare pecu- 40
niam, ita datam esse concedo. Quod si vel armis vel infirmitate
preventus pecuniam suam non dederit, nec dare disposuerit, uxor sua
vel liberi vel parentes, vel legittimi homines eius, pro anima sua eam
dividant, sicut eis melius visum fuerit. Si quis baronum vel aliorum
hominum meorum forisfecerit, non dabit vadium in misericordia 45
pecunie sue, sicut tempore patris vel fratris mei; sed secundum modum
forisfacti, ita emendabit sicut emendasset retro a tempore patris mei, et
tempore antecessorum meorum. Quod si perfidie vel sceleris*g* convictus
fuerit, sicut justum fuerit, emendet. Murdra autem ab ipso retro die in 50
quo in regem coronatus fui omnia condono; et ea que amodo facta
fuerint, juste emendentur secundum leges regis Eadwardi. Forestas

G i,317

fo.110v

---

b   +eq *del.C*
c   *corrected from* eas *C*
d   *D; lac.C*

e   +rebus *del.C*
f   *om.D; in margin R*
g   *D; celeris C*

exactions, out of reverence for God and the love which I have for all of
you I first of all set free the holy church of God, so that I shall neither
sell nor lease its property, nor at the death of an archbishop or bishop
or abbot shall I take anything from there, that is from the demesne of
the church or from its men until a successor enters into it. And I abolish
from there all the evil customs by which the kingdom of England used
to be unjustly oppressed. If any of the barons or earls or others who are
my tenants dies, his heir will not redeem the land, as they did in my
father's time, but he will redeem it by a lawful and just relief. Likewise
the men of my barons will redeem their lands from their lords by a
lawful relief. And if any of my barons or other of my men wishes to give
his daughter or sister or niece or kinswoman in marriage, let him speak
to me about it; but I shall neither receive anything from his property for
my consent nor shall I prevent him giving her [in marriage], unless he
wishes to unite her with my enemy. And if on the death of a baron or
any other man of mine a daughter remains as the heir, I shall give her
together with her land in marriage according to the counsel of my
barons. And if on the death of her husband a wife is left and is without
children, she will have her dower and marriage portion, and I shall not
give her [in marriage] except according to her wishes. If a wife is left
with children, she will have her dower and marriage portion, as long as
she has kept her body chaste, and I shall not give her [in marriage]
except according to her wishes. And either the wife or someone else
who ought to be justly [appointed] will be the guardian of the land and
of the children. And I command that all my barons shall conduct
themselves in the same way towards sons or daughters or widows of
their men. And as for the common mintage which was taken
throughout the cities and shires, and which did not exist in the time of
King Edward, I altogether forbid its existence from henceforth. If any
moneyer or anyone else is taken with counterfeit money in his
possession, let the appropriate justice be done for this. I forgive all
pleas and all debts which were owing to my father or brother except for
my own proper dues and those things that had been agreed to belong to
the inheritances of others or to those things that more justly belong to
others. And if anyone has promised anything from his own inheritance,
I remit that, and all reliefs which had been pledged for direct
inheritances. If any of my barons or other men of mine is ill, I allow his
property to be given away in accordance with his intentions for giving it
away. But if prevented by fighting or illness he does not dispose of his
property, and does not make a will, let his wife or children or parents or
his true men divide the property for his soul, just as seems best to them.
If any of my barons or other of my men incurs forfeiture, he will not be
obliged to give surety to an unlimited extent, just as in the time of my
father and brother; but according to the extent of his legal forfeiture he
will pay a fine just as he would have done in the time before my father
and brother and in the time of my ancestors. But if he is convicted of
breach of faith or a crime, he will pay such penalty as is just. I remit all
murder-fines incurred before the day on which I was crowned king; and
those that are incurred from henceforth will be justly paid according to
the laws of King Edward. By the common counsel of my barons I have
kept the forests in my own hands, just as my father had them. To the

communi consilio baronum meorum ita in manu mea retinui, sicut
pater meus eas habuit. Militibus qui per loricas terras suas defendunt,
terras dominicarum carucarum suarum quietas ab omnibus geldis et ab   55
omni opere, proprio dono meo concedo, ut sicut benignitas misericor-
G i,318   die propensior est in | eis, ita michi fideliores sint et ⟨sicut⟩[h] a tam
magno gravamine alleviati sunt, ita se equis et armis bene instruant, ut
apti et parati sint ad servicium meum et ad defensionem regni. Pacem
meam in toto regno meo pono, et amodo teneri jubeo legem regis   60
Edwardi cum illis emendacionibus quibus pater meus eam emendavit
consilio baronum suorum. Si quis autem de meo vel de rebus alicuius
post obitum regis Willelmi fratris mei cepit, [in] toto cito reddatur sine
emendacione. Et si quis inde aliquid retinuerit, ille super quem
inventum fuerit graviter inde emendabit. Presentis quoque ecclesie   65
monachi libertates, dignitates, regiasque consuetudines sibi per cartas
regum olim confirmatas concedo, hiis testibus c'.

    h   one word del. and replaced by sicut *C*

40

Adhuc de commendacione Matildis

Turgotus:

De dictorum regum Eadgari et Alexandri simul et David, de quo
dicetur, sororis regine Matildis Bone ammirabili gloria animique
virtute, quamque fuerit in officiis divinis sacrisque vigiliis assidua ac
devota, in tanta insuper potestate quam humilis, qui scribere voluerit,   5
alteram sibi Hester nostris temporibus declarabit. Quod facere nos[a]
omisimus, tum propter materie magnitudinem, tum propter harum
rerum minorem adhuc cognicionem. Unum tamen illius referam opus,
quod ex ore nominandi et numquam obliviscendi David regis audivi,
G i,291   per quod qualis fuerit circa pauperes | Christi satis, ut arbitror,   10
elucescet. 'Cum', inquit, 'adolescens adhuc in curia regis servirem,
nocte quadam in hospicio meo cum sociis meis, nescio quid agens, ad
thalamum regine ab ipsa vocatus, accessi. Et ecce domus plena
leprosis, et regina in medio stans, depositoque pallio, cum se lintheo
precinxisset, posita in pelvi aqua, cepit lavare pedes eorum et extergere,   15
extersosque utrisque constringere manibus, et devotissime osculari.
Cui ego: "Quid agis," inquam,[b] "O domina ? Certe si rex sciret ista,
numquam os tuum, tabe tali pollutum, suis dignabitur tangere labiis."
Tunc illa subridens: "Pedes", ait, "Regis Eterni quis nesciat labiis regis
morituri esse preferendos? Ego certe, frater amantissime, idcirco   20
vocavi te, ut exemplo meo talia discas operari." Sumpta deinde pelvi:

    a S; non *C*   *b S;* inquit *C*

60 knights who hold their lands through knight service, I grant as a gift
    from myself that the lands of their demesne ploughs shall be free from
    all gelds and from all labour service, just as kindness is more prone to
    mercy in these matters, so they will be more loyal to me, and inasmuch
    as they have been released from such a great burden, they will be better
65 equipped with horses and arms, so that they will be fit and ready for my
    service and the defence of the kingdom. I assert my peace over the
    whole of my kingdom, and I order that from henceforth the law of
    King Edward will be employed with those amendments with which my
    father amended it by the counsel of his barons. If anyone has taken
70 anything from my property or the property of anyone else since the
    death of King William my brother, let it be returned in full quickly
    without penalty. And if anyone keeps back any part of it, he on whom it
    is found will pay a heavy penalty for it. I also grant the privileges,
    dignities and royal customary dues of the present abbey church,
75 formerly confirmed to it by royal charters. With these witnesses...

40

More in praise of Matilda

Turgot says:

Anyone who wished to write about the admirable fame and virtuous
character of Queen Matilda the Good sister of the said kings Edgar and
Alexander and also of David, of whom more later, and how attentive
5   and devoted she was at divine services and holy vigils, moreover how
humble she was although in such a powerful position, would declare
that she was a second Esther of our times. We have omitted to do this
both because of the magnitude of the subject, and because there is still
too little knowledge of these matters. I shall however recount one deed
10 of hers which I heard from the lips of the renowned and never to be
forgotten King David, by means of which it will be sufficiently clear, I
think, how good she was towards the poor people of Christ. 'When', he
said, 'I was still a young man serving at the royal court, on a certain
night I was in my lodging with my companions, doing I know not what,
15 when I was summoned by the queen herself, and went to her bedroom.
And behold the house was full of lepers, and the queen standing in the
midst of them, had laid aside her cloak, tied a towel round herself,
placed water in a basin, and began to wash and dry their feet. When
their feet were dry she clasped them with both hands, and devoutly
20 kissed them. I said to her: "What are you doing, madam? Certainly if
the king knew about this, he would never condescend to touch with his
lips your mouth polluted with such corruption." Then she said with a
smile: "Who does not know that the feet of the Eternal King are to be
preferred to the lips of a mortal king? At any rate, dearest brother, I

"Fac", ait, "quod me facere^c intueris." Ad hanc vocem vehementer
expavi, et nullo modo id me pati posse respondi. Necdum enim sciebam
Dominum, nec revelatus fuerat michi Spiritus eius. Illa igitur ceptis
insistente, ego mea culpa ridens^d remeavi ad socios meos.'   25

[Hec ille.]^e Alexander quoque rex, etate et sensibus integer, quo nemo
devocior in clericos, in extraneos munificencior, in malefactores
severior, in bonos mansuecior, ab Incarnacione Domini anno m° c^{mo}
xxiiii^{to}, viii° kal. maii apud Strivelyne debitum humane carnis
persolvens, ab hac luce subtractus, spiritum celo reddidit, corpus   30
humo. Sepultus est autem apud Dunfermelyne honorifice die Sancti
Marci evangeliste prope patrem ante magnum altare, postquam in
regno xvii annos xxi dies perfecisset. | De quo sic habentur metra:

Scriptor

Regis Alexandri regnum duravit aristis
   quinque bis et vii, mensibus atque tribus.^{f} 35
In Scocia tota postquam pax firma vigebat,
   fertur apud Strivelyne mors rapuisse virum.

Autor

Anno hoc scilicet anno domini m^{mo} c^{mo} xvii° apud Italiam maximus
terremotus xl^a diebus duravit, plurimaque edificia corruerunt; villa
quoque^g quedam pergrandis de proprio loco mota est; [et]^h luna quasi   40
in sanguine versa est. Anno m° c° xix dompnus Norbertus auctoritate
pape Calixti ordinem Premonstratensem instituit. ⟨Anno domini m°
cxxi rex Henricus exercitum ducens in Walliam, incolas ad pacem
coegit. Et Ranulphus Dunelmensis episcopus castrum apud Norham
edificavit. Anno sequenti electus est in episcopum Sanctiandr'   45
Robertus prior de Scona. Cui successit in prioratum dominus
Nicholaus c'⟩ Anno domini m° [c]^i xxii° Sibilla regina Scocie, uxor
regis Alexandri, filia Henrici regis Anglie, apud Loughtey^j obiit.
Anno sequenti rex Jerosolim Baldwinus dolo a paganis capitur, cum

fo.103

quibus per duos annos | stetit captivus; sed tandem obsidibus et   50
redempcione datis, ad suos redire permittitur. ⟨Anno m° cxxv^k
monetarii tocius Anglie principales, deprehensi dolum fecisse in
coneta, jussu regis Henrici Wintonie congregati, amputatis dextris et
abscissis testiculis evirantur.⟩^{l}

c	+ nequis *del.C*	j	+ cella canonicorum de Scona *CA*
d	*S;* rediens *C*	k	*C,CA,R,H;* corrected to xvii *D;* xvii *E;*
e	*CA*		xxvii *B*
f	*corrected in margin to* iiii *D*	l	*this addition is not attached to the text by*
g	*CA* que *C*		*its signal C; placed at equivalent place to*
h	*CA*		*here CA; follows 'obiit' (l.42 above) R;*
i	*D; om.C*		*follows 'virum' (l.33 above) D,B,H,E*

25   summoned you for this reason that you would learn from my example
      to perform such deeds." Then taking the basin, she said, "Do what you
      see me doing." I was terribly frightened at these words, and replied that
      I could by no means endure it. For I did not yet know the Lord, nor had
      His Spirit been revealed to me. So while she went on with her task, I to
30   my shame returned laughing to my companions.'

King Alexander, while not yet old and in possession of all his
faculties, more devoted than anyone else to the clergy, more generous
to strangers, more strict with evildoers and kinder to the good, paid
the debt of human flesh on 24 April 1124 at Stirling. Withdrawn from   1124:
35 the light of this world, he delivered up his spirit to Heaven and his   24 Apr.
body to the earth. He was buried at Dunfermline with great honour
on St Mark the Evangelist's day near his father before the high altar,   25 Apr.
after completing seventeen years and twenty-one days in the kingship.
These verses are about him:

40   The reign of King Alexander lasted twice five
          and seven summers, and three months.
          After assured peace flourished in the whole of Scotland,
          death is said to have seized the man at Stirling.

In this year, that is in 1117, in Italy a huge earthquake lasted for forty   1117
45 days, and very many buildings collapsed, a certain very large country-
house was moved from its proper site, and the moon was turned to
blood.
      In 1119 sir Norbert instituted the Premonstratensian Order by   [1120]
authority of Pope Callistus.
50   In 1121 King Henry led an army into Wales, and forced the   1121
inhabitants to make peace. Ranulf bishop of Durham built a castle at
Norham.
      In the following year Robert prior of Scone was elected as bishop of   [1124: Jan.]
St Andrews. He was succeeded in the office of prior by sir Nicholas
55 etc.
      In 1122 Sibylla queen of Scotland wife of King Alexander,   1122
daughter of Henry king of England, died at Loch Tay.
      In the following year the king of Jerusalem Baldwin was   1123
treacherously captured by the pagans, with whom he remained as a
60 prisoner for two years; but at last when hostages and ransom had
been given, he was allowed to return to his own people.   [1125]
      In 1125 the chief moneyers of the whole of England were discovered   1125
to have cheated in the coinage, and by order of King Henry they were
brought together at Winchester, and had their right hands removed,
65 and were castrated by having their testicles cut off.

41

De successione benedicti regis David, et commendacione eius
et fratrum eiusdem

Quatuor mensibus rex Alexander ante mortem suam fecit eligi
dompnum Robertum priorem de Scona in episcopum Sanctiandr'.
Generis sui splendor David, filiorum Malcolmi et Margarite junior,
Alexandro fratri suo successit anno videlicet domini m° c° xxiiii^{to} quo
supra, et imperatoris Henrici quinti xviii^{to}, regnavitque annis xxix 5
duobus mensibus et tribus diebus. Erat enim in Deum religione pius,
in elemosinis largus, apud suos strenuus, in ampliando regno juste
sagax et sollicitus, et, ut breviter dicam, omnibus virtutibus emicuit
floridus; unde bonorum operum maturis semper fructibus habunda-
bat. Quique quam potentissimus erat rex, quanta super alios jure 10
conquisierit, quantasve abbacias et domos Dei fundaverat, Baldredus,[a] ut infra patebit,[b] pro morte sua lamentans, legentibus[c] veraciter
declarabit. Nichil vero superbum in moribus, nichil in verbis crudele,
nichil inhonestum dictis aut factis proferebat. Non erat ci rex similis
in regibus[d] terre diebus suis, quia hic pius, prudens, humilis, pudicus, 15
sobrius, castus fuit et quietus, vita dum presens vegitavit eius corporis
arctus. Willelmus:

> Neque vero umquam in acta historiarum relatum[e] est tante sanctitatis
> tres fuisse pariter reges et fratres, materne pietatis nectare redolentes.
> Namque preter victus parcitatem, elemosinarum copiam, oracionum 20
> assiduitatem, ita domesticum regibus vicium evicerunt, ut numquam
> [feratur][f] in eorum thalamos nisi legittimas uxores isse, nec eorum
> quemquam pelicatu aliquo pudiciciam contristasse legatur.[g]

Antequam idem rex David sublimatus esset in regnum, tradente rege
Anglorum sororis sue Matildis Bone regine marito, uxorem duxit 25
Matildem ⟨de Sant Lyce⟩ filiam et heredem Waldeofi sive Waldevi
comitis de Huntyngdon et Judith, que fuit neptis primi regis Willelmi,
⟨que prius fuit nupta Simoni Machald seniori sive Sant Lice,⟩ de qua
suscepit filium nomine Henricum, virum mansuetum et pium, ac
suavis spiritus, dignum per omnia qui de tali patre nasceretur. Interea 30

---

a	+abbas Rievall' *CA*	*e*	*CA*; elatum *C*
b	ut infra patebit *om.CA*	*f*	*S*; feretra [?] sive femina *C,D*
c	+suum codicem *CA*	*g*	*interlin.C*
d	regionibus *CA*		

41

The succession of blessed King David, and praise of him and his brothers

Four months before his death King Alexander caused sir Robert   1124
prior of Scone to be elected bishop of St Andrews. David the glory of
his race, youngest of the sons of Malcolm and Margaret, succeeded
his brother Alexander in 1124, as given above, and in the eighteenth   [24 Apr.]
5   year of the emperor Henry V. He reigned for twenty-nine years, two
months and three days. He was pious and Godly, lavish in alms,
energetic among his own people, wise and careful in the just extension
of his kingdom, and, in a nutshell, he blossomed brilliantly in all the
virtues; thus he always produced abundance of the ripe fruit of good
10   deeds. How powerful he was as a king, what great conquests he made
justly, or what great abbeys and houses of God he founded, Ailred, as
will appear below, will truthfully declare to readers, as he laments his
death. He revealed no haughtiness in his character, no cruelty in his
words, nothing that was dishonourable in what he said or did. There
15   was not a king like him among the kings of the earth in his own time,
since he was pious, wise, humble, modest, sober, chaste and tranquil,
while this present life animated his bodily frame.
    William [of Malmesbury] says:

Nor indeed has it ever been recorded in the annals of history that there
20   were three kings, all brothers, of such great sanctity, redolent of the
nectar of their mother's piety. For besides their frugal way of life, their
lavish giving of alms, and the constancy of their prayers, they so
thoroughly overcame the private vice of kings that it is never reported
that any but their lawful wives entered their bedrooms, nor is it said
25   that any of them stained his honour by keeping a mistress.

Before King David was elevated to the throne, from the hand of the
king of the English, the husband of his sister Queen Matilda the
Good, he received as his wife Matilda of Senlis, daughter and heir of   [1113-14]
Waltheof or Waldevus earl of Huntingdon and of Judith, who was the
30   niece of the first King William. She was previously married to Simon
Machald senior of Senlis. David had by Matilda a son Henry by
name, a gentle and pious man, of an agreeable spirit, in all respects
worthy to be born of such a father. Meanwhile the empress Matilda,
now that her husband the emperor was dead without children,   [1128:
35   returned to her father Henry king of England. He later gave her as   17 June]

Matildis imperatrix, imperatore marito sine liberis defuncto, rediit ad patrem Anglie regem Henricum. Quam postea Andigavie comiti Gaufrido dedit uxorem. Ex qua genuit Henricum futurum Anglie regem. Mortuo deinde Anglorum rege predicto Henrico ⟨anno domini m° cxxxv,⟩ invasit regnum Stephanus comes Bononie, nepos 35 eius ex sorore, contra jusjurandum, quoniam adjuratus est regnum, dicto rege Henrico vivente, unice filie sue Matildi imperatrici. Indignatus super hoc Gaufridus comes Andigavie,*h* sed parum aut |

G i,293
Scriptor

nichil sibi nocuit. | xi kal. januarii coronatus est, et in die coronacionis sue oblita est pax dari; unde nec fere in [tota]*i* vita sua habuit pacem. 40 Verum ante hoc David rex Scocie, dictus eciam Stephanus, et omnes archiepiscopi, episcopi, abbates, comites et barones tocius Anglie in presencia regis Henrici anno domini m^mo cxxvii in festo Circumcisionis Domini apud London' imperatrici regnum juraverunt.

h   *interlin.C*   *i*   *CA*

42

Scriba

De guerra mota inter reges David et Stephanum, et recuperacione Northumbrie et Cumbrie

Propter quod rex Scotorum David, avunculus eiusdem imperatricis, contra Stephanum ⟨Stentine⟩*a* continuo surrexit, et aquilonares Anglie regiones Northumbriam et Cumbriam vastare cepit, ⟨et sibi eas subjugavit videlicet a flumine Twede ex parte orientali usque ad flumen These, et a flumine Esk usque ad Rercors ex parte occiden- 5 tali.⟩ Et cum eas predando nunc hanc nunc illam sepius invasisset, circumvenerunt eum utriusque provincie nobiles, ingentibus vallati copiis, apud Allirton xii kal. septembris, ubi, commisso prelio, partis utriusque multi ceciderunt. Tandem Anglorum maxima multitudine perempta, fugerunt ceteri multique nobilium captivi sunt abducti. 10 Redierunt autem omnes circa festum Omnium Sanctorum redempcione liberi, redditis regi David Cumbria simul et Northumbria cum pertinenciis. ⟨In estate sequenti*b* iterum transiit rex David fluvium Thesam, et occurrit ei*c* exercitus Anglorum in Cutinemore, ubi commissum est*d* bellum quod dicitur Stanhard, ubi victi sunt Scoti, 15 captis multis et occisis. Anno domini m° cxxx Anegus comes Moraviensis cum gente sua interfectus est a Scotis. Anno m° cxxxii fundata est abbacia Rievallis die sabbati iii nonas marcii. Anno

a   +regni invasorem *CA*   *c*   Cui occurrit pergrandis *for* et occurrit ei
b   +nescio qua occasione *CA*   *CA*
                                          d   +formidabile *CA*

wife to Geoffrey count of Anjou. He had by her Henry, the future king
of England. Then when the aforesaid Henry king of the English died
in 1135, Stephen count of Boulogne, his nephew through his sister,   1135:
usurped the kingdom in violation of his oath, since during the lifetime   [1 Dec.]
40 of the said King Henry he had asserted under oath that the kingdom
would go to Henry's only daughter the empress Matilda. Geoffrey
count of Anjou was enraged at this, but did little or nothing to harm
him. He was crowned on 22 December, and on the day of his   22 Dec.
coronation they forgot to give the peace, so he had hardly any peace in
45 his whole life. But before this David king of Scotland, the said
Stephen also, and all the archbishops, bishops, abbots, earls and
barons of the whole of England took an oath in the presence of King
Henry in 1127 on the feast of the Circumcision of our Lord in London   1127: 1 Jan.
that the kingdom would go to the empress.

42

The war that broke out between Kings David and Stephen, and the recovery of Northumbria and Cumbria

Because of this David king of Scots, the uncle of the empress,
immediately rose against Stephen Stentine, and began to lay waste the   [1134]
northern regions of England, Northumbria and Cumbria. He
imposed his rule upon them from the river Tweed in the east right to
5 the river Tees, and from the river Esk right to Rey Cross in the west.
And when he had made numerous incursions now into one region,
now into the other, as he laid them waste, the nobles of both provinces
surrounded him, supported by huge forces, at Northallerton on 21   [1138:
August, where battle was joined, and many were slain on both sides.   22 Aug.]
10 At last when a very great number of the English had been killed, the
rest fled, and many of the nobles were led away captive. But they all
returned, after they had been freed by ransom, around about the feast
of All Saints, after both Cumbria and Northumbria with their   1 Nov.
pertinents were given back to King David. In the following summer
15 King David again crossed the river Tees, and was met by an army of
the English at Cowton Moor, where the battle of the Standard, as it is
called, was joined, in which the Scots were defeated, and many were
captured and killed.
      In 1130 Angus earl of Moray was killed along with his people by the   1130
20 Scots. In 1132 the abbey of Rievaulx was founded on Saturday 5   1132: 5 Mar.
March. In 1136 Northumbria and Cumbria were given back to King   1136: [5 Feb.]
David. But soon after the kings David and Stephen made peace on

domini m° cxxxvi Northumbria et Cumbria reddite sunt regi David.⟩
Sed statim pacificati sunt reges David et Stephanus*e* in hunc modum, 20
videlicet ut regi Stephano rediret Northumbria, Cumbria quoque
remaneret libere*f* regi David. Hec tamen pax inter eos inita modico
duravit tempore, David rege bellum parante Northumbrie. Qua-
propter Turstanus archiepiscopus Eboracensis ad castrum Marchi-
mond Roxburgh videlicet veniens, impetravit interim a rege ne 25
patriam ad tempus vastaret. Sed non multo post, solutis induciis, tota
Northumbria misere vastata est, eo quod rex Stephanus eam dare
noluit, sicut promisit, Henrico eiusdem regis David filio, quem genuit
ex Matilde predicta comitissa. Rex igitur Stephanus anno sequenti,
videlicet domini m° c*mo* xxxviii, capite jejunii cum exercitu magno 30
Roxburgh*g* adveniens, ubi subito pavore | territus, cum ignominia
statim rediit, ⟨cum paulo ante rex David miserabiliter vastavit
Northumbriam totam.⟩ Deinde anno sequenti venit idem rex
Stephanus*h* ad Dunelmum, ubi xv diebus pro pace tractanda
commoratus est, David rege in Novo Castro existente, habitoque 35
inter eos solempni de pace colloquio ad instanciam regine uxoris
Stephani Matildis neptis regis | David ex sorore Maria, concordati
sunt in hunc modum, ut videlicet Henricus filius regis David
homagium pro comitatu de Hontyngdon faceret regi Stephano, et
Northumbrie comitatum libere possideret. Erat enim mater istius 40
Henrici Matildis filia et heres Waldeofi*i* comitis Hontyndonie filii et
heredis Siwardi comitis Northumbrie.*j* Reversoque rege David de
Novo Castro venit Karleolum, in cuius opido arcem fortissimam
construi fecit, et urbis muros plurimum exaltavit. Ad quem*k* accessit
Henricus neptis sue Matildis imperatricis filius, et rex Anglie futurus, 45
a matre missus, et ibidem ab eo militare cingulum accepit, prestita
prius caucione quod nullam partem terrarum, que tunc in Scotorum
dominium ex Anglie*l* dissencione transissent, eius ullo tempore vel
mutilarent heredes. Isto eodem anno Albericus legatus Hostiensis
episcopus venit*m* Carleil ad regem David. 50

e + ut *del.C*
f *corrected from* libera *C;* libera *CA*
g + hostiliter *CA*
h *interlin.C;* om.*CA*
i + sive Walthevi *CA*
j sanctissimi martyris, qui fuit eciam comes
   Eboracensis et Northumbrie, cuius pater

fuit ille Swardus comes Northumbrie qui
in necessitatibus regi Malcolmo
opitulator fuit necesarius *for* filii ...
Northumbrie *CA*
k + ibi *CA*
l *CA;* Anglia *C*
m + ad *del.C*

these terms, namely that Northumbria should be given back to King
Stephen, while Cumbria should remain unconditionally with King
25 David. However this peace that was initiated between them lasted
only for a short time, as King David was preparing to do battle for
Northumbria. Therefore Thurstan archbishop of York came to
Marchmont castle, that is Roxburgh, and meanwhile obtained his
request from the king that he would not lay waste the country for the
30 time being. But not long afterwards the truce was broken, and the
whole of Northumbria wretchedly devastated, because King Stephen
refused to give it up, as he promised, to Henry son of King David and
the aforesaid Countess Matilda. So King Stephen in the following
year, that is 1138, on Ash Wednesday was coming to Roxburgh with a   1138:
35 great army, when he was suddenly gripped by panic, and ignomi-   16 Feb.
niously returned [home] straightway, when a little earlier King David
miserably laid waste the whole of Northumbria. Then in the following
year the same King Stephen came to Durham, where he stayed for
fifteen days to negotiate peace, while King David was in Newcastle. A
40 formal discussion concerning peace was held between them at the
insistence of Queen Matilda wife of Stephen and niece of King David
through his sister Mary, and they were reconciled on the following   1139:
terms, namely that Henry the son of King David should do homage to   [9 Apr.]
King Stephen for the earldom of Huntingdon, and should possess the
45 earldom of Northumbria unconditionally. For the mother of that
Henry was Matilda daughter and heir of Waltheof earl of Huntingdon, who was son and heir of Siward earl of Northumbria. King
David on his return from Newcastle came to Carlisle, in the town
centre of which he caused a very strong citadel to be constructed, and
50 he raised the city walls to a great height. To him came Henry the son of
his niece the empress Matilda and future king of England, sent by his
mother, and he there received the belt of knighthood from King   [1149: May]
David, after he had given a guarantee that his heirs would not at any
time curtail any part of the lands which had passed over to the
55 dominion of the Scots at that time through the dispute with England.
In that same year Alberic the papal legate and bishop of Ostia came to   [1138: Sept.]
King David in Carlisle.

43

De conjugio Henrici filii David cum Ada filia
Willelmi comitis de Warenna

Henricus regis David filius comes Northumbrie et Hontyndonie
uxorem duxit Adam filiam Willelmi senioris, sororem Willelmi
junioris comitis de Warenna, et sororem Roberti comitis Legecestren-
sis et Walranni comitis de Melent. Cuius mater fuit soror Radulphi
comitis de Perona, regis Francorum Lodovici consanguinea. Ex qua 5
suscepit tres inclitos filios, scilicet Malcolmum regem Scocie futurum,
et David qui fuit postea comes Hontyndonie et Gariawch, atque
Willelmum regem eciam futurum, et totidem filias, Adam videlicet,
que lege conjugii tradita fuit Florencio comiti Holandie, et Margaritam duci Britannie et comiti de Richemount Conano nuptam. Ex qua 10
genuit filiam nomine Constanciam, conjugio datam Gaufrido fratri
regis Anglie Richardi Primi. De qua ipse Gaufridus genuit filium
Arthurum nomine in mare postea mersum, unam eciam filiam
Aliciam nomine, que a Petro Mauclerk concepit, et peperit filium
nomine Johannem postea ducem Britannie, ac aliam filiam nomine 15
Alienoram, que cum Arthuro fratre mari periit. Necnon et tercia
comitis Henrici filia Matildis, eodem anno quo pater e mundo
decessit. Annis igitur florentissime juventutis | nondum completis,
elegantis speciei juvenis, paternis virtutibus viridescens, idem Henricus filius regis unicus comes Northumbrie et Hontyndonie anno 20
domini m^{mo} c^{mo} lii^o pridie idus junii ab hac luce substractus est. ⟨Cuius
filius Johannes Scotus est occisus in bello de Cothona ut in antiqua
repperi cronica sic:⟩

> ⟨Hic Henricus erat natus regis quoque David,
> quem rex is David ex Matilda generavit.   25
> Heres que fuerat Huntyndonie comitatus,
> cuius sic esset, si posset vivere, natus,
> qui bello moritur de Cothon; sed sepelitur
> in abbacia nomine Kalcovia.
> Hec Matilda datur de Sanlize, que tumulatur   30
> in Scona, cuius templum bustum tenet huius.⟩

⟨Hic Henricus⟩ adolescens speciosissimus, omnibus amabilis, successor regni speratus, modestissimi spiritus princeps, homo disciplinatus
et timoratus, Deo devotus, et pauperum^a procurator misericordissi-

---

a   + pror *del.*C

43

The marriage of Henry son of David to Ada the daughter of
Earl William de Warenne

Henry son of King David earl of Northumbria and Huntingdon
married Ada daughter of the older Earl William de Warenne, sister of [1139]
the younger Earl William de Warenne, and sister of Robert earl of
Leicester and Waleran count of Meulan. Her mother was the sister of
5 Radulf count of Peronne, cousin of Louis king of the French. By her
Henry had three sons, that is Malcolm the future king of Scotland and
David who was afterwards earl of Huntingdon and Garioch, and
William also a future king, and the same number of daughters, that is
Ada who was given to Florence count of Holland in lawful wedlock, [1162]
10 and Margaret who was married to Conan duke of Brittany and earl of [1160]
Richmond. Conan had a daughter by her called Constance who was
given in marriage to Geoffrey brother of Richard I king of England. [1181]
By Constance Geoffrey had a son called Arthur who was afterwards
drowned in the sea, also one daughter called Alice who was made
15 pregnant by Peter Mauclerc, and bore a son called John, afterwards
duke of Brittany, and another daughter called Eleanor who perished
in the sea with her brother Arthur. And Matilda the third daughter of
Henry departed this life in the same year as her father. So still in the 1152
full flower of his youthful years, a young man of handsome
20 appearance, beginning to show his father's virtues within him, Henry
the only son of the king, earl of Northumbria and Huntingdon, was
withdrawn from the light of day on 12 June 1152. His son John the 12 June
Scot was killed in the battle of Cowton Moor, as I found in an ancient
chronicle as follows:

25   This Henry was the son also of King David,
           whom King David had by Matilda.
           She was heir to the earldom of Huntingdon,
           of which her son also would have been heir,
           if he could have survived. He died in the battle of Cowton;
30   but is buried in the abbey Kelso by name.
           This Matilda was married to Simon de Senlis, and she is
               buried
           in Scone, whose temple contains her tomb.

This Henry was a most attractive young man, amiable towards
35 everyone, the expected successor to the kingship, a prince with a spirit

mus, et, ut breviter omnes eius virtutes commemorem, excepto quod 35
paulo suavior fuit, per omnia patri similis. Tres filios suos memoratos
et duas filias superstites relinquens, cum ingenti Scotorum simul et
Anglicorum luctu et ejulatu in monasterio de Calco secus Rokisburgh
sepultus est, quod pater eius a fundamentis construendo copiosis
possessionibus et magnis honoribus ditaverat, ⟨Hunc Henricum 40
infirmantem ad mortem Sanctus Malachias Ibernicus Ordinis Cisterciensis, sed episcopus, recedens de^b Claravalle a beato B[ernardo]
perfecte sanavit,^{c} sicut scribit Sanctus B[ernardus] qui composuit
vitam huius Sancti Malachie, qui eciam tumilatur cum Sancto
B[ernardo] in Claravalle. Anno domini m° cxl obiit Nicholas prior de 45
Scona cui successit Dionisius eiusdem loci canonicus.⟩
    Anno iiii^{to} regis David imperatori Henrico quinto successit
Lotharius electus, et imperavit annis xi. Eiusdem David anno vii°
regina Matilda uxor eius obiit, et apud Sconam sepelitur. Eodem

anno comes | Moraviensis Angusius apud Strucathrow cum gente sua 50
peremptus est a Scotis.^{d} Anno eiusdem David xv^{to} successit imperatori Lothario Coradus tercius et imperavit annis xv. Eodem anno
Johannes de Temporibus obiit etatis sue anno ccc^{mo} lxi°, qui fuit
armiger Magni Karoli. Hoc itaque tempore floruit magnus doctor
Richardus canonicus de Sancto Victore Scotus. Anno xviii regis 55
David natus est predicto Henrico filio regis filius nomine Malcolmus
cognomine Virgo rex futurus, et anno sequenti David postea comes
de Huntyndon et Garwach, ac anno xx° Willelmus eciam rex futurus
nati sunt.

    Anno m° cxx° viii° rex David fundavit monasterium Sancti Crucis 60
canonicorum de Edinburgh, et monasterium monachorum de Kelso.
Et anno m° cxxxii^e fundatur abbacia Sancte Marie Cistercii Ordinis in
Reyvalle. Et anno m° c^{mo} xxxvi^{to} monasterium de Melros Cistercii
idem fundavit,^{f} quo anno eciam dedicari^g fecit ecclesiam Glasguensem. Anno m° c° xl idem fundavit abbaciam monachorum de 65
Neubotil Cistercii Ordinis. Quo anno rex Stephanus capitur Lincolnie in prelio die Purificacionis Sancte Marie, et custodie mancipatur.
Et in festo Exaltacionis Sancte Crucis in septembri, contracto
numeroso exercitu militari de Anglia et de transmarinis partibus, per
sue regine instanciam omnino a vinculis liberatus et in regno 70
restitutus est.^{h} Et anno sequenti idem David^i rex fundavit monasterium de Dundranan' Ordinis Cistercii. ⟨Anno domini m° cxlii
Willelmus Cumyn cancellarius regis David Scocie per dacionem
imperatricis intravit castellum Dunelmense, et Sancti Cuthberti
possessiones per aliquod tempus vi optinuit, ceca ambicione volens 75

---

b interlin.over a del.C
c +scri del.C
d a Scotis interlin.C
e +idem del.C
f + unde versus: Anno milleno centeno ter

quoque deno/ et sexto Christi Melros
fundata fuisti CA
g dedicare C,D
h CA; om.C
i interlin.C

of moderation, a man well-schooled and reverent, devoted to God,
and a very compassionate protector of the poor; and to sum up all his
virtues in a few words, he resembled his father in everything except
that he was a little more agreeable. Leaving behind his three
40 aforementioned sons and his two surviving daughters, he was buried
to the great grief and lamentation of both Scots and English in the
monastery of Kelso near Roxburgh, which his father had built from
the foundations, and had enriched with abundant possessions and
great honours. When this Henry was mortally ill, he was completely [1140]
45 cured by St Malachy the Irishman, of the Cistercian order but a
bishop, as he was returning from visiting blessed Bernard at
Clairvaux. This is recorded by St Bernard who wrote a life of St
Malachy, who is also buried alongside St Bernard in Clairvaux. In
1140 Nicholas prior of Scone died, and Dionysius a canon of that 1140
50 same place succeeded him.

In the fourth year of King David's reign Lothair was elected as [1125]
successor to the emperor Henry V, and he reigned for eleven years. In
the seventh year of David his wife Queen Matilda died, and was 1131-2
buried at Scone. In the same year Angus the earl of Moray was killed
55 by the Scots along with his people at Stracathro. In the fifteenth year
of David Conrad III succeeded the emperor Lothair, and he reigned 1138
for fifteen years. In the same year John of the Times died at the age of
three hundred and sixty-one. He was a squire of Charlemagne. At this
time there flourished the great doctor Richard the Scot canon of St
60 Victor. In the eighteenth year of King David there was born to the [1141]
aforesaid Henry the son of the king a son called Malcolm surnamed
the Maiden, a future king, and in the following year was born David [1152]
afterwards earl of Huntingdon and Garioch, and in his twentieth year
was born William also a future king.   [1143]
65   In 1128 King David founded the monastery of canons of Holyrood 1128
in Edinburgh and a monastery of monks at Kelso. And in 1132 there 1132
was founded the abbey of St Mary of the Cistercian order in Rievaulx.
And in 1136 he founded the Cistercian monastery of Melrose. In this 1136
year also he brought about the dedication of the church of Glasgow.
70 In 1140 he founded the abbey of monks of the Cistercian order at 1140
Newbattle. In this year King Stephen was captured in battle at [1141:
Lincoln on the day of the Purification of St Mary, and was 2 Feb.]
imprisoned. And on the feast of the Exaltation of the Holy Cross in
September, after a large military force from England and parts
75 beyond the sea had been gathered together, at the insistence of his
queen he was altogether set free from prison, and restored to his [1 Nov.]
kingship. And in the following year King David founded the 1142
monastery of Dundrennan of the Cistercian order. In 1142 William
Comyn, chancellor of King David of Scotland through the gift of the
80 empress, entered the castle of Durham, and obtained by force the [1141]
possessions of St Cuthbert for some time, wishing in his blind

esse episcopus, quo ecclesiam illam graviter opprimente, recesserunt
de loco Rogerus prior et Ranulphus archidiaconus, et ceteri dispersi.
Ecclesia quoque a divino officio cessavit. Anno sequenti Willelmus de
Sancta Barbara decanus Eboracensis ecclesie electus est in episcopum
Dunelmensem. Consecrati sunt ambo Willelmi, unus in archiepisco-   80
pum Eboracensem, alter in episcopum Dunelmensem Wintonie ab
H[enrico] eiusdem loci episcopo apostolice sedis legato. Hic Willelmus Cumyn archiepiscopus Eboracensis ad missam suam, in ecclesia
Sancti Petri a ministris altaris pecuniis corruptis, veneno pocionatus
est. Qui licet venenum videret in calice, nichilominus fide fervens   85
sumpsit, et non diu post supervixit. Deo gracias.⟩ Et anno m° cl per
eundem David fundata sunt monasteria de Holmcultram et Kinslos
monachorum Cistercii. ⟨Eodem anno ad festum Sancti Martini Ordo
Premonstratensis venit ad Driburgh. Anno sequenti Alcwicius abbas
de Edenburgh cure renunciavit, cui successit Osbertus et eodem anno   90
obiit; cui successit Willelmus. Et Rogerus factus est primus abbas de
Driburgh.⟩

44

David nepotem suum circumduci fecit
per regnum

Scriba

G i,297 Rex autem David dissimulato merore super morte unici filii sui | tulit
continuo Malcolmum primogenitum filii predicti, dato ei rectore
Duncano comite de Fiffe cum exercitu copioso, quia ipse senuerat, et
sine detrimento corporis regnum peragrare non poterat, jubens
eundem suum nepotulum per provincias Scocie circumduci, ac   5
heredem regni proclamari. Juniorem quoque fratrem Willelmum rex
assumens venit ad Novum Castrum, et acceptis ibidem a principibus
Northumbrie obsidibus,[a] omnes eiusdem pueri dominio subditos
fecit. De tercio nepote David quid actum tunc, vel quo fuerit, scriptis
non reperi. Rediens autem rex grandevus, nichil tamen inordinatum,   10
nichil incompositum cunctis regni finibus relinquit. Anno deinde
sequenti post Pascha Carleolum adiit, ut et occidentis regni negocia
sicut orientis disponeret. Subito pius ipse rex et religiosus infirmitate
gravi pressus, cum regnum xxix annis et uno mense gloriose rexisset,
anno domini m° cliii° nono kal. junii, dominica ante Ascensionem   15
feliciter moriens, corpus terre, celo spiritum reddidit angelis socian-
dum. Sepultus est autem in ecclesia Sancte Trinitatis de Dunf'

a first -b- interlin.C

ambition to be bishop. As he grievously oppressed that church, Roger
the prior and Ranulf the archdeacon withdrew from the place, and the
rest were scattered. The church also ceased to perform the divine
85 office. In the following year William of Ste Barbe dean of the church
of York was elected bishop of Durham. Both Williams were   1143
consecrated, the one as archbishop of York and the other as bishop of
Durham at Winchester by Henry bishop of that place and legate of
the apostolic see. This William Comyn archbishop of York was
90 poisoned as he said mass in the church of St Peter by acolytes who had   [1154]
been bribed. Although he saw the poison in the chalice, he
nevertheless took it, fervent in faith, and not long afterwards he
recovered. Thanks be to God. And in 1150 the monasteries of monks   1150
of the Cistercian order at Holm Cultram and Kinloss were founded
95 likewise by David. In the same year on the feast of St Martin the   11 Nov.
Premonstratensian order came to Dryburgh. In the following year   [1150]
Alfwin abbot of Edinburgh renounced his charge, and was succeeded
by Osbert who died in the same year. He was succeeded by William,   [1152]
and Roger became the first abbot of Dryburgh.

44

David arranged for his grandson to be taken around the kingdom

Hiding his grief over the death of his only son, King David   1152
immediately took Malcolm the first-born of his aforesaid son, and,
giving him Duncan earl of Fife as his guardian together with a large
army, since he himself was an old man and could not travel around
5   the kingdom without injury to his health, ordered that his young
grandson should be taken around the provinces of Scotland, and
proclaimed as heir to the kingdom. The king also took the younger
brother William with him to Newcastle, and, having received
hostages there from the chief men of Northumbria, he made them all
10 subject to the boy's lordship. What was done concerning the third
grandson David, or where he was, I have not found in the records.
Returning [from there], the king, although advanced in years, left
nothing in disarray or out of order in the whole extent of his kingdom.
Then in the following year he went to Carlisle after Easter to put in   1153: Apr.
15 order the affairs of the western part of his kingdom, just as he had
done for the eastern part. Suddenly the pious and godly king was laid
low with a serious illness, and, after he had gloriously ruled the
kingdom for twenty-nine years and one month, met a happy death on
the Sunday before the Ascension day on 24 May 1153, giving his body   24 May
20 to the earth and his spirit to Heaven to consort with the angels. He

honorifice pavimento coram majore altari, quam[b] a patre et matre
primo fundatam, ab Alexandro[c] fratre possessionibus et edificiis
auctam, eciam ipse donis amplioribus et honoribus constructam   20
ditavit; et ibidem in senectute bona parentibus et fratribus est
appositus. Cuius memoria per omnes generaciones in benediccioni-
bus est, quia similis illius princeps, a tempore quo non extat memoria,
minime surrexit. Divinis devotus officiis, singulis diebus omnes horas
canonicas, eciam vigilias mortuorum, dicere non pretermisit. De quo   25
dicitur:[d]

> Bis deca rex annis David fuit atque novennis
>   in Scocia, caute provida prospiciens.
> Postquam castellis regnum munivit et armis,
>   rex[e] Carlville fertur obisse senex.   30

Predicabile quidem in eo fuit, quod in spiritu consilii et fortitudinis
gentis sue feritatem sapienter moderatus est, et quod in abluendis
pauperum pedibus frequentissimus, alendisque eis et vestiendis
misericors fuit. Qui eciam apud exteras naciones peregrinos,[f] et[g]
religiosos ac seculares, humilem se prebuit ac domesticum; ac eis   35
munera de suis munificenciis largissime donavit. Gloriosus enim rex
cotidiana frugalitate, victus sanctitate, vestitus honestate, conversacionis disciplina, et morum ingenuitate,[h] eciam viris religiosis
imitabilem se prebebat. Cuius nimirum vitam laudabilem, ymmo
cunctis admirabilem, mors preciosa secuta est. Quisquis igitur felici   40
morte se moriturum affectat, eiusdem Deo dilecti regis vitam, et
sequentem pro morte sua legendo lamentacionem, sue felicissime
mortis exemplo mori discat.[i]

b	+quidem ecclesiam CA	g	interlin.C
c	corrected from Allexandro C	h	interlin.C
d	+Inclitus in Scocia del.C	i	Qui licet dignum anime sue locum
e	+Eardville del.C		invenerit, mors tamen eius planctum
f	peregrinas C		nobis indicit for Quisquis ... discat CA

45

De prefacione lamentacionis Baldredi pro morte eius

Sequitur prefacio lamentacionis abbatis Baldredi Rievallis pro morte
regis David, quam ipse merens et ejulans scriptam Henrico, filio
imperatricis eiusdem David neptis, Anglorum regi futuro, transmisit,
ut eius exemplo juste vivendi[a] discat normam, simul et beate
moriendi: 5

a   S; vivendo C,D

was buried with great honour beneath the floor before the high altar
in the church of the Holy Trinity of Dunfermline, which was founded
first of all by his father and mother, enlarged by his brother Alexander
with possessions and buildings, and by himself enriched with
25 generous gifts and distinctions; and there in ripe old age he was placed
beside his parents and brothers. His memory is blessed throughout all
the generations, because no prince to equal him has arisen from time
immemorial. In his devotion to divine worship he took care to say all
the canonical hours each day including the vigils of the dead. He is the
30 subject of the following lines:

> David was king for twice ten years and nine
> in Scotland; he was far-sighted and cautious.
> After he had fortified the kingdom with castles and arms,
> the king is said to have died in old age at Carlisle.

35 It was indeed praiseworthy in him that he wisely moderated the
ferocity of his people in a spirit of wise counsel and resolution, and
that he was very constant in washing the feet of the poor, and
compassionate in feeding and clothing them. He also showed himself
to be unassuming and meek in the presence of foreigners and pilgrims
40 both religious and secular clergy, and lavishly gave them gifts from his
munificence. For the king was glorious in his everyday temperance,
the holiness of his way of life, his simplicity in dress, in his disciplined
behaviour; and in the nobility of his character he showed himself to be
a model even for men of religion. Assuredly his life deserving the
45 praise or rather the admiration of all was followed by a precious
death. Therefore whoever desires to die a happy death, let him learn
to die from the example of his most happy death by reading the life of
this king beloved of God and the lamentation for his death that
follows.

45

The preface to the lamentation of Ailred for his death

Here follows the preface to the lamentation of Ailred the abbot of
Rievaulx for the death of King David, which he wrote mourning and
wailing, and sent to Henry son of the Empress (who was David's
niece) and future king of the English, so that by his example he might
5 learn the rule for living righteously as well as for happy dying.

> To Henry the most illustrious duke of the Normans, count of the
> Aquitanians and Angevins, Father Baldred, also known as Ailred,

Illustrissimo duci Normannorum*b*, Aquitanorum et Andegavensium
comiti | Henrico, Frater Baldredus, alias Ethelredus, servus servorum
Christi qui Rivalle sunt, salutem et oraciones. Adeo secundum
naturam virtus est, et vicium contra naturam, ut virtutem laudet et
approbet eciam viciosus, vicium vero si humane racionis sequatur 10
judicium, nec viciosus excuset. Nam et vicium quasi semetipsum ob
innatam sibi turpitudinem erubescens, semper latebras querit*c* et optat
secretum; cum econtra virtus sue sibi pulcritudinis et honestatis
conscia ad omnem tripudiet et exultet aspectum, ob solam humilitatem
publicum fugiens et humanum testimonium horrens. Quoniam igitur 15
anime racionali naturaliter inest amor*d* virtutum, odium viciorum,
quicumque bonis moribus virtutique studuerit, facile sibi omnium
illicit et inclinat affectum. Hinc est, vir illustrissime, quod te multorum
qui te oculis non viderunt mentibus impressit fama virtutum, cum
ammiracioni sit universis nec minus delectacioni, in tali etate tanta 20
sapiencia, in tantis deliciis tanta continencia, in tantis negociis tanta
providencia, in tali sublimitate talis severitas, in tali severitate tanta
benignitas. Quis enim non obstupeat juvenem pro regno certantem
abstinere rapinis, cedibus parcere, cavere incendia, nullum gravamen
inferre pauperibus, pacem et reverenciam ecclesiis et sacerdotibus 25
conservare? Unde non immerito Andigavensium gloria, Normannorum tutela, spes Anglorum, Aquitanorum decus ab omnibus
predicaris. Hoc tantum superest, ut Christum Jhesum horum*e*
munerum largitorem agnoscas [et]*f* exoptes conservatorem. Ego vero
considerans de quorum progenie originem duxeris, gracias ago 30
Domino Deo meo quod pro talibus patribus talis nobis filius, quasi
novus quidam*g* splendor, illuxit. In quo cum omnium antecessorum
tuorum virtutes convenerint, maxime tamen in te spiritum Christianissimi regis David gaudeo quievisse. Unde divina providencia actum
existimo, ut illius mundissime manus baltheo*h* te cinxerunt militari, per 35
quas Christi gracia virtutem tibi castitatis illius, humilitatis et pietatis
infunderet. Quoniam autem recenti morte illius contristatus, vitam
eius et mores sicut nunc amor, nunc timor, nunc spes, nunc dolor
meum variant affectum, non historiando, sed lamentando, brevi stilo
collegi, te quasi pietatis illius heredem intimi cordis dileccione 40
suscipiens, ipsam tibi lamentacionem destinare curavi. In qua cum
laudabilem eius vitam et preciosam legeris mortem, illam imiteris ut
istam consequi merearis.

b   D; Narmannorum C   *f*   S
c   *corrected from* querat C   *g*   G; quidem S,C,D
d   S; mater C,D   *h*   -l- *interlin.*C
e   + universorum *del.*C

servant of the servants of Christ who are at Rievaulx, sends greetings
and prayers. Virtue is to such an extent natural and vice unnatural that
even a wicked man praises and approves of virtue, while not even a
wicked man would make excuses for vice, if he accepts the judgment of
human reason. For vice, as it were blushing at itself on account of the
wickedness innate within it, always looks for hiding-places, and longs
for secrecy; while on the contrary virtue conscious within itself of its
own beauty and integrity dances and revels at every glance, fleeing and
shrinking from the public testimony of men only from humility. Since
therefore love of virtues and hatred of vices is naturally inborn in the
rational soul, whoever studies good conduct and virtue easily entices
and inclines the affection of all to himself. This is why, most illustrious
sir, the fame of your good qualities has impressed you on the minds of
many who have not seen you with their eyes, since such great wisdom in
one so young is a wonder no less than a joy to all, such moderation in
the midst of such great pleasures, such great forethought in such
important transactions, such austerity in such high rank, such great
kindness in such austerity. For who would not be amazed that a young
man competing for a kingdom should abstain from plundering, refrain
from killings, avoid arson, inflict no hardship on the poor, observe
peace and reverence for the churches and the priests? Therefore not
undeservedly you are proclaimed by all as the glory of the Angevins,
the protector of the Normans, the hope of the English, the splendour of
the Aquitanians. Only this remains that you should recognise Christ
Jesus as the bestower of these gifts, and you should long for him as your
Saviour. I for my part, as I consider from whose lineage you derive
your origin, I thank my Lord God that in keeping with such ancestors
such a son has shone upon us like a new kind of radiance. Although the
virtues of all your ancestors meet together in you, I rejoice especially
however that the spirit of the most Christian King David has come to
rest in you. Therefore I think that it was the work of Divine Providence
that it was his hands that girt you with the belt of knighthood through
which the grace of Christ poured into you the virtue of his charity, his
humility and piety. Since, saddened by his recent death, I have
compiled a brief account of his life and character, not a historical
account but a lamentation, just as my feelings were swayed now by
love, now by fear, now by hope, now by grief, adopting you in the
affection of my innermost heart as the heir of his godliness, I have
undertaken to send the lamentation to you. When you read in it his
praiseworthy life and precious death, imitate the former in order that
you may deserve to attain the latter.

46

Lamentacio

Religiosus et pius David rex migravit e mundo, qui licet dignum anime
sue locum invenerit, mors tamen eius planctum nobis indicit. Quis
enim non lugeat virum tam necessarium mundo, rebus humanis
exemptum, nisi is qui rebus humanis pacem invidet et*ᵃ* profectum?
Juvenes et virgines, senes cum junioribus, induite vos ciliciis, et spargite 5
vos cinere. Audiatur in excelso clamor vester, et planctus vester in
celestibus. Inter vestibulum et altare plorate sacerdotes Domini,
ministri Dei vestri, quoniam recessit a vobis qui consolabatur vos, qui
vestiebat vos duplicibus, qui ditabat muneribus, et honoribus sublima-
bat. Verumptamen nolite flere super eum, sed super vosipsos flete et 10
super filios vestros. Amodo quippe iam dicit Spiritus, ut ipse requiescat
a laboribus suis. Opera enim illius secuntur eum. Nichil igitur mali viro
illi accidit; nobis accidit, si quid accidit. Sed ut quid dico: 'Si quid
accidit'? Heu! incredibile*ᵇ* dictu quantum accidit, qui eum amisimus,
virum qui non sibi vivebat sed omnibus, omnium curam agens, 15
omnium saluti prospiciens; rector morum, censor scelerum, virtutum
incentor, cuius vita humilitatis fuit forma, justicie speculum, castitatis
exemplar. Rex ergo mansuetus, rex justus, rex castus, rex humilis, quis
facile dixerit quid utilitatis humane vite contulit, quem mansuetudo
amabilem, justicia terribilem, compositum castitas, humilitas commu- 20
nem fecerat? Que omnia si in privato quolibet laude dignissima
judicantur, quanto magis in rege, cui potestas dat licere quod non libet,
cuius viciis facile favent inferiores, proni ad imitandum, prompti ad
adulandum, cum et | impunitas prestet audaciam, libido vero acuat et
accendat luxuriam? Laudatur enim peccator a peccatoribus in 25
desideriis suis, et qui inique agit benedicitur. Quis est igitur hic, et
laudabimus eum? Fecit enim mirabilia in vita sua. Qui*ᶜ* potuit enim
transgredi, et non est transgressus. Quis similis tui in regibus terre, O
rex optime, qui te in auro pauperem, in trono humilem, in armis*ᵈ*
mitem, castum in deliciis exhibebas, qui te modestum plebi, equalem 30
militibus, inferiorem sacerdotibus ostendebas, omnibus omnia factus,
ut omnibus consuleres ad virtutem? Merito igitur memoria nominis tui
dulcis in cordibus nostris, suavis in affectibus nostris, memorabilis in
sermonibus nostris, cui satis congruit, quod lectum est: 'Dilectus Deo
et hominibus, cuius memoria in benediccione est.' 35

a   + pp *del.C*
b   *S*; incredibili *C,D*

c   *R*; Que *S,C*; Que *corrected to* Qui *D*
d   + militem *del.C*

46

Lamentation   = Eulogy

The religious and pious King David has departed from this world.
Although he has found a place worthy of his soul, yet his death
demands our mourning. For who, apart from a man who grudges
peace and progress to human affairs, would not mourn for a man so
much needed in the world, when he has been removed from human
affairs? Youths and girls, old men and young, put on sackcloth, and
sprinkle yourselves with ash. Let your cry be heard on high, and your
mourning in the celestial regions. Weep between the porch and the
altar, priests of the Lord, the ministers of your God, since he who
comforted you, he who clothed you in twofold raiment, he who
enriched you with gifts and exalted you with dignities has departed
from you. Do not however weep for him, but weep for yourselves and
for your sons. Even now indeed the Holy Spirit pronounces that he
himself is resting from his labours. For his works follow him. So
nothing evil has happened to that man; if anything has happened, it has
happened to us. But why do I say: 'If anything has happened'? Alas, it is
beyond belief to say how much has happened, for we have lost a man
who lived not for himself, but for everyone, taking care of everyone,
taking thought for the welfare of all; director of morals, judge of
wickedness, encourager of virtues, his life was a pattern of humility, a
mirror of justice, an example of chastity. So a king who was gentle, a
king who was just, a king who was chaste, a king who was unassuming,
who could easily say what benefit he conferred on the lives of men,
whose gentleness had made him lovable, whose justice had made him
to be feared, whose chastity had made him tranquil, whose humility
had made him accessible to all? If all these qualities are considered to be
most praiseworthy in any private individual, how much more so in a
king whose power permits him to do what is unpleasing, whose vices
are readily encouraged by his inferiors, who are ready to imitate, quick
to applaud, since impunity bestows boldness, and lust sharpens and
kindles debauchery? For a sinner is praised by sinners in respect of his
desires, and the man who acts wickedly is blessed. So who is this, and
shall we praise him? For he performed wonders in his life. For he had
the power to transgress, and he did not transgress. For who among the
kings of the earth is like you, most excellent king, who showed yourself
a poor man while surrounded by gold, unassuming while seated on a
throne, gentle while engaged in warfare, chaste although surrounded
by luxuries, who showed yourself moderate to ordinary people, on an
equal footing to knights, and deferential to priests, having become all
things to all men, in order to consult the best interests of all on the path

47

De eodem

Vere dilectus a Deo, qui dirigit mansuetos in judicio, qui docet mites
vias suas. Dilexit quippe regem mansuetum et pium ille mitis Deus et
humilis corde, cuius optimos mores eciam in hac vita magna mercede
donavit, cuius in vita non pepercit offensis, nunc | puniens, nunc
remunerans, finem desiderii eius semper attendens, et ideo ad salutem   5
semper exaudiens. Ita tu, Domine Deus meus, exaudiebas eum. Deus,
tu propicius ei^a fuisti, et ulciscens in omnes adinvenciones illius. Nam in
eo eciam ad literam constat esse impletum quod in psalmo scriptum est:
'Mansueti autem hereditabunt terram, et delectabuntur in multitudine
pacis.' Scimus eum regnum non appetivisse, sed horruisse, magisque   10
illud^b ob alienam necessitatem suscepisse, quam dominandi libidine
victum avide invasisse. Unde et obsequia illa, que a gente Scotorum in
novella/regum promocione more patrio exhibentur, ita exhorruit, ut
vix ab episcopis ea suscipere cogeretur. Sublimatus autem in regnum,
nichil superbum in moribus, nichil in verbis crudele, nichil inhonestum   15
factis preferebat. Unde tota illa gentis illius barbaries mansuefacta,
tanta se mox benevolencia et humilitate substravit, ut naturalis oblita
sevicie, legibus, quas regia mansuetudo dictabat, colla submitteret, et
pacem, quam eatenus nesciebat, gratanter acciperet. Nec illa mansuetudo remissa videbatur aut segnis, cum in puniendis iniquis^c justicie per   20
omnia cederet, ne videretur gladium sine causa portare, et mansuetudi-
nem in corde teneret, ne videretur non exercere judicium, sed sue
pocius impaciencie satisfacere. Credo eum numquam sine magna
cordis contricione, eciam in eos qui prodicionis ipsius rei fuerant,
exercuisse vindictam. Vidimus eum sepe in penis latronum vel   25
proditorum pectus tundere, lacrimas fundere, ut manifestum fecerit^d se
in reis puniendis ut ministrum legum obedire justicie, non seviciam
exercere. Unde non immerito velut mansuetus hereditavit terram,
quantam nullus antecessorum suorum diebus nostris possidebat, et
delectabatur in multitudine pacis, quam inter barbaras gentes, et   30
diversitates linguarum et morum sibi contrarias, et propter mutuas
mortes et vulnera sibi invicem inimicissimas, tanta caucione composuit, tanta^e auctoritate servavit, ut inter cognatas gentes eiusdemque^f
generis et lingue homines, tale fedus tanto tempore vix aliquando
viderimus custodiri.

a   interlin.C   d   G; fecerat S,C,D
b   G; illam S,C,D   e   S,R; tante C,D
c   +et C,D; om.S   f   S; eiusdem C,D

to virtue? So deservedly the memory of your name is sweet in our hearts, pleasant in our affections, and celebrated in our conversations. The following text is appropriate to you: 'Beloved of God and men, remembrance of whom is blessed.'

47

The same

Beloved of God indeed, who directs the meek in judgment, who teaches the mild his way. That God mild and lowly of heart indeed loved the meek and pious king, whose excellent character he rewarded greatly even in this life, whose faults he did not spare while he was alive, now
5   punishing, now rewarding, always paying attention to the object of his desire, and on that account always ready to hear him for his salvation. Thus you, my Lord God, listened to him. You, God, were always favourable to him, although you punished all his innovations. For it is generally agreed that in him was fulfilled to the letter what is written in
10   the Psalm: 'The meek shall inherit the earth, and shall delight themselves in the abundance of peace.' We know that he did not seek the kingship, but shrank from it, and undertook it more for the needs of others than greedily usurping it because he was overcome by lust for mastery. Therefore he so much abhorred those ceremonies which are
15   offered by the people of the Scots according to the custom of the country at the inauguration of a new king that he was only with difficulty compelled by the bishops to accept them. When he was raised to the kingship he revealed no trace of haughtiness in his behaviour, no cruelty in his words, nothing dishonourable in his deeds. Accordingly
20   that total barbarity of that people was tamed, and soon overlaid with such great goodwill and humility that, forgetting its natural fierceness, it submitted its neck to the laws which the king's meekness dictated, and gratefully accepted peace, of which it knew nothing up to that point. Nor did that meekness seem negligent or slothful, since he
25   yielded to justice in all respects when punishing the wicked, so that he might not seem to wield the sword to no purpose, and since he kept meekness in his heart, so that it might not seem that he was failing to exercise judgment, but rather was satisfying his own intolerance. I believe that he never exacted punishment without great distress in his
30   heart, even from those who were guilty of treason against him. We saw him often when he was punishing robbers or traitors, beating his breast, shedding tears, to make it clear that he was obeying justice as an administrator of the laws in punishing the guilty, not practising cruelty. Therefore since he was meek, he deserved to inherit the earth, which he
35   possessed in our time to a greater extent than any of his predecessors, and he took delight in abundance of peace, which he brought about with such care and preserved with such authority between barbarous peoples with diversities of language and character that were opposed to

48

De eodem et fundacione episcopatuum et monasteriorum

Precellit hiis, ut michi videtur, quod talem servabat modum in utroque, ut in severitate justicie [ab omnibus amaretur, et in lenitate justicie]^a et misericordie ab omnibus timeretur, quamvis optaverit semper magis amari quam timeri. Unde non immerito dilectus Deo et hominibus videbatur. Dilectus plane a Deo, qui statim in regni sui iniciis ea que 5 Dei sunt diligenter exercuit, in ecclesiis construendis, in monasteriis fundandis, que et ampliavit possessionibus et diviciis, prout unicuique opus erat. Nam cum ipse in toto regno Scotorum tres vel iiii^{or} tantum invenerit episcopos, ecclesiis ceteris sine pastore tam morum quam rerum dispendio fluctuantibus, ipse tam de antiquis quas reparavit, 10 quam de novis quas erexit, decedens novem reliquit. Monasteria quoque diversorum ordinum Cluniacensis, Cisterciensis, Tironicensis,

G i,301

Arouensis, Premonstratensis, Belvacensis, videlicet | Kalcow, Melros, Jedwod, Neubotil, Holmcultrane, Dundranan, monasterium de Crag Sancte Crucis juxta Edinburgh, Cambuskineth, Kinlos, et juxta 15 Berwik monasterium sanctimonialium, et, ut quidam ferunt, monasterium monialium Sancti Bartholomei juxta Carleil, ⟨et canonicos Premonstratenses Novi Castri, et ibi monasterium nigrorum monachorum, et aliud monialium ibi, ut patet in prologo eius super Statutis Burgorum,⟩ et eciam ad Dunfermelyne ⟨xiii⟩ monachos^b introduxit de 20 Cantuaria,^{c} ac plura alia plena^d fratribus ordinata reliquit. Inter quos sic fuerat quasi unus ex ipsis, bona laudans, et si qua forte minus laudanda emergebant, verecunde dissimulans, substratus^e omnibus,

fo.105v

sollicitus pro omnibus, multa largiens, et nulla | exigens. O dulcis anima, quo abisti, quo recessisti? Querunt te oculi nostri, nec invenire 25 poterunt. Erigunt se aures nostre, ut audiant vocem jocunditatis tue, vocem humilitatis, vocem confessionis, vocem consolacionis; et ecce silencium! Ubi vultus ille suavissimus, qui se tam mitem pauperibus, sanctis tam humilem, sociis se prebuit tam jocundum? Ubi oculi illi pleni pietatis et gracie, quibus et congaudere gaudentibus, flere cum 30 flentibus, consuevisti? Quid agitis, O mei oculi, quid agitis? Quid dissimulatis emittere quod^f parturitis, producere quod intus reconditis?

---

a S; om.C,D	d + religiosis CA
b + scilicet conventum CA	e + pro del.C
c corrected from Cantibrigia C; + et religionem ibidem instituit CA	f S; quid C,D

40 each other and mutually hostile on account of slaughter and wounding inflicted on each other, that we have scarcely ever seen even among closely related peoples and men of the same race and language such accord being observed for such a long time.

48

The same, and the foundation of bishoprics and monasteries

He excelled in these matters, it seems to me, because he observed such moderation on each side that in the strictness of his justice he was loved by all, and in the leniency and mercy of his justice he was feared by all, although he always wished to be loved rather than feared. So
5 deservedly he was seen as beloved by God and men. Clearly beloved of God, since immediately at the beginning of his reign he diligently practised the things that are of God in building churches, in founding monasteries, which he also endowed with properties and riches according to the needs of each. For although he found only three or
10 four bishops in the whole kingdom of the Scots, while the rest of the churches were drifting aimlessly without a shepherd to the detriment of both morals and property, at his death he left nine bishoprics including both ancient ones that he had restored, and new ones that he erected. He also left monasteries of various orders, Cluniac, Cistercian,
15 Tironensian, Arrouaisian, Premonstratensian, order of Beauvais, namely Kelso, Melrose, Jedburgh, Newbattle, Holm Cultram, Dundrennan, the monastery of Holyrood Crag near Edinburgh, Cambuskenneth, Kinloss and a monastery of nuns near Berwick, and, as some say, a monastery of nuns of St Bartholomew near Carlisle, and
20 Premonstratensian canons of Newcastle and a monastery of Black Monks there, and another of nuns there, as appears in his prologue to the *Statutes of Burghs*, and he also introduced thirteen monks from Canterbury to Dunfermline, and left many other monasteries fully staffed with brothers. When he was with them, he was like one of
25 themselves, praising good deeds, and, if there chanced to emerge deeds less worthy of praise, modestly shutting his eyes to them, making himself available to all, concerned about everyone, giving generously, and asking nothing for himself. Oh sweet soul, where have you gone to, where have you withdrawn to? Our eyes search for you, but will not be
30 able to find you. Our ears are pricked up to hear the voice of your cheerfulness, the voice of humility, the voice of confession, the voice of consolation, and behold, silence! Where is that most pleasant face which showed itself so gentle to the poor, so humble to the holy, and so cheerful to its friends? Where are those eyes full of piety and grace with
35 which you would rejoice along with the joyful, and weep along with those who wept? What are you doing, my eyes, what are you doing? Why do you hesitate to give birth to what you are labouring with, to bring forth what you are hiding within you? Let the tears fall by day

Deducite lacrimas per diem et noctem, nolite parcere, quoniam hee delicie mee erunt in recordacione dulcissimi domini mei et amici. Nec solus lugeo. Scio quod lugent mecum sacerdotes et clerici, quos 35 venerabatur ut patres; lugent sanctimoniales et monachi, quos amplectabatur ut fratres; lugent milites, quorum se dominum nesciebat, sed socium; lugent vidue, quas tuebatur, orphani, quos consolabatur, pauperes, quos sustentabat, miseri, quos fovebat.

49

De eodem

Erat enim merencium consolator, pater orphanorum, et judex promptissimus viduarum. Nam cum alia regni negocia aliis committeret judicibus, pauperum semper, pupillorum et viduarum sibi negocia reservabat. Huiusmodi ipse auditor, defensor et judex, nec quisquam pauper, vidua vel orphanus, aliquid querimonie delaturus, ad eum 5 ingredi prohibebatur, sed statim ab ostiario introductus, eciam si in summis necessariisque*a* negociis et consiliis cum magnis eciam paucisque personis occuparetur, intermissis omnibus audiebatur. Vidi eciam ego oculis meis, cum aliquando paratus ire venatum, et in scansili pede posito, equm vellet ascendere, ad vocem pauperis audienciam sibi dari 10 postulantis, quod pedem retraxerit, relictoque equo et regressus in aulam ea die non reversurus ad propositum, judicia civilissimi sed et magnificentissimi Trajani principis exsuperans, vel saltem | imitans, causam pro qua fuerat appellatus benigne et paciencter audierit. Consueverat preterea, ad ostium aule regie sedens, pauperum et 15 vetularum, que certis diebus de singulis, quocumque veniebant, regionibus vocabantur, causas diligenter audire, et singulis cum multo labore satisfacere. Nam sepe litigabant cum illo, et ipse cum illis, cum contra justiciam personam pauperis nollet accipere, et ipsi racioni, quam ostendebat, nollent acquiescere. Taceo quam mira affabilitate et 20 morum suavitate omnium in se provocabat affectum, quomodo se omnium moribus coaptabat, ut nec gravibus lenis, nec lenibus durus crederetur. Denique si contingeret ut sacerdos vel miles, vel monachus, dives vel pauper, civis*b* vel peregrinus, negociator vel rusticus cum eo sermonem haberet, ita cum singulis de suis negociis et officiis 25 convenienter et humiliter disserebat, ut singulus*c* quisque sua eum tantum curare putaret. Et sic omnes jocundos et edificatos dimitteret. Ita enim populum illum rudem et agrestem ad mores compositos et edomitos illicere satagebat, ut non solum de magnis regni sui causis, verum et de minimis quibusque, utpote de ortis, edificiis et pomariis 30 curam gereret, ut eos ad similia suo exemplo provocaret.

G i.302

---

and by night, do not be sparing of them, since these will be my delight in
40 remembrance of my most sweet lord and friend. Nor do I grieve alone. I
know that priests and clerics whom he revered as fathers grieve along
with me; nuns and monks whom he embraced as brothers grieve;
knights grieve, whose friend rather than lord he knew himself to be; the
widows whom he protected grieve, as do the orphans whom he
45 comforted, the poor whom he supported, the wretched whom he
cherished.

49

The same

→ a beatitude

For he was a comforter of those who mourned, a father of orphans,
and a very ready judge of widows. For although he entrusted other
business of the kingdom to other judges, he always reserved for himself
the affairs of the poor, orphans and widows. He himself was auditor,
5 advocate and judge in cases of this sort, and no poor person, widow or
orphan, who intended to lodge some complaint, was ever forbidden
access to him, but was immmediately brought in by the doorkeeper.
Even if [the king] was engaged in the most important and pressing
business and consultations even with important and select persons, it
10 was all interrupted, and he or she was heard. I saw also with my own
eyes, when sometimes he was ready to go hunting, and with his foot
placed in the stirrup he was intending to mount his horse, that he
withdrew his foot, left his horse and returned to his hall at the voice of a
poor person demanding that audience be given to him, and he would
15 not return to what he had planned on that day, but exceeding or at any
rate imitating the judgments of the most civil and magnificent emperor
Trajan, he heard the case for which he had been called kindly and
patiently. It was his custom besides to sit at the door of the royal hall
and to listen attentively to cases of poor people and old women, who
20 were summoned on certain days from particular regions wherever they
came from, and to strive hard to give satisfaction to each one. For often
they argued with him and he with them, when he refused to accept the
legal standing of a poor person contrary to justice, and when they
refused to give assent to the reasoned argument which he demonstrated
25 to them. I say nothing of the wonderful courtesy and pleasant manner
with which he won the affection of all, or of how he adapted himself to
everyone's disposition, so that he was not thought to be soft to harsh
people, nor harsh to those who were soft. Finally if it happened that a
priest or a knight or a monk, a rich man or poor man, citizen or
30 foreigner, business man or countryman had conversation with him, he
discoursed suitably and unassumingly with each concerning his
business and duties in such a way that each one thought that he cared
only for his affairs. And thus he sent them all away cheerful and edified.
For thus he did his best to entice that rough and uncouth people to

50

Quod solicitus fuit discordantes pacificare

Super omnia autem solicitus erat, ut quemadmodum a forinsecis, ita
eciam et ab intestinis domesticis dissencionibus,^{a} feriarentur maxime
sacerdotes Domini et viri religiosi. Inter quos quocienscumque, sicut
est humana miseria, discordia oriebatur, non requiebat spiritus eius,
non caro quiescebat, donec precibus et blandiciis, ac aliquando 5
lacrimis, raro autem minis, eos in pacem pristinam revocaret. Nec
dedignabatur pro tali causa regium illud, caput ad eius genua, qui
forsan in hac parte durior appareret, cum/verbis^b humilibus humiliter
inclinare, ut vinceretur verecundia, qui vinci non poterat benevolencia.
Sane castitatem in eo laudare non est necesse, cum post initum semel 10
matrimonium fidem thori servaverit, adeo ut non solum non cognosceret aliam, sed numquam indecenter aspiceret; et sicut carne, ita et
mente, manu, motu, gestu, oculis, ac sermone pudicus. Nam ita
communis erat vita eius, ita in luce et in manifesto opera eius, ut
numquam in hac parte vel levi suspicione ureretur. Nullum ei secretum 15
preter consilia. Thalamus eius omnibus patuit | ad sessum, ad cubitum,
ad secessum. Unde, quod mirum est dictu, tantam ei graciam virtus
divina attulerat, ut numquam post mortem uxoris, cui supervixit
viginti tribus annis, vel in sompnis carnalis contagionis injuriam
pateretur. Quid trepidas, anima mea? Quid formidas, eciam ea que 20
displicent in medium proferre, cum non solum bonorum virorum sit
laudanda justicia, verum eciam si deliquerint penitencia predicanda?
Legimus Aaron primum sub lege pontificem populo idolum sibi fieri
postulanti | prebuisse consensum. Moises ipse ad aquas contradiccio-
nis pronunciatur celesti sentencia deliquisse. Mariam prophetissam, 25
ob murmur in Moysen,^{c} lepra fuisse percussam scriptura testatur.
David sanctus, post spiritualium graciarum munera innumera, quasi
divine bonitatis oblitus, primum servi sui fidelis adulteravit uxorem,
quem deinde mira prodicione peremit. Hii viri sancti in sacra scriptura
commemorantur non ad exemplum ruine sed ad rudimentum cautele. 30
Fateor, peccavit et noster David. Peccavit non seipso fedando aliquo
scelere, sed aliene crudelitati vires, plus quam oportuit, ministrando.
Nam post mortem Henrici regis Anglie sui sororii, cum exercitum

fo.106

G i,303

---

a D; dessencionibus C c $+$ in *del.C*
b S; vestris C

35 calm and civilised manners, so that he took care not only of the
important matters of his kingdom, but also of the most trivial such as
gardens, buildings and orchards so that he might encourage them to
similar interests by his example.

50

He was anxious to reconcile those that were
at variance with one another

He was above all anxious that priests of the Lord and men of religion
should be free not only from external dissensions but also internal and
domestic ones. As often as discord arose amongst them, human misery
being what it is, his spirit did not rest, his flesh had no repose until he

5 restored them to their former peace by entreaties and blandishments
and sometimes with tears, but seldom with threats. Nor did he disdain
for such a cause humbly to incline that royal head with humble words
onto the knee of him who perhaps appeared more obstinate on this
side, so that a man who could not be conquered by kindness might be

10 conquered by shame. It is not of course necessary to praise chastity in
his case, since from the beginning of his one marriage he was faithful to
his marriage vows, so that not only did he not make love to, but he
never as much as looked dishonourably at any other woman; and just
as he was chaste in his flesh, so also was he in his mind, his hand, his

15 movement, gesture, eyes and speech. For his life was so public, what he
did was so much in the full blaze of the light that he was never branded
in this respect by the slightest suspicion. He had no secrets apart from
[state] counsels. His chamber was open to all, whether he was sitting or
lying down or retiring. So, amazing to relate, divine goodness

20 conferred such grace upon him that never after the death of his wife,
whom he survived by twenty-three years, did he suffer harm from the
pollution of the flesh even in his sleep. Why are you in a state of alarm,
my soul? Why are you afraid to bring to light unpleasant facts as well,

25 since not only must the righteousness of good men be praised, but if
they transgress their repentance must also be proclaimed. We read that
Aaron the first high priest under the law gave his consent to the people
when they demanded that an idol be made for them. Moses himself was
pronounced by Heaven's decree to have erred at the waters of

30 contention. Scripture testifies that the prophetess Miriam was stricken
with leprosy because she murmured against Moses. The saintly David
after innumerable gifts of spiritual graces, as if forgetful of the divine
goodness, first of all committed adultery with the wife of his loyal
servant, whom he then put to death with amazing treachery. These

35 holy men are commemorated in sacred scripture not as an example of
downfall but to teach caution. Our David also sinned, I admit. He
sinned not by dishonouring himself with some crime, but by providing
the means for the savagery of others, more than he should have. For

egisset in Angliam, gens illa effera et Anglis inimicissima supra
humanum morem sevientes, in ecclesiam, in sacerdotes, in utrumque   35
sexum, in omnem etatem crudelia exercuere judicia. Que omnia, licet
eo nolente, ymmo eciam prohibente, facta sunt, quia tamen[d] poterat
eos non duxisse, poterat eos semel expertus non reduxisse, poterat eos
fortasse plus cohibuisse, et ipsum cum lacrimis peccasse confitemur.
Excusent eum alii, zelum justicie pretendentes, sacramentum quod   40
fecerat attendentes, regie hoc esse virtutis proclamantes, quod fidem
servavit, quod non violavit sacramentum, quod contra perjuros arma
tulit, quod ad heredes regnum, quod eis pater delegaverat, quod eis
clerus et populus, data juratoria caucione, firmaverant, revocare
temptavit. Habet forte aliquem[e] apud[f] tuam pietatem locum, bone 45
Jhesu, huius excusacionis elogium. Ego autem, sciens quod bonum est
confiteri tibi, elegi rogare, non excusare, misericordiam petens, non
presumens de judicio.

d   C,G; cum S   f   D; aput C
e   G; aliquam S,C,D

51

De eodem et quod abrenunciasset regno et Jerosolim peteret si non revocatus c'

Dico quod non intres in judicium cum servo tuo, Domine, quia nullus
apud te justificabitur homo, nisi per te omnium peccatorum tribuatur
remissio. Maluit enim se accusare quam excusare; maluit pectus
tundere quam exerere. Scimus eciam eum ita hoc horruisse peccatum,
et ad summa virtutum aspirasse studia, ut abrenunciasset regno,   5
sceptrum deposuisset, et in locis Dominice Passionis et Resurreccionis
eius ad spiritualem se miliciam contulisset, si non eum sacerdotum et
abbatum consilia,[a] lacrime pauperum, viduarum gemitus, plebis
desolacio, et tocius regni sui clamor et ejulatus revocasset, corpore non
mente aut voluntate detentus. Omnino religiosorum virorum consilio 10
se commisit, et de preclara milicia Templi Jerosolimitani optimos
fratres secum retinens, eos diebus et noctibus morum suorum fecit[b] esse
custodes.
    De elemosinarum largicione, de oracionum, missarum, psalmorum
frequentacione supersedeo, cum ab ipsa adolescencia in hac observa- 15
cione admiracioni fuerit universis. Hec sunt que me consolantur in
dolore meo, Jhesu bone, non ut dicam: 'Non | peccavit', sed quod
penituit, quod flevit, quod confessus est, quod consilium Danielis
secutus est, dicentis ad Nabugodonosor: 'Peccata tua elemosinis
redime, et iniquitates tuas misericordiis pauperum.' Preterea, O Fons 20

a   S; consilio C,D   b   + se C; om.S,CA

after the death of his brother-in-law Henry king of England he led an
40   army into England, and that fierce people most hostile to the English,
rampaging beyond the normal practice of human beings, wreaked
savage judgments upon the church, upon priests, upon men and
women, upon young and old alike. Although all of this was done
against his wishes or rather against his orders, yet because he had the
45   possibility not to have led them, he could after one such experience
have declined to lead them back again, he could perhaps have put more
restraint on them. We confess in tears that even he sinned. Let others
offer excuses for him by alleging his zeal for justice, by taking into
consideration the oath which he had taken, proclaiming that this is the
50   mark of royal virtue that he kept his word, that he did not break his
oath, that he took up arms against those who were forsworn, that he
tried to recover for the heirs the kingdom of England which their father
had assigned to them, which the clergy and people had confirmed to
them by giving their sworn pledge. This plea in his defence may have
55   some place in your pity, good Jesus. I for my part, knowing that it is
good to confess to you, have chosen to plead, not to make excuses,
asking for mercy, not anticipating judgment.

*a round-
about
excuse*

51

The same and the fact that he would have abdicated, and made for Jerusalem, if he had not been dissuaded etc.

I say: 'Do not bring your servant to trial, Lord, because no-one will be
found innocent before you', unless remission for all his sins were to be
granted through you. For [King David] preferred to accuse rather than
excuse himself; he preferred to beat his breast rather than to bare it. We
5   also know that he shrank from this sin to such an extent, and aspired to
the loftiest pursuits of virtues that he would have abdicated, laid down
his sceptre, and made his way to spiritual warfare in the places of our
Lord's Passion and his Resurrection, if he had not been dissuaded by
the advice of priests and abbots, the tears of the poor, the groans of
10   widows, the desolation of the people, and the outcry and lamentation
of the whole kingdom, held back as he was bodily, not by his mind or
his will. He was completely committed to the advice of men of religion;
and retaining for himself some excellent brothers from the famous
Knights Templar of Jerusalem, he saw to it that they were the
15   guardians of his morals by day and by night.

I make no mention of his lavish almsgiving, the frequency of his
prayers, masses and psalms, since he was the admiration of all from his
youth in his observance of these things. It is the following considerations that comfort me in my grief, good Jesus, not that I might say:
20   'He did not sin', but because he repented, he wept, he confessed,
because he followed the advice of Daniel, when he said to Nebuchad-
nezzar: 'Redeem your sins with almsgiving, and your wrong-doing by
having compassion on the poor.' Besides, oh Fount of Goodness and

Bonitatis et Pietatis Origo, nonne propicius fuisti ei cum ulciscereris in omnes adinvenciones illius? Corripuisti eum, Domine, corripuisti eum, ut pater filium, verumptamen in misericordia, quoniam non continuisti in ira tua misericordiam tuam. Dedisti enim ei filialem in flagellis affectum, ut non murmuraret, non recalcitraret, ymmo et in flagellis 25 gracias ageret, dicens cum propheta: 'Omnia que fecisti nobis, Domine, in vero judicio fecisti.' Hec vox eius, hic affectus eius, cum eius effunderetur exercitus, cum cedere necessitati a propriis militibus cogeretur. Hec vox eius cum immisisset ei Deus inimicum quendam pseudo-episcopum, qui se filium comitis Moraviensis menciebatur. In 30 quo satis apparuit divina pietas, in cuius manu sunt omnia jura regnorum, cuius nutu omnia disponuntur, ipse Dominus faciens pacem et creans malum. Non igitur glorietur sapiens in sapiencia sua, nec fortis in sua fortitudine, quoniam gressus hominis a Domino diriguntur, qui regem invictissimum, qui tot sibi barbaras subdiderat 35 naciones, qui de Moraviensibus et Insulanis parvo labore triumphaverat, ex monachi cuiusdam mendaciis flagellavit. Qui, licet statim dignam operibus suis mercedem invenerit, in hiis tamen omnibus rex Christianissimus manus Domini recognovit.

52

De eodem et quod Deus flagellavit illum in morte filii sui

fo.106v

Postremo, O Deus Ulcionum, ut paciencia illius omnibus innotesceret, effudisti super eum iram tuam, | et omnem iram furoris tui, castigans eum castigacione crudeli cum ei unicum filium abstulisti. Et qualem filium! Erat enim adolescens speciosissimus, amabilis omnibus et suavis, a quocumque videbatur dilectus, et ad omne bonum inclinatus. 5 O Domine Deus meus, quibus flagris doloris afflixisti cor eius, cum unigenitum suum, quem amantissimum et sibi similem fuerat expertus, ipse portaret ad tumulum, a quo simile speraret obsequium. Attamen ceteris flentibus et ejulantibus, vir ille, cui nichil defuit ad virtutem, tanta paciencia virgam Altissimi Patris excepit, ut et lacrimis parceret, 10 et cibum ipsa die oblitus sui cum familia sua regali more perciperet. Absit igitur ut hoc illi imputetur peccatum quod in presenti divina punivit justicia, quod ipse proprii oris confessione dampnavit, quod lacrimis lavit, quod redemit elemosinis, quod cotidiana cordis contricione purgavit. Ipse sui accusator, ipse contra se judex, ipse in se 15 carnifex. 'Nam si nosmetipsos judicaremus,' ait Paulus, 'non utique judicaremur.' Depone proinde, anima mea, sepone paulisper tristiciam, et hunc ultimum vite sue[a] annum quam religiose transegerit, cum

---

a   + animum del.C

Source of Pity, surely you were gracious to him when you punished all
his devices? You admonished him, Lord, you admonished him as a
father his son, but mercifully, since you did not in your anger withhold
your mercy. For you gave him the affection due to a son while
punishing him, so that he should not murmur, not be intractable, on
the contrary that he should give thanks while being punished, saying
with the prophet: 'All that you have done to us, Lord, you have done in
true judgment.' These were his words, this was his feeling, when his
army was turned to flight, when he was compelled to yield to the
inevitable by his own knights. These were his words when God sent
against him an enemy, a pseudo-bishop, who falsely claimed to be a son
of the earl of Moray. In this the Divine Pity was sufficiently apparent,
in whose hand are all the laws of the kingdoms, by whose nod
everything is ordered, the Lord himself who makes peace and creates
evil. So let not the wise man rejoice in his wisdom, nor the brave man in
his courage, since the steps of man are directed by the Lord, who
punished by means of the lies of a certain monk that most invincible
king, who had subdued to himself so many barbarous tribes, who with
little effort had triumphed over the men of Moray and the Isles.
Although the monk immediately found a reward worthy of his works,
nevertheless in all these things the most Christian king recognised the
hands of the Lord.

52

The same and the fact that God punished him
in the death of his son

Finally, oh God of Vengeances, in order that the king's patience might
become known to all, you poured out your wrath upon him and all the
wrath of your fury, chastising him with a cruel chastisement when you
robbed him of his only son. And what a son! For he was a very
handsome young man, amiable and pleasant to everyone, esteemed by
all who saw him, and inclined towards everything good. Oh Lord my
God, with what lashes of grief you afflicted the king's heart, when he
himself carried to the tomb his only begotten son whom he had found
most loving and resembling himself, and from whom he had expected a
like service. However while all the others were weeping and wailing,
that man whose goodness was absolute in every respect accepted the
rod of the Father most High with so much patience that he restrained
his tears, and, forgetful of himself, took food on the very day with his
household according to the royal custom. Therefore perish the thought
that it should be imputed to him as a sin for which divine justice
punished him in this present life, which he condemned himself by
confession from his own lips, which he washed with his tears, which he
redeemed by almsgiving, of which he purged himself by the daily
contrition of his heart. He himself was his own accuser, he himself the

G i,305

mentis alacritate revolve. In quo, toto corde conversus ad Deum, lumbis precinctis, cum lucernis ardentibus vigilans Domini prestolaba- 20 tur adventum. Vigilabat, qui nichil judicare, nichil discernere, nichil constituere, sine religiosorum et probatissimorum virorum consilio presumebat. Vigilabat, qui singulis diebus septies | laudem dixit Domino, et media nocte surgebat ad confitendum ei. Vigilabat, qui[b] elemosinam consuetam, hoc anno per omnia duplicatam, cotidie post 25 missarum et oracionum sacra solempnia propriis manibus pauperibus erogabat; et sic reliqum diei tempus[c] nunc inter clericos et religiosos fratres residens, ea que ad edificacionem erant aure humili audiebat. Vigilabat, qui testamentum suum, ante annum quo ab hac vita decessit, sapientissime fecit, et quod habebat thesauri in manus religiosorum 30 virorum tradens, eorum fidei ad parciendum, sicut ipse dictaverat, commisit. Vigilabat, qui omni die dominica peccata sua confitens Christi corpus percipiebat et sanguinem. Et sic ad vocem sponsi vocantis aures semper attonitas habens, cum solicitudine eius expecta- bat adventum. Denique hiis sacris diebus xl[e] cum pro quadam 35 necessitate domus nostre eius adissem presenciam, inveni fateor in rege monachum, claustrum in curia, in palacio monasterii disciplinam. Certis namque horis divinis vacabat officiis, et psalmis et oracionibus intendebat, certum itidem tempus pauperum obsequiis deputabat. Et ut nichil illi ad vitam honestam deesset, eciam hora convenienti 40 honesto alicui operi, id est herbis plantandis, vel surculis a sua radice excisis alieno trunco inserendis, operam dabat. Hora demum legitima sumpto cibo, cum fratribus religiosis et paucis viris honestioribus religioso quodam ocio mentem paululum relaxabat; sicque sole adhuc stante, cum pro defunctis consuetum officium persolvisset, lucernali 45 hora completa, cum summo silencio castum petebat cubile usque ad solis ortum nulli deinceps locuturus. O felix anima quam veniens Dominus invenit sic vigilantem! Ideo sic parata intravit cum eo ad nupcias! Sed ecce hanc exultacionem spiritus mei consideracio nostre infelicitatis[d] interpolat, et faciem quam fides et pietas Christiana 50 siccaverat, fructus lacrimarum, quas affectus educit, iteratis doloribus rigat. Quid enim facies, Scocia O desolata? Quis consolabitur te? Quis miserebitur tui? Versa est in luctum cithara tua, et organa tua in vocem flencium. Extincta est lucerna tua, cor tuum evanuit, elanguit virtus tua, nitor glorie tue emarcuit. Defecit ille qui illustrabat te, qui de terra 55 inculta et sterili gratam fecit et uberem.

b   S; quia C   d   infidelitatis D
c   S,D; temporis C

judge against himself, he himself was his own executioner. 'For if we were to judge ourselves,' says Paul, 'we would not be judged at all.' Therefore lay down, my soul, and set aside for a short while your sadness, and reflect with joyful mind on how devoutly he spent this last year of his life. In this year turning to God whole-heartedly, fastening his belt, keeping watch with lamps burning, he waited for the coming of the Lord. He kept watch, inasmuch as he took it upon himself to pass no judgment, issue no decree, come to no decision without the advice of men of religion and proven worth. He kept watch inasmuch as he uttered praise to the Lord seven times every day, and he used to rise in the middle of the night to profess his faith in Him. He kept watch inasmuch as he paid out to the poor with his own hands his accustomed alms (doubled in all respects in this year) every day after the sacred solemnities of the masses and prayers; and thus sitting down for the rest of the daytime now surrounded by clerics and brothers of religion, he listened with humble ear to those things that were for his edification. He kept watch inasmuch as he made his will very wisely the year before he departed this life, and handing over all the treasure he had into the hands of men of religion, he entrusted it to their good faith to distribute as he had himself dictated. He kept watch inasmuch as confessing his sins every Sunday he received the body and blood of Christ. And so with his ears always pricked up to hear the voice of the bridegroom calling to him, he anxiously awaited his coming. In short during these holy days of Lent when, because of some need of our house, I approached his presence, I found, I confess, in the king a monk, in the court a cloister, in the palace monastic discipline. For at the set hours he devoted himself to the divine offices, and gave his attention to psalms and prayers, and he allotted a certain time in the same way to his services to the poor. And to complete the picture of the good life he led, at a suitable hour he turned his hand to some honest toil, that is to planting herbs, and taking cuttings from a plant's own root and grafting them on to the stem of some other plant. Finally having taken food at the appropriate hour, he relaxed his mind for a little in a kind of religious leisure along with brothers in religion and a few good men; and so while the sun was still up, when he had completed the accustomed office for the dead, and dusk was over, he made for his chaste bed in utter silence without speaking to anyone thereafter until sunrise. Oh happy soul which the Lord when he came found keeping watch in this way! And so prepared in this way, it went in with him to the marriage. But look, consideration of our unhappiness interrupts this exultation of my spirit, and the face which Christian faith and piety had dried is drenched in the fruitful tears which are produced by my emotion, as my feelings of grief are renewed. For what will you do, Scotland, desolate as you are? Who will console you? Who will take pity on you? Your harp is turned to mourning, and your pipes to the sound of those who weep. Your lamp is extinguished, your heart has grown faint, your courage languishes, the splendour of your glory has faded away. He has gone who cast light on you, who made you, a land uncultivated and barren, pleasant and fruitful.

53

De eodem et quomodo in Scociam politicam induxit

Tu quondam ceterarum mendica terrarum, cespite duro famem incolis ingerebas, nunc ceteris mollior atque fecundior, ex tua habundancia vicinarum regionum inopiam allevabas. Ipse te castellis et urbibus decoravit, ipse excelsis turribus extulit, ipse portus tuos peregrinis mercibus fecundavit, et aliorum regnorum divicias | tuis deliciis 5 aggregavit. Ipse vero preciosis vestibus pallia tua pilosa mutavit, et antiquam nuditatem tuam bisso et purpura texit. Ipse barbaros mores | tuos Christiana religione composuit. Ipse tibi pudiciciam conjugalem, quam ferme nesciebas, indixit, et sacerdotes tuos honestiori vita donavit. Ipse te frequentare ecclesiam et sacrificiis interesse divinis 10 verbo simul et exemplo persuasit; presbyteris debitas oblaciones et decimas solvendas indicavit. Quid ergo retribues ei pro omnibus que tribuit tibi? Habes certe in quibus vicem rependas. Habes quibus pro beneficiis graciam inferas, quibus beneficium, quod ipse meruit, solvas. Habes eum in nepotibus[a] suis, quibus forte non ob aliud tam cito divina 15 providencia avitum subtraxit auxilium, nisi ut tua fides probaretur, et experiretur gracia. Infra annos sunt quidem, sed etas regis fidei militum estimatur. Solvite filiis quod patri debuistis; inveniant vos gratos beneficiis que accepistis.

a   + eum del.C

54

De eodem et quod Anglorum pericula docerent Scotos de cetero fidem regibus et mutuam servare concordiam

Doceant vos preterea Anglorum pericula fidem habere regibus, mutuam inter vos servare concordiam, ne regionem vestram coram vobis alieni devorent, et desoletur terra, sicut in vastitate hostili. Sicut enim in Sacra Scriptura legimus, Joas vii annorum erat cum regnare cepisset in Jerosolim, a pontifice Joiada consensu cleri et populi 5

fo.107

G i,306

53

The same and how he introduced civilised behaviour to Scotland

You who were formerly a beggar among all other countries used to inflict famine on your inhabitants from your harsh soil; now softer and more fertile than the others, you have relieved the poverty of neighbouring regions from your abundance. King David adorned you with castles and cities, he raised you up with lofty towers, he enriched your ports with foreign merchandise, and added the riches of other kingdoms for your delight. He exchanged your rough cloaks for expensive garments, and covered your long-customary nakedness with fine linen and purple cloth. He calmed your savage behaviour by means of the Christian religion. He imposed upon you chastity in marriage of which you were for the most part ignorant, and gave your priests a more honourable way of life. He persuaded you to go regularly to church, and take part in the divine sacrifices both in word and deed; he showed that the due offerings and teinds should be paid to the priests. So what will you give him in return for all that he has given you? You have assuredly the means to repay the debt. You have those to whom you may give thanks for his benefits, those to whom you may repay the kindness which he earned. You have him in the persons of his grandsons, from whom it may be that Divine Providence removed the support of their grandfather so soon for no other reason than that your loyalty might be tested, and your gratitude tried. They are indeed under age, but the age of a king is reckoned according to the loyalty of his knights. Pay to the sons what you owed to the father; let them find you grateful for the benefits which you have received.

54

The same and that the Scots should learn from the misadventures of the English to preserve loyalty to their kings and harmony with each other for the future

Learn moreover from the misadventures of the English to be loyal to your kings, to keep harmony with each other lest foreigners gobble up your region before your eyes, and the land becomes desolate as if devastated by enemies. For just as we read in Holy Scripture, Joash was seven years old when he began to reign in Jerusalem, having been

sublimatus in regem, melius consilio pontificis et procerum in
imbecilliori etate, quam in forciori suo consilio et virtute regnavit.
Sicut omne regnum in se divisum desolatur, ita concordia procerum
regni est stabilimentum. Mortuus quidem est rex, sed sit vobis pro rege
amor quem a vobis meruit; ipse amor dictet vobis leges, ipse 10
concordiam impleat; ipse vos ad fidem pueris et sociis amiciciam
servare compellat. Alioquin testes erunt contra vos celum et terra;
testes angeli qui castitatis illius fuerunt custodes; testes sancti quos fidei
vestre obsides super eorum reliquias jurando dedistis; testis ipse rex,
qui ab illa lucida celi plaga ob graciam puerorum hec terrena 15
prospiciens, singulorum convenit fidem et constanciam. Tu autem,
Domine Rex Sabaoth, qui juste judicas, et probas renes et corda,
memento, Domine, David et omnis mansuetudinis eius. Memento
illius in pueris quos dimisit; quoniam tibi derelicti sunt orphani,
pupillis tu eris adjutor. Et tu, rex dulcissime, convertere in requiem 20
tuam, quia Dominus benefecit tibi, quoniam eripuit animam tuam a
morte, oculos tuos a lacrimis, et pedes tuos a lapsu. Hoc de tua pietate
presumimus, Jhesu bone, a quo illi et recte credere et pie vivere, et
sancte mori donatum est. Nam vitam eius laudabilem, quam fides
Christiana formavit, tua[a] gracia operante, mors preciosa conclusit, ut 25
in sequentibus apparebit.

a   S; cuius C,D

55[a]

G i,307

De eodem et quomodo sui corporis dissolucionem
imminere presenciit

Tactus autem infirmitate qua fuerat carne solvendus, feria iiii[a] id est xiii
kal. junii, cum intellexisset sui corporis dissolucionem imminere,
vocatis familiaribus suis, quod de se ipse senciebat incunctanter
exposuit. At illi, more humano, consolabantur egrotum, vitam illi et
sanitatem penitus promittentes. Sed rex sapientissimus nullam omnino 5
consolacionem de longioris vite promissione suscipiens, ea pocius sibi
et dici et consuli precabatur que hore eius extreme necessitas
postulabat. Et quoniam non imparatus venit in horam hanc, testamen-
tum quod ante annum fecerat renovavit. Quedam eciam que fuerant
corrigenda correxit, et religiosorum consilio que de regni negociis 10
ordinanda videbantur, paucis sermonibus ordinavit. Deinde toto

a   D; liiii C

elevated to the throne by the high priest Jehoiada with the consent of
the clergy and people, and he reigned more successfully when he relied
on the advice of the high priest and nobles while he was young than
when he relied on his own counsel and courage when he was older. Just
as every kingdom divided against itself is brought to desolation, so the
harmony of the nobles is the firm foundation of a kingdom. The king
indeed is dead, but let the love which he merited from you stand for you
in the place of the king; let this love dictate laws to you, let it fulfil itself
in harmony; let it compel you to loyalty towards the young boys, and to
preserve friendship with his allies. Otherwise heaven and earth will be
witnesses against you; the angels who were the guardians of his chastity
will be witnesses; the saints whom you have given as hostages for your
loyalty by swearing on their relics will be witnesses; the king himself
who surveys these earthly scenes from that shining region of heaven
out of love for the young boys, and appeals for the loyalty and
constancy of each individual, will be a witness. Lord, King of Hosts,
you who judge justly, and test minds and hearts, remember, Lord,
David and all his gentleness. Remember him in the young boys whom
he has left behind; since they have been left to you as orphans, you will
be the champion of the fatherless. And you, most sweet king, turn to
your rest, because the Lord has blessed you, since he has snatched your
soul from death, your eyes from tears and your feet from slipping. We
assume this of your pity, good Jesus, who granted to him right belief,
and to live a godly life, and die a holy death. For his praiseworthy life
which was shaped by the Christian faith through the operation of your
grace, reached its end in a precious death, as will appear in what
follows.

55

The same and how he had a premonition that
the dissolution of his body was at hand

At the onset of the illness which was to bring about his release from the
flesh, on Wednesday, that is 20 May, when he realised that the
dissolution of his body was at hand, he called together his household,
and explained without hesitation what he felt about himself. But they
in kindly fashion comforted the invalid, unreservedly promising him
life and health. But the wise king utterly rejected any consolation that
promised prolongation of life, and begged rather that the words and
counsels which the requirements of his final hour demanded should be
given to him. And since he came prepared for this hour, he brought up
to date the will which he had made the year before. He also corrected
some points that had need of correction, and on the advice of men of
religion he arranged in a few conversations what seemed to need
arranging in the affairs of the kingdom. Then turning his thoughts
wholeheartedly to himself, he earnestly commended his departure to

1153:
20 May

corde conversus ad se, exitum suum Domino sedule commendabat. Ac licet omnia membra egritudinis pondere gravarentur, nichilominus tamen more suo tam ad missas quam ad horas canonicas oratorium ingrediebatur. Sed cum feria vi[ta] morbus ingravesceret, et ei standi 15 simul et incedendi facultatem vis langoris adimeret, accersitis clericis virisque religiosis, Dominici corporis sacramentum sibi dari postulavit. Parantibus illis afferre quod jusserat, prohibuit ille, dicens se ante sanctum altare misteria percepturum. Igitur clericorum ac militum manibus in oratorium deportatus, post missarum solempnia, venerandam 20 sibi Crucem quam Nigram vocant, produci sibi peciit adorandam. Est autem crux illa, longitudinem habens palme, de auro purissimo opere | mirabili fabricata, que in modum teche clauditur et aperitur. Cernitur in ea quedam Dominice crucis porcio, sicut sepe multorum miraculorum argumento probatum est, Salvatoris nostri imaginem 25 [habens][b] de ebore decentissime sculptam, et aureis distinccionibus mirabiliter decoratam. Hanc religiosa regina Margarita huius regis mater, que de semine imperatorum et regum Hungariorum[c] et Anglorum extitit oriunda, allatam in Scocia, quasi munus hereditarium transmisit ad filios. Hanc igitur crucem, omni[d] Scotorum genti non 30 minus terribilem quam amabilem, cum rex devotissime adorasset, cum multis lacrimis peccatorum confessione premissa, exitum suum celestium misteriorum percepcione munivit.

fo.107v

b   G; om.S,C   d   S; omnium C
c   -i- interlin.C

56[a]

De eodem et eius unccione

Deinde relatus in thalamum, venientibus sacerdotibus ut sacre unccionis sacramenta complerent, assurrexit ut potuit, ac de lectulo in terram sese deiciens, salutare illud officium cum tanta devocione suscepit, ut clericos paulo festinancius psallentes manu simul ac sermone compesceret, et singulis verbis ipse intenderet, ac singulis 5 oracionibus | responderet. Omnibus igitur rite peractis, cum maxima carnis ac mentis quiete diem expectavit extremum, suos diligenter obtestans, quatenus mox ut ipse discederet, mortem suam omnibus propalarent: 'Quanto cicius', inquit, 'mors mea innotuerit, tanto cicius amicorum meorum beneficiis, aliquid michi consolacionis pietas 10 divina prestabit.' Ita deinceps divinis laudibus intentus, fatiscentes artus spiritui subjugabat, quem tota die illa psalmis et oracionibus exitui preparabat. Die vero sabbati, et pridie quam[b] ab hac vita discederet, cum psalmum centesimum decimum octavum magna

G i,308

a   D; lv C   b   S; qua C

15   the Lord. And although his whole frame was oppressed with the
gravity of his disease, he nevertheless went into the chapel both for
masses and for the canonical hours according to his usual practice. But
when his illness became worse on the Friday, and his ability both to   22 May
20   stand and to walk was taken from him by the force of his exhaustion, he
summoned the clerics and men of religion, and asked that the
Sacrament of the Lord's Body be given to him. As they prepared to
bring what he had ordered, he forbade them, saying that he would
receive the mysteries before the holy altar. So he was carried into the
chapel by the hands of clerics and knights, and after the solemnities of
25   the Masses, he asked that the Cross, which is called the 'Black Cross',
which he revered should be brought to him for his adoration. It is that
cross a palm's breadth in length, wrought from the purest gold by
marvellous craftmanship, which can be shut and opened like a
cupboard. There is to be seen in it a fragment of the Lord's Cross, as
30   has often been proved by the evidence of many miracles, and it has in it
the likeness of our Saviour beautifully carved from ivory, and
marvellously decorated with golden adornments. It was brought to
Scotland by the devout Queen Margaret the mother of this king, who
was descended from the seed of emperors and kings of the Hungarians
35   and the English, and handed down by her to her sons as a family
heirloom. So when the king had devoutly adored this cross, equally
feared and loved by the people of the Scots as it was, he first of all made
confession of his sins with many tears, and fortified his departure by
receiving the divine mysteries.

56

The same and his unction

Then he was carried back to his bedroom, and as the priests came to
perform the sacrament of Holy Unction, he raised himself as best he
could, threw himself from his bed to the floor, and received that
salutary rite with such devotion that he checked the clerics both by
5   gesture and speech as they were reciting the Psalms a little too quickly,
and he himself missed not a single word, and gave the response to each
petition. So when everything had been duly performed, he awaited his
last day with the greatest peace of flesh and mind, carefully imploring
his people to make his death public as soon as he departed. 'The
10   sooner', he said, 'my death is known, the sooner will the divine pity
afford me some comfort through the good offices of my friends.' So
thereafter concentrating on praises of God, he subdued his failing
limbs to his spirit, which he prepared for death that whole day with
psalms and prayers. On Saturday, the day before he would depart this   1153:
15   life, when he was reflecting upon Psalm 118 with great contrition of   23 May
heart, and had come to the chapter of this psalm, which is sixteenth in
order of singing, groaning more deeply and grasping the force of the

cordis contricione revolveret, et ad decimum sextum^c huius psalmi 15
capitulum^d psallendi ordine perveniret, alcius ingemiscens et vim
verborum illorum spiritu profundiore concipiens, idem capitulum
septies repetivit, intimo affectu proclamans: 'Feci judicium et justiciam, non tradas me calumpniantibus me.' Sensit enim, ni fallor,
Spiritu docente, quid calumpniatori calcaneo nostro, id est fini, arccius 20
insistenti securius responderet, quas Judici preces pro sui defensione
porrigeret, et ait: 'Feci judicium' c'. Lenit quippe districti Judicis
sentenciam, qui contra se judicis fungitur officio, securusque post
mortem divinum expectat judicium, qui ante mortem in veritate facit
judicium. Unde cum devocione proclamat: 'Feci judicium', venit ad 25
Salvatorem nostrum calumpniator antiqus, sed in eo qui peccatum non
fecit nichil suum inveniens, confusus discessit. Quid igitur? Clamet
certe ad eum in quo nichil inveniet, et dicat: 'Feci judicium.' Est quippe
judicium cordis, est et judicium oris, et est judicium operis. Fecit corde
judicium rex Christianissimus, cum pro delictis suis interius compun- 30
geretur; fecit ore, cum adversum se peccata confiteretur; fecit et opere,
cum voluntaria afflixione puniretur. Fecit igitur judicium se accu-
sando; fecit justiciam aliorum miseriis miserendo.

c   decimum sextum S; nonum *written in a*   *written normally* D
    larger space formerly left blank C nonum   d   S; versiculum C,D

57^a

De eodem et quod in vite confinio reminiscebatur pauperum

Quid enim justius quam ut is, qui sibi postulat misereri, misericordiam
prestet egenti? Quam vero miserendo prestandoque pauperibus vir iste
profusus hac ipsa die satis innotuit, in qua cum omnem mundi
sollicitudinem, regni curam, filiorum insuper a suo pectore exclusisset
affectum, eam tamen quam circa pauperes habere consueverat curam 5
in tanta^b necessitate non deposuit. Inter psallendum quippe respiciens
Nicholaum clericum suum, quem in custodiendis thesauris suis
largiendisque elemosinis fidelissimum fuerat expertus, extenso brachio, cum eum ita ut lectulo accubabat complexus fuisset, quesivit
utrum elemosina quam ipse singulis diebus propriis consueverat 10
manibus erogare in Christi pauperes, ea die fuisset expensa. Cumque

fo.108   ille more solito omnia completa dixisset, gracias agens | Deo, psalmum
quem intermiserat repetivit. Quoniam igitur et judicium fecit pro
delictis suis semet puniendo, justiciam aliis miserendo, cum fiducia in
spe divine misericordie proclamat: 'Feci judicium et justiciam, non 15
tradas me calumpniantibus me.' Et cum huic principio reliqui ipsius |

G i,309   capituli versus conveniunt, in hiis nimirum libencius suaviusque

a   D; lvi C   b   D; tante C

words with greater profundity of spirit, he repeated the same chapter
seven times, proclaiming with the deepest emotion: 'I have exercised
judgment and justice; leave me not to my false accusers.' For he
realised, if I am not mistaken, through the prompting of the Holy Spirit
what he could reply more confidently to the false accuser treading on
our heels, that is death, as it pressed more closely, and what pleas he
could offer to the Judge in his own defence, and he said: 'I have
exercised judgment' etc. He indeed who performs the office of judge
against himself softens the sentence of the severe Judge, and he who
before his death exercises judgment according to the truth, after death
awaits confidently the divine judgment. Therefore he proclaims with
devotion: 'I exercised judgment'. The ancient adversary came to our
Saviour, but finding nothing of his own in him who committed no sin,
he departed in confusion. What then? Certainly let him in whom he will
find nothing shout out to him and say: 'I exercised judgment.' There is
indeed the judgment of the heart, there is the judgment of the mouth,
and there is the judgment of action. The most Christian king exercised
judgment in his heart when he felt deep remorse for his sins; he
exercised judgment with his lips when he confessed sins against himself;
he exercised it also in action when he was punished by voluntary
affliction. So he did judgment by blaming himself; he did justice by
taking pity on the misfortunes of others.

57

The same and the fact that he remembered the poor at the ending of his life

For what could be more just than that he, who asks for mercy for
himself, should show mercy to the needy? It is well known that that
man, lavish as he was in showing mercy and giving to the poor, on this
very day on which, having shut out from his heart all worldly anxiety,
the administration of the kingdom, as well as his affection for his sons,
in such an extremity however did not lay aside the concern which he
had always felt for the poor. While he was reciting the Psalms, he
looked up at Nicholas his clerk, whom he had found very trustworthy
in guarding his treasuries and bestowing his alms, and stretching out
his arm he embraced him, as he lay in bed, and asked whether the alms
which he himself had been accustomed to give each day with his own
hands to the poor of Christ, had been paid on that day. When the clerk
had said that everything had been accomplished in the usual way, he
gave thanks to God, and went back to the Psalm which he had
interrupted. So since he exercised judgment by punishing himself for
his sins, and justice by having mercy on others, he proclaims with
confidence in the expectation of divine mercy: 'I exercised judgment
and justice, do not hand me over to those who falsely accuse me.' And
since the remaining verses of the chapter are consistent with this
beginning, he predictably lingered over them with pleasure and delight.

morabatur. Cum igitur ad centesimum decimum nonum psalmum
perveniret, in isto quoque nescio quid suave vel salubre persenciens, et
ipsum, ut priorem, septies repetivit. Recolens forte quid tribulacionis   20
in peccatorum suorum recordacione fuerat paulo ante perpessus,ᶜ quid
consolacionis cum judicium justiciamque quam fecerat mente revolveret, in spe misericordie Christi fuerat expertus, cum magna
devocione proclamat: 'Ad Dominum cum tribularer clamavi, et
exaudivit me.' Sed ne iterum hastutus ille calumpniator adversus eum   25
fraudis commenta construeret, addidit quod in eodem psalmo conjun-
gitur. 'Domine, libera animam meam a labiis iniquis, et a lingua
dolosa.' Sed quid dabitur tibi, O anima Christiana, aut quid apponetur
tibi adversus linguam dolosam? Quid nisi 'sagitte potentis acute cum
carbonibus desolatoriis'. Clama ergo: 'Apprehende,ᵈ Domine, arma et   30
scutum et exurge in adjutorium michi.'

c   D; perpensus S,C   d   -hen- in margin C

58ᵃ

De eodem et continuis oracionibus

Retorquet ipse Deus in hostem sagittas acutas, lanceam simul et clavos
quibus in cruce confixus; et quasi sagittis acutis vulneribus quinque
confossus, vulnera nostra, que quinque sensuum delectacione nobis
hostis inflixerat, gratuita bonitate curavit. Quid igitur michi obiciet
versuti serpentis lingua dolosa, cum is qui peccatum non fecit peccati   5
penam pro me sustinuit, vulneratus propter iniquitates nostras,
attritus propter scelera nostra? Si itaque sagittis acutis, id est fidei tue
Passionis, Jhesu bone, addantur carbones, id est ignis tue dileccionis, et
hostis calumpnians cito repellitur, et peccati rubigo cito consumitur.
Sepe deinde alacriori virtute ad superiora respirans, et ob contempla-   10
cionem celestium hec terrena fastidiens, sequitur et dicit: 'Heu michi!
quia incolatus meus prolongatus est; habitavi cum habitantibus Cedar;
multum incola fuit anima mea.' Sed et hoc, quod sequitur, ei satis
arbitror convenire: 'Cum hiis qui oderunt pacem, eram pacificus; cum
loquebar illis, impugnabant me gratis.' Qui proditoribus suis tociens   15
pepercit, qui sepe hiis qui alios tradicionis sue convincere duelli
certamine spondebant audienciam denegavit. Nam cum ei familiares
dicerent: 'Si dimiseris^b istos sic, alii contra te simile scelus securius
attemptabunt', respondebat vitam suam non in hominis voluntate, sed
in Dei pocius consistere potestate. Unde sepe retribuebant ei mala pro   20
bonis, et cum ipse eis ea que pacis erant provideret,ᶜ ipsi eum et gratis
debellabant. Quod autem hos versus septies iteravit, quem numerum
legimus Spiritu Sancto consecratum, manifeste datur intelligi ipsum
Christi spiritum fuisse presentem, qui ei ipsorum versuum infusit
affectum, et animam fatiscentem sua virtute confovit. Cum igitur ab   25

a   D; lvii C   c   corrected from providebant C
b   corrected from dimiseros C

So when he came to Psalm 119, he went over it seven times as in the case of the previous psalm, perceiving in it also something delightful and beneficial. Happening to recall what anguish he had endured a short while before in remembering his sins, and what comfort he had found in the expectation of the mercy of Christ, when he pondered in his mind the judgment and justice that he had exercised, he proclaimed with great devotion: 'I called to the Lord in my distress, and he heard me.' But lest that cunning accuser might once again devise fraudulent lies against him, he added what follows in the same Psalm. 'Lord, save me from wicked lips and from a deceitful tongue.' But what will be given to you, Christian soul, or what will be provided for you against the deceitful tongue? Nothing less than 'sharp arrows of the mighty along with coals of desolation'. Shout therefore: 'Grasp shield and buckler, Lord, and rise up to help me.'

58

The same and his constant prayers

God himself sends his sharp arrows against the Enemy, the spear and the nails by which He was fastened on the cross; and pierced with five wounds as if by sharp arrows, by his freely-given goodness He has healed our wounds, which the Enemy had inflicted on us through our delight in the five senses. What then will the deceitful tongue of the cunning serpent taunt me with, when He who committed no sin endured the punishment for sin on my behalf, wounded because of our transgressions, bruised because of our evil deeds? Accordingly if hot coals, that is the fire of your love, were to be added to the sharp arrows, that is faith in your passion, good Jesus, both the Enemy that falsely accuses is quickly repelled, and the blight of sin is destroyed. Then often aspiring to higher things with keener virtue, and despising these earthly concerns as he contemplated the divine, he continues and says: 'Alas for me, that my stay has been prolonged; I have dwelt with the inhabitants of Kedar; my soul was long a dweller there.' But this which follows – 'With those whom hate peace, I was a peacemaker; when I spoke to them, they made war on me without a cause' – is also I think appropriate to him, who so often spared those who betrayed him, who often denied audience to those who promised to convict others of treason against himself through trial by combat. For when those close to him said to him: 'If you let these men go free in this way, others will with more confidence attempt a similar crime against you', he replied that his life did not depend on the will of man but rather on the power of God. Therefore they often repaid his kindness with evil; and when he himself bestowed on them those things that belong to peace, they gratuitously made war upon him. The fact that he repeated these verses seven times (the number seven, we read, is consecrated to the Holy Spirit) is clearly intended as proof that the actual spirit of Christ was

hiis qui aderant rogaretur, ut a labore psallendi spiritum paululum relaxaret: 'Sinite me', inquit, 'ea que Dei sunt pocius meditari, ut spiritus, ab hoc exilio profecturus ad patriam, verbi Dei viatico recreetur. Cum enim tremendo Dei judicio presentatus astitero, nullus | vestrum respondebit pro me, nullus vestrum me tuebitur, nec est 30 aliquis qui me de manu sua possit eruere.' In hac ei devocione dies clauditur, cui sequentem in magna tranqillitate continuavit et noctem.

G i,310

59[a]

De eodem et exitu anime

Die autem dominica que Christi Ascensionem precedebat, id est nono kal. junii illucescente, cum sol noctis tenebras radiis sue lucis abigeret, ipse a corporalibus tenebris e- | mergens, ad vere lucis gaudia commigravit, cum tanta tranquillitate, ut videretur non obisse, tanta eciam devocione, ut inventus sit utrasque manus junctas simul supra 5 pectus suum versus celum erexisse. Subvenite sancti Dei, occurrite angeli Domini, suscipientes animam[b] vestro dignam consorcio; et collocate eam in sinu Abrahe cum Lazaro, quem non despexit sed fovit; cum sanctis apostolis et martyribus, quorum memorias extruxit et coluit; cum Christi sacerdotibus et confessoribus, quos in suis 10 successoribus et basilicis veneratus est; cum sanctis virginibus, quarum pudiciam imitatus est; cum mundi contemptoribus, quos sibi de[c] mamona iniquitatis amicos constituit, quibus se pro Christi nomine cum omni humilitate substravit. Assit ei illa Misericordie Mater, que, quanto est ceteris potencior, tanto sit ei ipsius pietas efficacior. Ego 15 autem, licet peccator et indignus, memor tamen beneficiorum tuorum, dulcissime domine et amice, que michi ab ineunte etate mea impendisti, memor gracie in qua me nunc ultimo suscepisti, memor benevolencie qua me in omnibus peticionibus meis exaudisti, memor munificencie quam michi exhibuisti, memor amplexuum et osculorum in quibus me 20 non sine[d] lacrimis, omnibus qui aderant ammirantibus, dimisisti, libo pro te lacrimas meas, resolvo affectum meum, et totum refundo spiritum meum. Hoc pro te sacrificium offero, hanc beneficiis tuis vicissitudinem impendo, et quia hoc minimum est, ibi mens mea ex intimis medullis tui semper recordabitur, ubi pro omnium salute Patri 25 cotidie Filius immolatur.

    Explicit Lamentacio.

fo.108v

---

a   D; lviii C   c   interlin.C
b   + vestram del.C   d   S; om.C,D

30   there present, and it poured into him love for these verses, and nurtured
his fainting soul with its power. When therefore those who were present
begged him to rest his spirit for a short while from the exertion of
reciting the Psalms, he said: 'Rather allow me to ponder those things
which are of God in order that my spirit which is about to set out on its
journey from exile here to its own country may be refreshed by the
35   provision of the word of God. For when I am brought before God's
judgment, and stand trembling, none of you will reply for me, none of
you will protect me, nor is there anyone who could snatch me out of his
hand.' The day ended for him in this devotion, and the night which
followed he also spent in great tranquillity.

59

The same and the departure of his soul

As it grew light on the Sunday which preceded the Ascension of Christ,   1153:
that is 24 May, when the sun was driving away with the rays of its light   24 May
the darkness of night, the king emerged from physical darkness, and
passed over to the joys of true light with such great tranquillity that he
5   seemed not to have died, with so much devotion also that he was
discovered to have simultaneously raised both hands, which were
clasped together, above his breast towards Heaven. Come to his aid,
saints of God; run to meet him, angels of the Lord, receiving a soul
worthy of association with you; and place it in Abraham's bosom
10   along with Lazarus, whom he did not despise, but cherished; along
with the holy apostles and martyrs, monuments to whom he built and
revered; along with priests and confessors of Christ whom he venerated
in their successors and churches; along with the holy virgins whose
chastity he emulated; along with those who despised the world, whom
15   he set up as friends for himself by means of the mammon of
unrighteousness, to whom he made himself subservient in all humility
for the sake of the name of Christ. May the Mother of Mercy be at his
side, whose pity for him will be all the more effective, in proportion as
she is more powerful than all the rest.
20   I indeed although a sinner and unworthy, yet mindful of your
kindnesses, most sweet lord and friend, which you bestowed upon me
from my earliest years, mindful of the graciousness with which you
received me now for the last time, mindful of the courtesy with which
you listened to me in all my requests, mindful of the generosity which
25   you showed to me, mindful of the embraces and kisses with which you
sent me away in tears to the amazement of all who were present, I offer
a libation of my tears for you, I give free rein to my affection, and pour
out my whole spirit. I offer this sacrifice for you, in this way I repay
your kindnesses, and because this is very little, my mind will remember
30   you always in its innermost depths there where the Son is daily
sacrificed to the Father for the salvation of all.
The end of the Lamentation.

60[a]

De sua genealogia ex parte patris
ab eo deducta usque Japhet

Huius gloriosi regis David genealogiam ex parte patris, quam a
domino cardinale Scocie et legato, nobili doctore Galtero de
Wardlaw Glasguensi episcopo, dudum acceperam, hiis indere scriptis
puto conveniens, ut vobis, O reges moderni, cunctisque pateat
legentibus, de quam veteri, quam nobili, quamque forti processerit et 5
invicta stirpe regum, de qua vos ita processistis, qui pre ceteris
regibus, Altissimo Rege benedicti[b] (paucis dumtaxat, si qui sint,
exceptis) regiam | dignitatem tempore diucius, servitute liberius, et
(quod gloriosius est) fide catholica tenacius, expulsis a regno alienis
ipsum invadentibus, actenus observabant. | De quibus Scotis regibus 10
verificatur quod scriptum est:

G i,311

Scriptor

> Post Britones, Dacos, Pictos, Anglosque repulsos
> viriliter, Scoti jus tenuere suum.
> ⟨Et Romanorum spreverunt vim validorum.
> Exemplo quorum pensate preteritorum,   15
> inclita Scotorum proles, laudem genitorum.⟩

Autor   Erat enim ipse benedictus rex David filius Malcolmi nobilissimi
Scotorum regis, viri beate Margarite regine, filii Duncani filii Beatricis
filie Malcolmi victoriosissimi filii [Kenethi filii Malcolmi filii Dove-
naldi filii Constantini filii][c] Kenedi primi monarche, a quo quidem 20
linia regalis, ut patet supra nono capitulo libri iiii[ti], deducitur usque
regem strenuissimum Fergusium filium Erch, qui regnum per
Romanos et Pictos invasum et annis xliii detentum, ab eis nobiliter
eripuit. Et ille quidem Erch filius fuit Euchadii fratris Eugenii regis, a
Romanis et Pictis occisi, filii Angusafith filii Fethelmeth filii Angusa 25
filii Fethelmeth Romach filii Fencormach filii Crutliuch filii Findach
filii Akirkirre filii Echadii filii Fechrach filii Euchodii Ried filii Conere
filii Mogal filii Lugtach filii Corbre filii Dardremore filie Corbre
Finmore filii Coneremore filii Etherskeol filii Ewin filii Ellela filii Jair
filii Dethath filii Syn[d] filii Rosin filii Ther filii Rether filii Rwen filii 30
Arindel filii Manee filii Fergusii, qui Scotos ex Hibernia ducens
primus super eos regnavit in Scocia Britannica, cuius linie regalis

a   D; lix C   c   S; om.C
b   benedicto S,C,D   d   S; Fyn C

60

His genealogy on his father's side traced right back from him to Japheth

I consider it appropriate to include in these writings the genealogy on his father's side of this glorious King David, which I was given long ago by the lord cardinal of Scotland and legate, the noble doctor Walter de Wardlaw, bishop of Glasgow, so that it may be clear to you,
5   kings of the present day, and to all who read it, from what an ancient, what a noble, what a valiant and invincible line of kings he was descended, from which you also are descended, you who with the blessing of the Highest King (with only a few exceptions, if any) have beyond all other kings preserved the royal dignity up to now longer in
10 time, more freely in service, and, what is more glorious, more tenaciously in the catholic faith, after foreign invaders were driven out of the kingdom. This is shown to be true of these Scottish kings because it is written:

       After the Britons, Danes, Picts and English were driven back
15   manfully, the Scots were under their own jurisdiction.
       And they scorned the force of the mighty Romans.
       From the example of these deeds ponder the renown
       of your fathers of old, famous offspring of the Scots.

       For blessed King David was himself the son of Malcolm the most
20 noble king of Scots, husband of blessed Queen Margaret, the son of Duncan son of Beatrice daughter of Malcolm the most victorious son of Kenneth son of Malcolm son of Donald son of Constantine son of Kenneth the first monarch, from whom the royal line, as appears above in Book IV, Chapter 9, is traced right back to the most forceful
25 King Fergus son of Erc, who nobly wrested from the Romans and the Picts the kingdom which had been usurped by them, and held for forty-three years. And that Erc was indeed the son of Echadius brother of King Eochaid, who was killed by the Romans and Picts, son of Ōengus Fir son of Fedelmid son of Ōengus son of Fedelmid
30 Romach son of Cormac the Old son of Croithluithe son of Find Fēicce son of Acher Cerr son of Eochaid son of Fiachra son of Cairpre Rigfota son of Conaire son of Mug-lāma son of Lugaid son of Cairpre son of Dāire Dornmār son of Cairpre Findmōr son of Conaire Mōr son of Etarscēl son of Ēogan son of Ailill son of Iar son

series extenditur, ut in libri primi xxviii° capitulo superius patet,
usque ad | Simonem Brek, qui tronum regale lapideum secum ex
Hispania transtulit Hiberniam. Iste Simon Brek filius fuit Fonduf 35
filii*e* Etheon filii Glachus filii Nothachus filii Elchata filii Syrne filii
Deyn filii Demal filii Rothsaitha. Hic primus inhabitavit insulas
Scocie. Ipse fuit filius Ogmayn filii Anegus filii Fiathach filii Smyrnai
filii Synrecha filii Embacha filii Thyerna filii Faleg filii Etheor filii Jair
filii Fermon filii Micelii Espayn filii Bile filii Neande filii Bregan filii 40
Bratha filii Deatha filii Erchata filii Aldoth filii Node filii Nonael filii
Iber Scot filii regis Gaythelos et Scote, primi regis et regine gentis
Scotorum. Unde quidam:

> Illis Iber genitus primus cognomine Scotus.
> A muliere Scota vocitatur Scocia tota.   45

Iste Gaithelos fuit filius Neolos Athenar*f* filii Fenyas filii Ewan filii
Glonyn filii Lamy filii Etheor filii Athnemane filii Thoe filii Boyb filii
Reyn filii Mayr filii Ethech filii Abyur filii Arthech filii Aorth filii Jara
filii Esraw filii Rithaith filii Scot filii Gomer filii Japheth filii Noe.

---

e   changed to filius *C*; filii *D*   *f*   regis Athenarum for Athenar *S*

De prologo genealogie ex parte matris

'Quoniam', ut scribit Baldredus, 'de optimis moribus religiosi regis
Scotorum David pauca quedam lamentando descripsimus, dignum
duxi genealogiam eius ex parte matris breviter veraciterque subtexere,
ut cum videritis in quo vobis et sui successores quanta fuerit
antecessorum vestrorum eiusdem linie probitas, qualis in eis virtus 5
enituerit, qualis splenduerit pietas, agnoscatis eciam quam naturale
vobis sit habundare diviciis, florere virtutibus, victoriis illustrari, et
quod hiis omnibus prestat, religione Christiana et justicie prerogativa
fulgere. Est enim ad optimos mores optinendos maximum incenti-
vum, scire se ab optimis quibusque nobilitatem meruisse sanguinis, 10
cum ingenuum animum semper pudeat in gloriosa progenie inveniri
degenerem, et contra sit naturam de bona radice fructus malos
pullulare. Sicut enim veracissimis et antiquissimis hystoriis vel cronicis

---

a   *D*; lx *C*

35 of Dedad son of Sen son of Rosen son of Tríar son of Rothríar son of
Rogen son of Airndel son of Maine son of Fergus, who first led the
Scots from Ireland and ruled over them in Britannic Scotia, the
sequence of whose royal lineage extends as far as Simon Brecc, who
brought the royal stone throne with him across from Spain to Ireland,
40 as appears above in Book I, Chapter 28. That Simon Brecc was the
son of Ēn Dub son of Aedān Glas son of Nuadu son of Giallchad son
of Sīrnae son of Dēn son of Demal son of Rothechtaid. He was the
first to colonise the islands of Scotia. He himself was the son of Mōen
son of Ōengus son of Fiachu son of Smirgoll son of Smreth son of
45 Senboth son of Tigernmas son of Follach son of Ethrēl son of Iarēl
son of Hermonius son of Micelius Espayn son of Bile son of Reande
son of Bregan son of Brāth son of Deāith son of Aircid son of Aldōit
son of Nuadu son of Nōnael son of Hiber Scot son of King Gaythelos
and Scota, the first king and queen of Scots. As in the following verse:

50   Their son Hiber was the first to bear the name of Scot.
    The whole of Scotland is called after the woman Scota.

That Gaythelos was the son of Neolus [king] of Athens son of Fenius
son of Eogan son of Glūnfind son of Lāmfind son of Fethēr son of
Agnoman son of Tōe son of Banb son of Sēim son of Mār son of
55 Aurtecht son of Aboth son of Aoy son of Āra son of Iara son of Esrū
son of Rifad Scot son of Gomer son of Japheth son of Noah.

61

The prologue to his genealogy on his mother's side

'Since', as Ailred writes, 'we have in our lamentation described a few
details concerning the excellent character of David the pious king of
Scots, I considered it right to append briefly and accurately his
genealogy on his mother's side, so that when you have seen how great
5 has been the prowess of your ancestors in that line, what valour shone
forth in them, what dazzling goodness, you would recognise also how
natural it is for you to abound in riches, to flourish in virtues, to be
renowned for victories, and, what is better than all these, to shine with
Christian piety and the privilege of exercising justice. For it is a very
10 great incentive for preserving high moral character to know that one
has earned nobility of blood from all the best people, since a noble
mind is always ashamed to be found to be degenerate in a glorious
family, and since it is against nature for evil fruit to be produced from
good stock. For just as I have been able to find it in the most reliable
15 and ancient histories or chronicles, I shall briefly trace his ancestry,
beginning from King David himself, most illustrious of men, through

reperire potui, ab ipso rege David, virorum clarissimo, exordium
sumens, et per gloriosissimam matrem suam,' cum de patris 15
genealogia scribatur superius, ascendens breviter ad ipsum Adam
cunctorum patrem mortalium, liniam vestre[b] cognacionis Anglice
vobis ostendam, ut postmodum, omissis antiquissimis, quorum
historias vetustas ipsa delevit, per excellenciores Anglie reges, eorum
sublimiora gesta summatim tangendo, redeamus, ut cum videritis 20
tantam eorum gloriam morte ac vetustate perisse, eosque pro vite
meritis celeste premium, quod perire non poterit, meruisse, discatis
semper diviciis glorieque mundiali preferre justiciam, ut post vitam
temporalem perveniatis ad eternam.

b   nostre *S,C,D*

62[a]

De eadem genealogia ex parte matris secundum Baldredum

'Idem igitur excellentissimus rex David filius fuit gloriose regine
Scotorum Margarite, que nominis sui splendorem morum sanctitate
preferebat. Huius pater Eadwardus, qui fuit filius Eadmundi Irneside
regis invictissimi, cuius pater Ethelredus, cuius pater Eadgarus
pacificus, cuius pater Eadmundus, cuius pater Eadwardus senior, 5
cuius pater nobilis Alfredus, qui fuit filius Ethelwlfi regis, qui fuit
filius Egbrichty, cuius pater Alcherimundus, cuius pater Eaffa, cuius
pater Aeppa, cuius pater Ingels, cuius frater famosissimus rex Ine
nomine, quorum pater Ceonred, qui fuit filius Ceowold, qui fuit
Cutha, qui fuit Cuthwyne, qui fuit Ceauline, qui fuit Chinrik, qui fuit 10
Creodda, qui fuit Ceordik. Iste, transactis xlvi annis post primum
adventum Saxonum in Britannia, regnum in Westsax optinuit, cuius
successores processu temporis Anglorum cetera regna conquesierunt.
Ceordik fuit filius Elasa, qui fuit Eda, qui fuit Gewise, cuius pater
Wig, cuius pater Freawine, cuius pater[b] Freodegare, cuius pater[b] 15
Brand, cuius pater[b] Baldeger, cuius pater Woden, apud quosdam
Mercurius dictus est. Hic tante fuit auctoritatis apud suos, ut quartam
feriam suo nomine[c] dedicantes, diem Woden vocabant. Que consuetudo per Anglos eciam hodie servatur. Vocant enim eundem diem
Wodinsday. Gentiles vero Romani ipsum diem "diem Mercurii" 20
appellabant.' Ista vero Baldredi genealogia ab ea quam Willelmus
suis inscripsit cronicis quodammodo, sed parum, discrepat. Ideo cum

a   *D*; lxi *C*   c   +consecrantes *del.C*
b   cuius pater *S*; qui fuit *C,D*

his glorious mother back to Adam himself father of all mortals,
showing you the lineage of your English kinship,' since an account of
his father's genealogy is given above. Thus with the omission of the
20 most ancient [kings] whose histories have been destroyed by sheer
length of time, we may soon return by way of the more excellent kings
of England, touching briefly on their more glorious deeds, so that
when you see that their great glory has been lost through death and
lapse of time, whereas they have won their heavenly reward which
25 cannot perish in return for their good deeds during their life, you may
learn always to prefer justice to riches and worldly glory, so that after
this temporal life you may attain life everlasting.

62

The same genealogy on his mother's side according to Ailred

'So the most excellent King David was the son of the glorious
Margaret queen of Scots, whose saintliness of character outshone the
splendour of her name. Her father was Edward, who was the son of
the most invincible Edmund Ironside, whose father was Æthelred,
5 whose father was Edgar the Peaceful, whose father was Edmund,
whose father was Edward the Elder, whose father was the noble
Alfred, who was the son of King Æthelwulf, who was the son of
Ecgberht, whose father was Ealhmund, whose father was Eafa, whose
father was Eoppa, whose father was Ingild, whose brother was the
10 renowned king called Ine, whose father was Cenred, who was the son
of Ceolwald, who was the son of Cutha, who was the son of Cuthwine,
who was the son of Ceawlin, who was the son of Cynric, who was the
son of Creoda, who was the son of Cerdic. He obtained the kingdom
in Wessex forty-six years after the first arrival of the Saxons in Britain.
15 His successors in the course of time conquered all the other kingdoms
of the Angles. Cerdic was the son of Elesa, who was the son of Esla,
who was the son of Giwis, whose father was Wig, whose father was
Freawine, whose father was Frithogar, whose father was Brond,
whose father was Bældæg, whose father Woden was called Mercury
20 by some people. He was of such great standing with his own people
that they consecrated the fourth day of the week with his name,
calling it Woden's day. This custom is preserved by the English even
at the present day. For they call the same day *Wednesday*. The pagan
Romans indeed used to call the day "day of Mercury".' This
25 genealogy of Ailred differs to a certain extent but not greatly from the
one which William [of Malmesbury] inserted in his chronicles.

hec scripta superius ad propositum sufficere poterint, ulterius eam
prosequi pretermitto. Nam istius generacionis nullos preter istorum
legebam libros; si vero tercium vidissem, concordantes binos, omisso 25
discrepante, sequi finaliter voluissem.

Therefore since the account given above could suffice for my purpose, I decline to pursue the matter any further. For the only books that I have read concerning this genealogy were those of Ailred and William 30 [of Malmesbury]. If I had indeed seen a third, I should have wished in the end to follow the two that agreed with each other, leaving out the one which differed.

Notes

Chapter 1
pp.3-5

This chapter corresponds to *Fordun* (V c.1). See *Pluscarden*, V, c.1, and *Extracta*, 57-58. It continues the saga of Macbeth begun above IV c.49, l.57; see above IV c.51, l.1n. Fordun, it should be noted, concentrates attention on the figures of Macduff and Malcolm and ignores, or is unaware of, many of the details found in later and more familiar versions of the story – (a) the three witches; (b) the part played by Lady Macbeth; (c) the murder by Macbeth of the elderly Duncan, his guest; (d) the part played by Banquo and his son Fleance (supposed ancestors of the royal Stewarts); (e) the incident – the failure of a yoke of oxen provided by Macduff for work at the building of Macbeth's new castle at Dunsinane (modern Dunsinnan, between Perth and Coupar Angus PER) – which is the immediate occasion of Macbeth's hostility to Macduff and causes the flight of the latter to England; (f) the subsequent murder by Macbeth of Macduff's wife and children; (g) the prophecies that Birnam Wood (near Dunkeld PER) would come to Dunsinnan and that none born of woman would slay Macbeth; (h) the death at Dunsinnan of Macbeth at the hands of Macduff. As for (b), Gruoch, the historic original of Lady Macbeth, herself belonged to the royal line; she was grand-daughter either of Kenneth II or Kenneth III, and was married, first to Macbeth's cousin, Gillacomgain, by whom she had a son, Lulach, later briefly king, and second to Macbeth (*ES*, i, 580). In *Wyntoun* (iv, 274-5) she is the wife first of Duncan then of Macbeth, but plays no real part in the story. In the *Scottorum Historiae* (1527) of Hector Boece (R.W. Chambers, E.C. Batho and H.W. Husbands, *The Chronicles of Scotland Compiled by Hector Boece Translated into Scots by John Bellenden 1531*, 2 vols. [STS, 1938-41], ii, 151) she appears as Macbeth's unnamed wife who urges him to the murder of Duncan. (d) and (f) are also first found in *Scottorum Historiae* (ut cit., ii, 154-6; 157, 162). In *Wyntoun* (iv, 298-301) the apparent march of Birnam Wood fulfils one part of the prophecy (g) and causes Macbeth to abandon Dunsinnan and flee northwards where at Lumphanan ABD the second part is fulfilled when he is killed by an unnamed knight whose birth had been by caesarean section. The more familiar version, additionally involving (h), appears in *Scottorum Historiae* (ut cit., 161-2). (a) and (e) first appear in *Wyntoun* (iv, 272-301). It should perhaps be noted that (e) appears to be presupposed, but not directly expressed, in Macbeth's threat (above IV c.54, ll.11-12) to crush Macduff's neck under the yoke like an ox's in a waggon. Macduff reacts by his flight to England. In Boece (ii, 156-7) the building of Dunsinnan, without any specified incident, leads to the flight of Macduff. (c) is contributed by Shakespeare. In most other sources Duncan is a young man killed in some kind of direct encounter with Macbeth. Only in *Berchan's Prophecy* (*ES*, i, 582) is he described as old. He is not (*pace* B.T. Hudson, *Kings of Celtic Scotland* [Westport, Connecticut and London, 1994], 123) so described in the Verse Chronicle (*Cronicon Elegiacum*; see above Vol.2, xx-xxi).

In the light of this evidence, it seems probable that before Fordun the story of Macbeth, Macduff and Malcolm existed in a form which had already developed well away from historical reality, insofar as the latter is ascertainable. A number of points may now be taken as reasonably established. Macbeth was one of the kings mentioned (*ASC* (Plummer), 159 [MS E], s.a. 1031; *ASC*, 101) as accompanying Malcolm II to meet the English King Cnut. He was then probably king of *cenél Loairn* in succession to his cousin Malcolm son of Maelbrigte who died in 1029 (*ES*, i, 571, s.a. 1029; cf. Hudson, *Kings*, 135-6). In 1040 after defeating and killing Duncan I Macbeth succeeded to the Scottish throne. The land was prosperous during his seventeen-year reign. He and his wife were generous benefactors of St Andrews and St Serf's at Loch Leven. He suppressed (1045) a rebellion by Crinan, father of Duncan I (above IV c.43, ll.12, 13). The supposed defeat in 1046 at the hands of Siward earl of Northumbria is a misplaced version of the invasion of 1054 (Hudson, *Kings*, 140). In 1050 Macbeth was in Rome 'scattering money like seed to the poor' – perhaps in connection with the foundation of the monastery *Sanctae Trinitatis Scottorum* (ibid, 142). In 1052 he received two Norman exiles expelled with their followers from the court of the English king, Edward the Confessor (Simeon, *Kings*, 123). In 1054 an expedition by Siward succeeded in putting Malcolm III on the throne, though with authority over only part of Scotland – in all probability the area south of the Mounth (Duncan, *Kingdom*, 100; Hudson, *Kings*, 144). Macbeth's Norman allies fell in the course of this action (Simeon, *Kings*, 124). It is usually said that in 1057 Malcolm finally defeated and killed Macbeth at Lumphanan; there is some faint hint however that the latter was in fact the victor but died of his wounds at Scone soon afterwards (Hudson, *Kings*, 144). If there is any substance to the story that Macbeth built a castle at Dunsinnan or elsewhere, the building would probably have been a motte-and-bailey on the Norman model and Macbeth would have been the first Scottish king to make military and administrative use of such a construction. The building of mottes was at this time beginning in England and was already commonplace in Normandy and Anjou (*ASE*, 556-7, 562, n.1). Macbeth also employed cavalry in the Norman fashion. See above and cf. Duncan, *Kingdom*, 99-100; Barrow, *Unity*, 26; *ES*, i, 581-602.

For Macbeth's genealogy, which links him to *cenél Loairn* see O'Brien, *Corpus*, 330, 329; cf D.P. Kirby, 'Moray prior to 1100', *Historical Atlas*, 20-21; D. Sellar, 'Highland Family Origins – Pedigree Making and Pedigree Faking' in L. Maclean of Dochgarroch (ed.), *The Middle Ages in the Highlands* (Inverness, 1980), 104.

We find the evidence inconclusive for the identification of Macbeth with the Karl Hundason of *Orkneyinga saga* (see above IV c.51, l.1n.). For a contrary view see Barbara E. Crawford, *Scandinavian Scotland* (Leicester, 1987), 71-74. For Macbeth generally see E.J. Cowan, 'The Historical Macbeth' in W.D.H. Sellar (ed.), *Moray: Province and People* (Scottish Society for Northern Studies, 1993), 117-41. Cowan accepts the identification of Karl Hundason with Macbeth. See too K.D. Farrow, 'The Historiographical Evolution of the Macbeth Narrative', *Scottish Literary Journal*, 21, no.1 (May, 1994), 5-23. Farrow's Latin quotations are sadly inaccurate.

Obviously we are also much indebted to the discussion by B.T. Hudson cited above.

Shakespeare's *Macbeth*, it may be added, is based on an Anglicized version of Bellenden's translation of Boece printed in Raphael Holinshed's *Chronicles of England, Scotland and Ireland* (1578; 2nd edn, that probably used by Shakespeare, 1587).

For the story that Macbeth's mother conceived him by an incubus, see above IV c.51, l.1; *OBSV*, 19-22. Boece (*Scottorum Historiae*, ii, 152-3) gives a code of laws, probably apocryphal, which he attributes to Macbeth.

The dialogue between Malcolm and Macduff features in all versions of the story and has particular significance in terms of the power of 'enkinging' resident in the Macduff family (see above IV, c.54, l.4n). The discussion entails some analysis of the qualities necessary for, or adverse to, kingship. As a result, Macduff first finds Malcolm incapable, but in the end is forced to reverse his opinion. The effect is to enhance perception of Malcolm's kingly qualities. In effect the discussion becomes a brief Manual of Kingship which has relevance for times later than those of Macbeth. In the course of the dialogue it is also insinuated that Malcolm suspected Macduff of being an agent of Macbeth or possibly as someone who might himself be a candidate for the kingship in virtue of his descent from King Duff, suspicions which in due course are removed.

1. *Macduff*: see above IV c.54, l.4n. For the name and family see J. Bannerman, 'MacDuff of Fife' in A. Grant and K.J. Stringer (eds.), *Crown Lordship and Community in Medieval Scotland* (Edinburgh, 1993), 20-38.

Spurn Head YOE. 'Ravynsor', the form found in the Latin text (l.1) is derived from Old Norse *Hrafnseyri*, 'Hrafn's gravel bank' (*ODEPN*, 381-2)

2. *Malcolm*: i.e. the future Malcolm III (1057-93); see above IV c.49, l.13. The story referred to above IV c.49, l.2n, that Malcolm was Duncan I's bastard son by the miller's daughter of Forteviot PER, is to be found in *Wyntoun*, iv, 256-9; the two legitimate sons mentioned (presumably Maelmuir and Donald III *bàn*; see the genealogical table in Duncan, *Kingdom*, 628) are later said by Wyntoun to have fled like Malcolm to England, and to have refused to undertake an invasion of Scotland with Macduff. Reluctantly he then turned to Malcolm (*Wyntoun*, iv, 290):

> Than Makduf counsalit rycht thraly
> Malcome, the thrid brother thaim by,
> Set he wes nocht of lauchfull bed,
> As ye befor this has herd red,
> To pass with him, sen thai forsuke
> To follow thar rycht, and he vndertuke
> That he suld mak him of Scotland king.

This passage forms part of the introduction to Wyntoun's version of the conversation between Malcolm and Macduff which eventually leads to the expedition into Scotland. For the offer by Macduff to make Malcolm king, cf. the remarks above, introductory note.

Chapter 2
pp.5-7

This chapter corresponds to *Fordun* (V c.2). See *Pluscarden*, V c.2; nothing in *Extracta*. Dramatically it is a continuation of the speech begun by Malcolm in the previous chapter, but occasionally the mask slips to reveal Fordun, the 14c moralist and historian. In *Wyntoun* (iv, 292-3) Malcolm claims to be lecherous, but does not give the list of historical exempla conspicuous in this and the following chapter. These exempla have presumably been contributed by Fordun.

1. *I*: i.e. Malcolm.

3-12. *Tarquin ... over them*: cf. above III c.55, ll.28-60.

3. *Tarquin the Proud*: i.e. Tarquinius Superbus (534-510 BC), last king of Rome.

4. *you*: i.e. Macduff.

6. *Tarquin*: i.e. Sextus Tarquinius, son of Tarquinius Superbus.
Lucretia: i.e. the daughter of Spurius Lucretius Tricipitinus, prefect of Rome.
Collatinus: i.e. Lucius Tarquinius Collatinus, one of the founders of the Roman republic.

12. *Sardanapalus*: cf. above II c.18, ll.32-50.

17-22. *Childeric ... guarantee*: see *Liber Historiae Francorum*, MGH, *Scriptorum rerum Merovingicarum*, ii, 246-9.

17. *Childeric*: cf. above III c.20, l.21. By scribal or auctorial error the Latin text (l.13) reads 'Chilperic'.

18. *Merovech*: cf. above III c.20, l.20.
Clovis: cf. above III c.19, l.1.

22. *Eadwig*: cf. above IV cc.27, l.31; 29, ll.10-14.

23. *recent*: i.e. dramatically, from Malcolm's point of view. Eadwig reigned 955-9.

27. *Dunstan*: cf. above IV c.30, l.26.

31-33. *Culen ... daughter*: cf. above IV c.29, ll.1-31.

34. *Roderick*: i.e. Ruaidrì Ua Conchobair or Rory O'Connor (died 1198), king of Connacht and last person to be regarded as high-king of Ireland. He was later classified as one of the *righ co ffressabra*, 'kings with opposition', opposition especially from the king of Leinster, Diarmait Mac Murchada, and his Norman allies. Ruaidrì became high-king in 1166, and for much of his reign attempted to come to terms with the Norman invasion, which began with the return of the exiled Diarmait in 1167. In 1175 Ruaidrì concluded the Treaty of Windsor, in which he recognized the English king Henry II (1154-89) as his overlord. In 1186 he lost the kingship of Connacht to his son Conchobar Máenmaige. He died on pilgrimage. A brief account of his reign will be found in *Reim Riograide* (*Lebor Gabála* [Irish Texts Society, Dublin, 1956], v, 410-11). For an Anglo-Norman version see G.H. Orpen (ed.), *The Song of Dermot and the Earl* (Oxford, 1892). In Malcolm's mouth the reference to Ruaidrì is of course an anachronism.

descended ... stock: Ruaidri traced his descent by way of Brión son of Echu Mugmedón to Conn Cétchathach, who in turn was a descendant of Õengus Turbech Temra by way of the latter's elder son Énna Airgdech. The Scottish royal line traced its descent to Énna's brother Fiacha Fer Mara. See above I c.36, ll.8-9, and the genealogical tables in Byrne, *Kings*, 280, 299-301.

34-43. *who ... kingdom*: source not identified.

40-41. *to this day*: i.e. into Fordun's own time. He has again forgotten that Malcolm is the supposed speaker.

42-43. *now ... kingdoms*: the structure of Irish society before and after the Norman invasion involved a multiplicity of tribal and provincial kingdoms. 'There were probably no less than 150 kings in the country at any given date between the fifth and twelfth centuries' (Byrne, *Kings*, 7). Locally many dynasties remained in power until the end of the sixteenth century.

Chapter 3
pp.7-9

This chapter corresponds to *Fordun* (V c.3). See *Pluscarden*, V c.3, and *Extracta*, 58.

19. *give as examples*: cf. above c.2, ll.12-46. Macduff omits Eadwig and Culen.

Childeric: here the Latin text (l.15) has 'Chilperic'; cf. above c.2, l.16.

20. *Octavian*: cf. above II c.18, l.64.

21-23. *For ... seduced*: source not identified; cf. Suetonius, 'Divus Augustus', cc.68-71 (Loeb edn, i, 228-33).

25-26. *Oh that ... die*: source not identified; cf. above II c.24, l.24.

26-29. *He was ... acquired*: cf. above II c.24, ll.27-29 ('he would ... natural').

32. *I found ... marble*: Suetonius, 'Divus Augustus', c.28 (ut cit., i, 166).

38-40. *Previously ... peace*: source not identified.

Chapter 4
pp.9-11

This chapter corresponds to *Fordun* (V c.4). See *Pluscarden*, V c.4, and *Extracta*, 58. Cf. *Wyntoun*, iv, 292-5. Although Macduff (or Fordun speaking in his person) had regarded lechery as a mere monarchic peccadillo, he takes more seriously avarice leading to theft, but feels that personal self-control is always possible, and that in any case a king has no need to be avaricious.

27.: *The fickle ... leader*: cf. Walther, *Proverbia*, no. 14,986; the source is Claudian, *Panegyric on the Fourth Consulship of the Emperor Honorius*, l.302 (Loeb edn., 308).

31-32. *Thou ... steal*: Exodus 20:14-15.

35. *No one ... endure*: 1 Corinthians 10:13.

Chapter 5
pp.11-13

This chapter corresponds to *Fordun* (V c.5) and completes the analysis of unkingly qualities begun in c.1 above. See *Pluscarden*, V c.5, and *Extracta*, 58-59. Cf. *Wyntoun*, iv, 294-7.

39. *treachery*: for treachery as the supreme vice in personal and political life cf. above II c.19, ll.44-50; IV c.47.

41. *your adversary*: i.e. Macbeth.

Chapter 6
pp.15-17

This chapter corresponds to *Fordun* (V c.6). See *Pluscarden*, V c.6, and *Extracta*, 59. Cf. *Wyntoun*, iv, 296-7.

5-13. *since ... loyal*: the theme of treachery and its opposite, loyalty, is continued and concluded.

19-20. *first ... king*: cf. above IV c.54, l.4.

21-22. *country ... inhabit*: cf. Genesis 13:15; Exodus 6:8 etc. Fordun implies a parallel between the return of Malcolm from England to Scotland and the return of the Israelites from Egypt to the Promised Land.

29-51. *If ... battle*: source not identified; cf. Walther, *Initia*, 17,969.

Chapter 7
pp.17-19

This chapter corresponds to *Fordun* (V c.7). See *Pluscarden*, V c.7, and *Extracta*, 59. Bower has added ll.49-64 ('See also ... glory'). In this and the subsequent chapter Fordun's chronology is seriously distorted. Siward invaded southern Scotland in 1054, establishing Malcolm there, but leaving Macbeth in control of the north. In 1057, long after Siward's death in 1055, Malcolm defeated Macbeth at Lumphanan ABD, or alternatively was narrowly defeated by him. Macbeth was killed at Lumphanan or alternatively died soon afterwards, perhaps at Scone PER, of the wounds which he had received. Some time elapsed before Malcolm fully established his authority. See above c.1, introductory note; below c.8, l.34-45.

6. *Edward*: i.e. Edward the Confessor, king of England 1042-66; cf. above IV c.51, l.17.

17. *Siward*: Danish earl of Northumbria ca 1041-55 (*ASE*, 416-19).

28. *southern regions*: i.e. the area south of the Mounth. Moray, the territory hereditary to Macbeth and his kindred, lay to the north.

34. *5 December 1056*: Macbeth was in fact killed on 15 August 1057 (*ES*, i, 579, 602). Fordun (below c.8, ll.44-45) erroneously gives the date of the death of Macbeth's successor, Lulach, as 3 April 1057, after a reign of four months. He appears to have calculated the date for Macbeth's death in terms of this mistake for which we have not been able to find any source.

39-42. *Siward ... place*: *Malmesbury*, i, 237. The reference is to the invasion of 1054.

41. *Malcolm ... Cumbrians*: for Duncan as king of Strathclyde/Cumbria and thus heir-apparent of Malcolm II, see above IV c.46, ll.1-17. In Boece, *Scottorum Historiae*, ii, 150, and in Shakespeare, *Macbeth*, I.iv., ll.37-50, the proximate cause of Duncan's murder by Macbeth is the appointment of his son Malcolm as prince of Cumbria and so also as heir-apparent.

42-45. *See ... victory*: at least one Scottish source also gives the credit to Siward; see *Melrose*, 24, s.a.1054.

44-45. *Malcolm ... victory*: the reference to the standard-bearer may indicate that Fordun drew on some independent version of the battle, since lost.

51. *I*: i.e. Bower.

59. *observation ... Colman*: see above III c.46, l.2. The Latin text (l.50) reads 'Columbanum' for 'Colmanum'.

60. *Columba*: see above III cc.26-27, 29-30, 38; *ODS*, 95-96.
  Wilfred: see above III c.41, l.17; *ODS*, 435-7.

61-62. *If ... Columba*: based on *Bede*, (bk.3, c.25).

63-64. *Inglorious ... glory*: based on Alan of Lille, *De Planctu Naturae*, prose 7, 'prudentiae gloriam degloriet livor inglorius' (*PL*, 210, col.469).

Chapter 8
pp.21-23

This chapter corresponds to *Fordun* (V c.8). See *Pluscarden*, V c.8, and *Extracta*, 59. Bower has added ll.45-56 ('The following ... Judge'), replacing a final sentence in *Fordun*.

2. *tyrannous regime*: for medieval ideas on tyranny see, e.g., Aquinas, *De Regimine Principum*, c.3 (A.P. D'Entrèves [ed.], *Aquinas: Selected Political Writings* [Oxford, 1965], 14-19).

6. *rank*: Fordun ignores Macbeth's family claim to the throne; see above c.1, introductory note.

8-9. *in my opinion*: i.e. Fordun's opinion copied by Bower.

10-25. *head ... nature*: the idea of hierarchy by which the king stands to the state in the same relation as the head to the body is a medieval commonplace; cf. Aquinas, ut cit., c.1, 4-6: 'Multis enim existentibus hominibus et unoquoque id, quod est sibi congruum, providente, multitudo in diversa dispergeretur, nisi etiam esset aliquis de eo quod ad bonum multitudinis pertinet, curam habens; sicut et corpus hominis et cuiuslibet animalis deflueret, nisi esset aliqua vis regitiva communis in corpore, quae ad bonum commune omnium membrorum intenderet ... Propter quod et in omnibus, quae in unum ordinantur, aliquid invenitur alterius regitivum. In universitate enim corporum per primum corpus, scilicet coeleste, alia corpora ordine quodam divinae providentiae reguntur, omniaque corpora per creaturam rationalem. In uno etiam homine anima regit corpus, atque inter animae partes irascibilis et concupiscibilis ratione reguntur. Itemque inter membra corporis unum est principale, quod omnia movet, ut cor, aut caput. Oportet igitur esse in omni multitudine aliquod regitivum.' Fordun however develops the idea in the highly personal and deliberately grotesque figure of the foot (Macbeth) attempting to take over the function of the head (Duncan or Malcolm). The result is necessarily a tyranny.

26-36. *Gruffydd ... king*: cf.*Melrose*, 24, s.a.1055, where the exploits of Gruffydd are likewise erroneously juxtaposed with the reign of Lulach. This may indicate that Fordun's prime source was the lost chronicle, related to *Melrose*, discussed below vol. 5, p.xvii. Siward's return to England was not a consequence of Gruffydd's success; Siward died in spring 1055; Hereford HRE was captured and burned on 24 October; the death of Leofgar did not take place until 16 June 1056, when he rashly attempted to take reprisals on Gruffydd (*ASE*, 570-73). Fordun is probably attempting unsuccessfully to make sense of an already confused narrative.

26. *Gruffydd*: i.e. Gruffydd ap Llywelyn, king of Gwynedd and Powys 1039-63; of Deheubarth 1055-63 (*HBC*, 53). In 1055 he made a successful assault on Hereford in alliance with Ælfgar, the outlawed earl of East Anglia (*ASE*, 572-3; T.Jones [ed.], *Brut y Tywysogyon or the Chronicle of the Princes* [Cardiff, 1955], 25, s.a. 1056; cf. below c.12, ll.56-61).

27. *Radulf*: i.e. Radulf the Timid, earl of Hereford 1053-7; son of Godgifu (sister of Edward the Confessor) and the Norman, Drogo, count of the Vexin (*ASE*, 560, 569). 'He was the real founder of the system of organized castle-building which under the Norman kings made Herefordshire a principal bulwark of the midlands against assault from Wales' (*ASE*, 570). His failure at Hereford probably resulted from his attempt to make the Anglo-Saxon militia fight on horseback in the Norman fashion (*ASE*, 569).

Leofgar: bishop of Hereford March-June 1056; defeated and killed by Gruffydd near Glasbury-on-Wye RAD when he attempted to avenge the destruction of Hereford in the previous year (*HBC*, 217; *ASE*, 573). Fordun has compressed two separate events into one. The description of Leofgar given in *ASC* (Plummer), 186, *ASC*, 132, is satiric and almost contemptuous. Leofgar, for instance, did not remove his moustache, the mark of the Anglo-Saxon warrior, when he became a priest, but only when he was promoted to the episcopate. Even then his militaristic instincts came disastrously to the fore.

28. *Ælfnoth*: sheriff of Hereford, killed with Leofgar in 1056.

30. *As soon ... this*: as noted above, Siward had died in spring 1055.

33-56. *Immediately ... Judge*: cf. *Wyntoun*, iv, 304-7.

33-34. *certain ... family*: i.e. presumably members of the ruling house of Moray.

35. *Lulach*: i.e. Lulach, king of Scotland 1057-8, son of Gruoch by her first husband Gillecomgain (d.1032), mormaer of Moray. Gillecomgain was Macbeth's cousin, but with his brother Malcolm had killed Findlaech, Macbeth's father, in 1020. Gruoch married Macbeth shortly after the death of Gillecomgain. Lulach's claim to the throne was built on his descent through Gruoch from Kenneth II or Kenneth III, but Malcolm his uncle and Findlaech his great-uncle are both occasionally described as kings of Scotland (above IV c.43, l.8). For the idea that the house of Moray continued the line of *cenél Loairn* cf. above c.1, introductory note and the references there cited; cf too Hudson, *Kings*, 145-6.

Idiot: the nickname may be based on the resemblance of the name Lulach to Sc.Gaelic *lulagan, laoighcionn*, '[stuffed] calf-skin'.

Scone PER; cf. above IV c.48, l.5. Note the surprising ease with which the supporters of Lulach (presumably men of Moray) were apparently able to carry out the inauguration at Scone, far beyond the Moray boundaries.

39. *thanes*: for this term see especially Barrow, *Kingdom*, 41-53.

42. *Essie* ABD.

Strathbogie ABD.

44-45. *3 April*: according to the contemporary chronicler, Marianus Scottus, Lulach's reign came to an end on 17 March 1058 (*ES*, i, 602). In 1057 3 April *was* the Thursday in Easter Week, a fact which suggests that Fordun based his chronology on some earlier source now lost.

47-56. *... Judge*: see *Cronicon Elegiacum*, ll.71-80, for which see above, Vol. 2, pp.xx-xxi. Note the sympathetic attitude to Macbeth and Lulach.

55-56. *... Judge*: if Macbeth and Lulach were regarded merely as Moravian usurpers, their burials at Iona are as surprising as the inauguration of Lulach at Scone.

Chapter 9
pp.23-25

In this chapter ll.1-7 (... 'years') are based on the opening sentences of *Fordun* (V c.9). The remainder is the work of Bower. See *Pluscarden*, V c.9 (opening section), and *Extracta*, 59-60.

The abbreviated version of this chapter which appears in MS CA (VI c. 27) begins with ll.30-32 ('In the time ... Rome') and continues with an additional passage: 'Hiis enim temporibus diversi reges peregrinacionis optentu apostolorum limina visitabant, sicut et paulo ante, scilicet Anno domini M°. xxxi primo.' This is followed by ll.61-64 ('Cnut ... taxation'), which in turn is followed by a longer additional passage:

Nunc autem et, quod dolenter refero, reges et principes dediti sunt non
tantum bellis hostilibus ad extra, sed eciam intestinis et civilibus quod
raro vel numquam erigunt mentem ad Deum nec de misera anima que
in eternum vel in pena aut gloria victura erit excogitant, donec rei et
5   nudi peccatis onerati discendunt in locis penarum et de illis possunt
annumerari de quibus scriptum est Ecclesiastici xlix: 'Relinquentes
legem Altissimi potentes reges inde defecerunt quia contempserunt
timorem Dei. Dederunt regnum suum aliis, et est alienis.' Hec
propterea hic inserui ut sciatis quia quamvis isti duo reges Knuto
10   scilicet et Machabeda intrusores extiterant regnorum, tamen placare
Deum satagebant peregrinacionis sancte profeccione et elemosinarum
erogacione. De primo scriptum est Libro Revelacionum Brigitte, vj,
capitulo v quod in Roma sunt majores indulgencie quam homines
credere possunt, quas sancti suo sanguine meruerunt, et ibidem Libro
15   Celesti ad Imperatores et Reges, capitulo xiii: 'Rome compendium est
inter celum et mortem ad fugiendam penam purgatorii, quia ibi sunt
indulgencie que sunt elevaciones et redempciones animarum quas
sancti pontifices concesserunt, et sancti Dei suo sanguine meruerunt.'
Hec ibi. De ii° scriptum est: 'Peccata tua elemosinis redime', Danielis
20   iiii°. Super quo Augustinus: 'Si vis esse mercator optimus, fenerator
egregius, da quod non potes retinere ut recipias quod non poteris
amittere. Da modicum ut recipias centuplum. Da temporalem
possessionem ut consequaris hereditatem eternam.' Iste

This leads into ll.48-53 ('Cnut ... Romans'), after which the text jumps to
ll.33-35 ('In 1026 ... Bastard') and continues with c.10 below, ll.44ff.
('Harthacnut died' ...). The additions and abbreviations serve to emphasize
two themes – that of Macbeth and Cnut as usurpers, who nevertheless
recognized the compensatory potential of pilgrimage to Rome, and the
contrast of present-day rulers with those of the past. Bower also gives himself
the opportunity of further quotation from his favourite book, the *Heavenly
Revelations* of St Bridget of Sweden.

The passages referred to in the quotation are: ll.7-9 ('Relinquentes ...
alienis'), Ecclesiasticus 49:6-7; 14-15 ('in Roma ... meruerunt'), *Memoriale ...
B. Brigidae*, bk.6, c.105, para. D; 16-20 ('Rome ... meruerunt'), not identified;
20-21 ('Peccata ... redime'), Daniel 4:24; 21-25 ('Si vis ... eternam'), not
identified.

3.   *Scone*: cf. above c.8, 1.35.

5.   *1057*: the accession was in fact on 17 March 1058 (see above c.8,ll.44-45).

6.   *Henry IV*: cf. above IV c.55, l.11.
     or ... Henry III: 'I' here is Bower. Cf. above IV cc.39, 1.31; 51, 1.4.

7.   *almost fifty years*: i.e. 1056-1106.

8.   *three requests*: cf. *Wyntoun*, iv, 302-3.

10-11.   *place ... coronation*: cf. above IV, c.54, 1.4; Duncan, *Kingdom*, 114-15.
By an oversight in our note to IV c.54, 1.4 we stated wrongly that Professor
Duncan ignored Fordun's evidence for this Macduff (Duncan, ut cit., 115,
n.27).

13-14.   *Macduff law*: Bower has made a mistake; the law applied to cases in which a nobleman or yeoman was killed rather than in which he was himself a homicide. Wyntoun (ut cit., 302-4) has a more accurate and detailed account:

> Gif ony in suddand chadmelle
> Happinnit slane sa for to be
> Be ony of the thanys kyne
> Off Fife the kinrik within,
> Gif he sa slane were a gentil man,
> Xxiiii. markis than
> For kynbut the slaar suld pay,
> And he remyttit suld be for ay;
> And for yemen xii. merkis but mare
> Suld pay the slaare,
> And suld haif full remissioun
> Fra thin of all that actioun.
> Off that law are the thre capitale,
> That is the blak prest of Weddale,
> The thayne of Fiff, and the thrid syne
> Quha euer be lord of Abernethyne.
> Gif thare be ony that likis to se
> The law of this led, than may he
> Herkin quhen the day is set,
> As fallis to be done of det;
> To Cowper in Fyf than cum he;
> The law weill led thare sall he se.

The word 'chadmelle' means 'a sudden angry broil or affray' (*DOST*, s.v. 'Chaudmellé'). 'Weddale' is St Mary's church of Wedale at Stow MLO, a mensal church of the bishops of St Andrews. 'Abernethyne' is Abernethy PER, near the Fife boundary. 'Cowper' is Cupar FIF.

For further references see *Wyntoun*, i, 66; *DOST*, s.v. 'Law', 2b; Bannerman, 'MacDuff of Fife', ut cit. above c.1, l.1.

16. *kinbot*: 'a compensation for manslaughter, paid by the slayer to the kin of the slain person' (*DOST*, s.v. 'Kinbute').

18. *famine and plague*: cf. *ASC* (Plummer), MS E, 163 (s.a. 1041), 164-5 (s.a. 1043), 185 (s.a. 1054); MS C, 164 (s.a. 1044), 166 (s.a. 1047); MS D, 167 (s.a. 1049); *ASC*, 106-7, 108, 110, 111, 129; Simeon, *Kings*, 119 (s.a. 1048). All references are to England.

19-30. *a certain ... death*: see *Martin*, 468. For 'Idem dicitur cuidam principi Apollonie contigisse' (text ll.21-22), *Martin* has the more convincing reading 'Idem legitur cuidam principe Polonie [of Poland] contigisse.' The story is listed in F.C. Tubach, *Index Exemplorum* (Helsinki, 1969), no. 3280, with references; cf. Thomson, *Motif-Index*, Q415.2. For the story of the potentate (ll.19-25), cf. *Wyntoun*, iv, 244-5.

30-31. *great fertility*: cf. *Cronicon Elegiacum*, l.72.

31-32. *In 1050 ... Rome*: cf. *Melrose*, 23, s.a. 1050; Marianus Scottus, *Chronicle*, s.a. 1050 (*ES*, i, 588). Marianus, but not *Melrose*, includes the phrase 'to the poor' (*pauperibus*). Cross references here and in subsequent chapters to *Melrose* probably indicate that Bower as well as Fordun used the lost chronicle-source mentioned above c.8, ll.26-36.

33-35. *In 1026 ... Robert:* cf. *Melrose*, 21, s.a. 1026.

33. *Richard II:* i.e. Richard the Good, duke of Normandy 996-1026.

34. *Richard III:* duke of Normandy 1026-8, son of Richard II.

35. *Robert:* i.e. Robert I, duke of Normandy 1028-35, known as Robert the Magnificent or Robert the Devil. He is alleged to have gained the dukedom by poisoning his elder brother, Richard III. See above IV c.49, 1.7.

  William: i.e. William II and I, duke of Normandy 1035-87; king of England 1066-87. He was the bastard son of Robert I by Arletta, daughter of a tanner at Falaise, dép. Calvados, France.

38-44. *... Bastard:* source not identified.

39. *Rollo:* cf. above IV c.17, ll.42, 62-66. His fief was created in 911.

41. *William:* i.e. William I Longsword, duke of Normandy 933-42.
  Richard: i.e. Richard I the Fearless, duke of Normandy 942-96.

42. *Richard:* cf. above l.33.

43. *Robert:* cf. above l.35.

44. *William:* cf. above l.35.

45. *three ... stock:* cf. the passage from MS CA quoted above IV c.49, 1.6n.
  Cnut: Danish king of England 1016-35; cf. above IV c.45, 1.6.

46. *Harthacnut:* son of Cnut by his wife Emma, daughter of Richard I of Normandy; king of Denmark 1028-42; of England 1035-7, 1040-42.
  Harold: i.e. Harold I Harefoot, son of Cnut by his mistress Ælfgifu of Northampton; king of England 1037-40; cf. above IV c.49, 1.6.

47. *later:* see below c.10, ll.13-43, 72-77.

48-53. *In 1017 ... Romans:* cf. *Melrose*, 21, s.a. 1017. References there to the exile of the nephews of Edmund Ironside are here omitted.

48. *Swein:* see above IV c.38, 1.21.

49. *Emma:* see above l.46n. Her first husband was Æthelred, whom she married in 1002 and by whom she was mother of Edward the Confessor, Alfred (murdered in 1037) and a daughter Godgifu, whose second marriage was to Eustace count of Boulogne. By Cnut, whom she married in 1017, she was mother of Harthacnut and a daughter Gunhild (*HBC*, 27, 28).
  Richard: i.e. Richard I (above l.42).

50. *Æthelred:* king of England 978-1016; cf. above IV c.30, ll.12-13.

52-53. *Gunhild ... Romans:* the marriage took place in 1036; Gunhild (after her marriage called Kunigund), died in 1038. Henry was crowned German king in 1028 and later (1039-56) became Emperor as Henry III (above IV c.45, l.56).

53-64. *In 1028 ... taxation:* cf. *Melrose*, 21-22, s.a. 1027-31.

53. *1028:* in fact 1028-9.

55. *Olaf:* i.e. Olaf II Haraldsönn, king of Norway 1016-29, when he was exiled; on his return in 1030 he was defeated and killed at the battle of Stiklestad (*ODS*, 325-6).

57. *following year:* i.e. 1030.

59-60. *Harold ... Norwegians:* Harold was a descendant of Harold Fairhair (ca. 880-928), first king of Norway, but was himself no more than lord 'of a small district to the west of the Oslo Fjörd' (*ASE*, 402).

61. *following year*: in fact Cnut made his pilgrimage to Rome in 1027 on the occasion of the coronation of the emperor Conrad (above IV c.45, l.12; *ASE*, 407).

63. *Pope John*: i.e. John XIX, 1024-32 (*ODP*, 141-2).
English school: i.e. the fortified compound on the Vatican hill in Trastevere occupied by the English section or 'school' of the Roman militia; see W.H. Stevenson, *Asser's Life of King Alfred* (Oxford, 1904), 243-7; *ASE*, 466.

Chapter 10
pp.27-29

This chapter is the work of Bower. Not in *Pluscarden*, nor *Extracta*.

7-9. *Everything ... fall*: source not identified.

9-11. *In 1032 ... priests*: cf. *Melrose*, 22, s.a. 1032.

9. *church of St Edmund*: i.e. the abbey of Bury St Edmunds SFK; cf. above IV c.16, l.30.

12-13. *many ... put out*: cf. *Melrose*, 22, s.a. 1032. A fuller explanation will be found in *ASC* (Plummer), 159 (MS E, s.a. 1032), *ASC*, 102, where the fire is called 'wildefyr', i.e. 'a conflagration caused by lightning' (*OED*, s.v. 'wildfire').

13-20. *Before ... boy*: cf. *Melrose*, 22, s.a. 1035.

14. *Swein*: son of Cnut by his mistress Ælfgifu of Northampton; king of Norway 1030-35 (*ASE*, 405-6).
Harthacnut: see above c.9, l.45.

15. *Harold*: this is the MS reading. The marginal alteration to 'Edward' is a mistake, resulting perhaps from the description of Harold as 'Emma's son'. Harold was son of Ælfgifu. *Melrose* has 'super Danos Hardecnutum et Emme regine filium regem locavit, super Anglos Haroldum filium ex Hamtuensi Ælgiua procreatum.' Corruption of such a passage would be relatively easy.

16. *Shaftesbury* DOR; death-date is correct.

16-17. *Old Minster*: situated immediately to the north of the present Winchester cathedral.

17. *Winchester* HMP.

18. *Harold*: see above l.16n.
Harthacnut: about here in MS C the following note has been placed in the margin and later deleted: 'Hoc anno Johannes abbas de [ ] de Roma rediit [m]itratus.' It probably refers to some English abbey.
Robert: see above c.9, l.35.

19. *William*: see above c.9, l.35.

20-29. *In 1036 ... Normandy*: cf *Melrose*, 22, s.a. 1036. For the relatively rare word 'clitones' (Latin text 1.18), translated 'Æthelings', cf. below c.27, Latin text 1.3, where the form in the singular is glossed 'videlicet genere gloriosum'. The derivation may be from Greek κλειτός, 'famous, renowned, illustrious'.

20. *Alfred*: see above c.9, 1.49n.

Edward: i.e. Edward II the Confessor.

Richard: i.e. Richard II duke of Normandy (above c.9, 1.33), who died in 1026. He was Emma's brother. On the death of Æthelred in 1016, his sons Edward and Alfred had been entrusted to his care. Alfred alone returned to England in 1036, where he was murdered by Godwine (*ASE*, 421).

22. *mother*: i.e. Emma.

23. *Godwine*: earl of Wessex, one of Cnut's most influential retainers; a thorn in the flesh of succeeding kings until his death in 1053.

26. *Guildford* SUR.

27-28. *He ordered ... afterwards*: cf. *Wyntoun*, iv, 252-3.

29-34. *Harold ... Flanders*: cf. *Melrose*, 22, s.a. 1037.

34. *Baldwin*: count of Flanders 1036-67.

34-43. *In 1039 ... court*: cf. *Melrose*, 22-23, s.a. 1039, 1040, 1041. Bower has apparently omitted details, especially Harthacnut's savage treatment of his brother's corpse.

39. *gifts*: according to Simeon, *Kings*, 160-2, and Florence, *Chronicon*, 193-6, these consisted of a warship, magnificently equipped, together with a crew of eighty warriors.

44. *Harthacnut ... kingship*: cf. *Melrose*, 23, s.a. 1042, 1043. Bower has again apparently omitted much detail.

1043: in fact 8 June 1042 (*HBC*, 29).

44-51. *In 1047 ... envoys*: cf. *Melrose*, 23, s.a. 1047, 1048.

45. *Magnus*: king of Norway 1035-47.

Olaf: see above c.9, 1.55.

Swein: i.e. Swein Estrithson, king of Denmark 1043-74.

48. *Harold Hardrada*: king of Norway 1046-66; uterine brother of Olaf II. The reading 'Haroldus Harfahger' (text 1.44) indicates confusion with Harald Haarfager, 'Hairfair' (ca 870-ca 930), first king of a united Norway.

Sigurd king of the Norwegians: Harold's father was Sigurd Sow (d. 1018), provincial king of Ringariki in central Norway. Sigurd was a descendant of Harold Haarfager but he was never king of Norway as a whole.

51-67. *In 1050 ... home*: cf. *Melrose*, 23-24, s.a. 1051.

51. *1050*: in fact 1051 (*ASE*, 412).

51-52. *when Macbeth ... Scotland*: not found in *Melrose*.

52. *tax*: i.e. heregeld, also known as Danegeld, first imposed by Æthelred II in 1012; see *ASE*, 412; above IV c.11, ll.1-4; below c.39a, 1.62.

57. *count of Boulogne*: i.e. Eustace II, count of Boulogne 1049-93, husband of Godgifu, daughter of Æthelred and Emma. He was thus brother-in-law of Edward the Confessor.

58. *Dover* KNT.

63. *five sons*: i.e. Swein, Harold (the future King Harold II), Tostig, Gyrth and Leofwine.

64-66. *King Edward ... England*: William visited England in winter of 1051 or spring of 1052 (*ASE*, 565-6).

66-67. *back home*: here Bower in MS CA inserts cc.29-30 of Book VII.

72-77. *... last*: source not identified. It need hardly be added that the arithmetic of the verses is defective.

74. *prostitute*: i.e. Ælfgifu of Northampton (above c.9, l.46n).

75-77. *Edward ... last*: neither Edward the Confessor nor Harold II was of Danish origin.

Chapter 11
pp.31-33

This chapter corresponds to *Fordun* (V c.9), omitting the first sentence, already used as the opening of c.9 above. See *Pluscarden*, V c.9 (latter part); nothing in *Extracta*.

In this chapter ll.14-40, together with ll.1-37 of c.12 below, are attributed to 'Turgot', the English churchman, bishop of St Andrews 1107-15, and author of a *Life* of the English consort of Malcolm III Canmore, St Margaret (hereafter Turgot, *Margaret*). Material in later chapters is apparently drawn from the same source. The situation however is more complicated than the attribution in itself would suggest. The story of Malcolm and the traitor does not appear in the printed versions of Turgot *Margaret*. At a first glance it appears to be derived from *Genealogia regum Anglorum* (PL, 195, cols. 711-38; the story occupies most of col. 735), a work composed ca 1153-4 by Ailred of Rievaulx (1110-65), and addressed to the future English king, Henry II (1154-89), urging him to maintain the standards set by his predecessors and relatives, especially his recently deceased grand-uncle David I, king of Scotland 1124-53. In the present instance however Fordun derived the sentence 'We thought ... deeds' (ll.14-17), together with the story which it introduces, not from Ailred but, by way of his own *Early Gesta* (c.15; *Fordun*, 417), from an earlier version of the longer but as yet unpublished text of Turgot, *Margaret*, found in the late 15c Dunfermline MS [siglum 'DMS'] (Madrid, Royal Palace Library MS II 2097, fos.1-17v; the relevant passage will be found on fos.8-8v); see above Volume Introduction, pp.xvii-xviii. Ailred apparently knew Turgot, *Margaret* in this version, which he made one of the principal sources of his *Genealogia*. For ll.14-40 cf. *Wyntoun*, iv, 326-9.

That Fordun also knew Ailred, *Genealogia* itself is demonstrated by his Book VI (*Fordun*, 387-401), preserved in three Fordun MSS, which includes 'regum nostrae generationis caritatis opera, et actus bellicos, de Baldredi vel Ethelredi Rivallis abbatis chronicis [i.e. the *Genealogia*] breviter excerptos.' For the most part Book VI is an abbreviation of Ailred, *Genealogia*, cols. 717-34 ('Porro a Woden ... regnum obtinuit'), but a certain amount of extraneous material has been added. The story of Malcolm and the traitor does not appear. *Wyntoun* (iv, 326-33) includes a version of the story, but names no source.

1-4. *... follows*: source used by *Fordun* not identified.

4. *first nine years*: in fact only eight years, 1058-66; cf. above c.9, l.5n.
Edward: i.e. Edward II the Confessor.

5. *observed unbroken peace*: in fact Malcolm ravaged Northumbria in 1061 (Duncan, *Kingdom*, 118).

6-11. *In the thirteenth ... joyfully*: abbreviated from *Early Gesta*, cc.9, 10 (*Fordun*, 414); cf. DMS, fo. 6v.

6-7. *thirteenth ... Edward*: i.e. 1055. The date of this Edward's arrival in England was in fact 1057 (*HBC*, 28); see below VI c.22.

7. *brother*: in fact half-brother. Edmund II Ironside was son of Æthelred by Ælfgifu; Edward II the Confessor of Æthelred by Emma (*HBC*, 27).
Edmund: see above IV c.45, l.3.

8-10. *Edward ... Christina*: after Edward and Edmund, the two sons of Edmund II Ironside, had escaped the power of Cnut, it is generally believed that they were sent (by way of Sweden) to Hungary (above IV c.45, l.8). Edmund died young, but Edward survived and married Agatha, usually regarded as the daughter of St Stephen, king of Hungary 1001-38, and kinswoman of the Emperor Henry I (II), whose sister Gisela Stephen had married (above IV c.38, ll. 31-51; *HBC*, 28). Alternatively, Agatha may have been a member of the Russian royal family of Kiev (Barrow, *Unity*, 29). Of the children of the union, Edgar (the Ætheling) was chosen king of England after the battle of Hastings in 1066, but was never crowned. Margaret married ca 1069 Malcolm III Canmore. Christina died as a nun at Romsey HMP (*Malmesbury*, i, 278). Cf. below VI c.22; *Wyntoun*, iv, 314-15.

In a valuable but little-known article, to which Mr W.D.H.Sellar has kindly drawn our attention ('Agatha, Mother of Saint Margaret Queen of Scotland', *Duquesne Review* [1962], 71-87), Szabolcs de Vajay has suggested a more plausible sequence. On the death of Edmund Ironside, his sons were sent, first to Sweden, then in 1028 to the court of the Russian ruler Jaroslaw the Great (1015-54) at Kiev in the modern Ukraine. A slightly later exile who also took refuge in Kiev was Andrew son of Vassili, a disaffected cousin of St Stephen of Hungary. In 1043 or early in 1044 Edward married Agatha daughter of Liudolf, Margrave of Westfriesland, son, by her first marriage to Bruno of Brunswick, of Gisela of Swabia, whose third marriage was to the Emperor Conrad II (see above IV c.45, l.12), by whom she had another son, the Emperor Henry III the Salian (see above IV c.45, l.45). Liudolf and Henry III were thus half-brothers. The marriage of Edward and Agatha was the result of diplomatic negotiations between the courts of Edward the Confessor in England, Henry III in Germany and Jaroslaw in Russia. In 1046 Andrew son of Vassili set out from Kiev on a successful expedition to obtain the crown of Hungary, which he held until his death in 1060. Edward with his wife and Edmund accompanied the expedition. Edmund soon died, but Edward remained in Hungary, where his three children were born, until 1056 when the family removed to England.

12-13. *appropriate place*: see below cc.16-18.

14. *Turgot*: see above introductory note; cf. Watt, *Fasti*, 290.

14-40. *We thought ... with him*: see above introductory note.

15. *Canmore*: i.e. Old Irish *cenmar*, 'big-headed'.

18. *enemies*: Turgot does not say so, but these enemies may well have been members of the Moray royal family, which, in the persons of Macbeth and Lulach, claimed descent from *cenél Loairn*; cf. above c.1, introductory note; c.8, ll.33-34. The Moray dynasty retained power long after the death of Lulach. Under 1085 *AU* records that Maelsnechtai son of Lulach, king of Moray, ended his life happily. Under 1130 a battle is recorded between the men of Alban and the men of Moray, in which fell four thousand of the men of Moray with their king Oengus son of the daughter of Lulach (*Chron.Picts-Scots*, 370-2; cf. Duncan, *Kingdom*, 165-6; Hudson, *Kings*, 146-7; 170).

27. *Aurora*: Roman goddess of the dawn.

30-32. *plain ... hill*: the place formed an *eileirg*, 'ambush' – 'a defile, natural or artificial, wider at one end than at the other, into which the deer were driven, often in hundreds, and slain as they passed through' (*CPNS*, 489). The normal reflex of this Scottish Gaelic word in modern place-names is 'Elrick', the distribution of which extends from INV to WIG.

35-39. *allotted ... death*: the hunt is of the type described in the 14c English alliterative poem, *Sir Gawain and the Green Knight*, ll.1126-77. 'Men and hounds were stationed at various points around the area in which the game was to be hunted. Light greyhounds and other *taysours* [hounds for putting up and driving game] were slipped, and as they drove the deer the *stablye* or beaters belonging to the ring of stations, directed their course to where the lord and his party stood ready to shoot them. The men of the *stablye* also tried to strike down the deer if they came close enough, and at any of the stations there might be some larger greyhounds ("receivers") to pull the deer down' (J.R.R. Tolkien and E.V. Gordon [eds.], *Sir Gawain and the Green Knight*, 2nd edn, revised by N. Davis [Oxford, 1967], 106-7).

38. *Tristram*: i.e. Tristram (Tristrams, Tristan) of Lyonesse, an Arthurian warrior, best known for his tragic love-affair with Isolde (Isode, Yseult), but also particularly associated with hunting skills. Sir Thomas Malory, a younger contemporary of Bower, describes him thus: 'And aftir, as he [Tristram] growed in myght and strength, he laboured in huntynge and in hawkynge – never jantylman more that ever we herde rede of. And as the booke seyth, he began good mesures of blowynge of beestes of venery and beestes of chaace and all maner of vermaynes, and all the tearmys we have yet of hawkynge and huntynge. And therefore the booke of venery, of hawkynge and huntynge is called the booke of sir Tristrams' (E. Vinaver [ed.], *The Works of Sir Thomas Malory* [Oxford, 1954], 279-80). Cf. also the anonymous 13c, possibly Scots, romance, *Sir Tristrem*, ll.441-528 (G.P. McNeill [ed.], *Sir Tristrem* [STS, 1886], 13-15).

Chapter 12
pp.33-35

This chapter corresponds to *Fordun* (V c.10). See *Pluscarden*, V c.10; nothing

in *Extracta*. Cf. *Wyntoun*, iv, 328-33. Bower has added ll.38-61 ('About the same ... killed etc.') from a source resembling *Melrose*.

1-37. ... *matters*: see the introductory note to c.11 above.

8. *enemies*: see above c.11, l.18.

13. *lay siege to my bed*: note the contemptuous *double entendre*. Malcolm asks whether his opponent shamefully plans to murder him while he sleeps, and does so in terms which equate the scheme with the seductive approach of a loose woman to her intended lover. Cf. the same figure in *Wyntoun*, ut cit.

15. *knight*: Turgot assumes the universal acceptance of the code of knightly chivalry.

31. *hostages*: this may reflect the practice of early Gaelic society. 'Even when accepted by the *tuath* ['people, tribe', the basic unit of the early Gaelic polity] and his kindred, the new king usually found it prudent to insure against the aristocratic kindreds' swinging away from him later to support a rival; and the normal means of doing so was by taking from them hostages whose life would be forfeited by their kin's defection. So normal was this that to release one's hostages was regarded as equivalent to abdication' (G. Mac Niocaill, *Ireland before the Vikings* [Dublin and London, 1972], 56). At the beginning of Malcolm's reign, that is to say, his court maintained the traditional norms of Gaelic society.

38-61. *About the same ... killed etc.*: cf. *Melrose*, 24, s.a. 1052, 1054, 1055.

38. *Emma*: see above c.9, l.49; she died on 14 March 1052 (*HBC*, 28).

39. *Elguina*: i.e. Ælfgifu of Northampton, Cnut's mistress; see above c.9, l.46n. Confusion between the two ladies was usual among early historians; the main reference here is certainly to Emma.
    Winchester HMP.

40. *Edward*: i.e. Edward II the Confessor.
    Godwine and his sons: see above c.10, ll.23, 63.

41. *Normans*: i.e. the Norman knights and churchmen patronized by Edward II the Confessor in the earlier years of his reign (*ASE*, 425).

43. *Rhys*: nothing further is known of this Rhys.
    Gruffydd: see above c.8, l.26.

44. *Gloucester* GLO. The form in the text (l.34), 'Glawornam', is somewhat unusual.

45-48. *Godwine ... Thursday*: cf. VI, cc.21-22 below. This account is more detailed than the version in *Melrose* s.a. 1054, and reflects aspects of a late story, probably based on oral saga, according to which Godwine swore to King Edward that he had taken no part in the murder of the king's brother Alfred (above c.9, l.49n; c.10, l.20n): 'Tu rex, inquit, in omni memoria germani rugato me vultu video quod aspicias, sed non paciatur Deus, ut istam offam transglutiam, si fui conscius alicujus rei, quae spectaret ad ejus periculum vel tuum incommodum. Hoc dicto, quam in os miserat offa suffocatus, ad mortem oculos invertit, inde sub mensa per filium suum Haroldum extractus est et sepultus' ('Capitula ad Librum Sextum Parata', c.15 [*Fordun*, 401]), a passage not based on Ailred, *Genealogia*. Cf. *Huntingdon*, 195; Ailred, *Vita Sancti Edwardi Regis* (PL, 195, cols. 737-90),

col. 767. The death of Alfred is not a factor in Wyntoun's version (iv, 360-3), where the figure corresponding to Godwine is described simply as a traitor and remains unnamed. Wyntoun is however aware (iv, 252-3) of Godwine's responsibility for the death of Alfred. Bower seems unaware of the rash oath which led to Godwine's death.

45. *daughter*: i.e. Eadgyth or Edith (d.1075). The wedding was on 23 January 1045 (*HBC*, 29).

46-47. *Monday in Easter week*: i.e. 12 April 1053.

48-49. *Thursday in Easter week*: i.e. 15 April 1053.

49-50. *We will deal ... appropriate place*: this sentence was added by Bower. For the 'appropriate place' see below c.17, ll.43-48 ('I think ... rejected').

51. *earldom*: i.e. Wessex, in effect the entire south coast of England (*ASE*, 561).

Harold: i.e. the future King Harold II, defeated and killed at Hastings in 1066.

Harold's earldom: i.e. Essex, East Anglia, Cambridgeshire and Huntingdonshire (*ASE*, 561).

52. *Ælfgar*: d.1062. See above c.8, l.26n.; below ll. 55-61.

Leofric: earl of Mercia ca 1030-57.

53. *Siward*: see above c.7, l.17.

loyal ... Malcolm: this phrase is not in *Melrose* and was perhaps added by Bower.

54. *Tostig*: see above c.10, l.63. Tostig was earl of Northumbria 1055-65, when he was expelled. He allied himself with Harold Hardrada (above c.10, ll.48) and was killed at Stamfordbridge YOE in 1066.

55-61. *Ælfgar ... killed*: cf. above c.8, l.26n.

58. *Gruffydd*: cf. above c.8, l.26.

60. *Hereford* HRE.

Æthelbert: i.e. king of the East Angles, killed in 794 by Offa, king of Mercia, at Sutton Walls HRE. His body was afterwards translated to Hereford, where he became titular of Hereford cathedral (*ODS*, 147; *ASE*, 210). Æthelbert's cult was not wide-spread; unfamiliarity probably explains the corruption of his name in the form 'Alberti' (text l.47; so also *Melrose*, 24, s.a. 1055).

Chapter 13
pp.35-41

Apart from two additions at ll.21-25 (see below), Bower based ll.4-73 (... 'come in') on *Fordun* (V c.11). The remainder is his own work, in the form of an extended addition in the bottom margins of MS C, fos.93-95. Fordun based himself with a considerable degree of freedom on *Malmesbury*. Of ll.5-28, for instance, ll.5-12 correspond fairly closely to *Malmesbury*, i, 278 (bk.2, c.228, ll.1-7), with 'but Turgot ... emperor' (ll. 7-8), introduced by Bower. ll.12-14 ('then ... named above') are much abbreviated from the passage in *Malmesbury* immediately following; in particular Fordun omits the slighting reference to Edward the exile ('vir neque promptus manu, neque probus ingenio') and to Edgar ('qui post occisum Haroldi a quibusdam in regem electus, et vario lusu fortunae rotatus, pene decrepitum diem ignobilis ruri agit'). ll.17-20 are probably based on a corrupt version of *Malmesbury*, i, 280: 'nam recenti adhuc regalis funeris luctu, Haroldus, ipso Theophaniae die, extorta a principibus fide, arripuit diadema, quamvis Angli dicant a rege concessum'; one may suspect that for 'Angli' Fordun's source read 'alii'. The phrase in ll.20-21 ('which ... Bastard') is Fordun's own abstract of events described by *Malmesbury* at much greater length. Bower added in the margin ll.21-24 ('The king ... usurper of England'), based on *Malmesbury*, i, 281; to clarify the narrative he also added in the margin part of l.25 ('After ... Godwine'). ll.25-28 ('the nobles ... bishops') are expanded from a passage which in *Malmesbury* occurs considerably later (ii, 307): 'Ceteri proceres Edgarum eligerent si episcopos assertores haberent.' A confused version of the same events will be found in *Wyntoun*, iv, 312-17, where the probable source however is not *Malmesbury*, but Turgot as preserved in DMS, fos. 6v-7.

ll.59-69 (... 'pity them etc') are abbreviated from *Malmesbury*, i, 277 (bk.2, c.226). We have not identified an exact source for ll.71-73 (... 'to come in'), best perhaps regarded as a precis of various remarks made by Malmesbury in his account of the battle of Hastings (i, 281-2; ii, 302-3).

The passage by Bower immediately following (ll.73-125; 'William ... blessing'), although ultimately based on *Malmesbury*, as the marginal note in MS C suggests, takes its immediate derivation from *Vincent*, XXV: ll.73-80 ('William ... king') from c.39; ll.82-123 ('His foot ... stones') from the latter part of c.41; ll.123-5 ('For before ... blessing') from the beginning of c.41. ll.129-56 ('When Harold ... battle etc.') are taken from a different source, the 'Brevis Relatio de Origine Willelmi Conquestoris' (J.A. Giles [ed.], *Scriptores Rerum Gestarum Willelmi Conquestoris* [London, 1845]).

It should be noted that Bower uses 'scriba' (text l.3) rather than the more usual 'auctor' to refer to Fordun.

See *Pluscarden*, V c.11; two brief points only in *Extracta*, 60.

1-3. *In the one ... died*: cf. *Melrose*, 27, s.a. 1066.

6. *sons of Godwine*: see above c.10, l.63.

7. *king of the Hungarians*: i.e. Andrew (1046-60), cousin of King Stephen (see above c.11, ll.8-10n).

8. *Turgot*: see DMS, fo.6v; *Early Gesta*, cc.9-10 (*Fordun*, 414).

emperor: i.e. Henry III (1039-56). His successor, Henry IV, came to the throne when he was six years old; his minority came to an official end only in 1065. He died in 1106 (*ODCC*, 633).

Edward: see above c.11, ll.6-7; 8-10.

10. *Edmund Ironside*: see above c.11, l.7; IV c.45, l.3.

sons: the plural form, which occurs also in *Malmesbury*, is curious; Edgar the Ætheling is the only known son of Edward the exile.

13. *arrived ... died*: in 1057 (see the elegiac verse-passage in *ASC* (Plummer), 187-8 [MS D]; neither noted nor translated as verse, *ASC*, 133).

13-14. *Edgar ... above*: see above c.11, ll.8-10.

14-15. *The king ... kingship*: there is no equivalent of this sentence in *Malmesbury*.

15-16. *vigil of the Epiphany*: i.e. 5 January.

16. *not quite twenty-four years*: i.e. 8 June 1042-5 January 1066.

18. *Harold*: see above c.10, l.63.

20. *scarcely nine months*: i.e. 6 January-14 October 1066.

21. *William*: see above c.9, l.35.

21-22. *Harold surnamed Hardrada*: see above c.10, ll.48.

22. *Olaf*: see above c.9, l.55; c.12, l.54.
Tostig: see above c.10, l.63; c.12. l.54.

24. *Stamfordbridge* YON/YOE.

26-28. *chosen ... bishops*: cf. *Malmesbury*, ii, 307 (bk.3, c.247).

29-55. *... wills it*; Fordun's purpose in this passage is to indicate that the English sinfully abandoned their own hereditary royal line, whose rights were subsequently inherited by the Scottish kings through the marriage of Margaret to Malcolm III Canmore. Their daughter Matilda married Henry I king of England; see below cc.17 and 35.

29. *me*: i.e. Fordun.

42. *Eadric*: i.e. Eadric Streona, earl of Mercia 1007-17. For his treachery see especially *ASE*, 388-9, 399; cf. below VI c.16. He was not Godwine's father, but according to Florence (*Chronicon*, 160), Eadric's brother Æthelmær (Ægelmærus) was Godwine's grandfather. For Godwine see above c.10, l.23.

48-49 *... land*: Psalm 36:9 (*Vulgate*); 37:9 (*NEB*).

52-53. *united ... line*: i.e. in the marriage of Margaret with Malcolm III Canmore already mentioned.

68. *as did ... past*: cf. Jonah 3:5-10.

73-80. *William ... king*: cf. *Vincent*, XXV c.39.

74. *mother*: i.e. Arletta; see above c.9, l.35n.

77-81. *he filled ... two kingdoms*: it was assumed that by seizing the earth in his two hands the child was taking seisin or sasine – 'the acquisition of a real right in land by the transfer of symbols of the land itself at a public ceremony' (*Oxford Companion to Law*, 1103) – of two estates, Normandy and England.

82-121. *His foot ... illegally*: cf. *Vincent*, XXV c.41.

82-85. *His foot ... to be*: by stumbling and grasping the ground with his hand, William was taking seisin of England.

85. *battle*: i.e. Stamfordbridge YOE.

86. *king of the Norwegians*: i.e. Harold Hardrada; see above ll.21-22; c.10, l.48.

90-93. *almost everyone ... sprouting*: cf. above c.8, l.27n.

104. *song of Roland*: the reference is perhaps to an earlier version of the *Chanson de Roland*, the oldest French *chanson de geste*. The version now extant was composed very early in the 12c (*Oxford Companion to French Literature*, 115).

117. *mother*: i.e. Gytha sister of Ulf of Denmark who was the husband of Cnut's sister Estrith (*ASE*, 417; cf. 402-4). Gytha married Godwine ca 1020.

119. *Ealdred*: archbishop of York 1061-69 (*HBC*, 224).

120. *Stigand*: archbishop of Canterbury 1052-70. For the dubious circumstances of his appointment to Canterbury, see *ASE*, 465-6; cf. below c.14, l.17.

121-8. *William ... conquest*: cf. *Vincent*, XXV c.41 (beginning).

129-47. *... consequence*: cf. 'Brevis Relatio', ut cit., 3-4.

130. *Ponthieu*: the area around Abbeville, dép. Somme, France.

Guy: count of Ponthieu, brother and successor of Enguerrand or Isembard, count of Ponthieu, executed by William's men at the siege of Arques (dép. Seine-Maritime, France) in 1053. Guy himself, who had been captured by William's men at Mortemer (dép. Seine-Maritime, France) in 1054, ransomed himself in 1055 (*Malmesbury*, ii, 289, 290, 291). Enguerrand's wife was William's sister Adeliza.

132. *William's sister*: in *Malmesbury* (i, 280) and Simeon, *Kings*, 184, this lady is described as daughter not sister of William; in *Malmesbury* she is described as 'adhuc impubis'. Cf. below c.14, ll.9-10, 24 (where she is described as daughter); 29, 33 (where she is described as sister). If she was in fact William's sister, she is perhaps the same as the Adeliza mentioned in the previous note, and was certainly not 'impubis'. It may be significant that in 1066, immediately after his accession, Harold married Ealdgyth, daughter of Ælfgar earl of Mercia and sister of Edwin and Morcar, earls of Mercia and Northumbria respectively (*ASE*, 581). This is the only *regular* marriage of Harold admitted in *HBC*, 29, and served an obvious political purpose which may have outweighed any earlier agreement by Harold with William; cf. *ASE*, 581; M. Chibnall (ed.), *The Ecclesiastical History of Orderic Vitalis*, ii (Oxford, 1969), 136n.

134. *Bulls-eye*: cf. 'Brevis Relatio', ut cit., 4: 'Ei, sicut multi dicunt, super filacterium quod vocabant oculum bovis quod ei fidem et promissionem quam ei faciebat bene custodiret ...' The word 'phylactery' (*filacterium*), originally used of a small leather box containing sacred texts worn by Jews at morning prayer on weekdays, came in a Christian context to mean 'a vessel or case containing a holy relic' (*OED*).

141. *kinsman*: the mother of Edward II Confessor was Emma, daughter of Duke Richard I of Normandy, who in turn was William's great-grandfather. William, in other words, was Edward's first cousin once removed. See above c.9, ll.45n, 49.

147-55. *As William ... occur*: cf. 'Brevis Relatio', ut cit., 7. In ll.100-03 above the same incident is described, but the interpretation is less philosophical.

155-6. *Harold ... battle etc.*: cf. 'Brevis Relatio', ut cit., 8, where the phrase is added 'et cum iis maxima pars de nobilitate Anglorum.'

155. *two brothers*: i.e. Gyrth and Leofwine; see above c.10, l.63.

Chapter 14
pp.43-47

In this chapter ll.1-10 (... 'under-age'), 13-17, 39-42 (... 'October'), 48, 50, 68-84, correspond to *Fordun* (V c.12). Bower has added ll.10-12, 42-67 ('Then ... this day'), and in the margin ll.2-3 ('and that ... themselves'), 18-39 (... 'illegally'), and 49. See *Pluscarden*, V c.12, and *Extracta*, 60.

1-17. ... *French*: in DMS (fo.22v) the three causes given for the invasion are (1) that Godwine and his sons had murdered Alfred; (2) that they had brought about the expulsion of Archbishop Robert, Earl Odo and all the French from England; (3) that Harold had usurped the kingdom. In *Early Gesta*, c.11 (*Fordun*, 415) a phrase has been inserted under (3): '[Haroldus] filiam suam, in uxorem ductam, omittens.' In Book V Fordun gives primacy to (3), and the phrase he had added in *Early Gesta* is altered to become: 'quod itaque filiam suam adhuc impubem duceret uxorem promisit.' Bower makes the fate of William's daughter a separate cause for the invasion of England and adds some sensational details.

Note that according to c.13, 1.132 above it was William's sister rather than his daughter who was given to Harold in marriage. No earlier evidence suggests a marriage-alliance between Harold and William.

The passage in DMS is the work, not of Turgot, but of the anonymous 'Dunfermline Chronicler'. This suggests that Fordun used a MS which, although earlier than the Dunfermline MS, was similar in its contents.

5. *agreement*: see above c.13, ll.134-5 ('He swore ... William'). If the encounter in fact took place, the date was probably 1064 (*ASE*, 578).

6-8. *Harold ... England*: cf. *Malmesbury*, i, 278-80.

7. *Dover* KNT.

9-10. *Harold ... under-age*: cf. above c.13, 1.132.

10-12. *blinded ... this way*: there does not appear to be any truth in Bower's allegation.

13-15. *Godwine ... beheaded*: cf. above c.10, ll.20-28; below VI c.20, ll.39-45.

17. *Robert*: i.e. Robert, abbot of the Benedictine house of Jumièges (dép. Seine-Maritime, France), invited to England by Edward II Confessor, and made bishop of London (1044-51); archbishop of Canterbury 1051-2, when he was driven out by a popular rising; cf. above c.12, 1.41; *HBC*, 214; *ASE*, 465-6. He was replaced as archbishop by Stigand, on whom see above c.13, 1.120.

Odo: i.e. the Odo or Odda of Deerhurst GLO, 'comes' and kinsman of Edward II Confessor, who received the earldom of Somerset, Devon and Cornwall after the exile of Godwine and Harold in 1051, but lost it again on their restoration in 1053. The loss of his earldom may have given rise to the impression that he was one of the Frenchmen expelled at this time; he was in fact English and continued to be styled 'comes' until his death in 1056 (*DNB*, xli, 423).

20-27. ... *perjury*: extracted from *Huntingdon*, 196-7.

20. *Flanders*: a coastal county now divided between north-east France and Belgium.

21. *Ponthieu*: see above c.13, l.130.

23. *count of Ponthieu*: i.e. Guy; see above c.13, l.130.

28. *chronicle*: not identified.

39-42. ... *October*: a continuation of ll.1-17 above; see *Early Gesta*, ut cit., expanded from DMS, ut cit.

42-50. *Then ... comet*: cf. *Huntingdon*, 204.

44. *Ealdred*: see above c.13, l.119.

46. *comet*: i.e. Halley's Comet on one of its return visits to the neighbourhood of Earth (J. Mason, 'Halley through History', in N. Henbest [ed.], *Halley's Comet* [London, 1986], 17-18). The comet with the superscription 'Isti mirant stellam' is vividly portrayed in the Bayeux Tapestry (F.M. Stenton [ed.], *The Bayeux Tapestry* [London, 1957], plate 35).

51-56. ... *English*: cf. *Melrose*, 27, s.a. 1067, where the phrase 'divided up the land of the English amongst his knights' does not appear.

52. *Stigand*: see above c.13, l.120.

Edgar: see above c.11, ll.8-10; c.13, ll.26-28n.

53. *Edwin, Morcar*: see above c.13, ll.26-28n, 132n.

Waltheof: i.e. the son of Siward (see above c.7, l.17), in 1072 made earl of Northumberland; executed for treason 1076 (*ASE*, 610-12).

55. *divided ... knights*: cf. *Huntingdon*, 204; *ASE*, 625-6.

56. *tax*: see *ASE*, 599.

59-62. *This ... English*: cf. *Early Gesta*, ut cit. There is no corresponding passage in DMS.

62-67. *So he ... day*: cf. Robert Holkot, *Super sapientiam Salamonis* (Reutlingen: Johannes Otmar, 1489), lectio xi, B-b. The allegation that William intended to abolish the speaking of English has no foundation; it is a symptom of a wide-spread anti-Norman bias in 14c England (B. Smalley, *English Friars and Antiquity in the Early XIVth Century* [Oxford, 1960], 162-3, 325-6; A.C. Baugh, *A History of the English Language*, 2nd edn [New York, 1957], 138-9).

68-84. ... *cell*: cf. *Vincent*, XXV c.35.

68. *year ... above*: i.e. 1067.

69. *Henry IV*: see above c.13, l.8n.

tenth ... Malcolm: Malcolm III Canmore reigned 1057-93.

Paderborn: city, Westphalia, Germany.

71. *Paternus*: not identified.

74-84. *In a certain ... cell*: source not identified in the works of Peter Damian (PL, 144-5). The reference is taken from *Vincent*, ut cit.

Chapter 15
pp.47-49

This chapter corresponds to *Fordun* (V c.13). See *Pluscarden*, V c.13; nothing in *Extracta*. Bower has added ll.54-71.

3. *we*: in the Latin text the construction is impersonal, but the reference is clearly intended by Fordun for himself, and is accepted by Bower.

4-5. *our princes ... example*: i.e. one of the purposes of *Scotichronicon* is to be a Mirror for Princes; for the theme and some aspects of its development in medieval times and later see W. Farnham, *The Medieval Heritage of Elizabethan Tragedy* (Oxford, 1963), 69-172.

9-52. *... bad*: abbreviated and rearranged from *Malmesbury*, ii, 304-6 (c.245). Malmesbury's account of English decadence is much exaggerated; see, e.g., *ASE*, 545-54.

54-55. *... Northumbrians*: cf. *Melrose*, 27, s.a.1069; Earl Robert was killed on 29 January 1069 (*ASE*, 602).

55-71. *... St Peter*: see *Martin*, 434 (s.a. 1063).

55. *Alexander II*: pope 1061-73 (*ODP*, 152-3).

57. *Lucca*: city of Tuscany, Italy.
Cadalus: i.e. Peter Cadalus, bishop of Parma 1046-61; antipope Honorius II 1061-4 (*ODP*, 153-4).
Parma: city, Emilia-Romagna, Italy.

58. *Lombardy*: territorial division of northern Italy, centreing on Milan.
asserting: in l.48 of the text 'asserentes' disagrees grammatically with the antecedent 'episcopis'. Bower has copied this solecism from *Martin*, ut cit.

59. *parvis of Italy*: i.e. the porch or entry of Italy – in effect Lombardy (*OED*, s.v. 'parvis').

60. *twice*: i.e. in 1062 and 1063 (*ODP*, 154).

62. *Henry*: i.e. Henry IV; see above c.13, l.8n.

63. *council*: i.e. the council at Mantua, 1064 (*ODP*, 153).
Mantua: city, Lombardy, Italy.

64. *city*: i.e. Rome. Bower has here omitted some words in *Martin*, ut cit.: 'et ibidem defunctus. In Lateranensi ecclesia est tumulatus.'

64-65. *seized ... pope*: in 1053 Leo IX (1049-54) was defeated by the Norman, Robert Guiscard (ca 1015-85). In 1059 Nicholas II (1058-61) invested Guiscard with the duchies of Apulia and Calabria and the lordship of Sicily. At the same time he invested another Norman, Richard of Aversa, with the principality of Capua in Campania (*ODP*, 147-8, 152).

65. *Apulia*: i.e. Puglia, district of south-eastern Italy.

66. *Campania*: district of Italy south of Rome.
driven out: 1066 × 1069 (*CMH*, v, 45; cf.178).

67. *Godfrey*: i.e. Godfrey the Bearded (d.1069), duke of Lower Lorraine and second husband of Beatrice of Tuscany. In *Martin*, ut cit., he is called 'dux Spoletanus', a title granted to him by the pope (*CMH*, v, 31).
Countess Matilda: i.e. Matilda, *Grancontessa* of Tuscany 1055-1115. She was the daughter of Beatrice of Tuscany by her first marriage. It has often been assumed that Dante's Matilda, the type of the Active Life (*Purgatorio*, cantos 28, ll.40ff.; 33, ll.119ff.) is an idealization of this Matilda. She was too young in the later 1060s to join in resistance to the Normans, but was certainly very active for much of her life in the interest of St Peter, i.e. the papacy.

68.   *emperor*: i.e Henry IV; see above l.62; c.13, l.8n.

69.   *battle*: during the conflict of pope and emperor (the Investiture struggle), Matilda consistently opposed Henry IV. The celebrated penance (1077) of the emperor took place at the fief from which her family took their name, Canossa, near Reggio, Emilia-Romagna, Italy. See below c.19, ll.1-3.

70.   *made ... altar of St Peter*: the donation was made between 1077 and 1080, renewed in 1102, and revoked or modified in 1111, when she made the emperor Henry V her heir. This led to a long contest between the papacy and the empire (*CMH*, v, 104; I.S. Robinson, *The Papacy 1073-1198* [Cambridge, 1990], 246; cf. 449).

patrimony: her inheritance lay partly in Italy (northern Tuscany, Emilia and the lower Po valley) and partly north of the Alps in Lower Lorraine. For a map of the Italian estates see *Grosser Historische Weltatlas*, ii (Munich, 1970), 93.

71.   *Patrimony of St Peter*: the term is in fact much older than the 11c (cf. above II c.48, ll.139-43); it was sometimes used for the totality of papal landed possessions and rights (including claims to the Matildine lands), and more often for the lands immediately north and south of Rome which formed just one province within the whole (cf. D. Waley, *The Papal State in the Thirteenth Century* [London, 1961], 5n).

Chapter 16
pp.49-51

This chapter corresponds to *Fordun* (V c.14). See *Pluscarden*, V c.14; cf. *Extracta*, 61. In text l.1 'Scriba' rather than 'Auctor' is again used to refer to Fordun (cf. above c.13, introductory note). The entire chapter is abbreviated from a text resembling DMS, fos.7-7v, by way of *Early Gesta*, cc. 12-13 (*Fordun*, 415-16). The published text of Turgot, *Margaret* gives no account of the meeting of Malcolm and Margaret.

In *Melrose*, 27, s.a.1070, Malcolm is said to have met Edgar and his sisters, not in Fife, but at Wearmouth DRH when they were trying to make their way to Scotland. He gave them his peace and afterwards married Margaret.

2-3.   *land ... born*: i.e. Hungary.

5-15.   *Supreme ... God*: Turgot uses the traditional image of a storm at sea to indicate that apparently purposeless vicissitude may in fact be the benevolent operation of Providence. Cf., e.g., the sea-ordeals of the unhappy Constance in Chaucer's 'Man of Law's Tale' (F.N. Robinson, *The Works of Geoffrey Chaucer*, 2nd edn [Cambridge, Mass., 1957], 63-75). In the present passage the effect is heightened by the echo of the Psalm mentioned in the following note.

6.   *waves ... winds*: cf. Psalm 106:25 (*Vulgate*), 107:25 (*NEB*).

13.   *St Margaret's Bay*: i.e. St Margaret's Hope, Rosyth FIF. 'Hope' is Old Norse *hóp*, 'a sheltered bay' (H. Marwick, *Orkney Farm-Names* [Kirkwall, 1952], 25, s.v. 'Huip'). The use of this word in a Fife place-name is unexpected; cf. St Margaret's Hope, South Ronaldsay ORK.

14-15. *And we ... God*: cf. the passage, partly verse, in *ASC* (Plummer), 201-2 (MS D) (*ASC*, 146-8, with no indication of verse), where the idea that the direct intervention of divine providence brought Margaret to Scotland is more fully developed. As Stenton noted (*ASE*, 690), 'The emphasis, peculiar to this manuscript [i.e. MS D], which is laid on the English descent of Queen Margaret of Scotland suggests that its final form may have been destined for the Scottish court.' It is thus conceivable that the MS was actually used by Turgot.

18-19. *staying ... place*: i.e. probably at Dunfermline FIF, some three miles distant from the haven.

48-50. *as fluent ... years*: cf. above IV c.51, ll.6-22 (... 'fourteen years'). It is interesting, and in keeping with what is known of the court of Edward II Confessor, that Malcolm is said to have become fluent in French as well as English (cf. R.L.G. Ritchie, *The Normans in Scotland* [Edinburgh, 1954], 4-5).

50. *fourteen years*: DMS, fo.7v, makes no mention of years; *Early Gesta* has seventeem years; *Fordun* says fifteen years. Bower has fourteen probably to conform with IV c.51, l.22, above.

Chapter 17
pp.53-55

This chapter corresponds to *Fordun* (V c.15). See *Pluscarden*, V c.15; cf. *Extracta*, 61. Bower has added ll. 48-60. ll.1-25 are based, by way of *Early Gesta*, c.14 (*Fordun*, 417), on an earlier exemplar of DMS, fos.7v-8, 8v; the two parts are there separated by the story of Malcolm's encounter with the traitor (see above c.11, ll.14-40; c.12, ll.1-37.

1-5. *... God's command*: cf. especially *ASC* (Plummer), 201-2 (MS.D); *ASC*, 146-7; see above c.16, ll.14-15n.

2. *imperial*: see above c.11, ll.8-10.

4. *more ... desire*: i.e. Margaret had wished to be a nun.

5-7. *Esther ... countrymen*: see the Old Testament book of Esther; cf. above I c.8, ll.88-89.

6. *Ahasuerus*: i.e. probably Xerxes I, king of Persia 486-65 BC.

10. *Edward*: see above c.11, ll.8-10.
     uncle: i.e. Edward II Confessor.

11. *mentioned*: see above c.13, l.8.

16. *Black Cross*: this was a reliquary containing a fragment of the True Cross; cf. below c.55, ll.25-36; DMS, fo.8; *Early Gesta*, ut cit. According to Turgot (*Margaret*, c.4, para. 30 [Pinkerton, *Saints*, ii, 180]; cf. DMS, fo.16v), the queen kept it in a chest and had it brought to her on her death-bed. Cf. too Ailred, *Eulogium*, 281; *Genealogia*, col. 715.

19. *1070*: the date is uncertain; 1070 (*Melrose*, 27); ca 1069 (*HBC*, 57); not later than 1071 (Duncan, *Kingdom*, 119.
     Dunfermline FIF; cf. above c.16, ll.18-19.

25. *Not easy ... beasts*: source not identified.

27-41. *Malcolm ... opposed it*: the passage is a rearrangement, in some ways a distortion, of sentences taken from *Malmesbury* with the intention of magnifying the importance of Malcolm in the political situation. The source for ll.27-28 (... 'could') and 29-32 ('but Edgar ... arson') is *Malmesbury*, ii, 308 (bk.3, c.249), into which ll.28-29 ('Edgar ... York') have been interpolated from *Malmesbury*, ii, 309 (bk.3, c.251). For ll.32-37 ('King Malcolm ... individually') the source is *Malmesbury*, ii, 307-8 (bk.3, c.248); translation is difficult, but Fordun has made it appear that Malcolm rather than William besieged York. ll.37-41 ('These two ... opposed it') are loosely based on *Malmesbury*, ii, 307 (bk.3, c.247).

28. *Stigand*: see above c.13, l.120; c.14, l.17. Neither Stigand nor Ealdred was ever a refugee in Scotland.

29. *Ealdred*: see above c.13, l.119n.

31. *harried*: the reference is to Malcolm's invasion of northern England in 1070 (Duncan, *Kingdom*, 119).

33. *Morcar*: see above c.13, l.132n.
  Waltheof: see above c.14, l.55.
  Danes: i.e. the crews of the Danish fleet which reached England in 1069 (*ASE*, 602).

34. *breached ... York*: in autumn 1069 Edgar with Waltheof, Cospatrick (earl of Northumbria 1067-8 and 1070-72, when he fled to Scotland) and others joined the Danes in the capture of York. Neither Morcar nor Malcolm was directly involved (*ASE*, 603, 606). According to *Malmesbury*, ut cit., William later almost destroyed York, 'unicum rebellionum suffugium', when he recaptured it before Christmas; 'ibi enim rex Scottorum Malcolmus cum suis, ibi Edgarus et Marcherius [Morcar] et Weldeofus cum Anglis et Danis, nidum tyrannidis saepe fovebant; saepe duces illius trucidabant, quorum singillatim exitus si commemoravero, fortasse superfluus non ero, licet fastidii discrimen immineat.' Fordun has badly distorted the sense of this passage; particularly difficult is the meaning to be attached to 'fovebant' (text l.31), which in *Malmesbury* has its regular sense, 'nourished, nursed' ('nourished as a nest of tyranny'). A late 16c source gives 'pierce' as a possible meaning for 'foveo' (*Word-List*, 199); for want of anything better we have assumed a related meaning in the translation.

37-47. *These two ... rejected*: cf. above l.28n.

37-41. *These two ... opposed it*: cf. above c.13, introductory note and ll.26-28.

42-47. *I think ... rejected*: cf. above c.12, ll.49-50.

42. *I*: i.e. Fordun, copied by Bower.

44. *Judge ... men*: the text (ll.38-39) is a misquotation of Psalm 57:2 (*Vulgate*): 'recta judicate, filii hominum.'

46. *the man*: i.e. Edgar.

49. *old chronicle*: presumably the chronicle, related to *Melrose*, mentioned above c.8, ll.26-36.

49-60. *In 1070 ... Alexander*: cf. *Melrose*, 27-28, s.a. 1070, 1071.

50. *Cleveland* YON.

52. *Christina or Christiana*: see above c.11, ll.8-10.

54. *deposed*: in April 1070 (*ASE*, 659).

Pope Alexander: see above c.15, l.55.

55. *many other clerics*: i.e. Æthelmær, bishop of Elmham, Æthelric, bishop of Selsey and Leofwine, bishop of Lichfield. There is a 'vague report' that certain abbots were also degraded (*ASE*, 660-1).

55-56. *because ... king*: the phrase does not occur in *Melrose*, ut cit. The grounds for the depositions are not always clear, but it is unlikely that this was one.

56-78. *death ... Ealdred*: in 1069 (*HBC*, 281). The phrase does not occur in *Melrose*, ut cit.

57. *Thomas*: i.e. Thomas of Bayeux, archbishop of York 1070-1100 (*HBC*, 281).

Lanfranc: i.e. the Italian, Lanfranc, former abbot of Bec and Caen in Normandy, archbishop of Canterbury 1070-89 (*ASE*, 662-76).

59. *set out for Rome*: in the autumn of 1071 (*ASE*, 664).

Chapter 18
pp.55-59

In this chapter ll.8-41 ('King Malcolm ... horse-flesh') correspond to *Fordun* (V c.16), partly based on *Early Gesta*, c.16 (*Fordun*, 419). The opening (ll.1-8) differs substantially from the first two sentences in *Fordun* and is presumably the work of Bower, who also contributed ll.41-65. See *Pluscarden*, V c.16; cf.*Extracta*, 61.

1-2. *In 1070 ... Stephen*: see *Vincent*, XXV c.46. The Grandmontine Order, now extinct, was founded by St Stephen of Muret (ca 1054-1124); their mother-house was established at Grandmont, dép. Haute-Vienne, France. The monks were known as 'Bonshommes' (*ODCC*, 589; cf. *NCE*, vi, 694-5). Bower's reason for introducing this reference is not clear; no Grandmontine house was established in Scotland.

3-4. *In 1067 ... reign*: cf. *Early Gesta*, c.16 (*Fordun*, 419). There is no real equivalent in DMS. Cf. *Melrose*, 25, inserted folio 13.

3. *1067*: so *Early Gesta* and *Melrose*, ut cit. The date is apparently derived from *ASC* (Plummer), 201, MS E, or more probably MS D; *ASC*, 146. See above c.17, l.19.

4-8. *He laid ... married Margaret*: source not identified. The story is appreciably different from what is told above, cc.16, 17.

5. *Cleveland* YON.

5-6. *Wirwida ... Wearmouth* DRH; the form 'Wirwida' may be a corruption of Old English *Wiramuða* (*ODEPN*, 502).

8. *Culross* FIF. The burgh is some six miles west of St Margaret's Hope.

8-13. *King Malcolm ... individually*: see *Early Gesta*, c.16 (*Fordun*, 419), apparently derived from an exemplar of the text found in DMS, fo.23, the work of the 'Dunfermline Chronicler' rather than of Turgot as claimed both in *Early Gesta* and *Fordun*. Cf. *Melrose*, 25, inserted folio 13, s.a. 1056. Cf. *Wyntoun*, iv, 344-7.

The influence over Malcolm of Margaret 'is most strikingly exemplified in the names borne by her sons, of which four are those of her own ancestors of the royal house of Wessex: Edward, the eldest (after her father), Edgar (after her brother), Edmund (after her grandfather), Ethelred (after her great-grandfather). Alexander was named after Pope Alexander II or the Macedonian and David after the Welsh saint or the psalmist. Their daughters were called Edith (but later usually called Matilda) and Mary. Entirely absent are the names of the house of Alpin, names which, by recalling predecessors and ancestors, were a proud assertion of belonging to the royal race' (Duncan, *Kingdom*, 124).

9. *Edward*: d.1093, killed at Alnwick NTB with his father (see below c.25).

Edmund: possibly joint-king with Donald III 1093-7; became a monk in England (see below c.29, ll.10-12, 39-47).

Æthelred: earl of Fife 1097, and lay abbot of Dunkeld (see below c.29, ll.6-10).

Edgar: reigned 1097-1107 (see below cc.30, 34, 35).

Alexander: earl of Gowrie 1097-1107; reigned as Alexander I 1107-24 (see below cc.36-40).

10. *David*: i.e. David I, prince of Cumbria ca 1113-24; king of Scotland 1124-53 (see below cc.41-59).

Matilda: married Henry I of England 1100; d.1118 (see below cc.35, 39, 40).

11. *Mary*: married 1102 Eustace III, count of Boulogne 1093-1125; d. 1116 in Bermondsey SUR (see below c.39).

13-37. *The king ... them*: cf. *Early Gesta*, c.16 (*Fordun*, 419). Bower has omitted the sentence which in *Early Gesta* and *Fordun* separates this extract from ll.8-12 above: 'Qualis vero, vel quanti meriti fuerat illa beata regina Scociae Margareta apud Deum et homines, vitam ejus laudabilem, miracula et mortem preciosam liber inde confectus legentibus manifestat.' The reference is probably both to Turgot *Margaret* and to the unpublished collection of 'Miracles of Margaret' in DMS, fos.26- 41v; a version of the sentence will be found in DMS, fo.23, which otherwise contains nothing resembling this passage.

13. *often invaded*: i.e. in 1070, 1079, 1091, 1093 (Duncan, *Kingdom*, 119-21).

22-26. *who will be able ... slavery*: cf. Turgot, *Margaret*, 312 (para. 19).

29-30. *after Walcher ... Gateshead*: for the sequence of events see *ASE*, 613-14. Bishop Walcher d. 14 May 1080 (*HBC*, 241).

30. *Gateshead* DRH.

34. *twelve vills*: these have not been identified (see Duncan, *Kingdom*, 120).

35. *Northumbrians*: *Early Gesta* reads 'Anglos'; *Fordun* 'Northmannos.'

37-41. *Around ... human flesh*: cf. *Vincent*, XXV c.42. The text which we have used has no equivalent for the phrase 'and many of them horse-flesh', which is found in *Fordun*.

38. *fourteenth year of Henry IV*: i.e. 1070. Henry reigned 1056-1106.

39. *French*: i.e. the Normans.

41-48. *In 1072 ... Gregory VII*: cf. *Melrose*, 28, s.a. 1072, 1073, 1074.

41-46. *In 1072 ... withdrew*: cf. *Wyntoun*, iv, 346-7.

43. *Abernethy* PER.
for his lands in England: this qualification does not appear in *Melrose*, ut cit.

44-46. *King William ... withdrew*: for a more detailed account of this incident see Simeon, *Durham* i, 106 (bk.3, c.19).

45. *Cuthbert*: see above III c.51, l.5.
Durham DRH.

47. *Hildebrand*: pope as Gregory VII 1073-85 (*ODP*, 154-6).

48-53. *He was captured ... bounds*: see *Martin*, 434, s.a. 1074. Gregory was imprisoned at Christmas, 1075 (*CMH*, v, 66).

49. *Cenci*: see *CMH*, v, 44, 66ff., 179.

53-62. *This Gregory ... Ravenna*: see *Martin*, 468.

54. *Henry*: i.e. Henry IV (see above c.13, l.8n).

55. *split the unity*: i.e. by his support of an antipope during the Investiture conflict, which began in 1075 (*ODCC*, 710).

56. *council*: the council was summoned in January 1076.

57. *Worms*: city, Pfalz, Germany.

58. *council*: i.e. probably the council held at Rome during Lent 1076. There may be some confusion with the Lenten synod of 1080, which passed similar but more stringent decrees (*CMH*, v, 66-74).

58-59. *nine hundred bishops*: this is a considerable exaggeration. *Martin* (434) gives the number as 110.

60. *deposed*: the reference almost certainly is to June 1080, when Henry arranged the election of an antipope.

61. *Mainz*: city, Pfalz, Germany; this is probably an error for Brixen in Italy (see below c.19, l.9).

62. *Guibert*: i.e. Clement III, antipope 1080-1100 (*ODP*, 156-7).
Ravenna: city, Emilia-Romagna, Italy.

62-65. *And in ... killed*: source not identified. Henry besieged Rome from early 1083 to March 1084 (*CMH*, v, 68-69).

Chapter 19
pp.59-61

This chapter is the work of Bower. Nothing in *Pluscarden* or *Extracta*.

1-26. *... miracles*: this passage is an amalgam of *Martin*, 434 (Popes) and 468 (Emperors).

1. *After this*: note the chronological discrepancy; the last events mentioned in c.18 above occurred in 1083-84.

Lombardy: i.e. at Canossa, Emilia-Romagna, Italy, in January 1077 (*CMH*, v, 69-71).

3. *Forchheim*: town, Bavaria, Germany (between Bamberg and Erlangen).

4. *Rudolph*: duke of Swabia 1057-80; elected German anti-king March 1077; killed at Hohenmölsen, Saxony, Germany, 1080 (*CMH*, v, 141-2).

8. *him*: i.e. Rudolph. In *Martin* (468) the corresponding phrase is 'imperator cruento bello victoria contra Rodulphum habita.'

battle: i.e. Hohenmölsen; see above l.4n.

9. *Brixen*: now more usually known as Bressanone, Trentino, Italy (at the foot of the Brenner Pass).

10. *Guibert*: i.e. the antipope Clement III; see above c.18, l.62; he was elected 25 June 1080.

12-21. *coming to Rome ... emperor fled*: this was in 1084; the emperor was crowned on 31 March, Easter Day (*ODP*, 156).

12. *Bologna*: city, Emilia-Romagna, Italy.

16. *after ... vineyards*: the phrase does not occur in *Martin*.

18. *Capitol*: i.e. the ancient Roman citadel, built on the Capitoline Hill.

Leonine city: the part of the city on the right bank of the Tiber fortified by Pope Leo IV (847-55). St Peters is included (*ODP*, 104).

19. *castle of S. Angelo*: see above III c.36, l.55n. The castle is on the right bank of the Tiber, near the Vatican.

20. *Robert ... Apulia*: cf. above c.15, ll.64-65n.

22. *Siena*: city, Tuscany, Italy.

23-24. *Lateran palace*: cf. above II c.27, l.55; c.48, ll.59-60.

24-25. *there ... supporters*: this sentence is not found in *Martin*.

26. *Salerno*: city, Campania, Italy; Gregory died on 25 May 1085 (*ODP*, 154).

27-49. *Ambrose ... weeping*: this, together with c.20, ll. 1-40, is taken from 'Vita sancti Ambrosii', *Legenda Aurea* (Cologne, per Conradum de Hoemborch, 1478), 103v, col.1-104r, col.1; a shorter version will be found in *La Legende Dorée*, ed. J.-B. M. Roze (Paris, 1902), i, 439-40. An earlier version will be found in Paulinus, 'Life of St Ambrose', c.24 (F.R. Hoare [ed.], *The Western Fathers* [London and New York, 1954], 167-8). The incident took place in 390 (*OCD*, 1056).

28. *Tripartite History*: see above II c.53, l.22.

29. *Thessalonica*: city of northern Greece.

30. *Theodosius*: see above II c.62, ll.7-8, 9-10.

32. *Milan*: city, Lombardy, Italy.

Chapter 20
pp.61-63

This chapter is the work of Bower. Nothing in *Pluscarden* or *Extracta*.

1-40. ... *bishop*: this passage completes the extract from *Legenda Aurea* begun above c.19, l.27.

1. *Rufinus*: i.e. Flavius Rufinus, murdered 395 (*OCD*, 938; A.H.M. Jones and others, *The Prosopography of the Later Roman Empire*, i, [Cambridge, 1971], 778-81).

23. *chains*: i.e. the chains of excommunication mentioned above ll.7-8.

27. *David ... murder*: see 2 Kings, 11:2-12:15 (*Vulgate*); 2 Samuel 11:2-12:15 (*NEB*).

30. *public penance*: the parallel with Henry IV at Canossa is to be found here.

36. *Constantinople*: Theodore's capital was Constantinople (Istanbul, Turkey); see above II c.46, l.3n; c.48, ll.147-53.

39-40. *pontifex ... pontifex*: one of the official titles of the Roman emperor (*OCD*, 860) was *pontifex maximus*, 'chief priest', which in Christian terms might be rendered 'chief bishop' – a title first abandoned by Theodosius' predecessor Gratian (367-83). Theodosius contrasts his own role as *pontifex* with that of Ambrose.

41-42. ... *Dol*: cf. *Melrose*, 28, s.a. 1075. The correct date is 1076 (*ASC* (Plummer), 213 [MS E]; *ASC*, 158; *ASE*, 608).

41. *Philip*: i.e. Philip I, king of France 1060-1108.

42. *Dol*: i.e. Dol-de-Bretagne, town dép. Ille-et-Villaine, France.

42-45. *In 1077 ... him*: cf. *Melrose*, 28, s.a. 1077. For a brief account of the troubles between William I Conqueror and his son, starting in 1077 or early in 1078, see *ASE*, 608-9.

42. *Robert Curthose*: eldest son (1053-1134) of William I Conqueror (*HBC*, 35).

46-49. *In 1079 ... Robert*: cf. *Melrose*, 28, s.a. 1079.

46. *Tyne*: river NTB.

48. *Gerberoy*: near Beauvais, dép. Oise, France.

48-49. *William Rufus*: i.e. the future William II, king of England 1087-1100.

Chapter 21
pp.63-65

This chapter corresponds to *Fordun* (V c.17), partly based on *Early Gesta*, c.17 (*Fordun*, 419-20). Nothing corresponding in DMS. See *Pluscarden*, V c.17, and *Extracta*, 61. Bower has added ll.40-51; ll.40-41 ('1084 ... Teuton'), and 48-50 ('I have ... Newcastle-upon-Tyne') are added in the margin of MS C.

1-18.   ... *Newcastle-upon-Tyne*: based on *Early Gesta*, c.17 (*Fordun*, 419-20).

1-3.   ... *overseas*: Bower has omitted details (given in *Fordun* and *Early Gesta*, ut cit.) of the siege of Dol and the war between Robert Curthose and his father; see above c.20, ll.41-42, 42-45. Father and son were reconciled on 12 April 1080 (Douglas, *William the Conqueror*, 239).

3.   *lands overseas*: i.e. in France and Normandy.

3-8.   *And when ... back*: the reference is to the uprising in spring 1080 which led to the death of Bishop Walchere at Gateshead DRH; see above c.18, ll.29-30. Fordun has perhaps exaggerated Malcolm's power over the Northumbrians.

6.   *Odo*: i.e. Odo (1036-97), uterine brother of William I Conqueror, by whom he was made bishop of Bayeux in 1049. He fought at Hastings and was made earl of Kent in 1067 (*DNB*, xli, 424).

7.   *Bayeux*: town, dép. Calvados, France.

9.   *hostages*: cf. above c.12, l.31.

10-15.   *So Malcolm ... spoils*: there is no other evidence for this action on Malcolm's part.

16-18.   *sent ... Newcastle-upon-Tyne*: in autumn 1080 Robert invaded Scotland and reached Falkirk STL, where Malcolm submitted (see *SAEC*, 103-4; *ASE*, 614).

16.   *Robert*: see above c.20, l.42.

18.   *Newcastle-upon-Tyne* NTB; the castle was intended to hold Northumberland in subjection and to be a frontier-post against the Scots.

18-32.   *For a long ... behalf*: source not identified. But see *Life* of Waltheof, as in VI cc.3-4 below – presumably known to Fordun.

19-23.   *many nobles ... slaughter*: cf. above c.17, ll.32-35.

24.   *Waltheof*: see above c.14, l.55; c.17, l.33. Waltheof took part in the rebellion of 1075 against William and was executed in 1076. His body was interred in the chapter-house at Croyland LIN (l.29). In 1092 his relics were translated to the church and became the centre of a local cult (*ODS*, 429).
      Siward: see above c.7, l.17; c.12, l.53.

27.   *Judith*: daughter of William I Conqueror's sister Adelaide. She married Waltheof probably in 1072 (*ASE*, 610).

32-37.   *Waltheof ... strong*: cf. *Malmesbury*, ii, 311-12 (bk.3, c.253).

32-33.   *also known as Walderus*: this phrase does not occur in *Malmesbury*, ut cit.. The name 'Walderus' corresponds to Old English 'Waldhere', from which is derived the later form, 'Walter'.

33-34.   *battle of York*: see above c.17, l.34.

36.   *Digera*: i.e. Old Norse *digr*, 'big, stout'; cf. Earl Sigurd of Orkney (d. 1014), who was known as Sigurd *digri*, 'Sigurd the Stout' (Crawford, *Scandinavian Scotland*, 64).

37-39.   *King William ... Northumbria*: source not identified.

38.   *fifteenth year*: i.e. in 1081. William had in fact returned to England by Christmas 1080 (*HBC*, 34).

40-43. ... *surveyed*: this passage may be based on the lost chronicle referred to above c.8, ll.26-36.

40-41. *1084 ... Teuton*: source not certainly identified. St Bruno (ca 1032-1101) established the monastery of the Grande Chartreuse, dép. Isère, France, in 1084 (*ODCC*, 205, 244). Perth, founded by James I in 1429, was the sole Carthusian house in Scotland.

41-42. *William ... England*: cf. *Melrose*, 28, s.a. 1084; see *ASC*, 161; *ASC* (Plummer), 215, s.a.1083.

42. *hide*: a division of land, 'the tenement of a normal peasant, the holding which supported a ceorl and his household' (*ASE*, 279).

42-43. *in 1086 ... surveyed*: cf. *Melrose*, 28, s.a. 1086. The reference is to Domesday Book.

43-45. *In it ... 15,000*: the source for these figures is probably a corrupt version of a passage to be found in V.H. Galbraith (ed.), *The St Albans Chronicle 1406-1420* (Oxford, 1937), 55:

> Quot ecclesie, quot ville sunt in Anglia. In Anglia sunt ecclesie parrochiales quadraginta sex milia octingente viginti due. Item ville quinquaginta duo milia. Item episcopatus xvii. Item feoda militum triginta quatuor milia ducenta et quindecim. De quibus in manibus religiosorum sunt viginti octo milia et quindecim.

The context is an account of the English Parliament of 1410, when there was an attempt by some anti-clerical knights to get the government (then in the hands of Prince Henry while Henry IV was ill) to disendow the whole church in England by confiscating its temporalities. The value of these is itemised at considerable length in a document which has been copied into this chronicle (though there is no sign of it in the official Rolls of Parliament). It is argued that the king, earls, knights and men-at-arms could all benefit from such a redistribution of wealth. The clergy are expected to live on their spiritualities alone. Then comes the above statement, which appears to be separate from the document, and was presumably inserted by the St Albans chronicler (probably Thomas Walsingham) from some source available to him. The suggestion for disendowment was turned down by the government, with the comment that it was tainted with Lollardy (which no doubt it was).

The figures for the number of parish churches in both this and Bower's version are wildly wrong – the true total was under 10,000 (see J.C. Dickinson, *The Later Middle Ages* [London, 1979], 46). But there must have been a common origin for both statements that may have been readily available in a number of sources in which the numbers had come to be variable. The last words here ('viginti octo milia et quindecim') make sense of Bower's confused final words ('xxviii milites xv') where 'milites' appears to be a corrupt reading for 'milia et'. The numbers throughout are simple numerical totals unrelated to hide values.

We are much indebted to Dr C.J. Given-Wilson for help with this note.

45-51. *In this year ... Bari*: the ultimate source for this passage may be the lost chronicle referred to above c.8, ll. 26-36.

45-48. *In this year ... habit*: cf. *Melrose*, 28-29, s.a. 1086.

45. *Edgar*: cf. above c.11, ll.8-10.

47. *Apulia*: i.e. Puglia, district of south-eastern Italy, controlled by the Normans; cf. above c.15, ll.64-65.

Christina: see above c.11, ll.8-10.

48. *Romsey* HMP: see *VCH Hampshire*, ii, 126.

48-50. *I have found ... Newcastle-upon-Tyne*: cf. *Wyntoun*, iv, 345, where Agatha is not mentioned. For Agatha see above c.11, ll.8-10.

51. *In 1086 ... Bari*: cf. *Melrose*, 29, s.a. 1087.

Nicholas: see above II c.47, l.50.

Myra: town near the Mediterranean coast of Lycia, modern Dembre, Turkey.

Bari: city of Puglia, Italy. The transference of the relics took place when Myra and its shrine were taken by the Seljuk Turks. Bari, which had recently come into the hands of the Normans, had a largely Greek-speaking population for whom the cult of St Nicholas had a particular appeal (*ODS*, 315-17; *ODCC*, 970).

Chapter 22
pp.67-69

The greater part of this chapter is the work of Bower, using several sources, which included an exemplar of DMS. The opening sentence (... 'Rouen') and ll.23-34 are taken from *Fordun* (V c.19). Bower here does not follow Fordun's chapter-order; cc.23 and 24 below are based, or partly based, on *Fordun* (V c.18); in c.24 below Bower returns to the use of material from *Fordun* (V c.19). See the introductory notes to the chapters. See *Pluscarden*, V c.19; nothing in *Extracta*. Bower made a number of marginal additions in MS C, one substantial: l.15 ('and he granted ... son'); ll.20-22 ('His epitaph ... comet'); ll.44-45 ('For more ... following') and ll.46-76 ('In 1088 ... life').

At the start of the chapter and at two places within it MS CA adds material from VII c.31.

1. *thirty-first year*: i.e. in 1087.

2. *Rouen*: city, dép. Seine-Maritime, France.

3-20. *When ... gifts*: cf. *Melrose*, 29, s.a. 1087; *Early Gesta*, c.21 (*Fordun*, 423). The passage may be based on the lost chronicle referred to above c.8, ll.26-36.

4. *Mantes*: i.e. Mantes-la-Jolie or Mantes-Gassicourt, town, capital of the Vexin-Français, dép. Seine-et-Oise, France.

9. *Odo*: see above c.21, l.6. Odo had been arrested, forfeited and imprisoned in 1082 (*ASE*, 616).

Morcar: see above c.14, l.53. He had been imprisoned after the siege of Ely CAM in 1071 (*DNB*, xxxviii, 391).

10. *Roger*: i.e. Roger Fitzwilliam, earl of Hereford, imprisoned after his unsuccessful rebellion in 1075 (*DNB*, xix, 229).

Siward surnamed Barn: imprisoned after the siege of Ely CAM in 1071 (Simeon, *Kings*, 195, s.a. 1071).

Wulfnoth: described as a son of Earl Godwine, already in 1052 held by William as a hostage on behalf of Edward II Confessor; cf. *Malmesbury*, i, 245 (bk.2, c.200): 'Wulnodus a rege Edwardo Normanniam missus, quod eum pater obsidem dederat, ibi toto tempore Edwardi inextricabili captione irretitus, regnante Willelmo in Angliam remissus, in vinculis Salesbiriae consenuit.' He is not included in the list of Godwine's five sons above c.10, l.63.

13. *William*: i.e. William II Rufus, king of England 1087-1100

14. *Robert*: see above c.20, ll.42-45n; 42n.

15. *exile*: Robert had left England in or about 1081 (*DNB*, xlviii, 349ff.).

and he ... son: this phrase is paralleled in the work of the Dunfermline Chronicler (DMS, fo.22v, col.B) and in *Early Gesta*, ut cit., but is not found in *Melrose*. Bower added it in the margin.

Henry: i.e. Henry I Beauclerk, king of England 1100-35.

17. *twenty-one years and eleven months*: in fact he reigned from Christmas Day 1066 to 9 September 1087 (*HBC*, 34). *Melrose* and *Early Gesta*, ut cit., both read 'twenty years and eleven months'; the Dunfermline Chronicler, ut cit., has 'twenty-one years'.

19. *Caen*: town, dép. Calvados, France.

21-22. *... comet*: cf. the Dunfermline Chronicler, ut cit.; *Huntingdon*, 213 (bk.6, c.42). The reference is to the appearance of Halley's comet in 1066 (see above c.14, l.47).

23. *... Caen*: cf. *Malmesbury*, ii, 337 (bk.3, c.283): 'Corpus, regio sollempni curatum, per Sequanam Cadomum delatum.'

24-34. *Then one ... accusation*: see *Malmesbury*, ii, 337-8 (bk.3, c.283).

28. *knight*: In 'Excerpta de vita Willelmi' (J.A. Giles [ed.], *Scriptores Rerum Gestarum Willelmi Conquestoris* [London, 1845], 53-71), 69, he is called 'Ascelinus Arturi filius.'

32. *Henry*: see above l.15n. Henry had received an unusually good education, whence the later name 'Beauclerk' (see below ll.50, 64).

35-44. *... depart*: cf. *Melrose*, 29, s.a. 1087. The passage may be based on the lost chronicle referred to above c.8, ll.26-36.

36. *Winchester* HMP.

39. *Lanfranc*: see above c.17, l.57.

41. *Wulfnoth son of Harold*: not identified; perhaps a mistake for Wulfnoth brother of Harold; see above l.10.

42. *Duncan*: i.e. the future Duncan II, son of Malcolm III Canmore by his first wife Ingibiorg; king of Scotland 1094 (*HBC*, 57). He was probably given as a hostage by his father after William I's invasion of 1072 (*ES*, ii, 34; above c.18, ll.41-46).

46-60. *In 1088 ... Tinchebray*: this passage may be based on the lost chronicle referred to above c.8, ll.26-36.

46-47. *In 1088 ... unsuccessful*: cf. *Melrose*, 29, s.a. 1088 and *Early Gesta*, c.21 (*Fordun*, 423).

47. *king*: i.e. William II Rufus.

47-52. *In 1096 ... annually*: for the sequence of events see Poole, *From Domesday*, 110-16.

47-50. *In 1096 ... him*: cf. *Melrose*, 30, s.a. 1096, where the phrase 'for a crusade to the Holy Land' does not appear.

50-52. *In 1101 ... annually*: cf. *Melrose*, 30, s.a. 1101.

53. *and that ... to him*: source not identified. The statement has no historical foundation.

54-55. *In 1105 ... Normans*: cf. *Melrose*, 30, s.a. 1105, where however the entry is couched in terms more hostile to Henry: 'rex Henricus mare transivit, quem receperunt omnes fere barones Normannie, spreto fratre suo, cecati multe cupiditate pecunie, et Baiocas [Bayeux] incendit.' It is unlikely that Bower would have softened his entry in this way had he been using *Melrose* as his immediate source.

55-60. *In the following ... Tinchebray*: cf. *Melrose*, 30-31, s.a. 1106. There is no equivalent for l.57 ('Angered ... Bayeux'; Henry rather than Robert burned Bayeux in 1105; cf. preceding note) or for ll.58-59 ('and imprisoned'). There are also a number of minor, purely verbal, differences between *Melrose* and the present text.

57. *Bayeux*: see above c.21, l.7.

59. *Robert de Stuteville*: i.e. Robert Grundebeof, father of Robert de Stuteville who fought at the Standard in 1138, and grandfather of the justiciar Robert de Stuteville who died in 1186 (*DNB*, v, 139).

60. *William count of Mortain*: son of Robert, uterine brother of William I Conqueror, and thus cousin of Henry I (*DNB*, xxxix, 117). Mortain is in dép. Manche, France.

　Tinchebray: small town, dép. Orne, France. For the battle which was fought on 28 September 1106 see Poole, *From Domesday*, 120-1.

61. *chronicle ... 'Margaret'*: i.e. the work of the Dunfermline Chronicler (DMS, fos.21v, col.A-25v, col.A). The rubric, which begins 'De sancta Margarita regina', probably gave rise to the title.

61-75. *William ... imprisonment*: cf. DMS, fo.22v, col. B-fo.23, col.A. The phrase 'his conquest' (l.64), which does not appear in the DMS, is found in *Early Gesta*, ut cit. The text in the existing DMS is thus probably somewhat shortened from that used by Fordun and Bower. Alternatively Fordun may have expanded his exemplar when composing *Early Gesta*.

61-67. *William ... money*: cf. *Huntingdon*, 211; *Wyntoun*, iv, 339.

62. *three sons*: William in fact had four sons, the second of whom, Richard, died young (*HBC*, 35).

64. *conquest*: a pun; the word has its usual sense, as in the phrase 'Norman Conquest', but it is also used as a legal term: 'The personal acquisition of real property otherwise than by inheritance. Real estate so acquired as opposed to heritage' (*OED*).

65-67. *When Robert ... money*: early in the reign of William II Rufus, Robert sold the Cotentin and the Avranchin (dép. Manche, France) to his brother Henry. In 1091 William combined with Robert to drive Henry out of his new possessions (Poole, *From Domesday*, 104-7).

68-69. *Vengeance ... repay*: Romans 12:19; cf. Deuteronomy 32:35.

71. *Godfrey de Bouillon*: first Crusader to be ruler of Jerusalem (1099-1100, when he died). See below c.31, 1.13; c.32, 1.29. He was the second son of Eustace II, count of Boulogne (see above c.10, 1.57).

71-76. *refused ... life*: cf. below c.32, ll.27-34. Robert was a possible candidate in July 1099 but was never offered the kingship (Setton, *Crusades*, i, 338-9).

74-75. *take ... England*: see Poole, *From Domesday*, 115-16.

75. *everlasting imprisonment*: after the battle of Tinchebray (1.60), Robert was captured and imprisoned until his death in 1134.

Chapter 23
pp.71-73

Bower has divided *Fordun* (V c.18) into two separate chapters. Chapter 23 corresponds to the first part with some additions: ll.7-8 ('to confirm ... sanctified'); 14-21 (... 'devotion)'; 33-49 ('It was ... womb'). The greater part of *Fordun*'s contribution (ll.8-13, 22-33) is based on Turgot, *Margaret*, cc.2 and 3; note that Bower went independently to the same source for his additions. Note too how in the rubric Bower (not Fordun) calls Malcolm as well as Margaret saint. See *Pluscarden*, V c.18; nothing in *Extracta*.

1. *I*: i.e. Fordun, adopted by Bower.

3. *Turgot*: see above c.11, introductory note.

4-5. *In the company ... holy*: see Psalm 17:26 (*Vulgate*); 18:25 (*NEB*); cf. also 2 Kings 22:26 (*Vulgate*); 2 Samuel 22:26 (*NEB*).

7-8. *Through ... sanctified*: cf. 1 Corinthians 7:14. Bower has changed tense and word-order; the *Vulgate* text reads: 'Sanctificatus est enim vir infidelis per mulierem fidelem.'

8-21. *Not surprisingly ... devotion*: cf. Turgot, *Margaret*, c.2, para. 11 (Pinkerton, *Saints*, ii, 166); DMS, fo.10, col.B-fo.10v, col.A. Bower (ll.14-22, ... 'devotion') has expanded the quotation to include Turgot's reference to books.

22-27. *And he ... at prayer*: cf. Turgot, *Margaret*, c.2, para. 10 (Pinkerton, *Saints*, ii, 166); DMS, fo.10, col.B.

27-37. *During ... sleep*: abbreviated from Turgot, *Margaret*, c.3, para. 21 (Pinkerton, *Saints*, ii, 174); DMS, fo.14, cols.A-B. As noted below ll.28-29, 31, Fordun emphasised the role of Malcolm rather than that of Margaret, who is the dominant figure in Turgot, *Margaret*. Bower (ll.33-49) restores Margaret's dominance.

28-29. *unless ... business*: Fordun's phrase, found in MSS FB, FC, FD, FE, but in FA only in a corrupt form, has no equivalent in Turgot, *Margaret* or in DMS. Fordun introduced it to make it appear that the king had some part in the queen's spiritual exercises.

31. *king*: in Turgot, *Margaret* and in DMS the queen is the subject of the sentence. It is she who returns to her chamber where she is joined by the king.

33. *poverty*: after this MS C begins a new sentence with the words 'Inter hec tre[s]centos', the opening words of c.24 below, derived from a better exemplar of *Fordun* than that used by Skene, which for 'trescentos' read 'crescentes'. The scribe of MS C at first intended to continue with material taken from *Fordun*, but then decided to insert more material direct from Turgot, *Margaret*.

37-49. *When it ... womb*: cf. Turgot, *Margaret*, c.3, para. 22 (Pinkerton, *Saints*, ii, 174-5); DMS, fo.14, col.B-fo.14v, col.A.

47-49. *From my ... womb*: see Job 31:18 (*Vulgate*).

Chapter 24
pp.73-75

In this chapter ll.1-14 (... 'sobs') complete Bower's use of *Fordun* (V c.18); ll.27-31 ('at this time ... nothing') are related to *Fordun* (V c.19); ll.32-53 are taken directly from the middle of the same chapter. See *Pluscarden*, V cc.18, 19; nothing in *Extracta*. Bower has added ll.15-21 from Turgot, *Margaret*, and ll.22-30 (... 'land') from another source. The marginal 'Scriba' (text l.19) in MS C has been misplaced; it should be opposite 'quem rex' (text l.27).

1-14. *... sobs*: cf. Turgot, *Margaret*, c.3, para. 22 (Pinkerton, *Saints*, ii, 175); DMS, fo.14v, col.A.

1. *three hundred*: Bower's 'trescentos' (text l.1) corrects, or is based on a better exemplar than, Fordun's 'crescentes' (V c.18; cf. above c.23, l.33); cf. Fordun in V c.19 (quoting *Malmesbury*, ii, 366): 'pascebat pauperes, primo tres, mox novem, inde XXIIII, postremo trecentos.' Turgot, ut cit., had said that Margaret served three hundred poor persons with food and drink.

8-11. *For the king ... kingdom*: this sentence occurs in *Fordun*, but not in Turgot, *Margaret* or DMS.

15-21. *... herself*: cf. Turgot, *Margaret*, c.3, para. 22 (Pinkerton, *Saints*, ii, 175); DMS, fo.14v, cols.A-B.

15. *Hours*: i.e. the Offices for the canonical hours of the day – Mattins and Lauds, Prime, Terce, Sext, None, Vespers.

Trinity: i.e. Trinity Sunday, a variable feast which occurs on the Sunday following Pentecost.

Holy Cross: i.e. 14 September, 'Holy Cross Day'; cf. above III c.40, l.35n.

St Mary: the six principal Marian feasts observed in the Western church were the Conception (8 December), the Nativity (8 September), the Annunciation (25 March), the Purification (2 February), the Visitation (2 July), and the Assumption (15 August) (*ODCC*, 98-99, 692-3, 883).

17. *holy days*: i.e. the festival days listed in the note immediately preceding.

22-39. *... every year*: cf. *Melrose*, 29, s.a. 1088-91. This passage may be based on the lost chronicle referred to above c.8, ll.26-36. Note that Bower as well as Fordun appears to have used this chronicle.

22-23. ... *succeed*: this is a repetition of c.22, ll. 46-47 above; the reference is to the rebellion fostered by Odo of Bayeux after his return to England in 1087; cf. above c.21, l.6; c.22, l.9; Poole, *From Domesday*, 100-2.

24. *earthquake*: this event on 11 August 1089 was widely recorded; cf. *ASC* (Plummer), i, 225; *ASC*, 168; *Brut y Tywysogyon*, 33, s.a. 1090 (= 1089).

25. *Philip*: see above c.20, l.41.

26. *castle*: not identified (cf. *ASC* [Plummer], 225, s.a. 1090; *ASC*, 168).

27-31. *at this time* ... *nothing*: in fact Robert had already sold Mont St Michel and other territories in dép. Manche, France, to his brother Henry. In 1091 Robert and William combined to drive Henry out. Afterwards the three brothers returned together to England; see above c.22, ll.65-67; Poole, *From Domesday*, 107-8.

30. *Mont St Michel*: abbey on a fortified island, dép. Manche, France.

31. *achieved nothing*: as noted above, they captured Mont St Michel from Henry.

32. *At last* ... *them*: this sentence is not in *Melrose*. William returned to England in August 1091 (*HBC*, 35).

33. *with his two brothers*: the phrase is not in *Melrose*.

33-34. *met King Malcolm*: i.e. in 1091.

33-39. *met king Malcolm* ... *every year*: for this encounter see *SAEC*, 105-8; and for the implications of the agreement with which it ended see Duncan, *Kingdom*, 121.

34-35. *in the district of Leeds*: this phrase is not found in *Fordun*.

35. *Leeds*: *Melrose* too has 'Loidis', which is Leeds YWR (*ODEPN*, 293). It is usually rendered 'Lothian' (cf. Duncan, *Kingdom*, 120).

37. *twelve vills*: cf. above c.18, l.34.

38. *twelve*: in *Melrose* the reading is 'twelve thousand'.

41-53. ... *strength*: based on *Malmesbury*, ii, 365-6 (bk.4, cc.310-11).

44. *Welsh*: see *Malmesbury*, ii, 365 (bk.4, c.311).

51. *slain*: in 1093; see below c.25, ll.17-30 ('one man ... St Brice's day').

52. *men*: i.e. Morel of Bamborough, nephew of Robert de Mowbray, and Geoffrey en Gulevent (*ES*, ii, 51, 52; *SAEC*, 111).

Robert de Mowbray: created earl of Northumberland between 1080 and 1082; rebelled, captured and imprisoned 1095; d. ca 1125 (*DNB*, xxxix, 225; Poole, *From Domesday*, 109-10).

Chapter 25
pp.75-77

With the exceptions of ll.1-3 (... 'Bloet'), this chapter corresponds to *Fordun* (V c.20), where it is ascribed to Turgot. Nothing corresponding is to be found in the printed versions of Turgot, *Margaret*, but cf. DMS, fo.17, cols.A-B, fo.23v, col.A; *Early Gesta*, c.19 (*Fordun*, 421-2). Bower gives no indication in MS C that he is responsible for ll.1-3. See *Pluscarden*, V c.20, and *Extracta*, 62-63. Cf. *Wyntoun*, iv, 348-9.

1-6. ... *foundation*: cf. *Melrose*, 29, s.a. 1093. Fordun and Bower may have based this passage on the lost chronicle referred to above c.8, ll.26-36.

2. *Anselm*: i.e. St Anselm (1033-1109), born at Aosta, Valle d'Aosta, Italy. He became first (ca 1060) a monk, afterwards (1078) abbot, of Lanfranc's monastery at Bec. In 1093 he succeeded Lanfranc as archbishop of Canterbury (*ODS*, 19-21).

Bec: i.e. Bec-Hellouin, Brionne, dép. Eure, France.

3. *Robert Bloet*: chancellor of England by 1091; bishop of Lincoln 1093-1123 (*HBC*, 83, 255).

3-4. *Malcolm ... Durham*: Malcolm is also mentioned in the account of the founding of Durham Cathedral given in Simeon, *Kings*, 220. His presence however is not mentioned in Simeon, *Durham*, 128-9.

5. *William*: i.e. William of St Carilef, bishop of Durham 1080-96 (*HBC*, 241).

Turgot: see above c.11, introductory note. Turgot was prior of Durham 1087-1107.

7. *church* ... *Dunfermline*: the plan of this church in Fife is indicated on the paving of the nave of the present Dunfermline Abbey; it was served by Benedictine monks sent originally from Canterbury (*MRHS*, 58).

10. *Tees*: river DRH, YON, CMB, WML.
Cleveland: district YON.
Richmond YON.

11-32. *besieging ... Northumbrians*: cf. especially DMS, fo.17, cols.A-B; cf. *Wyntoun*, iv, 348.

11. *Alnwick* NTB.

12. *Murealden*: it has been supposed that this refers to a dale beside Alnwick called after Malcolm's killer Morel (Freeman, *William Rufus*, ii, 17; see below l.17). More probably it is a corruption of 'Inveralden', a Gaelic name for Alnmouth NTB rather than Alnwick (*KKES*, 51 and n.32).

17-30. *one man ... Brice's day*: cf. above c.24, ll.52-53.

17. *one man*: probably the Morel mentioned above c.24, l.52n; in one account he is described as an old comrade of King Malcolm (*SAEC*, 111, n.2; see Barrow, *Kingship*, 31).

29-30. *And thus ... Brice's day*: not in DMS, fo.17; fo.23v has 'ydus nouembris'. In *Early Gesta*, ut cit., the reading is 'Idus Novembris'; in *Fordun*, ut cit., 'Idus Novembris die Sancti Bricii'

31. *St Brice's day*: i.e. 13 November. After 'Bricii' (text l.24) Bower adds in MS CA: 'Vulgariter dictum est quod ille proditor regis mucrone dire lancie transfixit regem per oculum sive perforavit. et propterea dictus fuit percy quod anglice sonat perforare oculum sed in scriptis neque autenticis sive apocriphis hoc reperi. eadem facilitate contempnitur qua approbatur.'

32. *Edward*: see above c.18, l.9.

32-35. *He died ... Holy Cross:* cf. DMS, fo.23v, col.A., the work of the Dunfermline Chronicler.

33. *Edwardisle in Jedforest:* Cosmo Innes (*Origines Parochiales*, i, 384) identified Edwardisle as 'Long Edwardly near Jedburgh', now Long Edwardly in Jedburgh parish ROX (*RRS*, ii, 166). We have not been able to identify this place; perhaps it is the modern Langlee in Jedburgh parish. Jedforest was a royal forest in the valley of the river Jed ROX.

36-38. *After ... Alexander:* based on *Malmesbury*, ii, 309 (bk.3, c.250).

37. *Tynemouth* NTB: the Benedictine priory had been founded by Earl Robert de Mowbray ca 1088-9; it was he who supervised King Malcolm's burial there (*History of Northumberland*, viii, 46-47, 51).

afterwards: i.e. between 1107 and 1124, the reign of Alexander I.

38. *Alexander:* see above c.18, l.9. After 'deportatus' (text l.32) Bower adds in MS CA: 'Letatus est igitur rex Willelmus de morte dicti regis malcolmi quia semper crudelis et sevus habebatur. de quo scribit Helinandus quod', and continues with material from end of VII c.31 (text ll.22-46) below.

Chapter 26
pp.77-79

This chapter corresponds to *Fordun* (V c.21), based on *Early Gesta*, c.20 and the first part of c.21 (*Fordun*, 422-3). For ll.1-6 (... 'castle') the only close parallel to be found is in *Early Gesta*; with ll.7-23 ('While ... commanded') and ll. 31-43 (... 'right'), cf. also DMS fo.17v, col.B-fo.18, col.B, the work of the Dunfermline Continuator. Like *Fordun* MS C has 'Turgotus' in margin opposite text l.1. See *Pluscarden*, V c.21, and *Extracta*, 62-63. Bower has added ll.25-30 ('These verses ... Scotland').

1-24. ... *kingdom:* *Wyntoun* (iv, 348-51) has a similar story which however obscures the point by omitting all mention of the fact that at the time Edinburgh castle was under siege.

6. *given above:* see above c.25, l.1.

Edinburgh castle: here and in the rubric to the chapter the Latin phrase used is *Castrum Puellarum*, 'fort of the girls'. This corresponds to the more usual 'Castellum Puellarum' (see above II c.29, l.30n).

7-23. *While ... commanded:* for a discussion of the sources on Margaret's burial see Freeman, *William Rufus*, ii, 596-8, where it is concluded that Margaret was unpopular with the party headed by Donald *Ban*.

8. *Donald Ban:* i.e. Donald III *Ban*, brother of Malcolm III Canmore; reigned November 1093-May 1094; restored November 1094; finally deposed October 1097 (*HBC*, 57: see also above IV c.49, ll.12-14; c.51, ll.6-14; below c.29).

9. *invaded:* the magnates are said to have elected ('elegerunt') him as king (Simeon, *Kings*, ii, 222).

9-10. *with the help ... Norway:* this phrase, added by Bower in the margin of MS C, does not occur in DMS or *Early Gesta*. In IV c.51, ll.12-13, Donald is said to have fled from Macbeth to the Western Isles, which until 1266 formed part of the kingdom of Norway. This may at some stage have given rise to the idea that Donald had Norwegian help – the phrase may even reflect historic actuality.

14. *gates:* i.e. the gates corresponding to those at the head of the present day Castle Esplanade, east of the main castle buildings.

17-18. *postern ... side:* this gate was on the steep western side of the castle rock (cf. I. MacIvor, *Edinburgh Castle* [London, 1993], 27, 32-33).

26-30. *... Scotland:* see *Cronicon Elegiacum*, ll.81-84 which has the reading 'Malcolmus dictus' (l.82), rather than 'Malcolmus sanctus' (text, l.23); cf. above c.23, introductory note.

30. *in Scotland:* earlier Scottish kings had been buried on Iona.

31. *Edgar:* see above c.11, ll.8-10.

32-33. *There is ... kingship:* MS CA refers to Lucan; see Lucan, *The Civil War*, bk.1, l.92 (Loeb edn., 8).

33. *nephews:* cf. above c.18, ll.8-12.

38-39. *took them secretly:* another source states that they were expelled by King Donald (*ES*, ii, 89).

43-46. *And although ... against him:* the sentence may derive from a misunderstanding of DMS, or, more probably, the abbreviated version found in *Early Gesta*, ut cit. In both there is an acount of the alleged involvement of Edgar in the conspiracy against William II Rufus in 1098 (referred to above c.22, ll.46-47). The accusation leads to the judicial combat described in the next two chapters.

Chapter 27
pp.79-83

This chapter corresponds to *Fordun* (V c.22). The source is *Early Gesta*, cc.22, 23 (*Fordun*, 423-4), probably derived from the first part of the narrative as preserved by the Dunfermline Continuator (DMS, fo.18, col.B-fo.19, col.B). See *Pluscarden*, V c.22; nothing in *Extracta*.

The most recent discussion of the story here in cc.27-28 of a judicial duel at the court of William Rufus is in Freeman, *William Rufus*, ii, 114-18, 615-17, with a full analysis of the persons involved; the tale is not mentioned by any English chronicler, and is found only as here; Freeman argues that though the details may be legendary, they undoubtedly present 'real persons and a real state of things'; he accepts a date at end of 1093; the main interest lies in the use of the novel Norman procedure of a judicial duel between two Englishmen in place of the traditional English practice of judicial ordeal. The probably early date of the material in DMS supports Freeman's argument.

1-2. *degenerate English knight:* Bower follows most Fordun MSS with 'degener' (text l.1) here; but the version in *Early Gesta* and DMS has 'ex Anglorum genere', i.e. just 'of the English race'.

2. *Orgar*: i.e. perhaps Ordgar, king's thane, who in 1086 held two hides in Oxfordshire (*DNB*, xlii, 243, s.v. 'Ordgar or Orgar'). As was the man himself, the name is English.

3-4. *that is ... to him*: this is reasonably accurate; the word 'clito' is the equivalent of 'Æðeling' which is derived from Old English *æðel*, 'noble family' + -*ing*, 'belonging to'; in later writers it is often restricted as a historical term to a prince of the blood royal, or even to the heir-apparent to the throne (*OED*, s.v. 'Atheling'). In DMS and *Early Gesta* neither the word 'clito' nor the derivation are to be found; Edgar is described simply as 'ethelyng' or 'ethlinge'.

5-7. *The case ... law*: cf. above c.11, ll.8-10. During the reign of William II Rufus the succession to the throne remained a matter of some doubt; there is a faint possibility that Edgar was still regarded as potential heir. It is assumed that because Edgar was in some sense a member of the royal family, the charge of high treason could be heard only before the king himself.

18. *Winchester* HMP.

19. *Godwine*: not otherwise identified, save as father of the Robert mentioned below c.30, ll.22-23; just possibly he is the Godwine who was a tenant of Edgar's for lands in Hertfordshire (Freeman, *William Rufus*, ii, 616; *VCH Hertfordshire*, iv, 31, 70).

19-20. *mindful ... lineage*: i.e. as an Englishman he remembered Edgar's descent from the pre-Conquest royal line; cf. below ll.41-48 ('considered ... he had').

29. *duel*: i.e. the case was subject to trial by combat (G. Neilson, *Trial by Combat* [Glasgow, 1890], 46-50, 58-60).

49. *pledges*: see Neilson, ut cit.

50-51. *God ... hidden*: cf. Daniel, 13:42 (*Vulgate*): 'Deus aeterne, qui absconditorum es cognitor'; Daniel and Susanna, 42 (*NEB*).

Chapter 28
pp.83-85

This chapter corresponds to *Fordun* (V c.23), based on *Early Gesta*, cc.24, 25 (*Fordun*, 424-6), which in turn is derived from the second part of the narrative in the work of the Dunfermline Continuator, cited in the preliminary note to the previous chapter. See *Pluscarden*, V c.23; nothing in *Extracta*.

32-35. *For he ... weapons*: cf. Neilson, ut cit., 60.

42. *judgment of God*: cf. Neilson, ut cit., 6.

45. *attacker*: after this DMS (fo.19, col.B) and *Early Gesta* (c.25; *Fordun*, 425) insert the following words, not found in *Fordun*: 'odium vero regis, quod formidaverat, sibi cessit in contrarium'.

47. *lands and possessions*: cf. above c.27, l.2n.

48. *rights*: after 'possidendas' (text l.40) DMS (fo.19, col.B), *Early Gesta* and *Fordun* have a passage omitted by Bower: 'Sed et ipse Edgarus Etheling (Ethlinge), dum probatur regi fidelissimus, factus est ei etiam amicissimus, insuper et eum multis ditavit honoribus.'

Chapter 29
pp.85-87

This chapter corresponds to *Fordun* (V c.24), expanded from *Early Gesta*, cc.26, 28 (*Fordun*, 426, 427-8), and related to DMS, fo.23v, col.B-fo.24, col.A. See *Pluscarden*, V c.24, and *Extracta*, 63. Bower has added ll.24-35 ('He was ... bones').

1.   *Donald*: see above c.26, l.8.

2.   *Edgar, Alexander and David*: see above c.18, ll.9-10.

5.   *Edward*: see above c.18, l.9; c.25, ll.31-35.

6.   *I*: i.e. the Dunfermline Chronicler (DMS, fo.23v, col.B), taken over by Fordun and Bower. The Dunfermline Chronicler is the source only of ll.6-7 ('I have found ... died'); ll.7-8 ('he is ... Kilrymont') first appear in *Early Gesta*, c.26; ll.8-10 ('beneath ... visible') are found only in MS CA and presumably reflect Bower's own archaeological investigations.

7.   *Æthelred*: see above c.18, l.9.

8.   *Kilrymont*: i.e. St Andrews FIF; see above II c.60, l.62.

10-12.   *Edmund ... Montacute*: cf. the Poppleton MS (*KKES*, 255); *Wyntoun*, iv, 350-1.

10.   *Edmund*: see above c.18, l.9.

12.   *Montacute* SOM; as is indicated by the Poppleton MS, *Wyntoun* and *Early Gesta*, this was a Cluniac house (*MRHEW*, 98).

13.   *will appear*: see below ll.38-46.

13-24.   *Meanwhile ... Duncan*: cf. DMS, fo.23v, col.B-fo.24, col.A, the work of the Dunfermline Chronicler.

13-17.   *Meanwhile ... king*: see above c.22, l.42. As is there indicated, Duncan's birth was almost certainly legitimate; the Dunfermline Continuator (DMS, fo.19, col.B) describes him in the body of the text as 'Malcolmi regis filius sed non regine' (i.e. Margaret); Duncan appears to have been Malcolm's son by his first wife Ingibiorg; however in the colophon to the same passage he is called 'filius ... sed non legittimus'. The tradition that he was a bastard is found in *Malmesbury*, ii, 476; see also *Melrose*, 25, inserted folio s.a. 1056.

15-16.   *invested ... knighthood*: not in DMS, ut cit.

16-17.   *came into Scotland*: May 1094.

18.   *one year and six months*: in fact (as below l.30) he reigned for only six months, and was killed 12 November 1094 (*Liber Vitae* [Surtees Society, 13], 147, 152).

20-23. *slain ... three years*: cf. *Wyntoun*, iv, 352-3.

20. *Mondynes*: village south-west of Stonehaven KCD.

20-21. *mormaer ... Malpeder*: see *KKES*, 276, 284, 289; *ES*, ii, 89-91; Duncan, *Kingdom*, 125; cf.108-11. Malpetri or Malpeder is known only in the context of Duncan's death. The name represents Gaelic *maol Peadair*, 'servant of [St] Peter'. The name is not given by the Dunfermline Chronicler who calls him simply 'comes de Miernys'.

20. *the Mearns*: approximately the modern shire of Kincardine; cf. above IV c.9, l.2n.

21. *and ... Iona*: not in DMS, ut cit.
Iona: cf. above c.26, l.30.

23-24. *three years ... Duncan*: DMS, ut cit., has 'et tenuit annis tribus et dimidio'.

24. *as will appear*: see below cc.30, 34.

26-35. *... bones*: cf. *Cronicon Elegiacum*, ll.85-94. There are a number of variant readings: 'et totidem' for 'tot anno' (text, l.25); 'erat' for 'fuit' and 'Mernensibus' for 'per Merenez' (text, l.26); 'De male vivendo' for 'Malpeder comitem' (text, l.27); 'jura' for 'sceptra' (text, l.29); 'vita' for 'visu' (text, l.30).

27. *Albany*: i.e. Scotland.

31. *the whole ... against him*: Duncan II had come to power with the assistance of French and English troops. The rising against him 'is interesting for, unlike earlier revolts, it was not made in the interests of a rival; it seems to have arisen only from the strongest antipathy to the mail-clad knight and the foreign culture which he represented' (Duncan, *Kingdom*, 125). Initially Duncan was allowed to retain the kingdom, but his French and English followers were expelled. The successful revolt of Donald III *Ban* and his nephew Edmund followed.

35. *Rescobie*: lands near Forfar ANG.
Iona: Donald was the last Scottish king to be buried on Iona.

37. *five years*: in fact four years.

38-46. *... fratricide*: see *Malmesbury*, ii, 477 (bk.5, c.400).

40-42. *accomplice ... himself*: contrast above ll.10-12 ('Edmund ... Montacute'), where there is no suggestion that Edmund was Donald's associate; see Duncan, *Kingdom*, 125-6.

47-58. *So while ... interruption*: cf. *Early Gesta*, c.28 (*Fordun*, 427-8). There is no corresponding passage in DMS.

48-58. *Magnus ... interruption*: earlier chapters (e.g. IV c.16) refer to Scandinavian activities in mainland Scotland, but this is the first occasion on which Bower and Fordun mention Norse settlement and rule in the Isles. The reference is to the Norwegian expedition of 1098, for which see especially *ES*, ii, 101-18. Scandinavian domination of the Isles was of course much earlier; cf. Crawford, *Scandinavian Scotland*, 47ff.

48-51. *Magnus ... islands*: cf. also *Melrose*, 30, s.a. 1098, where however there is no equivalent of the poetic 'traversing ... seafarers' (ll.49-50), found in *Early Gesta*. Cf. *Wyntoun*, iv, 356-7.

48.   *Magnus*: i.e. Magnus III 'Barelegs', king of Norway 1093-1103.

49.   *Olaf*: i.e. Olaf III 'the Quiet', king of Norway 1066-93.
Harold: see above c.10, l.48.

51.   *Mevanian islands*: i.e. Anglesey (Welsh *Môn*) and the Isle of Man.
Magnus in fact reached Anglesey during the 1098 expedition; see *Brut y
Tywysogyon*, 37-38, s.a. 1094 (=1098). As Fordun seems to indicate,
Anglesey had at no time formed part of the Scottish kingdom. Bower may
have misunderstood the term to mean 'Man and the Hebrides'. Between 1264
and 1346 Man was subject to the Scottish kings (see above II c.10, ll.5-8n.).
Wyntoun, ut cit., has simply: 'Mawanys king of Norway than/ With his flote
the Out Ilis wan.'
Scotland: after this Fordun inserts 'et etiam Angliae'.

53-55.   *Eochaid ... islands*: see above I c.29.

57.   *Fergus son of Feradach*: see above I c.36, ll.8-9.

Chapter 30
pp.87-89

With minor verbal differences this chapter corresponds to *Fordun* (V c.25),
based on *Early Gesta*, c.27 (*Fordun*, 426-7), which in turn is probably derived
from the work of the Dunfermline Continuator (DMS, fo.19, col.B-fo.19v,
col.A). See *Pluscarden*, V c.25; nothing in *Extracta*.

1.   *Edgar the Ætheling*: note the primacy given to Edgar in the elevation of
his nephew and namesake; cf. and contrast the account given by the
Dunfermline Continuator and *Melrose*, 30, s.a. 1097, where William Rufus
appears to take the initiative against Donald *Ban* (cf. Barlow, *Rufus*, 371).

3-5.   *although ... friendship*: not otherwise recorded.

7.   *William*: i.e. William II Rufus.
he set out: this expedition is dated 'soon after Michaelmas', i.e. early
October 1097 (*SAEC*, 119), but young Edgar, with the help of the Ætheling, is
known to have exercised royal authority over lands in Scotland when acting
at Norham NTB as early as 1 August 1095 (Duncan, *Kingdom*, 125-6; Barlow,
Rufus, 353-4).

11.   *Cuthbert*: see above III c.51, l.5.

15.   *Durham*: Durham cathedral is the final burial-place of St Cuthbert to
whom it is dedicated. It is perhaps worth noting that Turgot was prior of
Durham for more than twenty years (1087-1109) before he became bishop of
St Andrews, and that he died at Durham (see Watt, *Fasti*, 290).

22-23.   *Robert ... Godwine*: cf. above c.27, l.19 and below c.34; see *DNB*,
xlviii, 361.

26-27.   *Before ... men*: the corresponding passage in DMS (fo.19v, col.A)
and *Early Gesta*, ut cit., reads '[Robertus] antequam Anglicus appropin-
quaret exercitus, Scotos in fugam convertit.' Fordun was uncomfortable with
the idea that the Scots army should have been defeated by a solitary

Englishman and amended the text. He further qualified the situation in ll.29-33 below.

27-29. *and in this way ... Cuthbert:* not in DMS.

29-34. *See ... father:* inserted by Fordun; these sentences are not in *DMS* or *Early Gesta.*

30. *as we ... Macbeth:* see above c.8, ll.1-25.

Chapter 31
pp.89-93

This chapter is the work of Bower. Nothing in *Pluscarden*; only ll.1-7 in *Extracta.* The section on the First Crusade (ll.5-54) is in effect an abstract of the primary authority, the anonymous *Gesta Francorum et Aliorum Hierosolymitanorum*, probably completed in 1099. We have used the edition by Beatrice A. Lees (Oxford, 1924), together with Steven Runciman, *A History of the Crusades*, i (Cambridge, 1951), and K.M. Setton, *A History of the Crusades*, vols.i-ii, 2nd edn (Madison, Wisconsin, 1969). See below VII cc.35-39, for another account of the First Crusade from different sources.

1. *... founded:* cf. *Wyntoun*, iv, 356-7.

Cîteaux dép. Côte-d'Or, France, some 16 miles south of Dijon; site of the mother-house of the Cistercian order.

Châlons: i.e. Châlons-sur-Saône, city, dép. Saône-et-Loire, France.

3-4. *... Robert:* source not identified.

4. *Cistercian ... Robert:* in 1098 Robert of Molesme (1027-1110) moved with some of his monks from his abbey of Molesme, dép. Haute-Marne, France, to Cîteaux, where he established a new monastery; see especially Jean-A. Lefèvre, 'Saint Robert de Molesme dans l'Opinion Monastique du XIIᶜ et du XIIIᶜ Siècle', *Analecta Bollandiana*, lxxiv (1956), 50-83. The third abbot, Stephen Harding (1109-34) probably made the first draft of the *Carta Caritatis*, the constitution which ensured the success of the new order (*ODS*, 372, 392-3). Eleven Scottish abbeys – Balmerino FIF, Coupar Angus PER, Culross FIF, Deer ABD, Dundrennan KCB, Glenluce WIG, Kinloss MOR, Melrose ROX, Newbattle MLO, Saddell ARG and Sweetheart KCB – belonged to the order.

5. *Urban II:* i.e. Odo or Eudo of Lagery, a French monk, pope 1088-99 (*ODP*, 158-60).

council at Turin: this is perhaps a confusion with the council held by the pope in March 1095 at Piacenza in northern Italy more than a hundred miles east of Turin (cf. Setton, *Crusades*, i, 229). The council mentioned met in fact at Clermont, the modern Clermont-Ferrand, dép. Puy-de-Dôme, France, in November 1095. It was during this council that Urban issued a summons to the First Crusade (*ODP*, ut cit.).

7. *aid of the Holy Land:* in 1071 Jerusalem had been captured from the more tolerant Arabs by the Seljuk Turks.

After 'subsidium' (text l.6) MS CA adds 'de quo infra dicemus' and then inserts material successively as follows: VII c.34, ll.1-71; c.41, ll.42-84; cc.42-43; c.44, ll.1-4; c.48, ll.43-80; c.49, ll.1-44; c.50, ll.2-14; c.35, ll.24-47; c.36, ll.1-9.

Henry: i.e. Henry IV (see above c.13, l.8n).

10. *Constantinople*: i.e. modern Istanbul, Turkey.

11. *Antioch*: i.e. modern Antakya, Turkey.

dividing ... contingents: cf. *Gesta Francorum*, 2, 5. The Crusaders travelled to Constantinople using three main routes.

12-17. *The army ... Hungary*: cf. *Gesta Francorum*, 2-3. Bower does not recognize the distinction between the army led by Godfrey and the earlier disastrous crusade of the people (1096), one commander of which was Rainald (see below l.14).

13. *Godfrey de Bouillon*: see above c.22, l.71. Henry IV made him duke of Lower Lorraine in 1082. His castle and county were at Bouillon in the Ardennes, Belgium.

13-14. *Peter the Hermit*: preacher of the First Crusade. He lived ca 1050-1115. He led the crusade of the people, but escaped the final massacre at Civitot, Turkey. He made a rather ignominious appearance at the siege of Antioch and was present at the capture of Jerusalem. On his return to Europe he became prior of Neufmoutier, Huy, Belgium (*ODCC*, 1072).

14. *Baldwin count of Hainault*: MS C reads 'comes de Monte' (text l.13). The apparent reference is to Baldwin of Hainault (*de Monte Henno*); cf. Setton, *Crusades*, i, 268. The brother of Godfrey, however, was Baldwin, youngest son of Eustace II, count of Boulogne 1049-93 (for whom see above c.10, l.57n). He became the first Latin king of Jerusalem 1100-18. See *Gesta Francorum*, 2, where both Baldwins are mentioned together. Bower or his source has combined the two into a single person.

Rainald: an Italian who became commander of the Italians and Germans in the crusade of the people. They were besieged by the Turks at the unidentified Xerigordon, where Rainald surrendered on the understanding that his life would be spared if he became a Moslem (see *Gesta Francorum*, 2-5).

15. *Lombards*: the people of north Italy.

Longobards: older form of the name Lombards. Here apparently the people of southern Italy; see *Gesta Francorum*, 101.

Alemanns; originally a Germanic people whose final settlement was in Alsace and northern Switzerland (*OCD*, 33). Here simply 'Germans'.

17-23. *The second ... Musio*: cf. *Gesta Francorum*, 5.

17. *territory of the Slavs*: i.e. by way of the modern Croatia, Serbia and Bulgaria; cf. *Gesta Francorum*, 5.

18. *Raymond*: i.e. Raymond IV, count of Toulouse, dép. Haute-Garonne, France, 1093-1105; previously count of Saint-Gilles (Saint-Gilles, dép. Bouches-du-Rhône, France); count of Tripoli (Tarābulus, Lebanon) 1103-5.

18-19. *bishop of Le Puy*: i.e. Adhémar, bishop of Le Puy, dép. Haute-Loire, France; appointed legate by Urban II 1095; d. August 1098, before the crusaders had reached Jerusalem.

20. *Via Egnatia*: i.e. the Roman road from Dyrrhachium, modern Durazzo,

Albania, to Thessalonica, modern Thessaloniki, Greece (*OCD*, 925); cf. *Gesta Francorum*, 5.

Bohemond: i.e. Bohemond I, eldest son of Robert Guiscard (see above c.15, ll.64-65n); prince of Antioch 1099-1111.

20-21. *Richard of the Principate*: i.e. Richard of Principato, Italy, son of Robert Guiscard's brother, William of Ferebrachia.

21. *Robert Curthose*: see above c.20, ll.41-42, 42-45; c.22, ll.47-52, 55-60, 65-76.

21-22. *Robert count of Flanders*: i.e. Robert II, count of Flanders 1093-1111.

22. *Hugh the Great*: i.e. Hugo Magnus, Hugh of Vermandois, younger brother of Philip I, king of France 1060-1108. Illness caused his return from the crusade in 1098.

Everard of Le Puits: i.e. Everard de Puisat, vassal of Stephen of Blois (see below l.29).

22-23. *Achard of Mount Merlay*: not otherwise identified.

23. *Isoard of Musio*: not otherwise identified.

23-27. *Tancred ... Scabioso*: cf. *Gesta Francorum*, 7.

23. *Tancred son of the Marquis*: i.e. Tancred (d.1112), nephew of Bohemond I and grandson on the female side of Robert Guiscard; prince of Galilee 1099-1100; count of Edessa, modern Urfa, Turkey, 1104-8; prince of Antioch 1105-12.

23-24. *Prince Richard*: i.e. Richard of Salerno, Bohemond's cousin, son of William prince of Salerno; in fact same as Richard of the Principate (Runciman, *Crusades*, i, 155).

24. *Rainulf*: brother of Richard of Salerno.

Robert of Sourdeval: Sourdeval is in Normandy (dép. Manche, France). Robert was a Frenchman who joined Bohemond's expedition.

24-25. *Robert son of Turstan*: not otherwise identified.

25. *Humphrey son of Radulph*: not otherwise identified.

25-26. *Richard son of Count Rainulf*; for Rainulf see above l.24.

26. *count of Rossignuolo*: not certainly identified; he may have come from southern Italy or from Roussillon in southern France.

26-27. *Boel of Chartres*: not certainly identified.

27. *Albered of Cagnano*: not otherwise identified. Cagnano is situated to the north-east of L'Aquila, Abruzzi and Molise, Italy.

Humphrey of Monte Scabioso: i.e. probably Godefridus de Monte Scabioso, Godfrey de Ribemont of Monte Scaglioso, near Matera, Murge, Italy (cf. Runciman, *Crusades*, i, 187).

29. *count of Blois*: i.e. Stephen Henry, count of Blois, dép. Loir-et-Cher, France, 1089-1102; son of Stephen, count of Blois-Chartres, and Adela, daughter of William I Conqueror (*HBC*, 35).

30. *Nicaea ... Rūm*: cf. *Gesta Francorum*, 13: 'Interea peruenimus ad Niceam, quae est caput totius Romaniae.'

Nicaea: i.e. modern Iznik, Turkey, east of the Sea of Marmara; capital city of the Seljuk Turks. It surrendered to the Emperor Alexius on 19 June 1097.

Rūm: i.e. the Seljuk sultanate in Asia Minor. In more general usage the word 'Romania' (text 1.29) signifies the territory subject to the Eastern Roman Empire.

31.   *emperor*: i.e. Alexius I Comnenus (1081-1118).

32.   *at that ... Christian*: the doctrine of the Double Procession of the Holy Ghost, accepted by the Western church, had in 1054 led to a major breach with Constantinople. Each branch of the church now regarded the other as schismatic. In his attempt to gain Western support against the Turks Alexius I sometimes appeared willing to give ground and so restore union. The agreement with the Greek bishops of south Italy to accept the *filioque* clause, reached by Urban II at the council of Bari in 1098, may have given rise to the impression that Alexius himself and the entire Eastern church had once more accepted unity with Rome.

33.   *Heraclea*: i.e. Heraclea-Cybistra, the modern town of Eregli north of the Taurus range, Turkey. It was captured in September 1097 (see *Gesta Francorum*, 22-23).

34.   *Tarsus*: city of southern Turkey, also captured in September 1097 (see *Gesta Francorum*, 23-24).

36.   *Caesarea of Cappadocia*: i.e. modern Kayseri, city of central Turkey. For the arrival there of the crusaders see *Gesta Francorum*, 24.

36-37.   *Raymond ... Saint-Gilles*: Raymond and the count of Saint-Gilles were one and the same person (see above 1.18n).

37.   *Rusia*: i.e. modern Ruiath, near Antioch. For its capture see *Gesta Francorum*, 26.
    Peter of Roaix: one of Count Raymond's knights (Setton, *Crusades*, i, 297). Roaix is in dép. Vaucluse, France.

38.   *Antioch*: see above 1.11. The city was captured June 3 1098, but the crusaders were themselves then besieged by Kerbogha, emir of Mosul, until his defeat on 28 June 1098.

40.   *Firouz*: an Armenian convert to Islam, who bore a grudge against Yaghi-Siyan, the Turkish governor of Antioch.

40-43.   *The seventh ... Pilet*: cf. *Gesta Francorum*, 70.

41.   *Tel-mannas*: now Tel Amania, Syria, captured mid-July 1098.

43.   *Raymond Pilet*: a Provencal who apparently took part in the siege of Nicaea and the defeat of Kerbogha. He was also present at the ordeal of Peter Bartholomew (see below c.32, ll.9-12).

44.   *Albara*: i.e. modern Kefr el Bara, Syria, south-east of Antioch. It was captured in September 1098 (see *Gesta Francorum*, 72).

46.   *Marra*: i.e. modern Ma'arat en Nu'mān, Syria, captured 11-12 December 1098 (see *Gesta Francorum*, 75-76).

47.   *Kephalia*: i.e. modern Kamāl-ad-Dīn, Syria, captured late January 1099 (see *Gesta Francorum*, 80).

48.   *Ibelin*: i.e. modern Yavne near Ramlah, Israel.

49.   *Jerusalem*: captured 15 July 1099.

51.   *Nablus*: city of occupied West Bank, Israel, captured ca 25 July 1099 (see *Gesta Francorum*, 91-92).

52. *Count Eustace*: i.e. Eustace III count of Boulogne, elder brother of Godfrey de Bouillon (Setton, *Crusades*, i, ad indicem).

53. *Ascalon*: i.e. modern Ashqelon, Israel. The battle took place on 12 August 1099 (see *Gesta Francorum*, 92-97).

Chapter 32
pp.93-95

This chapter is the work of Bower. Not in *Pluscarden* or *Extracta*. For the most part it is based on *Martin*, 468, which in turn is closely related to the *Historia Francorum qui ceperunt Jerusalem* (PL, 155, cols. 591-66), written by Raymond of Aguilers, a follower of Raymond IV count of Toulouse (see above c.31, l.18).

1-27. *... following year*: see *Martin*, 468, ll.15-29.

1-5. *... pierced*: cf. Raymond, *Historia Francorum*, c.14 (PL, 155, col.611).

1. *capture of Antioch*: see above c.31, l.38.

3. *Peter*: i.e. Peter Bartholomew, identical with the Bartholomew mentioned below l.10.

5. *lance*: see John 19:34. It is perhaps worth noting that this lance, together with the chalice of the Last Supper, figures prominently in the 12c romances of the Holy Grail; see especially J.D. Bruce, *The Evolution of Arthurian Romance*, 2 vols., 2nd edn (Baltimore, 1928), 257, 360-2.

5-8. *Inspired ... lance*: cf. Raymond, *Historia Francorum*, c.15 (PL, 155, col. 614).

7-8. *church of St Peter*: Peter was regarded as first bishop of Antioch (see above II c.25, l.6).

9-12. *While ... made*: cf. Raymond, *Historia Francorum*, c.28 (PL, 155, cols. 641-2). Here Peter Bartholomew is described as passing unharmed through the fire, but afterwards injured by the enthusiastic crowd of witnesses. In other sources his injuries are said to have been caused by his passage through the fire.

10. *Bartholomew*: cf. above l.3.

14. *Acre ... Ptolemais*: Acre is the modern 'Acco, coastal town north of Haifa, Israel. Originally Ace, it was renamed Ptolemais ca 261 BC by Ptolemy II Philadelphus (282-46 BC). It was not actually taken by the crusaders until 1104. The alternative name 'Ptolemais' is found in *Martin*, ut cit., but does not occur in Raymond, *Historia Francorum*. It may be found in the *Historia Hierosolymitana*, bk.1, c.17 (PL, 155, col.851) of Fulcher of Chartres, a follower of Baldwin I (see above c.31, l.14): 'Acon vero, id est Ptolemaida'.

14-20. *They came ... cities*: cf. Raymond, *Historia Francorum*, c.33 (PL, 155, col. 650).

15. *Caesarea*: i.e. modern Horbat Qesari, coastal site south of Haifa, Israel, formerly of great importance. It was not captured by the crusaders until 1101 (see below c.37, ll.46-47), when a chalice was found among the spoil, believed to have been that used at the Last Supper (see l.5 above).

17. *Accaron*: i.e. Acre.

21. *as ... before*: see above c.31, l.49.

23. *Siloam*: see above I c.27, ll.13, 18.

24-25. *destruction ... Vespasian*: see above II c.32.

25. *rebuilt ... Hadrian*: see above II c.34, ll.46-47.

26. *king*: the title accepted by Godfrey was 'advocate of the Holy Sepulchre'. His brother, Baldwin I, was first Latin king of Jerusalem (see above c.31, l.14).

27-36. *I have found ... valley*: in MS C the marginal additions at ll.27-34 and 35-36 are written in different inks.

27-33. *I have found ... English*: cf. *Melrose*, 30, s.a. 1099; cf. *Malmesbury*, ii, 461 (bk.4, c.389).

34-35. *imprisoned ... brother*: see above c.22, l.75.

35-36. *In 1102 ... valley*: a marginal note in *Melrose*, 30, s.a. 1102, reads: 'Ordo Tironensis cepit per abbatem Bernardum aput veterem Tironem in nemore.' Under 1109 (p.31) the foundation of the church at Thiron is mentioned. 1109 is generally accepted as the foundation date of the monastery (see *ES*, ii, 142). Six Scottish houses – Arbroath ANG, Fyvie ABD, Kelso ROX, Kilwinning AYR, Lesmahagow LAN and Lindores FIF – belonged to the Tironensian order.

35. *Bernard*: Benedictine monk of Poitiers whose resistance to the abbot of Cluny led him to retire to the solitude of the forest at Thiron near Nogent-le-Retrou, dép. Eure-et-Loir, France (see Geoffrey the Fat, *Life of Bernard of Thiron*, PL, 172, cols.1406-7, 1412).

37. *It is believed*: in MS C there is a marginal note here: 'De hoc passagio vide infra libro VII capitulo XXXV cum sequente.'

37-38. *... Holy Land*: see *Martin*, 468, ll.29-30. Runciman (*Crusades*, i, 335-41) calculates that there were probably 4500 knights, 30,000 infantry, and about 10,000 noncombatants.

46-61. *... suffer*: based on Peter of Blois, 'Epistula XCIV' (PL, 207, col.294). The phrase 'for the relief of the Holy Land' (l.53) does not appear in the published text; for 'who are subject to them' (l.59) appears 'who are subjects of Christ' (*subjectos Christi*).

46. *Vegetius Renatus*: i.e. Flavius Vegetius Renatus, who compiled *Epitoma rei militaris* probably ca 388-91 (*OCD*, 1110-11). For Vegetius as an authority during the Middle Ages see A. Murray, *Reason and Society in the Middle Ages* (Oxford, 1978), 127-9. Bower quotes him elsewhere in this work (see volume indices of Authorities Cited).

Chapter 33
pp.95-99

This chapter is the work of Bower. Not in *Pluscarden* nor *Extracta*.

1. *Bridget*: i.e. St Bridget of Sweden (1303-73). She made a pilgrimage to Jerusalem in 1371 (*ODS*, 62; *NCE*, ii, 799).

1-5. *as in ... receive*: *Memoriale ... B. Brigidae*, bk.5 (not 6), revelation 13, heading.

6-12. *... am*: ibid., summary.

6. *where Mary ... brought up*: for a discussion of early Christian traditions about where the Virgin Mary was born and brought up see *Dictionnaire d'Archéologie chrétienne et de Liturgie*, X, ii, cols. 1983-7; cf. description of Jerusalem below VII c.40.

13-16. *... purpose*: *Memoriale ... B. Brigidae*, bk.7, c.14, summary of heading.

16-17. *Where ... son*: ibid., bk.7, c.13, heading.

17. *Sir Charles*: Bridget had eight children by an early marriage before she became a nun; this one is specifically named in the source here.

18-19. *Sir William Lindsay of the Byres*: third son of Sir David Lindsay, eighth lord of Crawford (d.1357); not yet a knight when granted confirmation of the lands of the Byres, north of Haddington ELO in 1367 (*RRS*, vi, 399-400, no. 36); see *SP*, v, 391); Bower as a Haddington man is writing with local knowledge.

23-39. *... task*: see *Memoriale ... B. Brigidae*, bk.7, c.13 (not 14), 3rd sections F-H.

41-50. *... in them*: ibid., bk.7, c.14, section E.

56. *cities*: see above c.31, ll.29-54.

58. *miracle*: i.e. the discovery of the Holy Lance (see above c.32, ll.2-14).

59-60. *year mentioned above*: i.e. 1098. Bower has not in fact specifically identified the year.

61-63. *... captured*: these lines are quoted again below VII c.37, ll.20-22, and IX c.48 (in MS CA at l.44); see Fulcher of Chartres, *Historia Hierosolymitana* (PL, 155), col.847.

64. *following year*: i.e. 1099.

Chapter 34
pp.99-101

This chapter corresponds to *Fordun* (V c.26), based partly on *Early Gesta*, c.28 (*Fordun*, 427), but for the most part on *Early Gesta*, c.29 (*Fordun*, 428), the last probably derived from the Dunfermline Chronicler (DMS, fo.19v, col.B-fo.20, col.A). A passage corresponding to the extract from *Malmesbury* (ll.35-40) will be found in *Early Gesta*, c.28 (see above c.29, ll.48-59 ['So while ... interruption'; cf. *Fordun*, V c.24]). See *Pluscarden* V, c.26; nothing in *Extracta*. Bower has added ll.28-33 ('Robert ... sheep') in the text, and ll.41-55 in the top and right margins of fo.101 of MS C. This folio contains extensive marginal additions (see also below c.36, introductory note); MS R follows

MS C, but the scribe of MS D has, not implausibly, inserted ll.41-55 in c.36, between 'Saxony' (l.37) and 'King Alexander' (l.39), omitting ll.37-39 there ('After ... England') from the bottom margin of fo.101; MSS B, H and E follow MS D; these additions are not found in MSS CA and P.

1. *1098*: so the Dunfermline Chronicler (DMS, fo.24, col.A); in fact 1097 (*HBC*, 57).

emperor Henry's reign: see above c.13, l.8n.

Edgar: see above c.18, l.9.

2. *Donald*: see above c.26, l.8.

4. *Rescobie*: lands near Forfar ANG.

4-5. *put out ... imprisonment*: cf. the Dunfermline Chronicler (DMS, fo.24, col.A): 'Donaldo capto et cecitate perpetua dampnato', with no mention of Donald's death or place of burial, for which see *Cronicon Elegiacum*, l.94: 'Roscolpin obiit; ossaque Iona tenet.' *Cronicon Elegiacum* however says nothing about the blinding of Donald.

5. *buried*: the date of Donald's death is uncertain. *Wyntoun* (iv, 412-17) says that after the accession of Edgar he was blinded and gelded, but kept at the royal court where eventually he murdered his great-nephew, King David's eldest son, then 'a gangande childe'. The mother (presumably Queen Matilda), who was then pregnant, died of shock, but the child whom she carried, the future Earl Henry, was delivered by Caesarean section. Donald died of thirst and starvation in the dungeon to which he was subsequently confined. Variant versions of the story will be found in Ordericus Vitalis (*SAEC*, 156-7), where the murderer is described as a cleric, and in *Cronicon Elegiacum*, ll.105-12 (*Chron.Picts-Scots*, 181), where the murderer is described as 'quidam ... insidiator' and the victim is King David's daughter rather than his son. The variations in detail and improbabilities suggest that the story bears little relation to fact.

Iona: cf. above c.29, l.35.

6. *Dunkeld* PER.

Dunfermline FIF; Rescobie, Iona and Dunfermline are mentioned in *Early Gesta*, but not in *Fordun* V; for Dunkeld Bower must have had some other source. Neither Dunfermline nor Dunkeld is mentioned in *Cronicon Elegiacum*. If Donald had behaved in the way described above l.5n, it is not likely that he would have received honourable burial in any of the places mentioned.

8-9. *In the days ... times*: see Ecclesiasticus 11:27 (*Vulgate*); 11:25 (*NEB*).

9-10. *he did not ... Cuthbert*: cf. above c.30, ll.9-20.

10-15. *gave ... successors*: cf. *ESC*, 12-18 (charters no.XV-XXII); see A.A.M. Duncan, 'The Earliest Scottish Charters', *SHR*, xxxvii (1958), 103-35; I. Donnelly, 'The Earliest Scottish Charters?', *SHR*, lxviii (1989), 1-22; cf. G.W.S. Barrow, 'The Kings of Scotland and Durham', in *Anglo-Norman Durham 1093-1193*, ed. D. Rollason and others (Woodbridge, 1994), 315.

11. *Durham*: St Cuthbert's final resting place is in Durham Cathedral, where the Benedictine monastery had been founded in 1083 (*MRHEW*, 64).

Coldingham BWK.

14. *Berwick* NTB; the town then lay in Scotland; the gift probably related only to ecclesiastical rights in what was soon to become a Scottish royal burgh (Cowan, *Parishes*, 17; Pryde, *Burghs*, 3).

17. *Ranulf:* i.e. Ranulf Flambard, bishop of Durham 1099-1128 (*HBC*, 241). He 'shamefully abused' the bishopric of Durham (Poole, *From Domesday*, 171).

18. *William:* i.e. William II Rufus.

18-19. *Robert ... above:* see above c.30, ll.22-26.

32-33. *On November 3 ... sheep:* cf. *Melrose*, 30, s.a. 1099. These lines may be based on the lost chronicle referred to above c.8, ll.26-36; cf. below ll.41-55 (... 'Kelso').

35-40. *... killed there:* see *Malmesbury*, ii, 376 (bk.4, c.329).

35. *eleventh year:* i.e. 1098.

36. *Magnus:* cf. above c.29, l.48.

37. *Mevanian islands:* cf. above c.29, l.51.
other islands: i.e. the Hebrides.

39. *Hugh of Chester:* i.e. Hugh d'Avranches, earl of Chester ca 1077-1101 (*HBC*, 454).
Hugh of Shrewsbury: i.e. Hugh de Montgomery, earl of Shrewsbury 1094-8 (*HBC*, 482).

40. *killed them:* after this MS CA inserts material from VII c.41, ll.1-33, and then all of VII cc.32-33.

41-55. *... Kelso:* this passage may be based on the lost chronicle referred to above c.8, ll.26-36.

41-46. *... agency:* cf. *Melrose*, 31, s.a. 1109, 1110.

41. *Henry:* i.e. Henry I Beauclerk, king of England 1100-35 (*HBC*, 35).
Ely CAM: in 1108 Henry I and Anselm formed the see of Ely from part of the large diocese of Lincoln, with the prior and monks becoming the cathedral chapter. The first bishop, Hervey, was translated from Bangor CRN (*ODCC*, 454; *HBC*, 244).

42. *Thiron:* see above c.32, ll.35-36.

42-47. *In the following ... agency:* ca 1110 Godric, who had been pedlar, merchant, sea-captain and pilgrim to Rome and Jerusalem, finally settled as a hermit at Finchale DUR, some four miles north-east of Durham city. He remained there until his death in 1170. His *Life* was written by Reginald of Durham (*ODS*, 186-7).

47-55. *... Kelso:* cf. the marginal notes in *Melrose*, 31, s.a. 1109, 1114, and the somewhat confused note in the main text and margin s.a. 1119. According to Simeon, *Kings*, 247, s.a. 1113, the Tironensians were established in 1113 at Selkirk, where they remained for 15 years.

47. *preceding year:* as indicated immediately above, the Tironensian foundation at Selkirk is usually dated ca 1113 (see *MRHS*, 70).
Selkirk SLK.

48. *Radulph:* not otherwise identified.

49.   *Bernard*: see above c.32, l.35; he probably died in April 1116 (*ES*, ii, 160).

51.   *William*: had probably been brought by Earl David from Thiron in 1116 or 1117 to succeed Radulph as abbot of Selkirk, and returned to Thiron as abbot there in 1118 (Barrow, *Kingdom*, 203, 175).

52.   *Herbert*: abbot of Selkirk 1119-27; of Kelso 1127-47; bishop of Glasgow 1147-64; the move to Kelso had taken place by July 1127 (*Series Episcoporum*, VI, i, 58; cf. *MRHS*, 68; see also *ES*, ii, 163).

53.   *Kelso* ROX.

55.   *church of Kelso*: i.e. the present Kelso Abbey.

Chapter 35
pp.101-5

This chapter corresponds to *Fordun* (V c.27), related to *Early Gesta*, cc.30, 33 (*Fordun*, 429, 431). See *Pluscarden*, V c.27, and *Extracta*, 65. Bower has added ll. 62-65 ('These lines ... Edinburgh'). In the right-hand margin of MS C at fo.101 he has added ll.17-19 ('This Eustace ... Jerusalem'), and in the bottom margin ll.28-41 ('The following ... perished').

1-4.   ... *kindness*: the ultimate source of these words appears to be the work of the Dunfermline Chronicler (DMS, fo.20, col.A; fo.24, col.A); cf. Ailred, *Genealogia*, cols. 735-6. In the work of the Dunfermline Chronicler and in *Early Gesta*, c.30, they follow rather than precede the account of the death of William II Rufus, the succession of Henry I Beauclerk and the marriage of Matilda and Mary (*Fordun*, ut cit.; DMS, fo.23, col.A).

2.   *Edward*: i.e. Edward II Confessor.

4-21.   *In the fourth ... book*: cf. *Early Gesta*, c.30, opening sentences, and DMS, fo.23, cols. A and B.

4-8.   *In the ... beast*: see below VII c.34, ll.53-58 for a similar account. Cf. *Wyntoun*, iv, 356-7.

5.   *fourth year*: i.e. in 1100.

6.   *New Forest* HMP.

6-7.   *Walter Tirel*: lord of Poix, Ponthieu, dép. Somme, France, and of Langham ESX, the latter of which he held from Richard Fitzgilbert, founder of the house of Clare, whose daughter, Adeliza, he married (*DNB*, lvi, 414).

7-8.   *unintentionally ... beast*: this is doubtful. 'There is, at the least, enough evidence to arouse the suspicion that the sudden end of Rufus was the result of a conspiracy formed and organized among members of the house of Clare, a conspiracy of which Henry himself was cognizant' (Poole, *From Domesday*, 114).

9.   *many sins*: there is no parallel reference in *Early Gesta* or DMS, but see, e.g., *Malmesbury*, ii, 367-73 (bk.iv, cc.313-4); Simeon, *Kings*, 231-2; *Huntingdon*, 232-3 (bk, vii, c.22).

10. *more ... later on*: an addition by Bower to *Fordun*; see below VII, cc.31-34.

11-12. *carried off... tower*: not in DMS, save for a reference to Winchester as the place of Rufus' burial; cf. *Malmesbury*, ii, 379 (bk.4, c.333).

12. *Winchester* HMP.

13. *Henry surnamed Beauclerk*: see above c.22, ll.15, 32. The surname is not given in *Early Gesta* or DMS.

13-16. *In the same ... Day*: cf. Wyntoun, iv, 358-9.

14. *Matilda*: cf. above c.18, l.10.

Anselm: see above c.25, l.2. There is no reference to Anselm in DMS. According to *Wyntoun*, Matilda was crowned by the archbishop of York, presumably Gerard, transferred from Hereford in April 1100 during the lifetime of his predecessor Thomas of Bayeux, who died on 18 November 1100 (*HBC*, 281).

16. *St Martin's day*: i.e. 11 November 1100.

17-18. *Mary ... Boulogne*: see above c.18, ll.10-12.

17-19. *This Eustace ... Jerusalem*: a marginal addition by Bower; see above c.22, l.71; c.31, l.14.

21. *later*: see below cc.39, 40. A similar promise, mentioning 'this little book', is made in *Fordun*, *Early Gesta* and DMS. The 'little book' is probably the work of the Dunfermline Chronicler.

21-41. *Now Henry ... perished*: the White Ship episode appears in *Early Gesta*, c.33 (*Fordun*, 431), probably derived from an exemplar of DMS, fo.25, col. B-fo.26, col. A, part of a section devoted to Matilda and Mary. Cf. *Wyntoun*, iv, 382-3. The verse passage (ll.30-41) appears in DMS but not in *Early Gesta* or *Fordun*.

22. *William*: born before 5 August 1103; d. 25 November 1120 (*HBC*, 35). The death of William, the male heir-apparent, led ultimately to the anarchy which followed the death of Henry I Beauclerk in 1135 (see Poole, *From Domesday*, 126).

23. *with his father*; Henry was not aboard the White Ship, which set out from Normandy after the remainder of the fleet (see *Malmesbury*, ii, 496 [bk.5, c.419]).

24. *Richard*: see *CP*, xi, appendix D, p.107.

sister: i.e. Matilda, countess of Perche (*HBC*, 35)

25. *niece*: i.e. Matilda, wife of Richard earl of Chester, daughter of Stephen count of Blois by Adela, daughter of William I Conqueror (*DNB*, xxviii, 162).

Richard earl of Chester: son of Hugh d'Avranches (see above c.34, l.39), whom he succeeded in 1104 when he was seven years old (*HBC*, 454).

27. *Barfleur*: port, dép. Manche, France.

30-41. *... perished*: the verses are also quoted in *Huntingdon*, 243 (bk.7, c.32). Bower may have obtained them there or from an exemplar of the relevant part of DMS.

30. *victory*: i.e. the battle of Brémule (August 1119) in the Vexin, dép. Eure, France (Poole, *From Domesday*, 124).

42-58. ... *Christ*: in *Fordun*, ut cit., and *Early Gesta*, c.33 (*Fordun*, 431) this passage follows directly on the account of the White Ship (see above ll.22-28).

42-47. ... *apart from her*: cf. DMS, fo.25v, col.B, where the passage immediately precedes the account of the White Ship. Cf. too *Wyntoun*, iv, 378-9, 394-5.

42. *Matilda*: born ca February 1102; married (1) January 1114 Emperor Henry V; (2) 17 June 1128 Geoffrey count of Anjou; d. 10 September 1167 (*HBC*, 35). For her struggle with Stephen see Poole, *From Domesday*, 135-48.

44. *Henry IV*; in fact Henry V, emperor 1106-25.

45. *swear fealty*: i.e. in 1127 after the death of her first husband (see Poole, *From Domesday*, 131).

46. *before ... time*: in fact Henry went to Normandy on many occasions; the reference is perhaps to his departure on 26 August 1127 (*HBC*, 35).

47-58. *Now ... Christ*: cf. the account of Matilda and Mary given in the Poppleton MS (*KKES*, 255).

47-51. *Now the aforesaid ... stock*: cf. DMS, fo.26, col.A.

48. *Matilda*: daughter and heir of Eustace III count of Boulogne. She married Stephen in 1125.

49. *Stephen*: i.e. Stephen, king of England 1135-54, 2nd son of Stephen count of Blois and Chartres, and of Adela, daughter of William I Conqueror (*HBC*, 35).

50. *Mortain* dép. Manche, France. In addition to the county of Mortain Stephen held the honors of Lancaster and Eye in England, while 'by right of his wife he was also in possession of the county of Boulogne and the English honor of Boulogne' (Poole, *From Domesday*, 132).

51. *consular*: i.e. his male ancestors were counts.

51-52. *I ... I*; Bower here adopts the first personal pronoun found in both *Fordun* and *Early Gesta*.

52. *daughters*: i.e. the Empress Matilda and Matilda wife of Stephen.

53. *mothers*: i.e. Matilda, wife of Henry I Beauclerk, and Mary, wife of Eustace III count of Boulogne.

58-62. *After Edgar ... father*: cf. DMS fo.20, col.A and especially fo.24, col.A.

59-60. *as stated above*: see above c.18, l.9; c.34, l.1.

60-62. *he reached ... father*: this passage corresponds to the end of *Early Gesta*, c.30 (*Fordun*, 429); cf. DMS, fo.24, col.A.

60. *Dundee* ANG. So in *Early Gesta*, DMS and *Wyntoun*, iv, 368-9. Regnal list I (*KKES*, 284) also gives Dundee (*Dunde*) as Edgar's place of burial; regnal list F (*KKES*, 277) and *Cronicon Elegiacum* give Edinburgh (*Dunedin*). *Dunde* may be a corruption or misreading of *Dunedin*, but on the other hand it is certainly the *lectio difficilior*, and so perhaps to be adopted.

61. *8 January*: see below c.36a, l.1, where the date is given as January 10.

62. *Dunfermline* FIF.

father; i.e. Malcolm III Canmore.

64-65. ... *Edinburgh*: see *Cronicon Elegiacum*, ll.95-96, where l.95 reads 'Post hunc Edgarus regnavit ter tribus annis.' The reading 'Trimensis' (text, l.53) is ungrammatical as well as unmetrical.

Chapter 36
pp.105-7

This chapter corresponds to *Fordun* (V c.28), related to *Early Gesta* c.31 and c.34 (*Fordun*, 429-30, 431-2), which in turn seems derived, at least in part, from the work of the Dunfermline Chronicler (DMS, fo.24, cols.A-B); cf. *Wyntoun*, iv, 368-85. See *Pluscarden*, V c.28, and *Extracta*, 65-66. In MS C the chapter begins on fo.101. Bower has added in the bottom margins of fos.100v and 101, ll.2-27 ('He is called ... day'); in the bottom margin of fo.101 after the preceding, ll.28-29 (... 'and following'); in the bottom margin of fo.101 after both preceding additions, ll.37-39 ('After ... England'). In the right hand margin of fo.101v he has added ll.64-65 ('which ... St Andrews'), and in the left hand margin, opposite the last, appear the words 'et dedicatur per Turgotum Sancti Andree episcopum monachum Dunelmensem.' The scribe of MS D has miscopied this as 'et dedicatur per Turgotum Sancti Andree episcopum monasterii Dunelmensis', which he has inserted into the text after ll.64-65 ('which ... St Andrews').

1. *Alexander*: see above c.18, l.9.

Fierce: so in *Wyntoun*, iv, 370-71; not in *Early Gesta*, DMS, Ailred, *Genealogia*, the Poppleton MS or any regnal list (for the last see *KKES*, 255, 277, 284, 289).

2-27. *He is called ... day*: this is the origin legend of the Scrimgeour family, the head of which was hereditary royal Standard Bearer and Constable of the Castle of Dundee (see E.C. Batho and H.W. Husbands, *The Chronicles of Scotland compiled by Hector Boece*, ii [STS, 1941], 182; Black, *Surnames*, 715-16). A version of the story which differs in geographic detail and omits any reference by name to Scrimgeour will be found in *Wyntoun*, iv, 370-3. The ultimate source of the story has not been identified.

2. *uncle ... Gowrie*: not certainly identified. Gowrie was part of Perthshire, bounded to the south by the Firth of Tay, to the west by the river Tay and to the north by the river Isla; Dundee ANG was near the eastern limit. In the Poppleton MS (*KKES*, 242) Gowrie is associated with Atholl as a sub-region, with the probable implication that it had been governed by a *regulus* subject to the *rex* of Atholl. There is no evidence however for an early *mormaer* of Gowrie. If 'uncle' (*patruus*) is to be taken literally, Alexander's uncle was a brother of Malcolm III Canmore, perhaps Maelmuire, third son of Duncan I (*HBC*, 56). Professor Duncan (see *Kingdom*, 126) states that Alexander I was himself invested in the earldom of Gowrie during the reign of Edgar, but we have not found confirmation of this. Alexander was present at the exhumation of the body of St Cuthbert at Durham in 1104, where he is styled 'earl' (*comes*) by Florence of Worcester (*ES*, ii, 137) and Simeon (*Kings*, 236), but without territorial appellation.

3. *Liff and Invergowrie*: Liff ANG lies two miles north-west of Dundee; Invergowrie PER, ANG is now a western suburb of Dundee.

5. *ruffians ... Moray*: in *Wyntoun*, ut cit., they are 'Ylis men' (Wemyss MS) or 'Scottis men' (Cottonian MS).

Mearns: i.e. approximately the modern county of Kincardine.

Moray: see above II c.30, 1.47.

8. *Alexander Carron*: not certainly identified. Black suggests that he is the Carun of Cupar FIF whose grandson Alexander, called Schyrmeschur, obtained in 1293 a tack or lease of the land of Torr from Thomas de Kylmaron (Black, *Surnames*, 715, quoting *SP*, iii, 304). The period of almost two centuries between the reign of Alexander I and that of King John (1292-6) seems too great to be covered by three generations of a single family.

13. *Scone* PER. The priory of Scone, founded by Alexander I, was a house of Augustinian canons (*MRHS*, 97); see below c.36a; c.37, 1.1.

16. *Spey*: river INV, MOR, BNF. In *Wyntoun*, ut cit., the insurgents keep nearer the east coast, retreating to Stockford, near Beauly INV, then north of the Beauly Firth, which Alexander crossed at high tide to defeat them.

26. *Scrimgeour*: i.e. 'fencer', from Middle Scots *scrymmage*, 'a fencing bout'; cf. *Wallace*, bk.III, ll.358-68 (M.P. McDiarmid [ed.], *Hary's Wallace*, 2 vols. [STS, 1968-9], i, 44):

> Ane Inglisman on the gait saw he play
> At the scrymmage, a bukler on his hand.
> Wallace ner by in falouschipe couth stand.
> Lychtly he sperde, 'Quhi, Scot, dar thow nocht preiff?'
> Wallace said 'Ya, sa thow wald gif me leiff.'
> 'Smyt on,' he said.'I defy thine accioune.'
> Wallace thar-with has tane him on the croune.
> Throuch bukler, hand and the harnpan also,
> To the schuldyris the scharp suerd gert he go;
> Lychtly returnd till his awne men agayne.
> The wemen cryede, 'Our bukler player is slane!'

The quotation illustrates how Alexander Carron may have severed his opponent's hand – and also suggests that fencing bouts of this risky kind were regarded as a particularly English form of pastime.

27. *day*: after this MS CA inserts material from VII c.50, ll.15-55 and then VII c.53, ll.13-50.

28. *treason*: i.e. the murder of Malcolm I in 954.

31-39. *Henry ... England*: cf. *Wyntoun*, iv, 578-9.

31. *Henry V*: see above c.35, 1.44. His reign began in 1106.

31-32. *Matilda daughter ... married*: see above c.18, 1.10; c.35, 1.42.

32. *twenty years*: in fact 1114-25.

33-34. *When he ... prison*: see *Martin*, 468, 1.51-469, 1.1.

33. *father*: i.e. Henry IV (see above IV c.55, 1.11; V c.13, 1.8; c.15, ll.55-71 ('At this time ... Peter'). Henry IV did not die in prison. In 1104 the future Henry V declared that he owed no allegiance to an excommunicated father; in

1105 the emperor became a prisoner in the hands of his son and was forced to abdicate. He escaped and was engaged in gathering an army when he died at Liège, Belgium, on 7 August 1106 (*CMH*, v, 141-51).

34-37. *it is thought ... Saxony*: see *Martin*, 469, ll. 20-22.

37. *Lothair*: i.e. Lothair II or III, elected German king on the death of Henry V in 1125; crowned as emperor by Pope Innocent II in 1133; died 1137 (*CMH*, v, 334-45).

38. *Geoffrey ... Anjou*: see above c.35, l.42. Geoffrey was count of Anjou (approximately the modern dép. Maine-et-Loire) 1129-51. In 1144 he was crowned duke of Normandy, a title which he handed over to his son Henry in 1149 (*CMH*, v, 550-1). The name Plantagenet 'may have originated with ... Geoffrey, who planted brooms (*genistas*) to improve his hunting covers' (Poole, *From Domesday*, 129, n.2, referring to A. Cartellieri, *Historische Zeitschrift*, cxxxix [1928], 408).

39. *Henry II*: i.e. Henry Plantagenet, king of England 1154-89 (*HBC*, 36).

40-49. *He was ... clothing them*: related to part of *Early Gesta*, c.34; cf. DMS, ut cit.; Ailred, *Genealogia*, col.736.

49-69. *Following ... world*: cf. *Early Gesta*, c.31; there is nothing equivalent in DMS or Ailred, *Genealogia*. Cf. *Wyntoun*, iv, 372-7, where Scone and St Andrews, but not Dunfermline or Inchcolm, are mentioned.

51-52. *church ... Kilrymont*: see above II c.60; IV, c.14. Alexander's gifts included his Arab horse and Turkish weapons (see below VI c.24, ll.41-44; *Chron.Picts-Scots*, 190; *Wyntoun*, iv, 374-5). For the significance of Alexander's work at St Andrews see Barrow, *Kingdom*, 171-2.

52. *Dunfermline* FIF; see above c.25, l.7.
Scone: see above l.13.

56. *Boar's Chase*: cf. *Chron.Picts-Scots*, 190, 193. The area lies 'within the modern parishes of St Andrews and St Leonards, Cameron, Dunino, Ceres and Kemback [all FIF], forming a compact area about eleven miles by six' (M.O. Anderson, 'The Celtic Church in Kinrimund', in D. McRoberts [ed.], *The Medieval Church of St Andrews* [Glasgow, 1976], 7).

55-58. *It was he ... Inverkeithing*: Bower has compressed and altered the order of Fordun's text, which reads after 'erectam' (text l.48): 'ut posteri sui plus ab ipsis villicarint quam adjecerint. Fundavit etiam monasterium canonicorum de insula Emonia juxta Inverkeithin, excepto quod illustris David successor et frater ejus in bono statu tenuerit, et praecipue Dunferm lyn, ubi et ipse pausat, donis sustulerit et aedificiis ampliaverit. Ipse est, qui cursum apri beato Andreae contulit.' Professor Barrow (*Kingdom*, 170, n.23) comments: 'It is clear that the original endowment was held in trust until canons could be established on Inchcolm, and that this probably did not take place until after the end of David I's reign'; cf. *MRHS*, 91.

57. *Inchcolm* FIF: site of Bower's own house of Augustinian canons; for more detail see below c.37, ll.2-33. In the text the name is 'Emonia'; see above I c.6, l.41.

58. *Inverkeithing* FIF.

65. *Turgot*: see above c.11, introductory note.

67. *canons regular*: i.e. Augustinian or Black canons. The order, although claiming Augustine of Hippo as its founder (see above III c.3, 1.71), in fact dated from the early years of the papacy of Gregory VII (1073-85) (*ODCC*, 111).

68. *Oswald*: see above III c.42, 1.15.

Nostell: near Pontefract YOW. A community of Augustinian canons was established, perhaps by 1114 (*MRHEW*, 148), under Æthelwulf as prior. 'We can hardly over-emphasize the significance of King Alexander's action in bringing to serve its [i.e. Scone's] church members of an order of priests who represented the very vanguard of the Gregorian reform and of the new ideas at work in the western church' (Barrow, *Kingdom*, 171). Contrast however Duncan, *Kingdom*, 131-2.

69. *world*: after this MS CA inserts material from VII c.53, ll.11-13.

Chapter 36a
p.109

In MS C Bower inserted this untitled and unnumbered chapter at the beginning of VI (fo.110) after the contents list, with a caret mark indicating that it should be read here. Much of the material is paralleled in c.36. Not in *Pluscarden* or *Extracta*.

1. *10 January*: see above c.35, 1.61, where the date is given as 8 January.

9-12. *subtracted ... Lord*: cf. above c.36, ll.55-58n.

14. *Æthelwulf*: prior of Nostell YOW from ca 1114 X 1122 to 1153; also bishop of Carlisle 1133-1156 or 1157 (D. Knowles and others, *Heads*, 178).

18-19. *they came*: ca 1120 (*MRHS*, 97).

20. *Robert*: bishop of St Andrews 1124-59 (see below VI c.24, ll.37-58).

24. *Turgot*: see above c.11, introductory note.

26. *ancient little book*: not identified; apparently it is not an exemplar of DMS; ll.1-12 ('He ... Lord') are found also in *Early Gesta*, c.31, but then the two accounts diverge; see above c.36, ll.49-69.

27. *Sibylla*: illegitimate daughter of King Henry I Beauclerk (*CP*, xi, appendix D). *Malmesbury* (ii, 476; bk.5, c.400) says of her: 'defuerat enim foeminae, ut fertur, quod desideraretur, vel in morum modestia, vel in corporis elegantia.'

28. *island of Loch Tay*: see above II c.10, ll.97-98; Barrow, *Kingdom*, 171.

Chapter 37
pp.111-13

This chapter is the work of Bower; ll.2-35 ('about the year ... Heaven'), the foundation-legend of the abbey of Inchcolm, are presumably based on material preserved on the island. Not in *Pluscarden*; see *Extracta*, 66-67.

1. *1114*: in *Melrose*, 31, the foundation is recorded s.a. 1115. There are difficulties, either in accepting so early a date, or in rejecting it for a later. In 1114/15 the church of Nostell YOW, from which the king is said to have summoned clerics for his new church (see above c.36, 1.68; c.36a, ll.12-20), may not yet have been fully established as a house of canons regular. Turgot, on the other hand, died in 1115. The date ca 1120 has been favoured by recent commentators (*MRHS*, 97).

Scone: after this MS CA inserts material from VII c.54, ll.12-15.

2. *Turgot*: see above c.11, introductory note.

3. *1123*: the date is plausible, but as noted above, c.36, ll.55-58, the original endowment was probably held in trust until the end of the reign of David I in 1153 or even to a later date (*MRHS*, 91).

monastery ... Inchcolm: for the tradition, preserved in MS CA, that Columba had lived on Inchcolm while preaching to the Picts and Scots, see above I c.6, ll.34-42n.

7. *Queensferry* WLO.

10. *island hermit*: cf. the reference in Turgot, *Margaret*, c.3, para. 19 (Pinkerton, *Saints*, ii, 173): 'Quo tempore in regno Scottorum plurimi, per diversa loca separatis inclusi cellulis, per magnam vitae districtionem in carne non secundum carnem vivebant: angelicam enim in terris conversationem ducebant.'

11. *Columba*: see above III cc.26, 27.

19. *saint*: i.e. Columba.

25-29. *There was ... desire*: not in Turgot, *Margaret*. It is perhaps worth noting that Queen Margaret restored the abbey of Iona (M. Chibnall [ed.], *The Ecclesiastical History of Orderic Vitalis*, iv [Oxford, 1973], 272-3 [bk.8, c.22]).

30-35. *One thousand ... heaven*: source not identified.

36-48. *... whatsoever*: perhaps based on the lost chronicle referred to above c.8, ll.26-36; cf. *Melrose*, 30-31, s.a. 1100, 1101, 1104, 1107. .

36. *consecrated king*: 5 August 1100 (*HBC*, 35).

Maurice: bishop of London 1085-1107 (ibid., 258).

37. *Anselm*: see above c.25, 1.2. Disagreement with William II Rufus led to the exile of Anselm in 1097 (see *ODS*, 20; Poole, *From Domesday*, 172-6).

38-39. *He put ... London*: ibid., 170-2, 114.

38. *Ranulf*: i.e. Ranulf Flambard, bishop of Durham 1092-1128 (*HBC*, 241; cf above c.34, l.17).

39-40. *Robert count of Normandy*: see above c.20, ll.42-45; c.22, 1.75; c.32, ll.27-33. Robert invaded England in 1101, but recognized Henry I Beauclerk's claim to the throne in return for a pension of 3000 marks, which ended in 1103 (see Poole, *From Domesday*, 115-16).

40. *Robert count of Flanders*: see above c.31, ll.21-22.

Eustace count of Boulogne: i.e. Eustace III, count of Boulogne 1093-1125.

In 1102 he married Mary, daughter of Malcolm III Canmore and Queen Margaret (see above c.18, l.10; c.35, ll. 17-18, 48).

41. *following year*: i.e. 1101.

42. *Baldwin*: see above c.31, l l.13-14.
Godfrey: see above c.22, ll.71; c.31, l.13.

43. *Caesarea in Palestine*: see above c.32, l.15; the city was captured in spring of 1101 (Setton, *Crusades*, i, 382).

43-45. *In 1104 ... Durham*: cf. *Wyntoun*, iv, 366-9; for a full account of the translation in September 1104 see Simeon, *Durham*, 247-61; cf. *ODS*, 104-6.

43. *Cuthbert*: see above III c.51, l.5.

45. *new church*: i.e. Durham Cathedral (see above c.25, ll.3-4).

45-48. *In 1107 ... whatsoever*: cf. *Wyntoun*, iv, 376-7, referring to Scotland only. In England the problem of episcopal investiture by a lay person (prohibited by Pope Gregory VII in 1075) became acute on the return of Anselm from exile in 1100. As a consequence from 1103 to 1106 he was again in exile. At a council held in London in August 1107 King Henry gave up any right to the spiritual investiture with ring and pastoral staff, but appears to have retained that of investing a bishop or abbot with his *regalia*, his temporalities (D. Whitelock and others [ed.], *Councils and Synods*, i [Oxford, 1981], part II, 689-94; Poole, *From Domesday*, 179-84). Lay investiture was also a problem in France, and particularly in the Empire, where a formal settlement was reached by the Concordat of Worms (1122), the provisions of which were reasserted by the First Lateran Council in the following year (see *ODP*, 164-5).

Chapter 38
pp.113-15

This chapter is the work of Bower. Not in *Pluscarden* or *Extracta*.

1-16. *... Curia*: based on *Martin*, 435, ll.12-22.

1. *at this time*: i.e. in 1111.
Henry IV: i.e. the Emperor Henry V; see above c.35, l.44.
Teutons: i.e. Germans.

2. *Tuscany*: i.e. Toscana, province of central Italy; Henry was there in December 1110 (*CMH*, v, 102).

3. *Pope Paschal*: i.e. Paschal II 1099-1118 (*ODP*, 160-1).
investiture: cf. above c.37, ll.45-48.

4. *other emperors*: the primary reference is to Henry IV; see above c.15, l.68.

7. *the lord pope ... After*: Bower copies the imperfect syntax from *Martin*.

9. *St Peter's*: i.e. the basilican church erected by Constantine I, which during the 16c was replaced by the modern St Peter's, Rome (*ODCC*, 1225-6); this encounter took place on 12 February 1111 (*CMH*, v, 102).

13. *silver gate*: not identified.

16. *Curia*: i.e. 'the Papal court and its functionaries, especially those through whom the government of the RC Church is administered' (*ODCC*, 366).

16-18. *and deservedly ... chapter 36*: see above c.36, l.33. Bower's source (*Martin*) has confused Henry V, whom he calls Henry IV, with his father Henry IV. For the probable explanation see above IV c.38, ll.35-38; V c.9, l.6.

18-27. *Also ... that time*: see *Martin*, 435, ll.23-27.

19. *certain ... clerics*: i.e. adherents of the deceased antipope Clement III (see above c.18, l.62). It seems likely that the antipope Silvester IV (Maginulf; see below l.21) was elected by 'imperially minded malcontents belonging to the Roman aristocracy' (*ODP*, 162-3).

21. *hermits*: in *Martin*, ut cit., the reading is the more probable word 'heresiarchs'.

Albert: i.e. Albert or Adalbert, cardinal bishop of the Roman suburbicarian diocese of Silva Candida (i.e. Santa Rufina), who succeeded Theoderic (see below) as antipope briefly in 1101 (*ODP*, 162).

Arnulf: i.e. Maginulf, archpriest of S. Angelo; as Silvester IV antipope 1105-1111 (*ODP*, 162-3).

Theoderic: cardinal bishop of the Roman suburbicarian diocese of Albano; antipope September 1100-January 1101 (*ODP*, 161-2).

23-27. *the king of Hungary ... that time*: for this undated letter sent by an unnamed king of Hungary to Pope Paschal II see L.A. Muratori, *Rerum Italicarum Scriptores*, iii (Milan, 1723), 364-5; the king was Kálmán (1095-1114).

28-32. *In 1109 ... child*: perhaps based on the lost chronicle referred to above c.8, ll.26-36; cf. *Melrose*, 31, s.a. 1109, 1110, 1114.

28. *1109*: Turgot was nominated in 1107, and consecrated on 1 August 1109 (Watt, *Fasti*, 290; *Series Episcoporum*, VI, i, 81): cf. below VI c.24, ll.29-33.

Turgot: see above c.11, introductory note.

29. *comet*: this appeared over Europe 29 May 1110 (*Vistas in Astronomy*, v, 187, no.393; Hasegawa, 'Catalogue', 78, no.612).

30-32. *the river ... child*: cf. *Wyntoun*, iv, 380-1.

33-50. *Bernard ... living*: cf. *Sancti Bernardi Vita Prima Liber I Auctore Guillelmo*, PL, 185, cols.236, 244-5 (bk.i, cc.3.17, 6.30).

33. *Bernard*: i.e. St Bernard of Clairvaux (ca 1090-1153). In 1112 he became a monk of Cîteaux (see above c.31, l.4; W. Williams, *Saint Bernard of Clairvaux* [Manchester, 1935], 12). In 1115 he became founder and first abbot of the Cistercian abbey of Clairvaux (dép. Aube, France). During his lifetime, and as a result largely of his influence, Cistercian houses in Europe came to number more than 500 (*ODS*, 44-45; *ODCC*, 162).

Cîteaux: see above c.31, l.1.

34. *Stephen*: i.e. Stephen Harding (see above c.31, l.4n.).

36. *Tescelin Sorrel of Fontaines*: Burgundian nobleman. Fontaines is near Dijon, dép. Côte-d'Or, France.

Fontaines after this MS CA inserts material from VII c.54, ll.16-17.

37. *founding*: i.e in 1098 (see above c.31, l.4).

46.   *girl*: called Hombeline (Williams, ut cit., 29-30).

48.   ... *spikenard*: source not identified.
After this MS CA inserts material from VII c.54, ll.1-7.

49.   *one hundred and sixty*: by a modern count Bernard founded just sixty-eight monasteries after Clairvaux (Williams, ut cit., 92-95).

50.   *seven hundred monks*: i.e. the number of monks at Clairvaux on Bernard's death (*ODS*, 44).

Chapter 39
pp.115-19

This chapter corresponds to *Fordun* (V c.29), related to *Early Gesta*, c.32 (*Fordun*, 430-1), which in turn bears some relationship to DMS, fo.25v, col.A, and fo.26, col.A. *Fordun*, *Early Gesta* and DMS appear to share a common source with the passage devoted to Matilda and Mary in the Poppleton MS (*KKES*, 254-5). There are also less extensive parallels with *Huntingdon*, 241. Bower has added ll.24-50 (... 'book') in the bottom margin of fos.102 and 101v. See *Pluscarden*, V c.29, and *Extracta*, 67.

1.   *eleventh*: i.e. in 1118.

1-3.   *his sister ... London*: cf. DMS, fo.26, col.A, and the Poppleton MS (*KKES*, 255).

1.   *Matilda*: see above c.18, l.10.

2.   *the English ... Good*: cf. *Wyntoun*, iv, 358-9, 378; the phrase is not paralleled in the Poppleton MS.

3.   *church of St Peter*: i.e. Westminster Abbey, the Benedictine foundation of Edward the Confessor (*ODCC*, 1471-2).

4-6.   *In the middle ... workmanship*: this comment is in *Fordun*, but not in *Early Gesta*, DMS or the Poppleton MS. In 1163 the relics of King Edward were translated to a shrine in the choir (*ODCC*, 1471).

7-8.   *The following ... virtues*: *Early Gesta*, DMS and *Huntingdon*, 241, contain variants of the phrase which in DMS reads: 'De huius regine fascescia ('moral rule'; *variant* 'facetia') et morum prerogativa quidam sic ait versus.' The verse passage then follows as in MS C.

9-18.   ... *eternal day*: The verses appear in DMS and *Huntingdon*, but not in the Poppleton MS.

20-23.   ... *character*: in *Fordun*, but not in *Early Gesta*, DMS or *Huntingdon*.

21.   *Henry I*: see above c.18, l.10; c.22, l.15.
         Malcolm: i.e. Malcolm III Canmore.

22.   *1117*: in fact 1 May 1118 (*HBC*, 35).

24-25.   ... *advice*: the date is too early; 1123 is most probable (*MRHEW*, 132).

26-50.   *At that time ... book*: there is no historical foundation for this folktale, which is a variant of the ride through Coventry supposedly made by

Godiva (Godgifu), wife of Leofric earl of Mercia (see above c.12, l.52. The story is first recorded by Roger of Wendover [d.1237]). Motifs included are F553.3.1, Nude woman clothed in own hair, and H1054.2, Task: coming neither naked nor clad (Comes clothed in own hair) (Thomson, *Motif-Index*, iii, 137, 369). In the present version a third motif, usually present, is missing: C312.1.2. Tabu: looking at nude woman riding through town (ibid., i, 399). Bower is apparently the first to tell the story about Matilda, with the intention, presumably, of fabricating a link between her and the charter referred to below l.48. Norman courtiers who favoured the accession of Henry's brother Robert (see above c.37, ll.39-40) sneeringly gave Henry I Beauclerk and Matilda the English names Godric and Godiva (see *Malmesbury*, ii, 471 [bk.5, c.394]).

49-50. *See ... book*: Bower has copied this charter in MS C, fos.110-110v; see below c.39a.

52-67. *... six months*: abbreviated from *Malmesbury*, ii, 493-5 (bk.5, c.418).

68-81. *... Heaven*: cf. DMS, fo.25v, bottom margin, and the Poppleton MS (*KKES*, 255), in both of which the additional information is given that Mary died on 31 May 1116 (1115, DMS) and was buried by Petreus, prior of the Cluniac house of Bermondsey SUR, founded by William II Rufus in 1089 (cf. *MRHEW*, 95), and that her marble tomb was adorned with likenesses of kings and queens.

70-72. *She was ... rank*: in DMS, fo.26, col.A, and in the Poppleton MS these words occur in the context, not of Mary's death, but of her marriage to the count of Boulogne.

Chapter 39a
pp.119-23

This chapter is the work of Bower. In MS C (fos.110-110v) it is inserted at the beginning of Book VI, after the contents list and c.36a above. The text is based on the charter of liberties published by Henry I Beauclerk at his coronation on 5 August 1100, a date which preceded Henry's marriage to Matilda on 11 November 1100. Matilda, that is to say, had no such influence on the publication as was suggested in c.39 above. For the text see Stubbs, *Charters*, 116-19; a translation will be found in D.C. Douglas and G.W. Greenaway (eds.), *English Historical Documents*, ii (London, 1953), 400-2; see also R. Lane Poole, *Studies in Chronology and History* (Oxford, 1934), 308ff. Not in *Pluscarden* or *Extracta*.

4. *1210*: in fact, as noted above, 5 August 1100.

8. *oppressed*: i.e. during the reign of William I Conqueror and more particularly that of William II Rufus.

10-13. *set free ... into it*: the reference is to *regale*, regalian right, 'the right, on the part of the kings ... of enjoying the revenues of vacant bishoprics and abbacies, and of presenting to benefices dependent on these' (*OED*).

15-19. *If any ... relief*: the reference is to relief, 'in feudal law, an incident of tenure, the sum which the heir of a tenant had to pay to the lord so that he might succeed to his ancestor's property, in recognition of the lord's seignory. Hereditary right was recognized in return for the relief' (*OCL*, 1055; cf. J.A. Green, *The Government of England under Henry I* [Cambridge, 1986], 83-86).

16-17.   *my father's time*: i.e. the reign of William I Conqueror.

19-23.   *And if ... enemy*: cf. *OCL*, 810, s.v. 'Marriage in feudal law': 'The lord had an interest in the marriage of the widows and daughters of tenants to control who by marriage came to hold their lands'; cf. Green, ut cit., 83-86.

23-35.   *And if ... men*: the reference is to wardship, 'in feudal law, the right of a lord to take back land held on tenure of knight service or grand serjeanty by a tenant on the latter's death if the heir were an infant or a woman, and to have the wardship of the heir or the right to determine the woman's marriage' (*OCL*, 1290, s.v. 'Wardship and Marriage'; cf. Green, ut cit., 83-86, 178-80).

35.   *mintage*: a tax imposed when William I Conqueror stabilized the weight of the one coin in circulation, the silver penny. 'It was probably to compensate himself for the profit he might have expected to make by deliberately varying the penny's weight that he imposed a tax called the *monetagium*' (Green, ut cit., 88).

36-37.   *time of King Edward*: i.e. the reign of Edward II Confessor, regarded as a golden age for justice.

38.   *counterfeit money*: cf. below c.40, ll.62-65; cf. Green, ut cit., 89-91.

44.   *I remit that*: 'illud condono' (text l.38) introduced here from the text published by Stubbs.

45-46.   *If any ... giving it*: i.e. if he failed to make a will because of illness, but had previously made his testamentary intentions clear.

47-49.   *But if ... them*: i.e. if he died without making a will or otherwise making his testamentary intentions clear.

50.   *forfeiture*: i.e. 'the loss of some right, property, or privilege, by reason of some specified conduct' (*OCL*, 481; cf. Green, ut cit., 58).

52.   *brother*: i.e. William II Rufus.

56.   *murder-fines*: 'Legislation of William I required the hundred ... to pay a murder fine whenever a dead body was found within its limits which could not be proved to be that of an Englishman and the delinquent was not produced' (*OCL*, 861, s.v. 'Murdrum'; cf. Green, ut cit., 80).

59.   *forests*: the reference is to the harsh forest laws; see *OCL*, 480-1; Poole, *From Domesday*, 29-35; Green, ut cit., 124-30.

60.   *knight-service*: i.e. 'the main mode of tenure of land under feudalism whereby, after 1066, the King granted tracts of land to his followers to be held by them on terms of providing a stated number of knights, armed and accoutred, to serve in the army at their own expense for forty days in the year' (*OCL*, 706).

61.   *demesne ploughs*: in medieval law demesne lands were those 'retained by the owner of the manor and tilled [by his ploughs] at the cost and by the labour of the owner, and those held from him by villeins, but not including lands which belonged to the lord but which had been let by him as fiefs to vassals in return for services' (*OCL*, 349, s.v. 'Demesne lands').

62. *gelds*: i.e. heregeld or Danegeld, the tax first imposed by Æthelred II (see above IV c.38, ll.1-4), repealed by Edward II Confessor (see above c.10, l.52), but reimposed by the Norman kings (Poole, *From Domesday*, 418).
labour service: ibid., 19-21.

62-63. *just as ... loyal to me*: not in the Stubbs text.

66. *peace*: i.e. 'the quiet and security sought to be maintained by law and promised by the sovereign to be maintained' (*OCL*, 938, s.v. 'Peace, breach of the'; cf. *OCL*, 940, s.v. 'Peace, The King's [or Queen's]').

74. *abbey church*: not identified; ll.73-75 ('I also ... charters') are not in the Stubbs text. We may assume that Bower copied a version of this text sent to some monastery, but we cannot be sure which one.

Chapter 40
pp.123-5

This chapter corresponds to *Fordun* (V c.30), with ll.31-38 paralleled by the opening sentence of *Early Gesta*, c.34 (*Fordun*, 431); cf. above c.36, ll.40-49. See *Pluscarden*, V c.30, and *Extracta*, 67-68. Bower has added ll.39-43 ('These verses ... Stirling'). He attributes ll.44-65 (... 'cut off') to 'Autor', but they do not appear in *Fordun*; they contain a series of short entries probably from a lost chronicle.

1. *Turgot says*: Bower follows *Fordun* in attributing ll.2-30 to Turgot; in fact they are found in Ailred, *Genealogia*, col.736. The story is more likely to have been told to Ailred than to Turgot (see below l.9).

3-4. *Edgar ... David*: see above c.18, ll.9-10; cc.30, 34, 35; cc.36-40; below cc.41-59.

7. *second Esther*: the reference is to the Old Testament book Esther. Matilda is compared to the Jewish heroine because of the influence which she exercized over her royal husband, and for the service which she supposedly performed for the English people.

9. *I*: i.e. Ailred, who, as a boy, was in the service of David I (F.M. Powicke [ed.], *The Life of Ailred of Rievaulx by Walter Daniel* [London and Edinburgh, 1950], 2-9).

11. *David*: i.e. the queen's brother David I of Scotland.

13. *at the royal court*: i.e. the English court of King Henry I and Queen Matilda.

17-18. *laid aside ... feet*: cf. John 13:4-5.

31-38. *King Alexander ... kingship*: related to *Early Gesta*, ut cit.; cf. DMS, fo.24, col.B, where however there is no equivalent of ll.31-33 ('while not yet ... good'). Cf. too *Wyntoun*, iv, 382-5.

33. *more strict ... good*: not in *Early Gesta*, ut cit., nor in *Fordun*, c.30; both have 'in suos severior' instead.

40-43. *... Stirling*: see *Cronicon Elegiacum*, ll.97-100 (*Chron.Picts-Scots*, 181).

44-65.   ... *cut off*: this passage may be based on the lost chronicle referred to above c.8, ll.26-36.

44-47.   *In this year ... blood*: cf. *Melrose*, 31, s.a. 1117; *Wyntoun*, iv, 380-81. In MS C this item was added in the top margin of fo.102 (presumably in association with another item dated 1117 [see above c.39, l.21]), but then deleted, probably because of this entry in the text.

After this MS CA inserts material from VII c.54, ll.18-64.

48-49.   *in 1119 ... Callistus*: cf. *Melrose*, 32, s.a. 1119.

48.   *Norbert*: ca 1080-1134; founder in 1120 of the Premonstratensian order of canons regular at Prémontré, dép. Aisne, France; later (1126-34) archbishop of Magdeburg in Germany (*ODCC*, 980-1). Six Premonstratensian houses – Dryburgh BWK, Fearn ROS, Holywood DMF, Soulseat WIG, Tongland KCB and Whithorn WIG – were established in Scotland.

49.   *Callistus*: i.e. Callistus II, pope 1119-24.

50.   *In 1121 ... Wales*: see *Brut y Tywysogyon*, 104-9, s.a.1118 (= 1121); J.E. Lloyd, *A History of Wales* (London, 1911), ii, 465.

51-52.   *Ranulf ... Norham*: cf. *Wyntoun*, iv, 382-3.

51.   *Ranulf*: i.e. Ranulf Flambard (see above c.34, l.17; c.37, l.38).

52.   *Norham* NTB, on the river Tweed.

53-54.   *Robert ... St Andrews*: see above c.36a, l.20; cf. *Wyntoun*, iv, 376-9.

54-55.   *succeeded ... etc*: no equivalent in *Melrose*.

54.   *Nicholas*: not identified.

56-57.   *In 1122 ... Loch Tay*: cf. *Melrose*, 32, s.a. 1122, where the entry is less detailed; cf. *Wyntoun*, iv, 382-3.

56.   *Sibylla*: see above c.36a, l.27.

57.   *Loch Tay*: see above c.36a, l.28; II c.10, ll.97-98.

58-61.   *In the following ... people*: cf. *Melrose*, 32, s.a. 1123, 1126.

58.   *Baldwin*: i.e. Baldwin II (1118-31), cousin and successor of Baldwin I (see above c.31, l.14n; c.32, l.26n). He was held captive April 1123-June 1124, and returned to Jerusalem April 1125 (Runciman, *Crusades*, ii, 144, 162-73).

62-65.   *In 1125 ... cut off*: cf. *Melrose*, 32, s.a. 1125; Poole, *From Domesday*, 415; Green, ut cit., 89-90. *Wyntoun* (iv, 378-81) appears to preserve a distorted version of the incident.

64.   *Winchester* HMP.

65.   *cut off*: MS CA now adds material from Book VII successively as follows: c.55, ll.22-47, then ll.1-19; c.56; c.57, ll.1-11.

Chapter 41
pp.127-9

This chapter corresponds to *Fordun* (V c.31), related to *Early Gesta*, parts of cc.35 and 36 (*Fordun*, 432-3). In the margin Bower has added 'of Senlis' (l.28);

'She was ... Senlis' (ll. 30-31); 'in 1135' (l.38), and, in the body of the text, ll.1-2 and ll.48-49, perhaps based on the lost chronicle referred to above c.8, ll.26-36. See *Pluscarden*, V c.31, and *Extracta*, 68.

1-2. ... *St Andrews*: cf. *Melrose*, 32, s.a. 1124.

1. *Robert*: see above c.40, ll.53-54.

2. *prior of Scone*: see above c.36a, l.20.
David: see above c.18, l.10.

4. *as given above*: see above c.40, l.34.

5. *eighteenth ... Henry V*: see above c.35, l.44.

11. *Ailred*: see above c.11, introductory note.

19-25. ... *mistress*: see *Malmesbury*, ii, 477 (bk.5, c.400).

26-33. ... *father*: based on Ailred, *Genealogia*, col. 736, with modifications and additions by Fordun and Bower; cf. DMS, fo.24v, col.A, the work of the Dunfermline Chronicler who, as he appears to mention Ailred's work, must have written at a date later than 1153-4 when the *Genealogia* was composed (see below c.45, introductory note). Cf. *Wyntoun*, iv, 392-3.

26. *Before ... throne*: the date of the marriage is uncertain; Anderson suggests (*ES*, ii, 147, n.2) between the end of December 1113 and the beginning of February 1114.

27. *king*: i.e. Henry I Beauclerk.

28. *Matilda*: apart from the children whom she bore to Simon de Senlis and David I, almost nothing is known of this Matilda. She was born ca 1070 (*ES*, ii, 34) and thus was in her forties when she married David. Fordun gives the year of her death as 1131 (see below c.43, ll.53-55; c.50, l.20).
Senlis dép. Oise, France.

29. *Waltheof or Waldevus*: see above c.14, l.55; c.17, ll.34, 35; c.21, l.24. In *Wyntoun* he is erroneously called William.
earl of Huntingdon: Waltheof was created earl of Huntingdon and Northampton in 1065 (*HBC*, 466).
Judith: see above c.21, l.27.

30. *William*: i.e. William I Conqueror.

30-31. *Simon ... Senlis*: i.e. Simon de Senlis (d. ca 1111), created by 1090 earl of Huntingdon and Northampton; about the same time married Matilda daughter of Waltheof and of Judith who had claims to the earldom of Northumbria (see *DNB*, li, 248, and *CP*, vi, 640-1). The children of the marriage included Waltheof, abbot of Melrose 1148-59 (see below VI cc.4-8, 25, 28-34). On the death of Simon the earldom of Huntingdon and Northampton passed, first to his widow, and afterwards to her second husband, David I. This second marriage 'brought to the kings of Scotland hereditary claims to Northumbria, Cumbria, and the extensive lands pertaining to the honour of Huntingdon; claims which superseded the old vague claims to the northern counties; and which, when acknowledged, involved vassalage to the English king' (*ES*, ii, 148; cf. Duncan, *Kingdom*, 134-5).

31. *Henry*: i.e. Henry, earl of Northumberland and Huntingdon, Earl Henry, d. 12 June 1152 (*HBC*, 57).

33. *Matilda*: see above c.35, 1.42.

34. *emperor*: i.e. Henry V; see above c.35, 1.44.

35. *Henry*: i.e. Henry I Beauclerk.

36. *Geoffrey count of Anjou*: i.e. Geoffrey V Plantagenet, count of Anjou 1129-51; son and heir of Fulk V, count of Anjou 1109-29 and successor of Baldwin II (1118-31) as king of Jerusalem 1131-43. Geoffrey married Matilda 17 June 1128 (Poole, *From Domesday*, 128-9). See above c.35, 1.42n; c.36, 1.38.

39. *Henry*: i.e. Henry II Plantagenet; see above c.36, 1.39. He was born 5 March 1133 (*HBC*, 36).

38. *Stephen*: see above c.35, 1.49.

43-45. *He was crowned ... life*: cf. *Melrose*, 33, s.a. 1135.

44. *peace*: i.e. the Kiss of Peace or Pax, 'the mutual greeting of the faithful in the Eucharistic Liturgy, as a sign of their love and union' (*ODCC*, 784-5).

45-49. *But before ... empress*: cf. *Melrose*, 32, s.a. 1127.

45-46. *the said Stephen also*: not in *Melrose*, ut cit..

48. *feast of the Circumcision*: i.e. 1 January (*ODCC*, 294-5).

Chapter 42
pp.129-31

This chapter corresponds to *Fordun* (V c.32), related to *Early Gesta*, c.37 (*Fordun*, 433-4). Bower has added in the margin ll.2 ('Stentine'); 3-5 ('He imposed ... west'); 14-22 ('In the following ... David'); 36-37 ('when a little ... Northumbria'). In the main text he has added at 1.10 the words 'of the English' (text *Anglorum*) and ll.56-57, the last sentence. For the events of the period see Duncan, *Kingdom*, 219-21; Poole, *From Domesday*, 270-3; the chronology here is confused. See *Pluscarden*, V c.32, and *Extracta*, 68-70.

2. *Stephen*: see above c.35, 1.49.

Stentine: cf. *Wyntoun*, iv, 412-13, ll.1244/1232, where the form is 'Styntyng(e)', perhaps from 'stint: to cease action' (*OED*). The explanation is to be found in the king's character – 'to begin things vigorously and then to pursue them slothfully' (Poole, *From Domesday*, 138).

3-5. *He imposed ... west*: the phrase is taken from *Early Gesta*; it is not in *Fordun*.

5. *Tees*: river CMB WML DRH YON.

Esk: river DMF CMB.

Rey Cross YON; see above III c.29, 1.28.

7-14. *as he laid ... David*: the reference is to the battle of the Standard (22 August 1138) in which David was defeated by forces under the command of Thurstan, archbishop of York 1114-40. Fordun's Latin leaves the situation ambiguous; by the addition of the word 'Anglorum' (text 1.9) Bower has converted the defeat into a Scottish victory. In a marginal entry he then adds to Fordun's text a second account, apparently of a different battle, but actually named as the Standard (ll.14-18: 'In the following ... killed') in which the Scots were defeated. His source for this (with addition of the word *sequenti* [text l.13]) was the *Chronicle of Huntingdon* (*ES*, ii, 198, n.4; *Chron. Picts-Scots*, 212).

8. *Northallerton* YON. The use of this place-name rather than the more familiar Standard or Cowton Moor may have misled Bower into thinking that two battles had been fought.

8-9. *21 August*: according to John of Worcester, the continuator of Florence of Worcester's *Chronicle* (*SAEC*, 196), the battle took place on the octave of the Assumption of St Mary, 22 August.

13. *All Saints*: i.e. 1 November.

16. *Cowton Moor* YON, some eight miles NNW of Northallerton.

Standard: so called because the English forces marched under a standard or emblem consisting of a ship's mast mounted on a wagon on which were hung a silver pyx and the banners of St Peter, St John of Beverley and St Wilfrid (*SAEC*, 200).

19-57. ... *Carlisle*: probably based, with some additional material, on the lost chronicle referred to above c.8, ll.26-36.

19-20. *In 1130 ... Scots*: cf. *Melrose*, 33, s.a.1130.

19. *Angus*: see above c.11, l.18n.

20. *Scots*: note the distinction made between Scots and men of Moray.

20-21. *In 1132 ... March*: cf. *Melrose*, 33, s.a.1132; *Wyntoun*, iv, 394-5. The Wemyss MS of *Wyntoun* has the erroneous date 1122.

20. *Rievaulx* YON, some ten miles east of Thirsk; the abbey was Cistercian, founded from Clairvaux, and was the mother house of Melrose. Ailred was third abbot 1147-67 (*ODCC*, 1187).

21-25. *In 1136 ... David*: cf. *Melrose*, 33, s.a.1136; *Wyntoun*, iv, 396-7. The two kings met at Durham on 5 February 1136 (*SAEC*, 171-3); see above ll.1-5.

27-32. *Therefore ... David*: cf. *Melrose*, 33, s.a.1137; see also *SAEC*, 175, n.1.

27. *Thurstan*: see above ll.7-15.

28. *Marchmont*: see below VIII c.2, ll.14-15, and XVI c.26, l.12n.

32. *Henry*: see above c.41, l.31.

32-33. *and the aforesaid Countess Matilda*: not in *Melrose*.

33. *aforesaid*: see above c.41, l.28.

33-37. *So King Stephen ... Northumbria*: cf. *Melrose*, 33. s.a.1138. For an explanation of King Stephen's panic see Simeon, *Kings*, 290-1.

39-45. *A formal ... unconditionally*: cf. *Melrose*, 33, s.a.1139; *Wyntoun*, iv, 398-403. Though Stephen's wife was at Durham when agreement was reached on 9 April 1139, Stephen himself was then further south (*SAEC*, 214-15).

41. *Matilda*: see above c.35, l.42.

42. *Mary*: see above c.18, l.11; c.39, ll.67-80.

44-47. *earldom of Huntingdon ... Northumbria*: see above c.41, ll.30-31n.

48-50. *Carlisle ... height*: cf. *Chronicle of Huntingdon* (*Chron.Picts-Scots*, 212).

50-55. *To him ... England*: cf. *Wyntoun*, iv, 402-5; Roger of Howden (RS, 51), i, 211, s.a. 1148, but rightly May 1149 (*SAEC*, 221-2).

50-53. *To him ... David*: cf. *Melrose*, 35, s.a.1149.

50. *Henry*: i.e. the future Henry II, king of England 1154-89 (see above c.41, ll.33-37).

56-57. *In that same ... Carlisle*: cf. *Melrose*, 33, s.a.1138.

56. *Alberic*: cardinal-bishop of the Roman suburbicarian diocese of Ostia; papal legate to England and Scotland 1138-9; he was with King David at Carlisle 26-29 September 1138 (*SAEC*, 210-12).

Chapter 43
pp.133-7

This chapter corresponds to *Fordun* (V c.33), related to *Early Gesta*, c.38 (*Fordun*, 434-5). Bower has added ll.65-78 (... 'order'); 93-95 ('And in 1150 ... David'); and in the margin of MS C ll.22-24 ('His son ... as follows); 25-33 (... 'tomb'); 34 ('This Henry'); 44-50 ('When this ... succeeded him'); 78-93 ('In 1142 ... God'); 95-99 ('In the same ... Dryburgh'). The parallels with *Melrose* noted below suggest that much of the chapter is based on the lost chronicle referred to above c.8, ll.26-36. See *Pluscarden*, V c.33, and *Extracta*, 70-71.

1-5. *... French*: cf. *Melrose*, 33, s.a.1139.

1. *Henry*: i.e. Earl Henry; see above c.41, l.31.

2. *Ada ... Warenne*: i.e. Ada or Adelina, second daughter of William de Warenne, second earl of Surrey (d.1138); she married Henry in 1139 (*DNB*, lix, 375). She died in 1178 (see below VIII c.25, l.71). For the part played by de Warenne dependants in the Normanization of Scotland see Barrow, *Kingdom*, 328.

3. *younger earl William de Warenne*: i.e. William de Warenne (1119-48), third earl of Surrey (*HBC*, 484).

3-4. *Robert earl of Leicester*: i.e. Robert de Beaumont (1104-68), second earl of Leicester (*HBC*, 468), one of twins borne to Robert de Beaumont, first earl of Leicester (d.1118), by Elizabeth daughter of Hugh the Great of Vermandois (see above c.31, l.22), who later had an affair with the elder William de Warenne, by whom she had three sons and five daughters, and whom she married on the death of her husband (*DNB*, iv, 64-66; D. Crouch, *The Beaumont Twins* [Cambridge, 1986]). Robert was thus a half-brother of the younger William de Warenne.

4. *Waleran count of Meulan*: i.e. Waleran de Beaumont, twin brother of Robert earl of Leicester. He inherited his father's estates in France (*DNB*, iv, 69-70).
Meulan dép. Seine-et-Oise, France.
mother: i.e. the Elizabeth mentioned above ll.3-4n.

5. *Radulf*: not identified.

Peronne dép. Somme, France.

Louis: i.e. Louis VI, king of France 1108-37; son of Philip I (1060-1108), elder brother of Hugh the Great.

6. *Malcolm*: i.e. Malcolm IV Maiden, king of Scotland 1153-65.

7. *David*: i.e. David, earl of Huntingdon 1185-1215 × 1216 (*HBC*, 466). David was lord rather than earl of Garioch ABD (*RRS*, i, no.205; Duncan, *Kingdom*, 176-7; Barrow, *Kingdom*, 299-301). He was Earl Henry's youngest son. The order however in which the sons are introduced here, and more specifically in ll.60-64, suggests that David was born before William. Bower inserted a note, now almost illegible, in the top margin of MS C, fo.104, containing the words: '[David] senior fuit fratre suo dicto Willelmo.' The version in MS CA of the contrasting passage in VIII c.22, l.42 has after 'junior' (text l.31): 'quamvis supra libro iiii° capitulo xxxiiii [reference unexplained] dixerim eum seniorem Willelmo rege. Scitote quod ego non vario, sed sicut varianter reperio sic scribo.' For a discussion of this error about Earl David's place in the family see below VIII c.22, l.42n.

After 'filios' (text l.6) MS CA inserts: 'Anno xviij regis David natus est premisso Henrico filio regis filius nomine Malcolmus cognomine virgo rex futurus. Et anno sequenti David qui postea fuit comes de Hontyndona et de Garwiach', ac anno xx° Willelmus eciam rex futurus nati sunt. Ex quo patet quod David comes fuit senior Willelmo rege. Cuius contrarium in hoc libro ex ordine sepius reperies. Nemo ergo michi succensiat queso quasi michi ipsi videar contrarius quia sicut scriptum reperio hic cronicis intersero. Genuit eciam is Henricus ex premissa coniuge sua Ada.' Here Bower's explanation of his technique as a chronicler is virtually identical with that given in the passage from MS CA quoted in the preceding paragraph.

8. *William*: i.e. William I Lion, king of Scotland 1165-1214 (*HBC*, 58). William was Earl Henry's second son.

9. *Ada ... wedlock*: cf. *Melrose*, 36, s.a.1162. The marriage gave occasion for the claim made in 1291-2 by Florence V, count of Holland 1256-96, to the crown of Scotland (cf. below XI, c.7, l.17; Barrow, *Bruce*, 52-54).

Ada: second daughter of Earl Henry.

Florence: i.e. Florence III count of Holland, d.1190.

Holland: i.e. approximately the modern Dutch provinces of Noord and Zuid Holland.

10-17. *Margaret ... Arthur*: cf. below VIII c.7, ll.8-20; IX c.13, ll.11-15.

10-11. *Margaret ... Richmond*: cf. *Melrose*, 36, s.a.1160. There was no male issue of the marriage (*HBC*, 478).

10. *Margaret*: eldest daughter of Earl Henry. Her first marriage produced no male issue. On the death of her husband in 1171 she married Humphrey IV de Bohun (d.1182), by whom she had a son, Henry de Bohun, earl of Hereford and Essex (*DNB*, iv, 769). Margaret died in 1201 (*SAEC*, 326).

Conan: i.e. Conan IV, Conan le Petit, duke of Brittany 1156-71; earl of Richmond 1155-71 (*HBC*, 478).

11. *Constance*: married Geoffrey July 1181; in 1199 married Guy of Thouars as her third husband (*HBC*, 478); d.1201 (see below IX c.13, ll.11-15).

12. *Geoffrey*: fourth son of Henry II king of England; born 23 September 1158; count of Brittany 1169; married Constance July 1181; d. 19 August 1186 (*DNB*, xxi, 136-8).

Richard I: i.e. Richard I Coeur de Lion, 3rd son of Henry II; king of England 1189-99 (*HBC*, 36-37).

13. *Arthur*: see below IX c.8, l.14. Arthur was born 29 × 30 April 1187, after Geoffrey's death; baptized with the name Arthur to endear him to the Bretons; murdered by his uncle King John 12 April 1203 (*DNB*, i, 601-3; see also *Annales Monastici* [RS, 36], i, 27; W.L. Warren, *King John* [London, 1961], 82-83). The story of Arthur and Constance is best known from Shakespeare's *King John*, especially Act III, scene 1, and Act IV, scenes 1 and 3.

14. *drowned*: we have found no precise parallel to this version of the death of Arthur. According to the 'Annals of Margam' (*Annales Monastici*, ut cit., accepted by Warren, ut cit.) King John killed Arthur with his own hand and threw his body into the Seine, where it was afterwards discovered by a fisherman. The body was buried in secret at Bec, now Bec-Hellouin, dép. Eure, France.

Alice: half-sister of Arthur; see below IX c.13, ll.11-15.

15. *Peter Mauclerc*: i.e. Peter Mauclerc de Braine (or Dreux), who abdicated the dukedom of Brittany 1237; earl of Richmond 1215-50 (see below IX, c.13, ll.11-15).

John: i.e. John de Bretagne, duke of Brittany 1237-68; d.1286 (*HBC*, 479).

16. *Eleanor*: see below IX c.13, l.16. As there noted, Eleanor was in fact kept imprisoned by John until her death in 1241.

17. *Matilda*: cf. *Melrose*, 35, s.a.1152.

22. *12 June 1152*: see above c.41, l.31n.

John: as noted above ll.5-8, Earl Henry had three sons, none called John. There may be confusion with John, only son of Earl David and thus grandson of Earl Henry (Duncan, *Kingdom*, 629), who died in 1237, almost a hundred years after the battle of the Standard. Alternatively Bower may have misunderstood the verse-passage below (ll.25-33) which refers to a son, not of Earl Henry, but of of David and Matilda, killed at the Standard. The son however is identified as Earl Henry who in fact survived the battle. If Bower indeed misunderstood the passage, it is difficult to see why he gave to the son the name John. According to the list in *HBC*, 57, the eldest son of David and Matilda was Malcolm, a figure of whom we have found no mention elsewhere. If this Malcolm had been killed at the Standard, it is surely inconceivable that Ailred would have failed to commemorate the fact, or that the verse-chronicler would have called him Henry. Nor is it likely that Bower would have changed his name to John.

23. *Cowton Moor*: see above c.42, l.16.

25-33. *... tomb*: see 'Chronicon Rhythmicum', 152-9 (*Chron.Picts-Scots*, 337).

26. *Matilda*: see above c.41, l.28.

27. *She ... Huntingdon*: see above c.41, ll.28, 30-31.

28. *son*: the reference appears to be to Henry, although the verse-chronicler is mistaken in thinking that he died at the Standard; see above l.22n.

30. *Kelso* ROX. The abbey was founded by David I (see above c.34, ll.47-55).

31. *Simon de Senlis*: see above c.41, ll.30-31.

33. *Scone* PER.

38-39. *except ... agreeable*: an unexpected but convincing comment, which must surely originally have come from a contemporary of King David and his son.

40. *surviving*: the word implies that, when the passage was first written, Ada and Margaret were still alive, but that the death of Matilda in 1152 (see above ll.17-18) was still fairly recent.

44-48. *When this ... Clairvaux*: see R.T. Meyer (trs.), *Bernard of Clairvaux. The Life and Death of Saint Malachy the Irishman* (Kalamazoo, Michigan, 1978), 53-54; this episode is probably to be dated 1140.

45. *Malachy*: i.e. Máel Mádóc Ua Morgair, d.1148, archbishop of Armagh 1132-7. As a reformer he followed Pope Gregory VII (see above c.18, l.47; c.37, ll.45-48). Malachy was a friend of Bernard of Clairvaux (see above c.38, l.33), who wrote his *Life*. Malachy did not himself become a Cistercian, but introduced the order to Ireland at Mellifont, co. Louth. In Scotland he may have founded Saulseat WIG. He died at Clairvaux. See also *SEHI*, 764-7.

46. *Bernard*: see above c.38, l.33.

48-50. *In 1140 ... succeeded him*: source not identified, but would appear to have been a chronicle, probably with Scone or other Augustinian connections.

49. *Nicholas*: not identified; see above c.40, l.54.
Dionysius: not identified.

51. *fourth year*: i.e. in 1128. Lothair was in fact elected in 1125 and ruled until 1137 (see above c.36, l.37).

52. *Henry V*: see above c.35, l.44.

53. *seventh year*: i.e. in 1131; see above c.41, l.28.

54-55. *In the same ... Stracathro*: cf. above c.42, ll.19-20.

55. *Stracathro* ANG, north of Brechin.
fifteenth year: i.e. in 1139.

56. *Conrad III*: German king 1138-52. He never received the imperial crown.

57. *fifteen years*: in fact fourteen.
John of the Times: cf. above III c.31, l.87.

58. *Charlemagne*: see above III cc.61-62.

59. *Richard*: i.e. Richard of St-Victor in Paris (d.1173), author of *De Trinitate, Benjamin Minor* and *Benjamin Major* (*ODCC*, 1185-6; PL, 196). Richard may or may not have been a Scot.

60. *eighteenth*: i.e. April 1141 × April 1142.

61. *Malcolm*: see above l.6; in *Melrose*, 34, his birth is given s.a. 1141.

62. *following year*: i.e. April 1142 × April 1143.
David: see above l.7; 1152 is now the preferred date of his birth (K.J. Stringer, *Earl David of Huntingdon* [Edinburgh, 1985], 10).

63. *twentieth year*: i.e. April 1143 × April 1144.

64. *William*: see above l.8; his preferred date of birth is 1143 (*RRS*, ii, 3).

65-66. *In 1128 ... Kelso*: cf. the less detailed entry in *Melrose*, 32-33, s.a.1128.

65. *canons*: i.e. Augustinian canons.

66. *Kelso*: see above c.34, ll.47-55.

66-67. *And in 1132 ... Rievaulx*: cf. the less detailed account in *Melrose*, 33, s.a.1132.

67. *Rievaulx*: see above c.42, l.20.

68-69. *And in 1136 ... Glasgow*: cf. *Melrose*, 33, s.a.1136.

68. *Melrose* ROX.

69. *church of Glasgow*: i.e. Glasgow Cathedral.

70-77. *In 1140 ... kingship*: cf. *Melrose*, 33-34, s.a.1140.

71. *Newbattle* MLO.
Stephen: see above c.35, l.49. For his capture see Poole, *From Domesday*, 141-2.

72. *Lincoln* LIN.
Purification of St Mary; i.e. 2 February 1141.

73. *Exaltation of the Holy Cross*: i.e. Holy Cross Day, 14 September (see above III c.40, l.35). The correct date for Stephen's release is 1 November 1141 (Poole, ut cit., 145).

77-85. *And in ... office*: cf. *Melrose*, 34, s.a.1142, where the foundation of Dundrennan is made subsequent to the usurpation of the bishopric of Durham by William Comyn, but during the same year.

78. *Dundrennan* KCB.

78-79. *William Comyn*: chancellor of Scotland ca 1136-ca 1141 (*HBC*, 180). For his intrusion May 1141-October 1144 see Simeon, *Durham*, 143-8; Le Neve, *Fasti 1066-1300*, ii, 30; A. Young, *William Cumin: Border Politics and the Bishopric of Durham 1141-1144* (York, 1978).

80. *empress*: i.e. Matilda, widow of the Emperor Henry V; see above c.35, l.42.

82. *Roger*: prior of Durham 1137-49 (Le Neve, *Fasti 1066-1300*, ii, 33).

83. *Ranulf*: see Simeon, *Durham*, 143-8 and Le Neve, *Fasti 1066-1300*, ii, 39-40. Ranulf was nephew of Ranulf Flambard bishop of Durham 1099-1128; see Simeon, *Kings*, 312; above c.34, l.17.

85-89. *In the ... see*: cf. *Melrose*, 34, s.a.1143.

85. *William of Ste Barbe*: bishop of Durham 1143-52 (Le Neve, *Fasti 1066-1300*, ii, 30).

86. *both Williams*: i.e. William of Ste Barbe and St William of York (William FitzHerbert), archbishop of York 1143-7 and 1153-4 (*HBC*, 281). Bower resembles *Melrose* in wrongly assuming that the second William was William Comyn. These consecrations were held on 20 June and 26 September 1143.

88. *Winchester* HMP.

Henry: i.e. Henry of Blois, younger brother of King Stephen, bishop of Winchester 1129-71 (*DNB*, xxvi, 112-17).

90-93. *This William ... God*: cf. *Melrose*, 35, s.a.1154; see also below VIII c.2, ll.45-48. The rumour that William (i.e. St William of York) had been poisoned began immediately after his sudden death in 1154. The account given by Bower is unique in that it allows William to have survived the poison. See William of Newburgh, (bk.1, c.26); *ODS*, 439; *DNB*, xix, 173-6; D. Knowles, 'The Case of St William of York', in *The Historian and Character* (Cambridge, 1963), 76-97.

90. *church of St Peter*: i.e. York Minster.

93-96. *And in ... Dryburgh*: cf. *Melrose*, 35, s.a.1150.

94. *Holm Cultram* CMB.
Kinloss MOR.

95. *feast of St Martin*: i.e. 11 November.

96. *Premonstratensian*: see above c.40, l.48.
Dryburgh BWK.

96-99. *In the following ... William*: cf. *Chron. Holyrood*, 121-2, s.a.1150, 1152.

97. *Alfwin*: abbot of Holyrood 1128-50; d.1155 (ibid., 121, 128, s.a. 1150, 1155).
Edinburgh: i.e. Holyrood.

98. *Osbert*: d. 17 November 1150 (ibid., 121 s.a. 1150).
William: abbot of Holyrood 1152-71 (ibid., 122, 152-3, s.a. 1152, 1171).

99. *Roger*: abbot of Dryburgh 1152-77 (*Melrose*, 35, 42, s.a.1152, 1177)

Chapter 44
pp.137-9

This chapter corresponds to *Fordun* (V c.34), related to *Early Gesta*, cc.39, 40 (*Fordun*, 435-6). Bower has added ll.29-34 ('He is ... Carlisle'). See *Pluscarden*, V c.34, and *Extracta*, 71; thereafter the text in *Extracta* moves to VIII c.1 below.

1-10. *... lordship*: cf. *Wyntoun*, iv, 406-9.

1. *son*: i.e. Earl Henry. After 'filii sui' (text l.1) MS CA inserts:

Henrici. Erat enim sapiens valde et ex precedentibus futura cupiens precavere attendens idem Senece de moribus: 'Quicquid a sapiente diligenter providetur, cum ad rem agendam perventum fuerit, facilius superatur atque decernitur. Melius est enim ante tempus occurrere quam post vulnus datum remedium querere. Nam serum est cavendi tempus in medio malorum' Hec ipse. Timebat enim propter variebilitatem que emerserat in regno suo per patruum suum Dovenaldum Banum et fratrem suum Duncanum nothum rixantes pro regno et legitimos heredes exiliantes, et paulo post in Anglia in Stephanum regni sui nepotis Henrici filii imperatricis sororis sui invasorem: propterea.

The quotation from Seneca has not been identified: it occurs neither in 'De Moribus' nor in *Epistulae Morales*; cf. however *Thyestes*, 1.487: 'serum est cavendi tempus in mediis malis' (*Seneca's Tragedies* [Loeb edn], ii, 132-3); we are much indebted to Professor E.K. Borthwick for help with this reference.

For other fifteenth-century Scottish treatments of the theme of prudent foresight see James I, *The Kingis Quair*, ll.1016-43 (J. Norton-Smith [ed.], *The Kingis Quair* [Oxford, 1971], 37-38); Robert Henryson, 'The Preiching of the Swallow' (D. Fox [ed.], *The Poems of Robert Henryson* [Oxford, 1981], 64-75); cf. too above III c.17, ll.50-54. For the reference to Donald *Ban* and Duncan see above cc.26, 29-30; for Stephen, the Empress Matilda and her son Henry II of England see above c.41, ll.33-49; Matilda was David's niece rather than his sister.

2. *Malcolm*: see above c.43, 1.6.

3. *Duncan*: i.e. Duncan I, earl of Fife ca 1136-54 (*HBC*, 508). For the role of the earl of Fife in royal inaugurations see above c.9, ll.10-11; IV c.54, 1.4.

6. *taken around*: i.e. the heir followed the Celtic custom by making a circuit of the kingdom to establish his title. Originally the king was regarded as married to his kingdom, personified as the female figure of the Sovereignty; he thus became lord, indeed father, of its produce, possessing 'a right to maintenance and entertainment of himself and his suite during periodical circuits of his territory' (D.A. Binchy, *Celtic and Anglo-Saxon Kingship* [Oxford, 1970], 20). Of these circuits the most important was the first, the inaugural, which often involved the taking of hostages (cf. above c.12, 1.31; below 1.9). For a statement of the theme set in mythological times, see the circuit of Dyfed in south-west Wales made by Manawydan son of Llŷr when the consummation of his marriage to the Sovereignty in the person of Rhiannon had made him lord of Dyfed (I. Williams [ed.], *Pedeir Keinc y Mabinogi*, [Cardiff, 1930], 51). Cf. too the circuit of Ireland (with hostage-taking) made in 941, the year of his greatest military and political success, by Muircertach mac Néill (d.943), king of the Northern Uí Néill (E. MacNeill, *Phases of Irish History* [Dublin, 1919], 267), and that made in 1006 by Brian Bóramha, in the course of which he had recorded in the *Book of Armagh* his claim to be *imperator Scottorum* (K. Hughes, 'Introduction' in J. Otway-Ruthven, *History of Medieval Ireland* [London and New York, 1968], 32). In the present instance, the participation of the earl of Fife (see above 1.3) confirmed the position of Malcolm IV. In effect, and no doubt partly as a precaution, the eleven-year-old boy was inaugurated as king in the last year of his grandfather's reign.

8. *William*: see above c.43, 1.8.

Newcastle: i.e. Newcastle-upon-Tyne NTB. William succeeded to the earldom of Northumbria granted by Stephen to William's father, Earl Henry (see above c.41, ll.30-31n; c.42, ll.3-5). As a potential alternative candidate for the monarchy he was kept well away from the inaugural circuit made by his brother, while at the same time receiving a position of some power and authority.

9. *hostages*: cf. above c.12, 1.31.

11. *David*: see above c.43, 1.7.

I: i.e. Fordun, accepted by Bower.

14. *Carlisle* CMB.

15. *western part*: i.e. Cumbria, the former kingdom of the Strathclyde Britons which extended south of the Solway Firth. Before his accession King David had been prince of Cumbria (see above c.18, 1.10; cf. too above IV c.21, ll.30-31).

18. *twenty-nine years and one month*: i.e. from ca 25 April 1124 to 24 May 1153 (*HBC*, 57).

19. *Sunday before the Ascension day*: cf. *Chron.Holyrood*, 123. Ascension day is the sixth Thursday (i.e. the 40th day) after Easter (*ODCC*, 94).

20. *angels*: after this Fordun in Bk V has omitted two sentences found in *Early Gesta*, c.39 (*Fordun*, 435).

22. *church ... Dunfermline*: i.e. Dunfermline Abbey FIF.

22-24. *founded ... buildings*: cf. above c.25, ll.6-8; c.36, ll.52-53.

28-29. *all ... dead*: cf. above c.24, 1.15. For the Office of the Dead see *Catholic Encyclopaedia*, 16 vols. (London and New York, 1907-14), xi, 220-1.

31-34. *... Carlisle*: cf. *Cronicon Elegiacum*, ll.101-4 (*Chron.Picts-Scots*, 181).

35-45. *... religion*: based on Simeon, *Kings*, 330, s.a.1154.

39-40. *pilgrims ... secular*: the amendment (text 1.34) of 'peregrinas' (MS C) to 'peregrinos' agrees with the text found in *Early Gesta*, c.40 (*Fordun*, 436).

Chapter 45
pp.139-41

This chapter corresponds to *Fordun* (V c.35). ll.6-48 are based on the preface, the first section, of Ailred's *Genealogia*, (cols. 711-13). The chapters immediately following this (46-59) are based on an apparently different source, the *Eulogium Davidis Regis Scotorum* (Pinkerton, *Saints*, ii, 269-85). Fordun and Bower however regard the two as a single work. The text of the *Genealogia* contains some of the material found in the *Eulogium*; in what follows we indicate where this is so. Walter Daniel says of Ailred: 'uitam Dauid Regis Scocie sub specie lamentandi edidit cui genealogiam Regis Anglie Henrici iunioris uno libro comprehendens adiunxit' (F.M. Powicke [ed.], *The Life of Ailred of Rievaulx by Walter Daniel* [London and Edinburgh, 1950], 41). This may suggest that the 'life in the form of a lamentation' was composed separately, and only afterwards in 1153-4 expanded to make the *Genealogia* as it survives today (ibid., xcvii). The *Chronicon Angliae Petriburgense* (ibid., xcii, n.1) claims that in 1156 Ailred wrote an *Epitaphium regum Scotorum*, which may or may not be the same as the *Eulogium*. See *Pluscarden*, V c.35.

1. *preface*: see above, introductory note.

lamentation: i.e. the *Eulogium Davidis Regis Scotorum* (see above, introductory note).

1-2. *Ailred ... Rievaulx*: see above IV c.33, l.1; V c.11, introductory note; VI c.9, l.6 (text). We have no explanation of the form 'Baldred' (l.7) as an alternative to the correct 'Ailred'.

3. *Henry*: i.e. Henry II king of England (see above c.36, l.39). Henry was duke of Normandy and count of Anjou by inheritance from his father, Geoffrey Plantagenet (see above c.36, ll.37-39); he became duke of Aquitaine by his marriage in May 1152 to Eleanor, duchess of Aquitaine (*DNB*, xvii, 175-8).

Empress: i.e. the Empress Matilda (see above c.35, l.42).

6-48. *... latter*: see above, introductory note.

43-44. *his ... knighthood*: see above c.42, l.39.

Chapter 46
pp.143-5

This chapter corresponds to *Fordun* (V c.36 and the first sentence of c.37), based on Ailred, *Eulogium*, 269-70 (sect. I and the beginning of sect. II). ll.1-6 (...'affairs') and 21-31 ('So a king ... debauchery?') are to be found in Ailred, *Genealogia*, col.713. See *Pluscarden*, V c.36.

8-9. *Weep ... Lord*: cf. Joel 2:17.

12-13. *Do not ... sons*: cf. Luke 23:28.

13-14. *Even now ... follow him*: cf. Revelation 14:13.

39-40. *become ... men*: cf. 1 Corinthians 9:22.

43-44. *Beloved ... blessed*: Ecclesiasticus 45:1.

Chapter 47
pp.145-7

This chapter corresponds to *Fordun* (V c.37), the first sentence of which, as already noted, forms the conclusion of Bower's c.46 above. The chapter is based on Ailred, *Eulogium*, 270-71 (the latter part of sect. II and most of sect. III). ll.11-24 ('We know ... point') are to be found in Ailred, *Genealogia*, cols. 713-14. See *Pluscarden*, V c.37.

1. *Beloved of God*: see above c.46, l.43.

1-2. *directs ... way*: cf. Psalm 24:9 (*Vulgate*); 25:9(*NEB*).

2. *mild ... heart*: cf. Matthew 11:29.

10-11. *The meek ... peace*: Psalm 36:11 (*Vulgate*); 37:11 (*NEB*).

11. *We*: i.e. Ailred (editorial plural), accepted by Fordun and Bower.

14. *ceremonies*: see Duncan, *Kingdom*, 115-16.

20. *total barbarity*: Ailred's comment is at odds with the attitude generally adopted by Fordun and Bower.

34. *since ... earth*: cf. Matthew 5:5; above 11.10-12.

35. *greater extent*: Ailred knows nothing of such claims as those made above (IV c.17) for Giric.

36. *took ... peace*: cf. above 11.10-11.

38. *diversities ... character*: the primary reference is to differences between the Gaelic-speaking and English-speaking peoples of David's kingdom.

Chapter 48
pp.147-9

This chapter corresponds to *Fordun* (V c.38), based on Ailred, *Eulogium*, 271-2 (last sentence of sect. III and all but the final three sentences of sect. IV). A passage in Ailred, *Genealogia* (col.714) corresponds to 11.4-15 ('So deservedly ... Beauvais') and 23-36 ('and left ... wept'). Fordun has added 11. 16-18 ('namely ... Berwick'). Bower appears to have added 11. 18-23 ('and as ... Dunfermline'); 11.19-22 ('and Premonstratensian ... Burghs') appear in the margin of MS C. See *Pluscarden*, V c.38.

5. *beloved ... men*: cf. above c.46, 11.43-44; c.47, 1.1.

7. *things ... God*: cf. Matthew 22:21; Mark 12:17.

7-24. *building ... brothers*: cf. *Wyntoun*, iv, 384-7.

9-10. *three or four bishops*: i.e. St Andrews, Dunkeld, Moray and Glasgow (Watt, *Fasti*, 289, 94, 214, 143-4); see G. Donaldson, 'Bishops' sees before the reign of David I', in *Scottish Church History* [Edinburgh, 1985], 11-24. For the early history of all the mainland Scottish dioceses see *Series Episcoporum*, VI, i.

12. *nine bishoprics*: i.e. probably Aberdeen, Brechin, Caithness (Watt, *Fasti*, 1, 39, 58), Galloway (see above III c.9, 1.44; Watt, *Fasti*, 129), and Ross (see above IV c.44, 1.27; Watt, *Fasti*, 266), together with the four already noted. Bower keeps here to Ailred's figure of nine, abandoning the figure of twelve inserted by Fordun.

14. *Cluniac*: i.e. following the observance of Cluny, dép. Saône-ct-Loire, France, a monastery founded in 910 by William the Pious, duke of Aquitaine 893-918 (*ODCC*, 307-8). The only Cluniac houses in Scotland were Crossraguel AYR and Paisley RNF, both founded later than the reign of David I.

Cistercian: see above c.31, 1.4.

15. *Tironensian*: see above c.32, 11.35-36.

Arrouaisian: i.e. established from Arrouaise, dép. Pas-de-Calais, France, a house of Augustinian canons (*ES*, ii, 699; see also Barrow, *Kingdom*, 181-4).

Premonstratensian: see above c.40, 1.48.

Beauvais dép. Oise, France. For the possible connection between Jedburgh ROX and the Augustinian canons of Beauvais, see Barrow, *Kingdom*, 179-80.

16. *namely*: MS CA in place of 'videlicet' (text 1.13) has the following passage: 'multas eciam domus dei que Gallice Mesoñdew Latine hospitalia ad receptandum hospites debiles et pauperes necnon leprosorum domos magnis impendiis construxit. munificeque dotavit. que quasi omnia hodie in abusus secularium et speluncam vespilionum quod dolenter refero convertuntur. Fundavit nimirum monasteria de –.' The comment on the state of hospitals is of some importance for Bower's own time; cf. the slightly later commission of enquiry appointed by the parliament of March 1458 (Nicholson, *Later Middle Ages*, 386).

Kelso: a Tironensian house (see above c.34, ll.47-55).

Melrose: a Cistercian house (see above c.43, l.68).

Jedburgh ROX; an Augustinian house, established as a priory ca 1138; as an abbey 1154 (*MRHS*, 92-93; see also note on l.15 above).

Newbattle: a Cistercian house (see above c.43, l.71).

Holm Cultram: a Cistercian house (see above c.43, l.94). It received its foundation charter (1150 × 1152) from Earl Henry rather than King David.

16-17. *Dundrennan*: a Cistercian house (see above c.43, ll.77-85).

17. *Holyrood*: an Augustinian house (see above c.43, l.65).

17-18. *Cambuskenneth* STL. This Arrouaisian abbey (see above l.15) was founded ca 1140 (*MRHS*, 89-90).

Kinloss: a Cistercian house (see above c.43, l.94).

Berwick: i.e. the Cistercian nunnery of South Berwick NTB. The date of foundation is uncertain, but belongs to the reign of David I (*MRHS*, 145).

18-22. *as some ... Burghs*: not paralleled in *Wyntoun*.

18-19. *as some ... Carlisle*: no such nunnery is known (cf. *VCH Cumberland*, ii, 190, n.2).

20. *Premonstratensian ... Newcastle*: not identified.

20-21. *monastery of Black Monks*: this may refer to Tynemouth priory NTB, in favour of which David and his son Henry issued several charters (*History of Northumberland*, viii, 59-60, n.2).

21. *another of nuns*: see *MRHEW*, 215.

21-22. *prologue to the Statutes of Burghs*: not identified; there is no prologue to 'Leges Quattuor Burgorum' (*APS*, i, 329-56).

22-23. *introduced ... Dunfermline*: see *MRHS*, 58.

23. *many other*: for 'ac plura alia' (text 1.21) Ailred (*Eulogium* and *Genealogia*, ut cit.) reads 'non pauca, non parva'.

26-27. *making himself available*: for 'substratus' (text l.23) Ailred (*Eulogium* and *Genealogia*, ut cit.) reads 'subtractus', 'withdrawn (from all)', which in context seems meaningless.

35-36. *rejoice ... wept*: cf. Romans 12:15.

Chapter 49
pp.149-51

This chapter corresponds to *Fordun* (V c.39), based on Ailred, *Eulogium*, 272-4 (last three sentences of sect.IV together with sect.V entire). A passage in Ailred, *Genealogia*, col.714, corresponds to ll.10-15 ('I saw ... day'), 18-25 ('It was ... demonstrated to them'), and 28-33 ('Finally ... edified'). Fordun himself added ll.15-18 ('but exceeding ... patiently'). Given the eye-witness authority of Ailred as a some-time member of King David's court, the chapter provides evidence for the continuing importance of Gaelic language and institutions during the reign; cf. also above c.44, l.6. See *Pluscarden*, V c.39.

1.   *comforter ... mourned*: cf. Matthew 5:4.

2.   *judge of widows*: cf. Luke 18:2-5. Ailred (*Eulogium*, ut cit.) has the phrase 'vindex viduarum'; for 'vindex' Fordun substituted 'judex', the word used in Luke. See also following note.

2-5.   *For although ... sort*: the text (ll.2-4) is slightly expanded by Fordun and again by Bower from that in Ailred, *Eulogium*, which reads 'Nam cum alia regni negotia aliis committeret, pauperum et viduarum semper sibi negotium reservabat, ipse auditor, ipse defensor, ipse judex.' For the term 'judex' see Barrow, *Kingdom*, 69-82; the office 'formed a part of the older, Celtic order of society'. Under certain circumstances King David was prepared to take over the function of this important official.

7.   *doorkeeper*: an important court functionary in Gaelic and later Scottish society, Early Irish *dorsaid* or *dorsaire*. 'In the other half [of the hall], on the north, a warrior, a champion guarding the door: his spear in front of each of them to prevent a disturbance of the banqueting hall' (*Crith Gablach*, 'The Branched Purchase', an early 8c. Irish law tract quoted in Byrne, *Kings*, 33). The Scots version of the term was 'durward', a word which became attached as a surname to the Aberdeenshire family of de Lundin, the head of which held the hereditary office of 'ostiarius regis' or 'ostiarius Scocie' (Black, *Surnames*, 216-17; Barrow, *Kingdom*, 85, n.2). The doorkeeper may also have exercised some kind of preliminary judicial authority; it may not be coincidence that Alan Durward (d.1268) was appointed to the post of justiciar in 1255 (see below IX c.61, l.66), while in 1292 another man of the same name was deputy sheriff of Inverness (*CDS*, ii, no.560).

10.   *I*: i.e. Ailred.

16-17.   *judgments ... Trajan*: the legend of the Emperor Trajan's redemption through the prayers of Gregory the Great, first told in the early eighth century by an anonymous monk of Whitby YON (B. Colgrave [ed.], *The Earliest Life of Gregory the Great* [Cambridge, 1968], 127-9), was widely influential in medieval Europe. 'It was fabled of St Gregory that, passing through the forum of Trajan one day, he marvelled at its construction, which seemed rather worthy of a Christian than a pagan. For in the arch of Trajan was represented a scene in which Trajan going to the war was asked to do justice to a widow, but bade her wait till his return. "But," she answered, "Lord Trajan, if thou come not back, who will help me?" So he did her justice. So Gregory, passing into St Peter's, offered for Trajan's soul his wonted floods of tears, until by his deserts he obtained the salvation of the emperor's soul' (R. Flower, *The Irish Tradition* [Oxford, 1947], 6-7); cf., e.g., Dante, *Purgatorio*, canto 10, ll.73-96; *Paradiso*, canto 20, ll.43-48, 106-17; Langland, *Piers Plowman*, C-text (ed. D. Pearsall [London, 1978]), passus 12, ll.73-91; Johannes de Irlandia, *The Meroure of Wyssdome*, iii, ed. Craig McDonald (STS, 1990), 127-8; see also Curtius, *Latin Middle Ages*, 364. Fordun was probably most familiar with the version found in *Legenda Aurea* (*La Légende Dorée*, ed. J.-B. M. Roze, i [Paris, 1902], 337-8). Trajan's conduct corresponds closely to that of King David.

20. *from particular regions*: i.e. from different parts of Scotland, many of which in David's day were Gaelic-speaking. The narrative thus implies that David was able to speak, and argue a case, in Gaelic.

23. *legal standing*: 'personam' (text l.19), as used here, is a legal 'term of art': 'Persons are all mankind, but the law considers them only with respect to rights and their different state in that view: the civil law took notice only of the qualities affecting one's liberty, country or family, and the consequence of a change in any of these respects, and from thence distinguished the state of persons' ([Bankton], *An Institute of the Laws of Scotland in Civil Rights*, i [Edinburgh, 1751], 45). Stair (D.M. Walker [ed.], *The Institutions of the Law of Scotland*, 6th edn [Edinburgh and Glasgow, 1981], 630, 1035, 1077, 1082) uses the expanded form, *persona standi in judicio*. Cf. too *OCL*, 957 (s.v. 'Persons'), 1182-3 (s.v. 'Status').

34-35. *did his best ... manners*: cf. above c.47, l.20.

37. *gardens ... orchards*: i.e. David was an 'improving' king, anticipating on a smaller scale some of the work of 18c improving landlords. Ailred, followed by Fordun and Bower, fails to see the economic importance of such activities. See also below c.52, ll.49-51.

Chapter 50
pp.151-3

This chapter corresponds to *Fordun* (V c.40), based on Ailred, *Eulogium*, 274-5 (sect. VI, omitting the last two sentences). There is nothing to correspond in Ailred, *Genealogia*. See *Pluscarden*, V c.40.

1. *men of religion*: i.e. monks and regular canons.

20. *death of his wife*: i.e. Matilda, d. 1131 (see above c.41, l.28n.).

21. *twenty-three*: Ailred, *Eulogium*, ut cit., reads 'thirty-three', an improbable and therefore probably corrupt figure.

27-28. *Aaron ... for them*: see Exodus 32:1-4.

28-30. *Moses ... contention*: see Numbers 20:1-13; cf. Deuteronomy 32:51.

30. *contention*: i.e. Hebrew 'Meribah' (מְרִיבָה).

30-31. *the prophetess ... Moses*: see Numbers 12:1-13.

31-34. *The saintly ... treachery*: see 2 Kings 11:2-17 (*Vulgate*); 2 Samuel 11:2-17 (*NEB*).

34-36. *These ... caution*: added by Bower to the text of Ailred preserved by *Fordun*; it illustrates Bower's own thinking.

39. *his brother-in-law Henry*: see above c.18, l.10. The phrase 'his brother-in-law' appears in *Fordun*, ut cit., but not in Ailred, *Eulogium*.

39-40. *led ... England*: cf. above c.42, ll.7-14. The reference is to be read in the light of Ailred's rhetorical 'De Bello Standardii' (PL, 195, cols.701-12).

49-54. *the oath ... pledge*: cf. above c.41, ll.45-49; c.42, ll.1-18.

Chapter 51
pp.153-5

This chapter corresponds to *Fordun* (V c.41), based on Ailred, *Eulogium*, 275-6 (final two sentences of sect. VI and whole of sect. VII). Not in Ailred, *Genealogia*. See *Pluscarden* V c.41.

1-2. *Do not ... before you*: see Psalm 142:2 (*Vulgate*); 143:2 (*NEB*).

7-8. *spiritual ... Resurrection*: the reference is perhaps to the Second Crusade (1145-9), in support of which St Bernard wrote letters to Cistercian houses throughout Europe (Runciman, *Crusades*, ii, 256).

14. *Knights Templar*: the military Order of Knights Templar was established (1118) in a house near Solomon's Temple in Jerusalem. Other houses were soon established all over Europe (*ODCC*, 1345-6). In Scotland the foundation of Balantrodoch (Temple MLO) may date to the reign of David I (*MRHS*, 158).

22-23. *Redeem ... poor*: see Daniel 4:27.

30-31. *All ... judgment*: source not identified.

31-32. *When ... flight*: i.e. at the battle of the Standard (see above c.42, l.16).

33. *by his own knights*: see Ailred, *De Bello Standardii* (PL, 195), col.711.

34-35. *pseudo-bishop ... Moray*: i.e. Wimund, bishop of the Isles 1134 × 1140 – ca 1148. His unsuccessful rebellion occurred after 1142 (Watt, *Fasti*, 198; cf. *SAEC*, 223-6; *ES*, ii, 97; Duncan, *Kingdom*, 166; D.E.R. Watt, 'Bishops in the Isles before 1203: Bibliography and Biographical Lists', *Innes Review*, xlv (1994), 115-16).

35. *earl of Moray*: i.e. probably Angus (see above c.11, l.18n.), although the reference may be to Malcolm mac Heth, possibly son of an Aed or Heth who appears to have been earl of Moray early in the reign of David I. Malcolm mac Heth was captured and imprisoned 1134; released and created earl of Ross 1157; d. 1168 (see Duncan, *Kingdom*, 165-7; *ES*, ii, 232-3).

37-38. *the Lord ... evil*: cf. Isaiah 45:7.

38-39. *So let ... courage*: cf. Jeremiah 9:23.

40. *monk*: i.e. Wimund (see above ll.34-35).

42. *triumphed ... Isles*: see above c.11, l.18n. Wimund was apparently the protégé of Olaf I king of the Isles (see Watt, 'Bishops', ut cit.).

43. *reward ... works*: Wimund was blinded and castrated (*SAEC*, 226).

Chapter 52
pp.155-7

This chapter corresponds to *Fordun* (V c.42 and the opening of c.43), based on Ailred, *Eulogium*, 277-9 (sect. VIII and first half of sect. IX). Not in Ailred, *Genealogia*. See *Pluscarden*, V cc.42, 43.

4.   *son*: i.e. Earl Henry (see above c.41, 1.31).

20.   *judge*: the Latin word is 'judex' (text 1.15); cf. above c.49, ll.2-5. Ailred may well have associated the language of the Vulgate with the legal system known to him in his youth.

20-21.   *For if ... at all*: see 1 Corinthians 11:31.

24-25.   *fastening his belt*: cf. Exodus 12:11. The reference is to a detail in the narrative of the inauguration of the Jewish Passover, an inauguration which prepared for and immediately preceded the Exodus. In medieval Biblical exegesis the Exodus was held to signify on the anagogical level 'the passing of the sanctified soul from the bondage of the corruption of this world to the liberty of everlasting glory' (MacQueen, *Allegory*, 57, quoting Dante, 'Epistle 10', the letter to Can Grande della Scala). Ailred applies this anagogical sense to the last days of King David.

25-26.   *keeping ... Lord*: cf. Matthew 25:1-13; 26:40. The parable of the wise and foolish virgins underlies much of the language in this chapter. In medieval exegesis the virgins were held to represent the saved and the damned. The five wise ones 'symbolize the five forms of inner contemplation, which are, as it were, the five senses of the soul. Thus they are the perfect image of the Christian soul striving toward God. The oil burning in their lamps is the supreme virtue, Charity. The five Foolish Virgins symbolize the five forms of worldly concupiscence, the joys of the five senses, which cause the soul to forget all divine thought so that it allows the flame of love to die within itself. The bridegroom they all await at the door of the bridal chamber is Christ ... Their sleep ... symbolizes the waiting of the generations of man who sleep the sleep of death, and who will awake after long centuries at the hour of the second coming of Christ ... The frightening nocturnal cry is the voice of the archangel, the trumpet of God that will resound in the silence of the night when no one expects it [i.e. to herald the Last Judgement]' (Mâle, *Religious Art*, 202, figs. 255, 256). The relevance to King David is again obvious.

29.   *seven times*: i.e. at the canonical hours: Mattins and Lauds; Prime; Terce; Sext; None; Vespers; Compline. Cf. Mâle, ut cit. above, 12-13, on the various meanings of the number seven, to which God wished to give us the key by creating the world in seven days. 'Consequently the Church celebrates the sublimity of God's plan by singing his praises seven times a day.'

30.   *middle of the night*: Mattins and Lauds were sung at 2 a.m. (*ODCC*, 892).

35.   *those things ... edification*: cf. 2 Corinthians 10:8.

41-42.   *hear ... coming*: cf. Matthew 25:6.

43.   *Lent*: the forty days of fast before Easter; in this case between 4 March and 17 April 1153. David died 24 May 1153.

44. *I*: i.e. Ailred. The passage shows that he visited David, probably at Carlisle, shortly before the king's death. The visit is not noted by Powicke (*Life of Ailred*, xci).

45. *set hours*: i.e. the canonical hours (see above l.29).

50-51. *planting ... plant*: cf. above c.49, l.37.

53. *religious leisure*: i.e. the monastic concept of 'recreation'.

55. *office for the dead*: presumably at this time still celebrated primarily for Earl Henry. But cf. above c.44, ll. 28-29.

64-65. *Your harp ... weep*: cf. Job 30:31.

Chapter 53
p.159

This chapter corresponds to the latter part of *Fordun* (V c.43), based on Ailred, *Eulogium*, 279 (middle part of sect.IX). Not in Ailred, *Genealogia*. See *Pluscarden*, (part of) V c.43.

1-4. *... abundance*: i.e. as a result of the agricultural improvements introduced by David and the new monastic orders (see above c.49, l.37).

5. *castles*: i.e. mottes (see G. Stell in *Historical Atlas*, 28-29, 128).

cities: i.e. burghs (see Duncan in *Historical Atlas*, 31, 132; Duncan, *Kingdom*, 463-519; Barrow, *Kingdom*, 84-104). During David's reign eighteen burghs are known to have been certainly or probably established in dependence on the king; four were dependent on others (Pryde, *Burghs*, 3-10, 37-38).

6-9. *enriched ... cloth*: the reference is primarily to the wool trade with Flanders and Italy, in which monastic communities, especially the Cistercians, played an important part (Duncan, *Kingdom*, 427-31). Although wool was the most important export, a list (cited in Barrow, *Kingdom*, 96-97), referring to Berwick-upon-Tweed, probably during the 13c, includes among exports wool, woolfells, hides of various animals, herring, bacon, horses, oxen, sheep and pigs. Imports included wheat and other grains, beans, peas, salt, wine oil, honey, garlic, onions, pepper, cummin, alum, woad, teasels, metal pots, pans, basins, ovenware and tallow. But the emphasis here is on the import of fine cloth, for the most part, presumably, from Flanders, and manufactured from the wool exported from Scotland.

8. *nakedness*: the reference is probably to the fillebeg or kilt (cf. above II c.9, ll.12, 40).

10. *chastity in marriage*: Scottish and Irish marriage customs, the latter codified in the Brehon laws, had a common origin and differed sharply from the requirements of canon law. Cf. the canon against some of these customs passed at the Irish reforming synod of Cashel (1101). This 'forbade a man to marry his step-mother or step-grandmother, or his sister or daughter, his brother's wife, or any woman of similarly near kin' (K. Hughes, *The Church in Early Irish Society* [London, 1966], 264). For the text see S.H. O'Grady (ed.),

Caithréim Thoirdhealbhaigh, 2 vols, (Irish Texts Society, 1929) i, 174-5 (text); ii, 185-6 (translation). The canon said nothing however of the Irish practices of concubinage and divorce. Scottish Gaelic practices closely resembled Irish.

12. *more honourable*: the reference may be to the attempts to establish clerical celibacy as a norm, or simply to the consideration given by David to clerics.

12-13. *go regularly ... deed*: in Turgot, *Margaret*, c.2.15-16, the queen alleges that Scots failed to make Easter communion and to abstain from worldly occupations on Sunday. Such practices, it would appear, were still common during the reign of David I.

19. *grandsons*: i.e. Malcolm IV, William I and David earl of Huntingdon (see above c.43, ll.6-8).

Chapter 54
pp.159-61

This chapter corresponds to *Fordun* (V c.44), based on Ailred, *Eulogium*, 279-80 (latter part of sect. IX). Not in Ailred, *Genealogia*. See *Pluscarden*, V c.44.

1. *misadventures*: Ailred's reference is probably to the events leading up to the Norman Conquest, related in the form of a vision in Ailred's *Vita Sancti Edwardi Regis* (PL, 195, cols. 771-3), more directly but briefly in his *Genealogia* (col. 734). Cf. too above IV cc.39, 40; V c.13, ll.29-57.

4-9. *Joash ... older*: see 4 Kings 11:2-12:21; 2 Paralipomenon 24:1-26 (*Vulgate*): 2 Kings 11:2-12:21; 2 Chronicles 24:1-26 (*NEB*).

10. *every ... desolation*: cf. Matthew 12:25; Luke 11:17.

15-16. *heaven ... you*: cf. Deuteronomy 4:26.

17. *hostages*: with this metaphorical usage cf. above c.12, l.31; c.44, l.9.

22. *test ... hearts*: cf. Psalm 25:2 (*Vulgate*); 26:2 (*NEB*).

22-23. *remember ... gentleness*: cf. Psalm 131:1 (*Vulgate*); 132:1 (*NEB*).

Chapter 55
pp.161-3

This chapter corresponds to *Fordun* (V c.45), based on Ailred, *Eulogium*, 280-1 (most of sect. X). See too Ailred, *Genealogia*, cols. 714-15. See *Pluscarden*, V c.45.

2. *Wednesday ... May*: cf. above c.52, l.43n.

17. *canonical hours*: see above c.52, l.29n.

18. *Friday*: i.e. 22 May 1153.

21. *Sacrament ... Body*: i.e. the viaticum (*ODCC*, 1436).

25. *Cross ... Black Cross*: see above c.17, l.16.

30. *it has in it*: 'habens' (text l.26) is inserted by Goodall from the text in Ailred, *Eulogium*, 281, but is omitted in the text of Fordun which Bower was following.

34-35. *descended ... English*: see above c.11, ll.8-10.

Chapter 56
pp.163-5

This chapter corresponds to *Fordun* (V c.46), based on Ailred, *Eulogium*, 281-2 (end of sect. X and beginning of sect. XI). For ll.1-11 (... 'friends'), cf. also Ailred, *Genealogia*, col.715. See *Pluscarden*, V c.46, where the chapter-heading reads: 'Sequitur de eodem, et de ejus sacra unccione facta in civitate Carleali ubi spiritum reddidit Altissimo.' David I died at Carlisle (see above c.44, ll.14-20), but in this chapter or its source there is no mention of the city.

2. *unction*: i.e. extreme unction, the sacrament in which eyes, ears, nose, lips, hands and feet of a dying person are anointed (*ODCC*, 1406).

5. *Psalms*: i.e. probably the Seven Penitential Psalms, nos. 6, 32, 38, 51, 102, 130, 143 (*ODCC*, 1265; see also *NCE*, i, 575).

11. *good offices*: i.e. intercessory prayers to lessen the deceased's stay in Purgatory (*ODCC*, 1144-5).

14. *Saturday*: i.e. 23 May 1153.

15. *Psalm 118*: (*Vulgate*); 119 (*NEB*).

16. *chapter ... sixteenth*: Psalm 118 is acrostic; i.e. the initial word of each 8-verse section ('chapter') begins with the Hebrew letter which corresponds alphabetically to the position of the section in the psalm as a whole; these letters, Aleph, Beth, Gimel, and so on, are indicated in the Vulgate text and the Authorized Version, although not (unfortunately) in *NEB* (MacQueen, *Numerology*, 12). The sixteenth chapter, Ain (ע), occupies verses 121-8. The reading in MS C (text l.15) is not 'sixteenth' (*decimum sextum*) but 'ninth' (*nonum*), afterwards added where a gap had been left for a longer number; MS D copies *nonum* with normal word spacing. There is no apparent justification for the error. All Fordun MSS and the *Eulogium* read *decimum sextum*.

19. *seven*: for 7 as a mystical number in the context of Christian belief, see above c.52, l.9; below c.58, ll.26-30 ('The fact ... power'); Mâle, *Religious Art*, 12-13. The seven-fold repetition here is probably intended to ward off the Seven Deadly Sins and to gain the Seven Gifts of the Holy Ghost *in articulo mortis* (*ODCC*, 1264-5).

19-20. *I have ... accusers*: Psalm 118:121 (*Vulgate*); 119:121 (*NEB*).

29-31. *the ancient ... confusion*: cf. John 14:30.

29. *ancient adversary*: i.e. Satan; cf. 1 Peter 5:8.

Chapter 57
pp.165-7

This chapter corresponds to *Fordun* (V c.47), based on Ailred, *Eulogium*, 282-3 (middle part of sect. XI). Not in Ailred, *Genealogia*. See *Pluscarden*, V c.47.

1-2. ... *needy*: cf. Matthew 5:7.

5. *sons*: i.e. grandsons (see above c.53, l.19).

8. *Nicholas*: for Nicholas as clerk of King David see *ESC*, 165, 415, and *RRS*, i, 159-61. He had become royal Chamberlain by 1159 when he was despatched to Rome in an unsuccessful attempt to secure archiepiscopal status for the see of St Andrews. He was Chancellor from 1165 to his death in 1171 (*Chron. Holyrood*, 148; cf. Duncan, *Kingdom*, 159, 261).

17-18. *I exercised ... accuse me*: Psalm 118:121 (*Vulgate*); 119:121 (*NEB*); cf. above c.56, ll.19-20.

19. *chapter*: see above c.56, l.16.

21. *Psalm 119*: (*Vulgate*); Psalm 120 (*NEB*).
seven times: see above c.52, l.29; c.56, l.19.

23-24. *anguish ... sins*: cf. above c.52, ll.16-17 ('condemned ... tears').

27. *I called ... heard me*: Psalm 119:1 (*Vulgate*); 120:1 (*NEB*).

29-30. *Lord ... tongue*: Psalm 119:2 (*Vulgate*); 120:2 (*NEB*).

32-33. *sharp ... desolation*: Psalm 119:4 (*Vulgate*); 120:4 (*NEB*).

33-34. *Grasp ... help me*: Psalm 34:2 (*Vulgate*); 35:2 (*NEB*).

Chapter 58
pp.167-9

This chapter corresponds to *Fordun* (V c.48), based on Ailred, *Eulogium*, 283-4 (final part of sect. XI). The closing sentence (ll.38-39) appears in Ailred, *Genealogia*, col. 715. See *Pluscarden*, V c.48, where an additional clause, not derived from Ailred, appears after 'meditari' (text l.27): 'quia tempus meum prope est, et.'

1-11. ... *destroyed*: an exposition of Psalm 119:4 (quoted at the end of c.57), which is allegorical in the sense that an Old Testament text is regarded as prophetic of a New Testament event (MacQueen, *Allegory*, 18-22, 50-53). The sharp arrows prefigure the instruments of the redeeming Five Wounds of Christ – the nails of the Cross together with the lance which pierced Christ's side (for the latter see John 19:34). These instruments correspond to rather than prefigure the five bodily senses (taste, touch, smell, hearing, sight) which for human beings are the occasion of sin. The Five Wounds are redemption. The 'coals of desolation' (i.e. the desolation of the Cross; cf. Matthew 27:46; Mark 15:34) correspond to the 'hot coals' of Proverbs 25:21-22, Romans 12:20, and denote Charity, the supreme theological virtue. The combined strength of Charity and the Five Wounds is amply sufficient to drive away Satan and wipe out sin. For the symbolism of salvation and damnation inherent in the number 5, cf. also the parable (Matthew 25:1-13; 26:40) of the five wise and five foolish virgins discussed above c.52, ll. 25-26 note.

The exposition has a general as well as a particular application; general for humanity as indicated by the first-person plurals 'us' (l.4) and 'our' (ll.4,7,8), and particular for David as indicated by the corresponding singular 'me' and 'my' (ll.6, 7), and by the direct address of David to Christ indicated by 'your' and the vocative 'good Jesus' (l.10). Ailred makes a brief dramatic identification with the dying David, and so produces a kind of dramatic monologue. With ll. 11-12 ('Then often') historical narrative and the third person ('he', l.13) resume.

3-4. *by his ... wounds*: cf. 1 Peter 2:24.

5-6. *deceitful ... serpent*: cf. Genesis 3:1-6.

6. *He ... sin*: cf. 1 Peter 2:22-24.

7-8. *wounded ... deeds*: see Isaiah 53:5, a passage regarded as prophetic.

14-15. *Alas ... there*: see Psalm 119:5-6 (*Vulgate*); 120:5-6 (*NEB*).

15. *inhabitants of Kedar*: i.e. Kedar, a nomadic people living to the east of Palestine, regarded as the type of the barbarian (Hastings, *Dictionary*, 512).

16-17. *With those ... cause*: Psalm 119:7 (*Vulgate*); 120:7 (*NEB*).

18-20. *often spared ... combat*: reference not identified.

20. *trial by combat*: cf. above cc.27, 28.

27. *seven times*: cf. above c.52, l.29; c.56, l.19.

27-28. *the number ... Spirit*: based on Isaiah 11:2-3 (*Vulgate*), together with the so-called Lambda formula for the Anima Mundi, third after the One and Mind in the Neoplatonic Trinity, and so in a sense equated with the Holy Spirit. The formula consists of seven elements, the first three numbers (1, 2, 3) together with the squares and cubes of the latter two (4, 9, 8, 27) (Macrobius, *Commentarium*, ed. J. Willis [Leipzig, 1970], 26-27; MacQueen, *Numerology*, 31-36).

32-33. *things ... God*: cf. Matthew 22:21. It is appropriate that the first Scottish king to put his image and superscription on coins should use these words to reproach his attendants.

33-34. *set out ... own country*: cf. David's near contemporary Peter Abelard, significantly (see above c.56, l.14) in his hymn for Saturday at Vespers (*OBMLV*, 244):

> Nostrum est interim mentem erigere
> et totis patriam votis appetere,
> et ad Ierusalem a Babylonia
> post longa regredi tandem exsilia.

35. *provision*: for the word 'viaticum' (text l.28) see above c.55, l.21. Here the use is extended to include spiritual reading and meditation.

35-38. *brought ... hand*: standard details of the Last Judgment; see Honorius of Autun, *Elucidarium*, bk.3 (PL, 172); cf. the 6c 'Altus Prosator', attributed to St Columba (*OBMLV*, 66):

Stantes erimus pavidi
ante tribunal Domini
reddemusque de omnibus
rationem affectibus.

Cf. too the 13c 'Dies Irae' of Thomas of Celano (*OBMLV*, 393):

Quid sum miser tunc dicturus,
quem patronum rogaturus,
dum vix iustus sit securus?

Chapter 59
p.169

This chapter corresponds to *Fordun* (V c.49), based on Ailred, *Eulogium*, 284-5 (sect. XII). Cf. Ailred, *Genealogia*, cols. 715-16. See *Pluscarden*, V c.49. Bower has substituted the final phrase (1.32) for the more liturgical ending added by Fordun to Ailred's text: 'qui cum eodem Deo Patre suo et Spiritu Sancto vivit et regnat Deus per infinita seculorum secula. Amen.'

1. *Ascension*: see above c.44, l.19.

7-17. *Come ... Mercy*: particularly apposite to this call for aid from the orders of saints most closely associated with David's lifework – apostles and martyrs (l.11); priests and confessors (l.12); virgins (l.13); monks (ll.14-17), and finally the Blessed Virgin herself (l.17) – is the answer of the master to the disciple's question about Particular Judgment in the *Elucidarium* of Honorius of Autun (PL, 172, col.1166): 'D[iscipulus]. Qui sunt qui iudicant? M[agister]. Apostoli, martyres, confessores, monachi, virgines.' In Catholic doctrine Particular as opposed to General Judgment is passed on each individual soul immediately after death. The story of Lazarus (l.10; Luke 16:19-31) was often adduced in support of the doctrine (*ODCC*, 1035, s.v. 'Particular Judgment').

9-10. *Abraham's ... cherished*: see Luke 16:19-26. On the walls of many cathedrals the redeemed at the Last or General Judgment are depicted as being placed by angels in Abraham's bosom (see Mâle, *Religious Art*, 384, together with figs.246, 251 and especially 252). Note however that according to Scripture Lazarus and others were already in Abraham's bosom well before the General Judgment. Lazarus is also the type of the poor, whom David especially cherished.

12-13. *priests ... churches*: the reference is to the founders of the cathedral churches and monastic orders restored or introduced by King David into Scotland.

14. *those ... world*: i.e. monks and regular canons who have given up the world.

14-16. *whom ... unrighteousness*: see Luke 16:9, a difficult text: 'Et ego vobis dico: "Facite vobis amicos de mammona iniquitatis; ut, cum defeceritis, recipiant vos in aeterna tabernacula." Here the reference is to the monks and regular canons to whom David granted extensive temporal estates and so helped to ensure his own salvation.

17. *Mother of Mercy*: i.e. Mary as mother of Christ. The phrase 'Mater Misericordiae' occurs in 'Salve, Regina', the Antiphon of Our Lady used from First Vespers of Trinity Sunday to Advent.

22. *from my earliest years*: Ailred (1110-67) became a member of David's household at some time between April 1124 and ca 1132, when he became *dispensator* at court. He left to enter Rievaulx ca 1134 (*Life of Ailred*, xxxix-xli, xc).

23. *received ... time*: cf. above c.52, ll.44n.

Chapter 60
pp.171-3

This chapter corresponds to *Fordun* (V c.50). See *Pluscarden*, V, c.50.

1. *I*: i.e. Fordun, accepted by Bower.

3-4. *cardinal ... Glasgow*: see Watt, *Graduates*, 569-75. Wardlaw was archdeacon of Lothian 1357 × 1359-1367; bishop of Glasgow 1367-87; in 1383 created cardinal without a titular church in Rome by the Avignon Pope Clement VII. While archdeacon, he was also royal secretary to David II. He was D.Th. of Paris by September 1358. The words 'long ago' (ll.2-3) may imply that Wardlaw gave Fordun the genealogy before he became cardinal, or even bishop; perhaps when he was royal secretary.

5. *kings of the present day*: the somewhat ironical reference is to the sluggish Robert II (1371-90) and his son John, earl of Carrick, later (1390-1406) Robert III, who carried out much of the business of government 1371-88 (Nicholson, *Later Middle Ages*, 190-93, 199).

8. *few exceptions*: i.e. Culen and Constantine the Bald (see above IV cc.29, 37); later, John I Balliol (see below XI, c.18). Macbeth stands somewhat apart; Fordun scarcely acknowledges that he belonged to the royal line.

11. *tenaciously ... faith*: the reference is general, but probably includes Scottish adherence to the Avignon Pope Clement VII (1378-94) in the earlier stages of the Great Schism (see below XVI c.5, ll.31-41; Nicholson, *Later Middle Ages*, 190-3).

foreign invaders: i.e. the English. The reference is not only to the War of Independence, but to the campaigns called by Nicholson (*Later Middle Ages*, 194) 'a war of chivalry on the Borders', culminating (1388) in the battle of Otterburn NTB. The latest event mentioned by Fordun is the capture of Lochmaben Castle DMF in 1384 (*Fordun*, 383); for Bower's account of Otterburn see below XIV cc.53, 54.

14-18. *... Scots*: source not identified.

19-56. *... Noah*: cf. the shorter genealogies above I c.27, ll.22-31; IV c.9, ll.28-31 and that linking Alexander III to Fergus I below X c.2, ll.18-33. Neither Fordun nor Bower anywhere records the stages linking Fergus I to Simon Brecc; these are included however in Radulf of Diss, *Imagines Historiarum* (RS, 68, ii, 35; for translation with normalized name-forms see *SAEC*, 1-2); in the Poppleton genealogy of William I Lion (*KKES*, 256-8), and in *Wyntoun*, ii, 349 (Cottonian text only). In *Wyntoun* the genealogy from Noah to Fergus II occupies three sections: ii, 114-17 (Noah to Gaythelos); 210-13 (Gaythelos to Simon Brecc), and 349-51 (Simon Brecc to Fergus II). Where both MSS of *Wyntoun* contain a text, the Cottonian, though still corrupt, is generally better. The Irish *Genelach Ríg nAlban*, 'Genealogy of the kings of Scotland', has been preserved in two MSS, (1.) Bodleian MS, Oxford, Rawlinson B502, 162d, and (2.) the Book of Leinster (LL), Royal Irish Academy MS, H.2.18, 336a (O'Brien, *Corpus*, 328-9). In Rawlinson the genealogy extends through Feradach, father of Fergus I, to a certain Duach (Daui) Ladrach ('splay-footed'). He in turn (as may be shown, e.g., from *Genelach Osrithe*, 'Genealogy of the Osraige') was regarded as great-grandson of Simon Brecc (O'Brien, *Corpus*, 16). The LL version goes back only as far as Óengus Turbech Temra (see above I c.36, ll.8-9 note), but in general comes closer to the Scottish and English texts. Several names presuppose ancestral connections with the Érainn, an important pre-Goidelic Irish population-group, centred on Munster (Hogan, *Onomasticon*, 400).

The form of names in the translation and notes has been normalized, usually in terms of the head-words of O'Brien's 'Index of Personal Names' (*Corpus*, 493-750). Irish word-forms quoted are taken from the *Dictionary of the Irish Language* (Dublin, 1983).

21. *Duncan*: see above IV c.49.
Beatrice: see above IV c.43, where the name is given as 'Bethoc'.
Malcolm: i.e. Malcolm II (see above IV cc.36-38, 41, 43-44, 46-48).

22. *Kenneth ... son of*: the names of the four kings mentioned in this line, included in *Fordun*, have been omitted in the Bower MSS, perhaps as the result of haplography in MS C; for a similar, but not identical, omission cf. below X c.2, l.20.
Kenneth: i.e. Kenneth III (see above IV cc.30, 32, 35-36).
Malcolm: i.e. Malcolm I (see above IV cc.26-27).
Donald: i.e. Donald II (see above IV c.20).
Constantine: i.e. Constantine I (see above IV cc.15-16).

23. *Kenneth*: i.e. Kenneth I (see above IV cc.3-4, 9).

23-25. *royal line ... Erc*: see above IV c.9, ll.28-31.

27. *forty-three years*: ibid., ll.31-35.
Echadius: see above II c.57, l.40.

28. *Eochaid*: i.e. Eochaid Munremor (see above II c.57, l.34).

29-30. *Óengus Fir ... Romach*: the two Óenguses and two Fedelmids may originally have been a single pair with division made possible by differing epithets.

29. *Fir*: 'true': cf. Poppleton MS, ut cit., -'phir'; *Wyntoun*, '-Fire'.
Fedelmid: in the Poppleton MS he is given the epithet 'Aislingig'; in *Diss*, 'Aislingech'; in *Wyntoun*, 'Aslugeg', probably from Irish *aislinge*, 'dream'. The meaning is probably 'Fedelmid of the Dreams' or 'the Dreamer'.
Óengus: in the Poppleton MS he is given the epithet 'buiding'; in *Diss* 'buthini'; in *Wyntoun* 'Byntynyt'. The epithet is perhaps Irish *búdach*, 'triumphant'.

30. *Romach*: so in *Diss*, but meaningless; *Wyntoun* has 'Rephynek' as son of

'Fedomek' (Fedelmid). The Poppleton MS has 'Uamnaich', genitival form of Irish *uamnach*, 'terrible, causing fear'.

Cormac the Old: reading 'Senchormaic', as in the Poppleton MS, for 'Fencormach' in the text. Skene (*Fordun*, 251) has 'Sencormach'. *Wyntoun* has 'Syancormek' (Irish *sen*, 'old').

Croithluithe: the form is genitival; the nominative is uncertain.

30-31. *Find Fēicce*: literally 'white summit'.

Acher Cerr: i.e. 'Acher the left-handed'.

Eochaid: not otherwise identified.

Fiachra: in LL, the Poppleton MS and *Diss*, Fiachra *Cathmael*, 'battle-bald'. With the exception of LL, the Irish genealogies make Fiachra 'son of Fedelmid son of Cincce son of Guaire son of Cintae son of Cairbre Rigfota', for which there is no equivalent in the Scottish and English texts.

32-34. *Cairpre ... Conaire Mór*: see above I c.36, ll.8-9 note.

32. *Cairpre Rigfota*: with his brothers, Cairpre Musc and Cairpre Baschain, one of the three Cairpres, eponymous ancestors of three Érainn population-groups: the DálRiata (Co. Antrim; see Hogan, *Onomasticon*, 335); the Múscraige (Co. Cork and Co. Tipperary; ibid., 553), and Corcu Baiscind (Co. Clare; ibid., 293). They are described, sometimes as the sons of Conaire son of Mug-lāma, sometimes as the sons of his supposedly remote ancestor (in fact doublet), Conaire Mōr (O'Rahilly, *History and Mythology*, 202). The three were also known as Eochaid Riata (the form in which the name generally appears in the genealogies; see text l.27; below X c.2, l.28; *SAEC*, 1; *KKES*, 257, O'Brien, *Corpus*, 328, n.l), Ōengus Musc (ibid., 367), and Ailill Baschain (ibid., 372). Eochaid, Ōengus and Ailill are all originally divine names. Celtic divinities were often triple (Sjoestedt, *Gods and Heroes*, 17), and it is possible that in the final analysis the three Cairpres are in fact a single ancestor-figure, to be identified with Cairpre Cattchenn ('cat-head'), 90th mythical king of Ireland (*Reim Riograide*, 304-05), but 'ultimately a divine personage, the ancestor-deity of the Érainn' (O'Rahilly, *History and Mythology*, 159).

In *Wyntoun* (ii, 351, l.1124) Cairpre Rigfota appears as 'Cadak-Resedek-Corbre-Ridaga'. Two names would appear to have been combined, Cairbre Rigfota preceded perhaps by Cétach son of Conaire Mōr (O'Brien, *Corpus*, 45), eponym of Crinadegagh, Co. Offaly (Hogan, *Onomasticon*, 305). 'Resedek' is obscure – perhaps Irish *rescach*, 'talkative, loquacious'.

Conaire: i.e. Conaire Cóem, 'beloved' or 'beautiful', 100th mythical king of Ireland (*Reim Riograide*, 334-5). For his ultimate identity with Conaire Mór (below l.34), see previous note.

Mug-lāma: i.e. 'slave of the hands'; he is also known as Eochu Ilchrothach, 'Eochu the very shapely' or 'of many shapes' (O'Brien, *Corpus*, 190, where an obscure explanation of the name Mug-lāma is also provided). In *Wyntoun* the name is 'Magalame-Steg'; we have not identified the second element – perhaps *sleg*, 'javelin'. Mug-lāma does not appear as father of Conaire in any version of *Genelach Rīg nAlban* save that in LL.

Lugaid: the name is related to the name, 'Lug', of a well-known Celtic divinity; in the present instance Lugaid as grandson of Dāire Dornmār is probably a slightly disguised version of Lugaid son of Dāire ancestor of the Érainn, who is subdivided to become (O'Brien, *Corpus*, 155) five brothers,

Lugaid Leog, Cāl, Orc, Lon and Fer Corb respectively. Lugaid Leog became eponymous ancestor of the Corcu Loīgde (Co. Cork), who are described as rulers of Munster (O'Rahilly, *History and Mythology*, 189, n.2); Lugaid Cāl of the Callraige (Cos. Westmeath, Longford, Roscommon, Mayo and Sligo); Lugaid Orc of the Corcu Oirc (Munster). Fer Corb is the name of the 64th mythical king of Ireland (*Reim Riograide*, 280-1). We have no further information on Lugaid Lon. For the pedigree of the five see below l.33n, s.v. 'Daire Dornmár'.

In the genealogy of Alexander III Lugaid is called 'Lugchag (genitive) Etholoch'; in *Wyntoun* 'Lugnoys Allodeg'. In the Poppleton MS an intermediate figure, 'Ellatig', is inserted between Lugaid and Cairpre. These forms correspond to the 'Lugaid Allathach' or 'Allathag' of the Irish *Book of Lecan* and *Book of Ballymote* (*Genelach Mūscraige Tīre* in O'Brien, *Corpus*, 367). The meaning of the epithet is uncertain; O'Rahilly (*History and Mythology*, 192) suggests a corruption of *ollshuthach*, 'very prolific'.

33. *Cairpre, Cairpre Findmōr*: both are probably ultimately identical with Cairpre Rigfota (see above l.32, but see also immediately below, s.v. 'Dāire Dornmār').

Cairpre: i.e. Cairpre Cromchenn ('of the crooked head' or 'of the bowed head'); so in *Genelach Rīg nAlban* and *Diss*; in the genealogy of Alexander III 'Corbre Crangring'; in *Wyntoun* 'Corbre callit Congyn'; in the Poppleton MS 'Corpre Crumpchímí'.

Dāire Dornmār: (epithet, 'big-fisted'); so in *Genelach Rīg nAlban*; 'Dorn-mōr' in the Poppleton MS and *Diss*; in *Wyntoun* 'Dar-Dowrmer'. He is seven or eight generations below Dedad son of Sen. *Clanna Dedad*, 'Dedad's descendants or clan', is 'a frequent name for the Érainn' (*Dictionary of the Irish Language*, 198). Dāire Dornmār is thus probably a disguised version of Dāire son of Dedad son of Sen (O'Brien, *Corpus*, 16, 120, 154, 188, 189, 190), although it should be noticed that this Dāire does not figure in *Genelach Érend*, 'Genealogy of the Érainn' (ibid., 376). Dāire, father of the territorial Lugaids (above l.32), is son of Irēl Glūnmār, son of Conall Cernach, the Ulster hero, regarded as ancestor of an entirely different people, the Cruithnean Dāl nAraide of Cos. Ulster and Down (Hogan, *Onomasticon*, 330). An alternative offered is that Dāire son of Sidebolg son of Fer-Suilne was father of the five Lugaids. For the interesting suggestion that in this alternative version the true reading is *mac side Builg maic Fhir Shuilne*, 'He (Dāire) was the son of Bolg, son of Fer-Shuilne', and for a discussion of Bolg, taken to be the ancestor-deity of the Fir Bolg, equated with the Érainn, see O'Rahilly, *History and Mythology*, 48-57. Note in particular (p.49) 'the god Bolg was merely Dāire under another aspect'.

It is possible that Cairpre son of Dāire is a substitution for Cū-ruī (CúRoi) son of Dāire, the legendary Érainn king of Munster and shape-shifter (cf. Eochu Ilchrothach above l.33, s.v. *Mug-lāma*).

Findmōr: 'handsome and big'.

34. *Conaire Mōr*: so in *Genelach Rīg nAlban* and *Diss*; in Poppleton MS 'Conarremoir' (genitive); in *Wyntoun* 'Couer-Moer'. In *Reim Riograide* (pp.300-1) he is 86th mythical king of Ireland and reigned for seventy years before his death in Dá Derga's hostel (see above I c.36, ll.8-9 note). He is the central figure in the Irish tale *Togail Bruidne Dá Derga*, 'Destruction of Dá Derga's Hostel', on which see the edition by E. Knott (Dublin, 1936) and

O'Rahilly, *History and Mythology*, 117-30. Among the contemporaries of Conaire listed in *Reim Riograide* are 'Dedad son of Sen son of Daire son of Ailill son of Eogan son of Ailill son of Iar son of Ailill son of Dedad son of Sen' and 'Tigernach Tétbannach ['furiously lively'?] son of Dáire son of Ailill of the Érainn'. Both are described as rulers of Munster; the names in the genealogy self-evidently belong to the Érainn. Conaire Mór himself, like his father Etarscél, 84th mythical king of Ireland, was regarded as belonging to the Érainn: 'Etarscél Mór maccu Iar of the Érainn of Munster' (*Reim Riograide*, 298-9).

Eogan: probably the same as Eogan son of Ailill Aulomm ('bare-eared'), ancestor of the powerful Munster dynasty of the Eoganacht (see O'Rahilly, *History and Mythology*, 184-5).

Ailill: i.e. Ailill Án, 'fiery, brilliant, splendid, glorious'(*Genelach Ríg nAlban*). For this epithet and its superhuman connotation, see O'Rahilly, *History and Mythology*, 286-90. He is probably the same as the Ailill Aulomm and Ailill of the Érainn mentioned in the two previous notes, the same as *Ailill Erann Dē Bolgae*, 'Ailill of the Érainn, the god Bolga' (*Genelach Érand*, 'Genealogy of the Érainn' in O'Brien, *Corpus*, 376). O'Rahilly takes the name 'Bolga' to mean 'lightning'.

Iar: i.e. 'black, dark', in contrast to his brilliant son; cf. Seim son of Mar below l.54. For another Iar regarded as originator of *Iarnbélre*, 'the language of the Érainn', see O'Rahilly, *History and Mythology*, 85-91.

35.   *Dedad ... Rothríar*: on Dedad see above l.33n. If, as seems probable, the name was originally that of the divine ancestor of the Érainn, there was no need for any higher ancestral figures. The four who appear here – their names might be rendered 'Old son of Very Old son of Triad son of Supertriad' – are more obviously artificial than anything else in the genealogy; they have been created simply as a link between the Érainn and the overall Irish genealogical scheme. The sequence also appears in *Genelach Erand* (O'Brien, *Corpus*, 376). In *Genelach Ríg nUlad*, 'Genealogy of the kings of the Ulaid' [i.e. Dál Fiatach; see above I c.36, ll.8-9 note] (O'Brien, *Corpus*, 322), a certain Eochaid is called 'son of Sen son of Roshen'; in LL the line continues 'son of Tríar son of Rothríar' and so by way of Fergus I to Oengus Turbech Temra. Bodleian Library, Oxford, MS Laud 610 has the variant 'son of Tren son of Rothren' (son of Strong son of Very Strong) and continues to Fergus I. Again the names forge a link with the overall Milesian genealogical scheme. For 'son of Triad', cf. the figure of Lugaid Riab nDerg, 87th mythical king of Ireland, who was 'son of the three Finns of Emain' (*Reim Riograide*, 302-3; cf. O'Brien, *Corpus*, 121; O'Rahilly, *History and Mythology*, 486-7). As noted above l.32n, s.v. 'Cairpre Rigfota', Celtic divinities were often triple; the name Tríar may have been given as some indication of the fact.

36.   *Rogen, Airndel, Maine*: not otherwise known from early sources. Maine corresponds to Maynus in Boece, *Scottorum Historiae* (ut cit. above c.1, introductory note), i, 57-58. It is possible that Airndel corresponds to Dorvidilla (ibid., i, 58-59).

Fergus: i.e. Fergus I (see above I c.36, ll.8-9).

38.   *sequence ... Simon Brecc*: neither Bower nor Fordun anywhere gives this sequence. Versions will be found in *Diss*, the Poppleton MS and *Wyntoun*; as noted above ll.22-60 note, *Genelach Ríg nAlban* contains an incomplete version, which may be supplemented from *Genelach Osrithe* (O'Brien, *Corpus*, 329, 16). The number of monarchs in *Diss* and the combined Irish genealogy is 20; the Poppleton MS has 23, *Wyntoun* 22. As will be seen from the notes on individual figures, the differences are not significant. In *Wyntoun* individual names are exceedingly corrupt, although generally recognizable. The line is as follows:

1. *Feradach*, father of Fergus I.

2. *Ailill Ērann*, divided by *Wyntoun* into 'Ellala' and 'Caren'. Cf. above l.34n, s.v. 'Ailill'.

3. *Fiacha Fermara* (epithet, 'man of the sea'). The Poppleton MS and *Wyntoun* make him two individuals.

4. *Ōengus Turbech Temra* (epithet, 'enumerator of Tara'), 70th mythical king of Ireland; for him and his sons see above I c.36, ll.8-9 note.

5. *Eochaid Altlethan* (epithet, 'big-limbed'). In *Diss* and the Poppleton MS he appears as no.11; in *Wyntoun*, no.13.

6. *Fer Cetharraid*, (?'man of the four-wheeled chariot *cethairríad*'), known only from genealogical material. Originally perhaps a culture-hero?

7. *Fer Raith*, ('man of good luck'), known only from genealogical material.

8. *Fer Anaraith*, (?'man of ill luck'), known only from genealogical material.

9. *Fer Almach*, ('herdsman'), known only from genealogical material. Originally a culture-hero?

10. *Lāebchor*, 'crooked heart' or 'crooked cast'. In *Wyntoun* he becomes Cure son of Catan son of Eakak-Aldecen. The third corresponds to Eochaid Altlethan, no.5 above. It is possible that 'Cure' represents the second element in 'Lāeb*chor*'; 'Catan' is unexplained. In the Poppleton MS 'Labchore' (genitive of 'Lāebchor') is son of 'Echachaltlechin' (genitive of 'Eochaid Altlethan'). In the important *Genelach Clainne Colmāin*, 'Genealogy of Clann Cholmáin' (a branch of the Southern Ui Neill) Lāebchor is son of Eochaid Altlethan son of Ailill Casfiaclach (O'Brien, *Corpus*, 159).

11. *Ailill Casfiaclach* (epithet, 'of the crooked foot') known only from genealogical material. The name suggests that he may be the same as the various Ailills discussed above l.34n.

12. *Conlae*: i.e. Conlae Cāem (epithet, 'beloved' or 'beautiful', also known as *Cruaidchelgach*, 'rough and treacherous'). He is the 65th mythical king of Ireland, whose reign lasted five years (*Reim Riograide*, 282-3).

13. *Irero*: 63rd mythical king of Ireland, whose reign lasted seven years (ibid., 280-1).

14. *Meilge Molbthach* (epithet, 'praised, extolled, famed'); 60th mythical king of Ireland whose reign lasted 17 years (ibid., 278-81).

15. *Cobthach Cōel Breg* (epithet,'meagre one of Bregia' – i.e. the country between the rivers Liffey and Boyne). Cobthach was 58th mythical king of Ireland; he reigned for fifty years and, as narrated in the tale *Orgain Denna Ríg*, 'The Destruction of Dinn Ríg', was killed at Dinn Ríg, near Leighlinbridge, Co. Carlow (see D. Greene [ed.], *Fingal Rónáin and Other Stories* [Dublin, 1955], 18-23; Myles Dillon, *The Cycles of the Kings* [Oxford, 1946], 4-10; O'Rahilly, *History and Mythology*, 101-17).

16. *Augaine Mār* (epithet, 'great'); 56th mythical king of Ireland. He was also king of Alba (Britain) to the Sea of Wight, and of Europe – to the Caspian Sea in some versions. He is the common ancestor of the Leinstermen, the peoples of Conn's Half (i.e. the north of Ireland), and of Scotland (*Reim Riograide*, 266-75).

17. *Eochaid Buadach* (epithet, 'triumphant') known only from genealogical material.

18. *Dui Ladcra* (epithet, 'splay-foot') known only from genealogical material.

19. *Fiachu Tolgrath* (epithet, 'of warm love'). There is confusion here in the Poppleton MS. 'Duachlograich' (Dui Ladcra) is son of 'Fiachraig Duadach' (variant form of Fiachu Tolgrath) son of a repeated 'Duachlograich' son of another 'Fiachraig Tollgreich' (all genitive). Known only from genealogical material.

20. *Muiredach Balcc Rī* (epithet, 'strong king'); 39th mythical king of Ireland, who reigned for a month and a year (*Reim Riograide*, 252-3). In *Diss* and *Wyntoun* nos. 19 and 20 are combined: 'Fiacha Bolgrach' in *Diss*; 'Fiakak-Bolgeg' in *Wyntoun*.

37. *Scotia*: i.e. mainland Scotland north of the Forth-Clyde line together with Kintyre and the islands in the Firth of Clyde.

38. *Simon Brecc*: see above I c.27, ll.3-4.

41. *Ēn Dub*: see above I c.27, l.22.
   Aedān ... Giallchad: see above I c.27, l.24. This is the only Scottish genealogy to include Giallchad.

42. *Sīrnae ... Demal*: see above I c.27, l.25. The figure of another Ailill, Ailill Oalchlōen ('of the curving cheek'), is here omitted.
   Rothechtaid: see above I c.27, l.26.

43-44. *Mōen ... Ōengus*: see above I c.27, l.26.

44-45. *Fiachu ... Senboth*: see above I c.27, l.27.

45. *Tigernmas ... Ethrēl*: see above I c.27, l.28.
   Iarēl: see above I c.27, l.29.

46. *Hermonius*: see above I c.22, l.7; c.18, l.2.
   Micelius Espayn: see above I c.22, l.2.

46-48. *Bile ... Hiber Scot*: see above I c.21, l.2. It may be added that in *Wyntoun*, 210-13, eleven generations separate Gaythelos and Micelius Espayn. Where there is a difference, we give the names first as they appear in the Cottonian MS, second as in Wemyss: 1. Mile, Myla (i.e. Bile); 2. Neande, Weande (i.e. Reande); 3. Broge (i.e. Brīge; no equivalent in *Fordun*); 4. Brogen (i.e. Bregan); 5. Brata (i.e. Brāth; the Wemyss text is corrupt); 6. Doat, Daad (i.e. Deāth); 7. Arkada, Erbraida (i.e. Aircid); 8. Aldoyt, Alwyne (i.e. Aldoch); 9. Node (i.e. Nuadu); 10. Nouael, Nauaell (i.e. Nōnael); 11. Eber Stywut, Yber-Syowut (i.e. Hiber Scot).

46. *Bile*: 'ancient and venerable tree', 'hero'.
   Reande: cf. 'Neman', given as father of Bile in 'Pauca de Nominibus Laginensium', l.44. Neman's father is given as 'Brīge son of Bregan' (O'Brien, *Corpus*, 4).
   Bregan: see above I c.15, l.13n.

Brāth: 'judgment'; see above I c.13, l.12n; *Lebor Gabála*, ii, 24-27.

Deāith: the name is a compounded form of *fáith*, 'seer, prophet'; cf. Iarēl Fāith above I c.27, l.29.

Aircid son of Aldōit: known only from genealogical material, these two figures correspond to the Ercha and Allot of *Lebor Gabála*, ii, 76-77.

48.   *Nuadu*: for the etymology see above I c.27, l.24.

Nōnael: see above I c.21, l.2.

Hiber Scot: see above I c.18; c.21, l.1-2.

Gaythelos: see above I c.9, l.3.

49.   *Scota*: see above I c.9, l.11.

50-51.   ... *Scota*: source not identified; with l.51 cf. XI, c.49, l.58; c.62, l.9.

52-56.   *Neolus* ... *Noah*: see 'Pauca de Nominibus Laginensium', ut cit., ll.48-56; above II c.5, ll.9-15n.

52.   *Neolus*: see above I c.9, l.2.

Fenius: see above I c.18, ll.49-56.

Eogan: not otherwise known.

53-55.   *Glūnfind* ... *Esrū*: in *Lebor Gabála*, ii, 14-19, Esrū is the son of Gáedel Glas (i.e. Gaythelos). Glūnfind is son of Lāmfind son of Agnoman son of Tat son of Ogamain son of Boamain son of Eber Scot (i.e. Hiber Scot) son of Sru son of Esrū.

53.   *Glūnfind*: also known as Eber Glunfhind, 'Eber (i.e. Hiber) of the white knee', leader of the exiled Scots in the Maeotic Marshes, so called from the white marks on his knee (*Lebor Gabála*, ii, 18-19, 76-77).

Lāmfind: 'white hand', with his father Agnoman joint leader of the exiled Scots during their seven-year voyage on the Caspian Sea. He was so called 'because not greater used to be the radiance of a candle than his hands at the rowing' (*Lebor Gabála*, ii, 18-19, 74-75).

Fethēr: also 'Ethēr'; known only from genealogies.

54.   *Agnoman*: this may be Latin *agnomen*, 'surname, title, epithet', originally a gloss, later incorporated in the text. Agnoman, Tōe and perhaps Lāmfind, that is to say, may originally have been a single figure.

Tōe: 'silent' (see O'Rahilly, *History and Mythology*, 485). There is an uncertain but possible etymological parallel with the river-name Tay PER, ANG, FIF (*CPNS*, 50-51; Rivet and Smith, *Place-Names*, 470). In *Lebor Gabála*, ii, 18-19, the corresponding name is 'Tat' (i.e. the Egyptian god Thoth).

Banb: 'young pig, sucking pig'. The word is related to 'Banba', a poetic name for Ireland, ultimately the name of an ancient local goddess; cf. too the placename Banff BNF, which also occurs elsewhere in Scotland, and which may mean 'Ireland' (*CPNS*, 226-32).

Seim: 'thin, slender, slight'.

Mār: 'big, great'. Note the artificial balance of names between father and son. Cf. above l.34n.

55.   *Aurtecht, Aboth, Aoy, Āra, Iara*: known only from genealogies.

56.   *Rifad* ... *Noah*: cf. Genesis 10:1-3.

Chapter 61
pp.173-5

This chapter corresponds to *Fordun*, V c.51, based with some modifications on Ailred, *Genealogia*, col.716, the opening of the section entitled 'De genealogia regum Angliae, et regis David Scotiae'. See *Pluscarden*, V c.51.

1. *as Ailred writes*: not in *Fordun* (or Ailred).

we: i.e. Ailred (auctorial plural), accepted by Fordun and Bower.

4. *on his mother's side*: i.e. through Queen Margaret, wife of Malcolm III Canmore, mother of David and great-grandmother of Henry II of England (see above c.45, ll.3-4; c.36, ll.30-39).

you: i.e. the future Henry II to whom the *Genealogia* was addressed.

11-13. *a noble ... family*: a literary topos; cf. Henryson, *Orpheus and Eurydice*, ll.8-11 and note (Fox, *Henryson*, 132, 391-2).

13-14. *it is ... stock*: cf. Matthew 7:18.

16-17. *beginning ... mother*: in Ailred, *Genealogia*, the text reads: 'a te ipso, virorum clarissime [i.e. the future Henry II], exordium sumens, et per gloriosissimam matrem tuam [i.e. the Empress Matilda] aviamque clarissimam [i.e. Matilda, wife of Henry I, daughter of Malcolm and Margaret] ascendens.' Cf. below c.62, ll.1-3 note.

18-19. *since ... above*: not in Ailred, *Genealogia*.

19-21. *omission ... time*: in the next chapter Bower follows *Fordun* in taking the genealogy to Woden. Ailred continues by way of Scēaf, whom he calls Sem, son of Noah, to Adam. Between Woden and Adam there are twenty-two intermediate figures. The version in *Wyntoun* takes the line back to Sem son of Noah; Wyntoun divides it, as he divides his Scottish genealogy (see above c.60, ll.19-56 note), into three sections: 1. from Sem to Woden (ii, 134-7); 2. from Woden to Ine (ii, 210-11); 3. from Ine to Queen Margaret (iv, 306-11). Amours thinks (*Wyntoun*, i, 11) that this version is based, not on Ailred, *Genealogia*, but on the text found in *Malmesbury*, also mentioned by Fordun and Bower (see below c.62, ll.24-26).

Chapter 62
pp.175-7

This chapter corresponds to *Fordun*, V c.52, based on Ailred, *Genealogia*, cols. 716-17. Ailred gives first a continuous genealogy from the future Henry II of England back to Adam, then returns to discuss certain significant individuals who figure in it – Seth, Enoch, Noah, Shem, Melchizedec and Woden. His genealogy is based ultimately on that of the West-Saxon King Æthelwulf (839-56), preserved in *ASC* (Plummer), 66, s.a. 855; *ASC*, 44. On this in the context of other versions and other English royal genealogies see especially K. Sisam, 'Anglo-Saxon Royal Genealogies', in E.G. Stanley (ed.), *British Academy Papers on Anglo-Saxon England* (Oxford, 1990), 145-204. D.

Dumville, 'The West Saxon Genealogical Regnal List' (*Peritia*, 4 [1985], 21-66) is restricted to Cerdic and his successors, for whom a revolutionary chronological sequence is proposed. In translation and notes we have normalized the spelling of names above Æthelwulf in terms of Sisam's paper. Fordun begins with David and takes the line back only as far as Woden, adding directly to it Ailred's later discussion of Woden. See *Pluscarden*, V c.52.

For the 'English family' of the kings of Scots see also below VI cc.9-23 taken from *Fordun*, VI cc.1-15.

1-3. ... *name*: the corresponding passage in Ailred, *Genealogia*, reads: 'Tu igitur, vir optime [i.e. the future Henry II], filius es gloriosissimae imperatricis Mathildis [i.e. the Empress Matilda], cujus fuit mater christianissima et excellentissima Anglorum regina, Mathildis [i.e. Matilda wife of Henry I of England], filia sanctissimae feminae reginae Scotorum Margaretae, quae nominis sui splendori morum sanctitatem praeferebat.' Cf. above c.61, ll.16-17 note.

3. *splendour of her name*: the name 'Margaret' means 'pearl' (Latin *margarita*).

Edward: see above c.11, ll.8-10; c.13, ll.8-14; IV c.45, ll.8-10; *ASE*, 571.

4. *Edmund Ironside*: see above IV c.45, ll.3-5; *ASE*, 390-3.

4-5. *Æthelred ... Peaceful*: see above IV c.30, ll.12-13.

4. *Æthelred*: see above IV c.32, ll.39-47; c.36, ll.33-35; c.38, ll.1-29; c.45, ll.1-2; *ASE*, 372-90.

5. *Edgar*: see above IV c.30, ll.11-17; c.32, ll.35-36; cc. 33-34; *ASE*, 367-72.

Edmund: see above IV c.25, l.54; c.26, ll.10-47; *ASE*, 356-60.

6. *Edward the Elder*: see above IV c.20, l.41; c.21, ll. 14-19, 39; *ASE*, 319-39.

7. *Alfred*: see above IV c.18, ll.3-33; c.20, ll.20-23, 40-41; *ASE*, 248-50, 253-76.

Æthelwulf: see above IV c.13, ll.2-3, 33-36; c.14, ll.47-51; *ASE*, 244-5.

8. *Ecgberht*: see above IV c.13, ll.3, 39-49; *ASE*, 209-10, 231-5.

Ealhmund: perhaps the same as Ealhmund on record in 784 as king of Kent (see *ASE*, 207).

8-9. *Eafa ... Ingild*: otherwise unknown.

10. *Ine*: king of the West Saxons 688-726; see *ASE*, 71-73.

Cenred: the preface to Ine's law code shows that Cenred was alive and in a position of authority during his son's reign: 'Ic Ine, mid Godes gife Wesseaxna kyning, mid geðeahte ond mid lare Cenredes mines fæder –' (F.L. Attenborough [ed.], *The Laws of the Earliest English Kings* [Cambridge, 1922], 36).

11. *Ceolwald*: otherwise unknown.

11-13. *Cutha ... Cerdic*: this stage of the genealogy offers some difficulties. In *ASC* (Plummer), 18-19 (s.a.568); *ASC*, 13, Ceawlin and Cutha appear as fellow-campaigners. So later (s.a.577) do Cuthwine and Ceawlin. There is no hint, and indeed the entries make it seem improbable, that Cutha was Cuthwine's son and Ceawlin's grandson. Cutha was killed in 584; Ceawlin survived until 593 (*ASC* (Plummer), 20-21; *ASC*, 14). In *ASC* (Plummer), 20 (s.a.597); *ASC*, 14, a short genealogy makes Cutha son of Cynric son of Cerdic; there is no mention of Ceawlin or Cuthwine. The preface to the Parker MS (*ASC* (Plummer), 2; *ASC*, 3) makes Ceol (591-7) succeed Cynric son of Cerdic; there is no mention of Ceawlin, Cuthwine or Cutha, although elsewhere (ibid., 22, s.a.611; 15) Ceol is described as son of Cutha. The genealogy in Asser's *Life of King Alfred* (ed. W.H. Stevenson [Oxford, 1904], 2) corresponds to that given by Ailred and Fordun. These contradictory traditions begin to make sense if Myres' brilliant reconciliation of the literary, archaeological and topographical evidence (*Settlements*, 143-73) is accepted. According to this, Ceawlin, despite the fact that his name alliterates, did not belong to the line of Cedric; he was king of the Saxons of the upper Thames valley, whose military success brought him for a brief spell the title of Bretwalda, but whose reign ended in disaster. Cutha and Cuthwine were his associates; they may indeed have been a single person. In combination with the other evidence, Cerdic's Celtic name indicates that he was the part-Saxon, part-Romano-British ruler of Hampshire and Berkshire, who extended his power westward into Wiltshire. Cerdic's line was for some years subordinate to that of Ceawlin, but eventually recovered power by way of Ceol and his successor Ceolwulf (597-611). For a different view see Dumville, ut cit.

11.   *Cutha*: cf. above III c.28, l.20. The name is a shortened form, perhaps of Cuthwulf or Cuthwine (see Sisam, ut cit., 157; Myres, *Settlements*, 163, 169). The names Cutha and Cuthwine may refer to a single individual. Alternatively, Cutha may be the same as the Cutha or Cuthwulf mentioned (anachronistically according to Myres, *Settlements*, 168) in the annal for 571.
   Cuthwine: not otherwise identified.

12.   *Ceawlin*: king of the West Saxons 560-93 (*HBC*, 21; see above III c.21, l.44).
   Cynric: king of the West Saxons 534-?60 (*HBC*, 21). According to Myres (*Settlements*, 153-4) probably a ghost figure. See above III c.21, l.44.

13.   *Creoda*: does not appear in all sources (see Sisam, ut cit., 157; Myres, *Settlements*, 153, n.1; Dumville, ut cit., 59-60).
   Cerdic: king of the West Saxons 519-34 (*HBC*, 21; see above ll.11-13 note; *ASE*, 19-25).

13-16.   *He obtained ... Angles*: not in Ailred, *Genealogia*; based ultimately on the date for the arrival in Britain of Hengist and Horsa given (*ASC* (Plummer), 12-13; *ASC*, 10) as 449. Cerdic is said to have arrived in 495 (ibid., 14-15; 11), but it should be noted that *ASC* also contains traces of a variant tradition according to which the West Saxons arrived in 514 under the leadership, not of Cerdic, but of Stuf and Wihtgar. They arrive however at a place called *Cerdices ora*, where in the annal for 495 Cerdic is also said to have landed and presumably given it his own name. 'The gap of 19 years is likely to have arisen from the two versions being dated within two successive nineteen-year Easter cycles' (Myres, *Settlements*, 5, n.1, based on K. Harrison, 'Early Wessex Annals in the Anglo-Saxon Chronicle', *EHR*, lxxxvi [1971], 527-33; *Framework of Anglo-Saxon History* [Cambridge, 1976], 127-30). This of course would imply the early existence of two written versions of the annals. In 534 (*ASC* (Plummer), 16-17; *ASC*, 12) Cerdic and Cynric are said to have granted the Isle of Wight to their nephews, Stuf and Wihtgar. Stuf and Wihtgar are usually now regarded as Jutes rather than Saxons (*ASE*, 23-24).

16-19. *Elesa ... Woden*: H.M. Chadwick (*Origins of the English Nation* [Cambridge, 1907], 56-57) pointed out the relationship between this stage of the West Saxon royal genealogy and the corresponding stage of the Bernician. Sisam (ut cit., 159-63) goes so far as to suggest that the West Saxon genealogy is borrowed from the Bernician. As against this may be set the fact, noted by R.W. Chambers (*Beowulf, An Introduction*, 3rd edn. [Cambridge, 1959], 316-17), that the pedigree from Cerdic to Woden, including Giwis whom Sisam considers an intruder, forms a perfect alliterative poem, which may be of considerable antiquity. Sisam's dismissive comments are not therefore wholly convincing; cf. J.M. Wallace-Hadrill's comment on Sisam's treatment of the Kentish king-list (*Early Germanic Kingship in England and on the Continent* [Oxford, 1971], 44-45).

16. *Elesa ... Esla*: neither otherwise known. Elesa is perhaps related to the Alusa, Aluson or Aloc found in different versions of the Bernician royal genealogy (see Chadwick, ut cit., 57).

17. *Giwis*: the name is related to *Gewisse*, 'West Saxons', a term used on a number of occasions in *Bede*, but otherwise found only in Welsh and Irish sources; see, e.g. *Nennius*, 90, s.a.900. Giwis is the eponymous ancestor of the Gewisse; cf. *Asser's Life of King Alfred*, ut cit., 2: 'Geuuis, a quo Britones totam illam gentem Geguuis nominant.'

17-18. *Wig ... Freawine*: as Wigo and Frowinus both appear in Danish tradition as allies of Offa I, king of the continental Angles and ancestor of Offa II, king of Mercia (757-96). The sister of Wigo is said to have married Offa I (see Chadwick, ut cit., 111-36).

18. *Frithogar*: not otherwise identified.

18-19. *Brond ... Woden*: this sequence is common to the West Saxon and Bernician genealogies.

18. *Brond*: perhaps the eponymous ancestor of the Brondingas, a people mentioned (*Beowulf*, l.521) in connection with their king Breca, who competed with Beowulf in a swimming match. The Brondingas and Breca are also mentioned in *Widsith*, l.25. See F. Klaeber (ed.), *Beowulf and the Fight at Finnsburg*, 3rd edn. (New York, 1941), 20, 287.

19. *Bældæg*: not otherwise identified.

19-24. *whose father ... Mercury*: as noted above, in Ailred, *Genealogia* this passage does not immediately follow the first mention of Woden.

19. *Woden*: the principal divinity of the Anglo-Saxons and some continental Germanic peoples, regarded as an ancestor-figure for the royal line (Wallace-Hadrill, *Kingship*, ut cit., 12-14). Chadwick (ut cit., 56) notes that with the single exception of Essex all the Anglo-Saxon royal genealogies which have been preserved go back to him. In England south of Humber evidence for the cult is to be found in such names as Woodnesborough KNT, Wednesbury STF, Wednesfield STF and Wansdyke HMP, WLT, SOM (F. Stenton, 'The Historical Bearing of Place-Name Studies: Anglo-Saxon Heathenism', *TRHS*, 4th series [1941], 1-24). In the genealogy as given by Ailred Woden is euhemerized and regarded as an early king; cf. Jocelin, *Vita Kentegerni*, c.32 (Forbes, *Lives*, 217): 'Woden vero quem principalem deum crediderant, et precipue Angli de quo originem duxerant, cui et quartam feriam consecraverant, probabiliter affirmavit hominem fuisse mortalem, et regem Saxonum, secta paganum, a quo ipsi et plures nationes genus duxerant. Hujus inquid corpus multis annis transactis resolutum fuit in pulverem; et anima sepulta in inferno eternum sustinet ignem.'

called Mercury: based ultimately on Tacitus, *Germania*, c.9.1: 'Deorum maxime Mercurium colunt' (see the note in J.G.C. Anderson [ed.], *Cornelii Taciti De Origine et Situ Germanorum* [Oxford, 1938], 73-74).

24.   *day of Mercury*: cf. Italian *Mercoledi*, French *Mercredi*, 'Wednesday'.

24-32.   *This genealogy ... differed*: in this passage 'I' (ll.28, 30) is Fordun, accepted by Bower. The comment illustrates an important aspect of the historical method employed by both.

25-26.   *the one ... chronicles*: see *Malmesbury*, i, 120-21 (bk.2, c.116).

Book VI

Book VI

1

De bona prosapia sobolis regis David ex parte matris eius

Scriptor

*Sed quia^b sanctissimi regis David^c ex premissis constare poterit non solum sanctitudo, verum eciam generis et prosapie eiusdem claritudo, nunc superest ut^d de ipsius generose sobolis successione, et quam naturale inest eis parentum sequi vestigia, cum eciam ex parte matris eius,^e tamquam ex bona arbore, ut fieri assolet, dulces fructus et 5 generosos palmites comprobati sumus succrevisse, et eciam in futuris perpetue ut prosperari valeant velimus. Et quatenus confirmet Deus hoc quod incepit et operatus est in eis, fiat voluntas sua. Ut ergo sciatis qualis et quanta fuit domina regina uxor dicti regis David, ex sanctitate patris eiusdem Walthevi martyris, et sanctissimi filii 10 eiusdem Walthevi confessoris, patet per Jocelinum in libello nepotibus eius conscripto, ubi sic dicit:

Illustrissimis viris Willelmo regi Scocie et Alexandro filio eius et comiti David^f Jocelinus qualiscumque monachus Furnesii, utriusque hominis salute in Domino potiri, et utriusque vite felicitatem in Domino sortiri. 15 Sepius mente revolvens de cuius^g radice palmites producti pululastis, intueor ex summa et excellentissima dignitate tocius Europe vos originariam^h particulam traxisse carnis.ⁱ Sancte namque Margarite mater, Agatha nomine, filia fuit germani^j Henrici clarissimi Romanorum imperatoris (alii dicunt quod filia fuit Germanie imperatoris 20 Henrici), cuius posteritas Romanum illustrat imperium.^k Soror eciam eiusdem Agathe regina extitit Hungariorum, cuius uteri fructus successivus reges germinans, non solum eiusdem regni possidet^l principatum, sed eciam regnorum aliorum plurium nactus est sceptrum. Genitor nichilominus ipsius beate Margarite, dictus Eadwardus, 25 nepos et heres legitimus fuit sanctissimi confessoris^m Eadwardi regis Anglie, jure hereditario Anglici regni per linias rectas et directas successive generacionis in vos devoluto, vos sceptrigeros effecisset, nisi

---

a *decorated initial* S *C*	*f* +fratro *DMS*
b Antequam ad successorem nepotem et	*g* +vitis *DMS,AS*
heredem regis David Malcolmum aliquid	*h* originalem *CA*
descripturus accedam placet michi ex quo	*i* canis *CA*
ipsius *for* Sed quia *CA*	*j* +-e *interlin.C; not in D*
c +et *CA*	*k* Germanie et Romanorum imperatoris
d presentibus intitulare *for* nunc superest ut	Henrici *for* germani ... imperium *CA*
CA	*l* *AS*; possident *C,CA,DMS*; possideret *D*
e dicti heredis et regis futuri Malcolmi *for*	*m* +et *C,D; om.DMS,AS*
eius *CA*	

Book VI

1

The good lineage of King David's children on his mother's side

But it will be possible to establish from what has gone before not only the saintliness of the most saintly King David, but also the celebrity of the family and lineage of the same. In consequence, as regards the succession of his own noble offspring, and how natural it is for them
5 to follow in the footsteps of their forebears, since we have here proved on his mother's side also that sweet fruits and noble branches have been produced, just as from a good tree (as usually happens), it only now remains for us to wish that they may be able to thrive in the future also for ever. And seeing that God will confirm this that he has begun
10 and has worked in them, let his will be done. Therefore so that you may know the nature and greatness of the lady queen, the wife of the
- said King David, as a consequence of the sanctity of her father Waltheof the Martyr, and of her most saintly son Waltheof the Confessor, Jocelin makes it clear in the little book which he wrote for
15 David's grandsons, where he says:

> To the most illustrious William king of Scotland and Alexander his son
> and Earl David [his brother], Jocelin monk of Furness (such as he is)
> hopes for salvation in the Lord to be attained by both, and for felicity in
> the Lord to be their lot in both aspects of life. Often when thinking
20 about the root [of the vine] from which you have been produced and
> grown as branches, I reflect that you have derived a little piece of the
> origin of your flesh from the highest and most pre-eminent rank of all
> Europe. For St Margaret's mother, who was called Agatha, was a
> daughter of a brother of Henry the most celebrated emperor of the
25 Romans (others say that she was a daughter of Henry the Emperor of
> Germany), whose descendants give lustre to the Roman empire. Also a
> sister of the same Agatha was queen of the Hungarians, the successive
> fruit of whose womb by producing kings not only controls the same
> kingdom, but has also obtained sovereignty over many other
30 kingdoms. Likewise the father of the blessed Margaret, called Edward,
> was the nephew and legitimate heir of the most saintly Edward the
> Confessor king of England; and once the hereditary right to the
> English kingdom had passed down to you by rightful direct lines of
> descent in successive generations, he would have made you the rulers,
35 had not the violent plundering by the Normans (as God has allowed)
> prevented it until the appointed time. And not only have they been
> most powerful and pre-eminent in that glorious descent of the kings of

violenta Normannorum direpcio, Deo permittente, usque ad tempus
prefinitum prepedisset. Nec solum in illo glorioso stemate regum   30
Anglorum in diviciis et gloria in regno potentissimi prefulserunt, sed |

eciam in sanctitate et justicia magna Deo placentes in vita, et post
mortem miraculis multis modis magnifice claruerunt.

2

De avia eorum et avunculo

A sancto namque rege Adwlpho, qui totam Angliam decimavit,
[decimam*ᵃ*] Deo et ecclesie consecravit, novem numerantur reges
sancti, quorum posterior priori persona*ᵇ* prestancior in Christiana
religione emicuisse dinoscitur. In decimo vero, Sancto scilicet Eadwardo, cunctorum predecessorum summitas*ᶜ* quasi*ᵈ* transfusa con-   5
fluxit. Et sic ex illo,*ᵉ* tamquam fonte lucidissimo, vite religiose rivulus in
Sanctam Margaritam proneptem eius, et ex illa in filium eius regem
David avum vestrum, et ex eo in Malcolmum fratrem vestrum
emanavit. Ceterum avia vestra Matildis regina Scocie proneptis erat
Willelmi strenuissimi ducis qui debellabat Angliam, et comitis Wal-   10
thevi sancti martyris filia, ac mater sanctissimi Walthevi abbatis de
Melros patrui vestri. Ipse eciam decus et decor prosapie vestre, regni
tutor, tutela patrie, titulus pudicicie, gemma vite canonice, speculum
monastice discipline. Hic, inquam, degens in mundo fuit cleri
solacium, pauperum erarium, egenorum sustentaculum, infirmorum   15
remedium, et virtutum omnium*ᶠ* preclarum domicilium. Huius corpus
sanctissimum, tocius adhuc corrupcionis expers, future resurreccionis
preclarum prefert indicium, et fidei ac spei nostre probabile ac

palpabile prebet experimentum. | Cum ergo traduce nature a tam clara
et superexcellenti genealogia sitis*ᵍ* utrimque dirivati, ab illa vos esse   20
degeneres dedignemini,*ʰ* et sancte propaginis exsortes*ⁱ* fieri.

Hec Jocelinus regi Willelmo et fratribus. Placeat nunc lectori legere
quod non piget scriptori hic*ʲ* inserere, et aliquamdiu immorari in
conversacione huius almi confessoris Walthevi, quia nec erit lectori*ᵏ*
onerosum quod regno Scocie honorosum fuerit ad tractandum.   25

Congruum propterea duxi generositatem illius, maxime quia contu-
bernium Dei in pluribus personis utriusque sexus habet, in narracionis
exordio declarare. Sic profecto liquebit esse competens cunctis
discernentibus, quod de ingenua et sancta radice processerit surculus
optimus sanctitate conspicuus (Jocelinus).   30

a	decimam *AS; om.DMS*	*g*	sicut *CA*
b	*C,DMS*; par vel *AS*	*h*	*C,AS*; dedignamini *DMS*
c	*C,DMS*; sanctitas *AS*	*i*	*D,AS*; exortes *DMS*; extorres *C,CA*
d	+diffusa *del.C*	*j*	michi *for* scriptori hic *CA*
e	*DMS,AS*; illa *C,D*	*k*	+Scoto *CA*
f	*om.DMS,AS*		

the English in riches and glory in the kingdom, but they have also been
pleasing to God in their great saintliness and righteousness in life, and
40   have shone magnificently in many ways with miracles after their
deaths.

2

Their grandmother and uncle

Now, from the time of the saintly king Æthelwulf, who tithed the whole
of England, and consecrated the tithe to God and the church, nine
saintly kings are listed, of whom each successive person is perceived to
have been more conspicuously outstanding in the Christian religion
5   than the one before. In the tenth indeed, namely St Edward, the
[sanctity] of all his predecessors came together as if by transfusion. And
so from him, as from a pure spring, a stream of religious life poured
forth into his great-niece St Margaret, and from her into her son King
David your grandfather, and from him into Malcolm your brother.
10   Furthermore your grandmother Matilda queen of Scotland was a
great-niece of William the most vigorous duke who conquered
England, and the daughter of Earl Waltheof the sainted martyr, and
mother of the most saintly Waltheof abbot of Melrose your paternal
uncle. He indeed is the glory and adornment of your lineage, a
15   guardian of the kingdom, a protector of the country, a symbol of
chastity, a jewel of the canonical life, a mirror of monastic discipline.
This man, I say, during his lifetime was a comfort to the clergy, a
treasury for the poor, a support for the destitute, a remedy for the sick,
and a glorious dwelling-place for all the virtues. His most holy body,
20   still wholly incorrupt, offers a glorious sign of future resurrection, and
presents probable and palpable proof of our faith and hope. Since
therefore by your natural inheritance you are descended on both sides
from such a famous and super-excellent ancestry, you should refuse
with scorn to depart from its standards, and come to have no share in
25   your saintly lineage.

So writes Jocelin to King William and his brothers. I hope the reader
will now be pleased to read what the writer is not ashamed to insert
here, and to linger for a while on the life of this uplifting confessor
Waltheof, for a discussion of something which is an honour to the
30 kingdom of Scotland will not be tiresome for the [Scottish] reader.

On this account I have thought it suitable at the beginning of the story
to tell of the noble birth of that man, especially because it is given him
to live with God among many persons of both sexes. So undoubtedly it
will appear to all discerning people to be expected that the best shoot
35   notable for its saintliness will have grown from a noble and holy root
(Jocelin).

3

De nobili Walthevo comite Northumbrie patre Sancti Walthevi

Tempore igitur quo Willelmus dux Normannie, debellatis indigenis, Anglie sceptrum optinuerat, comes illustris Walthevus serenissimi Siwardi comitis filius comitatum Northanhumbrie et Eboracensis provincie principatum possidebat. Erat etatis floride, fortitudinis admirande, inter socios et domesticos mansuetudinis agnine,[a] erga 5
rebelles et hostes feritatis leonine. Diutino conflictu viriliter | Normannis resistens, plurimam stragem illis inferebat; preclaros triumphos de ipsis sepius reportabat. Animadvertens rex[b] animositatem et strenuitatem viri, post varios rotatus[c] fortune, factura nunciorum intercurrencium, datis dextris utrimque et acceptis, in graciam et pacem comitem 10
sibi federatum suscepit; et post hominium sibi factum, neptem suam Julictam[d] nomine, id est mecham, illi in matrimonium junxit, de qua unicam filiam Matildem nomine procreavit. Ipse vero inventus est in omnibus fidelis, ingrediens et egrediens ad imperium regis. Extitit nichilominus pauperibus munificus, in ecclesia devotus, clericis et 15
maxime religiosis acclinis, largus ac liberalis universis, hostibus tamen satis formidabilis. Cernens autem rex quod prosperatum esset regnum in manu eius, et siluisset terra in conspectu eius, perplures, ymmo fere cunctos,[e] nobilium Anglici generis[f] aut interemit, aut incarceravit, seu proscripsit, sive in miseram redegit servitutem. Videns autem quia 20
placeret Normannis, apposuit apprehendere comitem Walthevum. Et, ne videretur maculari prodicionis opprobrio, si sine causa innoxium condempnaret in nullo lesus ab eo, meditabatur et machinabatur qualiter id perficeret irreprehensibilis in conspectu humano. Tali ergo modo quesivit, et occasionem invenit non solum recedendi et 25
rescindendi vinculum dileccionis et pacis ab amico et fideli suo, verum eciam tollendi eum de medio. Fama namque volatilis in diebus illis resperserat per Angliam, Danos et Noricos in exterminium vel necem Normannorum conjurasse, et infinitam classem in unum collectam aure spirantis ad votum flatus expectare. Instillatum est auribus regis 30
ab emulis et malivolis adversariis Walthevi ipsum, velut fidefragum,[g] perjurum proditorem, conspiratorem, missis nunciis, sacramentis prestitis,[h] obsidibus datis, Danicam classem invitasse; adventantibus[i]

---

a	C,AS; agmine DMS	f	germinis DMS,AS
b	+ Willelmus CA	g	fedifragum DMS; foedifragum AS
c	AS; rogatus C,D,CA,DMS	h	sacramenta prestita C,D,DMS;
d	Julitam DMS,AS		sacramentis prestitis AS
e	CA,DMS,AS; cunctis C,D	i	advenientibus CA

3

The noble Waltheof earl of Northumbria, the father of St Waltheof

At the time therefore when William duke of Normandy had defeated the native inhabitants and obtained the sceptre of England, the famous Earl Waltheof, the son of the most serene Earl Siward, held the earldom of Northumbria and ruled the province of York. He was a man in the bloom of youth, with remarkable courage, with the mildness of a lamb among associates and servants, but the fierceness of a lion towards rebels and enemies. While resisting the Normans in manly fashion in a lengthy conflict, he inflicted a great deal of slaughter on them; and he often obtained splendid victories over them. King [William] recognized the man's spirit and vigour, and following various turns of fortune, after the work of intermediaries between them, and the exchange of right hands on both sides, he received the earl as his ally into his grace and peace. And after Waltheof had done homage to him, the king gave his niece called Judith (that is the adultress) to him in a marriage which produced just one daughter called Matilda.

Waltheof indeed turned out to be faithful in every way, coming and going as the king ordered. Besides he showed himself generous to the poor, devout in church, well-disposed towards the clergy and especially monks, lavish and liberal to all, yet quite formidable to enemies. But the king, observing that the kingdom had prospered under his rule, and that the land was quiet as he surveyed it, either killed, or imprisoned, or exiled very many (indeed nearly all) the nobles of English origin, or he reduced them to wretched slavery. When he saw that the Normans approved, he proceeded to arrest Earl Waltheof. And, lest he seemed to be tainted with the scandal of treachery if he condemned an innocent man without cause when he had in no way been harmed by him, he plotted and schemed how to achieve his aim while [appearing] blameless in men's eyes. He therefore searched in such a way, and found an opportunity not merely of withdrawing and cancelling the bond of love and peace from his faithful friend, but also of removing him from the scene. For a fleeting rumour had been spread throughout England at that time that the Danes and Norse had conspired to expel or kill the Normans, and that a vast fleet had been gathered together and was waiting in hope for a favourable wind to blow. It was instilled in the king's ears by Waltheof's rivals and ill-disposed opponents that as an oath-breaker, perjured traitor and conspirator he had invited the Danish fleet by sending messengers, taking oaths and giving hostages; and that he had promised advice and help as they approached in

illis pro viribus consilium et auxilium ad internicionem vel eliminacio-
nem Normannorum ab insula promisisse. Rex autem habens aures 35
accusacionis Anglorum bibulas, suspicioni pectus patulum, ad vindi-
candum cor ferocissimum, letus est effectus utpote materiam quasi
justam exercendi et explendi in Walthevum que corde conceperat
nactus.

4

De incarceracione et decollacione Sancti Walthevi martyris

Jussu itaque regis comes citatus simpliciter venit ad curiam, nil sibi
mali regem illaturum confidens, mundam et innocentem secum gestans
conscienciam. Hoc habet innocencia proprium ut sicut neminem ledere
contendit, sic a nullo se ledi confidit. Presentatus comes coram rege in
multis accusatur, in quibus omnibus, si justicia locum haberet, 5
inficiando et racionem reddendo erueretur, omnia objecta evacuando.
Verumptamen nulla responsione excusacionis oblate locum tenente,
G i,321   comes comprehenditur, compedibus ferreis vincitur, | incarceratur,
injuriis multiplicibus afficitur. Vir autem ingenuus, amplexans animo
divinum judicium vel permissionem, necessitatem vertit in virtutem; et 10
se totum ad Deum convertens crebra confessione peccaminum,
continua lacrimarum profusione, oracionibus assiduis et genuflexi- |
fo.112   onibus suam ipsius operabatur salutem. Quid plura? Post diutinum
carceris squalorem et multimodam affliccionem, regis sentencia
secundum voluntatem prolata, in urbe Wintonia capite truncatur, 15
eiusque corpus Crolande deportatum in ecclesia Sancti Guthlaci
tumulatur. Et quamvis juxta Salomonem ira regis ut fremitus leonis
adversus Walthevum sevierit, et de loco judicii eius procedens
prevaleret iniquitas, de vultu tamen Domini judicii producitur equitas.
Quem enim rex ferocissimus sustulit mundo, rex eternus et clemens 20
intulit celo. Quam grata enim Deo fuerat eius innocencia, quam
accepta penitencia,[a] mors in conspectu Domini preciosa – signa
proclamant insignia ante tumbam eius patrata. Quocirca processu
temporis evoluti, crebrescentibus miraculis, ossa eius que pululabant[b]
de loco suo, e terre gremio sunt translata, et in locello retro quoddam 25
altare reverenter recondita. Extat libellus in eodem cenobio conscrip-
tus[c] de miraculis eius, ex quibus probatur, quod[d] nomen ei martyris
ascribitur, attribuitur et decus.[e] Matildis vero filia eius prenominata,
cum pervenisset ad mundum muliebrem, oportuno tempore illustrissimo comiti de Hunteduna, scilicet seniori Simoni de Sainlize,[f] nupsit, 30
de quo votivo germine duos filios et filias edidit. Erat primogenitus

---

a   C,DMS; paciencia AS   d   +merito AS; om.DMS
b   que pululabant AS; depululabant C,DMS e   DMS,AS; ortus C
c   con- interlin.C   f   +sive Machald CA

40 accordance with his resources for the massacre or expulsion of the
Normans from the island. The king then, with ears ready to hear an
accusation against the English, a breast wide open to suspicion, and a
heart extremely fierce for vengeance, became happy, since he had
obtained an apparently just cause for putting into practice and
45 achieving what he had conceived in his heart against Waltheof.

4

The imprisonment and beheading of St Waltheof the Martyr

And so at the king's command the earl was summoned and came   [1075]
openly to the court, trusting that the king would do him no harm, since
his own conscience was clear and blameless. Innocence has this special
characteristic that just as it strives not to harm anyone, so it is sure that
5 it will not be harmed by anyone. Once the earl had been presented to
the king, he was accused of many things, on all of which (if justice had
been served) he would have been cleared by sweeping away all the
charges with a denial and an explanation. But no answer offered by
way of excuse was allowed, the earl was seized, fettered with leg-irons,
10 put into prison, and suffered all kinds of outrage. But this honourable
man embraced in his thoughts the divine judgment or permission [for
his condition], and made a virtue of necessity. Putting himself entirely
in God's hands with frequent confession of his sins, a continuous flow
of tears, and unremitting prayers and genuflexions, he devoted himself
15 to his salvation. Need I say more? After a long period of squalor in
prison and sufferings of many kinds, following a sentence pronounced
according to the king's wishes he was beheaded in the city of   [1076:
Winchester, and his body was conveyed to Crowland and buried in the   31 May]
church of St Guthlac. And although in the words of Solomon the wrath
20 of the king raged against Waltheof like the roaring of a lion, and
although unfairness arising from the king's place of judgment
prevailed, yet a fair judgment emerges from the presence of the Lord.
For the man whom an extremely fierce king removed from the world,
the eternal and merciful king has conveyed to Heaven. For the extent to
25 which his innocence has been pleasing to God, his penance welcome,
and his death a precious thing in the Lord's sight, is made clear by the
wonderful miracles performed at his tomb. In consequence as time
passed and miracles accumulated, his bones sent forth new life from
their resting-place, were moved from the bosom of the earth, and
30 reverently given a new place in a shrine behind one of the altars. A little
book is to be found in the same monastery which has been written
about his miracles, which shows how the name of martyr has [rightly]
been ascribed and honour attributed to him.
When Matilda his aforesaid daughter reached womanhood, at a
35 suitable time she married the most distinguished earl of Huntingdon,
namely the elder Simon de Senlis, and from this desirable stock she

paterni nominis et hereditatis successor, secundus vocabatur Walthevus aviti[g] nominis et sanctitatis renovator[h] [i]et successor.[j]

g   C,DMS; antiqui AS   i   + simul DMS; om.AS
h   AS; renator C,D,CA,DMS   j   possessor for successor DMS,AS

5

De preludio diversorum ludorum inter Walthevum et fratrem suum habitorum

Comes Simon prenominatus pater puerorum primogenitum, tamquam alter Isaac Esau suum, arccius amabat; mater vero mulier bona
Walthevum, velut Rebecca suum Jacob, affectu propensiori diligebat.
Cumque fratres in puerili[a] etate essent constituti, sapiebant, agebant,
ludebant ut parvuli. Prior natu Symon, collectis arbusculis seu   5
ramusculis secundum modulum suum castella construere consueverat,
et ascendens caballum[b] vel[c] sonipedem suum, et virgulam quasi
lanceam accipiens et vibrans,[d] cum coetaneis circa ficticii et imaginarii
castelli custodiam et defensionem solicitus miliciam simulabat. Walthevus vero puerulus ex virgulis et lapillis quasi ecclesias edificabat,   10
seque presbyterum tamquam missam celebrantem expansis manibus
representabat;[e] et quia[f] verba proferre non noverat, sonos cantum
simulantes edere solebat. Cumque parvuli huiusmodi lusui sepius
indulgerent, pluresque ad aspectum et risum converterent,[g] quadam
vice quidam religiosus et sapiens, astans et aspiciens cum ceteris, ait ad   15
intuentes: 'Quid vobis videtur de hoc ludo parvulorum?' Illi fatebantur
simplicem esse tantummodo, utpote quid sit inter dextram et sinistram
| ignorancium. Et ille: 'Non sic,' inquit, 'non sic! Est enim ludus iste
quoddam preludium vitam utriusque presagiens et exitum. Primus
namque vitam suam milicie usque ad mortem intricabit,[h] secundus   20
religiose vivens, dies suos in bonum[i] consummabit.' Nullum verborum
istorum in terram decidit; sed de utroque, quod conjecturando sive
vaticinando predixit, evenit. Simon namque paternum comitatum,
longe post patris decessum, cum multo labore tandem nactus, ac miles
strenuus effectus, tempore regis Stephani castella nova construxit, alia   25
ab aliis constructa conquisivit, et comitatui suo comitatus et civitates
conjunxit, et in seculari milicia, more tamen Christiano, vitam
terminavit. Walthevus vero, vitam virtutibus et eciam signis inclitam
ducens, demum obdormivit in Domino,

G i,322 (margin)

sicut libelli vite eius plenius declarat descripcio.[j]   30

a   AS; parili C,DMS   g   C,DMS; provocarent AS
b   canabum C,D,DMS,AS; canubum CA   h   C,DMS; iniciabit AS
c   velut DMS,AS   i   + communicabis del.C
d   AS; vibris C,D,CA   j   sicut plenius sequens nostra declarabit
e   re- interlin.C; presentabat DMS,AS   narracio for sicut ... descripcio DMS,AS
f   om.D

gave birth to two sons and daughters. The first-born boy was the
successor to his father's name and inheritance; the second was called
Waltheof as restorer of and successor to his grandfather's name and
40   saintliness.

5

*The prelude of different games played by Waltheof
and his brother*

The aforesaid Earl Simon the father of the boys loved the first-born
more dearly, like another Isaac loving his Esau; but their mother, good
woman, loved Waltheof with deeper affection, as Rebecca loved her
Jacob. And when the brothers were children, they understood,
5   behaved and played as children do. Simon the elder boy was in the
habit of collecting little twigs and branches to build castles to his own
little design, and mounting his horse or steed, and grasping and
brandishing a little stick like a lance, he painstakingly engaged in
pretend warfare with boys of his own age based on the guarding and
10   defending of a make-believe and imaginary castle. But Waltheof as a
small boy made buildings like churches out of small sticks and stones,
and stretching out his hands played the part of a priest celebrating
mass; and because he did not know how to pronounce the words, he
used to utter sounds in imitation of the chant. The boys would often
15   indulge in this kind of game, and they would cause many people to
watch and laugh. On one occasion a certain wise monk who was
standing and watching with the others said to the onlookers: 'What do
you make of this children's game?' They declared that he was merely a
simpleton, in that he was one of those who cannot tell their right hand
20   from their left. He said: 'Not so, not so! For this game acts as a kind of
prelude that foretells the life and end of each boy. For the first will
entangle his life with warfare until his death, while the second will live
as a monk and crown his days with good.' None of these words went
unfulfilled; but what he predicted in conjecture or prophecy came
25   about in each case. Simon indeed with great labour at length obtained
his paternal earldom long after his father's death. And after becoming
an active knight, in the reign of King Stephen he built new castles and
took over others built by other people; he added earldoms and cities to
his earldom, and ended his life in secular warfare, though in Christian
30   fashion. While Waltheof, after leading a life celebrated for his virtues
and also for his miracles, in the end fell asleep in the Lord,

as the account in the book on his life makes clear at greater length.

6

De bonis eius iniciis et morte patris sui

Cum autem Walthevus accepisset tempus habile ad discendum, traditur literis imbuendis cura parentum. Nimis tamen propere est ab earum studiis abstractus, ob varios rerum eventus et temporum status. Profecit tamen decenter in literatura secundum spacium temporis quo scolas frequentabat, multosque literaciores subtilitate sensus et acu- 5 mine ingenii, ac verborum elegancia, unccione magistra precedebat. Quo adhuc in puerili toga constituto, pater eius ob quandam offensam regis Henrici primi iram implacabilem incurrerat. A quo exheredatus, et iter versus Jerosolimam cruce signatus accipiens, in transmarinis partibus in fata concesserat. Mater vero eius, consobrina regis, ab 10 eodem rege traditur in matrimonium David regi Scocie, dato illi comitatu de Hontedune sub dotis nomine. Rex eciam prefatus Henricus duxerat in conjugium Matildem, sororem dicti regis David, filiam Sancte Margarite proneptis Sancti Eadwardi regis Anglie, genere et specie preclaram, quam ob vite sanctitatem et morum 15 graciam usque in presens Anglici cognominant 'bonam reginam'. |
David autem rex ex Matilde regina procreavit filium Henricum nomine, hominem, ut accepimus, mansuetum, pium et bene morigeratum, patrem duorum regum (Malcolmi videlicet viri sanctissimi et Willelmi preclarissimi), necnon et David comitis venerandi (ac eciam 20 tres inclitas filias de quibus infra loco suo patebit.) Walthevus bone indolis puer matrem, ex comitissa iam reginam*ᵃ* effectam que ipsum arccius amabat, secutus in curia regis David, nutriebatur, educabatur, crescebat et comfortabatur, et gracia Dei in eo evidentibus indiciis monstrabatur. In palacio namque clericum,*ᵇ* in turba monachum, inter 25 aulicos seipsum exhibuit solitarium. Inter cetera que possidebat insignia virtutum, illud singulare decus virginitatis videlicet candidatum, ex utero matris secum vexit ad celum. Rex autem ille non se victricum*ᶜ* sed patrem exhibebat, et quasi propriam prolem dilexit et excoluit; et dum iret venatum sepius illum advocans et secum 30 adducens, aliquociens archum | suum illi tradidit ad ferendum. Walthevus vero quam competenter potuit regis aspectibus se subducens, et alii archum regium commendans, opaca nemoris irrumpere, et infra condensa veprium aliquam planiciem querens et inveniens sedere, et in codice, ex industria ad hoc portato et de sinu prolato, consuevit 35 legere, aut oracioni incumbere. Quod cum crebrius actitasset, quadam

fo.112v

G i,323

a   *DMS,AS*; regina *C,D,CA*   *c*   *C,CA,DMS,AS*; nutricium *D*
b   clarum *DMS*; claustrum *AS*

6

His good beginnings, and the death of his father

When Waltheof had reached the age when he was ready for learning, his parents ensured that he was sent to be instructed in Latinity. Nevertheless he was withdrawn from his study of it all too soon because of the way various events turned out and the state of the times. Yet he made respectable progress in literacy in relation to the time which he spent at school; and he surpassed many who had studied for longer in the subtlety of his perceptions and the shrewdness of his intellect, the elegance of his speech, with the grace of unction as his teacher. While he was still a boy, his father had incurred the implacable wrath of King Henry I over some offence, and was disinherited by the king. After starting on a journey to Jerusalem as a crusader, he had submitted to his fate while overseas. Waltheof's mother, a cousin of the king, was then given in marriage by the same king to David [later] king [1113 × of Scotland, with a grant to him of the earldom of Huntingdon by way 1114] of dowry. Furthermore the said King Henry had married Matilda, a [1100: sister of the said King David, a daughter of St Margaret the great-niece 11 Nov.] of St Edward king of England, a lady notable for her ancestry as well as her beauty, whom the English up to the present time call their 'good queen' on account of the saintliness of her life and the charm of her character. King David then fathered a son by Queen Matilda called Henry, a man (as we have been told) who was mild, pious and virtuous, and who was the father of two kings (namely the most saintly Malcolm and the most distinguished William), and also of the venerable Earl David. He also had three famous daughters, regarding whom information will be given below.

Waltheof, a boy of innate good character, followed his mother (who loved him dearly), no longer a countess but now made queen, to the [1124: Apr.] court of King David. There he was nurtured and brought up. He grew big and strong, and the grace of God was demonstrated in him by clear signs. For in the palace he conducted himself as a cleric, in the crowd as a monk, among the courtiers as a hermit. Among the other virtuous qualities which he possessed, one unique distinction, the shining glory of chastity, travelled with him from his mother's womb to Heaven. King David did not behave as a step-father, but as a father, and loved and reared him as his own son. He often invited Waltheof to come with him when he went hunting, sometimes giving him him his bow to carry. Waltheof, however, escaped from the king's sight as best he could, and entrusting the royal bow to someone else, he used to penetrate the shady parts of the wood; and seeking and finding some clearing among the bushy thickets, he would sit and read a book

die fortuito rex illum consueta facientem reperit, et domum reversus,
regine que vidit enarrans, et sentenciose pronuncians, dixit: 'O regina,[d]
filius tuus non est de sorte nostra. Nichil illi et huic seculo. Aut cito de
hac vita in fata concedens demigrabit, aut secularibus abdicatis ad   40
aliquam religionem convolabit.' Quod autem ex ore regis Christianissimi connicientis, seu, Spiritu Sancto dictante, pronunciantis, egredie-
batur, non longe post effectui mancipabatur. Regina sapiens et optima
femina conservabat omnia verba hec, conferens in corde suo, gracias
agens et commendans filium suum omnia disponenti conditori suo.   45

d   *om.DMS,AS*

7

Quomodo seculum fugiens canonicus regularis efficitur et in priorem de Kirkhame preficitur

Processu dierum Walthevus vernantis juventutis limen attingens,
sperabatur a multis adepturus[a] nomen grande juxta nomen[b] magnorum qui sunt in terra, pontificalem videlicet gradum sortiturus in
Scocia vel in Anglia. Ipse vero intimis cordis medullis meditabatur
fugam a seculo, curans omnimodis ne contra Salvatoris prohibicionem   5
fieret fuga eius hyeme vel sabbato. Deliberabat autem super qualitatem
religionis et locum. Timebat enim ne forte si infra regnum regis Scocie,
vel infra terram comitis fratris sui, in aliqua domo religionis
susciperetur, diucius ibi morari non permitteretur; aut inde violenter
extractus, ad aliquod culmen honoris ecclesiastici, eciam invitus,   10
promoveretur. Hec ille mente pertractans, inspirante Spiritu Sancto
salubre consilium invenit: exiens de terra illa et cognacione sua,
veniensque ad locum Nostell' vocabulo extra regis et comitis dicionem,
in ecclesia Sancti Oswaldi regis et martyris habitum canonici suscepit.
Ubi ita religiose et disciplinate se habuit, ut liquide[c] claresceret   15
exhibitum in eius moribus et vita, quod scriptum invenerat in regula
clericorum a beato Augustino tradita. Ipse autem novicius et juvenis
proponebatur exemplar ad bene vivendum canonicis etate et conversacione annosis. Sed non potuit lucerna diucius, Deo disponente, vera
luce latere sub modio, quoniam canonici regulares de Kirkhame priore   20
privati Walthevum tunc temporis Sancti Oswaldi sacristam, licet
invitum et renitentem, verumptamen patris abbatis sui obedientem
imperio[d] constrictum, priorem et patrem suum spiritualem unanimi
assensu constituerunt. Qui sic in arce prelacionis[e] rector constitutus

a   adepturus *DMS*; ad episcopatus *AS*   *d*   patris abbatis sui ... imperio *om.DMS,AS*
b   *CA,DMS,AS*; numerum *C*   *e*   +constitucionis *del.C*
c   liquidum *DMS*; liduido *AS*

deliberately brought for the purpose and taken out from a fold in his
clothes, or devote himself to prayer. When he had been doing this
repeatedly, the king happened one day to find him following his usual
practice, and on returning home he told the queen what he had seen,
45   and speaking with great insight, he said: 'Your son, my queen, is not
one of us. He has nothing to do with this world. Either yielding to fate
he will soon depart from this life, or he will withdraw from secular
affairs and take refuge in some form of the monastic life.' Whether
these words were spoken by the most Christian king as a conjecture or a
50   pronouncement at the prompting of the Holy Spirit, they were carried
into effect not long afterwards. The queen as a wise and most excellent
woman treasured up all these words and pondered over them, giving
thanks and commending her son to her Maker who ordains everything.

7

How he fled from the world, became a regular canon
and was appointed prior of Kirkham

As time passed and Waltheof reached the threshold of the springtime
of youth, many hoped that he would acquire great fame like the fame of
the great ones of the earth, namely by obtaining the office of bishop in
Scotland or England. But he in the innermost depths of his heart
5   contemplated flight from the world, taking every care not to arrange
his flight during winter or on a Sabbath contrary to the Saviour's
prohibition. He debated then over what kind of religious life and the
place. For he feared that if he was received into some religious house
within the kingdom of the king of Scotland, or within the territory of
10   his brother the earl, he might perhaps not be allowed to stay there for
long, or would be forcibly removed from there and promoted to some
honoured position of ecclesiastical eminence, even though it was
against his will. On thinking over these matters carefully in his mind, he
was inspired by the Holy Spirit to come to a sound decision: leaving the
15   land of Scotland and his kinsmen, he approached the place called
Nostell, which lay beyond the jurisdiction of the king and the earl, and
there he received the habit of a canon in the church of St Oswald the
king and martyr. There he behaved with such monastic discipline that
what he had found written in the rule for clerics handed down by
20   blessed Augustine shone clearly revealed in his behaviour and life.
Indeed as a novice and a young man he was held up as a model of good
living to the canons who were senior in age and experience.
     But it was God's will that the lamp could not lie hidden from the true
light under a bushel for long, because the regular canons of Kirkham
25   (who had lost their prior) by unanimous assent elected Waltheof as   [× 1139]
their prior and spiritual father. He was sacristan at St Oswald at the
time, and although he was unwilling and resisted the offer, nevertheless
in obedience to the authority of his father abbot he was forced to

noluit extolli, sicut quibusdam moris est, sed quasi unus de subjectis 25
esse, nec dominari in clero, sed forma gregis fieri. Omnes bonas[f]

consuetudines et sacra | instituta que in diversis ecclesiis canonicorum
teneri cognovit, velut in fasciculum collecta, in domo cui prefuit
observari diligenter instituit. Quocirca benedixit Dominus domui illi

propter servum suum, crevit- | que possessio eius in terra, conferenti- 30
bus comite Henrico conterino eius et aliis magnatibus ecclesias et terras
in puram et perpetuam elemosinam ecclesie de Kirkhame possidendas.
Effloruit nichilominus intrinsecus religio sancta in regulari disciplina,
in hospitum suscepcione, ac multe humanitatis exhibicione. In hiis et
aliis sacris studiis vir iste quantam graciam invenerit in oculis Domini, 35
ipse Dominus declarare dignatus est revelacione ymmo apparicione[g]
satis admirabili.

---

f   +constu del.C   g   AS; operacione C,DMS

8

Quomodo in Natali Domini missam celebrantem amplexus est infans

Quadam die[a] sacratissimo Natali Domini missam celebrans in magna
cordis devocione et consueta lacrimarum profusione, cum infra
secretam canonis hostiam elevans deprompsisset verba sacramenti
effectiva, quando panis in corpus et vinum in sanguinem [Domini][b]
transubstanciatur, invenit in manibus infantulum speciosum pre filiis 5
hominum, coronam quasi auream in capite gestantem, gemmis
stelliferis rutilantem. Videbatur puerulus ille omni nive candidior, et
dulcifluo luminum risu, vultuque sereno, blandoque manuum
applausu caput et faciem eius tangens, contrectans, planansque
demulcebat; quandoque caput capiti, os[c] toto mundo preciosius eius 10
ori applicans, oscula crebrius imprimebat. Ille vero inebriatus a
torrente voluptatis domus Domini, utpote in cellam vinariam introductus, pedibus ac manibus et singulis membris huius Jhesuli nostri
oscula innumera[d] libavit: dilectum suum totum sibi desiderabilem,
dulcem ad ruminandum felici sensit experimento. Dilectus tandem 15
infantulus ille, elevatis manibus, eum crucis impressione benedixit, et
ab oculis eius evanuit, nilque in manibus nisi hostiam consuetam
conspexit. Quociens vir Dei huius deifice visionis medullitus recorda-
batur, inestimabili cordis jubilo repletus, lacrimarum placido proflu-
vio perfundebatur. Hec vir Dei diu celans, postea loquens, de secretis 20

a   die C,DMS; vice AS   c   AS; et C,D,CA,DMS
b   AS; om.DMS   d   innumerosa DMS,AS

comply. Once he had thus been made a ruler in the high position of a
prelate, he desired not to be exalted as is customary with certain people,
but to be as one of his subjects, nor to lord it over his charges, but to
become an example to the flock. He ordered scrupulous observance in
the house over which he presided of all the good customs and holy
ordinances which he discovered were being observed in various
churches with canons, after gathering them together as it were in a
bundle. As a consequence the Lord blessed that house on account of his
servant, and its landed property increased, with his half-brother Earl
Henry and other magnates conferring churches and lands on the
church of Kirkham to be possessed in pure and perpetual alms.
Likewise holy religious life flourished within the house in the discipline
of the rule, in the entertainment of guests, and in the display of
abundant philanthropy. How much grace in the eyes of the Lord this
man found by these and other holy pursuits, the Lord himself has
deigned to make known by a revelation, or rather an apparition, that is
quite remarkable.

8

How a baby embraced him when celebrating mass at Christmas

One most sacred Christmas Day he was celebrating mass in a spirit of
great devotion and with his usual shedding of tears. As he elevated the
Host in the secret part of the canon and uttered the operative words of
the sacrament when the substance of the bread is changed into the body
and the substance of the wine into the blood of the Lord, he found a
baby in his hands, surpassing all the sons of men in beauty, as if
wearing a golden crown on his head which was glowing brightly with
starry jewels. This little boy seemed whiter than any snow, with sweet-
flowing laughter in his eyes and a serene expression. He caressed
Waltheof's head and face by touching, stroking and smoothing them
with a delightful movement of his hands; and when placing his head
against Waltheof's head and, more precious than the whole world, his
mouth against Waltheof's mouth, he imprinted kisses over and over
again. Waltheof was indeed intoxicated by the torrent of pleasure in the
house of the Lord, as if he had been brought into a wine-cellar, and
planted innumerable kisses on the feet and hands and the various limbs
of this little Jesus of ours: he felt that his beloved was wholly desirable
for him, and delightful as he reflected on the happy experience. At
length the beloved baby raised his hands and blessed him with the sign
of the cross, and vanished from his sight; and he saw nothing in his
hands except the usual Host.

Whenever the man of God inwardly recalled this divine vision, he
was filled again with incalculable joy in his heart, and was drenched in a
quiet flow of tears. The man of God concealed all this for a long time,

anime sue cuncta confessori suo*e* revelavit; et ne hoc se superstite cuiquam propalaret, in virtute obediencie imperative perstrinxit. Ille vero imperanti obtemperans, vivente viro Dei verbum istud abscondit; sed post eius*f* deposicionem viris religiosis patefecit. Fatebatur eciam isdem homo Dei se non maius ponderis sensisse eciam*g* pueri ipsius 25 elevacione quam hostie altari supposite. Ex huius autem visionis mirifice contemplacione, non solum viri sanctitas agnoscitur, sed eciam fides catholica super vivificis sacramentis altaris roboratur, orthodoxorum patrum assercio confirmatur, et hereticorum misteria Dominici corporis et sanguinis denegancium detestabilis error confun- 30 ditur.

e   +canonico *CA*   *g*   in *DMS,AS*
f   carnis *CA*

9

G i,325;
Scriba

*Incipit prefacio autoris de recapitulacione
linie generose successionis regum Anglie
venustantis reges nostros*

Cum in vobis, Scotorum O reges,*a* vestre proprie generacionis simul et Anglice, prout scriptis superius clarissime patet et in hiis eciam infra patebit*b* sequentibus, linie regales globate conveniant, in quibus Scotici generis vestri quosdam actus regios ac virtutes legeritis, modo consequenter et hic itaque regum vestre generacionis Anglice caritatis 5 opera quedam, et actus bellicos de Baldredi Rivallis abbatis cronicis breviter excerptos, vobis inscribere placet, ut nunc illorum, nunc istorum veterum avorum ad placitum historias legendo, licet breves, letis cordibus exultantes Deum laudetis, quod ex gloriosis conjunctis radicibus processistis. Iste vero due regales linie, quibus inhabitan- 10 dum olim insule latitudo pace concordi non suffecerat, unius nunc persona principis, divina disponente gracia nulli dubium, in unum conjuncte requiescunt. Earum ergo radicum genite propagines vestrum est, ut non degeneres, quod absit, a radicibus acerbos et inutiles producere fructus, sed dulces et sapidos, ac victoriose 15 pugnatricis insule, Scotorum videlicet et Anglorum, rutilantis milicie prosequi vestigia studeatis. Primo quoque Deum, omnium regum

fo.113v   regem invictissimum, diligendo timere | devotasque sibi reddendo laudes illi soli servire; gladio proteccionis ab exteris invasoribus regnum defendere; justas et consuetas ecclesie Dei libertates illesas 20 servare; justicie sceptro subditum vobis populum benigne fovendo,

a   +incliti *CA*   *b*   +so *del.C*

25   but later spoke about it, revealing all the secrets of his soul to his
confessor, and peremptorily bound him by virtue of his obedience not
to divulge it to anyone while he was still alive. The confessor indeed
complied with the other man's instructions, and so long as the man of
God lived kept that story secret; but after his death the confessor
30   revealed it to some monks. The same man of God also declared that he
had felt no greater weight when actually lifting up the boy himself than
when elevating the Host placed on the altar. From reflection on this
wonderful vision then, not only does one acknowledge the sanctity of
the man, but also the catholic faith in the life-giving sacraments of the
35   altar is strengthened, the assertions of the orthodox fathers are
confirmed, and the detestable error of heretics who deny the divine
mystery of the body and blood of the Lord is confounded.

9

The beginning of Fordun's preface to a summary
of the noble line of succession of the kings of England
which is a decoration for our kings

Kings of the Scots! Since the royal lines of your own family as well as
of the English combine and meet together in you, as is abundantly
clear in what has been written above (and will also be clear in what
follows below), where you have read about certain royal actions and
5   virtues of your Scottish family, now as a consequence and here
accordingly we want to write to you about some charitable works of
the kings of your English family, and about some warlike activities
briefly excerpted from the chronicles of Ailred the abbot of Rievaulx,
so that by reading at leisure the histories first of one group of your old
10   ancestors and then of the other, even if they are brief, you may praise
God as with joyful hearts rejoicing exceedingly because you are
descended from glorious roots that have been joined together. Indeed
these two royal lines, for whom the size of the island was formerly
insufficient for living in peace and harmony, are now joined together
15   as one and are at peace in the person of one ruler by an ordinance of
divine grace as no one doubts. Therefore as the offspring produced
from these roots it is your duty to take care not to become degenerate
(God forbid!), and produce bitter and useless fruits, but rather sweet
and tasty ones, and to maintain the traditions of the brilliant fighting
20   force of a victorious fighting island, that is of the Scots and the
English. First also take care to love and fear God, the most invincible
king of all kings, and by rendering devoted praise to him to serve him
alone; and to defend the kingdom with a protective sword against
external invaders; and to preserve the just and customary liberties of

legibus regere; discordantes, si qui sint, proceres ad pacem humiliter invitare. Sed et regie majestati rebelles, eciam in populo malignantes, justum subire judicium cogantur, vel si non corrigibiles, ut prophete verbis utar, tamquam vasa figuli virga confringantur ferrea. Sed et 25 equitatis^c sit semper direccionis virga regni vestri. Quid vilius est, quid atrocius quam in caput membrum in regem insurgere militem? Ubi tocius corporis aut regni putatur imminere discrimen, numquid abscisione digni sunt ambo, vel subtili quodam et molli medicamine sanandi? Nam intestina, non solum contra regem, sed quelibet 30 discordie pernicies est cura diligenti cavenda. Si tamen contigerit, nequaquam est tarda, sed celeri reconsiliacione sedanda, sicut in carne vulnus tumescens habet repercussivis principio mederi, vel, si tumore majori turgescerit, tunc ex eo sanies ferro subtiliter extraha- tur. Sed optima, crede michi, discordiarum omnium curacio sive 35 morborum, et celerima, caute principiis est obstandum. Nunc ad propositum regrediamur.

c   +virga *del.*C

10

De computacione linealis successionis optimorum regum Anglie

G i,326

Sequitur Christianorum regum Anglie linealis computacio, cum suis quibusdam famosis gestis secundum scripta Baldredi breviter exe- quendis, quibus et regnandi pericia docetur, et sui propaginis a | regia majestate prodiciosa dejeccio palam a legentibus speculetur. Baldre- dus. Ab ipso quippe (de quo superius) pagano Woden^a vestre 5 generacionis Anglice linia regrediendo ducitur, usque quendam Saxonici generis paganum nomine Terdicium, qui cum familia sua vectus quinque navibus anno domini cccc^o nonagesimo quinto, Britanniam veniens, eodem die bello Britones vicit, et post adventum Horsi et Hingesti anno xlvii^o. Deinde paucis postmodum transactis 10 annis regnum in Westsax optinuit. A quo proceditur ad reges Christianos Ine et Ingels; quorum Ine, cum potentissimus regum tunc

a   Wodeñ pagano qui apud quosdam   dictum est *for* pagano Woden *CA*
     Mercurius dictus est. A quo Vodynsday

25 the church of God; and to govern with the laws by kindly cherishing
    with the sceptre of justice the people subject to you; and if there are
    any magnates at variance with each other, invite them humbly to be at
    peace. But at the same time rebels against the royal authority, and evil
    men among the people, should be compelled to submit to just
30 judgment, or if they will not accept correction, they should (to use the
    words of the prophet) like potter's vessels be shattered with a rod of
    iron. At the same time let the rod that gives direction to your kingdom
    be that of equity. What is more contemptible, what is more shocking
    than for a knight to rebel against the king, that is a limb against the
35 head? When a crisis for the whole body or kingdom appears to
    threaten, do both [body and kingdom] deserve mutilation, or a
    delicate and mild remedy for restoration to health? For an internal
    calamity, not only one affecting the king, but any kind of dissension,
    should be guarded against with attentive care. If nevertheless it comes
40 about, it should by no means be brought to an end by a slow
    reconciliation, but by a quick one, just as in the case of the flesh a
    suppurating wound has to be healed to begin with by medical
    applications, or if the swelling has increased, then the infected matter
    should be extracted from it skilfully with a knife. But believe me, the
45 best cure for all dissensions or illnesses, and the speediest, is to make a
    careful stand against them at the start. Now let us return to our main
    theme.

10

An account of the line of succession of the most excellent kings of England

An account of the succession of the most Christian kings of England
follows, along with some of their famous achievements, to be related
briefly according to the writings of Ailred, in which their skill as rulers
is shown, and readers may plainly observe the treasonable ejection of
5   their descendants from royal authority. Ailred says that the succession of your English family is derived by tracing from the pagan
Woden himself (see above) down to a certain pagan of the Saxon race
called Cerdic, who with five ships sailed with his family in 495, and on   495
coming to Britain defeated the Britons in a battle on the same day,
10 which was forty-seven years after the arrival of Horsa and Hengest.
Then after a few years had passed he obtained the West Saxon
kingdom.
        From him we proceed to the Christian kings Ine and Ingild.   [688-726]
Although Ine was the most powerful king in England at that time, he
15 left his kingdom and set out for Rome on pilgrimage; and there while

esset Anglie, relicto regno, Romam peregre profectus est, ibique feliciter peregrinans tandem ad celestem mansionem felicius conscendit. Ab Ingels vero linia tenditur ad Egbricht, qui totam Angliam ex 15 australi parte Humbri pene fluminis, que pluribus regibus eatenus divisa subjacuerat, suo subjugaret imperio. Huius filius fuit Ethilwlff, futuri generis sui caput, de quo sanctissimi fructus oriretur[b] radix preciosa. Hic in regno terreno semper meditabatur celeste, ut manifeste daretur intelligi non eum cupiditate[c] victum, sed caritate 20 provocatum, aliene necessitati regnando consulere, non sue voluntati dominando satisfacere. Elemosinis sane sic operam dabat, ut totam terram suam pro Christo decimaret, et partem decimam per monasteria divideret et ecclesias. Tandem cum apparatu multo Romam profectus, ibidem integro perhendinavit anno, loca sancta 25 frequentans, vigiliis et oracionibus vacans, ecclesiis beatissimorum Petri et Pauli, ipsique summo pontifici, pro regia munificencia plurima largitus est munera; et sic cum multarum virtutum stipendiis in Anglia est reversus. Post biennium vero regnum inter filios sapienter divisit, et sic in senectute bona collectus est ad patres suos, 30 regnum non amittens sed mutans, temporale deserens et eternum adipiscens.

---

b orirentur *S,C,D,CA*   *c* *CA*; cupidate *C,D*

11

De rege Alfredo quam maximam reverenciam ecclesiasticis exhibente

Huius Ethilwlfi filius fuit illud Anglorum decus Alfredus, ceteris fratribus suis etate junior, sed annosior virtute. Unde eum pater, cum adhuc puerulus esset, cum multis militibus magnisque donariis Romam misit, ut sanctissimorum apostolorum precibus commendaretur, et a summo pontifice benediceretur. Venerabilis autem summus 5 sacerdos Leo, qui tunc Romane prefuit ecclesie, tempus et etatem regnandi regie unccionis sacramento preveniens, sicut quondam | sanctus Samuel puerum David, ita eum[a] in regem sanctissimus presul devote consecravit. Cum vero post mortem fratrum suorum, cum quibus aliquo tempore regnavit, ad eum totum regnum hereditario 10 jure transisset, sublimior omnibus factus est omnium servus, ut posset dicere cum propheta: 'Exaltatus[b] autem humiliatus sum.' Ita se bonis amabilem, impiis terribilem, ecclesiarum ministris pavidum, amicis et sociis jocundum, pauperibus mitem et largum exhibuit. Quod igitur

---

a *S; corrected to* ante *C;* ante *D*   *b* -x- *interlin.by rubricator C*

happily a pilgrim, he at length more happily embarked for the
heavenly mansion. From Ingild indeed the line is extended to
Ecgberht, who subjected to his rule nearly all of England south of the   [802-39]
river Humber, which hitherto had been divided and was under the
20   rule of many kings. Ecgberht's son was Æthelwulf, the head of his   [839-56]
future family, from whom the precious root of a most holy fruit would
originate. While in his earthly kingdom, he was always contemplating
the heavenly one, so that we can clearly appreciate that it was not
bcause he had been overcome by greed, but because he was moved by
25   charity that in ruling he took account of the needs of others, not
seeking satisfaction for his own wishes as a tyrant. Certainly he gave
attention to alms, so that he tithed all his land for Christ, and divided
this tenth share among monasteries and churches. At length he set off
for Rome amid great pomp, and stayed there for a whole year, visiting   [855-6]
30   the holy places, devoting himself to vigils and prayers; he bestowed
very many gifts on the churches of blessed Peter and Paul and on the
supreme pontiff himself with royal munificence; and so he returned to
England having acquired many virtues. Then after two years he
wisely divided his kingdom between his sons, and thus in a good old
35   age he was gathered to his fathers, not losing his kingdom but   [858]
exchanging it, leaving the temporal one and acquiring an eternal one.

11

King Alfred, who displayed the greatest possible
respect for the clergy

Alfred, the glory of the English, was a son of this Æthelwulf. He was
younger than his other brothers in age, but older in virtue. For this
reason his father, when he was still a small boy, sent him to Rome with   [853]
many knights and expensive gifts, so that he might be commended to
5   the prayers of the most holy apostles and receive the blessing of the
supreme pontiff. So Leo the venerable high priest, who presided over
the Roman church at that time, anticipated with the sacrament of
royal unction the time and age for him to be king; and just as at
another time the holy man Samuel had done for the boy David, so the
10   most holy bishop [of Rome] devoutly consecrated him as king. After
the deaths of his brothers, with whom he had reigned for some time,
when the whole kingdom passed to him by hereditary right, more   [871]
exalted than all he became the servant of all, so that he could say with
the prophet: 'Being exalted, I have been humbled.' So he behaved
15   amiably to the good, terrifyingly to the profane, deferentially towards
the ministers of churches, congenially with his friends and associates,
kindly and generously to the poor. Therefore he believed something

raro nunc^c invenitur in terris, illam maximam regis credidit dignita- 15
tem | nullam in ecclesiis Christi habere potestatem. 'Illa est', inquit,
'vera regnantis dignitas, si se in regno Christi, que est ecclesia, non
regem sed civem cognoscat, si non in sacerdotes legibus dominetur,
sed Christi legibus quas promulgaverint sacerdotes humiliter subicia-
tur.' Porro Constantini piissimi imperatoris imitabatur exemplum, 20
qui cum urbi prefuisset et orbi, et ad Christi fidem conversus fuisset,
tantam sacerdotibus reverenciam exhibuit ut cum ad eum aliquando
episcopi scriptas cartulis^d querimonias adversus invicem detulissent,
convolvens eas in sinu, jusserit igne consumi, 'Non est meum',
inquiens, 'de sacerdotibus judicare.' Vocans interim episcopos, 25
inquit: 'Patres sanctissimi, nolite judicio contendere, presertim apud
nos, de quorum erratibus vestrum est judicare. Sed si quid inter vos
ortum fuerit questionis, modeste tractetur in ecclesia; nec aliquid
quod vestram dedeceat sanctitatem ad eorum qui foris sunt noticiam
transferatur. Ego certe, si quempiam de sancto ordine vestro 30
cernerem cum muliere peccantem, proprio eos operirem pallio, ne
qua religioni vestre impiis daretur occasio detrahendi.'

---

c *S*; ut *C,D* 　　　　　　　　*d* *corrected from* cartulas *C*

12

De eodem et filio eius Eadwardo

Huius itaque et aliorum regum sanctorum Alfredus secutus exemplum, ipsius mundi principis adversum se provocavit invidiam. Nam
idem omnium bonorum inimicus Sathan immisit ei^a inimicos
pessimos, Dacos scilicet et Frisones, a fide Christi alienos. Qui cum
multa classe venientes in Angliam, maximam regni porcionem, 5
rapinis et incendiis ⟨auxilio^b et proditorio consilio Edrici ducis
Merciorum⟩ consumunt. Quos cum rex sepius repulisset, permissi
sunt tandem prevalere, totamque in tantum occupare provinciam, ut
rex Christianissimus, tamquam alter Job temptatus, fugam sibi
consulens, exutus regno, cum paucissimis familiarum suarum in silvis 10
ac paludibus dilitesceret, ubi suam suorumque vitam piscium captura
transigeret. Postea tamen, transactis novem annis, 'Dominus dedit
virtutem et fortitudinem plebi sue. Benedictus Deus,' adeo ut arreptis
armis in hostes irruunt, et mox, sicut fluit cera a facie ignis, sic
perierunt pagani a facie sua Christo duce. Sternuntur, fugantur et 15

---

a *corrected from* eis *C* 　　　　　*b* instincti *CA*

which is nowadays rarely found in the world – that the greatest
authority of a king has no power over the churches of Christ. 'A ruler
20 is held in true esteem', he said, 'if he recognizes that he is in the
kingdom of Christ (which is the church) not as a king, but as a citizen,
if he does not claim jurisdiction over priests, but is humbly subjected
to the laws of Christ which the priests have proclaimed.' Furthermore
he followed the example of the most pious emperor Constantine,
25 who, when he had control of the city and the world, and had been
converted to the Christian faith, showed such reverence towards
priests that when on one occasion bishops lodged written complaints
with him against each other, he tucked them into a fold in his
garment, and ordered them to be burnt in the fire, saying: 'It is not for
30 me to pass judgment concerning priests.' At the same time he
summoned the bishops and said: 'Most holy fathers, do not engage in
lawsuits, especially before us, whose sins it is up to you to judge. But if
any problem arises among you, let it be dealt with in the church with
propriety; and let nothing which might bring disgrace to your holiness
35 be brought to those who are outside. Certainly if I come across any
member of your holy order sinning with a woman, I shall cover them
with my own cloak, lest wicked people be given any chance of
disparaging your ascetic way of life.'

12

The same [king] and his son Edward

And so for following the example of this and other saintly kings,
Alfred aroused the ill-will of the Prince of the World against him. For
the same Satan, the enemy of all good men, sent against him the worst
of enemies, namely the Danes and Frisians, who were strangers to the
5 Christian faith. When these men came to England with a large fleet,
they destroyed a very large part of the kingdom with pillage and fire,
with the help and treasonable advice of Eadric the ealdorman of the
Mercians. After the king had repeatedly driven them back, they were
at length allowed to have the upper hand, and to occupy the whole
10 province to such an extent that the most Christian king (afflicted like
another Job) decided to flee, and abandoned the kingdom. With a   [878]
very few of his friends he lay hidden in woods and marshes, where he
spent his time and that of his companions in fishing. Yet later, once
nine years had passed, 'the Lord gave power and strength to his
15 people. Blessed be God', to such a great extent that seizing their arms
they rushed on their enemies, and soon, just as wax melts when
confronted by fire, so did the pagans perish when confronted by them
with Christ as their leader. They are struck down, they are routed, and

dissipantur, relicto nominatissimo vexillo suo, quod, quia demoniaco instinctu effigie corvina deformaverant, 'Ravyn'*c* vocabant. Quotquot manus persequencium evadere poterant, silvarum quesiere latibula. Ab illa die et deinceps erat Alfredus vir in cunctis prospere agens, quoniam Dominus erat cum illo et omnia opera dirigebat. Rex 20 igitur Alfredus cum regnasset annis xxix et mensibus sex, de regno terreno ad regnum celeste transcendit, Eadwardum filium suum regni morumque relinquens heredem. Erat autem in sciencia literarum patre minor, sanctitate vero non multum inferior, sed potestate superior. Impiissimam namque Dacorum gentem, quam pater eius 25 non expulerat, rebellantem sibi, multis contritam preliis, vel fugavit penitus, vel misera servitute compressit, et totam regni faciem in antique pulcritudinis speciem reformavit. Igitur rex Eadwardus, vir

G i,328   mansuetus et pius, omnibus amabilis et affabilis | omnium in se provocavit affectum. Regnavit annis xxiiii et genuit filios et filias. Ex 30 nobili femina Egwiva filium genuit nothum Athelstanum; et ex regina nomine Aedgina tres filios, scilicet Eadwinum, Eadmundum et Eadredum, et quatuor filias, quarum prima Eadburga in Christi sponsam eligitur, altera ab imperatore Othone in matrimonium sumitur, tercia ad Karolum regem Francorum ducenda destinatur, 35 quartam regulus Northumbrie Dacus nomine Sithricus duxit uxorem.

c   + ipsum *CA*

13

De Athelstano, [Eadmundo,] Edredo et Eadwino

fo.114v   Dormivit autem cum patribus suis rex Eadwardus, et regnavit filius eius Adelstanus pro eo. Rebellaverunt ei Daci Northumbrenses; atque Cumbrenses fedus quod cum eo pepigerant prevaricati sunt. Regnavit annis xvi, et mortuus est. Et regnavit Eadmundus frater eius pro eo. Qui erat Eadwardi patris sui in omnibus imitator. Promotus 5 autem in regnum, zelo zelatus est pro fide Christi, egre ferens paganorum reliquias idolorum cultura regni sui fedare decorem. Quinque nobilissimas civitates, Lincolniam scilicet, Leicestriam, Standfordiam, Notynghame et Derby, quas eatenus incoluerant, de manibus eorum potenter extorsit, omnique infidelitate abrasa, 10 Christiane fidei lumine illustravit. Purgato autem ab alienigenis regno, et sibi per omnia pace subjecto, monasteriorum et ecclesiarum maxime curam habuit; consilioque Sancti Dunstani et statuenda

they are scattered, leaving their most famous banner behind, which
20   they called 'The Raven', because at the prompting of the Devil they
had designed it with the likeness of a raven. As many as managed to
escape the hands of their pursuers sought hiding-places in the woods.
From that day and thereafter Alfred was a man who prospered in all
that he did, since the Lord was with him and guided all his activities.
25   When therefore King Alfred had reigned for twenty-nine years and
six months, he passed over from the earthly kingdom to the heavenly   [899]
kingdom, leaving his son Edward as heir to his kingdom and
character. He was indeed a lesser man than his father in knowledge of
literature, not much inferior to him indeed in saintliness, but his
30   superior in power. For when the irreligious Danish people whom his
father had not driven out rebelled against him and had been crushed
in many battles, he either put them utterly to flight, or subdued them
into wretched slavery, and he transformed the whole appearance of
the kingdom into a semblance of its former beauty. King Edward
35   therefore, a gentle and pious man who was amiable and affable to
everyone, aroused affection for himself in everyone. He reigned for
twenty-four years, and fathered sons and daughters. By the noble-   [899-924]
woman 'Ecgwynn' he fathered his natural son Athelstan; by his queen
called Eadgifu he had three sons, namely Edwin, Edmund and
40   Eadred, and four daughters, of whom the first Eadburh was chosen as
a bride of Christ, the second [Eadgyth] was taken into matrimony by
the Emperor Otto [I], the third [Eadgifu] was destined to be married to
Charles king of the Franks, and the Danish sub-king of Northumbria
called Sigtryggr took the fourth as his wife.

13

Athelstan, [Edmund,] Eadred and Eadwig

So King Edward slept with his fathers, and his son Athelstan reigned   [924-39]
in his place. The Danes and Northumbrians rebelled against him; and
the Cumbrians violated the treaty which they had concluded with
him. He reigned for sixteen years and died.
5   And his brother Edmund reigned in his place. He followed the   [939-46]
example of his father Edward in everything. Indeed when he was
promoted to the kingdom, he was zealous with zeal for the Christian
faith, being pained that the remains of pagan idols polluted with their
cult the honour of his kingdom. He was strong enough to wrest from
10   their hands five most noble cities, namely Lincoln, Leicester,
Stamford, Nottingham and Derby, which they had inhabited until
then, and once all paganism had been erased, he illumined them with
the light of the Christian faith. Indeed once the kingdom had been rid

statuit, et corrigenda correxit. Cum igitur Anglia sub tanto patre, magis quam rege, floreret, immatura morte, exactis in regno annis 15 quinque et mensibus vii, et passione inopinata emarcuit. Sibi successit in regnum frater eius Edredus, et ambulavit in viis fratris sui in omnibus beati Dunstani consiliis et mandatis acquiescens, ac justissimis legibus subditos regens. Huius vitam laudabilem, postquam annis novem et dimidio rexisset, mors preciosa conclusit. Post 20 quem suscepit regnum Eadwinus filius regis Eadmundi, nec ambulavit in viis patrum suorum, sed in illa sancta progenie novus quidam Herodes surrexit. Qui cuiusdam mulieris, Herodiadis videlicet impie, contra Domini leges et contra ipsius jura nature*a* adulterinis abutebatur amplexibus, et consilia nequissima sequebatur. Nec defuit 25 spiritus Johannis in Sancto Dunstano, quin regem argueret adulterantem. Que, Jezabelitico spiritu incitata, nostri Helie moliebatur interitum, fuissetque voti sui compos, si non sanctus Dei, premunitus a Spiritu, exilium patrie pretulisset. Rex vero cum, huius nequissime mulieris deceptus consiliis, nec juste nec prudenter regnasset, maxima 30 regni sui parte exuitur, que mox ad fratrem suum Eadgarum transfertur. Tandem, cum Sancti Dunstani reprehensionibus, tum admonicionibus, tum precipue apud Deum pro illo piis obsecracionibus compunctus, | renunciavit adultere cui adheserat inconsulte, et consiliis utebatur sanioribus. Recordatus est enim Dominus patrum 35 suorum, regum scilicet Christianorum, et, ne quis de illa sancta stirpe periret, occasionem qua salvaretur adinvenit. Cum rex Eadwinus nature debitum persolvisset in fata cedendo, et ab immundis spiritibus, quorum suggestionibus in carne positus satisfecerat, traheretur ad penam, Sanctus Dunstanus, nichil de morte eius adhuc 40 sciens, et ecce cohors tartarea sub eius aspectu, veluti de capta preda, letas cepit victorias agere. Perscrutatur itaque*b* causam leticie, audit regem obiisse, atque eius animam penis traditam esse. Qui mox resolutus in lacrimas,*c* tam diu ante misericordem Jhesum pro illo supplicans et plorans procubuit, donec a demonibus liberatus 45 veniam, quam sanctus peciit, optineret.

G i,329

---

a   corrected from natura C   *c*   corrected from lacrimis C; lacrimis CA
b   sanctus DMS

of foreigners and subjected to him with peace everywhere, he took
15 particular care over monasteries and churches; and with the advice of
St Dunstan enacted what needed enacting, and corrected what
needed correcting. When therefore England was flourishing under
such a father rather than a king, it withered away at the unexpected
occurrence of his early death after a reign of five years and seven
20 months had passed.

He was succeeded in the kingdom by his brother Eadred, who   [946-55]
walked in the ways of his brother, with complete trust in all the blessed
Dunstan's advice and instructions, and ruling his subjects with very
just laws. A precious death brought this man's praiseworthy life to an
25 end, after he had reigned for nine and a half years.

After him Eadwig son of King Edmund took over the kingdom,   [955-9]
and did not walk in the ways of his fathers, but a new Herod arose in
that holy family. He spent his time in the adulterous embraces of a
certain woman, an unholy Herodias in fact, against the laws of the
30 Lord and against the sanctions of nature itself, and followed wicked
plans. And the spirit of John [the Baptist] was not lacking in St
Dunstan, that he should fail to censure the adulterous king. This
woman was roused by a spirit like that of Jezebel to bring about the
extinction of our Elijah, and her prayer would have been granted if
35 the saint of God, warned by the Spirit, had not regarded exile from his
country more desirable. Since the king, deceived by the advice of this
wicked woman, did not reign justly nor prudently, he was deprived of
the greater part of his kingdom, which was soon transferred to his
brother Edgar. At last, when moved by the reproaches and warnings
40 of St Dunstan, and especially by pious prayers to God on his behalf,
the king renounced the adulteress to whom he had clung inadvisedly,
and followed more sensible plans. For the Lord remembered his
fathers (that is the Christian kings), and devised an opportunity by
which he might be saved, lest any member of that sainted lineage
45 perish. When King Eadwig had paid his debt to nature by yielding to
fate, and was being dragged to punishment by diabolical spirits, to
whose suggestions he had been responsive when in the flesh, St
Dunstan, not as yet knowing of his death, saw a crowd from the
infernal regions beginning to celebrate happy victories over a
50 captured prize. Accordingly he enquired into the cause of this
happiness, heard that the king had died, and that his soul had been
handed over for punishment.

Dunstan soon dissolved into tears, and prostrated himself for a
long time before the merciful Jesus, interceding and lamenting on
55 Eadwig's behalf, until he was released by the evil spirits and obtained
the pardon which the saint requested.

14

De Eadgaro pacifico et filiis eius

Defuncto igitur rege Eadwino, frater eius Eadgarus successit in regnum, qui fuit filius Eadmundi nobilissimi regis, qui fuit Eadwardi senioris Christianissimi principis, qui fuit Alfredi victoriosissimi ducis filius. Erat enim Anglis non minus memorabilis quam Cirus Persis, Romulus Romanis, Karolus Francis. In ipsius nativitate 5 audivit beatus Dunstanus angelos cantantes et dicentes: 'Pax Anglorum ecclesie huius pueri qui natus est tempore.' Iste Eadgarus per Angliam quadraginta construxit monasteria. Cunctis predecessoribus suis felicior fuit, et in morum suavitate prestancior. Tanta enim in verbis, in vultu, moribus, interioris suavitatis indicia 10 preferebat, ut, Deo cooperante, tocius insule sibi reges et principes, Scocie videlicet Cumbrie et Wallie, ad veram amiciciam attractaret. Hyeme et vere infra regnum suum usquequaque per singulas provincias transire solitus erat, judicia mores et actus ministrorum et principum diligenter explorare, quomodo legum jura et suorum 15 statuta decretorum servarentur subtilius investigare, et ne pauperes a potentibus prejudicium passi opprimerentur solicite precavere. Inter hec semper et de hiis cum episcopis et viris doctissimis, ac de lege Dei ac sacris literis conferebat. Sed nichil in terrenis eternum, nichil in caducis stabile, nichil in mortalibus immortale. Translato ad celestia 20 Eadgaro, in regno terreno filius eius successit Eadwardus, qui ab impiis interfectus injuste, tum ob vite sanctitatem, tum ob necis acerbitatem, nomen et meritum sancti Deo donante promeruit. Cui frater eius Athelredus Eadgari filius et regine successit in regnum, et a Sancto Dunstano archiepiscopo inungitur et consecratur. Regnante 25 igitur rege predicto, Daci supervenientes magnam terre partem igne ferroque vastaverunt. Tunc rex, missis in Normanniam nunciis,

fo.115

Emmam filiam | Richardi ducis in uxorem sibi dari peciit et accepit, cum iam de filia Thoreti nobilissimi comitis filium suscepit Eadmundum. Ex Emma deinde duos habuit filios, Alfredum videlicet et 30 Eadwardum.

G i,330

⟨Istum Alfredum sive Ethelredum Godwinus proditor nephanda prodicione apud Heli | [interemit; et Eadwardus,]ᵃ qui ob vite meritum nomen sancti accepit, et Westmonasterium Londonie fundavit.⟩ᵇ 35

ᵃ　D; lac.C　　　　　　　　ᵇ　Istum ... fundavit *om.*CA

14

Edgar the Peace-maker and his sons

Therefore after King Eadwig's death his brother Edgar succeeded to [957-75] the kingdom. He was a son of the most noble King Edmund, the son of the most Christian prince Edward the Elder, the son of the supremely victorious leader Alfred. He was indeed no less remem-
5 bered among the English than was Cyrus among the Persians, Romulus among the Romans, and Charlemagne among the Franks. At his birth the blessed Dunstan heard the angels singing and saying: 'The peace of the church of the English will be in the time of this boy who has been born.' This Edgar built forty monasteries throughout
10 England. He was more fortunate than all his predecessors, and surpassed them in the charm of his character. He displayed such splendid traits of his inner sweetness in his speech, expression and character that with God's help he won over to true friendship for himself the kings and princes of the whole island, namely of Scotland,
15 Cumbria and Wales.

During the winter and spring it was his custom to move around everywhere in his kingdom through each province, to enquire thoroughly into the judgments, character and actions of his servants and princes, to make a minute investigation into how the rights laid
20 down in the laws and the statutes containing his decrees were being observed, and to take anxious care to prevent the poor from being oppressed by suffering injustice at the hands of the powerful. He always conferred with bishops and learned men concerning these activities while he was engaged in them, and regarding the law of God
25 and the sacred writings.

But no earthly things are eternal, no perishable things are permanent, no transient things are immortal. Once Edgar had been carried off to Heaven, his son Edward succeeded to his earthly [975-8] kingdom, who after being unjustly killed by wicked men, earned as a
30 gift from God the title and reward of saint, for both his saintly life and his cruel death.

His brother Æthelred the son of Edgar and his queen succeeded to the kingdom, and was anointed and consecrated by the archbishop St [979: Dunstan. So during the reign of the aforesaid king the Danes arrived 4 May]
35 and laid waste a large part of the land with fire and sword. Then the king by sending envoys to Normandy sought and acquired Emma the [1002] daughter of Duke Richard as his wife, when he had already

15

*De exilio regis Ethelredi, morte Swani,
et revocacione regis ad regnum*

Tunc rex, solito forcior effectus, omnes per Angliam Dacos una die
sabbati, eadem hora, die videlicet Sancti Bricii, missis epistolis jussit
interfici. Quod et ita factum est. Quod Daci transmarini audientes in
furorem versi sunt; et anno sequenti duce Swano cum innumerabili
exercitu Angliam intrantes, non ordini vel sexui aut etati parcentes, 5
sed nec ab ecclesiarum vel monasteriorum incendiis manus sacrilegas
continuerunt. Quibus cum strenuissimus Ethelredus sepius restitisset,
tandem prodicione suorum factus inferior, reginam cum puerulis filiis
suis misit Normanniam, quos ipse postmodum exutus regno secutus
est. Willelmus: 10

> Sed non diu sivit propicia Divinitas Angliam fluctuare. Nam pervasor
> ille Swanus Dacus in Purificacione Sancte Marie, subita morte
> preventus, vel a Sancto Eadmundo invisibili pena percussus, pro eo
> quod terram eius depopulanti sanctus martyr eidem per visum
> apparuerit, leniterque de miseria conventuum suorum conquerens, 15
> insolenciusque respondentem in capite percusserit, quo dolore tactum
> in proximo*a* dictum est obisse.

Baldredus:

> Cum Swanus sic subita morte preventus, apud inferos crudelitatis sue
> stipendia recepisset, revocatus ab Anglis Ethelredus infulis regni 20
> reinduitur, et iterum contra Dacos, virtute qua poterat, erigitur.
> Contra quem Knowt filius Swani rex Dacorum effectus paternum
> odium non desiit exercere. Ethelredus, cum laboriosissime sed
> strenuissime xxxvii annis regnasset, Londoniis obiit, Eadmundum
> filium suum primogenitum laboris et regni relinquens heredem. 25

Sed, morte regis nondum propalata, fertur a quibusdam reginam
Emmam, ut erat mulier summe calliditatis, pepigisse clam fedus cum
ipso Knowt, ut ei regem et regnum traderet, si eam cum liberis et suis
abire libere atque permitteret repatriare. Quo facto, et hinc inde
prestita omni securitate, rem regina retulit, et regem mortuum 30
detexit. Sic plerumque solet ars arte deludi.

a + ut *del.C*

acknowledged Edmund as his son by the daughter of the most noble ealdorman Thored. By Emma he then had two sons, Alfred and
40 Edward. The traitor Godwine killed this Alfred (or Æthelred) at Ely   [1036]
by an abominable act of treachery; and Edward, who received the title of saint for his meritorious life, founded Westminster at London.

15

*The exile of King Æthelred, the death of Swein,
and the recall of the king to the kingdom*

Then the king became more forceful than usual, and sent out letters ordering that all the Danes throughout England were to be killed on one Saturday, St Brice's Day, at the same hour. This was done as   [1002:]
planned. When the Danes across the sea heard of this, they were   13/14 Nov.
5   moved to fury; and the next year they entered England with a vast   [1003]
army under the command of Swein. They spared neither rank nor sex nor age, and what is more did not restrain their sacrilegious hands from setting fire to churches and monasteries. Though Æthelred often countered them most energetically, at length he came off second
10 best as a result of treachery among his own men. He sent the queen and their young sons to Normandy, and followed them himself later   [1013: Dec.]
when he had been stripped of the kingdom.
William [of Malmesbury] says:

> But the beneficent Deity did not allow England to be tossed about for
15 > long. For on the Purification of St Mary the Danish Swein, the invader,   [1014:
> was forestalled by sudden death, and struck down with an invisible   3 Feb.]
> punishment by St Edmund, inasmuch as while he was plundering the
> saint's land, the saintly martyr appeared to him in a vision, and while
> mildly remonstrating about the wretched condition of his monastic
20 > houses, he struck Swein on the head as he answered back arrogantly.
> He is said to have died soon afterwards from the effect of this affliction.

Ailred says:

> When Swein was forestalled in this way by sudden death, and had
> received the rewards for his savagery in Hell, Æthelred was recalled by   [1014:
25 > the English and donned the emblems of kingship again; and again he   Spring]
> was roused against the Danes with as much courage as he could
> command. Cnut son of Swein, who had become king of the Danes, did
> not cease from keeping his father's hatred going against him. After
> reigning with the greatest difficulty and vigour for thirty-seven years,
30 > Æthelred died at London, leaving his eldest son Edmund as heir to his   [1016:
> struggle and his kingdom.   23 Apr.]

But while news of the king's death had not yet been spread around, it is said by some that Queen Emma, a woman of supreme shrewdness

16

De successione Eadmundi Irneside in regnum Anglie

Regina vero cum filiis et omnibus ad se pertinentibus in Normanniam transvecta, regnum et regni proteccio in Eadmundum accidit, sed et ipsum pondus belli insedit. De cuius mirabili fortitudine quicquid dicerem minus esset. Unde ob invincibile robur corporis *Irneside* (id est Ferrei Lateris) nomen accepit. Sagitta eius numquam abiit 5 retrorsum, et gladius eius inanis non est reversus. Contra hostes leonine feritatis fuit, erga suos columbine simplicitatis, quo nemo forcior, sed[a] quo nemo suavior; quo nullus audacior, sed quo nullus caucior; quo in adversis nemo securior, et quo in prosperis nemo temperancior. | Strenuissimus vero rex Eadmundus cum exercitu suo, 10 sicut leo rugiens terram circumiens, regiones plurimas, quas occupaverant Dani in dedicionem, obstante nullo, redegit. Porro Dani et qui a rege defecerunt Angli Knowtum sibi in regem elegerunt. Verum quociens cum eo pugnavit, quociens eius fuderit exercitum, quociens vocatam a partibus transmarinis validam manum cum paucis, ymmo 15 pene solus, prostraverit, quociens denique nephandam illam gentem exterminasset, et in nichilum redigisset, nisi quidam patrie proditores, quorum Edericus precipuus fuerat, obstitissent? ⟨In illo quo regnaverat anno sepcies commisit bellum contra Dacos et vicit; et semel contra Knutum, et dimidiarunt regnum; sed Eadmundo remansit 20 regni Anglie corona.⟩[b] Willelmus:

G i,331

> Eadmundus rex mox acclamatus, exercitu congregato apud Penhame et Gylmehame diebus Rogacionum Danos fugavit. Post festum Sancti Johannis apud Scortstane eisdem[c] congressus equis manibus discessit, Anglis suis inicium fuge facientibus, auctore Edrico, qui in parte 25 adversariorum stans, et gladium in manu tenens quem in pugna, quodam rustico impigre ceso, cruentarat. 'Fugite', inquit ille vafer Edericus. 'O fugite, miseri Angli. En rex vester hoc ense occisus est! Fugissent continuo Angli, nisi cognita re in eminenciori colle infra exercitum ascensus processisset, et ablata casside caput suum nudatum 30 hilari vultu commilitonibus suis ostendisset. Nox prelium diremit |

---

a   S; se C,D,R; se forcior *for* forcior se quo   b   In illo ... corona *om.*CA
    CA   c   G; eiusdem S,C

as she was, had secretly concluded an agreement with Cnut himself to
35 hand over the king and kingdom to him if he would allow her with her
children and servants to leave freely and go back home. Once this was
done and both sides had offered complete warranty, the queen
reported the truth of the matter, and disclosed that the king was dead.
So most often is cunning deceived by cunning!

16

The succession of Edmund Ironside to the kingdom of England

Once indeed the queen with her sons and all her household had
crossed over to Normandy, the kingdom and the protection of the
kingdom fell to Edmund, and the burden of the war lay heavily on   [1016: Apr.]
him. Whatever I might say about his wonderful courage would be
5 inadequate. From this he got the name 'Ironside' on account of his
invincible bodily strength. His arrow never went astray back into the
quiver, and his sword was not sheathed unused. Against enemies he
was as fierce as a lion; towards his own men he was as open-hearted as
a dove. No one was braver than he, nor anyone more charming; no
10 one was more bold, nor anyone more cautious; no one was more
confident in adversity, nor anyone more self-controlled in prosperity.
In the most energetic fashion indeed King Edmund with his army
prowled around the land like a roaring lion, and brought about the
surrender of many districts which the Danes had occupied, without
15 any opposition. Next the Danes and the English who defected from
King Edmund elected Cnut as their king. But as often as Edmund
fought with Cnut, so many times did he scatter Cnut's army, did he
overthrow a strong force brought over from across the sea, with a few
men, indeed almost alone. How often finally would he have destroyed
20 that abominable people and reduced it to nothing, had not certain
traitors to their country (of whom Eadric was the most important)
been a hindrance? During the one year of his reign he joined battle   [1016]
against the Danes seven times and won; and [he himself fought] once
against Cnut, and they divided the kingdom; but Edmund retained
25 the crown of the kingdom of England.
William [of Malmesbury] says:

> Edmund was soon acclaimed king, and after gathering an army
> together put the Danes to flight at Penselwood and Gillingham during   7-9 May
> the Rogation Days. After the feast of St John he joined battle with   24 June
> 30 these same Danes at Sherston and came off with equal advantage as his
> English troops at first turned to flee. Eadric was responsible for this,
> standing on the enemy's side, and holding a sword in his hand which he
> had stained with blood in the fight by quickly killing one of the

Anglis tamen victoriam sperantibus. Non multum postmodum obsidentes Daci Londonias, audito regis adventu, fugam per prona invadunt. Subsecutus est eos rex a vestigio, et transito vado quod Brentford dicitur, eos victoriosa strage delevit, ac insigni cede 35 profligavit. Conantem ulterius Eadmundum tendere, ut reliquias predonum ad internicionem persequeretur, vafer[d] ille et pessimus Edericus revocavit, ficto dudum animo in graciam regis reversus, ut eius meditaciones Knowtoni renunciaret. Ultimus ille dies Danis profecto fuisset si perseverandum rex putasset. Sed preventus, ut dixi, 40 susurrio proditoris, qui nichil hostes ultra ausuros [affirmaret],[e] maturum et sibi exicium et toti paravit Anglie.

d S; vefer C,D,CA   e G

17

De duello inter Eadmundum regem et Knowtum Dacum

Baldredus:

Pertesus est tandem uterque exercitus, quorum proceres ad colloquium tractaturi convenientes dixerunt: 'Insensati cotidie pugnamus, nec vincimus, sed nec vincimur. Que est ista insolencia, ymmo violencia, quin ymmo insania? Anglia quondam septem aut octo regibus subiecta 5 fuit, et gloria floruit et diviciis habundavit. Quare ergo ad presens non duobus[a] sufficit, que septem aut eo pluribus satis fuit? Quare si tanta inest eis dominandi libido ut Eadmundus parem habere dedignetur, et Knowt nullum habere velit superiorem, pugnent soli qui soli cupiunt dominari; certent pro corona soli qui soli cupiunt insigniri. Aut 10 pugnent ipsi, aut componant.' Delatam ad ipsos sentenciam procerum reges approbant. | Convenientibus autem utrisque cum exercitu super ripam Sabrine fluminis; Eadmundus cum suis in occidentali, Knowt cum suis in orientali plaga consedit.

Willelmus: 15

Ita cum infestis signis constetissent, Eadmundus singularem peciit pugnam ne duo homunculi propter ambicionem regnandi tot subjec-

a D,CA; duobis C

peasants. 'Run for it', said the cunning Eadric. 'Run for it, you
35   miserable English! Look, your king has been killed by this sword.' The
English would have fled without more ado, if Edmund had not grasped
the situation, climbed a conspicuous small hill in the middle of the
army and stepped forward. There he removed his helmet and cheerfully
showed his bare head to his fellow-soldiers. Night broke off the battle,
40   though the English were still hoping for victory.

Not long afterwards, while the Danes were besieging London, they
heard that the king was coming and plunged headlong into flight. The
king followed them immediately, and after crossing the ford which is
called Brentford, he obliterated them with victorious bloodshed, and
45   overwhelmed them with memorable slaughter. While Edmund was
trying to proceed further with pursuing the rest of the plunderers to
their total destruction, that cunning and evil Eadric restrained him; he
had returned to the king's favour a little earlier with deceitful intention,
in order that he might report Edmund's plans back to Cnut. That
50   would undoubtedly have been the final day for the Danes if the king
had thought that he must press on. But, as I said, he was prevented by
the whisper of a traitor, who maintained that the enemy would not
engage in any further venture; and thus he paved the way for early ruin
for himself and all of England.

17

The duel between King Edmund and Cnut the Dane

Ailred says:

At length both armies became weary, and when their chiefs met
together to discuss negotiations, they said: 'We are stupid to fight
today, for we neither conquer nor are conquered. What is this
5   arrogance, indeed violence, or rather madness? England in former
times was subject to seven or eight kings, and flourished gloriously with
abundant wealth. Why therefore does it not now have sufficient
resources for two, when it used to be enough for seven or more than
that? Therefore if they have such a lust for being the master that
10   Edmund scorns to have an equal and Cnut wishes to have no superior,
let those who alone want to be master fight alone; let those who alone
want to be adorned with the crown contend for it alone. They should
either fight themselves or settle their differences.' The kings approved
of the chiefs' opinion when it was reported to them. The two sides then
15   gathered with their forces on the banks of the river Severn; Edmund
with his men took up his position on the west shore, and Cnut with his
men on the east shore.

William [of Malmesbury] says:

So when they came to a halt in hostile array, Edmund sought for single
20   combat, so that as two mere men they should not be held responsible

torum sanguine culparentur, cum possent sine dispendio fidelium
fortunam experiri; magnam utrilibet laudem futuram qui, suo potissi-
mum periculo, tantum regnum nancisceretur.   20

Baldredus:

Est autem insula in ipsius fluminis medio sita, que Eleney ab illis
gentibus appellatur; in quam reges transvecti, armis protecti splen-
didissimis, utroque spectante populo, certamen ineunt singulare. At
ubi hastarum robur, tam virtute impingencium, quam fortissimorum   25
objectu clipeorum, deperiit, extractis gladiis sese cominus impetunt.
Pugnatum est acriter, dum Eadmundum virtus virium juvaret, et
Knowtum foveret fortuna. Circa galeata capita gladii tinniunt,
collisione metallorum scintille prosiliunt. Ubi vero robustissimum
illud pectus Eadmundi, ex ipso, ut assolet, bellandi motu, ira incanduit, 30
calescente sanguine factus robustior, dextram elevat, vibrat ensem, ac
tanta vehemencia in caput obstantis ictus iterat, ut spectantibus non
tam percutere quam fulminare videretur. Ad singulos enim ictus inter
ensem et galeam ignis prorumpens, non modo apparere sed incendere
videbatur.   35

18

De unanimi concordia inita per se solum in duello

Senciens autem Knowt breviori hanelitu*a* sibi vires deficere, cogitat de
pace juvenem convenire. Sed ut erat hastutus sibi precavens, timuit ne
si defectus suus juveni innotesceret, pacis verbum non audiret. Igitur
totum in se spiritum colligens, quicquid virium habuit omni conatu
intendens, virtute mirabili uno impetu irruit in Eadmundum, ac   5
flectere quodammodo fecit; et mox se paululum retrahens, rogat
juvenem subsistere modicum, et sibi dicere volenti prestare auditum.
Ille autem, ut erat suavis animi, dimissa ad terram inferiori parte scuti,
leniter procubuit in superiori, ac supinato in dextra gladio ad verba
loquentis intendit. Tunc Knowt: 'Actenus', inquit, 'regni tui extiti 10
cupidus, sed nunc, virorum fortissime, tui certe ipsius cupidior sum,
quem non dico Anglorum regno, sed universo utique orbi video
preferendum. Michi Dacia cessit, michi succubuit Norgwegia, michi
rex Suavorum manus dedit, et mei conatus impetum, quem nullum
mortalium sustinere posse | credebam, tua mirabilis virtus iam plus 15

a   *corrected from* halitu *C*; haneletu *D*

for the blood of so many of their subjects on account of their selfish desire to rule the kingdom, since they could put their fate to the test without cost to their followers. Great would be the glory for whichever of the two obtained such a kingdom, especially with risk to himself.

25 Ailred writes:

There is an island situated in the middle of the river which the people there call Alney. Once the kings had crossed over to it, protected by the most superb arms, they engaged in single combat while both crowds watched. But when the effectiveness of their spears was shattered, as a
30 result both of the valour of the men wielding them and of the resistance of extremely strong shields, they drew their swords and attacked each other at close quarters. It was a spirited fight, with Edmund helped by the force of his strength, and Cnut by the favour of fortune. The swords rang on the helmeted heads, sparks shot out from the clash of metals.
35 When indeed that most powerful breast of Edmund's blazed with anger, as was usual from the very motion of fighting, and becoming more powerful as his blood grew heated, he raised his right hand, brandished his sword, and dealt repeated blows to the head of his opponent with such strength that he seemed to the spectators to be not
40 so much dealing blows as striking with lightning. For at each blow between sword and helmet fire broke out, and seemed not only to appear but to inflame as well.

18

The unanimous agreement they reached on their own in the duel

As Cnut realised from his shorter breathing that his strength was fading, he decided to make an agreement for peace with the young man. But as he was astute in watching out for his own interests, he feared lest the young man would not listen to a proposal for peace if he
5 noticed Cnut's weakness. Therefore summoning up all his courage and exerting whatever strength he had with all possible effort, he rushed against Edmund in one attack with wonderful courage, and made him step back a little; and soon he drew back himself a short distance, and asked the young man to stop for a while and pay attention to what he
10 wanted to say. Then Edmund, being a good-natured man, lowered the bottom part of his shield to the ground, and leaning lightly on the top part and reversing his sword in his right hand, paid attention to the speaker's words. Then Cnut said: 'So far I have been eager for your kingdom; but now, bravest of men, I am without any doubt more eager
15 for you yourself, whom I see must be preferred not just to the kingdom of the English, but certainly to the whole world. Denmark has submitted to me, Norway has given in to me, the king of Sweden has surrendered to me; but with your wonderful valour you have more

semel illisit.[b] Quocirca licet ubique me victorem futurum fortuna
promiserit, ita tamen tua me mirabilis probitas illexit ad graciam ut
supra modum te amicum cupiam, et regni consortem exoptem. Utinam
ut et tu mei cupidus sis, ut ego tecum in Anglia, tu mecum in Dacia
regnes. Certe si fortune mee tua virtus accesserit, pavebit Norgvegia,   20
tremebit Swavia, et ipsa bellis assueta Gallia trepidabit.' Quid plura?
Annuit Eadmundus, ut vir benigne mentis, et Knowt de regni
participio consentit. Cessit enim verbis, qui non cesserat gladiis;
oracione flectitur, qui armis flecti non poterat. Depositis itaque armis, |

G i,333

in oscula ruunt, utroque exercitu exultante. Deinde in signum federis   25
vestes mutant, reversique ad suos, modum amicicie pacisque prescri-
bunt. Et sic cum gaudio exultantes et Deum in omnibus collaudantes
ad sua universi revertuntur.

---

b   elisit *CA*

19

De prodiciosa morte regis Eadmundi per Edericum
propter hoc extinctum

Hiis itaque gestis, quidam proditor Anglice nacionis, eodem anno
scilicet incarnacionis dominice m° xviii festo Sancti Andr',[a] volens se
Knowto gratum prestare, Eadmundo regi et domino suo liegio
molitur insidias; nec oportunum, quo regem occideret, locum
inveniens, nephandissimum ac turpissimum insidiarum genus excogi-   5
tat. Nam apud Oxenfordiam sub purgatoria domo sese occultans,
regem ad requisita nature nudatum inter celanda veruto sive cultello
bis acuto percussit; et inter viscera ferrum figens reliquit, et ad
Knowtum scelestissimus ac turpissimus sicarius confugit. ⟨Repperi
in quadam antiqua cronica quod cum rex ivissset ad requisita nature,   10
'filius Ederici ducis Mercie in fovea secretaria, consilio patris,
delitescens, regem inter celanda cultello bis acuto percussit, et inter
viscera ferrum figens reliquit'. Hec ibi.⟩[b] Stans autem coram rege
inquit: 'Salve rex solus!' Sciscitanti cur eum tali theumate salutasset,
regi retulit. Qui cum omnia rei geste denudasset, respondit rex: 15
'Unusquisque secundum suum laborem mercedem accipere debeat.
Et quia te michi tali obsequio pre ceteris graciorem exhibuisti, et me
tuis acquiescere credidisti factis, ecce sustollam caput tuum super

---

a   + Edericus nomine dux Merciorum *CA*   *b*   Repperi ... ibi *om.CA*

than once crushed the onset of my attack which I believed could not be
20   withstood by any mortal. Therefore although fortune has promised
that I shall be victorious everywhere, nevertheless your wonderful
prowess has so seduced me to look favourably upon you that I have an
immoderate desire for you to be my friend, and I long for you as my
partner in the kingdom. If only you would want me, so that I may rule
25   in England with you, and you rule in Denmark with me! There is no
doubt that if your valour is added to my good fortune, Norway will be
terrified, Sweden will tremble, and Gaul itself, accustomed as it is to
warfare, will panic.' To make a long story short – Edmund as a man of
kindly disposition agreed, and Cnut consented to sharing the kingdom.
30   So he who had not yielded to swords, yielded to words; he who could
not be swayed by arms, was swayed by speech. Laying down their arms
therefore, they fell into an embrace, while both armies were exultant.
Then as a sign of their agreement they exchanged clothes, and on
returning to their followers set out the manner of their friendship and
35   peace. And so with everyone exulting with joy and praising God for
everything, they returned to their own affairs.

19

The treasonable murder of King Edmund by Eadric,
who perished on account of this

So after these events a certain traitor belonging to the English nation
[called Eadric ealdorman of the Mercians] on the feast of St Andrew
1018, wishing to ingratiate himself with Cnut, devised a treacherous   [1016:]
trap for Edmund his king and liege lord. Finding no suitable place   30 Nov.
5   where he might kill the king, he thought up a most wicked and
disgraceful kind of trap. For hiding himself at Oxford under cover of
a privy, he struck the king when bared for the needs of nature in the
private parts with a spit or a doubly-sharp knife; he fixed the iron
implement in the vital organs and left it there, and fled to Cnut, the
10   most villainous and disgraceful murderer that he was.
        I have found in an old chronicle that when King Edmund went for
the needs of nature, 'it was a son of Eadric ealdorman of Mercia who
was hiding in a privy on his father's advice, and who struck the king in
the private parts with a doubly-sharp knife and left the iron
15   implement fixed in the vital organs'.
        Then standing before King Cnut he said: 'Greetings, sole king!'
When the king asked why the traitor was greeting him with such a
phrase, he told the king his story. Once he had disclosed all that had
happened, the king answered: 'Everyone ought to receive a reward in
20   keeping with his labour. And because by such deference to me you
have shown yourself more anxious to please than the others, and you

omnes proceres Anglie. Sed et in ulcione talis facinoris perennis
memorie decus, et in caucione proditorum omnium dedecus sempiter- 20
num.' Hiis dictis, jussit rex abscidi caput eius, et in sublimiori porta
Londonie in rememoracionem debite mercedis suspendi. Sic periit rex
Eadmundus regum strenuissimus atque fortissimus; et apud Glasin-
biry cum avo suo Eadgaro Pacifico sepelitur. Willelmus:

> Edericus eodem anno jussu regis, arte qua multos circumvenerat, ipse 25
> quoque circumventus[c] putridum spiritum transmisit ad inferos. Nam,
> nescio qua simultate inter ipsum et regem orta, dum asperius
> colloquerentur, ille, fiducia meritorum, beneficia regi sua quasi
> amicabiliter improperans, ait: 'Eadmundum pro te primo deserui, post
> eciam ob fidelitatem tuam extinxi.' Quo dicto, Knowtoni facies 30
> immutata iram rubore prodidit. Et continuo prolata sentencia: 'Merito
> ergo', inquit, 'tu morieris, cum sis lese majestatis reus in Deum et in me,
> qui dominum proprium et fratrem michi federatum occideris. "San-
> guis tuus super caput tuum, quia os tuum loqutum est contra te, quod
> misisti manus in christum Domini."' Mox, ne tumultus fieret, in eodem 35
> cubiculo proditor elisus, et per fenestram in Thamensem fluvium
> precipitatus, perfidie meritum habuit.

Scriptor Alibi sic scriptum reperi. Anno m° xviii 'in Nativitate Domini rex
Knowtus perfidum ducem Merciorum Edericum Sanctonas in
palacio jussit occidi, qui timebat insidiis ab eo quandoque circumve- 40
niri, sicut priores domini sui Alfredus et Eadmundus frequenter sunt
G i,334 circumventi. | Corpus vero illius super murum civitatis proici ac
insepultum precepit dimitti.' Ceteri vero tres filii eius sine culpa sunt
interempti.

---

c   *G*; conventus *S*,*C*; *changed from*
conventus *to* circumventus *D*

20

De exilio fratrum et filiorum regis Eadmundi
de regno

Autor Volens igitur Knowt tam fratres Eadmundi, qui Normannia exula-
bant, quam filios eius puerulos Eadmundum et Eadwardum privare
penitus spe regni, anno domini m° xix magnum consilium apud
Cirecestre tenuit, ubi jubet adesse summos regni proceres in Pascha,
queritque ab eis que fuerat inter ipsum et regem Eadmundum in regni 5

have believed that I would take satisfaction from your actions, take
note – I shall raise your head high above all the leading men of
England. But the honour of everlasting remembrance lies in the
25 retribution taken for such a crime, and perpetual disgrace lies in an
indemnity for all traitors.' With these words the king ordered the
traitor's head to be cut off, and to be hung on a lofty gate at London in
remembrance of his due reward. So died King Edmund, the most
active and brave of kings; he is buried at Glastonbury with his
30 grandfather Edgar the Peacemaker.
   William [of Malmesbury] writes:

> In the same year on King Cnut's orders Eadric, with the skill with   [1017]
> which he deceived many, was himself deceived, and sent his rotten
> spirit to join the inhabitants of the underworld. For when a quarrel
> 35 arose between him and the king for reasons unknown to me, and they
> were talking angrily, Eadric, relying on his meritorious services, was
> reproachful in a friendly enough way over the favours he had done the
> king, saying: 'First I deserted Edmund for you, and afterwards I killed
> him out of loyalty to you.' On hearing this Cnut's face changed and
> 40 betrayed his anger by turning red; and he immediately pronounced
> sentence, saying: 'Well then, you deserve to die, since you are guilty of
> treachery to God and myself for having killed your own lord and my
> brother by alliance. "Your blood be on your head, for out of your own
> mouth you condemned yourself, [by saying] that you have laid hands
> 45 on the Lord's anointed."' To prevent a riot the traitor was soon
> battered to death in the same room, and flung out of the window into
> the river Thames, so gaining the reward of treachery.

   I have found the following account elsewhere: 'at Christmas 1018   [1017:
King Cnut ordered the killing in the palace of the traitor Eadric   25 Dec.]
50 Streona ealdorman of the Mercians, for he feared being tricked by
one of Eadric's treacherous attacks some day, just as his previous
lords Æthelred and Edmund had often been tricked. Indeed Cnut
ordered that his body should be thrown over the wall of the city and
left without burial.' In fact his three remaining sons were killed, even
55 though they were blameless.

20

The exile of the brothers and sons of King Edmund
from the kingdom

With the desire therefore of entirely depriving both Edmund's
brothers (who were in exile in Normandy) and his young sons
Edmund and Edward of any hope of becoming king, Cnut in 1019   [1020:
held a great council at Cirencester. He ordered the chief nobles of the   17 Apr.]
5 kingdom to attend there at Easter, and asked them what had been the

divisione convencio, quem eciam sibi designaverat heredem, quem-
que filiis adhuc infantibus custodem deputaverat, et quid de fratribus
Alfredo et Eadwardo prescripserat. At illi, ut regi placerent,
mendacium preferunt veritati, oblitique | justicie, obliti nature,
insurrexerunt in innocentes testes iniqui, et mentita est iniquitas sibi. 10
Quoniam igitur adulantes regi mentiti sunt in caput suum, gladius
eorum intravit in corda ipsorum, et ab eodem rege quem alienigenam
dominis suis naturalibus preferebant, non immerito arcus eorum est
confractus. Itaque proprii sanguinis proditores dicunt regem Eadmundum ipsi Knowto pocius regni et filiorum suorum curam 15
delegasse, cum ipse fratres suos heredes designaverit, et puerorum
custodiam eis deputaverit. Cum igitur eorum mendaciis Anglie
monarchiam, illis faventibus, optinuisset, omnes qui affuerant in illo
consilio exterminavit; et quotquot de regio semine superstites reperit
vel e regno repulit vel occidit. At filios Eadmundi ferire pre pudore 20
metuens, ad regem Swavorum socerum suum transmisit quasi
alendos, sed pocius interficiendos. Ille vero nobilium puerorum
miseratus, eorum erumpnam miseram in misericordiam convertit, et
ad eius confederatum regem Hungariorum eos destinavit fovendos
alendos et in hiis que eos decebat instruendos. Quos ipse benigne 25
suscepit, benignius fovit, et benignissime sibi in filios adoptavit.
Processu vero temporis cum adulti fuissent, Eadmundo filiam suam
dedit in uxorem, et Eadwardo Agathen filiam germani sui Henrici
silicet imperatoris in matrimonium copulavit. Sed paulo post
Eadmundus de temporalibus ad eterna transfertur, et Eadwardus 30
sospitate et prosperitate perfruitur. Interea mortuo Knowto et filiis
eius Haroldo et Hardknowto qui post eum regnaverunt, accersitur ad
regnum Anglorum Eadwardus, frater Eadmundi Irneside, filius
Æthelredi, qui in Normanniam, sicut diximus, exulabat. Nam frater
eius Alfredus alias Æthelredus prodicione Godwini in Anglia dum 35
matrem suam Emmam, quam Knowt in uxorem duxerat, visitaret,[a]
crudeli morte [perierat].[b] Apud Gillinghame[c] ⟨sive Heli,⟩[d] ut premisimus, luminibus orbatus, ubi omnibus comitibus preter decimos
decapitatis, quos sors a morte liberavit. Non tamen impune. Nam[e]
tempore sequenti cum idem rex quadam die que populo celebris 40
habebatur, presente eodem comite Godwino proditore, cuius filiam
ipse duxerat in uxorem, cum virgine tamen permanens virgo, mensis
regalibus assideret, accidit ut inter prandendum unus | ministrorum
in obicem aliquem uno pede immoderacius impingens, pene lapsum
incurrit, quem tamen pes alius, recto gressu procedens, iterum in 45
statum suum nichil injurie passum sustinuit. De hoc autem casu
pluribus inter se loquentibus, et quod pes pedem sustinuerit

a insitaret D
b CA,S; interierat DMS; interemit del., with
   perierat interlin. and del.C; perierat om.D
c Gollynghame CA
d marginal addition in text D; om.CA
e +eodem del.C

agreement between himself and King Edmund about the division of
the kingdom, whom also had [King Edmund] named as his heir, and
whom had he appointed as guardian while his sons were still children,
and what had been laid down about his brothers Alfred and Edward.

10   But they, to please the king, preferred a lie to the truth; and unmindful
of justice, unmindful of nature, they rose up as unjust witnesses
against the innocent and injustice lied for them. Since therefore in
flattering the king they lied against their own interests, their sword
pierced their own hearts, and their bow was deservedly shattered by

15   the same King Cnut, whom they preferred as a foreigner to their
native lords. So as traitors to their own blood they said that King
Edmund had entrusted the care of the kingdom and of his sons to
Cnut himself, when [in fact] he had named his brothers as his heirs,
and had assigned the guardianship of his boys to them. When

20   therefore Cnut had secured the sole rule of England by their lies and
with their support, he banished all those who had attended that
council, and however many survivors of royal descent he found, he
either thrust out of the kingdom or killed.

But out of shame he was afraid to execute Edmund's sons, and so he
25   sent them to his father-in-law the king of the Swedes, ostensibly to be
cared for, but really to be killed. But he felt sorry for the noble boys,
and gave them mercy in place of misery; he sent them to his ally the
king of the Hungarians to be fostered, cared for and instructed in
matters which were right for them. He received them kindly, fostered

30   them with more kindness, and with extreme kindness adopted them as
his sons. Then in due time when they were adults he gave his daughter
in marriage to Edmund, and arranged the marriage of Edward to
Agatha, the daughter of his brother (that is the emperor Henry). But
soon afterwards Edmund was transported from the temporal state to

35   the eternal, and Edward enjoyed health and happiness.

Meanwhile following the deaths of Cnut and of his sons Harold   [1035]
and Harthacnut who had reigned after him, Edward, the brother of   [1040, 1042]
Edmund Ironside and a son of Æthelred, who was in exile in
Normandy as we have said, was invited to be king of the English. For

40   his brother Alfred (or Æthelred) had through Godwine's treachery
met with a cruel death while visiting his mother Emma (whom Cnut   [1036]
had married) in England.

He had been blinded at Gillingham (or Ely) as we have said, when
all his companions were decapitated, except for ten who were fated to
45   escape death. This did not, however, go unpunished. For afterwards
when the same king [Edward the Confessor] was sitting at the royal
tables on a day which the people held as a festival, and the same Earl   [1053:
Godwine the traitor was present (whose daughter the king had   12 Apr.]
married, though he remained a virgin with a virgin), it happened that
50   during the meal one of the servants carelessly tripped on some
obstacle with one foot and nearly had a fall. His other foot however

jocantibus, comes quasi ludendo subintulit: 'Sic est frater fratrem adjuvans, et alter altri in necessitate subveniens.' Et rex ad ducem:*f* 'Hoc', inquit, 'michi meus frater fecisset, si Godwinus permisisset.'   50

f   comitem *CA*

21

De vindicta et subita morte proditoris

Ad hanc itaque regis vocem, male mentis conscius, Godwinus expavit; et tristicia vultum pallidum pretendens subintulit. 'Scio,' inquit, 'scio, O rex, quod adhuc de morte fratris tui tuus me apud te animus accusat, nec eis adhuc estimas discredendum qui vel eius, vel tuum, me menciuntur proditorem. Sed secretorum omnium conscius 5 Deus rem veram inde judicet; et sic buccellam hanc, quam gluciendam manu tenes,*a* guttur meum pertransire faciat, et me servet illesum et non suffocatum, sicut nec de tua prodicione reum me sencio, nec de fratris tui interitu michi conscius existo.' Dixit, et buccellam a rege benedictam intulit ori, et usque in medium gutturis attraxit. Tunc 10 ulcione divina inibi firmiter hesit sed inhesit. Temptat interius semisuffocatus attrahere, sed adhesit firmius; temptat emittere, sed cohesit firmissime. Quid plura inde? Mox meatus, quibus ducebatur spiritus,*b* obcluduntur, evertuntur oculi, brachia cum tibiis rigescunt, totum corpus frigescit et denigrescit. Intuetur rex infeliciter morien- 15 tem, et ulcionem divinam in eum senciens processisse, astantibus dixit: 'Extrahite istum canem hinc, extrahite. Manifestavit Deus opera sua que, Deo teste, negando eciam detestatus est in internicione fratris mei vel prodicione mea.' Accurrunt filii mortui patris cadaver,*c* protractumque de sub mensa thalamis inferunt, ubi post modicum 20 intervallum debitum proditori finem sortitus est.

Autor   〈Willelmus: 'Frater Eadmundi regis ex matre Edwius, non aspernande probitatis adolescens, per proditorem Edericum jubente Knowtone Anglia cessit.'

Scriptor   Hic Godwinus habuit prius uxorem Knoutonis sororem, ex qua 25 puerum genuit, qui dum evo puerili jactancia superbiret, ab eodem portatus in Themensem fluvium suffocatus interiit. Mater quoque eius ictu fulminis exanimata est. Hec dicebatur agmina mancipiorum in Angliam 〈de〉 Danemarchia solere mittere, maxime puellas

a   *CA; altered from* teneo *C*; tenens *D*   *c*   *interlin.C*
b   + obducuntur *del.C*

moved correctly to restore his balance, and he suffered no harm. Then
as many people discussed this incident among themselves, joking that
a foot had saved a foot, the earl playfully added: 'Thus does a brother
55 help a brother, and one comes to the support of the other when there
is an emergency.' And the king said to the [earl]: 'My brother would
have done this for me, if Godwine had allowed it.'

21

The punishment and sudden death of the traitor

So at these words of the king Godwine, having a guilty conscience,
became frightened. And with a pale face and a pretence of grief he
added: 'I know, I know, your majesty, that in your mind you still
accuse me of your brother's death, and that you still do not consider
5 that no trust should be put in those who falsely accuse me of being a
traitor to him or you. But let God who knows every secret judge the
truth of the matter; and so may God cause this morsel of food, which
you are holding in your hand to swallow, to pass down my throat, and
preserve me unharmed and not choked, so surely do I feel that I am
10 not guilty of treachery against you, and I do not have a guilty
conscience over the violent death of your brother.' He said this, and
put the morsel after it had been blessed by the king into his mouth,
and swallowed it half-way down his throat. Then by divine
retribution it stuck firmly and remained there. Half-choking he tried
15 to force it down, but it adhered the more firmly; he tried to spew it out,
but it stuck in place very firmly indeed. Need I say more from then on?
Soon the passage-ways for his breathing were blocked, his eyes were
closed, his arms and legs became rigid, his whole body grew cold and
turned black. As the king watched the man dying miserably, he felt   [1053:
20 that divine retribution had operated against him, and said to the   15 Apr.]
bystanders: 'Drag this dog away from here, drag it away. God has
disclosed Godwine's deeds, which he denied under oath, calling God
to witness, in killing my brother and in treachery to me.' Godwine's
sons hurried to the body of their dead father, dragged it from under
25 the table, and carried it to the bedrooms, where after a short time he   [1053:
received the due end for a traitor.   15 Apr.]
  William [of Malmesbury] says: 'Eadwig, the brother of King
Edmund with the same mother, a young man of appreciable integrity
that should not be despised, withdrew from England on Cnut's   [1017]
30 instructions through the influence of the traitor Eadric.'
  This Godwine had Cnut's sister as his first wife, by whom he
fathered a son, who while still a boy was haughty and ostentatious. He
was carried by Godwine to the river Thames and drowned. His

pulcras.⟩ Sed nunc ad narracionem nostram revertamus,*d* | de qua 30
paulisper digressi sumus.

d corrected from revertamur *C*

22

Quomodo imperator misit regi E[adwardo] nepotem
cum uxore et filiabus

Scriba

G i,336

Veniens igitur in Angliam Eadwardus, ab universo clero et populo
cum exultacione maxima suscipitur; et Wintonie die sancto Pasche ab
archiepiscopis (scilicet Cantuariensi et Eboracensi) | cunctisque fere
regni episcopis in regem ungitur et consecratur ⟨anno domini m°
[xliii.]*a*⟩ Et ambulavit in viis avi sui Eadgari, homo mansuetus et pius, 5
magis pace quam armis regnum protegens. Habebat animum ire
victorem, avaricie contemptorem, expertem superbie. Qui cum
pacem tam a suis quam ab extraneis optinuisset, et vicinis regibus ac
principibus amabilis et gratus extitisset, dirigit nuncios ad Romanum
imperatorem, rogans ut nepotem suum, filium fratris sui Eadmundi 10
Irneside, debiti sibi*b* regni futurum heredem mittere dignaretur.
Imperator autem regis nuncios gratanter accipiens, non parvo
tempore summo cum honore detinuit. Tandem paratis navibus, et
omnibus que navigaturis necessaria videbantur illatis, Eadwardum
cum uxore sua Agatha germani sui filia et liberis eius Eadgaro 15
Ethlyng, Margarita atque Cristina, cum magna gloria atque diviciis,
sicut rex pecierat, ad Angliam misit. Qui prospero cursu in Angliam
veniens, tam regem quam populum suo letificavit adventu; sed post
paucos dies vita decedens, gaudium in luctum, risum mutavit in
lacrimas.   20

Scriptor

Nonnullis croniographis vertitur in dubium, cuius quidem*c* filia
fuerit ista domina Agatha mater Eadgari Ethlyng, id est junioris, et
Sancte Margarite*d* regine, necnon et Cristine sanctimonialis. Quorum
quidam, ut est Baldredus, dicit quod Eadwardus filius Eadmundi
Irneside filiam germani imperatoris Henrici, scilicet Agathen, duxit 25
uxorem. Willelmus vero Malmesbiriensis dicit eum duxisse uxorem
Agathen sororem regine Ungariorum. In alio autentico scripto, si
autenticum dici poterit propter antiquitatem scripture, repperi sicut
supra scriptum est xx capitulo huius libri sic: 'Hic rex Ungariorum
Eadmundo filiam suam dedit in uxorem, et Eadwardo filiam germani 30

a   D; lac.C   *c   ambiguous C;* quidam *D,CA*
b   +regni del.C   *d   +postea Scotorum CA*

mother also was killed by a thunderbolt. This lady was said to have
35 been in the habit of sending slaves to England from Denmark,
especially pretty girls.

But now let us return to our narrative, from which we have
digressed for a short while.

22

How the emperor sent to King Edward his nephew
with his wife and daughters

Edward therefore came to England and was received by all the clergy
and people with the greatest rejoicing; and he was anointed and
consecrated as king at Winchester on Easter Day 1043 by the 1043:
archbishops (that is of Canterbury and York) and nearly all the 3 Apr.
5 bishops of the kingdom. And he walked in the ways of his grandfather
Edgar, being a gentle and pious man, who protected his kingdom
more by peace than by arms. He had a spirit that mastered anger,
despised greed and was free from pride. When he had secured peace
both from his own people and from foreigners, and had become well-
10 liked and popular among neighbouring kings and princes, he sent
envoys to the Roman emperor asking him to agree to send his [1054]
nephew, the son of his brother Edmund Ironside, as future heir to the
kingdom that was due to him. The emperor received the king's envoys
joyfully, and had them stay for a long time with the highest honours.
15 At length, once ships had been got ready and everything brought
aboard that seemed necessary for those going on the voyage, he sent [1057]
Edward with his wife Agatha (the daughter of his brother) and his
children Edgar the Ætheling, Margaret and Christina to England,
with great honour and riches, just as the king had requested.
20 Edward's arrival after a favourable voyage to England delighted both
king and people; but his death a few days later, caused joy to turn to
grief, and laughter to tears.

It is a matter of debate and doubt among chroniclers who indeed
was the father of this lady Agatha, the mother of Edgar the Ætheling
25 (that is the Younger), and of St Margaret the queen, and also of
Christina the nun. One of them, namely Ailred, says that Edward the
son of Edmund Ironside married a daughter of a brother of the
emperor Henry [II], namely Agatha. But William of Malmesbury
states that he took as his wife Agatha a sister of the queen of the
30 Hungarians. In another authoritative text (if it can be called
authoritative because of the antiquity of the writing), I have found it
as written above in Chapter 20 of this Book, namely: 'This king of the
Hungarians gave his daughter in marriage to Edmund, and joined in

sui, Henrici scilicet imperatoris, in matrimonium copulavit.' Alibi
eciam reperi Eadwardum filiam Germanie imperatoris Agathen in
matrimonium duxisse. ⟨Hanc sentenciam duorum concordancium
amplector, videlicet quod Eadwardus duxit filiam imperatoris
Germanie,[e] sicut clare patet capitulo xx huius libri supra, hoc est dictu 35
filiam imperatoris germani videlicet regis Ungariorum, qui vocabatur
Salomon, frater dicti imperatoris.⟩ ⟨In antiquo libro Sancte Margar-
ite de Dunfermel' sic repperi quod rex Salomon Ungarie dedit
Eadmundo filiam suam in uxorem, Eadwardo vero Agatham filiam
fratris sui Henrici Rome imperatoris in matrimonium copulavit.⟩ 40
Alibi sic repperi, et concordat cum Martiniano,[f] quod Otho dux
Saxonum genuit Henricum imperatorem Alemannie. Qui quidem
Henricus genuit ex Mathilde filia Theodorici regis Saxonum Otho-
nem primum imperatorem, et Henricum ducem Bajoarie; et idem
Otho imperator genuit Othonem tercium. Henricus vero dux 45
Bajoarum genuit Henricum[g] imperatorem electum primum, Gillam et
Agathen. Qui Henricus dedit sororem suam Gillam Salomoni regi
Hungariorum,[h] per quam fidem Christi suscepit cum omni regno suo.
Qui in baptismo, mutato nomine, vocatus est postea Stephanus. Cui
destinati sunt illis diebus per regem Swavorum duo filii regis Anglie 50

G i,337

Eadmundi Irneside, | Eadmundus scilicet et Eadwardus. Eadmundo
quoque filiam suam uxorem, et Eadwardo sororem regine dedit
Agathen.[i] Ex qua Eadwardus genuit filium Eadgarum, Margaritam
reginam Scocie et Cristinam sanctimonialem. Neptem vero eiusdem
Henrici electi Corradus, qui sibi successit in imperium, uxorem duxit, 55
ex qua genuit Henricum secundum qui dictus est Pius, quamvis
Jacobus Januensis et Martinus ipsum, ut superius scriptum est, fuisse
filium Lupoldi comitis asseverant. Elige que vis c'.

e	-e *interlin.*C		Martiniano *CA*
f	Ad hoc confirmandum audivi notabilem	g	*interlin.*C
	virum fatentem se legisse cronicam istam	h	*CA*; Hungarum *C,D*
	in Gallico, ubi expresse Eadvinum filiam	i	+ Iste Henricus dux Bajoarum dicebatur
	Germanie imperatoris in conjugem		imperator, sed quia non electus, ideo
	accepisse. Istud bene concordat cum		cronice vocant eum sepius ducem quam
	Martiniano *for* Hanc sentenciam ...		imperatorem *CA*

23

De successione Haroldi filii Ederici proditoris et de perfida prodicione regni

Autor

Nec multo post ipse Eadwardus, cum nobile monasterium, quod ad
occidentalem partem Londonie in honorem beati Petri fundaverat,
cum maxima gloria dedicari fecisset, vigilia Epiphanie felici morte
vitam terminavit. Quo ibidem tumulato, proceres Eadgarum Ethling,

marriage to Edward the daughter of his brother, that is the emperor
35 Henry.' Elsewhere also I have found that Edward married Agatha, a
daughter of the emperor of Germany. I understand this to be the
meaning of two views that are in agreement – that Edward married
the daughter of an emperor of Germany (as appears clearly above in
Chapter 20 of this Book), that is to say a daughter of the emperor who
40 was a brother of the king of the Hungarians called Salomon, the
brother of the said emperor [Henry II]. In an old book of St Margaret
of Dunfermline I have found that King Salomon of Hungary gave his
daughter to be the wife of Edmund, and joined Edward in marriage to
Agatha the daughter of his brother Henry the emperor of Rome. I
45 have found it so elsewhere, and it agrees with Martin that Otto duke
of the Saxons fathered Henry [I] emperor of Germany. This Henry
fathered by Matilda daughter of Theoderic king of the Saxons the
emperor Otto I and Henry duke of Bavaria; and the same emperor
Otto fathered Otto [II]. But Henry duke of Bavaria fathered Henry
50 [II] the first elected emperor, Gisela and Agatha. This Henry gave his
sister Gisela to Salomon king of the Hungarians. Through her he was
converted to the Christian faith along with all of his kingdom,
changed his name at his baptism, and was afterwards called Stephen.
It was to him that the two sons of Edmund Ironside king of England,
55 that is Edmund and Edward, were sent at that time by the king of the
Swedes. Also he gave his daughter to Edmund as a wife, and Agatha
the queen's sister to Edward. By her Edward fathered his son Edgar,
Margaret the queen of Scotland, and Christina the nun. The Conrad
[II] who succeeded the same Henry the elected emperor married his
60 granddaughter, by whom he fathered Henry II [III], called the Pious,
although James of Genoa and Martin assert (as is written above) that
he was a son of a Count Lupold. Choose as you like, etc.

23

The succession of Harold son of the traitor [Godwine]
and the treacherous betrayal of the kingdom

Soon afterwards Edward himself, after he had arranged the dedi- [1065:
cation with the greatest splendour of the noble monastery which he 28 Dec.]
had founded to the west of London in honour of St Peter, ended his [1066:]
life with a happy death on the eve of Epiphany. After he had been 5 Jan.

si clerum assertatorem haberent, [in regem erigere molirentur;][a] sed et 5
quia puer tanto oneri minus idoneus videbatur, Haraldus comes filius
superioris Godwini proditoris, cuius erat et mens hastucior et
crumena fecundior, ac miles copiosior, intelligens quia 'semper nocuit
differre paratis', viribus et potencia extorta fide a majoribus, regnum
indebite invadens, diadema regium sinistro omine capiti proprio 10
imposuit.

Ecce quomodo prodicione proprie gentis regnum ab Anglicis
deperiit! Quod utique Eadgari Pacifici diebus et Eadwardi filii sui
regum prosperitate pacifica vigebat, donec malignus spiritus Ead- |

wardi novercam Alfricht in eius prodicionem excitans, ipsum 15
visitando fratrem suum patris[b] filium Ethelredum, qui statim
regnavit, malefica proditrix occidi nequiter procuravit. Hac autem
prodicione regnum decrescere cepit, quia prodicioni prodicio, proditores proditrici succedentes, nec a prodicione cessantes, quousque
regiam liniam in mortem et exterminium, seipsos in servitutem 20
miseram, et totum regnum exteris gentibus in possessionem redigis-
sent. Eadwardo martirizato successit idem Ethelredus, ut premissum
est; cui per Sanctum Dunstanum die coronacionis dictum est: 'Quia
per mortem tui fratris ad regnum aspiras, non delebitur peccatum
ignominiose matris tue et virorum qui interfuerant illius consilio 25
nequam, nisi multo sanguine miserorum provincialium. Et venient
super gentem Anglorum mala, qualia non passa est usque tempus
illud.' Nec multo post, Dacis regnum destruentibus, predicta
ceperunt exoriri. Quodam postea tempore rex Ethelredus adversus
hostes classem paravit, cuius admirallum preposuit proditorem 30
Elfricum, qui, nocte que diem pugne precesserat, transfuga vilis cum
xxx navibus ad hostes concessit.[c] Proceres quidem hiis diebus ad
consilium si convenissent, pars hoc, pars illud eligentes, numquam in
bonam convenerunt sentenciam. Magis vero de simultatibus domesticis quam necessitate rei publice consultabant. Sed quid utile vel 35
archanum decrevissent, ad Danos statim per proditores deferebatur.

Nam preter | proditorem Elfricum, fuit in arte[d] prodicionis Edricus
comes Merciorum improbe perfectus,[e] fex hominum c', ut supra. In
eius autem loco surrexit et alter potens proditor comes Godwinus,
qui, sicut Edericus regem Eadmundum ad mortem prodidit, apposuit 40
et iste fratres[f] eius Ethelredi filios ut Danis placeret, eciam de mundo
delere, vel a regno protinus exterminare. Rex eciam Eadwardus de
prodicione habuit Haroldum filium suspectum Godwini, quod sui
generis heredes per illum debita successione regni post suum obitum
privarentur. Quod utique factum est. Nam eodem die quo sepultus est 45
rex, Haroldus, ut premittitur, diadema regni suo proprio capiti

a   S   d   + pro d del.C
b   S; fratris C,D,CA   e   profectus CA
c   S,E; consessit C,D   f   fratris S

5 buried there, the magnates would have sought to raise Edgar the
Ætheling to the kingship if they had had the support of the clergy; but
because as a boy he seemed unsuitable for so heavy a burden, Earl
Harold, the son of the traitor Godwine mentioned above, whose mind
was cunning and whose purse copious, and who was a well-endowed
10 knight, understood that 'it always does harm to put off what has been
planned'; once he had secured the adherence of the magnates through
his strength and power, he seized control of the kingdom improperly,
and with evil omen placed the royal crown on his own head.   [6 Jan.]

See how by the treachery of their own people the kingdom was
15 destroyed by the English! There is no doubt that in the days of the
kings Edgar the Peace-maker and Edward his son the kingdom
flourished in peaceful prosperity, until a malign spirit aroused
Edward's step-mother Ælfthryth to treachery against him, and the
wicked traitress villainously arranged for his death while he was   [978:
20 visiting his brother Æthelred the son of his father, who immediately   18 Mar.]
became king. With this act of treason the kingdom began to decline,
because with treason succeeding treason, the traitors who succeeded
the traitress did not abandon their treachery until they had brought
the royal house to death and destruction, themselves to wretched
25 slavery, and the whole kingdom into the possession of foreign
peoples. After Edward had been martyred, he was succeeded by the
same Æthelred, as has been said. St Dunstan is said to have addressed
him on the day of his coronation thus: 'Because you aspire to the   [979:
kingdom as a result of the death of your brother, the sin of your   4 May]
30 shameless mother and of the men who were implicated in her wicked
plot will not be wiped out without much bloodshed among the
wretched provincials. And misfortunes such as they have not suffered
previously will befall the English people.' And not much later when
the Danes were destroying the kingdom, these predictions began to
35 come about.

Sometime afterwards King Æthelred was preparing a fleet against
his enemies, over which he appointed the traitor Ælfric as admiral,   [992]
who on the night before the fight went over to the enemy with thirty
ships as a contemptible deserter. When the magnates in these days
40 gathered for a council, some chose one way and some another,
without ever agreeing on a good decision. They were indeed more
concerned with private rivalries than with the needs of the state. But
anything useful or secret that they decided was immediately reported
by traitors to the Danes. For besides the traitor Ælfric, Eadric
45 ealdorman of the Mercians was shamelessly proficient in the art of
treachery, the dregs among men that he was (see above). In his place
yet another influential traitor emerged, Earl Godwine, who just as
Eadric had betrayed King Edmund to death, contrived in order to
please the Danes to efface Edmund's brothers the sons of Æthelred
50 from the world or banish them forthwith from the kingdom. King

imposuit, anno domini m° lxvii°. Quem Willelmus Bastard, ut
premittitur, simul vita privavit et*g* regno. Cetera usque mortem regis
David*h* supra patent. Hucusque scriba clare. Cetera sunt scriptoris.
Anno domini m° c.*i*   50

> Actenus actorem de Fordon sume Johannem;
> hinc opus auctoris et scriptoris superextat.
> Alternative scriptor nonnulla priori
> immiscit parti, protractu marginis apte
> intitulata tamen. Quos Christus protegat! Amen.*j*   55

g   + egi *del.C*
h   + present' *del.C*
i   Anno ... m° c *C,D;* Nunc ad annalia

j   redeamus *for* Cetera ... m° c *CA*
j   Actenus ... Amen *in large bookhand C,D;*
    om.R,CA

fo.118

De episcopis Sanctiandree post Kenedum Alpini

24

De episcopis Kilreymonth id est Sanctiandr' a tempore
expulsionis Pictorum usque huc

Scriptor

*a*Sed quia, ut premissum est, sanctissimus rex David episcopatus
ampliavit et*b* fundavit, visum est michi conveniens etsi non distincte
de aliis saltem de episcopis Sanctiandr' hic aliqua successive a
tempore regis Kenedi filii Alpini primi Scotorum monarche*c* qui
Pictos et eorum gesta evacuavit usque presentem diem inserere, 5
potissime cum quilibet eorum qui pro tempore fuerat*d* non tamquam
primas sed primus et precipuus in regno habeatur, ne si sparsim juxta
annales inserantur, eorum noticia tepidius a querentibus inveniatur.
Primus ut reperi fuit*e* Fothad qui*f* ab Indolff rege expulsus fuit, et
post expulsionem ab episcopatu vixit octo annis.*g* De quo sic reperi in 10
circumferencia textus argentei evangeliorum adhuc in Sanctoandr'
servati insculptum:

a   *Decorated initial* S *C*
b   + regnavit *del.C*
c   utriusque regni Pictivie videlicet et Scocie
    que nunc unum Scotorum scilicet regnum
    efficiunt *for* Scotorum monarche *CA*
d   + et erit *CA*

e   + Kellach. Secundus *CA*
f   + postquam magno tempore
    episcopizavit *CA*
g   + et obiit quarto nonas maii. Quidam
    tamen tenent quod fuit primus episcopus
    CA

Edward also suspected Harold son of Godwine of treachery, on the grounds that the heirs of his own family would be deprived by Harold of their rightful succession to the kingdom after Edward's death. This is certainly what happened. For on the same day as the king was buried in [1066], Harold (as has been said) placed the crown of the kingdom on his own head. William the Bastard (as has been said) deprived him at the same time of his kingdom and his life.

The rest up to the death of King David is set forth above.

So far this has clearly [been the work of] the scribe; the rest [is the responsibility] of the writer.

Assume that John de Fordun is the author so far;
from here it is the work of the author and of the writer.
The writer in his turn has added some material
to the earlier part, which has nevertheless been appropriately
    identified
by a marginal note. May Christ protect them both! Amen.

The bishops of St Andrews after Kenneth son of Alpin

24

The bishops of Kilrymont (that is St Andrews) from the time of the expulsion of the Picts until now

But because (as has been stated) the most saintly King David increased the number of bishoprics by [new] foundations, it seems to me appropriate (even if I do not deal separately with the other bishops) at least to insert something here about the succession of the bishops of St Andrews at least from the time of King Kenneth son of Alpin, the first monarch of the Scots (who swept away the Picts and their achievements) down to the present day, especially since each of them in his own time was regarded not as primate, but as the first and foremost [bishop] in the kingdom, lest if this information were to be scattered through the annals, enquirers would find a notice about [each of] these bishops less readily.

I find that the first was [Kellach [I], and the second] Fothad [I], who was driven out by King Indulf; and after his expulsion from the see he lived for eight years. Regarding him I have found this inscription round the edge of the silver cover of a gospel book which is still preserved at St Andrews:

Fothad, who is the leading bishop among the Scots,
made this cover for an ancestral gospel-book.

Hanc evangelii thecam construxit avites
Fothad, qui primus Scotis episcopus est.

Deinde Kellach, post quem[h] Malisius qui octo annis stetit episcopus. 15
[Iste Malisius, ut legitur in vita gloriosi ac eximii confessoris beati
Duthaci, discipulus fuit beato Duthaco in Hibernia. Cui beatus
Duthacus vaticinando futurum episcoporum Scotorum se dixit; quod
et adimpletum est.][i] Dehinc secundus[j] Kellach filius Ferdlag' qui fuit
primus qui adivit Romam pro confirmacione, et post confirmacio- 20
nem vixit xxv annis. Dehinc successive Malmore, Malisius secundus,
Alwinus qui tribus annis stetit episcopus, Maldwinus filius Gillandris,
Tuthald quatuor annis, Fothald,[k] Gregorius, Cathre, | Edmarus et
Godricus obierunt electi.

Anno m° c. ix Turgotus prior Dunelmensis electus est in Transla- 25
cione Sancti Augustini, et consecratus stetit episcopus fere septem
annos.[l] Anno m° c ⟨xvii⟩ Eadmundus Cantuarie monachus electus
est, sed deposita voluntate episcopandi ad claustrum suum reversus
est. ⟨Hic tamen in vita Sancti Anselmi vocat se Eadmerum, qui eciam
dictavit et scripsit vitam[m] Anselmi.⟩   30

Anno m° centesimo xxii electus est Robertus prior de Scona in
episcopum ad instanciam regis Alexandri.[n] Et[o] terram que Cursus
Apri dicitur que ab ecclesia Sanctiandr' ablata fuerat ex integro
restituit, ea condicione ut inibi constitueretur religio ut per regem
Alexandrum preordinatum fuerat, et per regium equm Arabicum 35
cum proprio freno et sella, opertum pallio grandi ct precioso, cum
scuto et lancea argentea que nunc est[p] hasta crucis, que omnia
precepit rex coram magnatibus terre usque ad altare adduci, et de
predictis libertatibus et consuetudinibus regalibus ecclesiam investiri
fecit et sasire.[q] Quam donacionem David frater eius tunc comes ibi 40
presens confirmavit. Consecratus fuit idem a Thurstino Eboracensi
archiepiscopo sine professione, salvis[r] utriusque ecclesie dignitate et
apostolice sedis auctoritate. Stetit electus per bienium,[s] consecratus
stetit xxxv annis et sic electus et episcopus stetit xxxvii annis. Alibi sic
reperi scriptum: 'Stetit electus per biennium et consecratus stetit xxxii 45
annis, et sic electus et episcopus stetit xxxiiii annis.' Et obiit anno
domini m° centesimo lix et sepultus in antiqua ecclesia Sanctiandr'
tempore Malcolmi regis.

G i,340

---

h Tercius *for* Deinde ... quem *CA*
i *H only*
j Quartus sanctus *for* Dehinc secundus *CA*
k +secundus, Girich alias *CA*
l +Hic scripsit libellum de sanctitate
   Sancte Margarete regine et de virtutibus
   sobolis eius. Qui eciam fuit confessor eius
   CA

m +eiusdem *CA*
n +primi *CA*
o Qui *CA*
p *interlin.C*
q *altered from* saisire *C*
r +ut ibi protestatum fuit *CA*
s +et *CA*

Then Kellach and Maelbrigde, who was bishop for eight years. [This
20 Maelbrigde, as we read in the *Life* of the glorious and excellent
confessor the blessed Duthac, was a pupil of the blessed Duthac in
Ireland. The blessed Duthac prophesied that he would be one of the
bishops of the Scots; and this was fulfilled.] Then came Kellach II, son
of Ferdlag', who was the first to go to Rome for confirmation; he lived
25 for twenty-five years after his confirmation. Then in succession came
Malmore, a second Maelbrigde, Alwin who held the see for three
years, Maelduin Makgillandris, Tuthald for four years, Fothad [II],
Giric, Cathre, Edmar and Godric, who died as bishops-elect.

In 1109 Turgot prior of Durham was elected on the day of the   [1107]
30 Translation of St Augustine, and served as a consecrated bishop for
about seven years. [He wrote a little book about the saintliness of St
Margaret the queen and about the virtues of her offspring. He was
also her confessor.] In 1117 'Edmund' a monk of Canterbury was   [1120]
elected, but on renouncing his desire to become a bishop, he returned
35 to his cloister. (But this man in the *Life* of St Anselm calls himself
Eadmer. He it was who also dictated and wrote the *Life* of Anselm.)

In 1122 Robert prior of Scone was elected to the see on the urging of   [1124]
King Alexander. He [the king] restored in its entirety the land called
the Boar's Chase, which had been taken away from the church of St
40 Andrew, on condition that a religious community was established
there, as had been previously arranged by King Alexander [in a
ceremony involving] the king's Arabian steed with its special harness
and saddle, covered with a voluminous and precious caparison, along
with a shield and silver lance (which now forms the shaft of a cross) –
45 all these things the king in the presence of the magnates of the land
had brought up to the altar, and he had the church invested with, and
given sasine of, the said liberties and royal customs. David his
brother, then an earl, was present there and confirmed this gift. This
same [Robert] was consecrated by Thurstan archbishop of York   [1127]
50 without a profession of obedience, saving the privileges of each
church and the authority of the apostolic see [as was then specified].
He remained a bishop-elect for two years, and once consecrated
served for thirty-five years, and so as elect and as bishop he served for
thirty-seven years. (Elsewhere I find it written thus: 'He served as elect
55 for two years, and after consecration served for thirty-two years, so
that as elect and bishop he served for thirty-four years.') He died in
1159, and was buried in the old church of St Andrew during the reign   1159
of King Malcolm.

25

De eleccione Sancti Walthevi abbatis de Melros ad episcopatum Sanctiandr'[a]

*b*Roberto mortuo, ut scribit Jocelinus monachus Furnesii,

vacabat[c] sedes episcopalis Sanctiandr' in Scocia, populique peticio, cleri eleccio, principum[d] assensus sanctum abbatem Walthevum Melrocensem elegerunt in pastorem et episcopum animarum suarum. Venerunt igitur clerici capitanei cum magnatibus terre satis instructi[e] 5 Melros, gracia sumendi et educendi secum electum suum; paterque abbas Rievallis, qui tunc casu affuit, injunxit eidem ut obtemperaret eleccionem, subiret onus, susciperet et[f] officium. Ille vero pretendebat imbecillitatem virium et impotenciam sustinendi tanti ponderis negocium, indicavitque secrecius abbati Rievallis se non diu super terram 1(
victurum. Illis autem persistentibus in eleccionis facte perficiendo proposito, et patre abbate in imperio suo, respondit Sanctus spiritu vatidico et ore veridico: 'Expoliavi me tunica mea; quo modo induam illam? Lavi pedes meos; absit ut iterum pulvere secularis sollicitudinis inquinem eos.' Et adiciens, 'Credite michi,' inquit, 'quoniam eligetis et 1!
habebitis alium pontificem quam me.' Extensoque digito exteriori capitulari domo Melrocensi, designans ibi sue sepulture locum, 'En[g] hec', inquit, 'requies mea. Hic habitabo quamdiu Domino placuerit, quoniam elegi | eam in filiorum meorum consolacionem.' Hiis dictis, negocium suspenditur, et suspensum sub induciis differtur, | dilatum 2(
ad effectum non perducitur. Illo denique eleccioni nullatenus consenciente, alius, id est abbas Kalcoensis de quo post dicetur, eligitur, et Walthevus in tempore a Domino constituto in loco premonstrato dormiens[h] sepelitur.

Hec Jocelinus.   2:

G i,341
fo.118v

---

a this word added after the number of the chapter C	*d* C,DMS; principis AS
b capital R unusually decorated with a clover-leaf and a fleur-de-lys C	*e* corrected from instiucti C
c +ad C; om.D,CA	*f* interlin.C; om.DMS,AS
	g C,DMS; om.AS
	h +in Domino DMS,AS; del.C

25

The election of St Waltheof abbot of Melrose to the see of St Andrews

After Robert's death, as Jocelin the monk of Furness writes,

the episcopal see of St Andrews in Scotland was vacant, and by the
request of the people, the election of the clergy and the assent of the
princes Waltheof the saintly abbot of Melrose was chosen as pastor   [1159:
5   and bishop of their souls. Therefore the leading clergy came with some   × May]
magnates of the land to Melrose with sufficient authority to embrace
the man they had elected and bring him away with them; and the father
abbot of Rievaulx, who happened to be present then, ordered
Waltheof to comply with the election, assume the burden, and
10   undertake the office. But he excused himself on account of the
weakness of his physical powers and his inability to undertake so
weighty an employment; and he privately informed the abbot of
Rievaulx that he had not much longer to live on this earth. Replying to
those who persisted in carrying through the plan for his election which
15   had been conducted, and as the father abbot persisted in his command,
the saint spoke truthfully in a prophetic spirit: 'I have put off my robe;
how can I put it on again? I have bathed my feet; God forbid that I dirty
them again with the dust of worldly care.' And he added, saying:
'Believe me, you will elect and have a bishop other than me.' Pointing
20   his finger outside the chapter-house at Melrose, indicating his burial-
place there, he said: 'This is my resting place. Here I shall dwell as long
as the Lord pleases, since I have chosen it as a consolation for my sons.'
After these words the business was suspended; once it had been
suspended it was adjourned by a stay of proceedings, and once delayed
25   it was not carried through into effect. Once he had finally and utterly
refused to consent to the election, another (namely the abbot of Kelso,
who will be mentioned later) was elected, and Walthcof was buried at
the time chosen by the Lord, lying asleep in the place which he had   [Aug.]
pointed out.

26

De canonico nolente eleccioni de se consentire

Scriptor Quid dicemus ad hec? 'Nichil', inquit Augustinus, 'in hac vita facilius
maxime hoc tempore et lecius ac hominibus acceptabilius episcopi
dignitate aut officio presbyteri.' Sed vide quid sequitur: 'Si perfunc-
torie atque adulatorie res agatur, nichil apud Deum miserius. Nichil
est', inquit qui supra, 'in hac vita difficilius laboriosius periculosius-   5
que episcopi aut presbyteri officio. Sed nichil beacius apud Deum si eo
modo militetur quo noster imperator jubet.' Hec ille. Non ergo
mirum si^a Sancti unccione Spiritus edocti^b senciant se in pontificali
dignitate proficere posse vel ne, sicut diversimode^c in diversis exemplis
subsequentibus demonstratur. Scribit enim Barbason libro suo De   10
Apibus quod

> apud Sanctum Victorem Parisius erat quidam canonicus vita genere et
> literis precellens. Electus ergo in episcopum renuit, et pertinaci
> constancia contra plurimorum et majorum prelatorum consilium se
> substraxit. Moriturus autem post multos annos, socius quidem eius qui   15
> eum multum dilexerat adjuravit eum quatenus ad ipsum, si Deus
> permitteret, resolutus morte rediret. Annuit ille, statimque defunctus
> est. Nec dies multi post mortem eius effluxerant cum ecce anima
> secundum quod promiserat rediens, eminus in pariete signum crucis
> impressit dicens: 'Ne dubites aut vacilles in visu, sed quere quid vis, et   20
> me sinas ad pociora transire.' Mox socius ad visionem exultans,
> 'Solicitus,' inquit, 'valde fui ne gravissimam ad minus penam in
> Purgatorio sustineres, quia vitasti contra majorum consilium tam
> pertinaciter presulatum, in quo ad salutem anime tue tot et tanta facere
> potuisses.' Cui anima, 'In me', ait, 'hoc ordinavit clementissima   25
> bonitas Salvatoris, quia ex tunc timui et nunc scio [quod]^d si
> episcopatus cathedrem^e ascendissem, in perpetue dampnacionis peri-
> culum incidissem.' Et hoc dicens quasi ingenti coruscacionis lumine
> pertransivit.

Hec ille.   30
⟨Simile legimus de quodam priore Clarevallis Galfrido nomine,
qui, cum electus esset in episcopum Tornacensem et^f ab Eugenio papa
et abbate suo beato Bernardo cogeretur onus episcopatus subire,
prostratus ad pedes abbatis et clericorum qui eum elegerant in

a	+juri *CA*	*d*	*CA*
b	+senciant *del.C*	*e*	+suscepissem *del.C*
c	diversimodi *C,D*	*f*	*interlin.over* ut *del.C*

26

A canon who did not wish to consent to his own election

What shall we say about this? 'Nothing in this life', says Augustine,
'especially at this time is more bearable, more pleasing and more
acceptable to men than the dignity of bishop or the office of priest.'
But note what follows: 'If something is carried out carelessly in a
5 fawning manner, nothing is more distressing to God. Nothing', says
the same writer, 'is more difficult, burdensome and dangerous in this
life than the office of bishop or priest. But nothing gives God more
pleasure if someone serves in the way which our general directs.' It is
therefore not surprising if after instruction by the unction of the Holy
10 Spirit they feel that they can advance in the episcopal office or not, as
is demonstrated in various ways in the various examples which
follow.

For Brabantinus writes in his book *On Bees* that:

15   at St Victor in Paris there was a canon outstanding for his conduct,
        family connections and learning. Then on being elected a bishop, he
        turned it down, and with unyielding firmness withdrew against the
        advice of very many important prelates. When he was near death many
        years later, one of his friends who had a high regard for him urged him
        to pay him a visit when released by death, if God would allow it. He
20   agreed, and immediately died. Not many days had passed after his
        death when see! his spirit, returning as he had promised, imprinted the
        sign of the cross on a wall from a distance, saying: 'Do not wonder or
        hesitate at what you see, but ask for what you want, and allow me to
        move on to better things.' Soon the friend, excited at the vision, said: 'I
25   have been greatly worried lest at the least you are suffering a very heavy
        penalty in Purgatory because you so stubbornly against the advice of
        people of importance shunned a bishopric, in which you could have
        done so many great things for your salvation.' The spirit said to him:
        'The most merciful goodness of the Saviour has ordained this for me,
30   because I was fearful then, and now I know that if I had mounted the
        throne of the bishopric, I should have incurred the danger of perpetual
        damnation.' So saying, he passed right away as if with a great flash of
        light.

I have read something similar about a prior of Clairvaux called
35 Geoffrey who, when he had been elected to the see of Tournai and was
being constrained by Pope Eugenius and the blessed Bernard his
abbot to take on the burden of episcopal office, prostrated himself in
the shape of a cross at the feet of the abbot and of the clergy who had

modum crucis ait: 'Monachus fugitivus, si me eicitis, esse potero: 35
episcopus numquam ero.' Isti laboranti in extremis, quidam monachus ei carus assidens ait: 'Care frater, quia nunc corpore separ-
[amur],^{g} oro te, si potes salva Dei voluntate, ut statum tuum michi
post mortem reveles.' Cui oranti post mortem eius coram altare
apparuit Galfridus dicens: 'Ecce assum frater tuus.' Cui ille: 'Care 40
socie, quomodo est tibi?' 'Bene', inquit, 'est; sed revelatum est michi a
Sancta Trini-[ta-]te^g quod si promotus fuissem in episcopum, fuissem

G i,342   de | numero reproborum.' Nec mirum quia honores ut frequenter in
peius mutant mores. Unde dicitur:

> Plurima cum soleant hominum corrumpere mores,   45
> alcius evertunt femina,^{h} census et honores.⟩

Nec hec propterea scribimus ut presulatum condempnemus, sed, ut
in suo Pastorali scribit Ambrosius:^{i} 'Magna sublimitas magnam debet
habere cautelam, honor grandis grandiori debet solicitudine circum-
vallari, quia cui plus creditur plus ab eo exigitur, sicut scriptum est: 50
"Scienti legem et non facienti peccatum est grande; et servus sciens
voluntatem domini sui, si non fecerit eam, vapulabit multum."' Ex
quo patet quod quando constare poterit electo, quod eius ad
presulatum assumpcio placeat Deo, quamvis alias onus prelacionis
fugeret, subire debet.   55
Sicut legimus quod:

> quondam ecclesia Cinomanensis multo tempore sine vere vite pastore
> languerat, et mortuo episcopo eleccionis dies instabat. At quoniam vix
> est congregacio aliqua in personis adeo desolata, quin unum saltem
> habeat qui filiali pietate de materno defectu ecclesie doleat, et gaudeat 60
> de profectu,

---

g   D; lac.C   i   G. for Ambrosius CA
h   + se del.C

27

De canonico per inspiracionem consenciente

quidam ipsius ecclesie vere canonicus ad quandam famosissime
sanctitatis reclusam pro digno episcopo eligendo petiturus accessit.
Cuius precibus illa commota ab oracione conversa dixit: 'Carissime,
ego rapta in Celum vidi quia beata Virgo^a Maria patrona ecclesie^b

---

a   D; Virga C   b   Carissima Carissime ego quidem rapta in
                                            celum vidi quia beata Virgo Maria del.C

elected him and said: 'If you banish me, I can exist as a fugitive monk:
40 a bishop I shall never be.' When this man was at the point of death, a
monk who was dear to him sat down beside him saying: 'Dear
brother, since we are now being parted in the bodily life, I beg you, if
you can and if it is the will of God, to reveal to me your condition after
death.' Geoffrey appeared before the altar after his death to the man
45 who had made this request, saying: 'See, I your brother am here.' The
monk said to him: 'Dear companion, how is it with you?' 'I am
content,' he said, 'but it has been revealed to me by the Holy Trinity
that if I had been promoted bishop, I should have been among the
damned.' This is not surprising, because it is frequently the case that
50 honours change conduct for the worse. Hence the saying:

> Although many things commonly corrupt the conduct of
> men,
> a woman, property and honours may ruin them more
> profoundly.

55   We do not write this in order to condemn the office of bishop, but,
as Ambrose writes in his *Pastoral Care*: 'Great elevation ought to take
great care, weighty honour ought to be hedged around by weighty
concern, because the more that is entrusted to a man, the more is
expected of him, as it is written: "It is a weighty sin for someone to
60 know the law and not keep it; and if a slave who knows his master's
wishes does not follow them, he will be severely beaten."' From this it
is clear that when it becoms plain to an elect that his acceptance of a
bishopric is what God wants, he ought to give in, although he would
otherwise flee from the burden of a prelate's office.
65   We have similarly read that:

> at one time the church of Le Mans had languished for a long time
> without a pastor of integrity; and after the bishop's death the day for an
> election came round. But since scarcely any group of clergy is so short
> of persons that it does not have at least one man who out of filial piety
70   grieves at the mother church's failure and rejoices at its success,

27

The canon who was inspired to consent

one of the canons of this church indeed approached a certain recluse
who was very famous for her sanctity to ask how a worthy bishop
might be elected. Moved by his entreaties, turning from prayer she
said: 'Dear brother, I was transported into Heaven and saw that the
5   Blessed Virgin Mary, the protector of the church, when the subject was
raised, advanced to the feet of her son to ask for an answer. The son,
courteously rising to his feet, said to her: "It will be for you, my lady

prolato negocio ad pedes filii rogatura processit. Cui filius dignanter 5
assurgens, "Tuum", inquit, "erit,^{c} mater et domina, statuere quem-
cumque volueris." Secedens ergo mater Christi cum angelis sanctis
quasi de negocio tractatura, tandem reversa dixit: "Placet michi, fili, de
consilio beatorum Mauricium quondam archidiaconum Trecensem^d in
episcopum prefici Cenomannis." Et filius, "Digne", inquid, "elegisti; 10
sic fiat.'" Et mox reclusa canonico: 'Vide ergo, carissime, ut secretum
habeas quousque^e factum sit quod vidisti.'

fo.119
Hic | Mauricius archidiaconus circuibat diocesim pedes, et eam in
solo baculo predicacionis [officio] visitabat. Archidiaconatu postmodum derelicto, monasterium nigrarum monialium (quarum elemosinis 15
nutritus fuerat adhuc puer) expeciit, ut eas ad emendaciorem vitam
corrigeret, et rudem pro tempore terre populum predicacionibus
erudiret. Nec eum fefellit effectus. Quid plura? Ad eleccionem ventum
est Cenomannis. Electi sunt duo, prepositus scilicet et decanus,
quorum primus vir sensatus est et nobilis, alter vero literatus et dives. 20
Neutro igitur altri volente cedere, dixit decano prepositus: 'Michi
quidem episcopatum expedire non video, sed nec tibi. Michi sufficit
honor, tibi divicie. Cedere tibi nolo, nec tu michi. Nichil ergo restat nisi
iam in parte dilapidatam ecclesiam per nostrum litigium funditus

G i,343
enervari. Vellem igitur, | si velletis et vos, ut inter nos virum probatum 25
et humilem concorditer postulemus, qui confusionis nostre ruinas velit
et valeat restaurare. Ecce venerabilis ille Mauricius, vir in omni norma
justicie singulariter decoratus, qui eciam totum mundum posset divina^f
providencia gubernare. Presto sum cum meis omnibus tantum
hominem postulare, et credo cercius quod Deo et saluti sue adversabi- 30
tur contradicens.' Mox decanus subridens, 'Sic fiat,' inquit. 'sed hac
condicione: si idem episcopatum acceptare noluerit, michi cedat.' Cui
mox prepositus exultabundus inclamat: 'Ratificetur et fiat.' Et mox
facta postulacio consensu omnium est firmata. Decanus presumebat
numquam acceptare^g Mauricium presulatum: prepositus vero dignius 35
presumebat sanctum virum, Christi amore coactum propter salutem
multorum, non audere respuere tantum oblatum. Missi ergo duo
canonici invenerunt eum secundum quod solebat in via^h peditem ad
predicandum euntem. Literis sue vocacionis ostensis, respondit ille:
'Ibitis ad hospicium vestrum. Vespere facta predicacione redibo, et 40
mane quod Dominus dederit respondebo.' Factum est sic. Redeunti-
bus illis ad hospicium, processit ille, predicavit, audivit impransus
confessiones usque ad vesperam, redit domum, salutat hospites,
incenatus oratorium petit, pernoctat celebs in precibus, respondit
mane canonicis: 'Consilium Dei et matris eius est: Negare non convenit 45
quod offertis.' Quid plura? Condigno honore receptus cathedratur,
consecratur, et tanto regimine claruit ut infra quingentos annos
preteritos similis ei fuisse non creditur.

c   + et *del.C*
d   Trecacensem *C,D,CA*
e   adusque *corrected from* adhusque *C*

f   digna *C,D,CA*
g   *corrected from* accaptare *C*
h   + peditum *del.C*

mother, to appoint whomsoever you wish." Christ's mother therefore withdrew along with some holy angels to discuss the business; and at length returned saying: "My son, on the advice of the blessed ones, it is my wish that Maurice formerly archdeacon of Troyes be appointed bishop of Le Mans." And the son said: "You have made a worthy choice; so be it."' And next the recluse said to the canon: 'See therefore, dear brother, that you keep what you have seen secret until it is achieved.'

This Maurice as archdeacon used to go round the diocese on foot, and visited it as a preacher bearing just his staff. Later, after abandoning the archdeaconry, he sought out a convent of black nuns (by whose charity he had been brought up while still a boy), so that he might admonish them in the direction of a more perfect life, and so that he might through his preaching teach the ignorant people of the district in accordance with the needs of the time. And the outcome did not disappoint him.

To be brief – the election came round at Le Mans. There was a double election, namely of the provost and the dean, of whom the first was intelligent and of noble birth, and the other was well-read and rich. When therefore neither was willing to give way to the other, the provost said to the dean: 'I appreciate that the bishopric is not useful for me, nor for you. I have honour enough, and you have wealth. I am unwilling to give way to you, and you to me. The only outcome therefore now in this matter is that an already partly devastated church is being completely weakened as a result of our dispute. I would prefer therefore, if you also were willing, that between us we would agree on postulating a man of good reputation and modest standing, who would be willing and able to restore our disastrous and confused situation. Such a man is the venerable Maurice, a man singularly honoured by every standard of holiness, who could rule even the whole world under divine providence. I am ready to postulate such a man with all my resources, and I certainly believe that anyone who objects will be acting contrary to God and his own salvation.' Then the dean smiled and said: 'So be it, but with this condition: if this man declines to accept the bishopric, he should make way for me.' Then the provost triumphantly shouted to him: 'Let this be ratified and carried out.' And soon the postulation was made and confirmed with everyone's consent. The dean assumed that Maurice would never accept the bishopric: the provost to be sure assumed more worthily that the saintly man, motivated by love of Christ for the salvation of many, would not dare to reject so great an office when it was offered.

Two canons therefore were sent and found him according to his habit walking on the road on his way to a preaching engagement. When he had been shown the letter containing his call, he replied: 'You will go to your lodging. I shall return this evening after my preaching, and in the morning I shall give the answer which the Lord has provided.' So it was done. They returned to their lodging; he went on his way; he preached; while still fasting he heard confessions until the evening; he returned home and greeted his guests; dinnerless he made for his oratory and spent the night alone at prayer; and in the morning he gave his answer to the canons: 'This is the advice of God and his

28

Quomodo Walthevus episcopari renuit

Scriptor

Sicut igitur ut estimo iste Mauricius Spiritu Sancto revelante prescivit se non debere restitisse vocacioni sue et canonicus de Sancto Victore cum salute propria consentire dedignasse,*a* sic Walthevum eodem Spiritu informatum reor de non acceptando episcopatum, sed illum pocius fugiendo meliorem contemplacionis partem cum Maria 5 elegisse ab eodem nequaquam auferendam; quia juxta dictum Jocelinum cum isdem Walthevus canonicus existens regularis prioris adhuc officio in Kirkhame sine querela fungeretur,

crevit et crebuit circumcirca eiusdem religionis fama, aromatizans salutaris suavitatem odoris. Huius haustu attracti clerici Eboracensis 10 ecclesie et diocesani magnates illius provincie, cum vacaret episcopalis sedes, in archiepiscopum illum libenter eligerent, si principis assensum haberent. Rex enim Stephanus licet eum diligeret et veneraretur, sciens eum virum justum et sanctum, timuit tamen ne, si archipresul efficeretur, regi David faveret, et cum eodem secundum posse foveret 15 partes Henrici adversarii eius, cui sceptrum Anglie jure hereditario competebat. Hac de causa non solum eleccioni eius assensum*b* non prebuit, sed ne id fieret omnino prohibuit. Quidam tamen optimatum |

G i,344

qui erant a secretis regis ipsum super hoc sepius convenerunt, et ad hoc ipso priore ignorante*c* inclinare studuerunt. Unde quadam vice comes 20 Albemarlie consanguineus eius conveniens virum interloquendum dixit ad eum: 'Quamdiu latitando in antro claustri tui prosapiam nostram inhonoras abjeccione tui? Effer te in publicum frequenter. Donis et promissis nancisci satage familiaritatem et amorem regis, graciam consiliariorum eius et auxilium, ut ad decus et exaltacionem 25 generis tui episcopatum acquiras. Qualemcumque caucionem volueris, prestabo me tibi impetraturum a rege Eboraci archiepiscopalem cathedram, si michi concesseris villam Schireburniam tantum in vita

fo.119v

mea de te tenendam.' Quo audito vir | sanctus in spiritu vehementi prius comitem redarguens, et de periculo heresis simoniace insinuans 30 inter cetera correptoria subintulit dicens: 'Non ob consanguinitatem mee promocionis queris sublimitatem, sed pocius tuam transitoriam utilitatem, nec honorem meum, sed tuum lucrum. Fixum ergo teneas,

---

a   noluisse *CA*   *c*   + regium animum *AS*
b   *corrected from* assū *C*

60   mother: It is not becoming to decline what you offer.' Need more be
          said? He was received with appropriate honour, enthroned and
          consecrated; and was so famed for the conduct of his office that there is
          thought to have been no one like him in the last five hundred years.

28

How Waltheof refused to become a bishop

In my view therefore, just as that Maurice knew beforehand by a
disclosure of the Holy Spirit that he should not reject his call, and the
canon of St Victor knew to refuse to consent for his own salvation, so
I think that Waltheof was instructed by the same Spirit not to accept
5   the bishopric, but rather by fleeing from it to have chosen with Mary
the better part of contemplation, which was by no means to be taken
away from him, because, according to the said Jocelin, when the same
Waltheof as a regular canon discharged the office of prior while still at
Kirkham without complaint,

10   the fame of his religious life increased and spread all around, wafting
          the sweet fragrance that brings eternal bliss. Attracted by the scent of
          this man, the clergy of the church of York and the magnates of the
          dioceses of that province, when the episcopal see was vacant, would
          willingly have elected him as archbishop, if [only] they had had the   [1140]
15   consent of the prince. For although King Stephen loved and respected
          him, knowing him to be a just and saintly man, he nevertheless feared
          lest, if he were made archbishop, he would show partiality to King
          David, and with him give as much support as he could to the party of
          Stephen's adversary Henry, to whom authority over England belonged
20   by hereditary right. For this reason he not only did not offer his consent
          to Waltheof's election, but he entirely forbade its taking place.
          Nevertheless some of the nobles who were in the king's confidence met
          with him often on this matter, and while the prior himself remained in
          ignorance, worked to incline his mind towards it.
25   Hence on one occasion the count of Aumale, Waltheof's kinsman,
          on meeting the man spoke to him by way of conversation: 'How long,
          by hiding in your cave of a cloister, are you to dishonour our family by
          your self-abasement? Get out and about frequently. Apply yourself to
          obtain the friendship and love of the king with gifts and promises, the
30   goodwill and help of his counsellors, so that you may acquire a
          bishopric and bring honour and glory to your family. Whatever kind of
          security you may require, I shall make it my business to obtain for you
          from the king the archiepiscopal throne of York, if you will grant me
          the township of Sherburn to be held of you just for my lifetime.' On
35   hearing this the saintly man in a spirited and forceful way first refuted
          the count, then hinted at the danger of simoniacal heresy, and among
          other things added reproaches saying: 'You are not seeking my high

te numquam me visurum cathedre pontificali presidentem' Comes,
vatidico hoc verbo velut telo percussus, cum^d rubore recessit, et verbum 35
ex ore sancti prolatum perpetua veritate subnixum stetit.

d + ro *del.C*

29

Quomodo, ne episcopus fieret, monachum se fecit Hugo c'

Scriptor   Ne igitur blandientis seculi alluderetur episcopalis dignitatis fastigiis
tumentibus, arcciorem regulam statuit in animo experiri (sicut infra
dicetur), et ad modum

> venerabilis Hugonis Cameracensis decani, viri in omnibus honestate et
> generis nobilitate clarissimi, qui,^{a} cum in diversarum ecclesiarum 5
> episcopatibus se principari formidaret,^{b} nec posset subterfugere sedis
> apostolice jussioni, derelictis omnibus monasterium ordinis Cister-
> ciensis in Vacellis ingredi cogitavit. Cumque proposito declarato,
> ancipitrem peroptimum quem habebat multi nobiles peterent, mira
> curialitate dissimulavit; et veniens ad portam cenobii monachus mox 10
> futurus, ancipitrem pedum vinculis solvit, et ad auras^c libere avolare
> permisit, dicens:

> Hic te dimitto laxum, placidaque^d remitto
> libertate frui pro bonitate tui.

> Nec mora; multi dimissum ancipitrem capere vel revocare conantes 15
> frustrati sunt quia nusquam comparuit. Et hoc quidem in moribus
> aliquando dispensacione Dei permittitur perfectis, ut in avibus celi
> ludant horis et temporibus congruis, ne temptacionum diversorum
> fluctibus subruantur. Hic receptus in monachum, sed et in mensa
> novicius sedens, passerem advolantem ad manus eius panis minuciis 20
> pascere solebat. Super quo a magistro noviciorum lepide semel
> redargutus, hiis versibus passerem secundum consuetudinem secum
> garrientem alloquitur dicens:

G i,345   Passer abi, nec habe mirum quod abire rogaris.
> Etas, ordo jubet me michi, non tibi me.   25

> Hic in antea forma et speculum conversandi factus consociis, maluit
> esse novissumus et abjectus in domo Domini, et sub regula latere^e

a	*interlin.C*	d	placid'que *C,D*
b	formidavit *C,D*	e	+ sub *del.C*
c	*corrected from* aures *C*		

promotion out of family feeling, but rather because of its passing
advantage to you, not as an honour for me, but as profit for you. You
40   may therefore regard it as certain that you will never see me presiding
from a bishop's throne.' The count was struck by this prophetic
statement as by an arrow, and retired shamefacedly; and the statement
which the saint uttered has remained confirmed as a true prophecy for
ever.

29

How Hugh became a monk to avoid being made a bishop etc.

To avoid therefore being the plaything of a flattering world for the
inflated heights of an episcopal dignity, Waltheof made up his mind to
try out a stricter rule (as is mentioned below). This was in the manner

5   of the venerable Hugh dean of Cambrai, a man honest in everything
and a noble from a most distinguished family, who, since he dreaded
ruling as bishop of various churches, and could not escape from a
command of the apostolic see, planned to leave everything behind and
enter the monastery of the Cistercian order at Vaucelles. And when,
10   after he had declared his intention, many nobles sought an excellent
hawk which he possessed, he disguised his purpose with wonderful
courtesy; and when he came to the gate of the monastery on the point of
becoming a monk, he freed the hawk from the chains on its feet, and let
it fly away aloft freely, saying:

15   Here I let you loose, and I set you free
to enjoy your liberty in peace, as a reward for your good
conduct.

No time was lost; many who tried to capture and recall the freed hawk
were disappointed because it was not found anywhere. And this indeed
by a divine dispensation is sometimes allowed to those who are perfect
20   in their behaviour, that they play at suitable times and seasons among
the birds of the sky lest they be overwhelmed by the waves of various
temptations.
When Hugh had been received as a monk, but was still at the novices'
table, he used to feed a sparrow that flew on to his hands with little
25   pieces of bread. Once when he was mildly rebuked for this by the
master of the novices, he addressed the sparrow who was chattering
with him as usual wih these lines of verse:

Go away sparrow, and do not wonder that you are asked to
go away.
30   Superior age and rank give me orders for myself, but not for
you.

He who had once been a model and mirror of behaviour for his fellows
preferred to be the most junior and unimportant in the house of the

habitu monachali, quam in tabernaculis potentum et peccatorum
pontificali infula decorari.

Sic et noster Walthevus fugiens prelacionem, nesciens et invite subivit   30
eam, sicut in sequentibus declarabo. Jocelinus:

Augebatur de die in diem contemptus mundialis pompe in corde viri,*f*
et desiderium celestis patrie accrescens*g* animo; statuit,*h* desiderio
diutino circumspecte*i* diliberato libramine, religionis arccioris se velle
viam arripere.   35

---

f   contemptus ... viri C *follows word-order of*   *h*   animoque statuit fixum *for* animo statuit
      DMS rather than AS   *DMS,AS*
g   om.*DMS,AS*   *i*   *DMS,AS*; cirspeccionis *C*;
                                                              circumspeccionis *D*

30

Quomodo Walthevus de canonico se monachum fecit

Velle sibi adjacebat de minoribus ad majora conscendere, et cum beato
Job per singulos gradus suos Deum pronunciare. Desiderabat de
canonicatu ad monachatum, et maxime Cisterciensis ordinis, qui sibi
videbatur ceteris austerior et arcior habitu et actu progredi. Sed
verebatur, ut referre solebat, virium suarum imbecillitati, tali et tanto   5
oneri nimis incompetenti. Consuluit*a* ergo crebro*b* super hoc magni
consilii angelum devote, ut spiritu consilii et fortitudinis illustraret et
corroboraret spiritum suum, ad eligendum sapienter et tenendum
fortiter, quod salubrius*c* foret anime sue. Timebat ne forte angelus
Sathane, qui se sepe transfigurat in angelum lucis, in calice aureo   10
venenum sibi propinaret, et sub ascensus annisu, quod in pluribus
perpendit et prospexit, precipicium palliaret. Sed cum columpna cordis
staret immobilis*d* in tali proposito, intellexit vir spiritualis ad hoc corde
conceptum se visitatum et invitatum a Domino. Et sicut cervus
desiderat ad fontes aquarum, sic anima eius ad*e* Deum fontem vivum.   15
Et continuo Wardoniam se transtulit, ingressu monachatus petito et
impetrato, habitum mutavit, et probatorium intravit. Quod audiens
comes Simon germanus eius ira totus incanduit, et illum sibi et cunctis
amicis suis pronuncians perditum, totique cenobio de Wardonia cum
fo.120   juramento terrifico | consumptorium,*f* si illum ulterius retinerent*g*,   20
minabatur incendium. Abbas autem et conventus de Wardonia,
agnoscentes comitem prefatum ad malum proclivem, et iram eius ut

---

a   +que *del.C*   *DMS*; immobilis *AS*
b   *D*; crebe *corrected to* crebo *C*   *e*   *interlin.C*
c   -lu- *interlin.C*   *f*   *AS*; consentorium *C,D,DMS*
d   *corrected from* immolabilis *C*; immolabilis   *g*   *C,DMS*; retineret *AS*

35   Lord, and to live in obscurity in a monastic habit under a rule, rather than be adorned with episcopal insignia in the dwellings of the powerful and of sinners.

So also our Waltheof, while avoiding a prelate's office, unknowingly and unwillingly assumed it, as I shall explain later.

Jocelin says:

40   Contempt for worldly pomp was intensified in the man's heart from day to day, as the desire for his heavenly home grew in his mind. After carefully weighing his long-felt desire in the balance, he decided that he wanted to adopt the way of a stricter religious life.

30

How Waltheof became a monk instead of a canon

In addition he wanted to climb from lesser to greater things, and like the blessed Job to proclaim God at each of his steps. He longed to progress from being a canon to being a monk, and especially one of the Cistercian Order, which seemed to him to be more austere and strict
5   than the others in its apparel and activities. But he viewed with apprehension (as he used to say) the weakness of his physical powers, as too inadequate for a burden of this kind and magnitude. He therefore frequently and faithfully consulted the Angel of Great Counsel to enlighten and strengthen his spirit with the spirit of counsel
10   and fortitude in the matter of choosing wisely and upholding courageously what would be salutary for his soul. He was afraid lest by chance an angel of Satan (who often masquerades as an angel of light) might give him poison to drink in a golden chalice, and conceal a precipice under the effort of the ascent, something which he [Waltheof]
15   considered and foresaw in many things. But since his heart stood firm as a pillar regarding such a plan, the spiritual part of the man understood that he had been visited and invited by the Lord to this heartfelt idea. And just as a deer longs for springs of water, so did his soul long for God as a living spring.
20   Without more ado Waltheof moved to Warden after requesting and   [1143: Aug.
being granted entry to the monastic life, he changed his habit, and   × 1145:
entered the novices' quarters. When his brother Earl Simon heard of   Aug.]
this, he became extremely heated with anger. Pronouncing Waltheof as
lost to himself and all his friends, he threatened destruction by fire to
25   the whole monastery of Warden with a terrifying oath, if they kept him
any longer. Now the abbot and convent of Warden knew of the said
earl's inclination towards evil and of his wrath as the roaring of a lion,
and feared that they were going to incur severe damage to their house at

leonis fremitum, formidabant sese incursuros per illum sue domus
dampnum perniciosum. Communicato[h] tandem consilio prudentum,[i]
ipso consenciente ob temporis maliciam mitigandam, donec transiret   25
iniquitas miserunt eum Rievallem, suam videlicet matrem, in quo loco
vel eius vicinia prefatus comes nullam nocendi vel efficacem habuit
prohibendi potestatem. Cum itaque in probatorio peregisset aliquanti
temporis spacium, antiquo serpente sibilante, ordinis arrepti observan-
cia vertebatur illi in fastidium. Videbatur illi potus et cibus insipidus,   30
asper et vilis vestitus, labor manualis durus, vigiliarum et psalmodie
protelacio[j] gravis, | ac totus ordinis tenor nimis austerus. Recogitans
autem annos pristinos in canonicatu vel prioratu suo, persuasum
habuit in mente instituciones illorum licet leniores discrecioni tamen
viciniores esse, ac per hoc salvandis animabus apciores. Cum autem in   35
corde huiusmodi serpere sensisset venenum, jugis ac devote oracionis
opposuit antitodum. Sed cum nec sic minueretur temptacio, sed pocius
cresceret, ita ut ordinem Cisterciensem deserere et ad canonicatum
reverti deliberasset, tandem[k] respiciente Domino, in se confusus
erubuit, et contra faciem suam se statuit.   40

G i,346

h C,DMS; convocato AS	j om.AS
i prudencium DMS,AS	k om.AS

31

Quomodo de temptacione ereptus abbas efficitur

Quadam namque die, pulsante[a] signo ad horam canonicam, egressis
secundum ritum noviciis ceteris, solus in cella remansit, et impetu
Spiritus ductus in ostii limine[b] se proiciens, caput, scapulas, brachia,
ventrem intro, nates, coxas, tibias ac pedes extra posuit, et orans cum
lacrimis dixit: 'Deus omnipotens, omnium conditor, omnium et   5
dispositor, utrum voluntati tue placeat, ut in monachatu maneam aut
ad canonicatum redeam, da ostensionem; et aufer a me animam meam
affligentem temptacionem.' Cum hec et huiusmodi proferendo Deum
deprecaretur, subito, nullum videns, nullum tactum senciens, divina
tantummodo gracia et virtute vectus[c] ad sedem in qua meditari et legere   10
solebat transponitur. Ab illa hora quamdiu vixit, tali temptacione
caruit, et quicquid austerum et grave videbatur in ordine sibi leve ac
levius[d] deinceps fuit, quia jugum Domini suave ac onus eius leve sensit.
Sic, sic Christus noster Heliseus quicquid in olla cordis electi sui
amarum sapuit, injecta farinula gracie sue dulcoravit. Miro modera-   15
mine mirabilis Deus hunc, quem ad regimen animarum provehere
disposuit, hac[e] temptacione fatigari[f] permisit ad corone videlicet

a C,DMS; pulsato AS	e +temperacione fatigacionis del.C
b C,DMS; limen AS	f temptacione fatigari C,AS; fatigacione
c C,DMS; tractus AS	temptans DMS
d C; dulce DMS; bene AS	

his hands. At length, after discussion with some men of experience, and
30   with his agreement, with a view to alleviating the evil threatening at
that moment, they sent him to their mother-house at Rievaulx until the
difficulty blew over. There and in its vicinity the said earl had no
effective means of doing harm or interfering.

When therefore he had spent a considerable time in the novices'
35   quarters, with the old serpent hissing, he developed a distaste for the
observance of the order which he had adopted. The drink and food
seemed insipid to him, the dress rough and cheap, the manual labour
hard, the prolonged vigils and psalm-singing wearisome, and all the
aims of the order too austere. Then reflecting on his earlier years as a
40   canon or prior, he became persuaded in his own mind that the
arrangements associated with these activities, although easier, were
nevertheless nearer to prudence, and for this reason more appropriate
for the saving of souls. But when he felt this kind of poison creeping
into his heart, he responded with the antidote of constant and devout
45   prayer. Yet when the temptation did not lessen in this way, but rather
increased to the extent that he considered leaving the Cistercian Order
and returning to being a canon, in the end as the Lord looked on he
blushed in confusion at himself, and judged himself to his own face.

31

How he was delivered from temptation and was made an abbot

For one day, when the bell was ringing for a service, and the other
novices had left in the usual way, he remained alone in his cell; led by
the urging of the Spirit he prostrated himself on the threshold of the
door, placing his head, shoulders, arms and belly inside, and his
5   buttocks, hips, legs and feet outside. Then he prayed tearfully saying:
'Almighty God, maker of all things, and disposer of all things, show me
whether it is your will that I remain as a monk or return to being a
canon; and take from me the temptation that is distressing my soul.'
While he was praying to God expressing these and similar words,
10   suddenly, seeing nothing and feeling no touch, he was transported to
the seat where he usually meditated and read, conveyed only by divine
grace and power. From that hour as long as he lived, he was free from
such temptation, and whatever seemed hard and oppressive in the
order was henceforth light for him, and all the lighter because he felt
15   the yoke of the Lord to be easy to bear and his load light. Thus, thus,
whatever tasted bitter in the pot of the heart of the man he had chosen,
Christ as our Elisha has sweetened by the insertion of a little meal of his
grace. By a strange management of affairs God, the source of wonder,
allowed this man, whom he intended to advance towards the rule of
20   souls, to be troubled by this temptation as if to increase his crown; and
his own experience would teach him how he ought to have compassion
and pity for the tempted and afflicted. Therefore after the rubble of

augmentum, et qualiter temptatis et afflictis compati ac misereri
deberet, proprium edoceret experimentum.*g* Venerabilis igitur Walthevus, erutis ruderibus temptacionum, instar jugeris optimi, opimum   20
fructum in agro dominico deinceps protulit; et tractus a sponso in
odorem unguentorum eius, velociter et delectabiliter cucurrit. Post
anni ergo circulum in probatorio expletum, juxta*h* regulam beati
Benedicti habitu et actu induit monachatum;*i* et, ut breviter dicam,
tocius sanctitatis in se evidens expressit exemplum. Circa idem tempus   25
Richardus primus abbas de Melros vir vite insignis abbacie renunciavit, et Walthevus unanimi consensu cunctorum electus, quamvis
nimium renitens, virtute tandem obediencie a patre abbate constrictus,
in pastorali cura illi successit ⟨anno domini m° c° xlviii.⟩ Dilectus et
electus Domini Walthevus abbas effectus nomen re*j* et officium opere et   30
veritate adimplevit, quia non in eo magni umbra nominis, sed veritas
apparuit. Comes vero Simon frater eius, cum ab eo sepius corriperetur

G i,347

ob nimios excessus eius, rubore salubri | perfusus,*k* vitam correctoriam
arripuit, pro preteritis piaculis perpetratis penitens, et a perpetrandis
abstinens, pro eorum expiacione, consultacione sui fratris, monachis   35
ordinis Cluniacensis monasterium Sanctiandree Northamtonie,*l* et
monasterium sanctimonialium*m* extra opidum fundavit, redditus
ampliavit, atque multa bona contulit. Cenobium eciam Cisterciensis
ordinis, scilicet Saltreiam, fundavit; abbatem et conventum de
Wardonia, ab abbate Simone sancto viro directum, ibidem locavit.   40
Tandem more Christiano facto testamento, in dicta ecclesia Sanctiandr', quam fundaverat, humatus requiescit. Cuius epitaphium hiis
versibus quidam, eo quod miles in armis strenuus, sapiens et pulcher
erat, describens sic ait:

fo.120v

Dantur item fato, casuque ruunt iterato,   45
Simone sublato, Mars, Paris atque Cato.

---

g operimentum *D*	*k* *C,DMS*; suffusus *AS*
h *om.AS*	*l* *first* -t- *interlin.C*
i *C,DMS*; monachum *AS*	*m* +Sancte Marie *DMS,AS*
j *C,DMS*; rem *AS*	

32

Quod hortatu Walthevi Henricus comes
et Malcolmus filius eius fundaverunt cenobia

Alius autem germanus sancti abbatis, Henricus comes de Huntyndon
filius David regis, optemperans eius hortatui preclaram abbaciam
vocabulo Holcoltran, quam pater eius fundavit, amplis possessionibus
locupletavit; conventum de Melros assumptum per abbatem Walthevum illuc destinavit, cui virum vite venerabilis Everardum nomine ab   5
eis electum abbatem prefecit. Erat isdem Everardus a puericia divinis
obsequiis mancipatus in canonicatu, virum Dei pre ceteris canonicis
arccius amans in Christo, et ad monachatum secutus, in Melrosensi

temptation had been cleared away, the venerable Waltheof like the best
acre of ground henceforth brought forth rich fruit in the Lord's field;
25   and drawn by the Bridegroom he ran speedily with delight towards the
fragrance of His perfumes. After completing a full year in the novices'
quarters, therefore, he assumed the monastic life in dress and
behaviour according to the rule of the blessed Benedict; and (to cut a
long story short) he exhibited in himself a clear model of utter sanctity.
30   About the same time Richard, the first abbot of Melrose, a man of
distinguished life, resigned the abbacy, and Waltheof was elected by
the unanimous consent of everyone. Although extremely resistant, he
was in the end compelled by the father-abbot by virtue of his
obedience, and succeeded to that pastoral charge in 1148. Beloved and   1148
35   chosen of the Lord, once he had become abbot Waltheof lived up to his
name in fact, and to his office in deed and in truth, because in him it was
not the shadow of a great name that appeared, but the reality. His
brother Earl Simon, indeed, after being often rebuked by him for his
excessive sins, embraced a reformed life suffused with salutary blushes.
40   Repenting for the sins he had previously committed, and refraining
from committing more, on the advice of his brother he founded St
Andrew's monastery for monks of the Cluniac Order at Northampton
and a monastery for nuns outside the town as expiation for these sins.   [ca 1145]
He increased the revenues [of these houses] and conferred many goods
45   [on them]. He founded also a monastery of the Cistercian Order at   [1147]
Sawtry, and settled there an abbot and convent sent from Warden by
the saintly Abbot Simon. At length as a good Christian he made his
will, was buried and rests in the said church of St Andrew that he had
founded. Because he was a knight vigorous in arms, wise and
50   handsome, his epitaph contains these lines describing him thus:

When Simon died, martial prowess, beauty and integrity
die also, and perish in a second misfortune.

32

With Waltheof's encouragement Earl Henry
and his son Malcolm founded monasteries

Another brother of the saintly abbot, Henry earl of Huntingdon the
son of King David, in obedience to his encouragement enriched with
extensive possessions the splendid abbey called Holm Cultram, which
his father founded; he sent there a community from Melrose chosen by   [1150]
5   Abbot Waltheof, for which he appointed as abbot a man of venerable
life called Everard after he had been elected by them. The same Everard
had been from boyhood destined for divine service as a canon; he loved
the man of God in Christ more profoundly than the other canons, and

cenobio eiusdem capellanus conscius secretorum sancti est effectus.
Hic multis annorum circulis*a* vivens, domum cui prefuit interius ad   10
magne religionis culmen erexit, et exterius prediis et possessionibus
ditatam in altum provexit; sicque plenus dierum et virtutum in
senectute bona ibidem in Domino requievit.*b* Rex autem David,
diversorum ordinum ac multiplicium religionum in terra sua fundator
devotus, ac multorum monasteriorum plantator egregius, eodem   15
sancto abbate ipsius privigno*c* persuadente, in Morevia cenobium
construxit*d* Kinlos nomine, et abbatem ac conventum de Melros illuc*e*
adduxit. Sed priusquam locum illum, sicut disposuerat, attolleret in
sublime, mors festina nimis*f* regem de medio tulit. Ada*g* eciam
comitissa conjunx*h* fratris sui Henrici post obitum mariti ad instigacio-   20
nem, ut dicitur,*i* ⟨eiusdem⟩ abbatis Walthevi, Cisterciensis ordinis
fundavit monasterium monialium de Hadyngtona. Malcolmus vero
rex nepos abbatis sancti in puericia et juventute ante regnum et in regno
constitutus, monitis ipsius et imperio obsecundans, vitam suam ad eius
arbitrium ac mores composuit, domum ac regnum disposuit. Extans   25
enim equivolus, justicie judicium equilibre inter virum et virum tenuit,
censuram legum inflexibilem adversus | latrones predones et proditores
exercens, secundum apostolum se non sine causa gladium portare
opere probavit. Ceterum quod*j* religionis, quod sanctitatis, quod
morum, quod virtutis sub habitu seculari exercuit, virginitatis decus   30
usque ad tumulum perseverans, Deo presentavit. Hic ad nutum abbatis
sancti patrui sui abbaciam ordinis Cisterciensis fundare promisit,
locum providit,*k* et Cupram vocabulo assignavit. Sed tamen, ob
quedam negocia inevitabilia emergencia, aliquantulum opus differre
comodum duxit. Quocirca abbas interim metas vivendi faciens, illuc   35
abbatem et conventum non direxit, sed succesori suo illud peragendum
reliquit. Fundatur enim anno domini m° c lxiiii*to*. Nullatenus sanctus
iste Walthevus in hac parte a participio*l* premii privatur, cuius
hortamento, sive incitamento, hii preclari principes premissi ad opera
tam*m* commemorabilia perficienda efficaciter inducebantur. Hic qua-   40
tuor cenobia, quasi quatuor flumina de Paradiso, Cisterciensis ordinis,
in ablucionem*n* peccatorum et animarum refrigerium, produxit Fons
Vite per huius servi sui Walthevi ministerium.

G i,348

a	C,DMS; curriculis AS	*h*	D; conjux C
b	C,DMS; requiescit AS	*i*	+ dicti del.C
c	AS; privilegio C,D,DMS	*j*	+ erat DMS,AS
d	+ in del.C	*k*	D; previdit C
e	+ conduxit del.C	*l*	DMS,AS; principio C,D
f	C,DMS; om.AS	*m*	+ mirabilia del.C
g	Adam C,D	*n*	DMS,AS; ablucione C,D

followed him into the monastic life; as his chaplain in the monastery of
Melrose, he became privy to the saint's inner thoughts. This Everard,
as he lived through the changing seasons of many years, brought the
house over which he presided to a high standard on the spiritual side
and in the conduct of the religious life, and advanced it to a peak on the
material side, enriched by lands and possessions; and thus, when full of
days and virtues, he rested in the Lord at a great age.

King David indeed, as the pious founder of numerous religious
houses of various orders in his land, and an outstanding planter of
many monasteries, on the urging of the same saintly abbot his stepson
built a house called Kinloss in Moray, and brought there an abbot and   [1150]
community from Melrose. But before he could raise that place to the
level he had planned, too premature a death bore the king away from
this world.

The Countess Ada also, the wife of Waltheof's brother Henry, after
the death of her husband, and at the instigation (it is said) of the same
Abbot Waltheof, founded the monastery at Haddington for nuns of   [× 1159]
the Cistercian Order.

King Malcolm moreover, the nephew of the saintly abbot, both
during his boyhood and youth before he became king and when he was
in office, in compliance with the abbot's advice and bidding organized
his life and managed his household and kingdom in accordance with
his wishes and his ways. Being by nature fair-minded, he maintained
impartial judgment in matters of justice between man and man; and
applying the inflexible sentence of the laws against robbers, brigands
and traitors, he proved by his deeds (in the words of the apostle) that he
did not hold the power of the sword for nothing. Moreover what
quality of religious observance, what holiness, what habits, what virtue
he displayed as a layman, he offered to God, persisting in the glory of
virginity until the grave. At the suggestion of the saintly abbot his uncle
he promised to found an abbey of the Cistercian Order, he provided a
site and made it over under the name of Coupar. Yet when some   [1159]
unavoidable business arose, he thought it desirable to delay the work
for a little, and in consequence, since the abbot was meanwhile
reaching the end of his life, it was not he who arranged for an abbot and
convent to go there, but it was left to his successor to complete the
arrangements. This foundation was in 1164.   1164

This Saint Waltheof should on no account be deprived of a share in
the reward in this connection, for it was by his encouragement and
stimulus that these aforesaid distinguished princes were sufficiently
persuaded to achieve such praiseworthy undertakings. The Fountain
of Life through the agency of his servant Waltheof brought into
existence the four monasteries of the Cistercian Order mentioned here,
like the four rivers of Paradise, for the washing away of sins and the
refreshment of souls.

33

De elomosinarum^a eius opere

Licet predictarum et aliarum virtutum conventus in hoc Dei homine*^b*
sue mansionis stabile construxerat habitaculum, misericordia erga
pauperes et infirmos ipsum sibi*^c* sic vendicavit totum, quasi natus ad
eius solius obsequium exercicium et*^d* usum fuisset. Merito proinde illi
congruit quod beatus Job de se sentenciose pronunciando dicit: 5
'Mecum crevit miseracio, et ex utero egressa est mecum.' Unde vir
sanctus non solum sanus, verum eciam multociens*^e* laborans in
infirmitate, quandoque baculo innixus, quandoque filiorum ulnis
sustentatus, infirmitoria non solum monachorum et conversorum, sed
et pauperum et hospitum visitare*^f* cotidie consuevit; et a singulis 10
sciscitatus*^g* quid appeterent, quo indigerent,*^h* et unicuique que necessaria erant, utroque*ⁱ* homini diligenter amministrari fecit. Omni
tempore, et maxime famis prevalentis super terram, cum innumera
multitudo pauperum vite sue consultura conflueret ad Melros ob vite
necessaria sive victualia percipienda, vir Dei, non parcens bobus et 15
ovibus vel porcis, omnium inopie prout potuit subvenire solebat. Unde
et cum egencium victualia deficerent abbatis sufficiencia, ipse Fons
Misericordie sepius copiosa sui largiflui muneris miraculose satis
adimplevit affluencia, sicut sequens declarabit narracio. Quodam
tempore, ingruente extinctorie famis calamitate, con- | fluxerat ad 20
Melros inopum turba copiosa ut putabatur numero*^j* quatuor milium,
construxeruntque*^k* sibi tugurria seu tabernacula in campis et silvis circa
cenobium ad spacium duorum miliarium. Abbas more solito cum
quibusdam fratribus et cellerario, nomine Thoma*^l*, re et cognomento
Bono, exiit ut videret multitudinem hanc magnam. Quam ut vidit, 25
letabundus ait: 'Quam terribilis est locus iste! Vere castra Domini sunt
hec.' Et subjungens: 'Misereor, | inquit, 'super turbam hanc, et quid
ponam ante eos, ad manum non habeo. Magnopere curandum est, ut
usque autumpnum victualia*^m* habeant, ne, quod absit, inedia defi-
ciant.' Spiritus induit predictum cellerarium utpote virum misericordie 30
et ideo abbati carissimum, taleque sancto dedit responsum: 'Habemus,
pater carissime, pecora plurima, boves pascuales, oves, verveces, et
porcos pingues, casei et butiri non modicam quantitatem. Mactabimus
animalia, apponemus et reliqua libenter, et liberaliter in victu eorum

fo.121

G i,349

---

a	elimosinarum *D*	*g*	scicitans *DMS,AS*
b	*C,DMS*; honore *AS*	*h*	quo indigerent *C,AS; om.DMS*
c	*om.AS*	*i*	*C, D, DMS*; utrique *AS*
d	+fi *del.C*	*j*	+quasi *DMS; om.AS*
e	+multiplici *AS*	*k*	*C,DMS*; construxeratque *AS*
f	-ta- *interlin.C*	*l*	*AS*; Tina *DMS*; Tyna *C*
		m	alimenta *AS*

33

Waltheof's alms-giving

Although the conjunction of the aforesaid and other virtues in this man
of God had built a lasting dwelling-place for his abode, compassion for
the poor and sick made its claim on his whole being as if he had been
born for the service, exercise and practice of that alone. Accordingly
5 the saying of the blessed Job when making a pithy statement about
himself is deservedly appropriate for him: 'Mercy grew up with me, and
it came out with me from my mother's womb.' It follows that the
saintly man, not only when healthy, but also often when suffering from
illness, sometimes leaning on a staff, sometimes supported by the arms
10 of his sons, was in the habit of making daily visits to the infirmaries not
only for the monks and lay-brothers, but also for the poor and guests;
and after ascertaining from each of them what they would like, and
what they lacked, he carefully arranged for each man in both directions
to be given what were the needs of each. At all times, but especially
15 when the land was stricken by a famine, when an innumerable crowd of
the poor in order to preserve their lives gathered at Melrose to obtain
the food necessary for life, this man of God did not spare their cattle,
sheep and pigs, but regularly provided relief for everyone's needs so far
as he could. In these circumstances when an adequate supply of the
20 abbot's food for those in need ran short, the very Fountain of Mercy
often miraculously provided supplies from the copious abundance of
His overflowing bounty, as the following story will reveal.
    On one occasion when the calamity of a deadly famine threatened, a
vast crowd of destitute people reckoned to number four thousand
25 gathered at Melrose, and erected huts and tents for themselves in the
fields and woods around the monastery to a distance of two miles. The
abbot in his usual way went out with some of the brothers and the
cellarer (called Thomas, who in fact and nickname was Good), to
survey this great multitude. As he saw it, he joyfully said: 'What an
30 awesome place is this! Truly this is the camp of the Lord.' And next he
said: 'My heart goes out to these people; but I do not have to hand
anything to set before them. We must see to it that they have food until
the autumn, lest (God forbid!) they succumb to starvation,' The Spirit
filled the aforesaid cellarer since he was a man of compassion, and was
35 for that reason very dear to the abbot, and he gave this answer to the
saint: 'Dearest father, we have a great deal of livestock, cattle at
pasture, sheep, wethers, and fat pigs, and no small amount of cheese
and butter. We shall slaughter the animals, serve the rest of the
products gladly, and dole it all out generously as food for them. Yet the
40 shortage of bread touches and pains my heart, because with our corn

expendemus omnia. Panis tamen penuria cor meum tangit et angit, 35
quia, frugibus nostris pene cunctis expensis, porcio permodica in orreis
duarum grangiarum, scilicet Heldwn tritici usui conventus pertinentis,
et Gattaneside siliginis[n] familie reservande, adhuc remansit.' Pius ergo
pater cellerarii verbis adgaudens, obstipo capite gracias multas egit
illi,[o] et benedixit illum in nomine Domini.   40

n   + victualibus *AS*   o   *C*,*AS*; *om.DMS*

34

Quomodo sanctus orrearum fruges sequestratas benedixit et ipsas multiplicavit

Perrexit deinde abbas comitante cellerario ad grangiam de Heldwn, et
ingressus orreum, baculum quem manu gestabat gelimario infixit,
genua flexit, signo crucis edito messem[a] illam benedixit, et recessit.
Deinde ad Galtanside abiit, et eodem modo quod ante fecerat iteravit,
cellerarioque dixit: 'Disperge nunc, et da nobis et pauperibus secure,   5
quia Deus incrementa dabit et augebit et multiplicabit sufficienter
necessaria nostrorum et pauperum usibus.' Res miraque[b] rara! Fruges
que in utriusque horrei angulis continebantur, non censebantur
sufficere victualibus duarum ebdomodarum circulo, trium mensium
protendebantur spacio velut inconsumptibiles et in eodem [statu][c] suo 10
permanentes, speciem farinule vidue Saraptene preferentes, usque ad
novorum fructuum[d] delibatam percepcionem. Ex quo vero novarum
frugum suffecit assumpcio, prescriptarum frugum apparuit consump-
cio. Sic quondam manna, quod filios Israel quadraginta annis in
deserto pavit, post ingressum illorum in Terram Repromissionis et   15
novorum percepcionem illis defecit.

Dehinc post memorabilium, ymmo mirabilium, miraculorum perpe-
tracionem, ut patet in libro vite sue, et post mortem conscripto,

iii° nonas augusti, die scilicet qua Invencio Sancti Stephani prothomar-
tyris celebratur, anno domini m° centesimo[e] sexagesimo transivit de   20
mundo ad Patrem, de fide ad faciem, de spe ad speciem, de umbra ad
veritatem, de stadio ad bravii coronam, et de presentis vite miseria ad
indefective vite gloriam eternam. Gaudeat nunc sancta mater ecclesia
Scoticana super filio suo post nature debitum solutum,[f] future iam
resurreccionis simulacrum representando preferente, fidem incorrup-   25
cionis post mortem predicante, hereticorum resurreccionem corporum
negancium[g] vesanam assercionem destruente. Glorietur, ut dignum
est, Dunelmensis ecclesia eiusdem matris ecclesie Scocie[h] olim |

a   *C*,*DMS*; metam *AS*   e   + xl *del.C*
b   *C*,*DMS*; mira, quia *AS*   f   solitum *D*
c   *DMS*,*AS*; *om.C*   g   *corrected from* negante *C*
d   *om.AS*   h   *om.D*

nearly all exhausted, [only] a very small supply is still left in the barns of
two of our granges, namely some wheat at Eildon kept for the use of the
abbey community, and some rye at Gattonside reserved for the
servants.' The good father was delighted at the cellarer's words; with
45   bent head he gave him many thanks, and blessed him in the name of the
Lord.

34

How the saint blessed the corn stored in the barns and multiplied it

The abbot then made his way to the grange of Eildon along with the
cellarer, and entering the barn he thrust the staff which he was carrying
in his hand into a heap of sheaves; he genuflected, made the sign of the
cross, blessed the crop there, and withdrew. Then he went away to
5   Gattonside, and entered in the same way as he had done before, saying
to the cellarer: 'Make a distribution now, and give both to us and to the
poor with confidence, for God will make it grow, he will increase and
multiply it to the extent necessary for our use and that of the poor.'
What a remarkable event and a rare one! The corn which was stored in
10   the corners of each barn and was thought to provide sufficient food for
scarcely two weeks, stretched out for three months, as if it was
inexhaustible. It remained at the same level (in imitation of the widow
of Zarephath's handful of flour) until the gathering of the new harvest
had been accomplished, From the time when the harvesting of the new
15   corn produced enough for them, the depletion of the aforesaid corn
became apparent. In the same way at a former time the manna, which
sustained the Children of Israel in the desert for forty years, failed them
after their entry into the Promised Land and the gathering of new
crops.

20 Then after performing remarkable, indeed marvellous, miracles, as
appears in the book on his 'Life' written after his death,

on 3 August, that is when the feast of the Invention of St Stephen the
first martyr is celebrated, 1160, he moved over from this world to the   [1159]:
Father, from faith to the presence, from hope to sight, from the   3 Aug.
25   semblance to the truth, from the contest to the crown of the prize, and
from the miseries of the present life to the eternal glory of the life
everlasting.
The holy mother Scottish church should rejoice over her son now
that his debt to nature has been paid, already portraying and
30   displaying a reflection of the future resurrection, proclaiming the faith
in incorruptiblity after death, destroying the insane claim of heretics
who deny the resurrection of the body. It is appropriate that the church
of Durham, which [as part of] the same mother church of Scotland was

fidissima fide a regibus Scotorum fundata dotata et ditata, super
corpore, omni corrupcione carente, sanctissimi confessoris atque 30
pontificis Cuthberti. Sic et Melrocensis abbacia ex incorrupta gleba[i]
Sancti Walthevi abbatis eiusdem sancti presulis socii. Sanctus namque
Cuthbertus in Melros monachatum subiit, quem religione et moribus
Sanctus Bosilus abbas Melrocensis docuit et instituit, ubi post hoc
Sanctus Walthevus abbatis officio prefuit.[j] Uterque operibus[k] miseri- 35
cordie fuit[l] deditus, in religione perfectus, sanctitate perspicuus,[m]
virtutibus plenus, miraculis mirificatus, theoriis sublevatus, corporis et
incorrupcione glorificatus. Exultet Scocie genus regium[n] universum
habendo talem tantumque cognatum parentem et patronum. Sed et
vos omnes Melrocenses cenobite[o] gaudete in Domino, qui, iam melle et 40
rore perfusi celico, mellifluum patrem presentem habetis quodammodo pre oculis, similiorem soporato quam defuncto. Iterum dico
'Gaudete', quia pater vester (ymmo et noster), inductus[p] in[q] splendori-
bus sanctorum, similis illis[r] in gloria, potencior effectus est ad
impetrandum que nobis[s] necessaria ad salutem.[t] 45

Ergo:

> Melros mellita sic est non fellea vita;
> jure vocatur ita, patre pociori potita.

i AS; glebe C; glebe *altered to* gleba D; geba DMS
j C,DMS; praefulsit AS
k om.AS
l om.DMS
m C,DMS; conspicuus AS
n regium eiusque regnum *for* genus regium AS

o in Melros degentes cenobio *for* Melrocenses cenobite DMS,AS
p introductus DMS,AS
q +gloria del.C
r om.DMS; illis factus AS
s C,DMS; vobis AS
t sunt salubria *for* necessaria ad salutem DMS,AS

35

De eleccione ad episcopatum Sanctiandr'[a] Ernoldi abbatis Kalcoviensis

Anno domini m° c° lx electus est Ernoldus Kalcoviensis abbas in festo
Sancti Bricii, quod dominica die evenerit,[b] in sequenti die dominica
consecratus est in veteri ecclesia eiusdem a Willelmo Moraviensi
episcopo sedis apostolice legato astante rege Malcolmo. Cui ad
abbaciam de Kalko successit Johannes eiusdem cantor [in][c] vigilia 5
Sancti Andr' electus; et in die Epiphanie a Glasguensi Hereberto
benedictus. Eodem anno episcopus Ernoldus[d] cum rege Malcolmo
fundavit ecclesiam magnam Sanctiandr'. Qui stetit episcopus per

a +epi del.C
b in festo ... evenerit CA, *for* in episcopum Sanctiandr' que hoc anno dominica die

evenit fest' Sancti Bricii C,D,R
c CA
d +factus domini pape legatus CA

35   long ago founded, endowed and enriched by the kings of the Scots with
      most devoted faith, should glory in the body of Cuthbert, the most
      saintly confessor and bishop, entirely incorrupt as it is. So also the
      abbey of Melrose should glory in the incorrupt remains of the abbot St
      Waltheof as an associate of the same saintly bishop. For St Cuthbert
      became a monk at Melrose; it was St Boisil [prior] of Melrose who
40   guided and instructed him in the religious life and customs, where later
      St Waltheof held the office of abbot. Each of them was devoted to
      works of mercy, perfect in the religious life, conspicuous for saintliness,
      full of virtues, exalted by miracles, lofty in their philosophic specula-
      tions, and made glorious by the incorruption of their bodies. The whole
45   royal house of Scotland should rejoice in having such a great kinsman,
      ancestor and protector. And rejoice in the Lord all you monks of
      Melrose, who, already drenched with honey and heavenly dew, have
      with you your honey-sweet father before your eyes as it were, more like
      a man sleeping than dead. Again I say 'Rejoice!', because now that
50   your father (and indeed ours) has been installed in the brightness of the
      saints, and made equal to them in glory, he has become more
      influential in securing what is necessary for our salvation.

Therefore:

      Honeyed Melrose is thus not a life full of gall;
55   it is rightly so called, having acquired a more powerful father.

35

The election of Arnold abbot of Kelso
to the see of St Andrews

In 1160 Arnold abbot of Kelso was elected [as bishop of St Andrews]   1160:
on the feast of St Brice, which fell on a Sunday, and he was   13 Nov.
consecrated on the following Sunday in the old church of St Andrew   20 Nov.
by William bishop of Moray as legate of the apostolic see in the
5 presence of King Malcolm. He was succeeded as abbot of Kelso by
John, the precentor of that community, who was elected on the eve of
the feast of St Andrew, and blessed by Herbert [bishop] of Glasgow   29 Nov.
on the Epiphany. In the same year Bishop Arnold [was made legate of   1161: 6 Jan.
the lord pope and] with King Malcolm founded the great church of St
10 Andrew. He served as bishop for one year, ten months and seventeen
days, and died on 13 September 1162.   1162:
   He was succeeded by Richard, a chaplain of King Malcolm, who   13 Sept.

unum annum et decem*e* menses et xvii dies, et moritur idus septembris*f*
anno domini m° c° lxii.   10

Cui successit Richardus regis Malcolmi capellanus. Electus anno
domini m° c lxv*to*, et consecratus apud Sanctumandr' ab episcopis
regni dominica in Ramis Palmarum v*to* scilicet kal' aprilis astante
rege. Electus stetit per biennium, et confirmatus xii annis et uno
mense, et iii° non' maii obiit in infirmitorio canonicorum in dierum   15
plenitudine et vite sanctitate. Unde de hiis tribus precedentibus in
antiqua ecclesia tumulatis tabularis scriptura sic se habebat:

> Qui peregrinus ades, sta, respice primo Robertum,
> Ernoldum reliqum; circumdat tumba Richardum
> ultima, pontifices quondam, celi modo cives.   20

Eodem anno magister Johannes dictus Scotus electus est ad
episcopatum Sanctiandr', scilicet anno domini m° c° lxxvii. Rege

Willelmo totis viribus renitente, | Hugonem capellanum suum regis
fretus potestate in ecclesia Sanctiandr' ut voluit*g* episcopum consecrari fecit. Hinc inde gravis contencio et periculosa divisio emersit,   25
sicut in sequentibus patebit, quia quamvis Scotus sic vocatus, tamen
in veritate Anglicus natus fuit in villa que dicitur Podoth infra
comitatum Cestrie. Qui artibus liberalibus primitus Oxonie deinde
Parisius vacabat. Et non solum in artibus liberalibus sed eciam in
phisica postremum in theologia a cunctis regere dignus videbatur.   30
Cum autem a scolis reversus esset et per aliquantulum temporis in
domo paterna cum suis moram fecisset, Scociam personaliter adire et
limina Sanctiandr' apostoli disposuit visitare, ubi ab episcopo
honorifice susceptus, iam non hospes et advena, sed ut civis et
indigena, post mortem archidiaconi archidiaconatum est adeptus. Et   35
non post multos annos post decessum episcopi, statuto eleccionis die
congregatis omnibus qui interesse tenebantur, presente eciam legato
domino Johanne de Celio Monte cardinali a latere domini pape in
Scocia specialiter directo, Spiritus Sancti invocata gracia, vota sua
tam singuli quam universi in archidiaconum*h* transtulerunt,*i* et eum   40
communiter sine aliqua contradiccione*j* in episcopum elegerunt.

e	*D; lac.C*	*h*	archidiaconem *C,D,CA*
f	novembris *CA*	*i*	*D*; transulerunt *C*
g	+de facto *CA*	*j*	+prius Scoticatum *CA*

was elected in 1165, and consecrated at St Andrews by the bishops of [1163]
the kingdom on Palm Sunday, that is 28 March in the presence of the 1165:
15 king. He served as bishop-elect for two years, and as a confirmed 28 Mar.
bishop for twelve years and one month. He died on 5 May in the [1178:]
canons' infirmary in good old age and in saintliness of life. An 5 May
inscription on wood about these three foregoing bishops buried in the
old church reads as follows:

20   You who come as a pilgrim, pause, and first look on Robert,
        then on what remains of Arnold; the last tomb covers
            Richard;
        they were once bishops, now they are citizens of Heaven.

In the same year, that is 1177, Master John called Scot was elected [1178]
25 to the see of St Andrews. King William was totally opposed, and
confident in the royal power had Hugh his chaplain consecrated as
bishop in the church of St Andrew in accordance with his wishes. On
both sides a serious dispute and dangerous rift arose, as will be clear in
what follows, because although Scot was so called, nevertheless he
30 had in truth been born an Englishman in the township which is called
Budworth in the county of Chester. He had spent some time as a
student of the liberal arts first at Oxford and then at Paris; and it was
not only in the liberal arts, but also in physics and finally in theology
that he seemed to everyone good enough to teach as a master. Then
35 when he had returned from the schools and had stayed for some time
with his relatives in his family home, he decided to go in person to
Scotland and visit the church of St Andrew the Apostle, where he was
taken up as an honoured protégé by the bishop. Now regarded not as
a guest and a foreigner, but as a citizen and a native, after the death of
40 the archdeacon he obtained the archdeaconry. And not many years
later on the death of the bishop, when the day for an election had been
arranged and everyone had gathered who was supposed to attend,
and in the presence also of sir John de Monte Celio, the cardinal who
had been appointed a legate from the lord pope's side in Scotland in
45 particular, the grace of the Holy Spirit was invoked, and all and
sundry cast their votes for the archdeacon, and jointly elected him as
bishop with no dissent.

36

Quo modo rex Willelmus eum ab episcopo expulit
et curiam Romanam propterea appellavit Johannes

Tunc temporis Willelmus rex Scocie, audito quod archdiaconus ipso
inconsulto et nullum prebente consensum vel assensum in episcopum
eligeretur, egre tulit, et rancorem animo conceptum dissimulare non
sustinens in hec verba prorupuit: 'Per brachium Sancti Jacobi' (sic
enim jurare consueverunt) 'me superstite episcopatum Sanctiandr'   5
numquam gaudebit, nec in ea sede principatum optinebit.' Mox ergo
res et redditus episcopi confiscantur, et tam ipsum quam omnes alios
eum quovis consanguinitatis vel familiaritatis titulo contingentes
exilio rex jussit addici. Quid igitur ageret, vel quo se verteret, servus
Christi non habebat. Nam cum infra patriam non permitteretur   10
remanere, necessario compellebatur exulare. Solum igitur et
singulare sibi superesse refugium perpendit sedem apostolicam*a*
appellare, et tam se quam causam suam proteccioni domini pape
committere. ⟨Exilium subiit iiii anno post exilium Sancti Thome
Cantuar'.⟩ Limina igitur apostolorum, iter suum Domino dirigente,   15
visitavit, et domino Alexandro tunc temporis summo pontifici
causam suam utpote vir gnarus et urbane eloquencie satis sapienter et
efficaciter exposuit, de contingentibus nichil pretermittens, nec
falsitatis quicquam admiscens, sed geste rei seriem ei seriatim
exponens. Quibus auditis dominus papa non mediocri admiracione   20
percellitur, quia vir talis et tante discrecionis et canonice electus tam
facile sine causa racionabili repudiaretur, insuper et exulare compelli-
tur. Causam ergo suam justam tuendam suscepit, et consilium et
G i,352   auxilium fidele | secundum cause sue merita promittit. De mandato
igitur pape Alexis, sancte Romane ecclesie subdiaconus et apostolice 25
sedis nuncius ut de facto ecclesie Sanctiandr' cognosceret, Scociam
cum Johanne electo et ab eodem papa prius confirmato rege Willelmo
vix permittente intravit, concesso dicto confirmato ut pro dignitate
fo.122   ecclesie Sanctiandr' et regis honore in sede episcopali | a quibus vellet
episcopis consecrari. Quem Alexis domini pape nuncius, post multa   30
consilia et multa gravamina, excommunicatis eciam quibusdam regis
clericis, insuper episcopatu Sanctiandr' interdici comminato, sed id
fieri Johanne nequaquam consenciente, convocatis quasi omnibus

a   *D*; appostolicam *C*

36

How King William drove John out of the bishopric
and how John appealed to the Roman court because of this

At that time William king of Scotland, on hearing that the
archdeacon had been elected bishop without him being consulted or
giving any consent or approval, took it badly; and unable to hide the
anger aroused in his mind, he burst out with these words: 'By the arm
5   of St James' (for this was his usual oath) 'as long as I live he will never
enjoy the bishopric of St Andrews, nor will he exercise episcopal
authority in that see.' Soon therefore the property and revenues of the
bishop were seized, and the king ordered that both John and all the
others connected in any way with his family or household be
10 condemned to exile. This servant of Christ therefore did not know
what to do or where to go, for since he was not allowed to remain in
his own country, he was necessarily forced to live in exile. He
calculated therefore that the one and only refuge left to him was to
appeal to the apostolic see, and to commit both himself and his case to
15 the protection of the lord pope. He underwent exile four years after
the exile of St Thomas of Canterbury. With the Lord guiding his
journey therefore, he went to visit the apostolic see, and as one might
expect in a man of experience and polished eloquence he set forth his
case to the Lord Alexander who was then the supreme pontiff very
20 intelligently and effectively. He omitted none of the circumstances,
nor added anything untrue, but set forth the sequence of events in the
matter to him stage by stage. On hearing this, the lord pope was struck
with very considerable surprise that a man of such character and
discernment who had been canonically elected should have been so
25 readily rejected without reasonable cause, and in addition forced into
exile. Therefore he undertook to defend his just case, and promised
reliable advice and assistance in accordance with the merits of his
case.
By order of the pope therefore Alexis, a subdeacon of the holy
30 Roman church and nuncio of the apostolic see to find out the facts
about the church of St Andrews, entered Scotland along with John
the bishop-elect, who had previously been confirmed by the pope,
though King William was reluctant to allow the visit. The said
confirmed man had secured agreement that in conformity with the
35 dignity of the church of St Andrews and the king's honour he was to
be consecrated to the episcopal see by whatever bishops he wanted.

episcopis abbatibus et notabilioribus clericis dignitate constitutis
apud Edenburgh' in ecclesia monasteriali Sancte Crucis, die Sancte   35
Trinitatis vi^to idus junii, a Matheo episcopo Aberdonensi ex mandato
domini pape Alexandri ad prenominatam sedem in antistitem
magnifice^b consecrari fecit. Qui sic consecratus et absque episcopatu
se esse intelligens, extimplo pre timore regis et indignacione regalium
provinciam^c merens reliquid, et Romanam curiam repedando peciit.   40

---

b   in ... magnifice *om.CA*   c   regnum *CA*

37

Quomodo septennio exul in Romana curia stetit

Ubi cum^a aliquantulum temporis in curia papa consulente et
precipiente stetisset, timens ne forte domino pape vel alicui suorum
oneri esset, licenciam postulat ad horam recedendi, et alibi quo
Dominus permiserit perhendinandi. Cui papa: 'Mane nobiscum; ne
timeas, et nusquam a curia divertere presumas, ne forte te absente   5
superveniant adversarii tui a latere regis Scocie directi, qui te super
multis articulis accusent, et non sit qui pro te se murum defensionis
opponat, vel exprobrantibus tibi pro te verbum respondeat. Quod si
tibi necessaria deesse conquereris, non super hiis aliquatenus
solliciteris vel perturberis. Que enim tue desunt necessitati, nostre   10
habundant et superhabundant potestati. Marsupium unum sit
omnium nostrum.' Interea dominus papa regi literas transmittit
monitorias et deprecatorias ut episcopum repatriare concedat, et
revertentem affectu filiali sicut decet honorifice recipiat. Alioquin ne
tam justa causa ecclesie per eius neclectum deperire videatur, se   15
severius acturum in brevi comminatur. Voluit enim papa micius se
habere, quia rumor de veteri fecit eundem circumspecte futura
precavere, ne scilicet contingeret inter regem et episcopum sicut paulo
ante ad quatuor annos,^b quando isdem de justicia fulminavit censuras
contra Henricum regem Anglie, cognatum ipsius regis Willelmi, ipse   20
tamen contemptibiliter Thomam Cantuarie archipresulem in gremio
matris ecclesie, cuius jura tuebatur presul, et crudeliter passus est
occidi. Ad modum igitur aspidis surde obturantis aures suas ne vocem
sapientis incantantis^c exaudiat, sed nec rex monitis flexus, nec minis

---

a   + aliquo tempore *del.C*   c   *D,CA*; incantatis *C*
b   quatuor annos *om.CA*

After many discussions and many troubles, with even the excommunication of some of the king's clerks and a threat of interdict over the
see of St Andrews besides (though John by no means agreed to this
40 being done), when nearly all the bishops, abbots and eminent clergy
designated by high office had been called together at Edinburgh in the
church of the monastery at Holyrood, Alexis had John splendidly
consecrated as bishop for the aforesaid see on Holy Trinity Sunday, 8   [1180:
June, by Matthew bishop of Aberdeen by virtue of a mandate of the   15 June]
45 lord pope Alexander. The man thus consecrated, realizing that he was
without a bishopric, immediately left the province sadly for fear of the
king and the wrath of the king's men, and sought to return to the
Roman court.

37

How he remained an exile at the Roman court for seven years

When he had stayed at the Roman court for a fair amount of time
while the pope was taking advice and on his instructions, fearing that
he was perhaps a nuisance to the lord pope or any of his court, he
sought permission to leave immediately and stay somewhere else
5 where the Lord would allow it. The pope spoke to him: 'Stay with us;
don't be afraid, and do not take it on yourself to go anywhere away
from the court, lest it happen that in your absence your adversaries
sent from the king of Scotland's side arrive, to accuse you on many
points, and lest there is no one here to set himself up as a wall of
10 defence on your behalf, or speak up for you against your accusers. But
if you are complaining that you are short of the necessities of life, do
not worry or be upset in any respect about these things, for we, by
reason of our power, possess in abundance and superabundance what
is lacking for your needs. Let there be one purse for all of us.'
15   Meanwhile the lord pope sent a letter to the king admonishing and
requesting him to allow the bishop to come home, and to receive him
honourably on his return with proper filial affection. Otherwise lest so
just a case for the church appear to be lost by his neglect, the pope
threatened to act more severely soon. For the pope wanted to pursue
20 peaceful means of action, because a report of long standing made him
cautiously take care for the future, that is lest a situation arise between
the king and the bishop like that four years earlier when the same
pope issued thunderbolts of judicial censures against King Henry of
England (a relative of King William himself), who had nonetheless
25 contemptuously and cruelly allowed Thomas archbishop of Canterbury to be killed in the bosom of mother church, whose rights the
bishop was protecting. Therefore in the manner of a deaf snake

G i,353

perteritus, in priori sentencia*d* immobilis perseverat, et minas 25
comminantis contempnens, et preces | supplicantis*e* surda aure
pertransiens. Unde summus*f* pontifex non modice permotus interdicto totum regnum Scocie supponere diffinivit, nisi rex sine more
dispendio ad emendacionem redeat, et episcopum cum honore debito
se suscepturum promittat. Quo audito, ante pedes domini pape 30
episcopus prosternitur, obnixius obsecrans ut animum ab hac
intencione revocare dignetur, ne ob aliquam causam ipsum con-
tingentem ecclesia Scoticana suspendatur, et in ea more solito
graciarum acciones Domino non exsolvantur. 'Malo,' inquit, 'pater
sancte, juri modo cedere, et in manus vestras honorem episcopalem 35
cum onere honori adjuncto resignare, quam misse pro redempcione
animarum in Purgatorio existencium celebrande pro quacumque
dignitate michi collata vel conferenda saltem una die obmittantur.'
Papa eius lacrimosis precibus effractus, videns eum pocius episcopatui velle cedere quam*g* pro conservacione justicie sue procedi pati, non 40
sine magna ammiracione se continuit, et ab illa die et deinceps tantam
graciam in oculis ⟨summi⟩ pontificis factum est ut inveniret, quod
quicquid ab eo postulasset, quod de jure concedi potuisset, confestim
assequeretur, nec peticionis juste et racionabiliter petite repulsam
pateretur.*h* Per septennium igitur continuum sicut Thomas de 45
Cantuaria compulsus est exulare, ita ut nec per literas domini pape vel
cardinalium satis affectuose pro eo scribencium repatriandi licenciam
potuit impetrare.

d	pertinacia *CA*	*g*	*corrected from* tam *C*
e	exhortantis *CA*	*h*	nec ... pateretur *om.CA*
f	sumus *CA*		

37a*a*

Quomodo promotus est ad episcopatum Dunkeldensem et receptus in graciam regis

Vir autem Domini pacienter omnia sustinuit, sciens scriptum: 'Beati
qui persecucionem paciuntur propter justiciam' c'. Unde istud poete
sepius in ore, semper tamen in corde*b* habuit:

a	*chapter number* 37 *is here repeated without comment C,R; chapter is numbered* 38 *with subsequent chapters re-numbered also*		*E;* capitulo vii [*sic*] *D, with subsequent numbering as in C*
		b	mente *CA*

closing his ears lest he hear the voice of a wise man casting a spell, the
king neither yielded to warnings nor was frightened by threats, but
30   persisted unmoved in his earlier purpose; he despised the menaces of
the man who was issuing threats, and passed by with a deaf ear the
prayers of the suppliant. Thereupon the supreme pontiff was much
angered, and determined to place an interdict on the whole kingdom
of Scotland unless the king without excessive delay were to make
35   amends and promise to take the bishop under his protection with due
honour. When he heard this, the bishop prostrated himself at the feet
of the lord pope, vehemently imploring him to deign to cancel his
intended purpose in this matter lest the Scottish church should be
suspended on account of any case affecting him, and lest prayers of
40   thanksgiving be not offered in it to the Lord in the usual way. 'I prefer,
holy father,' he said, 'to surrender my right now, and resign the
episcopal rank into your hands with the responsibilities attached to
this rank, rather than that the masses being celebrated for the
redemption of souls lying in Purgatory should be discontinued for
45   even one day on account of any dignity conferred or to be conferred
on me.' The pope's resolution was broken by his tearful entreaties,
seeing that he wanted to surrender the bishopric rather than allow
proceedings for the maintenance of his suit; and full of great
admiration he restrained himself, and from that day forward it turned
50   out that John found so much goodwill in the eyes of the supreme
pontiff that whatever he asked of the pope which could legally be
granted, he immediately acquired, and he did not suffer the rejection
of the request which he had justifiably and reasonably made. He was
compelled to stay in exile for seven years continuously, like Thomas
55   of Canterbury, so that not even by letters from the lord pope and the
cardinals, who wrote very warmly on his behalf, was he able to obtain
permission [from the king] to return home.

37a

How he was appointed to the see of Dunkeld
and received into the king's favour

The man of the Lord then patiently endured all this, knowing the
Scripture: 'Blessed are those who are persecuted in the cause of right'
etc. Hence he often had these lines of the poet on his lips, and always
at least in his heart:

5   Patience the greatest of the virtues fights without weapons,
and often is accustomed to prevail over armed men.

Maxima virtutum paciencia pugnat inermis,
armatosque viros vincere sepe solet.   5
Nobile vincendi genus est paciencia. Vincit
qui patitur. Si vis vincere, disce pati.

Hiis itaque se habentibus, contigit sedem Dunkeldensem vacare. |
Quo in tempore, ob rumorem et metum interdicti, turbatus est rex et
omnis^c Scocia cum eo. Sed audita morte Dunkeldensis episcopi, rex 10
nactus oportunum tempus, ut sibi videbatur, quo exulem suum
revocaret, reverenter scripsit episcopo per notabiles nuncios literas
regias satis efficaces secum deferentes, ut sine cunctacione et
hesitacione repatriaret, nec quicquam machiacionis sinistre contra
ipsum ex parte regis vel alicuius suorum formidaret. Susceptis igitur 15
et perlectis literis domini regis tam pape et cardinalibus^d quam
episcopo directis, in communi Domino gracie referuntur, qui non
permittit servos suos temptari supra id quod possunt, sed facit eciam
cum temptacione proventum ut possint sustinere. Episcopus autem
post tam diuturnum^e exilium cum plenaria gracia tam pape quam 20
cardinalium, literis ad votum impetratis, in Scociam revertitur, et a
rege et regni proceribus cum magno | honore suscipitur, tam singulis
quam universis de eius reversione gaudentibus, et eidem ad multip-
lices graciarum acciones assurgentibus,^{f} quod cum dominum papam,
sicut eis a comeantibus fidedignis innotuerat, adeo propicium 25
haberet, ut eum in quamlibet partem qua vellet, racione tamen previa,
inclinaret, non est passus ut regnum Scocie interdicto supponeretur,
sed ad eius supplicacionem de die in diem per septennium sentencia
suspenderetur. Cum igitur^g pace reformata,^{h} venia petita, et rege ab
episcopo absoluto, ac omni offensa hinc inde remissa, dominus rex 30
sicut sepius asseruit libenter assensum in primis prebuisset, ut ad
episcopatum Sanctiandr' ad quem canonice electus fuerat, si tamen
juramentum regium non obstetisset, per quod se rex frequencius
astrinxerat et inadvertencius, quod illi eleccioni numquam consen-
tiret. Indecens insuper sibi videbatur, si quavis occasione perjurii nota 35
notaretur, et sic fama sua perpetuo denigraretur. Ecce secundario
juramentum Herodis qui, ne perjurus videretur, Johannem Baptistam
occidere non veretur. Sed debuit rex scivisse quod juramentum
institutum non est,^{i} ut esset iniquitatis vel cuiuscumque criminis
vinculum, ut xxii questione iiii, 'Inter cetera', sed quodcumque 40
juramentum debet habere tres comites, scilicet veritatem, judicium et
justiciam, qui omnes defecerunt in rege. Habet enim veritatem
quando non aliter corde sentitur quam ore juratur; et tamen si in isto
concurrat comes veritas, tamen attenta temeritate juramenti debuit se

c   *corrected from* omnia C
d   + ipsi CA
e   + consilium *del.C*; + auxilium *del.CA*
f   + potissime CA

g   + super *del.C*
h   CA; reformanda D; reformanda *corrected*
     to reformanta C
i   non est *interlin.C*

Patience is a noble kind of prevailing. Someone who suffers
prevails. If you wish to prevail, learn to suffer.

So in these circumstances it happened that the see of Dunkeld was
10   vacant. At that time, on account of the report and fear of an interdict,
the king was alarmed and all Scotland with him. But when he heard of
the death of the bishop of Dunkeld, the king took it as an opportune
time (as it seemed to him) to recall the man he had exiled. He wrote
respectfully to the bishop by eminent messengers, who carried with
15   them a royal letter that was sufficiently effective, saying that he might
return home without delay or hesitation, and that he should have no
fear of any sinister plot against him on the part of the king or any of
his men. Once therefore letters from the lord king addressed to the
pope and the cardinals as well as the bishop had been received and
20   studied, thanks were given by all to the Lord, who does not allow his
servants to be tested above their powers, but also along with the test
provides a way out so that they can sustain it. Thus after that long
period of exile the bishop returned to Scotland with the full support of
both pope and cardinals, once he had obtained letters as he wished,
25   and was received with great honour by the king and magnates of the
kingdom. All and sundry rejoiced at his return, and stood up to offer
him many expressions of thanks [especially] because when (as was
made known to them by some trustworthy travellers) he had the lord
pope so well-disposed that he might influence him in whatever
30   direction he wished (provided, however, that it was reasonable), he
did not allow the kingdom of Scotland to be put under an interdict,
but on his pleading the sentence had been suspended from day to day
for seven years. When therefore peace was restored, pardon had been
requested, and the king had been absolved by the bishop, and every
35   offence on both sides had been forgiven, the lord king (as he often
claimed) would right away have willingly given his assent that John
might have the see of St Andrews (to which he had been canonically
elected), if only his royal oath had not stood in the way, by which the
king had often thoughtlessly bound himself never to consent to that
40   election. Besides it seemed to him unseemly if on any occasion he were
branded with the stigma of perjury and his reputation permanently
blackened in this way.
Remember secondly the oath of Herod, who did not scruple to put
John the Baptist to death, lest he appear to be perjured. But the king
45   ought to have known that the swearing of an oath has not been
devised to be a bond of injustice or of any kind of crime (as [stated in
the *Decretum*, cause] 22, question 4, 'Inter cetera'), but that any oath
ought to have three companions, namely truth, judgment and justice,
in all of which the king was deficient. For an oath has truth when it is
50   not felt in the heart differently from the way it is sworn by the mouth;
and yet if truth goes along with it as a companion, once the

reformasse, quia illicitum juramentum maius est peccatum implere　45
quam perjurium incurrere, ut in premissa causa et questione capitulo
'Unusquisque'. Et ideo debet omnis Christianus specialiter advertere
quod omne juratum est servandum, nisi in pejorem vergat exitum et in
salutis detrimentum, ut ibi capitulo 'David' et capitulo 'Dilecti filii',
de hiis qui vi metusve c'. Item illicitum juramentum non est　50
adimplendum, ut D. xiii, 'Duo'. Illicitum est ex persona cui juratur, ut
cum clericus laico jurat, quod non licet. Item ex re, ut si res per quam
juratur non est sacra. Item ex fine, ut si juretur ante eleccionem, ne N.
eligatur. Item ex causa obligatoria, scilicet ad hoc impellente, ut^{j}
exemplum de Herode. Item si temere vel indiscrete vel sine necessit-　55
ate, ut hic juravit rex, et exemplum de Jepte, qui indiscrete juravit.
Hec omnia probantur sparsim in premissis causa et questione. In
judicio juratur, quando cum discrecione et cautela juratur, et in licitis.
In justicia, quando licitum et justum est quod juratur, non tendens ad
mortale peccatum. Et ideo notandum quod juramentum licitum fit　60
tantum in sex casibus; unde:

> Pax et fama, fides, reverencia, caucio dampni,
> defectus veri, sibi possunt sacra tueri.

j　　+ hic rex juravit vel verius *del.C*

38

G i,355

Quod perjurus est multipliciter detestandus

Non moveatur lector licet aliquantulam hic faciam digressionem,
quia cotidie video quod dolenter refero, quamplures tam in assisis
quam in testimoniis perhibendis modicum vel nichil curare de
irritacione juramentorum.^{a} Et ideo, ut perjurium caveatur, aliqualis
sermo de eodem hic inseratur. Est enim omnis perjurus prodiciosus　5
per infidelitatem quo ad Deum, injuriosus per falsitatem quo ad
proximum, perniciosus per iniquitatem quo ad seipsum. Quo ad
primum: prodicio foret magna si cancellarius,^{b} vel ille qui haberet

a　-rum *interlin.C*　　　　　　　　　*b*　*first* -l- *interlin.C*; cancelarius *D*

recklessness of an oath was observed, he ought to have put things
right, because to fulfil an unlawful oath is a worse sin than to incur
perjury (as stated in the aforesaid cause and question at the chapter
55 'Unusquisque'). And for that reason every Christian ought to take
special note that everything that has been sworn must be kept, lest he
sink to a worse fate to the detriment of his salvation (as in the same
place in the chapter 'David' and the chapter 'Dilecti filii' concerning
those who by force or fear etc.). Again, an unlawful oath should not
60 be fulfilled (as in the *Decretum*, distinction 13, 'Duo'). It is unlawful
because of the person to whom the oath is made, as when a cleric
swears to a layman, which is not allowed. Again, because of the
object, as happens if the object on which the oath is taken is not
sacred. Again, because of its purpose, as happens if an oath is taken
65 before an election not to elect N. Again, because of some compelling
reason, namely one that drives [the person swearing] towards it, like
the example of Herod. Again, if the oath is sworn rashly or
indiscreetly or unnecessarily, as the king swore in this case, and as in
the example of Jephthah, who made an indiscreet oath. All these are
70 demonstrated at various points throughout the aforesaid cause and
question. An oath is made with judgment when it is made with
discrimination and caution, and in lawful circumstances. It is made
with justice when the oath is lawful and just, not tending towards
mortal sin. And for that reason it should be noted that a lawful oath
75 occurs in only six kinds of circumstance, namely:

> Peace and good reputation, faith, respect, avoidance of harm
> and of lies – these can uphold oaths for themselves.

38

How a perjurer is abhorrent on many counts

I hope that the reader will not be annoyed if I here make a little
digression, for I see every day something that grieves me, that very
many people both when serving on juries and when bearing witness
take little or no care over making their oaths void. And for this
5 reason, as a warning against perjury, some sort of account of this
topic is included here. For every perjurer is a traitor by his disloyalty
as far as God is concerned, causes harm by his deceit as regards his
neighbour, and is destructive by his wickedness as regards himself.

As to the first point: it would be a great act of treason if a chancellor
10 (or the person who had the custody of the king's seal) were to seal an
agreement which the king particularly disliked. Even if he did this in

custodiam sigilli regis, signaret literam paccionis quam rex maxime
detestaretur. Eciam si hoc faceret de sigillo pape, esset excommunica- 10
tus ipso facto et brachio seculari tradendus. Nomen Dei est nomen
commissum nobis, quasi quoddam sigillum ad testificandum et ad
veritatem confirmandum. Unde: 'Dominum Deum tuum timebis et
illi soli servies, et per nomen eius jurabis' (Deuteronomii vi^{to}). Et ideo
dicit apostolus quod 'omnis controversie finis ad confirmacionem est 15
juramentum'. | Falsitas autem est illud quod Deus summe odit, sicut
sibi contrarium quia ipse est veritas; et ideo qui nomen Dei assumit ad
confirmandum falsitatem Dei proditor est. Hoc idem patet ii^o quia qui
castrum domini regis suo fidelitati commissum traderet hostibus
regis, proditor regis esset. Castrum est nomen Domini quod 20
invocamus et ad quod confugimus in omni necessitate. Unde in
Proverbiis ait Salomon: 'Turris fortissima nomen Domini;' ad eam
qui confugerit salvabitur. Istud castrum traditur hosti quando
demonibus et falsis hominibus committitur ad probacionem falsitatis. Hoc idem patet iii^o quia qui dominum suum diffamat maliciose et 25
involvit in crimine, proditor suus est; sed qui Deum inducit tamquam
testem falsitatis, involvere nititur Dominum in crimine et auferre sibi
nomen bonum quo vocatur^c et est summa veritas, proditor suus est.
Unde quantum in eo est, plus contempnit Christum quam crucifix-
ores Christi, nam ipsi non intulerunt Christo nisi malum pene, et iste 30
nititur eum involvere in malo culpe. Diabolus adjuratus in nomine
Domini dicere veritatem non mentitur communiter, nec invenitur
quod ipse addat suis mendaciis juramentum, licet ipse sit mendax et
pater omnis mendacis; et ideo non est mirum si Deus eis ulcionem
promittat, qui dicit Malachie iii^o: 'Ero testis velox maleficis, adulteris 35
et perjuris.'^{d}

   ii^o perjurus est injuriosus per falsitatem quo ad proximum. Decipit
enim judicem et spoliat jure suo bone fidei possessorem, et ideo
restituere tenetur quilibet detentum in solidum. Si tamen unus
solverit restituendo complete, alii deobligantur. 40

   iii^o est perniciosus per iniquitatem quo ad seipsum, quia qui
scienter perjurans manum libro supponit^e qua tangit Evangelium,
illam Diabolo commendat nisi dicat veritatem. | Unde illa manus
efficitur manus Diaboli, et post hoc et deinceps manu Diaboli se
signat, cibat et operatur. Unde per illam manum tenet eum Diabolus 45
donec fructuose peniteat. In missali vero super quod jurat iiii^{or} scripta
sunt, consecracio scilicet corporis et sanguinis Christi, suffragia
sanctorum, beatitudo beatorum, et dampnacio reproborum.^{f} Est
igitur sensus juramenti sui, quasi diceret: 'Nisi verum sit quod modo
juro, non me juvet missarum celebracio, nec sanctorum deprecacio; 50
sed priver omni beatitudine sanctorum, et veniat super me malediccio

---

c D,R; vacatur C e supposuit D
d + Narra $del.C$ f + ac dampnacio reproborum $del.C$

accordance with the papal seal, he would be *ipso facto* excommunicated and would have to be handed over to the secular arm. God's name is a name entrusted to us as a particular seal for bearing witness
15 and confirming the truth. Hence: 'You are to fear the Lord your God; and serve him alone, and take your oaths in his name' (Deuteronomy 6). This is why the apostle says that 'an oath provides a confirmation to end all dispute'. Deceit indeed is something that God dislikes intensely, as it is the opposite of him, because he himself is truth; and
20 therefore whoever takes on himself God's name to confirm a piece of deceit is betraying God. This same point is clear secondly because if anyone was to hand over to enemies one of the lord king's castles that had been entrusted to his loyalty, he would be a traitor to the king. The Lord's name is a castle which we invoke and to which we flee at
25 every time of need. Hence Solomon says in Proverbs: 'The Lord's name is a tower of great strength;' whoever flees to it will be saved. This castle is handed over to an enemy when it is entrusted to demons and deceitful men as support for deceit. This same point is clear thirdly because if anyone was to slander his lord maliciously and
30 implicate him in a crime, he is a traitor to him; but anyone who brings God to bear as a witness to deceit, who endeavours to involve the Lord in a crime and to deprive him of the good name by which he is invoked and which is the supreme truth, he is a traitor to God. Hence so far as he is concerned, he is more insulting to Christ than were those
35 who crucified Christ, for they did not inflict on Christ anything more than the evil of a punishment, but such a man is endeavouring to involve him in the evil of a sin. When the Devil has been required under oath in the Lord's name to tell the truth, he does not ordinarily lie, nor do we find that he adds an oath to his lies, even if he is
40 untruthful and the father of all liars; and so it is no wonder if God promises them retribution, as he says in Malachi 3: 'I shall be quick to testify against sorcerers, adulterers and perjurers.'

Secondly, a perjurer causes harm by his deceit as far as his neighbour is concerned. For he deceives a judge and deprives a bona
45 fide owner of his right, and on that account is bound to repay what has been kept back in full. If however one man pays by making complete restitution, the others are released from their obligation.

Thirdly, a perjurer is destructive by his wickedness as far as himself is concerned, because anyone who knowingly commits perjury when
50 placing his hand on the book (by which means he touches the Gospel) is entrusting that hand to the Devil unless he speaks the truth. Hence that hand becomes the Devil's hand, and henceforth and thereafter he signs himself, eats and works with the Devil's hand. Hence by that hand the Devil holds on to him until he repents with good effect. In the
5 missal indeed upon which a man swears are written four passages – that is the consecration of the body and blood of Christ, the intercession of the saints, the blessedness of the blest, and the

reproborum.' Similiter quando homo scienter vadit ad pejerandum,
abrenunciat omnibus bonis gressibus, quos pedibus suis peregrinando ⟨iverat⟩, vel alias infirmos vel ecclesiam visitando, nisi dicat
veritatem; extendendo eciam manus ad librum, abrenunciat omnibus 55
bonis operibus elemosine, si que fecit. Similiter osculando librum,
omnibus bonis verbis et oracionibus quas Deo fecit. Propter quod
scriptum est: 'Vir multum jurans replebitur iniquitate; et non recedat
de domo eius plaga.'

39

Quomodo episcopus episcopatum Dunkeldensem partitur

Ut revertatur[a] ad ea de quibus ad propositum: quamvis multum
timuit rex notari de voto quo temere se astrinxit juramento, tamen
sibi precavisse debuerat, quod votum de malo est semper rescinden-
dum. Unde: 'In malis promissis rescinde votum', et illud: 'Quod
incaute vovisti, vide ne reddas', quia antequam quis voveat, debet tria 5
attendere, videlicet quid liceat secundum equitatem, quid deceat
secundum honestatem, et quid expediat secundum utilitatem, ut
capitulo 'Magne', 'De voto et voti [redempcione]'. Tandem ut omnis
contencionis materia tolleretur, et pax stabilis firmaretur, rege pariter
et clero hilariter consensientibus, Johannes in episcopum Dunkelden- 10
sem eligitur,[b] et a cunctis summa devocione suscipitur. Sed quoniam
multas expensas et fatigabiles labores et dampna illo septennio exul
passus est, et episcopatus Dunkeldensis episcopatu Sanctiandr' longe
inferior erat redditibus et possessionibus, communi consilio in
aliqualem recompensacionem decretum est, ut omnes redditus quos 15
in episcopatu Sanctiandr' tempore archidiaconatus sui possederat in
suo perpetuo sibi plenarie remanerent, post obitum suum ad
episcopatum Sanctiandr'[c] sine contradiccione revocandi. In episcopum igitur Dunkeldensem concorditer electus, a domino papa
confirmatur, et eius auctoritate consecratur. In illo tempore tota 20
Ergadia episcopo Dunkeldensi parebat et eius jurisdiccioni sicut ab
antiquo subjacebat. Est autem Ergadia terra lata et spaciosa, et multis

---

a   revertar D   c   + re del.C
b   preficitur CA

damnation of the condemned. This then is the meaning of his oath, as
if to say: 'If what I now swear is untrue, may the celebration of masses
60 be of no help to me, nor the prayers of the saints; but deprived of all
the blessedness of the saints, may the curse of the condemned come
over me.' Similarly when a man knowingly rushes into perjury, he
renounces all the good steps which he has taken when going on foot as
a pilgrim, or when at other times visiting the sick or going to church,
65 unless he speaks the truth; also by placing his hands on the book, he
renounces all good works of alms-giving, if he has done any. Similarly
in kissing the book, he renounces all the praise and prayers which he
has made to God. On this account Scripture has it: 'A man given to
oaths will be wicked to the core; and the rod will never be far from his
70 house.'

39

How the bishop divided the see of Dunkeld

To return to matters relating to the point: although the king was very
afraid of being censured for the vow with which he had rashly bound
himself with an oath, yet he ought to have been aware that a vow
regarding something evil must always be annulled. Hence: 'Annul a
5 vow concerned with evil promises', and: 'You should not discharge a
vow made when off your guard', because before anyone makes a vow,
he ought to consider three things, namely what would be equitably
allowable, what would be honestly fitting, and what would be usefully
expedient, as in the chapter 'Magne' under the heading 'De voto et
10 voti redempcione'.

At length John was elected bishop of Dunkeld, so that all grounds
for dispute would be removed, and a lasting settlement achieved, with
both king and clergy cheerfully consenting, and he was accepted by
everyone with the greatest devotion. But seeing that he had suffered
15 much expense and wearisome hardships and damages while an exile
for seven years, and the see of Dunkeld was far inferior to the see of St
Andrews in revenues and estates, it was decreed in common council as
some compensation that all the revenues which he held in the diocese
of St Andrews when he held his archdeaconry were to remain
20 permanently with him in full, and after his death they were to be
returned to the diocese of St Andrews without argument. He was
therefore harmoniously elected bishop of Dunkeld, confirmed by the
lord pope, consecrated by his authority.

At that time the whole of Argyll was subject to the bishop of
25 Dunkeld and his jurisdiction as it had been from long before. Argyll is
an extensive and spacious region, and containing in many places

in locis multis et diversis bonis referta, sed a seva*d* gente et barbara ac eciam indomita usque ad illa tempora possessa. Preterea solam linguam maternam in qua | nati et nutriti fuerant tantum noverunt, 25 Scoticam scilicet et Hibernicam, nec aliam preter intel- | ligebant. Quid igitur ageret vir Domini ignarus? Quia periculosum sibi videbatur oves proprias, quarum curam susceperat, sine pastore disserere, minus eciam sibi tutum judicabat super eorum raciociniis in suppremo judicio Summo Pastori respondere, cum alter alterius 30 linguam adinvicem ignoraret, sed in quavis poscenda vel reddenda racione, et populus pastori et pastor populo, pro barbaro reputaretur. Majorem autem questum reputans episcopus salutem animarum quam dilatacionem possessionum, et quantum in se fuit studuit et seipsum exonerare, et Deo et populo satisfacere, nullomodo illis 35 consenciens preesse, quibus quasi sibi barbaris non sperabat prodesse. Capellanum igitur Heroldum nomine, virum prudentem et honestum et*e* in utraque lingua peritum et expeditum, cum literis suis ad sedem apostolicam transmittit, domino pape subnixius supplicans ut episcopatum Dunkeldensem in duas sedes divideret, Ergadiensem 40 scilicet et Dunkeldensem, et, episcopatu Dunkeldensi ad opus suum retento, Heroldum capellanum suum in episcopum Ergadiensem consecraret. Asseruit namque confidenter quod uterque episcopatus ad proprii pontificis et suorum sustentacionem satis honeste et habundanter sufficeret respondere, et omnia necessaria sine aliqua 45 indigencia copiose ministrare, si tamen ipsi tales fuerint qui neque sint prodigi, nec stirpatores patrimonii Crucifixi, sed nec nimis avari, sed modum et mediacionem modestam in omnibus servantes, neque nimis ad dextram vel ad sinistram declinantes; unde:

Est modus in rebus, sunt certi denique fines 50
ultra quos citraque nequit*f* consistere*g* rectum.

Audiant ista episcopi diciores, qui habentes beneficia prepinguia impetrant ecclesias et monasteria in commenda, qui non solum non minuere sed augere student

Si possint recte, si non quocumque*h* modo rem. 55

Audiant quid pauper episcopus egerit, beati Martini imitatus exemplum, qui clamidem, quam solam habuit, algenti pauperi dimidiavit.

---

d silvestri *CA*

e magne literature et egregie predicacionis
    for et *CA*

f citra que nescit *for* citraque nequit *CA*

g + virtus *del.C*

h quoquomodo *CA*

many and various goods, but owned by a ferocious and savage people
who were in fact untamed up to that time. Besides they knew only one
mother tongue into which they had been born and brought up, that is
30   Scottish or Irish Gaelic, and they understood no other except that.
What therefore was the man of the Lord who did not know this
language to do? Because it seemed to him dangerous to abandon his
own sheep, whose care he had undertaken, without a shepherd, even
less did he judge it safe for himself to answer to the Chief Shepherd at
35   the Last Judgment on their reckonings, since one party did not
reciprocally understand the language of the other; but in any account
that was to be demanded or rendered the people thought the pastor
savage, and the pastor the people. Considering the salvation of souls
to be more profitable than the increase of possessions, the bishop
40   sought as much as he could to relieve himself of a burden and give
satisfaction to God and the people. In no way did he agree to have
charge of those to whom he had no hopes of being of assistance, since
they were like savages to him. Therefore he sent his chaplain called
Harold, a discreet and honourable man who was knowledgeable and
45   skilful in both languages, with his letter to the apostolic see, humbly
requesting the lord pope to divide the bishopric of Dunkeld into two
sees, namely Argyll and Dunkeld, and to consecrate his chaplain
Harold as bishop of Argyll, with the bishopric of Dunkeld retained
for his own service. For he confidently claimed that each bishopric
50   would have sufficient resources to match the support needed for its
bishop and his staff at a suitably honourable and affluent level, and to
provide abundantly for all their needs without any shortage, provided
they were the kind of men who were not extravagant, nor destroyers
of Christ's patrimony, and not too greedy, but following moderation
55   and the middle way within due limits in all things, not inclining too
much to right or left; hence:

> There is a measure in affairs; there are, in fact, fixed bounds,
> beyond and short of which right can find no place.

Richer bishops should pay attention to this, those who with
60   exceptionally fat benefices obtain churches and monasteries in
commend, who busy themselves not only with avoiding decrease but
with increase of

> Their property, legally if they can, but if not, in any kind of
> way.

65   They should note what a poor bishop has done, following the example
of the blessed Martin, who divided the only cloak he had with a poor
man who was cold.

40

Quod papa miratur conscienciam episcopi et postulata concedit

Summus vero pontifex, perceptis et perlectis literis a Johanne
episcopo Dunkeldensi sibi transmissis, vehementer obstupuit, admir-
atus in viro Dei consciencie puritatem, mentis devocionem et spiritus
paupertatem. Et circumspiciens astantibus dixit: 'Advertite fratres,
advertite   5

> Rara avis in terra, nigroque simillima cigno,
> sepe quesita multum, minimeque reperta.

In Johanne episcopo Dunkeldensi, licet absente corpore, nobis hodie
literatorie presentatur.*ᵃ* Qui, quod ceteri moliuntur prolongare, solus
| nititur breviare. Nam cum ceteri redditus et predia studeant   10
ampliare, hic solus preter morem ceterorum unicum episcopatum, et
ipsum satis tenuem, quem nobis consensientibus nuper assecutus est,
annisu conatur dimidiare. Nec cessabit, scimus, a ceptis donec
affectus animo conceptus optatum per nos consequatur effectum.'
Accersito ergo predicto Heroldo, summus pontifex ei secundum   15
peticionem Johannis episcopi Dunkeldensis episcopatum Ergadie
dedit, et consecratum in Scociam cum literis apostolicis remisit. Unde
factum est a diebus illis et in posterum, quod dictus Heroldus
episcopus et successores sui Ergadiensem, predictus eciam Johannes
et sibi succedentes Dunkeldensem rexerunt episcopatum. Qui episco-   20
patu exoneratus Ergadiensi, non modicum onus humeris suis
quondam impositum se gratulatur excussisse, licet quamplures
moderni episcopi tale onus in usus proprios retinuissent, jacturam
maximam reputantes si episcopatui suo quavis occasione justa vel
injusta tantum subtraxissent. Hic vero Johannes in senectute bona   25
decidens lecto egritudinis qua mortuus est apud Neubotil, accersitisᵇ
abbate et conventu, ait: 'Testis michi est Deus, cui secreta patent
animorum, qui eciam judex est non solum operum sed intencionum,
quod ex quo michi perfeccio vestre sancte religionis operibus magis
quam sermonibus innotuit, semper ordinem vestrum in tantum   30
zelatus sum, ut pridem habitum et vestrum induissem, nisi quidam
domesticorum meorum quibus propositum meum secrecius revelavi

G i,358

---

a quia *for* [*second*] advertite ... presentatur   *b*   *D*; accisitis *C*
CA

40

*The pope admires the bishop's conscience and grants
what was requested*

The supreme pontiff indeed, after receiving and reading the letter sent
to him by John bishop of Dunkeld, was very much amazed,
marvelling at the man of God's pure conscience, pious mind and
humble spirit. And looking around, he said to the bystanders: 'See,
5 brothers, see

> A bird that is rare on earth, and most like a black swan,
> that is often much sought after, and seldom found.

In John bishop of Dunkeld it is presented to us today in his letter, even
if he is absent in the flesh. He is one who, although others strive to
10 extend things, alone endeavours to make them smaller. For when the
others concentrate on augmenting their revenues and estates, he alone
contrary to the ways of the others is strenuously trying to halve the
one see (and that a pretty modest one) which he has recently acquired
with our consent. And he will not desist from his undertaking, we
15 know, until the wish he has conceived in his mind achieves the effect it
desires through us.' The said Harold was therefore summoned, and
the supreme pontiff gave him the see of Argyll in accordance with the
request of John bishop of Dunkeld, and after consecration sent him
back to Scotland with an apostolic letter. Hence it turned out that
20 from that time forward the said Bishop Harold and his successors
governed the see of Argyll, and the aforesaid John and those
succeeding him governed that of Dunkeld. Once he had been relieved
of the see of Argyll, he was thankful to have shaken off no small
burden that had previously been placed on his shoulders, although
25 very many bishops today would have held on to such a burden for
their own use, thinking it a serious loss if only they had detached what
was or what was not their due from their see under any circumstances
whatsoever.
　　This John, indeed as he was dying in good old age on the bed of
30 sickness which led to his death at Newbattle, summoned the abbot
and convent and said: 'God be my witness, to whom the secrets of
men's minds are open, who also is the judge not only of actions but
also of intentions, that since I have learned about the perfection of
your holy religious life from actions rather than words, I have always
35 been so zealous for your order that I would have donned your habit

affectu permoti carnali quam spirituali penitus restitissent, et
lacrimosis precibus ne hoc aliquatinus attemptarem dissuasissent.
Falsa enim quadam suspicione decepti, me quasi mortuum se   35
credebant perdidisse, quem habitum episcopalem pro monachili
cernerent commutasse, trepidantes timore ubi non erat timor. Quod
igitur in bona prosperitate constitutus necligenter, ymmo nimis
insipienter, ad quorundam suggestionem, omisi, saltem iam in
vespere vite mee positus, ulterius effectu prosequente complere non 40
differam.' Dixit, et ut habitus sibi daretur, caritative cum magna
devocione supplicavit, quem humiliter induit, et monachus in
Domino obdormivit, sepultusque est in choro^c ex parte^d aquilonali
altaris, ubi claret^e miraculis, sicut testatur libellus de eius vita inibi

fo.124   habitus, | eleganter compositus per quendam monachum^f dominum 45
Willelmum Benyng eiusdem domus tunc priorem, postea vero de
Cupro abbatem. Dictus vero dominus Hugo, accessor eius ad
episcopatum Sanctiandr', stetit ibi episcopus^g decem annis et totidem
mensibus, ⟨qui cum pro ipsa causa inter ipsum et Johannem
Dunkeldensem sedem Romanam adiret, et in favorem^h pape accep- 50
tus, et de intrusione ad episcopatum^i absolutus,^{j} sexto miliario^k cis
urbem⟩ mortuus est pridie non' augusti anno domini m° c lxxxviii°.^{l}

c	+eiusdem *CA*	h	+tandem non sine difficultate *CA*
d	+al *del.C*	i	+indicta sibi gravi penitencia *CA*
e	clarere dicitur *for* claret *CA*	j	+mortuus est *del.C*
f	+eiu *del.C*	k	+in redeundo *CA*
g	+more suo *CA*	l	+et sepultus in veteri ecclesia *del.C*

41

G i,359   *De successione Rogeri^a et Willelmi episcoporum eiusdem*

Anno domini m° c° lxxxix post obitum Hugonis episcopi Rogerus
filius nobilis viri et comitis Leycestrie, cognatus domini regis Willelmi
et cancellarius, electus est ad episcopatum Sanctiandr' idus aprilis
feria vi; et anno dominice incarnacionis m° c° xc° viii° consecratus est
a Richardo episcopi Moravie prima dominica xl^e in ipsa sui 5
episcopatus sede, astante rege c'. Et stetit electus decem annis, et
consecratus tribus cum dimidio; mortuus est apud Cambuskeneth
non' julii anno domini m° cc° ii°, sepultusque in veteri ecclesia
Sanctandr'. Quo anno quidam legatus Johannes nomine in Scociam
destinatus Willelmum episcopum Glasguensem ad instanciam regis 10
Willelmi transferens ecclesie Sanctiandr' prefecit antistitem. Cuius

a   *interlin.over* Hugonis *del.C*

some time ago, had it not been that some of my household to whom I
privately revealed my intention had offered heartfelt resistance
(moved by fleshly rather than spiritual affection), and had with tearful
prayers to some extent advised me against attempting this. For they
40 were misled by a false suspicion when they believed that they had lost
me as if in death, when they saw that I had changed my episcopal garb
for a monk's habit, trembling with fear where there was no fear. What
therefore when I was at the height of my powers I negligently, indeed
too foolishly, failed to do at the prompting of some people, at least
45 now that I am in the evening of my life, I shall not put off fulfilling any
longer with immediate effect.' So he spoke; and with great piety he
begged that out of charity he might be given the habit, which he
donned with humility; and as a monk he fell asleep in the Lord, and   [1203]
was buried in the choir to the north of the altar. There he shines forth
50 by reason of his miracles, as is testified by a book on his life kept there,
which was skilfully composed by a certain monk, sir William Bening,
who was then prior of the house [of Newbattle] and later abbot of
Coupar.

The said sir Hugh, his successor in the see of St Andrews, remained
55 as bishop there for ten years and as many months, and when he went
to the Roman see regarding the case between him and John of
Dunkeld, and had been received into the pope's favour and absolved
regarding his intrusion into the see, died [while returning] six miles
from the city on this side on 4 August 1188.   1188:
                                                                        4 Aug.

41

The succession of Roger and William as bishops of the same

In 1189 after Bishop Hugh's death Roger, a son of the nobleman who   1189:
was earl of Leicester, and a kinsman and chancellor of the lord king   13 Apr.
William, was elected to the bishopric of St Andrews on 13 April (a
Friday); and in 1198 he was consecrated to his episcopal see by   1198:
5 Richard bishop of Moray on the first Sunday in Lent, in the presence   15 Feb.
of the king, etc. And he served as bishop-elect for ten years, and as a
consecrated bishop for three years and a half. He died at Cambuskenneth on 7 July 1202, and was buried in the old church of St Andrew.   1202: 7 July

In this year a certain legate called John who had been sent to
10 Scotland translated William bishop of Glasgow at the request of King   20 Sept.
William, and appointed him bishop of the church of St Andrews. His
postulation and translation took place at Scone on 20 September (a
Friday). He ruled the church of St Andrews with vigour and
distinction through many misfortunes for thirty-five years, ten

postulacio et translacio apud Sconam celebrata est xii kal' octobris
feria vi. Hic rexit ecclesiam Sanctiandr' fortiter et egregie in multis
adversitatibus xxxv annis decem mensibus et duabus ebdomadis.
Dispersa namque et alienata pervigili cura in pristinum statum   15
studuit revocare, congregata et usibus ecclesie deputata sagaci[b]
industria conservare, hilari vultu et mente jocunda largiter dispen-
sare. Abstulit tamen a domo de Dunf' voluntarie, ut dicitur,
collacionem vicariarum de Kinglassi et de Haleʒ, quia quadam vice,
dum apud Dunfermelyne pernoctaret, defecit sibi potus vini ad   20
collacionem in camera post cenam. Et hoc non defectu ministrorum
monachorum, sed suorum, qui diliberata sibi ad sufficienciam minus
caute expendendo ante tempus consumpserunt. Et tandem vii idus
julii feria vi anno domini m° cc^{mo} xxxviii° apud Inchemurthauch
moritur, et in nova ecclesia Sanctiandr' sepelitur.   25

Anno domini m° cc° xxxviii[c] Gaufridus Dunkeldensis episcopus
fuit postulatus, sed graciam domini pape et regis Alexandri secundi
non fuit consecutus. Et anno sequenti, Gaufrido cifrato, et licencia
tam a rege quam a papa optenta, ut in altrum sua vota electores
dirigerent, David de Bernhame camerarium regis iii non' junii per 30
viam compromissi concorditer elegerunt; et a venerabilibus patribus
Glasguensi, Catanensi, Brechinensi episcopis per literas apostolicas
potestate eis commissa in die Sancti Vincencii consecratus est. Hic
collegio suo durus et inhumanus extitit; diversis exaccionibus angariis
et extorsionibus fatigavit, et ecclesiam de Incheture, quam[d] pie 35
memorie rex Willelmus canonicis ante dederat, injuste et de facto
abstulit; sed inde modicum lucri reportavit, quia subito post hoc
incidit in egritudinem incurabilem, per quam ad extremam horam
perveniens ⟨restituta tamen eis ecclesia⟩ mortuus est vi kal' maii apud
Narthanthira; et sepultus in Kalco contra protestacionem et prohibi- 40
cionem ecclesie Sanctiandr'. Stetit episcopus xiii annis tribus mensibus et ix diebus, et mortuus est[e] anno domini m° cc° liii°.

b   + -que *interlin.C; om.CA*
c   xxviii *C,R*; xxvii *D*; Eodem anno *for*
    Anno ... xxviii *CA*

d   + eis *del.C*
e   et mortuus est [?] *marked for deletion C;*
    om.D

42

De Abel, Gamelino et Willelmo Wischard
successive episcopis

Anno quo supra electus fuit Robertus de Stwtevile decanus Dunkeldensis, vir sciencia et moribus preclarus, per viam compromissi in

15 months and two weeks. For he devoted himself with ever-watchful
attention to restoring property that had been dispersed and alienated
to its original condition, to preserving with discerning purposefulness
what had been gathered together and assigned for the church's
purposes, and with cheerful countenance and jovial disposition to
20 making generous distributions. Yet he arbitrarily took from the
house of Dunfermline, it is said, the right to nominate to the vicarages
of Kinglassie and Hailes, because on one occasion when he was
spending the night at Dunfermline he had insufficient wine to drink
for refreshment in his room after supper. And this was not the fault of
25 the monks' servants, but of his own, who by reckless serving of the
amount of wine which had been calculated as sufficient for his needs
used it up earlier than expected. And at length he died at Inchmurdo
on 9 July 1238 (a Friday), and is buried in the new church of St   1238: 9 July
Andrew.
30   In 1238 Geoffrey bishop of Dunkeld was postulated [to the see of St
Andrews], but he did not win the favour of the lord pope and King
Alexander II. And in the following year, once [the election of]
Geoffrey had been quashed and permission had been obtained from   1239:
both king and pope for the electors to vote for someone else, they   [12 Feb.]
35 amicably elected David de Bernham the king's chamberlain on 3 June   3 June
using the compromise procedure; and he was consecrated on St
Vincent's Day by the venerable fathers the bishops of Glasgow,   [1240:]
Caithness and Brechin on the strength of authority granted to them   22 Jan.
by apostolic letters. This man behaved with harshness and inhu-
40 manity towards his [cathedral] community; he harassed them with
various exactions, tolls and extortions, and took from them unjustly
and *de facto* the church of Inchture, which King William of blessed
memory had previously given to the canons; but from that he
obtained modest profit, for suddenly after this he fell ill with an
45 incurable disease. It was this that brought him to his life's end. He had
however restored the church to them, and he died on 26 April at   1253:
Nenthorn. He was buried at Kelso despite the protest and prohibition   26 Apr.
of the church of St Andrews. He served as bishop for thirteen years,
three months and nine days, and died in the year 1253.

42

Abel, Gamelin and William Wischard who
succeeded each other as bishops

In the same year on the eve of the feast of St Peter and St Paul Robert   1253:
de Stuteville dean of Dunkeld, a man distinguished for his learning   28 June

vigilia*a* Apostolorum Petri et Pauli. Unde facta est magna dissencio,
archidiacono Sanctiandr' impedimentum prestante, et eiusdem
mediis ipso*b* electo per dominum regem non admisso. Prior cum   5
canonicis Sanctiandr', facta appellacione, electum domino pape
direxerunt; ex altera parte rex per nuncios suos cum dicto archidiacono magistro Abell ad curiam Romanam transmisit. Ubi factum est
ut, succumbente veritate per sinistram suggestionem, prevalente
falsitate, electus graciam pape non est assecutus, sed archidiaconus   10
Abel de eodem episcopatu ex provisione apostolica infulatus repatriavit. Qui cum ecclesiam Sanctiandr' primo visitaverit, propria
manu in*c* porta creto scripsit:

> Hec michi sunt tria, lex, canon, philosophia.

In crastino consimili scriptura, nescitur tamen a quo,*d* sic subscribe-   15
batur:

> Te levent absque bria fraus, favor, vana sophia.

Qua scriptura comperta,*e* ira incanduit, furia infremuit, et scriptori
ultimi versus exterminium comminatur. Sed, ut dicit Beda: 'Ubi est
fervida vindicta, | non est temperata justicia.' Presul in premissis   20
canonicos*f* habuit suspectos, et propterea non tantum, sed quia sibi
consensum in eleccione denegarunt, indignatus quamplurimum, in
despectum et dedignacionem*g* eos quoad vixit procuravit. Quare cito
Deus delevit memoriam eius e terra, ne pastoris officio fungeretur,
cuius*h* justo judicio facti sunt dies eius pauci, et episcopatum eius   25
accepit alter. Nam stetit episcopus decem mensibus et duabus
septimanis, et in crastino Sanctiandr' anno m° cc° liiii*to* mortuus, et in
nova ecclesia sepultus est. ⟨De quo require infra libro x capitulo viii.⟩
Quo anno prima dominica xl*e* postulatus est Gamelinus domini regis
Alexandri tercii cancellarius; ac secundo die Natalis Domini, que   30
dominica habebatur, anno sequenti*i* a Willelmo episcopo Glasguensi
consecratus, quodammodo rege invito, licet consiliarii regis reclamantibus et missis nunciis ad papam appellantibus prohiberent.*j* Iste
episcopus satis provide gubernavit ecclesiam pacificus et amatus; et in
crastino Sancti Vitalis martyris apud Inchemurthawch anno domini   35
m° cc° lxxi° mortuus, et in nova ecclesia juxta magnum altare
honorifice, postquam stetisset electus et*k* episcopus xvi annos,
sepultus. ⟨De ipso vide infra libro x capitulo xxii cum sequente.⟩ Quo
anno postulatus*l* est Willelmus Wischart*m* ⟨electus Glasguensis⟩, vir

fo.124v (margin, left of line 19)

a	corrected from via C	*g*	corrected from indignacionem C
b	episcopo D	*h*	+eciam CA
c	+prop del.C	*i*	+id est domini m° cc lv° CA
d	+dissimili tamen manu a quo nescitur *for*	*j*	quodammodo ... prohiberent om.CA
	nescitur tamen a quo CA	*k*	electus et om.CA
e	+episcopus CA	*l*	interlin.over electus del.C
f	interlin.C	*m*	spelled Wischard in margin C

and character, was elected by means of the compromise procedure.
Thereupon a major dispute arose, with the archdeacon of St Andrews
5 raising an objection, and in the middle of this the [bishop-] elect was
not admitted by the lord king. The prior and canons of St Andrews
appealed, and sent the elect direct to the lord pope; on the other side
the king sent his account of the case to the Roman court by his envoys
along with Master Abel, the archdeacon. There the truth yielded to
10 improper hints, and falsehood prevailed; and it turned out that the
elect did not win the pope's favour, but Abel the archdeacon returned
to Scotland vested with episcopal insignia for the same see by [1254:
apostolic provision. When he first visited the church of St Andrews, 1 Mar.]
he wrote in chalk in his own hand on the door:

15   Law, the Bible, philosophy – these three are mine.

The next morning in similar writing there was written underneath (it
is not known by whom) as follows:

    Deceit, partiality, illusory wisdom without measure may raise
        you up.

20 When this writing was discovered, his wrath became red-hot, his
frenzy roared, and expulsion was threatened against the writer of the
last line of verse. But, as Bede says: 'Where vengeance is passionate,
justice is not controlled.' The bishop suspected the canons in this
affair, and in his extreme indignation, not only on that account, but
25 because they had denied him an agreed election, he regarded them
with contempt and disdain as long as he lived. Therefore God soon
expunged memory of him from the land. To prevent him exercising
the office of pastor, Abel's days by God's just judgment were made
few, and another took over his see. For he served as bishop for [only]
30 ten months and two weeks; and he died on the day after St Andrew's 1254:
Day 1254, and was buried in the new church. (For him see below [31 Aug.]
Book X, Chapter 8.)
        In this year on the first Sunday in Lent Gamelin the chancellor of 1254/5:
the lord king Alexander III was postulated; on the day after 14 Feb.
35 Christmas of the following year (which was a Sunday), he was 1255:
consecrated by William bishop of Glasgow. This was to some extent 26 Dec.
against the king's wishes, although the king's councillors had
impeded those who objected and were appealing to the pope by
sending envoys. This bishop ruled the church quite wisely as a beloved
40 peacemaker; and he died on the day after the feast of St Vitalis the
Martyr 1271 at Inchmurdo, and was buried with honour in the new 1271:
church next to the high altar, after serving as elect and bishop for 29 Apr.
sixteen years. (For him see below Book X, Chapter 22 ff.)
        In this year William Wischard, bishop-elect of Glasgow, a man of
45 great nobility and reputation, was postulated on 2 June. He was then [3] June
consecrated at Scone on 15 October 1273. The Culdees had been 1273:
                                                                15 Oct.

magne nobilitatis et fame iiii^{to} non' junii. Consecratus est autem apud 40
Sconam idus octobris anno domini m° cc° lxxiii, Keldeis tunc ab
eleccione exclusus. Qui ecclesiam | suam et collegium affectuose
diligens, occidentalem partem eiusdem ecclesie violencia cuiusdam
ventose tempestatis ad terram dejectam, de eschaetis suis notabiliter
et sumptuose reedificavit. Huius temporibus nemo magnatum Scocie 45
causam contra ecclesiam Sanctiandr' movere, vel cum ipso contendere, voluit aut valebat. Mortuus est autem apud Merbotil quinto kal'
junii anno domini m° cc° lxxix, et sepultus est apud Sanctumandr' in
nova ecclesia ante altare iiii^{to} non' junii, revolutis annis eadem die qua
fuit electus. ⟨De ipso vide infra libro x capitulo xxviii et capitulo xxxi 50
cum sequenti.⟩ Stetit autem electus per biennium iiii^{or} menses et xxiii
dies; episcopus autem per quinque annos et octo menses; et sic electus
et episcopus stetit per septem annos vi menses et ix dies.

43

De Willelmo Fraser et Willelmo Lambirton' episcopis

Anno domini m° cc° lxxix pridie non' augusti electus Willelmus
Fraser cancellarius regis, exclusis eciam Keldeis tunc sicut et in
eleccione precedenti. Consecratus est autem in curia Romana a
domino papa Nicholao xiiii kal' junii anno gracie m° cc lxxx. Stetit
electus decem mensibus et vi diebus, episcopus autem xvii annis 5
mensibus tribus et octo diebus; electus autem et episcopus annis xviii
et diebus xv. Qui tirannidem Eadwardi de Langschankis regis Anglie
et Anglicorum inimicicias cupiens declinare, ad partes Francie
secessit, et apud Artuyl xiii° kal' septembris anno domini m° cc°
nonagesimo septimo fatis cessit, Parisiusque sepultus in ecclesia 10
Fratrum Predicatorum. Cor autem eius post aliquantulum temporis
delatum est in Scociam, et per successorem suum Willelmum de
Lambirdon est reconditum in pariete ecclesie Sanctiandr' juxta
tumbam episcopi Gamelini. Interim vero dum dictus episcopus
Willelmus in Francia perhendinaret, anno scilicet domini m^{mo} cc° 15
xcv^{to}, propter evidentissimas causas suspicionis prodicionis, et
probabilia argumenta conspiratorie pravitatis contra regem et statum
regni,^{a} omnes Anglici beneficiati in episcopatum Sanctiandr' omnibus beneficiis per magistros Willelmum de Kingorn et Petrum de
Campania sentencialiter pro perpetuo^b sunt ejecti. Similiter reliqui 20
omnes et singuli Anglici tam clerici quam laici propter suas
conspiraciones per consilium regis de eiusdem regno sunt expulsi,
⟨cuius executor fuit Willelmus Wales.⟩

---

a +tunc acephali *CA* b +similiter reliqui omnes et singuli *del.C*

excluded from this election. He had an affectionate love for his church
and cathedral community, and when the western part of the same
church fell to the ground as a result of the violence of a certain storm
50 of wind, he rebuilt it in remarkable fashion and at great expense out of
his escheats. In his day none of the magnates of Scotland wished or
had the power to start a case against the church of St Andrews or to
dispute with him. But he died at Morebattle on 28 May 1279, and was   1279:
buried at St Andrews in the new church in front of the altar on 2 June,   28 May
55 the same date with the passing of the years as that on which he had
been elected. (For him see below Book X, Chapters 28 and 31 ff.) He
served as elect for two years, four months and twenty-three days, then
as bishop for five years and eight months; and so as elect and bishop
he served for seven years, six months and nine days.

43

Bishops William Fraser and William Lamberton

On 4 August 1279 William Fraser, the king's chancellor, was elected,   1279:
with the Culdees again excluded then as in the preceding election. He   4 Aug.
was consecrated in the Roman court by the lord pope Nicholas on 19   1280:
May 1280. He served as bishop-elect for ten months and six days, as   19 May
5   bishop for seventeen years, three months and eight days; and so as
elect and bishop for eighteen years and fifteen days. Wanting to avoid
the tyranny of Edward Longshanks king of England and the hostile
acts of the English, he withdrew to France and met his end at Auteuil
on 20 August 1297; and he was buried in the church of the Friars   1297:
10 Preachers at Paris. Then after a little while his heart was brought to 20 Aug.
Scotland, and was buried by his successor William de Lamberton in
the wall of the church of St Andrew next the tomb of Bishop Gamelin.
In the meantime in 1295 indeed, while the said Bishop William was   [1296]
staying in France, all Englishmen holding benefices in the diocese of
15 St Andrews were ejected permanently from all their benefices by
judicial decree of Master William de Kinghorn and Master Peter de
Campania on account of the clearest grounds for suspicion of
treason, and credible proofs of criminal conspiracy against the king
and state of the kingdom. In like manner all and sundry of the rest of
20 the English, both clerics and laymen, were expelled by the king's
council from his kingdom on account of their plotting, William
Wallace being the man who put their decree into effect.   [1297]
William Fraser was succeeded by William de Lamberton, who was
then chancellor of Glasgow. He was elected on 5 November 1297,   1297:
25 with the Culdees then entirely excluded as in the two previous   5 Nov.

Willelmo Fraser successit Willelmus de Lambirton tunc cancellarius Glasguensis. Electus est non' novembris anno domini m° cc° 25
xcvii°, exclusis penitus Keldeis tunc sicut in duabus eleccionibus
precedentibus. Propter quod Willelmus Cumyne tunc Keldeorum
prepositus huic eleccioni se opponens Romam adiit, et in presencia
domini pape Bonifacii viii omnibus modis quibus potuit eleccionem
predictam et ipsum electum impugnavit; sed nichil profecit. Nam non 30
obstantibus ipsius excepcionibus, dominus papa ipsam eleccionem

G i,362

approbavit, electum | confirmavit, ipsumque electum kal' junii anno
domini m° cc° xcviii° more debito consecravit. Et notandum est quod
jurisdiccio sedis, ipsa vacante, penes capitulum totaliter remansit.
Quam quidem jurisdiccionem^c magister Nicholaus de Balmile officia- 35
lis curie Sanctiandr' per eiusdem loci capitulum constitutus per totam
diocesim efficaciter exequebatur, et plenarie quatenus de jure potuit
nomine capituli exercebat. Iste Willelmus canonicos suos affectuose
diligens multa bona in vita sua fecit. ⟨Circa reparacionem edifi-
ciorum monasterii valde intentus, et multa exponens, pauca de 40
propriis reparavit mansis. Qui postquam steterat episcopus quasi
xviii annis, dum a suis familiaribus redargutus quod non edificaverat
maneria propria, sic eum semel fertur commote respondisse: 'Tanta et
tam valida, Dei cooperante gracia, intendo edificia erigere, quod
multi, quasi michi^d succedentes, pro magno ducent ipsa in congruo vel 45
statu consimili sustinere.' Dehinc quasi omni anno perfecit satis
sumptuose^e ⟨videlicet proprium palacium in Sanctoandr' fortaliza-
tum⟩^f manerium videlicet^g Inchemurdach, Monymell, Dersi, Torry,
Mukkardi, Ketnes, Mwnymusk, Lynton, Leswad, et le Stow in
Wedal', ac eciam⟩ capitulum novum suis sumptibus construxit. 50

fo.125

Magne ecclesie trabes tabulis | dolatis et celaturis solempniter
ornavit, preciosumque vestimentum rubeum imaginibus contextum^h
cum mitra et baculo pastorali ac plures libros valde bonos eisdem
canonicis reliquit. Ecclesiam suam sapiencia et prudencia ac omni
morum honestate laudabiliter rexit; jura et libertates ecclesiasticas 55
cunctis diebus conservavit intactas, ac aliis virtutum insigniis ipsam
multipliciter decoravit. Stetit autem vii mensibus et duabus septimanis electus, episcopus autem xxx annis et vi diebus; et sic electus et
episcopus per xxx^{ta} annos xxx^{ta} septimanas et sex dies. Post hec decidit
in egritudinem, qua ex hac luce substractus est in monasterio 60
Sanctiandr' camera domini prioris loci eiusdem; sepultusque est in
magna ecclesia ad borealem partem altaris vii idus junii anno domini
m° ccc^{mo} xxviii°.

c	+ Rich *del.C*	*f*	*in margin of marginal addition C*
d	*corrected from* mei *C*	*g*	manerium videlicet *om.CA*
e	+ unum de maneriis *CA*	*h*	+ cum imaginibus contextum *del.C*

elections. On this account William Comyn who was then provost of
the Culdees opposed this election. He went to Rome, and in the
presence of the lord pope Boniface VIII challenged the said election
and the man who had been elected in every way that he could; but to
30 no effect. For notwithstanding his objections, the lord pope approved
the election, confirmed the bishop-elect, and on 1 June 1298   1298:
consecrated him in due fashion.   1 June

It should be noted that episcopal jurisdiction during a vacancy rests
entirely with the chapter. This jurisdiction was effectively adminis-
35 tered throughout the whole diocese by Master Nicholas de Balmyle,
the official of the court of St Andrews appointed by the chapter of the
same place, and was exercised in the name of the chapter as fully as
possible under the law.

This William had an affectionate love for his canons, and did many
40 good things during his lifetime. While extremely concerned with the
repair of the monastery buildings and making much available [for
that], he repaired little on his own estates. After he had served as
bishop for some eighteen years, when shown by members of his
household to be guilty of not building his own manor-houses, he is
45 said to have once replied in some agitation: 'With the help of the grace
of God, I intend to erect buildings of such size and of such strength
that many as my successors, will think it important to maintain them
in a suitable or similar condition.' From then on he completed [one of
his manor-houses] nearly every year at quite considerable expense,
50 namely his own fortress palace at St Andrews, his manor-houses at
Inchmurdo, Monimail, Dairsie, Torry, Muckhart, Kettins, Monymusk, Liston, Lasswade and Stow in Wedale; he also built a new
chapter-house at his own expense. He splendidly adorned the beams
of the great church with shaped boards and carvings, and left to the
55 canons of the same a valuable red vestment adorned with [embroi-
dered] pictures, along with a mitre and pastoral staff and a great many
books. He ruled his church in a praiseworthy manner with wisdom
and foresight and complete integrity of character; he preserved its
rights and ecclesiastical liberties intact all his days, and adorned it in
60 many ways with other signs of his virtues. He served as bishop-elect
for seven months and two weeks, and as bishop for thirty years and six
days; so he served as elect and bishop for thirty years, thirty weeks and
six days. Then he fell ill with the complaint by which he was carried off
from this life in the monastery of St Andrews, in the room of the lord
65 prior of that place; and he was buried in the great church to the north   1328:
of the altar on 7 June 1328.   7 June

44

De domino Jacobo Ben, Willelmo Bell electo, et Willelmo Laundalis episcopis

Anno premisso*ᵃ* xiii kal' julii processerunt ad eleccionem canonici Sanctiandr', exclusis penitus Keldeis sicut in eleccionibus precedentibus. Aliquibus concordantibus per viam scrutinii in dominum Jacobum Ben*ᵇ* archidiaconum tunc Sanctiandr', aliquibus in dominum Alexandrum de Kyninmonth tunc archidiaconum*ᶜ* Laudonie, 5 discordia facta est in eleccione. Sed dominus Jacobus, tunc personaliter in curia Romana existens, antequam ad eum pervenit noticia de eleccione facta optinuit episcopatum ex collacione domini Johannis pape xxii, qui quasi omnes episcopatus mundi ad collacionem suam reservavit. Dominus autem Alexander curiam Romanam adiens, 10

provisione | domini pape effectus est episcopus Abirden'. Contra autem eleccionem dominus Willelmus Cumyne tunc prepositus capelle regie se opposuit, sed suam appellacionem veluti fingebat; propter hoc curiam Romanam adire non est persecutus. Qui postea gracia domini pape ad archidiaconum Laudonie est promotus. Hic 15 dominus Jacobus episcopus, timens feritatem et seviciam intolerabilem Anglicorum post bellum de Dupplyne in regno Scocie usquequaque fremencium, coronato prius per eum rege David puerulo, de Lacu de Levin nocte venit apud Sanctumandr'; et valedicens priori et conventui nocte sequenti cum paucis ibidem navem ingressus,*ᵈ* non 20 multis interjectis diebus in Flandria applicuit incolumis, et in villa de Brugis moratus x kal' octobris ab hac luce migravit, ⟨sepultusque in monasterio de Akewod canonicorum regularium Brugis.*ᵉ*⟩ anno domini m° ccc° xxxii.*ᶠ* Stetit autem episcopus quatuor annis duabus septimanis et totidem diebus. 25

Quo anno xiiii kal' septembris electus est Willelmus Bell decanus Dunkeldensis, exclusis tunc penitus Keldeis, nullumque jus in dicta eleccione vendicantibus seu impedimentum facientibus, per viam compromissi. Qui curiam que tunc Avinione erat adiit, ubi multos contradictores et adversarios invenit, quibus eius expedicio usque 30 promocionem domini Willelmi de Laundalis*ᵍ* finaliter fuit impedita.

---

a   +electus est Jacobus Ben *del.C*   *e*   *om.CA*
b   Benedicti *CA*   *f*   +nescitur tamen quo die *CA*
c   *CA*; archidiaconem *C,D*   *g*   +ad episcopatum *CA*
d   +est *D; del.C*

44

The bishops sir James Ben, sir William Bell elect, and William Laundels

On 19 June of the said year the canons of St Andrews held an election, 1328:
with the Culdees entirely excluded as in previous elections. The 19 June
method of a general vote was used, and with some agreeing on sir
James Ben who was then archdeacon of St Andrews, and some on sir
5 Alexander de Kininmund who was then archdeacon of Lothian, the
election was a disputed one. But sir James, who was then staying at
the Roman court in person, before news of the outcome of the
election reached him, obtained the bishopric by appointment of the [1 Aug.]
lord pope John XXII, who had reserved for his own appointment
10 nearly all the bishoprics in the world. Sir Alexander then went to the
Roman court and was made bishop of Aberdeen by the lord pope's [1329:
provision. Sir William Comyn, who was then provost of the Chapel 21 Aug.]
Royal, challenged this election, but this was a pretence of an appeal,
as it were; and on this account he did not follow it up by going to the
15 Roman court. Later he was promoted archdeacon of Lothian by [11 Nov.]
favour of the lord pope. This bishop sir James, in fear of the ferocity
and intolerable cruelty of the English, who were on the rampage
everywhere in the kingdom of Scotland after the battle of Dupplin, [1332:
for the young boy David had earlier been crowned by him, came to St 11 Aug.]
20 Andrews by night from Loch Leven; bidding farewell to the prior and
convent he boarded a ship there the next night with a few
companions. Not many days later he landed safely in Flanders, and
while staying in the town of Bruges he departed this life on 22 1332:
September 1332, and was buried at the Eeckhout monastery of 22 Sept.
25 regular canons of Bruges. He served as bishop then for four years, two
weeks and as many days.
  In this year on 19 August William Bell dean of Dunkeld was elected 19 Aug. [?]
by means of the compromise procedure; the Culdees were then
entirely excluded, claimed no right in that election, and raised no
30 objection. He went to the curia which was then at Avignon, where he
encountered many opponents and adversaries, by whom the processing of his case was in the end held up until the promotion [as bishop] of
sir William de Laundels. Smitten indeed by various afflictions, and in
the end overtaken by old age and stricken with blindness, he resigned [× 1342]
35 his right of election. After returning from the curia in the company of
the said William de Laundels who had now been promoted to the see,

Hic vero variis molestiis afflictus, tandem autem etate depressus cecitateque percussus, juri eleccionis cessit. Qui rediens de curia in predicti Willelmi de Laundalis ad episcopatum iam promoti comitiva, et in monasterio Sanctiandr' habitum suscipiens regularem[h] 35 canonicorum, vii° idus februarii diem clausit extremum[i] anno domini m° ccc° xlii°,

Anno precedenti kal' marcii[j] xii[k] dominus Willelmus de Laundalis rector ecclesie de Kinkel promotus est ad episcopatum ex provisione domini pape Benedicti xii, ac xvii° die marcii consecratus; quem 40 multiplicium precum suffragia illustrium regum Francie et Scocie necnon aliarum venerabilium personarum apud summum pontificem et venerabile eius collegium dignum episcopatu pro vite meritis commendarunt. Sed precipue litere capituli Sanctiandr' tam patentes quam clause, diversis vicibus directe ad eandem sedem et pro eodem, 45 cognita renunciacione dicti magistri Willelmi Bell, expeditum ipsius negocium reddiderunt; sine quibus litere alie quevis supplicatorie expedicionis effectu penitus caruissent, quod in ipsius domini pape bullis patentibus plenius declaratur. In quibus non tamquam cuiuscumque precibus commendatus, sed eiusdem ecclesie electus 50 patenter nominatur. Cuius sedes a morte domini Jacobi Ben usque promocionem domini Willelmi Laundalis vacavit novem annis quinque mensibus et viii diebus.

h   cum magna et admiranda devocione se canonicum fieri a priore et fratribus efflagitavit et accepit habitum regularem *for* habitum ... regularem *CA*

i   + in infirmaria eiusdem *CA*
j   maii *CA*
k   + kal' marcii *CA; and del.C*

45

De eodem et domino Galtero Treyle

fo.125v
G i,364

Hic Willelmus Laundels fuit vir magne generositatis, dapsilis et benignus, dominus et heres omnium terrarum et possessionum de[a] Laundalis, lepidus, munificus, hilaris, mitis,[b] modestus, | pulcher et | pacificus, diligens[c] canonicos tamquam natos proprios. Qui cum graciose[d] rexisset xliiii annis, in[e] senectute bona in monasterio 5 Sanctiandr' diem clausit extremum. ⟨In festo Sancte Tecle Virginis[f] anno vii° et anniversario combustionis ecclesie Sanctiandr' obiit anno domini m° ccc° lxxxv[to],⟩ et in pavimento coram ostio vestibuli in magna ecclesia sub artificioso lapide humatur.

a   + le *CA*
b   *interlin.over* benignus *del.C*
c   + viscerose *CA*
d   + x *del.C*

e   xliiii annis in *corrected from* xxii annis in *with* -iiii *interlin.C*
f   + sive Adamnani *CA*

and assuming the habit of the regular canons in the monastery at St
Andrews, he breathed his last [in the infirmary there] on 7 February   1343: 7 Feb.
1342.

40   On 18 February of the previous year sir William de Laundels rector   1342:
of the church of Kinkell was promoted to the bishopric by provision   18 Feb.
of the lord pope Benedict XII, and on 17 March he was consecrated.   17 Mar.
The support which came in many requests to the supreme pontiff and
his venerable college [of cardinals] from the illustrious kings of
45 France and Scotland and also from other venerable persons
recommended him as worthy of a bishopric on the strength of the
merits of his life. But it was especially the letters (both public and
private) of the chapter of St Andrews, sent on various occasions to the
same see on his behalf, and taking into account the resignation of the
50 said Master William Bell, which achieved the processing of his
business. Without them any other letters in the form of petitions
would have entirely failed to achieve processing, a fact that is more
fully made clear in the public bulls of the lord pope himself. In these
William is not recommended as if by the request of some individual,
55 but he is openly named as the elect of the same church. This see from
the death of sir James Ben to the promotion of sir William Laundels
was vacant for nine years, five months and eight days.

45

The same [William Laundels] and sir Walter Trayl

This William Laundels was a man from a leading family, generous
and kind, the lord and heir of all the lands and estates of Laundels,
witty, generous, cheerful, gentle, forbearing, handsome and peace-
able, a [sincere] lover of the canons as his own sons. When he had held
5 office for forty-four years, he met his end at a good old age in the
monastery of St Andrews. He died on the feast of St Tecla the Virgin
[or St Adomnan] 1385, on the seventh anniversary of the burning of   1385:
the church of St Andrew, and he is buried in the paved floor in the   23 Sept.
great church opposite the door to the sacristy under a finely carved
10 stone.
     He was succeeded by Walter Trayl, a champion of the church, a
knight of civil law, a doctor of canon law, and a man equipped with all
the liberal arts, who was, however, not elected, but [appointed] by

Cui successit pugil ecclesie, miles legum, doctor canonum, et 10
omnibus artibus liberalibus preditus, Walterus Treyle, non tamen
electus, sed ex spontanea provisione domini Clementis pape^g – ⟨hic
papa linealiter descendit de Maria comitissa Bolonie, filia Margarete
regine et Malcolmi regis Scocie⟩ – cuius^h tunc in curia referendarius
Avinione erat familiarissimus et auditor^i precipuus.^{j} Ad cuius eximie 15
commendacionis titilum, audita vacacione episcopatus Sanctiandr',
fertur de eo sic papam retulisse quod isdem Walterus judicio suo
dignior erat papatu quam episcopatu. De cuius provisione longe
inferius provideretur persone quam loco. Post mortem tamen dicti
domini Willelmi de Laundelis,^{k} electus fuit per capitulum dominus 20
Stephanus Pa prior Sanctiandr',^{l} qui pro confirmacione assequenda,
cum eleccionis decreto et literis commendaticiis regis et capituli, ad
curiam iter arripiens, casu incidit mare in manus piratarum, et
Anglie^m captivus adducitur. Et quia sciebat monasterio Sanctiandr'
onere sue redempcionis, ⟨et^n infortun-[io]^o incendii ecclesie, paulo 25
ante combuste,⟩^{p} dispendium imminere, elegit pocius vitam finire in
Anglia quam occasione huiusmodi redempcionis episcopatum et
monasterium nimium dampnificare.^{q} Unde, Deo disponente, egritudinem incurrit ⟨apud Alnewik⟩ qua ex hac luce substractus; eius
anima de habitaculo corporis^r egressa, in gaudium Domini, ut 30
speratur, est ingressa.^{s} Post cuius, ut premissum est, exitum dictus
Walterus Trayl ad episcopatum accessit. Qui, quamvis de mediocri
prosapia genitus, nobilitate tamen^t morum genus excessit. Episcopus
igitur effectus, et a domino papa graciose bullis expeditus et
confirmatus, properans ad natale solum, satis suum implevit offi- 35
cium;^{u} constitutus a papa super gentes et regna,^{v} id est suos
diocesanos gentiliter viventes, et^w majores regni, ut evellat peccatorum plantaciones, et destruat hereticorum municiones, et disperdat
iniquorum consultaciones, et edificet in moribus, et plantet in fide.
Talem enim decuit tali ecclesie prefici, ad cuius quasi arbitrium tocius 40
regni in arduis pendebat gubernaculum. Impendit^x unicuique, quod
sua intererat, regi et curie consilium, ecclesie sue propendium: et sic
curis curie admixtus, quia cura sibi de omnibus erat, in neutra
administracione reliquit locum incurie. Sic seipsum ubique exornans

g   + vii *del.C*; + vii assumptus *CA*
h   Huius pape *for* cuius *CA*
i   + causarum *CA*
j   + Ipse magister *CA*
k   + quo die nescitur *CA*
l   + vir multum dapsilis et libertati acclivis,
    statura procerus et intuentibus gratus et
    valde graciosus *CA*
m   in Angliam *for* Anglie *CA*
n   Ubi ad tempus detentus perpendens
    monasterio suo Sanctiandr' onere sue
    redempcionis operante ad hoc *for* Et quia
    ... et *CA*

o   D; *lac.C*
p   + maximum *CA*
q   -ific- *interlin.C*
r   carceris *CA*
s   + ii die marcii anno domini m° ccc°
    lxxxv^{to} *CA*
t   *interlin.C*
u   + sacerdos et pontifex, et virtutum artifex
    bonus pastor in populo *CA*
v   et regna *om.CA*
w   + regna id est *CA*
x   Impendebat *CA*

provision at the wish of the lord pope Clement [VII]. (This pope was   [29 Nov.]
15 in the straight line of descent from Mary countess of Boulogne, the
daughter of Margaret the queen and Malcolm the king of Scotland.)
Walter was then a referendary in the court [of this pope] at Avignon,
one of the inner circle of his household and a distinguished auditor [of
cases]. As a mark of the pope's exceptional esteem for this man, it is
20 said that when news came of the vacancy in the bishopric of St
Andrews, the pope suggested concerning him that in his judgment the
same Walter was more worthy of the papacy than of a bishopric. By
his provision the person [i.e. Trayl] would be far worse provided for
than the place.
25   Despite this, after the death of the said sir William de Laundels the
chapter [on some unknown day] elected sir Stephen Pay prior of St
Andrews [a very generous man inclined to plain speaking, lofty in
stature, attractive to onlookers and extremely popular]. Making a
rapid start on a journey to the Roman court with his election decree
30 and letters of recommendation from the king and the chapter to
acquire confirmation, he accidentally when at sea fell into the hands
of pirates, and was taken as a captive to England. And because he
knew that the monastery of St Andrews was threatened by the [great]
expense of the burden of his ransom and the unfortunate fire which
35 had burnt their church not long before, he chose rather to end his life
in England than through a ransom of this kind do too much harm to
the bishopric and monastery. There by God's will he took ill at
Alnwick, as a result of which he was borne away from this world; his
soul departed from its bodily dwelling-place and, it is hoped, entered
40 into the joy of the Lord [on 2 March 1385].   1386: 2 Mar.
   After his death, as has been said above, the said Walter Trayl
succeeded to the bishopric. Although he belonged to a family of
middling status, nevertheless by the nobility of his character he
surpassed his lineage. Once he had been made bishop therefore, with
45 his appointment graciously expedited and confirmed by bulls of the
lord pope, he hurried to his native land and satisfied the demands of
his office well enough; [as priest and bishop, and a good skilled master
of the virtues, a good pastor among his people,] he had been given
authority by the pope over peoples and kingdoms, that is those of
50 good birth living in his diocese and the magnates of the kingdom, to
eradicate deeply-rooted sins, and tear down the ramparts of heretics,
and destroy the deliberations of the wicked, and build on the
foundation of morals and plant on faith. For it was suitable for such a
man to be put in charge of such a church, on whose judgment
55 depended the government of almost the whole kingdom in matters of
difficulty. He bestowed on everyone what was of advantage to them –
advice to the king and court, cash payments to his church: and being
thus involved in the concerns of the court, because he had concern for
everything, he left room for neglect in neither of his administrative

virtutum ornamentis, populum eo amplius spiritualibus instituit 45
documentis. Ita in seipso vicia subegit, ne regnarent; carnem domuit,
ne dominaretur; spiritum extulit ut preesset; non quasi dominans in
clero, sed forma factus gregis, circa omnes seipsum bonorum operum
prebuit exemplum. Censura ecclesiastica in ecclesiam malignantes
corripuit seculares; a secularibus negociis et negociacionibus compes- 50
cuit^y ecclesiasticos; et ab omni lenocinio per totam suam diocesim

restrinxit focarios, et^z | eliminavit, ut ibi nequaquam esset infra sacros
clericus qui perceptibiliter vel publice concubinam tenuit, quin eum,
cuiuscumque preeminencie foret, aut carceribus humiliaret, aut
beneficio privaret, aut alias sagacissime divorcium perpetuum cele- 55
braret. Hic igitur censor morum [et]^{aa} corrector viciorum, quo nullus
severior in corripiendo, mansuecior in miserendo, profusior in
expendendo, affabilior in loquendo, prompcior in subveniendo,^{bb}
fractus senio^{cc} moritur in castro Sanctiandr' quod ipse a fundamentis
construxit, [   ] die [   ] anno domini m° cccc^{mo} i. Sedit 60
⟨episcopus xvi annis,⟩ et sepultus honorifice in sepulcro pontificum
juxta magnum altare ecclesie Sanctiandr' ad aquilonem intra^{dd}
pulpitum. De quo ibi fuit scriptum:^{ee}

> Hic fuit ecclesie directa columpna, fenestra
> lucida, thuribulum redolens, campana sonora.   65

---

y *corrected from* corripuit *C*
z +ab huiusmodi vili spurcicia *CA*
aa *CA*
bb +Non timebat minas magnatum, nec
    acceptor erat personarum, nec fuit
    inventus similis illi qui conservaret legem

Excelsi *CA*
cc +quasi septuagenarius *CA*
dd *corrected from* infra *C*
ee juxta suos predecessores in choro ecclesie
    magne cuius epitaphium *for* in sepulcro ...
    scriptum *CA*

46

De Henrico Wardlaw episcopo

Post mortem domini Walteri Treile, electus est Thomas Stewart filius
Roberti regis senioris, frater Roberti tercii regis,^{a} patruus regis Jacobi
primi, archidiaconus Sanctiandr', modestissimi spiritus vir et colum-
bine implicitatis. Qui postquam eleccione admissa, cum decretum
eleccionis fuisset curie transmittendum, eleccionem renunciavit; et 5

a +avunculus *del.C*

60 functions. By thus adorning himself everywhere with the embellishments of the virtues, he inculcated spiritual lessons in the people all
the more on that account. Thus he suppressed vices in himself, lest
they held sway; he tamed the flesh, lest it be in control; he raised up the
spirit to take the lead; not as it were lording it over the clergy, but
65 having become a model for his flock, he presented himself as an
example of good works towards everybody. He reproached laymen
who maligned the church with ecclesiastical censure; he curbed clerics
from worldly affairs and commerce; and he restrained priests with
concubines from all brothel-keeping throughout the whole of his
70 diocese, and banished them [from vile filth of this kind], so that there
was no cleric there at all among the men of holy church who obviously
and openly kept a concubine without Walter either humbling him,
however eminent he might be, with imprisonment, or depriving him
of his benefice, or otherwise very shrewdly sanctioning a permanent
75 separation.

This severe critic of morals therefore and corrector of faults, than
whom no one was more severe in his rebukes, more gentle in his
compassion, more lavish in his expenditure, more friendly in his
conversation, more ready with his assistance, [had no fear of the
80 threats of the magnates, nor was he a respecter of persons, nor was
anyone found like him in maintaining the law of the Most High.]
Broken by old age [when he was about seventy] he died in the castle at
St Andrews which he had himself built from the foundation on
[   ] 1401. He served as bishop for sixteen years, and was   1401:
85 honourably buried in the burial place of the bishops next to the high   [25 Mar.
altar in the church of St Andrew on the north side within the screen.   × 1 July]
There it was written of him:

This man was an upright pillar of the church, a bright
window,
90 a scented censer, a resounding bell.

46

Bishop Henry Wardlaw

After the death of the said Walter Trayl, Thomas Stewart was elected.   [1401:
He was a son of the elder King Robert, a brother of King Robert III, a   1 July]
paternal uncle of King James I, archdeacon of St Andrews, a man of
very retiring disposition and dove-like innocence. After his election
5 had been approved and the election decree was about to be
transmitted to the curia, he renounced his election; and Master
Walter Danielston was postulated, who took possession of the fruits   [1402:
of the see until his death.   ca June]

postulatus est magister Walterus Dan3elston, qui occupavit fructus episcopatus usque ad ipsius mortem. ⟨Hic Walterus Dan3elston cum ingenti copia armatorum stetit tamquam dominus in castro de Dumbretan, non sine magna displicencia regis et regni. Vir multum facti, qui aliter non potuit excludi de castro regis nisi per talem 10 translacionem. Qui tamen obiit castellanus. De utroque Waltero, Trail scilicet[b] et Dan3elston, quidam sic scripsit, et primo de primo:

> O vas virtutis! alimentum lux tabidorum,
> egrotos refovens ubere salvifico.

Ad secundum vertit stilum sic dicendo: 15

> Que quia non facis, nomen mutabis et omen.

Ethemologia facta per antithesim:

> O viciorum vas! alimentum luxuriei,
> trux egros reprimens verbere sulphureo.⟩

Post quem[c] postulatus fuit[d] [e]magister Gilbertus Grenlaw episcopus 20 Aberdonensis et cancellarius Scocie.[f] [g]Sed interim ex provisione domini Benedicti xiii repatriavit a curia Avinione scilicet vir clari | sanguinis magister Henricus de Wardlaw, precentor Glasguensis,[h] doctor juris, nepos magistri Walteri de Wardelaw cardinalis Glasguensis episcopi. Hic vir mansuetus,[i] omnibus in bono placere 25 affectans, magnarum expensarum ultra vires cotidianus hospes, sed et hostilarius gratis[j] graciosus, qui in civitatem Sanctiandr' primus fundator universitatem introduxit, le Garebrig multis impendiis construxit, et duas partes | magne custume Sanctiandr' a rege Roberto tercio, qui ante hoc habuit nisi solum terciam partem, sibi et 30 succedentibus sibi episcopis pro perpetuo impetravit. Inter ipsum tamen et dictum dominum Walterum Treyl vacavit episcopatus tribus annis et dimidio. Hic stetit episcopus fere annis quadraginta, et in decrepita etate, post presentis vite stadium, sepultus est in ecclesia Sanctiandr' in pariete medio chori et capelle nostre Domine 35 honorificencius antecessoribus suis. Obiit in castro post Pascha vi die aprilis anno domini m° cccc^mo quadragesimo. Ulteriorem eius laudem perpende per epitaphium:

> Heu quem sarcofago pressum terit anxia petra.
> Ecce doloris ago patris lugubria metra. 40
> Nobilis Henrici Wardlaw caro sic tumulata:

---

b   videlicet *CA*
c   Post mortem huius Waltheri Dan3elston *for* Post quem *CA*
d   *interlin.C*
e   + venerabilis pater omnium morum gravitate suffultus *CA*
f   regni, justicie tenax et omni accione sua

solidus et compositus *for* Scocie *CA*
g   + sed *del.C*
h   precentor Glasguensis *interlin.C*
i   + dapsilis et liberalis, pulcher facie et moribus pulchrior, modicus statura sed decens persona *CA*
j   viendarius *for* hostilarius gratis *CA*

This Walter Danielston with a large force of armed men set himself
10 up as lord in Dumbarton castle, causing great annoyance to the king
and the kingdom. A man of action, he could not be prised away from
the king's castle other than by a transfer of this kind. Yet he died as
keeper of the castle. Someone has written this about both Walters,
that is Trayl and Danielston, first about the former:

15   Vessel of Virtue! food and light for the emaciated,
        who revives the sick with life-saving abundance.

He changes his style for the latter, saying thus:

        Because you fail to do these things, you will change your
        name and fame.

20 An etymology arising from the contrast:

        Vessel of the vices! food of indulgence,
        who without pity holds the sick in check by a sulphurous
        lash.

[After the death of this Walter de Danielston, the venerable father]
25 Master Gilbert Grenlaw was postulated. [A man supported by the   [1403: early]
dignity of all the virtuous habits,] he was bishop of Aberdeen and
chancellor [of the kingdom] of Scotland, [tenacious for justice, firm
and calm in all his conduct.] But meanwhile following a provision of
the Lord Benedict XIII there came home from the curia at Avignon a   [10 Sept.]
30 man of distinguished blood, that is Master Henry de Wardlaw,
precentor of Glasgow, doctor of civil law, nephew of Master Walter
de Wardlaw the cardinal bishop of Glasgow. This man was gentle,
[kind and liberal, handsome in appearance and more handsome in his
character, slight of build but pleasing in personality.] In his
35 endeavour to please everybody in doing good, he entertained daily at
great cost beyond his means, but was an agreeable inn-keeper who
charged nothing. It was he who as the prime founder brought the
university to the city of St Andrews, who built the Guardbridge at
great expense, and who obtained from King Robert III two-thirds of
40 the great custom of St Andrews for himself and his successors as
bishops for ever, while previously he held no more than one-third.
Between him, however, and the said sir Walter Trayl the see was
vacant for three and a half years. He served as bishop for nearly forty
years, and when worn out by age after this present life's course, he was
45 buried in the church of St Andrew in the wall between the choir and
the Lady Chapel with greater honour than that given to his
predecessors. He died in the castle after Easter on 6 April 1440.   1440: 6 Apr.
Consider his further praise on his epitaph:

        Alas for the one whom the fretful stone presses upon as he is
50   weighed down by the tomb.

Res jubet ut modici spacio fit id unde creata.
Junge, Camena gemens, gemitus geminando dolores,
Cum necis ira fremens cunctos sic sternit honores.
Vertitur in cineres cinis hac latitans libitina.   45
Subdit par proceres et viles ecce ruina.
Dux cecis, claudis fuit hic pes, causa salutis
Egrotis, laudis titulis dans dogma secutis.
Vestivit pietas, bonitas, hunc legis honestas,
Virtus, pax, probitas; pestes tulit ipse molestas.   50
Arbitriis equs, lancem libraverat eque.
Regula, forma, decus populi, cleri patrieque.
Doctor jure pia decreta serens documento.
Laus sua sunt studia Rymonth fundata fluento.
Ad rivuli laticem bibit huius Scocia tota.   55
Vernat pontificem scola post hunc undique nota.

Si quis quesierit de quo sunt hec reperire,
versibus hic poterit mox per capitalia scire.

47

De Jacobo Kenedy episcopo Sanctiandr'

In sequenti[a] xxii[ab] die mensis aprilis anno domini m⁰ cccc xl
postulatus[c] est nobilis vir magister Jacobus Kenedy[d] nepos domini
regis Jacobi primi ex sorore sua comitissa de Angus, episcopus[e]

a   +Quadragesima R; del.C   d   second -e- interlin.C
b   xxix R   e   +tunc del.C
c   interlin, over illegible word del.C

See, I commence my mournful verse expressing my grief for a
    father.
The earthly flesh of the noble Henry Wardlaw is thus buried:
the cirumstance demands that, within a short space of time, it
55   becomes that from which it was created.
My Muse, groaning, add in your lamentations, redoubling
    your grief,
since the rampant rage of death thus lays low all honours.
Dust is turned to dust hidden here in this burial.
60 See, equal desolation subdues high and low alike.
This man was a guide to the blind and a foot to the lame; a
    source of salvation to the sick,
by his outstanding fame giving teaching to those who
    followed him.
65 He was clothed in piety, goodness, the integrity of the law,
virtue, peace and probity; he in person removed harmful
    scourges.
Fair in his judgments, he balanced the scales of justice with
    impartiality.
70 He was a model, an example, and the glory of the people, of
    the clergy and of his country.
As a teacher he rightly propagated God's decrees by his
    example.
The schools founded on the Rymont stream are his noble
75   achievement.
The whole of Scotland drinks at the waters of this stream.
The school flourishes in the wake of this bishop everywhere
    renowned.

If someone seeks to find out who is the subject of these verses,
80 he will soon be able to find out by looking at their initial
    letters.

47

James Kennedy bishop of St Andrews

On the following 22 April 1440 the nobleman Master James Kennedy,   1440:
the nephew of King James I by his sister the countess of Angus, and   22 Apr.
bishop of Dunkeld, was postulated by the method of [accepting the
guidance of] the Holy Spirit. He was then at the curia at Florence with
5 the lord pope Eugenius, from whom in the previous year he obtained   1439:
the monastery of Scone in commend. But before his election decree   [23 Sept.]

Dunkeldensis, per viam Sancti Spiritus. Qui tunc erat cum domino
papa Eugenio Florencie in curia, a quo anno precedenti consecutus 5
est monasterium de Scona in commenda. Sed antequam pervenirent
ad curiam decretum eleccionis et litere regales commendaticie,
provisum est sibi de episcopatu Sanctiandr'. Qui primam missam cum
magna solennitate celebravit apud ecclesiam suam in festo Sancti
Jeronimi*f* anno domini m° cccc° xlii°.   10

f   + que dominica contigit *CA*

49

fo.127;
G i,367

*De prioribus Sanctiandr' usque nunc*ᵃ

Cum igitur*b* majoribus*c* regni prelatis*d* preeminet, ut premisimus,
Sanctiandr' episcopus, restat ut de majore prelato post pontifices,
priore videlicet*e* Sanctiandr', cronicas presentes aliqualiter stipare et
ornare curemus. Et*f* quamvis quisque religiosus prior rite ac eciam
debite subsequi debet abbatem ex ordine, dominus tamen prior 5
Sanctiandr' ex speciali prerogativa abbates Scocie antecellit univer-
sos, tum ob honorem Sanctorum mitissimi Andr' apostoli protectoris
regni et patroni,*g* vocacione eciam ad apostolatum primi, tum ob
dignitatem ipsius ecclesie precipue et prelate, universique*h* regni
domine et magistre. Et ideo de omnibus prioribus Sanctiandr' 10
successive usque ad presentem diem, et ad eos specialiter, stilum
nostrum vertere non nocebit. Et quamvis dominus abbas de Kalco ex
antiquis, ut allegare solebat, privilegiis in parliamentis et consiliis
sepius posuit, se omnibus abbatibus et prioribus regni prestare et
preesse, de consuetudine tamen prescripta non solum eum sed et 15
omnes alios abbates prior Sanctandr' antecedit. Nam cum semel in
parliamento coram rege Jacobo primo super prioritate status et
sessionis premissorum prioris et abbatis grandis altercacio oriretur,
auditis allegacionibus hinc inde propositis, et decreto trium statuum
consilii interpositis, sic fertur dictum dominum regem conclusisse: 20
'Prior', inquit, 'Sanctiandr' judicio meo inferior est episcopo, et si
fuisset alius prior ab eo inferior eciam abbate. Sed in hoc non
inconvenienter potest assimilari prior marchioni, qui dignitate
inferior est duce, et prestancior comite. Sic forte et quidam judicarent
de isto priore, nam prior est ex ordine, temporis scilicet prioritate, 25

a   + et eorum successoribus *and another*   *e*   *interlin.C*
      word del.C   *f*   *corrected from* Qui *C*
b   + post *del.C*   *g*   + va *del.C*
c   *corrected from* majorebus *C*   *h*   *corrected from* universeque *C*
d   *corrected from* prelatos *C*

and the royal letter of recommendation reached the curia, he was
provided with the bishopric of St Andrews. He celebrated his first   [1440:
mass with great splendour in his church on the feast of St Jerome   1 June]
10   [which fell on a Sunday] in 1442.   1442:
                                                                   [30 Sept.]

49

The priors of St Andrews until now

Since therefore the bishop of St Andrews takes precedence over the
greater prelates of the kingdom, as we have already mentioned, it
remains for us to take care to fill out and enhance the present
chronicles in some way concerning the greater prelate below
5   episcopal rank, namely the prior of St Andrews. And although each
monastic prior ought correctly and properly to come next in order
after an abbot, nevertheless the lord prior of St Andrews by a special
privilege takes precedence over all the abbots of Scotland, both by
reason of the honour paid to the saints [and especially] to the gentlest
10   apostle Andrew the protector and patron of the kingdom, who was
also the first to be called as an apostle, and at the same time by reason
of the standing of that exceptional and prestigious church, the lady
and mistress of the whole kingdom. And therefore it will do no harm
for us to turn our pen to all the priors of St Andrews in succession
15   down to the present day, and to them individually. And although the
lord abbot of Kelso often claimed in parliaments and councils by
ancient privileges (as he customarily alleged) that he took precedence
and a lead over all the abbots and priors of the kingdom, nevertheless
by prescriptive custom the prior of St Andrews has a prior claim not
20   only over him but also over all the other abbots. For when on one
occasion in a parliament in the presence of King James I an intense
dispute arose over the priority in the status and seating of the
aforesaid prior and abbot, the allegations put forward on both sides
were heard and were made the pretext for a decree of the council of the
25   three estates; and so it is reported that the said lord king made an end
to the matter by saying: 'The prior of St Andrews in my judgment is
inferior to a bishop, and if he had been prior of another place, he
would have been inferior also to that abbot. But in this case it is not
inappropriate to consider the prior as the equal of a marquis, who is
30   inferior in rank to a duke, and more important than an earl. So

quia clarum est quod monasterium Sanctiandr' prius fundatum est et prestancius monasterio Kalcoensi. Et in hoc verificatum est de eo illa juris regula videlicet: "Qui prior tempore pocior est jure.'" Hec ille. Exemplum ad hoc habemus de Sancto Columba, qui tocius Hibernie describitur archiabbas, et qui in tanta preeminencia apud incolas 30 habebatur ut omnes[i] sui temporis Hibernie episcopos confirmare et consecrare[j] dicebatur.

i +quasi *CA*   j benedicere *CA*

50

De prioribus Roberto, Galtero, Gilberto et Thoma ac Simone

Anno dominice incarnacionis m° c^{mo} xl^{mo} Robertus prior of Scona ad monasterium Sanctiandr' per episcopum Robertum eiusdem vocatus, suscepit curam et custodiam prioratus ecclesie Sanctiandr'. Qui quam notabiliter et vigorose ac eciam virtuose pro tempore quo steterat rexit conventum sibi creditum, libro[a] relacionum eius plenius 5 attestatur. Stetit autem prior xxii^{bus} annis, et in senectute bona ac vite sanctitate obiit anno domini m° c^{mo} lxii°.

Cui successit Walterus eiusdem ecclesie cantor, qui xxiiii annis laudabiliter se gerebat. Qui post tantum tempus propter corporis invalitudinem prioratui cessit. Cui | successit sive accessit venerabilis 10 vir eiusdem domus Gilbertus canonicus, qui post duos annos in officio laboriose decursos, tactus infirmitate apud Clakmanan in hostilagio monasterii, ibidem vitam finivit, adhuc vivente et convalente dicto Waltero priore premisso. Qui post obitum Gilberti, resumptis viribus, in conventum rediens, officium prioratus prout 15 potuit exercere conabatur. Sed modico tempore superfuit; nam infra eundem annum viam universe carnis ingressus appositus est ad patres suos in senectute bona anno scilicet m° cc^{mo}.

Cui successit dominus Thomas eiusdem loci supprior, vir bone conversacionis et tocius religionis exemplar. Cumque quosdam de 20 fratribus contra ipsum esse commotos propter tamen zelum quem habuit ad observanciam[b] regularem, et ipsius sanctitatem moleste ferentes conspexisset, elegit magis ipsorum societatem deserere quam cum ipsis ad viam veritatis non reversis sub silencio periclitari. Anno igitur dominice incarnacionis m^{mo} cc^{mo} xi° dignitatem prioratus 25 relinquens, et fratribus invitis et reclamantibus, quibusdam vero ubertim flentibus et plangentibus, valedicens de patre et prelato

G i,368

a liber *CA*   b -b- *interlin.C*

perhaps also some would conclude regarding this prior, for he is sequentially prior, that is by priority in time, because it is clear that the monastery of St Andrews was founded earlier and is more important than the monastery of Kelso. And in this case the matter is proved by
35 that rule of law namely: "He who is prior in time has the stronger right." We have a relevant example in St Columba, who is described as archabbot of all Ireland, and who was regarded by the inhabitants as [occupying a position of] such pre-eminence that he was said to confirm and consecrate [nearly] all the bishops of Ireland in his day.

50

Priors Robert, Walter, Gilbert and Thomas and Simon

In 1140 Robert prior of Scone was called to the monastery at St   1140
Andrews by Robert the bishop there, and undertook the charge and guardianship of the priory of the church of St Andrew. He ruled the convent entrusted to him in an extremely remarkable and vigorous
5 manner, and also most virtuously for the time during which he held office (as is more fully attested in the book of stories about him). He served as prior indeed for twenty-two years, and died in a good old age and in sanctity of life in 1162.   [1160]
His successor was Walter, the precentor of the same church, who
10 carried on in a praiseworthy manner for twenty-four years. He gave up the priory after such a long time because of ill-health. Gilbert, a   [1195
venerable man who was a canon of the same house, succeeded and   × 1198]
took over from him. After two years of busy activity in office had passed, he was stricken with illness in the monastery's lodging at
15 Clackmannan, and ended his life there, while the said Walter who has been mentioned as prior was still alive and in better health. On Gilbert's death Walter returned to the convent on regaining his   [ca 1199]
strength, and endeavoured to fill the office of prior as best he could. But he survived for [only] a brief period; for within the same year, that
20 is 1200, he went the way of all flesh in good old age and was placed   [1199]
beside his fathers.
He was succeeded by sir Thomas, the subprior of the same place, a   [1199:
man of good behaviour and a pattern for all monastic life. And when   × 6 June]
he noticed that certain of the brothers had been stirred up against him
25 (on account nonetheless of the zeal which he had for the observance of the rule), and were finding his holiness irksome, he chose rather to leave their fellowship than stay silent and be at risk with them when they had not returned to the way of truth. In 1211 therefore he   1211
relinquished the dignity of prior, and as his brothers showed their
30 reluctance by crying out in protest – with some indeed weeping and

canonicorum vi^to idus decembris factus est in Cupro humilis
discipulus et novicius monachorum.

Cui successit Simon eiusdem ecclesie canonicus, vir honeste vite et　30
laudabilis conversacionis. Qui in fornace^c tribulacionis decoctus,
quoniam dies mali erant, malignancium insidias et invidencium
detracciones declinans, anno domini m° cc^mo xxv^to curam et custodiam prioratus de quorundam consilio dereliquit, et prioratum de

Louchlevyn de consensu fratrum et episcopi auctoritate | suscepit. Et　35
sic prior stetit annis xiiii,

Cui successit Henricus de Norhame canonicus eiusdem ecclesie
eodem anno, et per xi annos stetit prior; et tandem ipso renuncians
anno domini m° cc^mo xxxvi, domum desolatam expensis et debitis
innumeris oneratam et impeditam dereliquit.　　　　　　　　　　　40

　　c　　two letters del. after -e C

51

De Johanne Qwhite, Gilberto, Johanne de Hadyngton et c'

Anno quo supra Johannes Qwhite canonicus eiusdem electus est in
priorem. Cuius industria et providencia omnium bonorum largitor
bona ecclesie et possessiones, ante distracta et dissipata, in pristinum
statum redacta misericorditer ampliavit. Suscepit autem curam et
custodiam prioratus anno domini m° cc xxxvi^to xii kal' junii, et stetit　5
annis xxii. Qui dormitorium, refectorium et magnam aulam hospitum
nobiliter, ut nunc patet, fecit edificari. Post hec et multa alia bona
opera obiit die Sancti Kenelmi regis anno domini m° cc^mo lviii°.

Cui successit Gilbertus terrarius eiusdem domus, vir religiosus et
graciosus in temporalibus, licet non evidenter literatus. Suscepit　10
autem curam prioratus in crastino Sancti Agapiti Martyris anno
supradicto; et obiit anno domini m° cc° lxiii xvi kal' aprilis. Et sic stetit
prior quinque annis.

Cui successit Johannes de Hadyngtona camerarius eiusdem domus
vii° idus aprilis per eleccionem anno sequenti, die videlicet lune festo　15
Sancti Ambrosii. Qui inter cetera opera laudabilia fecit magnam

cameram in orientali parte monasterii | juxta cimiterium situatam. Et
cum ipse xl^a annis mensibus tribus diebusque duobus cursum officii
sibi commissi fideliter peregisset, universe carnis viam ingressus est
quinto non' julii anno domini m° ccc° iiii^to, sepultusque est in capitulo.　20
Cuius epitaphium sic erat:

wailing copiously – he said farewell to being the canons' father and
prelate, and on 8 December became a humble pupil and novice of the   8 Dec.
monks at Coupar Angus.

35   He was succeeded by Simon, a canon of the same church, a man of   [× 1212]
honourable life and praiseworthy behaviour. Consumed in the
furnace of tribulation, since these were evil times, and avoiding the
plots of the spiteful and the slanders of the envious, in 1225 on the   1225
advice of certain persons he abandoned the charge and guardianship
of the priory, and with the consent of the brothers and the authority of
40   the bishop undertook the priory of Loch Leven. Thus he served as
prior for fourteen years.

     He was succeeded in the same year by Henry de Norham, a canon
of the same church, who served as prior for eleven years; in the end he
gave up office in 1236, leaving the house devastated by expenses and   1236:
45   burdened and embarrassed with innumerable debts.   [× 21 May]

51

John White, Gilbert, John de Haddington, etc.

In the same year John White, a canon of the same, was elected prior.   1236:
By his hard work and care this generous provider of all good thngs   21 May
restored to their original state the goods and possessions of the church
which had previously been dissipated and scattered, and through his
5   concern he enlarged them. He undertook the charge and guardianship of the priory on 21 May 1236, and served for twenty-two years.
He arranged the building of the dormitory, refectory and the great
hall for guests in noble fashion, as may be seen today. After these and
many other good works he died on St Kenelm's Day 1258.   1258:
10   He was succeeded by Gilbert the terrar of the same house, an   17 July
ascetic man who was well-regarded in worldly affairs, though
manifestly not a man of learning. He undertook the charge of the
priory on the morrow of the feast of St Agapitus the Martyr in the   19 Aug.
same year; and he died on 17 March 1263. And so he served as prior   1263/4:
15   for five years.   17 Mar.
     He was succeeded by John de Haddington the chamberlain of the
same house by an election on 7 April of the following year, namely the   1264:
Monday [after] the feast of St Ambrose. Among his other praise-   7 Apr.
worthy works he built the great chamber on the eastern side of the
20   monastery sited next the cemetery. And when he had faithfully
performed the round of activities of the office entrusted to him for
forty years, three months and two days, he went the way of all flesh on
3 July 1304, and was buried in the chapter-house. This was his   1304: 3 July
epitaph:

Corporis efficitur custos hec petra Johannis
quadraginta domus prior huius qui fuit annis.
*Felix certamen ⤬ concedat ei Deus. Amen.
Pace frui celi ⤬ certavit fine fideli.   25

Cui successit canonicus huius domus Adam videlicet Mauchan
tunc temporis Sanctiandr' archidiaconus, canonice electus vi^{to} kal'
augusti videlicet sequenti die lune in festo vii Dormiencium anno quo
supra. Qui postquam prioratum annis novem et diebus septem inter
varias angustias et procellas guerrarum laboriosissime rexisset, obiit 30
xix° kal' septembris anno domini m° ccc^{mo} xiii°, sepultusque est juxta
predecessorem suum priorem Johannem a dextro latere tumuli
eiusdem.

a   + Pace frui celi *del.C*

52

De successione Johannis, Johannis et Willelmi

Supradicto anno successit eidem Adam dominus Johannes de Forfare
canonicus eiusdem, tunc temporis vicarius de Lothrise et camerarius
domini Willelmi de Lambertoun episcopi, per viam Sancti Spiritus
electus in festo Decollacionis Sancti Johannis. Qui edificavit
cameram claustro annexam quam priores habere consueverunt. 5
Quam postmodum Willelmus de Laudonia prior munitissimo muro
circumquaque vallavit. Dictum autem prioratum rexit in bona pace et
prosperitate digne et laudabiliter novem annis xxiiii^{or} diebus, et obiit
nono kal' octobris, sepultusque in novo capitulo primus anno domini
m° ccc^{mo} xxi°.   10
Cui successit Johannes de Gowry terrarius eiusdem domus eodem
anno electus. Qui multa adversa tempore guerre per octo annos et
amplius sustinuit. Et licet impedicioris lingue fuerit et minus cautus in
loquendo, officium tamen prioratus omni tempore quo prefuit cum
magna industria et pericia regebat, multas adversitates prudenter 15
precavebat, et illatas quandoque cum magna cautela depellebat.
Stetit autem prior xviii annos, et mortuus est viii die decembris anno
domini m° ccc^{mo} xl^{mo}, sepultusque in novo capitulo. ⟨Hic compulsus
per regem Edwardum Wyndesore et Edwardum de Balliolo exposuit
in construccione unius turris porte de Perth ducentas et octoginta 20
marcas.⟩
Anno et mense supradictis xv die eiusdem Willelmus de Laudonia
supprior electus est in priorem per viam scrutinii sede vacante. Cuius
laudabilia opera per ipsum quo stetit intus et extra facta dignum
extitit memorie commendare. Nam dormitorium monasterii ex omni 25

25   This stone is constituted as guardian of the body of John
who was prior of this house for forty years.
He fought the good fight with a faithful end.
May God grant him enjoyment of Heavenly peace. Amen

He was succeeded by a canon of this house, namely Adam
30   Mauchan, then the archdeacon of St Andrews, who was canonically
elected on the following 27 July, namely on Monday the feast of the   27 July
Seven Sleepers in that year. After ruling the priory with very great
difficulty for nine years and seven days amid the various restrictions
and disturbances of wars, he died on 14 August 1313, and was buried   1313:
35   next to John his predecessor as prior on the right side of the grave of   14 Aug.
the same.

52

The succession of John, John and William

In the aforesaid year the same Adam was succeeded by sir John de   1313:
Forfar a canon of the same, at that time vicar of Lathrisk and   29 Aug.
chamberlain of sir William de Lamberton the bishop. He was elected
by the method of [accepting the guidance of] the Holy Spirit on the
5   feast of the Decollation of St John [the Baptist]. He built the chamber
next the cloister which was customarily used by the priors. Afterwards the prior William de Lothian surrounded it on all sides with a
very safe wall. He ruled the said priory in satisfactory peace and
prosperity in a fitting and praiseworthy manner for nine years and
10   twenty-four days, and died on 23 September 1321. He was the first to   1321:
be buried in the new chapter-house.   23 Sept.

He was succeeded by John de Gowrie the terrar of the same house,
who was elected in the same year. He faced many troubles at a time of
war for eight years and more. And although he had a speech
15   impediment and was careless when speaking, he nonetheless conducted the office of prior for all the time when he was in charge with
great diligence and skill; he was clever in taking precautions against
many adversities, and averted them at any time when they did come
with great care. He served as prior for eighteen years, and died on 8
20   December 1340. He was buried in the new chapter-house. He was   1340: 8 Dec
compelled by King Edward of Windsor and Edward de Balliol to
expend two hundred and eighty marks on the construction of a tower
for a gate at Perth.

In the aforesaid year on the fifteenth day of the same month   15 Dec.
25   William de Lothian the subprior was elected prior by the method of a

parte, subtus cum tabulis dolatis, et supra cum plumbo, sumptuosa tectura vestivit. Veterem ecclesiam, cameram orientalem, quatuor partes claustri, australem partem refectorii, et alia plura edificia magnis expensis tegebat. Velum eciam magnum ecclesie inter altare |

et chorum[a] | Quadragesimali expansum artificio opere compositum, 30 diversis imaginibus et bestiis subtiliter consutum, sumptibus monasterii fieri demandavit. Novam eciam ustrinam maximo opere et labore et expensis suo tempore constat esse factam. Ecclesias monasterii in Fife et alibi in diversis partibus habitas, quando et quociens necesse erat, cum bordis operiebat, inspectis aliis necessitati- 35 bus et reformatis. Ecclesiam eciam de Rossiclerach in Gowery cernens insufficientem et vetustam, solo penitus dirutam et in alio loco remotam, reedificavit sumptuose. Iste Willelmus statura brevis erat, literarum sciencia et eloquencia preditus. Magnatum dedignaciones propter utilitatem monasterii equanimiter tolerabat, regularis institu- 40 cionis observanciis inter fratres et consocios ad decorem religionis primitus custoditis. Ad voluntatis libitum sibi temporalia succedebant. Et sic feliciter monasterium xiiii annis non solum rexit, sed decenter erexit; ac ipsum bordis ferro sale et aliis necessariis, exutum omni debito cum centum libris in deposito, nobiliter instauravit. Et 45 quinto die augusti festo Sancti Oswaldi anno domini m° ccc^mo liiii^to in Domino obdormivit. Sepultus juxta predecessorem suum Johannem de Gowry[b] in novo capitulo.

a   + De prioribus Sanctiandr' usque nunc   b   de Gowry *interlin.over* Johannem *del.C*
    del.C

53

De aliis

Anno eodem per viam scrutinii xii die augusti electus est vir nobilis progenie sed moribus nobilior dominus Thomas Biset, nepos domini Thome Biset comitis de Fife, supprior eiusdem domus. Qui fratres suos et subjectos valde diligens, et ab illis multum dilectus, ymmo generaliter omnium oculis amabilis videbatur; et per consequens a 5 Domino commendatus gregem sibi commissum pro qualitate temporis commendabiliter regebat. Denique Dominus erat cum eo, et omnia opera eius dirigebat. Pre omnibus semper observanciam

general vote while the see was vacant. It is appropriate to record for
posterity the excellent works done by him inside and outside while he
was in office. For he clothed the dormitory of the monastery all over
with a costly covering, with hewn boards underneath and with lead
30　above. At great expense he roofed over the old church, the eastern
chamber, the four sides of the cloister, the southern section of the
refectory, and many other buildings. Also he ordered the construction at the monastery's expense of a great veil for the church that was
hung during Lent between the altar and the choir; it was woven by
35　craftsmen, and exquisitely embroidered with various figures and
animals. It is well known that a new malt-kiln was built in his time
with a very great deal of work, toil and expense. He roofed over with
boards the churches held by the monastery in Fife and in various parts
elsewhere, when and as often as it was necessary, once other needs had
40　been inspected and put right. Observing that the church of Rossie in
Gowrie was in poor condition and very old, he rebuilt it at great
expense after pulling it down completely to the ground and moving it
to another site. This William was short in stature, and equipped with
knowledge of letters and eloquence. He bore with equanimity the
45　magnates' scorn in the interests of the benefit to the monastery,
provided that the observances of the monastic institution among the
brothers and the other members of the community had first been
protected in accordance with the dignity of the religious life.
Temporal matters went well for him according to his will and
50　pleasure. And so he not only ruled the monastery successfully for
fourteen years, but he built it up with good taste; and he was notable
for restoring it with boards and ironwork, with stores of salt and other
essentials, free from all debt with a hundred pounds on deposit. And
he fell asleep in the Lord on 5 August 1354 on the feast of St Oswald,　1354:
55　He was buried next to his predecessor John de Gowrie in the new　5 Aug.
chapter-house.

53

Other [priors]

In the same year on 12 August a man was elected by the method of a　1354:
general vote who was noble by descent but more noble in character.　12 Aug.
This was the subprior of the same house, sir Thomas Biset, a nephew
of Sir Thomas Biset earl of Fife. He was extremely loving towards his
5　brothers and those under him, and much loved by them, or rather he
seemed universally lovable in everybody's eyes; and in consequence as
a man commended by the Lord he guided the flock entrusted to him in
a commendable fashion considering the times [he lived in]. In short,

regularem et sanctorum patrum instituta habebat pre oculis. Quorum
erat amator et custos, ammonens fratres suos ea*a* quam sedule 10
observare, eorum mores et actus diligenter reformans, excessus et
errata benigne corrigens, honeste viventes nutriens et amplectens,
sciens se ad hoc precipue esse propositum. Cumque sic per novem
annos non tam ferventer quam feliciter rexisset, decidit in egritudinem et invalitudinem nimiam; timensque domui sue propter impoten- 15
ciam corporalem dispendium imminere, in manibus domini Willelmi
Laundelis episcopi sui, salubriori pro tunc usus consilio, quibusdam
sociis plangentibus et reclamantibus 'Cur nos, pater, deseris?' aut
'Cui nos desolatos relinquis? Propicius tibi esto, ne fiat quod
protendis', honori pariter et oneri predicti prioratus pure et simpli- 20
citer resignavit, provisione honesta sibi per predictum episcopum de
consensu fratrum ordinata ac provisa, anno videlicet domini m° ccc°
lxiii°.

Post quem eodem anno in festo Sancti Columbe abbatis electus fuit
venerabilis vir et omni morum honestate predictus dominus Stepha- 25
nus Pai subprior eiusdem ecclesie per viam Spiritus Sancti, qui per
dictum dominum episcopum confirmacionem et munus benediccio-
nis accepit. Hic fuit | statura largus, corpore procerus, vultu jocundus
et hilaris, cunctis largus et munificus, omnibus se amabilem exhibuit.
Qui magnam ecclesiam, infortunio casualis incendii tempore suo 30
combustam, anno scilicet domini m° ccc° lxviii°, in tecturis et opere
lapideo ligneo et plumbeo infra sequentis anni spacium in tantum
reparavit, quod in sumptus et expensas reformacionis eiusdem, cum
reedificacione duarum columpnarum a parte australi dicte ecclesie
juxta altaria Sanctorum Michaelis et Laurencii marcarum exposuit 35
duo milia et ducentas. Qui xxᵗⁱ annis stetit prior et in Anglia electus ad
episcopatum captivus, ut premisimus, mortuus est ⟨ii die marcii anno
c' lxxxv.⟩

---

a   corrected from eas C

54

De Roberto^a *de Monte Rosarum*

Post hunc ad prioratum electus est persona religiosissima dominus
Robertus de Monte Rosarum eiusdem domus canonicus, ⟨prior

---

a   + et Jacobo bino prioribus Sanctiandr' c
       liiii *del.*C

the Lord was with him, and directed all his activities. Before all else he
10 always kept the observance of the rule and the ordinances of the
sainted Fathers before his eyes. He was a devotee and guardian of
these, warning his brothers to observe them as carefully as possible,
thoroughly reforming their habits and actions, correcting in kindly
fashion their transgressions and faults, encouraging and cherishing
15 those who lived with integrity, knowing that he had been appointed
especially for this. And when he had been in charge for nine years,
creating happiness rather than displaying fervour, he became ill and
exceedingly infirm, and fearful that the cost arising from his bodily
weakness was a threat to his house, he took the more beneficial advice
20 in the circumstances (while some of his fellow-canons lamented and
protested 'Father, why are you abandoning us?' or 'To whose care are
you leaving us, forsaken as we are? Kindly desist, we beg you, from
doing what you have in mind'), and resigned the honour together with
the burden of the said priory purely and simply into the hands of sir
25 William Laundels his bishop in 1363, once a proper allowance had   1363
been arranged and provided for him by the said bishop with the
consent of the canons.

After him in the same year on the feast of St Columba the Abbot the   9 June
said sir Stephen Pay the subprior of the same church, a venerable man
30 of complete integrity in character, was elected by the method of
[accepting the guidance of] the Holy Spirit. He received confirmation
and the favour of blessing from the said lord bishop. He was of broad
build and tall in body, with an agreeable and cheerful appearance;
liberal and generous to everybody, he proved to be a lovable man to
35 all. When the great church was in 1368 during his time unfortunately
burned in an accidental fire, he repaired the roofing and stonework,   [1378:
the woodwork and the lead within the space of the year following, to   23 Sept.]
such an extent that he paid out two thousand and two hundred marks
in outlays and expenses in the restoration of the same, with the
40 rebuilding of two pillars on the south side of the said church near the
altars of St Michael and St Laurence. He served as prior for twenty
years, and after election to the see died as a prisoner in England, as we   1385/6:
have said, on 2 March 1385.   2 Mar.

54

Robert de Montrose

After him a very religious man was elected prior, namely sir Robert de
Montrose a canon of the same house, prior of Loch Leven and official
of the court of St Andrews. He was a very knowledgeable man,
distinguished for his eloquence, warily circumspect, a ruler with
5 foresight, and an outstanding preacher. Intent as he was on the

Lacus de Levin⟩[b] et officialis curie Sanctiandree, vir magne sciencie et
eloquencie insignis, circumspeccione cautus, gubernacione providus,
ac predicator egregius, observanciis regularibus intentus, forma 5
gregis factus | in claustro, bonus pastor in populo, et sic placuit Deo.
Nam populum non sprevit, sed docuit, et singula singulis reddidit.
Divites non palpavit, nec minas magnatum expavit; pauperes non
gravavit, sed fovit; crimina subditorum non dissimulavit, sed
correxit. In omnibus et per omnia exhibens se devotum senioribus, 10
blandum junioribus, religiosis fratribus placidum, superbis rigidum,
humilibus benignum, penitentibus misericordem, et inflexibilem
obstinatis. Dum sic se omnia haberent, cum patre suo Augustino
prior veraciter dicere potuit et sentire; qui Augustinus[c] in epistola
scribens ad Donatistam Vincencium sic ait: 'Michi arrogare non 15
audeo, ut domus mea melior sit quam archa Noe, ubi tamen inter tot
homines unus reprobus inventus est; aut melior sit quam domus
Abrahe, cui dictum est: "Eice ancillam et filium eius"; aut melior sit
quam domus Isaac, cui de duabus geminis dictum est: "Jacob dilexi,
Esau autem odio habui."' 'Simpliciter autem fateor. Ex quo Deo 20
servire cepi, quomodo sicut difficile sum expertus meliores quam qui
in monasteriis profecerunt, ita non sum pejores expertus quam qui in
monasteriis defecerunt.' Hec ille. Et scribuntur transsumptive D. xlvii
'Quantumlibet'. Unde accidit eundem[d] priorem habere in claustro
quendam fratrem nomine Thomam Platar minus disciplinatum, 25
correcciones supprioris et ordinis contemptibiliter aspernantem.
Quem propterea, cum ad morum rectitudinem et regule omnibus viis
accomodis nunc minis nunc blandiciis retorquere prior niteretur,
quicquid sategit ad emendam, induratus tetendit ad noxam. In se
tandem prior reversus, ad illud proverbii attendebat quod: 'Qui non 30
corrigit resecanda committit, et facientis culpam habet, qui quod
potest corrigere, necligit, sciens utique quod impunitas incurie
soboles, insolencie mater, radix petulancie, et transgressionum est
nutrix.' Dum ipse animo revolveret quomodo fratrem lucraretur,
perversus proprio patri mortem machinatur. Nam | instinctu maligni 35
spiritus sero quodam, cum prior solus, ut solitus erat, dormitorium ad
pernoctandum ascenderet, oportunitate explorata, prelatum suum
aggreditur, et, extracto de sub cuius capa ferreo pugione, priorem
letaliter ⟨in claustro⟩ vulneravit. Qui triduo supervixit; et fratribus
valefaciens obdormivit in Domino, et positus est[e] apud patres suos in 40
novo capitulo. Patricida, post scelus perpetratum fuge consulens,
statim apprehenditur, et post biduum sepelicionis prioris, stelatus et
mitratus, post solempnem sermonem a domino Waltero Treyl
episcopo factam ad clerum et populum, perpetuis carceribus manici-

---

b marginal entry replacing vicarius de   d -dem interlin.C
    Lochris del.C   e interlin.C
c interlin.C

observances of the rule, he became a model for his flock in the cloister,
a good pastor among the people, and thus was pleasing to God. For
he did not disdain the people, but was their teacher, and gave
individual attention to each person. He did not flatter the rich, neither
10 did he take fright at the threats of the magnates; he did not harass the
poor, but cherished them; he did not turn a blind eye to the offences of
those subject to him, but corrected them. In every situation and in
everything he did he showed himself obedient to his elders, charming
to his juniors, kindly to his brothers in religion, stern to the proud,
15 generous to the humble, compassionate to the penitent and unbend-
ing to the incorrigible. All this being so, the prior could truthfully
express and share the opinion of his father Augustine, who when
writing a letter to Vincent the Donatist said this: 'I do not dare to
claim for myself that my house is better than the ark of Noah, where
20 among so many men one back-slider was nonetheless found; or better
than the house of Abraham, to whom it was said: "Put away your
slave-girl and her son"; or better than the house of Isaac, to whom it
was said regarding his twin sons: "I have loved Jacob, but hated
Esau."' 'I honestly acknowledge that from the time when I began to
25 serve God, just as I have had difficulty in finding men better than
those who have had success in monasteries, so I have not found men
worse than those who have been failures in monasteries.' And so it is
written with a transferred meaning in the *Decretum*, xlvii, 'Quantumlibet'.
30 Hence it happened that the same prior had in the cloister a certain
brother called Thomas Platar, who was not fully responsive to
discipline as he spurned with contempt the corrections of the subprior
and the order. On this account, when the prior endeavoured in all
suitable ways to direct him back to proper behaviour and to the rule,
35 now with threats, now with blandishments, whatever effort he made
to achieve improvement, this man hardened his heart and tended [all
the more] to evil doing. At length the prior turned his thoughts to
himself, noting the proverbial saying that: 'He who does not correct
what ought to be curbed, commits an offence, and he who neglects
40 what he is able to correct is as guilty as the one who commits the fault,
for he knows without doubt that exemption from punishment is the
offspring of indifference, the mother of insolence, the root of
impudence, and the nurse of transgressions.' While the prior was
considering how to win over the brother, the misguided man was
45 plotting the death of his own father. For one evening when the prior
by himself (as was his custom) was mounting the stairs to spend the
night in the dormitory, at the prompting of an evil spirit the man
seized the chance to approach his prelate, and taking an iron dagger
from under his cloak wounded the prior mortally in the cloister. He
50 survived for three days; then saying farewell to the brothers he fell [1394:
asleep in the Lord, and was buried with his fathers in the new chapter- 24 Mar.]

pandus truditur, ubi pane doloris et aqua tristicie languide libatis, 45
infra breve moritur, et in sterquilinio sepelitur.

55

De eodem, et binis^a Jacobitis prioribus

Hic domum suam, dum vixerat, nobiliter reformavit, et notabiliter
exstruxit. Novum opus^b in corpore magne ecclesie usque ad tigna et
tecturas, non sine maximis expensis, erexit et perfecit; ac xxiiii^{toc} die
marcii presentem vitam finivit anno domini m° ccc^{mo} xciii°. Qui stetit
prior xiii annis.   5
   Cui successit decus morum et virtutis speculum dominus Jacobus
Biset canonicus eiusdem domus licenciatus in decretis, spectabili satis
quod solet esse incitamentum bonitatis prosapia genitus, nobilitate
morum genus vicit et seculum. Hic nepos ex sorore religiosissimi et pii
patris domini Thome Biset prioris suprascripti, cuius actus religiosos^d 10
in proximis imitatus, nulli precedencium priorum in suo operandi
genere invenitur secundus. Siquidem vere vitis palmes a generoso^e
surculo crevit in arborem electam, et multiplici fructuum propagine,
Christi bonus odor in omni loco inventus est Deo et hominibus. Hic
eciam super ceteros humilis affabilis et benignus, fratribus et   15
indigentibus compaciens et viscerosus, tam in spiritualibus quam
temporalibus solus, quasi ceteros suos decessores^f supergressus,
navem ecclesie magne, similiter et claustrum, ex omni parte tignis et
tecturis solemniter consummavit; chorum in stallis et claustra- ⟨le
tetragonum tam tecturis quam⟩ pavimentis decenter reparavit.   20
Totum eciam monasterium | et singulas eiusdem officinas innovacio-
nibus et edificiis, ⟨unacum⟩ granariis, molendinis, ustrinis, porcinis,
horreis et bostaribus^g redintegravit; quorum quedam ex integro, alia
in sartatectis et tecturis, sicut et aulam hospitum, quam in columpnis
et fenestris vitreis cum binis eiusdem cameris honorifice perfecit.   25
Curiam eciam tocius monasterii tam inferiorem quam exteriorem
petrinis pavimentis placide composuit et polivit. Omnes eciam

fo.129

---

a	interlin over premissis *del.C*	*e*	corrected from generosa; + propagine
b	+co *del.C*		*del.C*
c	xx- *interlin.C*	*f*	predecessores *D*
d	corrected from religiosus *C*	*g*	bostralibus *D*

house. The parricide sought to flee after committing this crime, but he
was immediately seized, and after the two days of the prior's funeral,
when wearing his vestments and a mitre, and after the customary
55 sermon by sir Walter Trayl as bishop had been delivered to the clergy
and people, he was hurriedly made over to perpetual imprisonment,
where he feebly tasted the bread of sorrow and the water of affliction.
He died shortly afterwards, and was buried in the midden.

55

The same, and the pair of priors called James

This man restored his house in noble fashion as long as he lived, and
built it up in notable fashion. He raised and completed new work in
the main body of the great church up to the rafters and the roof
covering at very great expense. And he ended his life here on 24 March
5   1393, after holding office as prior for thirteen years.   1393/4:
He was succeeded by that man of distinguished character and   24 Mar.
mirror of virtue sir James Biset, a canon of the same house and
licentiate in decrees. Born into a quite notable family, which is usually
a stimulus for good, by the nobility of his character he surpassed his
10 family and his times. He was a nephew as sister's son to the most
devout and pious father sir Thomas Biset the prior mentioned above.
In his close copying of his uncle's religious practices, he is identified as
second to none of his predecessors as prior in the kind of way in which
he worked. Inasmuch as a branch of the true vine developed from a
15 choice side-shoot into a special tree, and with a numerous progeny of
fruits, the fine fragrance of Christ was found everywhere for God and
men. He was also humble, friendly and kind beyond all others,
sympathetic and sincere to his brothers and the needy, unique both in
matters spiritual and temporal, surpassing practically all his other
20 predecessors; he completed the nave of the great church properly, and
likewise the cloister, in all respects with rafters and roof covering; he
renewed the choir [enclosure] tastefully with stalls, and the cloister
quadrangle with both roofing and paving. He also restored the whole
monastery and each of its domestic buildings with alterations and
25 new buildings, along with granaries, mills, malt-kilns, piggeries,
barns and byres; some of these were new buildings, with others it was
a matter of covering and roofing; likewise also the guest-hall, which
he constructed in an appropriate style with columns and glazed
windows with its two apartments. The courtyard also of the whole
30 monastery, both at the lower level and outside, he pleasingly constructed and finished with stone paving. He refurbished at a good
standard all the churches attached to his office, and whichever others

ecclesias suas commensales, et alias quascumque monasterio annex- as, in structuris et vestimentis ecclesiasticis decenter refecit. Impendi- dit[h] enim quod sua intererat, utrique ecclesie forinsecam materialibus 30 decorans ornamentis, et conventualem spiritalibus instituens docu- mentis. Plurima illi sollicitudo si niterent altaria, si lucerent lumi- naria, si ministri idonei, si moribus compti canonici, vasa munda, vestimenta candida, si divina ex ordine celebrarentur officia. Sciebat

enim in hiis esse Dei honorem, domus eius decorem, | sacramentorum 35 multiplicem significacionem, ministrorum exercitacionem, populi devocionem, et indistincte omnium erudicionem. Sed et sui primo et conventus precipue operam agens, quicquid de decimis, debitis, redditibus vel annuis pensionibus, aliisve justis questibus habere poterat, totum preter stipendia vite in exaltacionem ecclesiastice 40 fabrice, in sumptus hospitum et usus pauperum servavit et dedit. Sustinuit insuper multa tam extera quam civilia et domestica bella, que omnia pro communi fratrum utilitate et viriliter pertulit et fortiter reppulit. Quis non tumeret tipo tot virtutum[i] insignibus adornatus? Proxima solet semper surripere bonis superbia, et que pulul021arunt 45 germina necare virtutum. Credidi, inquam, et scivi, propter quod locutus sum. Ipse autem humiliatus est valde, quia semper et ubique fodit in se fundamentum humilitatis, quo perventum fuit ad fastigia caritatis. Quis fratrum eius languesceret et ipse non infirmaretur? Quis scandalum pateretur et ipse non ureretur? Ut paucis multa 50 comprehendam, omnibus fratribus omnia factus est, ut omnibus proficeret ad salutem.

h   corrected from Impendit C
i   + in s del.C

56

Adhuc de eodem

Hic prior statura erat procerus, moribus compositus, et in cunctis agibilibus circumspectus. Nam oculo cautele imminentes pacienter sustinuit injurias, et manu prudencie celerius detersit irruentes; et (ut de ceteris eius virtutibus taceam) corde erat humilis, verbis gravis, animi prudens, loquendi affabilior, ulciscendi tardior,[a] remittendi 5 paracior; multum amabat humiles, corripuit arrogantes. Non fuit

a   second -r interlin.C

were annexed to the monastery, as regards the buildings and the
ecclesiastical vestments. For he expended on each church what was
35 important to it, decorating the outside with material adornments, and
establishing the conventual part with spiritual texts. He took very
great care that the altars sparkled, the lamps shone, the clergy were
suitable, the canons were adornments morally, the altar-vessels clean,
the vestments laundered, and that the divine offices were celebrated in
40 due order. For he knew that in [care for] these matters lay the honour
of God, the seemliness of his house, many kinds of meaning in the
sacraments, the performance of the clergy, the devotion of the people,
and the instruction of all without distinction. But also when taking
thought first for himself and then especially for the convent, from
45 whatever he could raise from teinds, dues, rents or other annual
payments, or other legitimate profits, he saved and gave the whole
amount (save support for living expenses) towards the erection of
ecclesiastical buildings, expenditure on guests, and the needs of the
poor. In addition he withstood many assaults both from outside and
50 of a civil and domestic nature, all of which he both endured in manly
fashion and fended off with vigour for the common benefit of the
brothers. Who adorned with so many signs of the virtues would not be
swollen with pride? When pride is an adjunct to good qualities, it
tends to detract from them, and kills the shoots of the virtue that they
55 sprout. I believe, I say, and I know; and because of this I have spoken.
But he was assuredly humbled, because always and everywhere he
dug within himself a foundation of humility, by which he was brought
to the heights of charity. Which of his brothers would fall ill and he
would not himself lose his strength? Who would not experience
60 scandal and and he would not himself be painfully affected? To put it
briefly: he became all things to all the brothers, so that he might help
them all to salvation.

56

Still the same man

This prior was tall in stature, placid in character, and circumspect in
all his actions. For he patiently withstood impending injustices with
the eye of caution, and speedily wiped out attackers with the hand of
prudence; and (not to mention his other virtues) he was humble at
5 heart, thoughtful in what he had to say, judicious in his opinion,
courteous in conversation, slow to take revenge, ready to forgive; he
had a great love for humble people, he rebuked the conceited. He was
not feeble in his gestures, careless in his gait, nor heedless in his
speech; but the appearance of his body and bearing offered the

gestis fraccior, non incessu dissolucior, nec voce petulancior; sed ipsius corporis et habitus species intuenti fuerat simulacrum mentis, et figura probitatis. Quid in singulis morer? Cui quam vigil sensus, discreta racio, docile ingenium, precellens clerimonium, herens 10 memoria,[b] sciencia diserta, commendabilis operacio – facta adhuc clamant, eciam si nostra silescat oracio. Qui eciam qualis quantusve et quam religiosus fuerit, regendique policia preditus, lector a canonicis et aliis circumvicinis qui eum in vita noverant ediscat. Sed et de eo haud dubium filii Dei, qui exurgent in hoc monasterio, 15 enarrabunt fratribus suis, ut cognoscat generacio altera, et ponant in Deo spem[c] suam, et non obliviscantur opera prioris, sed et scemata eius exquirant. Nam plures sui discipuli sub eius disciplinatu imbuti, virtutum apices assecuti, confestim post eius decessionem ad alia loca famosa assumpti sunt in patres et pastores, quorum unus episcopus 20 Rossensis, alii duo in Scona et Emonia abbates intitulantur, tres eciam successive in priores de Monymusk preficiuntur. Nec mirum quia provisione[d] prioris duo eorum magistri in theologia, quorum unus sibi in prioratu successit, alter in Scona prefectus; duo eciam licenciati, et quinque bachallarii in decretis extiterunt. | Sanctiandree 25 tunc claustralis paradisus ad suavem spirantis austri clemenciam, quasi tot floribus vernabat, | quot virtutum viris insignibus[e] habundabat, quando in claustralibus cerimoniis,[f] in diebus huius prioris viguit monastica compago. In Marthe sollicitudinibus refloruit juristica propago, et in scienciis theologicis efferbuit seraphica indago. In 30 primis pax et concordia morum, in secundo pax et proporcionabilitas studiorum, in tercio pax et progressus meritorum, in conspectu Dei suavem et in auribus hominum dulcem[g] melodiam reddiderunt. Multa quidem et alia bona fecit in vita sua, nam terras tempore casus incendii ecclesie impignoratas redemit, et sine debitis cum stauro 35 ferri, plumbi, asserum, lignorum, bituminis, salis et auri in deposito monasterium liberum, cum numeroso fratrum collegio in pace dimisit. Et in magno senio vitam finivit in camera prioris crastino Sancti Johannis Baptiste Nativitatis anno domini m° cccc^mo xvi, Seditque prior annis xxiii, et in capitulo novo repositus est ad patres 40 suos, in future resurreccionis gloria cum justis,[h] ut speratur, premia percepturus, quia non est veresimile quod Summi liberalitas Conditoris non respondeat eius laboribus religiosis recompensacione condigna, qui de sue pietatis habundancia merita suplicum excedit et vota. [Unde:][i] 45

fo.129v

G i,374

Hic Jacobita, fulgens velut gemma polita,
in claustri vita vixit velut vir heremita.

b   + lingua d *del.*C
c   + suam *del.*C
d   + huius pii *CA*
e   theocris *CA*

f   + reviguit *del.*C
g   + ditorum *del.*C
h   + premia *del.*C
i   *CA*

10 onlooker a likeness of his mind, and an expression of his integrity.
Why should I take time over the details? His deeds still proclaim how
alert was his mind, how prudent his understanding, how responsive
his temperament, how outstanding his knowledge of the church, how
retentive his memory, how skilfully expressed his learning, how
15 commendable his good works – these facts still resound even if our
discourse were to fall silent. Also the extent of his character and
ability, and of his life in religion, and of how he was endowed with
finesse as an administrator – the reader may learn about these from
the canons and other neighbours who knew him when he was alive.
20   But there is also no doubt that the sons of God who will arise in this
monastery will give an account to their brothers so that a second
generation may be informed, and they may place their hope in God,
and not forget the prior's deeds, but also examine his ideals. For many
of his novices, who had been instructed under his training and had
25 attained to the pinnacles of the virtues, were soon after his death
employed in other celebrated places as fathers and pastors. One of
these was the bishop of Ross; another two were appointed as abbots
at Scone and Inchcolm; and three were in succession appointed priors
of Monymusk. This is not surprising because the prior arranged for
30 two of his canons to become masters of theology, one of whom
succeeded him as prior, and the other was appointed at Scone; two
also qualified as licentiates and five as bachelors of decrees. At that
time, touched by the delightful mildness of a breeze from the south,
the paradise of a cloister at St Andrews was experiencing spring with
35 as many flowers as it abounded in distinguished men of virtue, when
during the time of this prior the monastic company flourished in the
sacred rites of the cloister. In the sphere of the preoccupations of
Martha the scion of legal studies bloomed again, and the seraphic
enclosure reached boiling point in the theological branches of
40 knowledge. In the first place peace and harmony of conduct, secondly
peace and a just proportion of studies, thirdly peace and progress in
meritorious actions produced a man who was pleasing in the sight of
God and a sweet melody in the ears of men. He did many other good
things indeed during his lifetime, for he redeemed lands which had
45 been mortgaged at the time of the accidental burning of the church,
and he left the monastery free of debt with a stock of iron, lead, timber
planks, wooden beams, pitch, salt and gold on deposit, and in peace
with a numerous company of brothers. And he ended his life at a great
age in the prior's apartment on the morrow of the feast of the Nativity
50 of St John the Baptist 1416. He served as prior for twenty-three years, 1416:
and was buried with his fathers in the new chapter-house. He will 25 June
receive, it is hoped, his rewards as one of the righteous in the glory of
the future resurrection, because it is not likely that the generosity of
the Supreme Creator would not respond to his religious works with

57

De Willelmo electo et Jacobo priore

Huius post decessum et eodem anno electus est per viam Spiritus
Sancti in priorem honestissima et benigna persona dominus Willelmus de Camera supprior eiusdem domus. Qui cum decreto eleccionis
et pro*a* confirmacione ad Romanam curiam accedens, et Bruʒeʒ
denuo confirmatus rediens, bullis suis ad partes remissis, ibi navigium 5
expectans, infirmitatem incurrit, qua presenti luce subtractus est. Et
in ecclesia Sancti*b* Egidii ante altare Sancti Andr' sepultus; nescitur
quoto die, sed sequenti anno sue eleccionis.

Quo eciam anno, audita eius morte, vir venerabilis et religiosus
dominus Johannes Lysstar licenciatus in decretis, dignissimus eius- 10
dem domus canonicus, qui tunc forte erat cum electo ultra partes
marinas, adiit Paniscoley curiam tunc Benedicti xiii, et faciliter*c* per
bullas suas sibi provisum fuit de prioratu. Sed interim sive cito post
dominus Jacobus de Haldenston magister in sacra pagina, vir
eloquentissimus et eiusdem domus canonicus et electus, accessit 15
Rome ad curiam domini Martini quinti, et ante substraccionem
confirmatus ab eo repatriavit, et prioratum optinuit, lite adhuc inter
bullatos dependente. Sed quia ipse magister Jacobus nuncius (et
collega ⟨dominorum⟩ Willelmi permissione divina episcopi Dunbla-
nensis et Johannis Scheveʒ decretorum doctoris ac officialis Sanc- 20
tiandr', nunciorum et ambassatorum) a domino Roberto Stewart
duce Albanie et gubernatore regni, cum consensu trium statuum
eiusdem constitutus, bonum*d* nuncium de substraccione a Benedicto
et adhesione Martino portan',*e* quicquid defuit electo in primis,
supletum est in secundis. Novissime autem omnium regnorum facta 25
est Scotorum substraccio. | Et hoc eis ad magnam fidei constanciam et
singularem laudem ab omnibus predicatur. Facta est hinc inde
substraccio et adhesio uno et eodem anno, scilicet domini m*mo* cccc*mo*
xviii°. Hic dominus Jacobus Haldenston magister in theologia
eloquens multum*f* erat, et decens persona in apparatu et habitu 30

G i,375

a interlin.*C*
b +Andr' del.*C*
c +de probably del.*C*
d +et acceptabile *CA*
e *C,D*; contulit *CA*
f singulariter *CA*

55 appropriate recompense. God in the abundance of his holiness
exceeds the merits and prayers of those seeking mercy. Hence:

> This man called James, shining like a polished jewel,
> lived in the life of the cloister like a hermit.

57

William the prior-elect, and Prior James

After this man's death and in the same year sir William de Camera the   1416
subprior of the same house, a most honourable and kind person, was
elected prior by the method of [accepting the guidance of] the Holy
Spirit. He went to the Roman court with his election decree to obtain
5 confirmation, and when at Bruges again on his way back after   [1417:
confirmation (after his bulls had been sent home [for implemen-   5 June]
tation]), and he was waiting for a ship there, he contracted an illness
which led to his death. And he was buried in the church of St Giles
before the altar of St Andrew; the date is unknown, but it was in the
10 year following his election.

In that year also, on hearing of William's death, sir John Litstar,
licentiate in decrees, a venerable and religious man who was a most
worthy canon of the same house, who then happened to be with the
prior-elect beyond the seas, went to the court of Benedict XIII who
15 was then at Peñiscola, and easily obtained a provision of the priory   [1418:
with his bulls. But meanwhile or soon afterwards sir James de   10 Mar.]
Haldenston master of the sacred page, a most eloquent man and
canon of the same house, had been elected, and went to Rome to the   [1417: end]
court of the Lord Martin V. He was confirmed by him before the   [1418:
20 withdrawal [from Benedict XIII], returned home, and got possession   17 Feb.]
of the priory, though litigation between those who had obtained bulls
was still pending. But because Master James had been appointed an
envoy (as a colleague of the envoys and ambassadors William, by
divine permission bishop of Dunblane, and John Scheves doctor of
25 decrees and official of St Andrews) by Sir Robert Stewart duke of
Albany and governor of the kingdom, with the consent of the three
estates of the same, bearing the good [and acceptable] news of the
withdrawal from Benedict and adherence to Martin, whatever as
prior-elect he lacked to begin with was made good subsequently. Of
30 all the kingdoms indeed, the withdrawal of the Scots was the last to be
made; and everyone speaks well of them for the great firmness of their
loyalty and for their uniquely praiseworthy action. The withdrawal
and adherence on both sides were made in one and the same year,
namely 1418.   [Oct.]
35   This sir James Haldenston master of theology was a man of great

compta satis^g et honesta. Qui postquam domum suam xxiiii^{or} prior vixerat bene regens, apud monasterium^h diem clausit extremum xviii die julii, et in pariete aquilonali capelle Nostre Domine infra ecclesiam cathedralem honorifice tumulatus anno domini m° cccc^{mo} xliii°. Cuius epitaphium est: 35

> Qui docui mores, mundi | vitare favores,
> inter doctores sacros sortitus honores,
> vermibus hic donor; et sic ostendere conor
> quod sicut [hic]^i ponor, ponitur omnis honor.

Fuit enim vir multum hilaris et jocundus, facie rubicundus et   40
complexione sanguineus, comis canus, et statura mediocris; severus in corripiendo, mansuetus^j in miserendo, liberalis in exponendo,^{k} affabilis in colloquendo, et pronus in compaciendo.^{l} Multum enim fuit miseris et egenis misericors, propter quod dispersit et dedit pauperibus, quibus, ut quidam ⟨interpretati sunt,⟩ non tam intencio-   45
ne^m caritatis quam respectu vanitatis^n distribuit. Sed caveant sibi temere judicantes, quia scio quod dedit largiter et habunde indigentibus et petentibus; nec interest cui petenti erogetur, quia non^o requirit Deus utrum mereatur ille qui postulat, sed querit qualiter prestet qui donat. Hilaris enim erat conviva; et quos escis laucioribus non   50
poterat, erogacione panis Christi et vultus hilaritate saciabat. Ecclesiam suam monasterialem mera et specabili pulcritudine tam in^p sculpturis stallorum quam picturis imaginum decoravit. Cuius navem ecclesie per recolende memorie dominum Jacobum Biset predecessorem suum tignis et tectura sumptuose erectam, intus tamen   55
tamquam vacuam amplam^q et solitariam sinagogam, luminariis vitriis per totum unacum construccione altarium, imaginum et ornamentorum ac politis pavimentis decenter perlustravit. Gabellum orientale a fundamentis unacum arcuali volta eiusdem construxit. Revestiarium cum reliquiis, et earum^r reparacionibus et clausuris,   60
non sine magnis impendiis placenter perornavit. Universum larem, tam chori quam transversarum capellarum, ecclesie cum duobus lateribus sive panis claustri, ac eciam inferius capitulum,^{s} pavimentis placidis complanavit. Pulcrum et spectabile palacium infra curiam hospicii prioris cum decencioribus oratorio et camera inibi situatis.   65
necnon domestica maneria in suis locis perhendinalibus, utpote Ballon, Pylmore, Segy et^t Kynmoth, quasi a fundamentis reedificavit. Insignia pastoralia, videlicet mitram, baculum et anulum, primus prioribus usuris impetravit. Servicium divinum in solemnizacione

---

g	multum *CA*	*n*	+sive humane laudis *CA*
h	*interlin.over* Ballon *del.C*	*o*	+tantum *CA*
i	*CA*	*p*	+superioribus *CA*
j	sed cito flexus *for* mansuetus *CA*	*q*	+vastam *del.C*
k	expendendo *CA*	*r*	+caris *del.C*
l	et pronus in compaciendo *om.CA*	*s*	+lucidis lateribus *CA*
m	intuitu *CA*	*t*	*interlin.C*

eloquence, and a person of pleasing appearance, quite elegant and
becoming in his dress and bearing. After he had served as prior ruling
his house well for twenty-four years, he ended his final day at the
monastery on 18 July 1443, and was honourably buried in the north
40 wall of the Lady Chapel in the cathedral church. His epitaph is:

> I, who have taught virtuous habits, and how to avoid
>   the world's favours,
> after acquiring honours among the sacred doctors
> am here consigned to the worms; and so I try to show
45
> that just as I am placed [here], all honour is laid aside.

He was a very cheerful and congenial man, red of face and with a
ruddy complexion, his hair turned white, and of medium build; he
was severe in his rebukes, gentle in showing pity, lavish in spending,
courteous in conversation, disposed towards compassion. Indeed he
50 was extremely tender-hearted towards the unfortunate and the needy,
and on this account he distributed and gave to the poor. Some people
have inferred that he made a distribution to them not so much with
charity in mind as with regard to vanity [or human praise]; but those
who judge him rashly should take care, for I know that he gave
55 generously and in large measure to the poor and to beggars; and it
makes no difference who was the beggar to whom a payment is made,
because God does not ask whether someone who is making a request
is deserving, but inquires about the spirit in which the giver gives. He
was indeed a cheerful table-companion, and those whom he could not
60 [feed] with sumptuous food, he satisfied with a distribution of the
bread of Christ and a cheerful expression.

He embellished the church of his monastery with sheer beauty of
outstanding quality, both in the [upper] carvings of the choir-stalls
and in the painted statues. The nave of this church had been built at
65 great expense by his predecessor sir James Biset (whose memory
should be recalled) up to the rafters and roof covering; but inside it
was like an empty, vast, deserted synagogue. This he tastefully lit with
glass lamps throughout, along with the erection of altars, statues and
[other] embellishments, and with smooth paving. He built the east
70 gable from the foundations, along with an arched vault for the same.
He greatly and pleasingly adorned the vestry with the relics,
refurbishing and enclosing them [in reliquaries], not without great
expense. He levelled the whole expanse of the church with agreeable
paving, both in the choir and the flanking chapels, along with two
75 sides or sections of the cloister, and also the lower chapter-house. He
rebuilt almost from the foundations the beautiful and attractive hall
within the courtyard of the prior's lodging with a tasteful oratory and
private room contained in it, and also the living-quarters of the
manors at his dwelling-places, namely Balone, Pilmore, Seggie and
80 Kinninmonth.

misse Nostre Domine in capella eius, ad ipsorum laudem, insigniter 70
ampliavit. In facultate sacre pagine precellenter rexit, et in theologia
decanus graduandos cathedrizavit. Hereticos et Lolardos et in fide
devios ipse[u] inquisitor diebus suis[v] objurgando acriter confutavit.
Collector eciam annatarum olim sedis apostolice infra regnum, et
capellanus honoris, in senectute bona ad Dominum transmigravit. In 75
cuius eciam | diebus dominus[w] Willelmus Bowar vicarius[x] Sanctiandr'
altare crucifixi in nave ecclesie cum solio eius solido et ymaginibus
sumptuosis adornatum, similiter Willelmus de Balbothy supprior
ipsius,[y] dicto[z] priore suffragante, larem dormitorii per lateres et alia
pavimenta perpulcre et decenter perfecerunt. In diebus eciam 80
predecessoris sui dominus Willelmus de Camera, tunc supprior sed
postea electus, ut premittitur,[aa] pavimentis polivit refectorium.
Quorum propterea anime eterna fruantur requie.

u	+suppremus *CA*	*y*	ipsis *C,D; om.CA*
v	+maxime obstinatos *CA*	*z*	de *CA*
w	*CA*; dm̄ *C,D*	*aa*	+lateranis *CA*
x	+et canonicus *CA*		

He was the first to obtain the pastoral insignia (namely the mitre, staff and ring) for the use of the priors. He markedly augmented [the provision of] divine service by the celebration of the mass of Our Lady in her chapel with general approval. He directed the faculty of the
85 sacred page in an outstanding fashion, and as dean he chaired those who were to graduate in theology. As inquisitor too for his time he bitterly refuted with censure heretics and Lollards and those who had strayed from the faith [especially the obstinate ones]. He was also a former collector of annates for the apostolic see in the kingdom, and
90 an honorary papal chaplain; he passed away to the Lord at a good old age.

In his time also sir William Bower vicar [and canon] of St Andrews erected the rood altar in the nave of the [cathedral] church on its substantial loft and adorned with costly statues; and likewise William
95 de Balbuthy the subprior of the same with the support of the said prior tastefully and handsomely floored the dormitory with tiles and other paving materials. Also in the time of his predecessor, sir William de Camera, then the subprior and later the prior-elect (as previously mentioned), levelled [the floor of] the refectory with [brick] paving.
100 On this account may their souls be blessed with eternal rest.

Notes

Chapter 1
pp.291-3

None of this chapter (or cc.2-8 that follow) is derived from the two mid-15c MSS of *Fordun* which contain cc.9-23 below (i.e. MSS FG and FA), though it is found in MS FC, into which 1480 x 1496 cc.1-8 here were copied along with other material from the Bower MSS that were by that date available for copying (see general introduction above p.xv); instead, after a brief introduction (ll.1-15), Bower from l.16 onwards through to the end of c.8 below includes lengthy extracts from the *Life* of Waltheof by Jocelin of Furness, selected from the following parts of that work: Prologue; c.I, paras.6-9, 11-15; c.II, paras.18-24; then in c.25 and cc.28-34 below he offers further extracts from c.VI, paras.79-80, 90; c.II, paras.29-30; c.III, paras.31, 33-37; c.IV, paras.48-53; c.IX, paras.135-6 of the same work. In this chapter ll.16-41 come from Jocelin's Prologue, paras.1-2. There is nothing in *Pluscarden* to correspond with cc.1-8 and 24-57 of this Book; *Extracta* ignores the whole Book.

This *Life* was probably available to Bower in a lost exemplar of the late 15c MS belonging to Dunfermline Abbey which is now in Madrid, Royal Palace Library, MS II. 2097, fos.41v-68, and has not been published (see general introduction p.xvii); a printed version, which appears in *Acta Sanctorum*, August, I, 242-78, was taken from a copy (now lost) included in a 15c MS collection of saints' *Lives* kept in the monastery of Boeddeken in Westphalia, Germany; a text similar to that in *Acta Sanctorum* with minor emendations was included in 'An Edition and Translation of the Life of Waldef, Abbot of Melrose, by Jocelin of Furness', by G.J.McFadden, Columbia University thesis 1952 (University Microfilms edn); in this edition the Latin text is broken into numbered paragraphs as in the *Acta Sanctorum* edition, but the translation is additionally divided into the Prologue, then Book I in 26 chapters, and Book II in 11 chapters; since this modern edition is not widely available, the references here are given to the chapters and paragraphs of the *Acta Sanctorum* edition (the Dunfermline MS is divided into similar but unnumbered paragraphs); but the translation here is indebted for some renderings of difficult Latin passages to McFadden's suggestions, and his identification of biblical references has proved useful; for a summary of his views on this source see George McFadden, 'The *Life of Waldef* and its author, Jocelin of Furness', *Innes Review*, vi (1955), 1-13; for a critical assessment of this *Life* and of its subject (based on the *Acta Sanctorum* text only) see D.Baker, 'Legend and reality: the case of Waldef of Melrose', in *Church, Society and Politics*, ed. D.Baker, *Studies in Church History*, xii (1975), 59-82.

Here Bower's extracts have been collated selectively with photographs of the Dunfermline MS now in Madrid (using the siglum 'DMS'), and with the text printed in the *Acta Sanctorum* (using the siglum 'AS'); there are many more variants compared with the *Acta Sanctorum* text than with the Dunfermline MS, and this is why it is highly likely that the exemplar of the latter was Bower's main source; but he may have had access to another text to find a very small number of words which do not appear in the Dunfermline MS, but are in the *Acta Sanctorum* version (e.g. see below c.33, l.13).

Waltheof died in 1159 (cf. below c.34, ll.22-24); Jocelin composed this *Life* 1207 × 1214, probably ca 1207 (Baker, 'Legend', 62).

19.   *both aspects of life*: apparently a reference to the 'two lives', man's life in the spirit and his life in this world (McFadden, 'Edition', 201, n.2).

23.   *Agatha*: for a discussion of the identity of this lady see above V c.11, ll.8-10 note, and below c.20, ll.31-35 and c.22, l.23 ff..

25-26.   *others ... Germany*: added by Bower to Jocelin's text.

30.   *Edward*: see below c.20, ll.24-35; c.22, ll.10-22.

34.   *he would have made you the rulers*: this is still addressed to King William, his son and brother, who by hereditary right from Margaret's father would have been rulers in England.

36.   *until ... time*: cf. Galatians 4:2.

39.   *saintliness and righteousness*: cf. Luke 1:75.

Chapter 2
p.293

ll.1-21 ('hope') continue to come from the *Life* of Waltheof, Prologue, paras.2-3; ll.21-25 from Prologue, para.4; and ll.31-35 from c.I, para.6.

1.   *Æthelwulf*: see below c.10, l.20.

5.   *St Edward*: i.e. Edward the Confessor 1042-66.

10.   *Matilda*: see above V c.41, l.28, and below c.6, ll.12-15.

12.   *Earl Waltheof*: see below c.3, l.3.

13-14.   *Waltheof ... uncle*: MS C has a side-note here: 'De S. Walthe-[vo] Scoto'; in 15c thinking apparently he was an adopted Scot. In fact he was only a stepson of King David (see below c.4, ll.38-40, and c.6, ll.34-35).

20.   *still wholly incorrupt*: Jocelin is here relying on the report of an opening of Waltheof's tomb in May 1171 (*Melrose*, 39; *Life*, c.IX, para.121), and a second inspection conducted probably in 1206 (*Life*, c.IX, paras.133-4; cf.Baker, 'Legend', 62, n.9 for date); both these examinations were probably connected with abortive plans of the monks of Melrose to have Waltheof recognized as a saint; but when the tomb was opened again in 1240, the body had disintegrated (*Melrose*, 87).

26-30.   *... reader*: Bower reveals his motive for these extracts from the *Life* of Waltheof; cf. Baker, 'Legend' (above c.1, introduction) for the argument that Waltheof was in fact a more conventional figure than either Jocelin of Furness or Bower suggests.

26. *his brothers*: in fact Jocelin was addressing King William and his son and brother (see above c.1, ll.16-17).

31. *I*: i.e. Jocelin.

32-33. *it is ... God*: cf. Wisdom 8:3.

35. *holy root*: cf. Romans 11:16.

Chapter 3
pp.295-7

This whole chapter follows on c.2 above in being taken from the *Life* of Waltheof, c.I, paras.6-8.

3. *Earl Waltheof*: see *ODS*, 429; *DNB*, lix, 265-6.

15. *adultress*: 'mecham' (text l.12) i.e. 'moecham', 'adultress', is presumably a reference to the central character in the Book of Judith in the Apocrypha; AS has 'victam', but it is 'mecham' in DMS.

17-18. *coming and going*: cf. Deuteronomy 28:6.

24-25. *When ... arrest*: cf. Acts 12:3.

Chapter 4
pp.297-9

This chapter continues from c.3 above, comprising the *Life* of Waltheof, c.I, paras. 8-9.

5-10. *Once ... outrage*: the truth was more complicated; see information collected in *ES*, ii, 39-40.

18-19. *Crowland ... St Guthlac*: a Benedictine abbey near Spalding LIN, where St Guthlac had lived as a hermit in late 7c (*MRHEW*, 63; *ODS*, 198-9).

19-20. *wrath ... lion*: cf. Proverbs 19:12.

22. *a fair ... Lord*: cf. Psalm 16:2 (*Vulgate*); 17.2 (*NEB*).

26. *death ... sight*: cf. Psalm 115:15 (*Vulgate*); 116:15 (*NEB*).

28. *and miracles accumulated*: 'crebrescentibus miraculis' (text l.24) added by Bower to Jocelin's text.

28-29. *his bones ... resting-place*: Ecclesiasticus 46:14 (*Vulgate*); 46:12 (*NEB*).

30-33. *A little book ... to him*: these *Miracles* were edited by F.Michel, *Chroniques Anglo-Normandes*, ii (Rouen, 1836), 131-42, and by J.A.Giles, *Vitae quorundam Anglo-Saxonum* (Caxton Society, 1854), 23-30; see also *ES*, i, p.lxxvi.

34-36. *Matilda ... Simon de Senlis*: Matilda and Simon de Senlis I married about 1091, when he first occurs as an earl, apparently by right of his wife; he died ca 1111; she lived (as queen of Scots from 1124) until 1131 (*CP*, vi, 640-2; see above V c.41, 1.28n.).

34.   *reached womanhood*: the phrase 'mundum muliebrem' (text 1.29) is found in Esther 2:9 (*Vulgate*); but here it is used metaphorically.

Chapter 5
p.299

This whole chapter (except 1.32) follows the *Life* of Waltheof, c.I, paras.11-12.

2-4.   *Isaac ... Jacob*: cf. Genesis 25:28.

10-14.   *But ... chant*: it is suggested that this picture is the product of Jocelin's imagination as a hagiographer (McFadden, 'Edition', 215n.); but it has been pointed out that Gerald of Wales tells the same story of his brothers and himself (Baker, 'Legend', 60, n.5).

19-20.   *who cannot ... left*: Jonah 44:11.

23-24.   *None ... unfulfilled*: cf. 1 Samuel 3:19.

25-30.   *Simon ... fashion*: see notes on his biography in *ES*, ii, 150-3; cf. *CP*, vi, 643; *DNB*, li, 248-9; he died in 1153.

Chapter 6
pp.301-3

Nearly all of this chapter is selected from the *Life* of Waltheof c.I – ll.1-9 ('teacher') from para.13; ll.9-31 ('hermit') from para.14; and ll.31-53 from para.15.

8-9.   *with the grace ... teacher*: McFadden refers to 1 John 2:27; 'unction' or 'anointing' is used here in the figurative sense of spiritual influence; the implication is that though Waltheof did not have much instruction from human teachers, the special grace which he had from God made up for the deficiency.

11-12.   *he ... overseas*: see McFadden, 'Edition', 218 for notes about Simon's death, which took place ca 1111 (*HBC*, 466; *CP*, vi, 640-1).

13.   *marriage*: this took place Dec.1113 × Feb.1114 (*ES*, ii, 147).

15.   *married Matilda*: 11 Nov. 1100 (*HBC*, 35).

21.   *we*: i.e. Jocelin.

23.   *William*: Bower omits Jocelin's statement that William was still living and 'much to be praised'.
   venerable: McFadden translates 'venerandi' (text 1.20) as 'worshipful'.

24-25. *He also ... below*: an addition by Bower to Jocelin's text.

28-29. *He grew ... in him*: cf. Luke 2:40.

30-31. *For ... hermit*: McFadden ('Edition', 220) notes that this 'conceit' goes back to Sulpicius Severus, *Vita Martini*, c.2.

43-53. *the king ... everything*: McFadden regards this story as an invented incident, but an effective one ('Edition', 221n.).

52. *treasured ... over them*: cf. Luke 2:19.

Chapter 7
pp.303-5

The whole chapter is taken from the *Life* of Waltheof c.II – ll.1-13 ('will') from para.18; ll.13-22 selected from para.19; ll.23-32 ('flock') summarized from para.20; ll.32-45 selected from para.21.

2-3. *like the fame ... earth*: cf. 2 Samuel 7:9.

5-6. *arrange ... Sabbath*: cf. Matthew 24:20.

10. *his brother the earl*: this implies a date sometime after 1138-9, when Waltheof's brother Simon was recognized by King Stephen as an earl (*HBC*, 466; cf.474); this date is probably in fact several years too late, though it is argued that 'it is impossible to date either his entry into Nostell, or his promotion to Kirkham, with any accuracy' (Baker, 'Legend', 75); he may have been born ca 1100 (ibid., 74); and since his father had died ca 1111 (see above, c.6, ll.11-12), Waltheof was apparently not a young novice, as McFadden notes ('Edition', 223n.).

14-15. *leaving ... kinsmen*: cf. Genesis 12:1.

16. *Nostell*: an Augustinian house near Pontefract YOW founded ca 1114 and dedicated to St Oswald (*MRHEW*, 148; *VCH Yorkshire*, iii, 231); King Alexander I had drawn the first canons of Scone PER from this house (Barrow, *Kingdom*, 170-1), and their leader Robert served as bishop of St Andrews 1124-59 (see below c.24, ll.37-58). It has been argued indeed that in contrast to Jocelin's explanation here of Waltheof's choice of Nostell, it is likely that he went there at King David's suggestion (Baker, 'Legend', 75, 77-78).

23-24. *the lamp ... bushel*: cf. Luke 11:33.

24. *Kirkham*: an Augustinian house near Malton YOE founded ca 1122 (*MRHEW*, 142; *VCH Yorkshire*, iii, 219); Waltheof is found as its prior in 1141 and 1143 (Knowles and others, *Heads*, 168); he may have assumed office by as early as ca 1134, as he certainly did by 1139 (Baker, 'Legend', 75).

31-32. *nor ... flock*: cf. 1 Peter 5:3, which is the source of the specialized meaning of 'in clero' (text l.26) here.

35-36. *as it were in a bundle*: McFadden ('Edition', 226n.) explains this as a reference 'to the old tale of the father who used a bundle of sticks to illustrate for his sons the maxim "in union there is strength".'

36-37.   *the Lord ... servant*: cf. Genesis 39:5.

37.   *landed property increased*: cf. Job 1:10.

Chapter 8
pp.305-7

This chapter is all taken from the *Life* of Waltheof, c.II – ll.1-24 ('tears') from para.22; ll.24-30 ('monks') from para.23; and ll.30-37 from para.24.

1-37.   *... confounded*: McFadden ('Edition', 229n.) observes that the story told here, familiar in art as 'The Mass of St Gregory', is told of many saints, including St Hugh of Lincoln. See also 'Miracula Nynie Episcopi', ed. W.MacQueen, *TDGAS*, xxxvii (1959-60), where in c.13 (p.48) the priest Plecgils experiences the same miracle at the tomb of St Ninian at Whithorn.

6.   *surpassing ... beauty*: Psalm 44:3 (*Vulgate*): 45:2 (*NEB*).

14-15.   *intoxicated ... Lord*: cf. Psalm 35:9 (*Vulgate*); 36:8 (*NEB*).

30.   *some monks*: Bower omits the next sentence in the *Life* where Jocelin identifies one of these monks as Everard, a canon of Kirkham, later a monk of Melrose, and subsequently the first abbot of Holm Cultram CMB 1150-92 (see below c.32, l.6); cf. Baker, 'Legend', 69, 71-72.

Chapter 9
pp.307-9

Bower now moves with a warning side-note 'Scriba' in the margin of MS C (indicating that he was now following Fordun again) to the chapters numbered cc.9-23 here which are found also in three of the Fordun MSS (FG, FA, FC) as having been prepared by Fordun for a sixth book of his work that was never completed (and which were printed by Skene as his Appendix I in *Fordun*, 387-401; cf. below c.23, ll.61-67); hence the mention of 'prefacio autoris' (text rubric), meaning a preface compiled by Fordun (VI c.1), which Bower follows word for word to make up this chapter. Cf. amended version in *Pluscarden* VI, c.1.

    The style of the bold advice offered to the king is in fact more characteristic of Bower's approach as an experienced, if disillusioned, royal councillor rather than of the work of Fordun, the humble scholar and man of the study (see Prologue to the whole work in Volume 9 below). Yet Bower is clear in his attribution of the text from the beginning of this chapter to Fordun (whether as 'Scriba' or 'Autor'; cf. above Vol.2, p.xv).

5-7.   *your Scottish family ... your English family*: The *Fordun* text has 'our' in both cases for 'your' here; but Bower's 'your' makes better sense.

8.   *chronicles of Ailred*: for Ailred abbot of Rievaulx 1147-67 see below c.25, l.8; the reference is to his *Genealogia Regum Anglorun*, printed in PL, 195, cols.711-38, composed in 1153-4 for the young Henry II just before he became king of England (Walter Daniel, *The Life of Ailred of Rievaulx*, ed. F.M.Powicke [London and Edinburgh, 1950], pp.xci-ii, xcvii, 41); Fordun had already made use of Ailred's book in his Book V c.35 ff. (cf. above V c.45 ff.; c.62).

14-15. *now joined ... one ruler*: these are Fordun's words taken over by Bower; it is not clear to which period 'now' refers, for there certainly was no single ruler of England and Scotland in the later 14c when Fordun was writing; from the ending with King David I below (c.23, 1.58) it may be that Fordun was echoing a mid-12c view of the Scottish court that David was the rightful heir to both kingdoms since he had the blood of both royal families in his veins (cf. *Life of Ailred*, p.xlii); 'are now' therefore probably means 'were by then'.

31-32. *like potter's vessels ... iron*: cf. Psalm 2:9.

Chapter 10
pp.309-11

Bower in this chapter follows *Fordun* (VI c.2), where the text is said to be based on Ailred, *Genealogia*; but see details below. See also *Early Gesta*, c.1 for a shorter version derived from DMS, fos.1v-2. See general introduction (above p.xviii) for the relationship betwen these sources. See *Pluscarden* VI, c.2.

5-12. *Ailred says... kingdom*: this summary does not in fact correspond to Ailred's text (col.717), where Woden is mentioned, but not Cerdic.

6. *your*: Bower again substitutes 'your' for 'our' in *Fordun* (cf. above c.9, ll.5-7).

7. *Woden*: the chief deity of pagan Germanic mythology (cf. *ASE*, 19, 100); the additional information provided in MS CA about Woden's name being given to Wednesday perhaps indicates Bower's direct familiarity with Ailred's text, where the same fact is mentioned in different words.

see above: this cross-reference is taken over from *Fordun*.

8. *Cerdic*: came to Britain in 495 as stated here, and was later regarded as the founder of the West Saxon dynasty (*ASC*, 11, s.a.; *ASE*, 19-25; *HBC*, 21; see above III c.20, 1.74; c.21, 1.44).

10. *Horsa and Hengest*: see above III c.12, 1.6; these leaders are traditionally supposed to have arrived in Britain in 449 (*ASC*, 10, s.a.; *ASE*, 16-17); therefore the calculated 'forty-seven years' is perhaps not quite accurate.

13-20. *... kings*: adapted by Fordun from Ailred, *Genealogia*, cols.717-18.

13. *Ine*: king of the West Saxons 688-726 (*HBC*, 22; *ASC*, 24, 27).

17-18. *Ingild ... Ecgberht*: Ecgberht king of the West Saxons 802-39 was a great-grandson of Ingild a brother of Ine (*HBC*, 23); see above IV c.13, 1.39.

20-36. *Ecgberht's son ... eternal one*: copied (with omissions) by Fordun from Ailred, *Genealogia*, col.718.

20. *Æthelwulf*: king of Wessex 839-56, died 858 (*HBC*, 23); see above IV c.13, 1.3.

27-28. *tithed ... churches*: in fact it was the 10c before English rulers put clerical wishes for payment of tithe to them into effect by laying down penalties for non-payment (*ASE*, 154-5).

29-32. *Rome ... munificence*: Æthelwulf's pilgrimage to Rome took him abroad from early 855 to autumn 856 (*ASE*, 245; see above IV c.14, ll.47-51).

33-34. *Then ... sons*: Æthelwulf had to agree to share his kingdom with his eldest son Æthelbald in 856; another son Æthelberht succeeded to Æthelwulf's share at his death in 858, and on Æthelbald's death in 860 he reunited his father's whole kingdom (*ASE*, 245). Ailred's account here is similar to that in Asser's *Life of Alfred* (*Alfred the Great*, ed. S.Keynes and M.Lapidge [Harmondsworth, 1983], para.16, pp.72-73).

Chapter 11
pp.311-13

This chapter follows *Fordun* (VI c.3); it is all taken (with minor omissions) from Ailred, *Genealogia*, cols.718-19. See also shorter account in *Early Gesta*, c.2, shortened from DMS, fos.2-2v. See *Pluscarden* VI, c.3.

1. *Alfred*: king of Wessex 871-99 (see above IV cc.18-20).

3. *still ... Rome*: Alfred was only four years old when sent to Rome in 853 by his father (*ASC*, 43, s.a.).

6. *Leo*: Pope Leo IV 847-55 (*ODP*, 104-5).

7-8. *anticipated ... king*: Leo in fact invested him with just the honorary dignity of a Roman consul, which was confused by the compiler of the Anglo-Saxon Chronicle and later writers (as here) with consecration to the kingship, when in 853 he was still very much a younger brother in his family (cf. *ASE*, 271, n.3); see discussion of the significance of this error in *Alfred the Great*, 14; 211, n.7; 232, n.19.

9. *Samuel ... David*: 1 Samuel 16:13.

10-23. *After ... proclaimed*: Ailred's source for these details about Alfred has not been traced.

14. *... humbled*: Psalm 87:16 (*Vulgate*).

18. *nowadays*: 'nunc' (text 1.15) is the reading in *Fordun* and Ailred, *Genealogia*; MS C is ambiguous.

22. *but*: 'sed' (text 1.19) follows Ailred's text, while Fordun has 'si'.

23-38. *Furthermore ... life*: Dr L.M.Whitby advises that the kernel of this story about the Emperor Constantine the Great can be traced back to accounts of the Council of Nicaea in 325 (cf. A.E.Burn, *The Council of Nicaea* [London, 1925], 26-28); by the ninth century it was being elaborated more like the form in which it is found here (e.g. *Theophanis Chronographia*, i (Corpus Scriptorum Historiae Byzantinae, 1839), 32, section AM 5816; *Georgii*

Monachi Chronicon, ii [Teubner edn, 1904], 508, ll.4-16); it is an example of a legendary story which came to be used for political purposes in terms of later ideological developments (A. Kazhdan, '*Constantin imaginaire*. Byzantine legends of the ninth century about Constantine the Great', *Byzantion*, lvii [1987], 196-250, especially 246-7); but it is not known where Ailred found this story for use here.

32. *to judge*: 'vestrum' (text l.27) follows Ailred's text, while Fordun has 'nostrum'.

Chapter 12
pp.313-15

This chapter corresponds to *Fordun*, VI c.4, which had been compiled from selected passages in Ailred, *Genealogia*, cols. 719, 721, 722 and 723; cf. brief accounts in *Early Gesta*, c.2 and DMS, fo.2v. See *Pluscarden*, VI, c.4.

7-8. *with the help ... Mercians*: this marginal addition by Bower in MS C is clearly misplaced, for Eadric lived in the early 11c (see below c.19, l.2).

10-11. *afflicted ... Job*: added by Bower to *Fordun*; cf. Ailred, *Genealogia*, col.719, where the simile is included at a neighbouring part of the text.

11. *abandoned the kingdom*: Alfred withdrew to Athelney SOM in 878 (*ASE*, 255; *Alfred the Great*, 21-22).

12. *his friends*: Bower has 'familiarum suarum' (text l.10) as in *Fordun*; but Ailred had written 'familiarium suorum'; the translation here is based on Ailred's choice of words rather than Fordun's.

13-14. *once nine years had passed*: 'transactis novem annis' (text l.12) added by Fordun in a bridge-passage between two widely-separated parts of Ailred's text; the words are perhaps derived from *Malmesbury*, i, 124. By 886 Alfred's forces had occupied London and he was accepted in some sense as overlord of the whole English nation (*ASE*, 258-60).

14-15. *... God*: Psalm 67:36 (*Vulgate*); 68:35 (*NEB*).

19. *famous banner*: for the origin of this Raven-banner, which bore a raven as the emblem of the pagan god Odin, and which supposedly had miraculous qualities, see various explanations in *Asser's Life of King Alfred*, ed. W.H.Stevenson (Oxford, 1904), p.44. para.54b, and notes on pp.265-7.

25-26. *twenty-nine ... months*: in fact twenty-eight years and six months by modern computation.

27. *Edward*: Edward the Elder, king of Wessex 899-924 (see above IV c.20, l.41).

37-44. *By the noblewoman ... wife*: for details of Edward's children and their mothers see *HBC*, 24-25.

38. '*Ecgwynn*': this name is doubtful, since it is attested only by post-Conquest writers.

 natural son: 'nothum' (text l.31) substituted by Fordun for 'primogenitum' in Ailred's text, *Early Gesta* and DMS.

41.   *bride of Christ*: i.e. a nun.

42.   *Otto*: Otto I king of Germany 936-73, also emperor from 962.

43.   *Charles*: Charles the Simple, king of the Franks 898-929.

44.   *called Sigtryggr*: added by Fordun to Ailred's text; he ruled at York 921-7 (*HBC*, 7).

Chapter 13
pp.315-17

Most of this chapter (ll.1-39 and 53-56) is taken from *Fordun* (VI c.5), where the text was compiled from passages selected from Ailred, *Genealogia*, cols.724, 725, 726; but at ll.39-52 Bower rejects a single sentence in *Fordun* and three sentences in *Ailred* in favour of a longer passage taken directly from DMS, fo.3. The brief account in *Early Gesta*, cc.2-3 is also based on DMS, fo.3. See *Pluscarden* VI, c.5.

1.   *Athelstan*: king of Wessex 924-39, first effective king of England as a whole from 927 (*HBC*, 25); see above IV c.21, l.4.

2-3.   *The Danes ... the Cumbrians*: for 'Daci Northumbrenses atque Cumbrenses' (text ll.2-3) taken from *Fordun*, Ailred has 'Northymbri et Scoti'; the Scots were among the force that fought against Athelstan at Brunanburgh in 937 (*ASE*, 342-3; see above IV cc.21, 24, 25).

5.   *Edmund*: Edmund I king of England 939-46 (see above IV c.25, l.54; c.26, ll.44-47).

10-11.   *Lincoln ... Derby*: Edmund in 940 lost these so-called Five Boroughs (which had for twenty years been obedient to the king of England) to a Norse king of Dublin, and then regained them in 942 (*ASE*, 357-8).

14.   *with peace everywhere*: for 'per omnia pace' (text l.12) in *Fordun*, Ailred has 'in omni parte'.

16.   *St Dunstan*: abbot of Glastonbury SOM and successively bishop of Worcester (957), bishop of London (959) and archbishop of Canterbury (960-88) (*ODS*, 122-4; *ODCC*, 431-2; see above IV c.30, l.26).

18-19.   *it withered ... death*: Bower has simplified Fordun's text here, which was itself an abbreviation of Ailred's text.

21.   *Eadred*: king 946-55 (see above IV c.26, l.47).

24.   *A precious death*: i.e. in the religious sense of 'a holy death'.

25.   *after ... years*: added by Fordun to Ailred's text.

26.   *Eadwig*: king 955-9, but with his authority confined to south of the river Thames from 957 (*HBC*, 27); see above IV c.27, l.31.

28-36.   *He spent ... desirable*: this story in explanation of Dunstan's exile has 'invited legendary accretions' by later writers (*ASE*, 365-6).

39.   *Edgar*: see below c.14.

39-52.   *At last ... punishment*: while Fordun was content with simple extracts from Ailred, *Genealogia*, though adding the information that Dunstan was in exile when ignorant of the king's death (cf. 1.48), Bower chooses to expand this account with an extract from DMS; ll.47-52 are ultimately derived from the *Life* of St Dunstan by Osbern (*Memorials of St Dunstan, Archbishop of Canterbury* [RS, 63], 104, para.30); cf. different account in *Malmesbury*, i, 164.

53. *prostrated himself*: 'procubuit' (text 1.45) is taken from Ailred's text, though the word had been omitted in *Fordun*.

Chapter 14
pp.319-21

Most of this chapter has been copied from *Fordun* (VI c.6), with the omission of two cross-references to IV cc.33-34 and 39 above; the Fordun text is based on extracts from Ailred, *Genealogia*, cols.726-7, 729-30, but adds ll.10-15 from a source that has not been identified; Bower inserts at ll.4-10 three sentences probably taken directly from DMS, fos.3-3v, since they are found together there, but only separately in Ailred (cols.726-7), and since in *Early Gesta*, cc.3-4 only the first and third sentences were included among the material copied from DMS; Bower then adds a marginal tailpiece at ll.40-42; see also brief extracts in *Early Gesta*, cc.3-4. See *Pluscarden* VI, c.6.

1. *Edgar*: king of the Mercians and Northumbrians from 957, then of all England 959-75 (*ASE*, 366-72).

7-9. *At his ... born*: cf. *Malmesbury*, i, 164 for another version of Dunstan's supposed words on this occasion.

10-15. *He ... Wales*: Fordun's source for this addition to the material from Ailred is unknown; cf. above IV c.30, ll.23-26.

25. *writings*: Bower omits here Fordun's cross-reference to the sermon attributed to King Edgar (see above IV cc.33-34).

28. *Edward*: King Edward I the Martyr, succeeded his father 975, assassinated 978 (*HBC*, 27; *ODS*, 135-6); see above IV c.32, ll.36-38.

32. *Æthelred*: King Æthelred the Unready 978-1016, consecrated 4 May 979 (*HBC*, 27); cf. above IV c.39, ll.1-12 (a cross-reference inserted by Fordun, but omitted by Bower). His mother was King Edgar's third wife (see below c.23, 1.18).

36. *Emma*: daughter of Richard I duke of Normandy, married Æthelred in 1002 (*HBC*, 27); after his death she married King Cnut in 1017, and lived until 1052 (ibid., 28; *DNB*, xvii, 360-1).

38. *Edmund*: i.e. King Edmund II Ironside (see below c.16).

38-39. *daughter ... Thored*: Ælfgifu, daughter of Ealdorman Thored (*HBC*, 27); see above IV c.45, ll.3-4).

39-40. *Alfred and Edward*: Alfred (d.1036), and King Edward the Confessor (see below).

40-41. *The traitor ... treachery*: see below c.20, ll.39-42.

Chapter 15
pp.321-3

This whole chapter follows *Fordun* (VI c.7), where ll.1-12 and 23-31 here are based on Ailred, *Genealogia*, col.730; Fordun takes some additional words ('sabbati' [text l.2], 'die videlicet Sancti Bricii' [ibid.], 'Quod et ita factum est' [text l.3], 'anno sequenti' [l.4], and 'incendiis' [l.6]) from his shorter version in *Early Gesta*, c.4 (derived from its source, DMS, fo.3v); ll.32-39 are found in Fordun, VI c.7, *Early Gesta*, c.4, and DMS, fo.4, but not in Ailred's account. Fordun has looked further afield for ll.14-21, which are based on *Malmesbury*, i, 212; Bower in his turn amends this paragraph by introducing 'vel ... percussus' (text l.13) either from Ailred's book (col.730) or from its probable source DMS, fo.3v. See *Pluscarden* VI, c.7.

1-8. *... monasteries*: see above IV c.38, ll.20-29; The extra information which Fordun added to Ailred's account here provides dates. The massacre is dated 1002 (*ASC*, 86, s.a.) where St Brice's Day is taken to be 13 Nov., which was a Friday in that year; but in some churches this saint's day was held on 14 Nov; or Fordun may have been mistaken about the day of the week (see *ASE*, 380).

6. *Swein*: Swein Forkbeard, king of Denmark ca 988-1014 (*ASE*, 375, 386).

11-12. *followed ... kingdom* late Dec. 1013 after Christmas (*ASC*, 93, s.a.).

15. *Purification ... Mary*: the date 3 Feb. 1014 in *ASC* (93, s.a.) is usually preferred to the date here (2 Feb.) taken from *Malmesbury*.

16-18. *struck down ... saint's land*: for St Edmund, king of East Anglia and martyr (d.869) see *ODS*, 131-2; his body was preserved at Bury St Edmunds SFK; the later great abbey came to enjoy extensive lands and jurisdiction; Swein in fact died at Gainsborough LIN.

24. *recalled*: Æthelred returned in Spring 1014 (*ASC*, 93, s.a.).

27. *Cnut*: king of England 1016-35; also king of Denmark from 1019 and of Norway from 1028 (*HBC*, 28).

30. *Æthelred died*: 23 Apr. 1016 (*ASC*, 95, s.a.).
Edmund: see above c.14, l.38.

Chapter 16
pp.323-5

All of this chapter (except the marginal addition at ll.22-25 [see below]) is taken from *Fordun* (VI c.8); Fordun takes the initial sentence (ll.1-4) either from his other version in *Early Gesta*, c.5 or direct from its source DMS, fo.4, and then ll.4-22 ('Whatever ... hindrance') from Ailred, *Genealogia*, cols.730-1; ll.27-54 are selected and summarized from *Malmesbury*, i, 215-16. See *Pluscarden* VI, c.8.

3. *Edmund*: King Edmund II Ironside, Apr.-Nov. 1016 (*HBC*, 27-28; *DNB*, xvi, 403-5); see above c.14, l.38; c.15, l.30.

4. *I*: 'dicerem' (text 1.4) was taken over by Ailred from his source, for it is found in DMS, fo.4; both Fordun and Bower in turn adopt this first person statement.

12-15. *In the most ... opposition*: in Ailred's text this sentence comes after the one which here follows it. Presumably Fordun thought that this placing of it made better sense (cf. *ASE*, 390-3).

16. *elected ... king*: Cnut secured the allegiance of England bit by bit 1015-16 (*HBC*, 28).

21. *of whom ... important*: added by Fordun to Ailred's text. For Eadric Streona, ealdorman of Mercia 1007-17 (*ASE*, 381-2, 399; *DNB*, xvi, 415-18) see above IV c.38, l.24; c.44, l.16.

22-25. *During ... England*: this marginal addition by Bower is probably summarized from *Huntingdon*, 183-5, where the supposed seven battles are separately described.

23-24. *fought once against Cnut*: see below cc.17-18.

24-25. *they divided ... England*: at Alney Island in the river Severn near Deerhurst GLO, Oct.-Nov. 1016 (*ASC*, 96, s.a.; *ASE*, 392-3); this marginal addition is placed out of chronological order.

28. *Penselwood*: near Wincanton SOM.
Gillingham DOR.

29. *Rogation Days*: 7-9 May 1016.
feast of St John: 24 June.

30. *Sherston*: near Malmesbury WLT.

35-39. *The English ... fellow-soldiers*: Fordun's text is close to *Malmesbury* here, with 'rex' added after 'nisi' (text 1.29); but Bower has re-written the two sentences, though still largely to the same effect, adding 'hilari vultu' (text 1.31).

41-45. *... slaughter*: see also *ASC*, 95-96, s.a.1016.

44. *Brentford* MDX: now in West London; it is usually assumed that here a crossing of the river Thames is meant, but the matter is ambiguous; 'The name Brentford is recorded from 705, and has generally been assumed to refer to the ford over the Brent [a tributary of the Thames] ... although it may have referred to the crossing of the Thames' (*VCH Middlesex*, vii, 113).

51. *as I said*: i.e. as William of Malmesbury had said..

52. *maintained*: 'affirmaret' (text 1.41) is a necessary verb which Fordun had omitted from the *Malmesbury* text.

Chapter 17
pp.325-7

For the story about a supposed duel between Edmund and Cnut in this chapter and the next one, Bower is following *Fordun* (VI cc.9-10); in this chapter Fordun followed Ailred, *Genealogia*, cols.731-2 for ll.2-17 and 26-42, but inserted also at ll.19-24 a short parallel passage from *Malmesbury*, i, 217; see also version in *Early Gesta*, cc.5-6, dervived from DMS, fos.4v-5. See *Pluscarden* VI, c.9.

There is no mention of this duel in the earlier account in the Anglo-Saxon Chronicle (*ASC*, 96, s.a.1016); this imaginary legend was in circulation by the mid-12c in time for both Ailred and Malmesbury to include it (cf. *DNB*, xvi, 405).

3. *they said*: in Ailred's text the speech that follows was made by one speaker.

3-13. *We are stupid ... differences*: Fordun has much abbreviated this invented speech, and altered the references to the earlier numbers of English kings. 'Insensati' (text l.2) is copied from *Fordun* VI, and is found also in *Early Gesta* c.5, but not in either Ailred's text or DMS.

15. *river Severn*: at Alney Island (see above c.16, ll.24-25).

19-24. *... himself*: Fordun introduces this parallel passage to explain Edmund's supposed motives for a duel; but he fails to include the next sentence in Malmesbury's account where it is stated that Cnut refused the offer of a duel.

Chapter 18
pp.327-9

This chapter continues from c.17 the story of an imaginary duel, taken from *Fordun* (VI c.10), based on Ailred, *Genealogia*, cols.732-3; Bower follows Fordun in including the following phrases which are not found in Ailred's text: 'sibi precavens' (text l.2), 'ac flectere quodammodo fecit' (ll.5-6), and 'ut vir benigne mentis' (l.22); they come from the text in DMS, fos.4v-5, and are found also in the version copied into *Early Gesta*, c.6 (which in other details is closer to the DMS text than is the Ailred text that is followed here). See *Pluscarden* VI, c.18.

16-18. *Denmark ... surrendered to me*: this supposed speech of Cnut is anachronistic here, for in 1016 he was not yet ruler of Denmark, Norway or Sweden (*HBC*, 28).

Chapter 19
pp.329-31

Most of this chapter is taken from *Fordun* (VI c.11); Fordun had already for *Early Gesta*, c.7 produced a version of his own about King Edmund's death, supposedly drawn specifically from Ailred (*Genealogia*, col.733), but in fact based more on the much longer earlier version in DMS, fos.5-5v, with details drawn from *Huntingdon*, 185-6; for his version in VI c.11 Fordun had added other details, and the long passage at ll.32-47 here from *Malmesbury*, i, 219.

Bower adds two passages with material which he had found in other chronicles – first ll.48-55 in the body of MS C, and then ll.11-15 as a marginal addition to that MS (see below for details). See *Pluscarden* VI, c.11.

1-2. *belonging ... Mercians*: Ailred followed DMS in not naming the supposed traitor, but says that he was on the Danish side ('partis Danicae'); Fordun omitted these two words in his account in *Early Gesta*, and then positively suggested differently by inserting 'Anglicae nationis' in his version in VI c.11; Bower follows this change from the DMS tradition, and goes further in MS CA by introducing the name of Eadric; this is probably a misreading of *Huntingdon* (186), where it is 'filius Edrici ducis' that is said to have been involved (see below l.12), though it was still Eadric himself who approached Cnut afterwards: Fordun had introduced 'filius Edrici' to his *Early Gesta* version, but deleted it from VI c.11; cf. account in *Malmesbury*, i, 217, where it is suggested that 'rumour implicates Eadric' in this connection; see above IV c.45, l.5; in fact Edmund probably died of natural causes (see discussions in E.A.Freeman, *History of the Norman Conquest*, 2nd edn [Oxford, 1870-5], i, 694-8, and *DNB*, xvi, 405).

3. *1018*: Fordun had added the feast-date to his VI c.11 text; Bower has then added the year-date; in fact the king died on 30 Nov. 1016 (*ASC*, 97, s.a.1016); Bower also adds 'and liege lord' (1.4) to heighten the enormity of the supposed treason.

6. *at Oxford*:Fordun had first included this fact from *Huntingdon* (185) in his *Early Gesta* version.

8. *spit ... knife*: Fordun had also first introduced the detail about a doubly-sharp knife to his *Early Gesta* version from the same source (186), and Bower adds the alternative of a spit (source unknown).

11-15. *... organs*: in this addition Bower is in his turn quoting *Huntingdon* (186) directly.

18. *phrase*: meaning of 'theumate' (text l.14) is not clear – perhaps equals rather 'title' or 'salutation'.

27. *head to be cut off*: this cannot refer to Eadric, who lived until 1017 (see below l.32).

29. *Glastonbury* SOM: see also *ASC*,97, s.a.1016.

32. *Eadric*: his death took place sometime in 1017 (ibid.; *ASE*, 398-9), perhaps at Christmas (*DNB*, xvi, 418).

33. *was himself deceived*: though the text (l.26) has 'conventus', and this word-form occurs in the *Malmesbury* (i, 219) source as well as in *Fordun* and MS C, the correct form must surely be 'circumventus' as some user of MS D seems to have realised.

43-45. *... anointed*: cf. 2 Samuel 1:16.

48-55. *... blameless*: most of this paragraph is taken from Florence, *Chronicon*, i, 181-2, where it is included correctly under the year 1017, and the place is said to be London.

Chapter 20
pp.331-5

The first part of this chapter (ll.1-42) is taken from *Fordun* (VI c.12), to the text of which Bower has added some insertions; the material in *Fordun* is drawn from Ailred, *Genealogia*, cols.733-4, to which Fordun has added only a few words here and there; but he reversed the order of the sentences now found as ll.12-16 and 16-19, restoring them to the order (but not the shorter form of words) found in DMS, fo.5v and *Early Gesta* c.8. After a bridging sentence at ll.43-45, Bower leaves *Fordun* for the rest of this chapter and most of c.21, preferring to follow DMS, fos.6-6v (cf. shorter version in *Early Gesta*, c.9). Fordun (398) had included only a brief account of Earl Godwine's death from *Malmesbury*, i, 240. See *Pluscarden* VI, c.12.

1-2.   *Edmund's brothers*: Alfred and Edward (see above c.14, l l.39-40).

3.   *Edmund and Edward*: see below ll.24-35, and c.22.

3-5.   *in 1019 ... Easter*: Bower has added 'anno domini ... ubi' and 'in Pascha' (text ll.3-4) to Fordun's text. This council was celebrated at Cirencester GLO on 17 April (Easter) 1020 (*ASC*, 98, s.a.1020).

6.   *agreement*: in 1016 (see above c.16, ll.24-25).

13-14.   *their sword ... shattered*: cf. Psalm 36:15 (*Vulgate*): 37:15 (*NEB*).

25-26.   *to his father-in-law ... cared for*: Fordun added 'socerum suum ... quasi alendos sed pocius' (text ll.21-22) to Ailred's text from DMS, fo.5v; The king of the Swedes was not Cnut's father-in-law (cf. *HBC*, 28). In fact the two boys were not sent abroad by Cnut, but found refuge in Hungary as a country where Cnut's murderous agents could not reach them (*ASE*, 397).

26-29.   *But he ... for them*: For this sentence (text ll.22-25) Fordun had followed the shorter text in *Ailred*; but Bower restores the more elaborate text found in DMS,fo.5v and *Early Gesta*, c.8.

27-28.   *his ally ... Hungarians*: St Stephen was king in Hungary 997-1038; it is Fordun's speculative addition that he was an ally of the king of the Swedes.

31-42.   *Then ... England*: in this section (text ll.27-37) Fordun had followed Ailred, but added 'sororem reginae' from *Malmesbury* (i, 218) to explain 'filiam germani'(text l.28); Bower has preferred to follow DMS (fos.5v-6) by inserting several extra phrases, while retaining the lady's name from *Fordun*.

31-35.   *Then ... happiness*: see below c.22, l.23 ff. for a commentary on these marriages.

36-37.   *the death ... after him*: Cnut died 12 Nov.1035; Harold I Harefoot reigned until 17 Mar.1040, and then Harthacnut until 8 June 1042 (*HBC*, 28-29).

37-39.   *Edward ... English*: King Edward the Confessor 1042-66 had in fact been resident in England as associate king since 1041 (ibid., 29).

39-41.   *For his brother ... death*: Alfred was mutilated and died at Ely abbey CAM in 1036 (*ASC*, 104, s.a.); cf. above c.14, ll.40-41; the share of Godwine earl of Wessex in this event is regarded as inconclusive (*DNB*, xxii, 50-55, especially 51-52; cf. *ASE*, 421). It is not clear what sources Bower was using when he made an addition to Fordun's text here; but the accounts in

Florence, *Chronicon* (i, 191-2) and *Huntingdon*, 191 mention Guildford SUR rather than Gillingham (KNT or DOR); see above V c.10, ll.20-28.

41. *Emma*: see above c.14, l.36.

45-57. *For afterwards ... allowed it*: a shorter version of the full story here and in c.21 was included by Ailred of Rievaulx, in his *Vita S. Edwardi Regis* (PL, 195, cols.766-7), composed 1162 × 1163 in association with the translation of the relics of Edward the Confessor in Oct. 1163 (*Life of Ailred*, pp.xciii and xcvii).

47. *day ... festival*: Easter Monday, 12 April 1053; see *ASC* (127, s.a.) where it is clear that Godwine simply had a stroke, became speechless, and died three days later.

48-49. *whose daughter ... married*: Edward married Eadgyth, daughter of Earl Godwine, 23 Jan.1045 (*HBC*, 29).

Chapter 21
pp.335-7

Bower starts (ll.1-26) with a continuation of the story from DMS begun in c.20 above – it is noteworthy that two words copied into MS C and then corrected (see textual notes a and d) were taken from DMS, fos.6 and 6v. This is followed by two items in the margin of MS C; the first (ll.27-30) picks up a short excerpt from the end of *Fordun*, VI c.12 which had not been included in c.20 above (it came from *Malmesbury*, i, 217-18); the second (ll.31-36) completes the story of Godwine's death with a passage from *Malmesbury*, i, 245. Only ll.27-30 here are taken into *Pluscarden* VI, end of c.12 (see above c.20 introduction).

19. *dying miserably*: he died on 15 April 1053 (see above c.20, l.47n.).

23-24. *Godwine's sons*: these are listed as Harold, Tostig and Gyrth in the account in Florence, *Chronicon*, i, 211.

27-30. *... Eadric*: this was in 1017, and Eadwig was later killed on Cnut's instructions (*ASC*, 97, s.a.). This item is intruded into the story of Godwine's death out of chronological order.

31. *first wife*: Malmesbury is in error here; Godwine married Gytha, a sister of Earl Ulfr, who was the husband of Cnut's sister Estrith (*DNB*, xxii, 51).

32. *a son*: in *Malmesbury* this boy is described separately from the known sons of Godwine, who are wrongly supposed to have been born to a second wife.

37-38. *But now ... while*: Bower takes over this sentence from DMS, fo.6v, where 'we' means Turgot.

Chapter 22
pp.337-9

The first paragraph (ll.1-22) is taken from the first part of *Fordun*, VI c.13, which is drawn explicitly from Ailred, *Genealogia*, col.734; cf. the different text in *Early Gesta*, cc.9-10, which follows DMS, fo.6v. The rest of the chapter is a discussion by Bower based on extracts from various sources. See *Pluscarden* VI, c.13.

3. *Winchester* HMP.

    1043: date added correctly by Bower to Fordun's text (cf. *HBC*, 29).

6. *Edgar*: see above c.14, l.1.

10-11. *sent envoys ... emperor*: the bishop of Worcester was sent to the Emperor Henry III in 1054 (*ASE*, 571).

16-22. *he sent ... tears*: in 1057 (*ASC*, 133, s.a.).

17. *Agatha*: see below.

18. *Edgar the Ætheling*: uncrowned king of England after death of King Harold at battle of Hastings in 1066; still alive ca 1125(*HBC*, 29; *DNB*, xvi, 371-3; see above V ad indicem).

    Margaret: St Margaret, queen of King Malcolm III (see above V ad indicem).

    Christina: became a nun 1086; lived until after 1100 (*DNB*, x, 289-90).

23-28. *... Agatha*: cf. above c.1, l.23 and c.20, ll.31-35; see also above V c.11, ll.8-10 note.

26-28. *One of them ... Agatha*: this is not in fact what Ailred says (see above, c.20, ll.32-33); Bower seems to be referring here to Florence, *Chronicon*, i, 181, where a note suggests that this brother was called Bruno.

29-30. *took ... Hungarians*: *Malmesbury*, i, 218; the queen of the Hungarians was Gisela, sister of the future emperor Henry II, married to St Stephen in 996 (*NCE*, vi, 498).

30-35. *In another ... Henry*: i.e. some other source agrees with Ailred's statement above c.20, ll.32-33. Henry was in fact the brother-in-law, not the brother, of St Stephen, so that 'germani' (text l.30) i.e. 'full brother' is surely a mistake here.

35-36. *Elsewhere ... Germany*: source not identified.

40. *Salomon*: presumably a wrong extension for S[tephen], whose pagan name before his baptism was Vajk (*NCE*, xiii, 697), and could scarcely have been a biblical name; see below l.53; see also above IV c.38, ll.46-51.

41-42. *In an old ... Dunfermline*: presumably a reference to an exemplar of DMS, which bears the title (fo.1): 'Sancte Margarite de Dunfermlyn liber iste.' For ll.42-44 here see DMS, fo.22.

45. *agrees with Martin*: apparently a reference to Martin of Troppau, *Chronicon Pontificum et Imperatorum*, in MGH *Scriptores*, xxii, which Bower uses as a source elsewhere (e.g. above IV c.38, ll.32-33). Most of the information which follows here is accurate, but is not taken from any particular passage in Martin's book, and intrudes into Bower's discussion of Agatha's exact family connections.

The shortened text found in MC CA has an interesting reference to a chronicle in French which Bower has not himself seen, but which he has heard about from a 'distinguished man'. It is not the *Scalacronica*, but has not been identified.

49-50. *Henry ... fathered Henry [II]*: in fact Henry II was the grandson of this earlier Henry (see above IV c.38, ll.30-51).

50. *first elected emperor*: after the death of Otto III in 1002, Henry II obtained the throne only after a contested election (*CMH*, iii, 215-17).

50-51. *Henry gave his sister Gisela*: Martin, 466; but Agatha is not mentioned as a sister of Gisela.

54-57. *It was to him ... Edward*: see above c.20, ll.24-33. Bower here seems to be concluding his discussion by identifying Agatha as the sister of Gisela queen of the Hungarians, whilst in c.20 above he regarded her as her niece. The agnostic statement in *ASC* (133, s.a.1057) that she was 'a kinswoman of the emperor' is the best resolution of this problem of contradictory sources (cf. *DNB*, xvi, 371), though it has been argued in modern times that she was a daughter of King Stephen and Queen Gisela (*ASE*, 571n), and more plausibly that her father was Liudolf Margrave of Westfriesland, a son of Gisela of Swabia, who was later the mother of the Emperor Henry III (see above V c.11, ll.8-10 note)..

57. *Edward*: the extra sentence in MS CA after 'Agathen' here (text 53) appears to be misplaced; it probably refers to the Henry duke of Bavaria who is identified above as the father of the Emperor Henry II, Gisela and Agatha (see above ll.49-50).

60. *granddaughter*: Conrad II's wife Queen Gisela was a member of the royal house of Burgundy, a niece of Rudolf III there (*CMH*, iii, 256).

61. *James of Genoa*: i.e. James de Voragine, archbishop of Genoa; see his *La Légende Dorée*, ed. J.-B. M. Roze, iii (Paris, 1902), 464-6.
Martin: i.e. Martin, 466-7.
as is written above: see IV c.45.

Chapter 23
pp.339-43

ll.1-13 are taken from *Fordun* (VI, end of c.13), where the source is a last extract from Ailred, *Genealogia*, col.734; see also short version in *Early Gesta*, c.10, related to DMS, fo.6. Though the text from l.14 onwards is marked in the margin of MS C as having been compiled by Bower himself, nearly all of it (ll.15-56) is in fact selected from *Fordun* (VI cc.14-15), where the author recapitulates some of the preceding chapters; nothing coresponds to this in *Early Gesta* or DMS. See *Pluscarden* VI, c.14.

1-13. *... head*: Fordun changed 'quidam' in the Ailred text to 'proceres' (text l.4), added the phrase 'si clerum assertatorem haberent' (l.5), added 'intelligens ... regium' (ll.8-10), and changed 'regnum obtinuit' to 'capiti proprio imposuit' (ll.10-11); Bower took over these changes, but omitted 'in regem erigere molirentur' (l.5) which is necessary for the sense, and restored 'et quia ... videbatur' (ll.5-6) which is found in the Ailred text, but with 'oneri' for 'honore', which matches more the *Early Gesta* and DMS versions; he also omits 'cui regnum hereditario jure debebatur' which Fordun had inserted after 'haberent' (text l.5).

1-3. *dedication ... St Peter*: Westminster Abbey was consecrated with a dedication to St Peter and All Saints, 28 Dec. 1065 (*ASC*, 138-9, s.a.).

5. *buried*: Edward the Confessor was buried at Westminster on 6 Jan. 1066 (ibid).

5-6. *Edgar the Ætheling*: see above c.22, l.17.

6. *if ... clergy*: it is not known where Fordun found this evidence for clerical opposition to Edgar.

Bower's apparent suppression of the phrase about Edgar's hereditary right is probably part of the scribal omission of a necessary part of Fordun's text that immediately follows.

8. *Harold ... Godwine*: see above c.21, ll.23-24; he was king of England from 6 Jan. 1066 until his death in the battle of Hastings on 14 Oct. 1066 (*HBC*, 29). Fordun has developed to greater length Ailred's unfavourable account of Harold; Bower goes further by adding 'viribus et potencia' (text l.9).

10-11. *it always ... planned*: Lucan, *The Civil War*, bk.I, l.281 (Loeb edn, 22), cited (not from here) in Walther, *Proverbia*, no.27,978; it is unusual for Fordun (as opposed to university-educated Bower) to insert a literary allusion of this kind.

16. *Edgar the Peace-maker*: see above c.14, l.1.
Edward: see above c.14, l.28.

18. *Ælfthryth*: third wife of King Edgar (*HBC*, 27).

19-21. *wicked traitress ... decline*: cf. *Malmesbury*, i, 183 for an account of Edward's murder on 18 Mar. 978; 'there is nothing to support the allegation, which first appears in writing more than a century later, that Queen Ælfthryth had plotted her stepson's death' (*ASE*, 373).

20. *Æthelred*: see above c.14, l.32.
father: Bower has attempted with 'fratris' (text l.16) to correct 'patris' in *Fordun*; but 'patris' must surely be correct here, for Æthelred was the half-brother of Edward on their father's side.

25-26. *possession ... peoples*: i.e. the Norman Conquest of 1066 (see below ll.56-57).

27. *St Dunstan*: see above c.13, l.16.

28. *day of his coronation*: 4 May 979 (*HBC*, 27).

28-33. *Because ... people*: Fordun is here quoting *Malmesbury*, i, 186; see above IV c.39, ll.5-12.

36-39. *... deserter*: for the treachery of Ælfric ealdorman of Hampshire in 992 see *ASC*, 82, s.a.; the text here has similarities to that in *Malmesbury*, i, 187 (though no number of ships is mentioned there).

44. *Eadric*: see above c.19, l.2.

47. *Godwine*: see above c.20, ll.39-57; c.21, ll.1-26.

49. *Edmund's brothers*: see *HBC*, 27.

50-56. *King Edward ... head*: in fact Edward the Confessor appears to have nominated Harold as his successor in preference to his great-nephew Edgar the Ætheling (*ASE*, 580); see above ll.4-13.

56. *William the Bastard*: see above V cc.13-14.

58. *set forth above*: i.e. in Book V.

59-60. *... writer*: see ll.61-66 below.

60. *writer*: the date 1100 which ends the chapter in MS C is copied into the other MSS (sometimes with 'etc.' added), but has no obvious implications.

61-66. *... Amen*: these five lines in the large bookhand of the text-writer in MS C fill in a blank half-page on fo.117v; they are not copied into MS R and so were probably added to MS C after MS R was copied and before MS D was copied; they are also not in MS CA; then on fo.118 of MS C (which is the opposite page of the centre of a section of the pages of that MS) Bower makes a new start in the middle of Book VI with quite different material.

Bower (or perhaps his scribe after his death) here makes one of his two specific references to John de Fordun as the 'author' (i.e. main authority) for the first five books of this work, together with the chapters of Book VI so far. This is proof that cc.9-23 above must have been found by Bower as part of the Fordun corpus; but see the alternative definition of the division of responsibility at the end of the whole work (XVI c.39). ll.63-66 here explain Bower's policy so far in the work of identifying separately passages based on Fordun and additions of his own. Elsewhere (XII c.34, ll.46-47) he mentions that he has used the word 'scribe' as an alternative to 'author' when referring to Fordun. Now he explains that the greater part of the rest of the work is to be his own. In fact he alone is responsible for the rest of Book VI and the whole of Book VII, and it is only in Books VIII – XIII that he makes occasional use of the notes which Fordun had collected separately, and which are called by Skene the *Gesta Annalia* (*Fordun*, i, 254-383); and since Bower often alters these notes from *Fordun* as he fits them into his own story, it is not surprising that he ceases to include the marginal signals of authorship which he had so far (as is stated here) dutifully inserted in the margins of MS C.

Chapter 24
pp.343-5

The first rubric before the chapter-number introduces a separate section of Book VI; in MS C it is written in the text-hand in the top margin of fo.118; since it is not found in MS R, it was presumably added after that MS was copied; but it is found in MSS D, B, H and E. In the margin opposite this rubric in MSS C, D and R is this note: 'Ulterius non fiant limares protracciones' ('Let there be no more extended revisions'), which is brought into the text of MSS B, H and E, with this addition in MS H: 'Cetera sunt scriptoris primevi non ultimi' ('The rest is the work of a recent writer, not the last one' [meaning uncertain, but the implication must surely be that Bower rather than Fordun is now the author]). In MS CA cc.24-57 here are included under the title 'Liber Alius' at the end of Book XVI.

Bower here introduces an account of the bishops and priors of St Andrews which was not part of Fordun's plan; to some extent at any rate he must have followed for the bishops an account (now lost) drawn up at some earlier date at St Andrews, for the same source was followed earlier in 15c by Wyntoun, who had scattered entries from it about particular bishops throughout his chronicle at the appropriate chronological places (cf. below ll.9-11); any differences between the two versions drawn from the same source are noted below.

This account of the bishops of St Andrews is parallelled in Scotland by only two other accounts of episcopal succession, both compiled in lasting form in the early 16c; see for Dunkeld, A.Myln, *Vitae Dunkeldensis Ecclesiae Episcoporum*, 2nd edn (Bannatyne Club, 1831), and for Aberdeen,*Hectoris Boetii Murthlacensium et Aberdonensium Episcoporum Vitae* (New Spalding Club, 1894).For modern accounts of these bishops from 9c to 1115 see Haddan & Stubbs, *Councils*, II, i, 173-4; from 9c to 1202 see *Series Episcoporum*, VI, i, 75-91; and from 1109 to 15c see Dowden, *Bishops*, 1-72.

For Kilrymont as the name for St Andrews in use in 12c, see above IV c.11, l.21.

1-2. *... foundations*: see above V c.48, ll.9-13. In MS CA Bower introduces this section differently:

> Fiat hic in nomine Domini primus liber extravagans separatim et per se de episcopis Kylremonth, id est Sanctiandr', qui semper in suis titulis dicebantur episcopi Scotorum usque tempora regis nostri Willelmi.

In St Andrews tradition a succession of bishops with varying titles suggesting general authority over the Scots were believed to have all been associated with St Andrews in some way (G.Donaldson, *Scottish Church History* [Edinburgh, 1985], 15-17; *Series Episcoporum*, VI, i, 75-76).

5-6. *Kenneth son of Alpin*: ruled Pictavia as well as DálRiata (Scotland) from 842 until his death in 858 (see above IV c.3, l.1n, and c.15, l.3n).

8. *primate*: the title of a bishop regarded as the chief bishop of a state or people (*ODCC*, 1124; cf. *DDC*, vii, col.214); when Bower was writing in the 1440s there was still no archbishop in Scotland, but it is likely that the bishop of St Andrews was customarily regarded as 'first and foremost' among the Scottish bishops, and Bower's addition of 'and will be' in MS CA (text l.6, note d) shows his confidence in this special status. Only in 1472 was the see of St Andrews raised to a metropolitan archbishopric.

12. *first was Kellach I*: see above IV c.17, l.36, where this bishop holds office under King Giric (878-89), a fact noted in *Wyntoun* (iv, 184-5); still in office in 906 (*KKES*, 251); for MS C Bower followed a source which mentioned this Kellach as coming after Fothad I, but he corrected this for MS CA, while still noting that some sources said that Fothad came first; see *Series Episcoporum*, VI, i, 77-78.

Fothad I: King Indulf reigned 954-62 (see above IV c.26, l.34); Fothad may have been ousted in 955, and lived until 963 (*Series Episcoporum*, VI, i, 78); the month-date of his death is given in MS CA, but not the year; cf. *Wyntoun*, iv, 192-3.

14-18. *Regarding ... gospel-book*: the inscription copied here was noted by a St Andrews writer before 1153 in the Great Register of St Andrews Cathedral Priory (*Chron.Picts-Scots.* 190; for date see Barrow, *Kingdom*, 172, n.32); there the last word in the first line ('avites' [text l.13]) is given as 'aviti', which more closely matches the word-forms given by Wyntoun, and is translated here as 'ancestral' (cf. *DML*, s.v. 'avitus'). Though both Wyntoun and Bower attribute this inscription to Bishop Fothad I, it may perhaps relate rather to the 11c Bishop Fothad II (M.O.Anderson, 'St Andrews before Alexander I', in *The Scottish Tradition*, ed. G.W.S.Barrow [Edinburgh, 1974], 4).

19-23. *Maelbrigde ... fulfilled*: he died in office during the reign of King Culen 966-71 (*KKES*, 252); Wyntoun (iv, 244-5) associated his episcopate with the pontificates of Popes Benedict VIII and IX; this is impossible, for their dates were 1012-24 and 1032-45; but there were earlier Popes Benedict V (964) and VI (973-4) about his time (*ODP*, 128-30). The late addition only in MS H associating Maelbrigde with St Duthac (d.1065) is erroneous (cf. *Series Episcoporum*, VI, i, 72).

23-25. *Kellach II ... confirmation*: Wyntoun (iv, 244-7) appears to suggest that he became bishop while Culen was still king; but he makes no mention of confirmation by Rome; Bower's authority for this assertion is unknown; possibly it has some substance (M.O.Anderson, in McRoberts, *St Andrews*, 5).

26-27. *Malmore ... Tuthald*: no more is known about these five bishops in *Wyntoun* (iv, 246-7, 318-19), where it is stated that Maelbrigde preceded Malmore; but from an Irish source it is known that Maelduin died and was succeeded by Tuthald in 1055 (*Series Episcoporum*, VI, i, 79-80), and the latter may have continued in office until the pontificate of Nicholas II (elected Dec. 1058 [*ODP*, 151]) as Wyntoun suggests.

27. *Fothad II*: Wyntoun (iv, 345) mentions him as performing the marriage ceremony for King Malcolm III and Queen Margaret ca 1070 (see above V c.17,ll.17-20); he lived until 1093 (*ES*, ii, 49); for further details see *Series Episcoporum*, VI, i, 80.

28. *Giric ... Godric*: not mentioned in *Wyntoun*; there is no evidence to prove that any bishop of St Andrews was consecrated between 1093 and 1109 (cf. *Series Episcoporum*, VI, i, 80).

29-33. *... confessor*: Bower has more detail about this bishop than Wyntoun (iv, 354-5), who mentions only that Turgot had been prior of Durham DRH and acted as the queen's confessor; but Bower's date for Turgot's election in 1109 (11 October) is wrong: he was in fact consecrated at York on 1 August, after election in June 1107 (see above, V c.38, ll.28-29); he died 31 August 1115 (*ES*, ii, 159); for his *Life* of St Margaret see above V c.16.

33-36. *In 1117 ... Anselm*: Bower is here following an inaccurate source, which he partly corrected in a marginal addition in MS C; it was Eadmer, a monk of Canterbury, who wrote the *Life* of Anselm archbishop of Canterbury (1093-1109); but his election to St Andrews with the support of King Alexander I did not take place until 29 June 1120, and he resigned and returned to Canterbury by early 1121 (*Series Episcoporum*, VI, i, 82).

37-38. *Robert prior of Scone ... Alexander*: for this Robert see above V c.36a, l.20; he was elected to St Andrews in January 1124, four months before King

Alexander's death (*ES*, ii, 166); Bower has the wrong date also above V c.40, ll.53-54; Wyntoun (iv, 372-3) is unspecific; see *Series Episcoporum*, VI, i, 83-84.

38-48. *He ... gift*: selected from the account composed for the Great Register of St Andrews before 1153 (as above ll.14-18), with addition of 'as had ... Alexander' (l.41), and 'which now ... cross' (l.44) by Bower (cf. *Chron.Picts-Scots*, 190);Wyntoun (iv, 374-7) follows the same source, and includes some details omitted by Bower.

39. *Boar's Chase*: an area of about eleven miles by six around St Andrews, which in 12c was believed to have been given to the church there by the Pictish King Hungus (M.O.Anderson, in McRoberts, *St Andrews*, 7; see above II c.60, ll.49-52, and IV c.13, l.1).

47-48. *David his brother*: i.e. King David I 1124-53.

48-51. *This same Robert ... specified*: the delayed consecration took place at Roxburgh ROX on or before 17 July 1127 (*Series Episcoporum*, VI, i, 83); Bower and Wyntoun (iv, 376-9) both follow the account in the Great Register here which gives no date (*Chron.Picts-Scots*, 191).

49. *Thurstan*: archbishop of York 1119-40 (*HBC*, 281).

52-56. *He remained ... thirty-four years*: Bower has found two sources now lost for the length of Robert's episcopate, both inaccurate; *Wyntoun* (iv, 378-9) is different, but erroneous also.

56-58. *He died ... Malcolm*: Wyntoun (iv, 426-7) is no more precise about the date of death; burial place is the church now known as St Rule's, which came to be called the 'old church' once the great new cathedral came to be built in the later 12c (see below c.35, ll.3, 9-10).

Chapter 25
p.347

For this chapter Bower returns to the *Life* of Waltheof by Jocelin of Furness (see above c.1, introduction), following here c.VI, para.79 for ll.1-13 ('earth') and para.80 for ll.13-29.

3-4. *assent .... princes*: King Malcolm is likely to have given his consent before leaving Scotland for France at the end of May 1159 (*Series Episcoporum*, VI, i, 85).

4. *abbot of Melrose*: Waltheof had held this office since 1148 (*Melrose*, 34); Bower has not yet explained how he moved from the Augustinian to the Cistercian Order (cf. above c.8). See biographical notes in *DNB*, lix, 267-8 and *ODS*, 429-30.

5. *souls*: Bower omits after 'suarum' (text l.4) 'voto unanimi communi consensus conniventia' (AS text; DMS text has 'consensu' for 'consensus conniventia') i.e. 'by unanimous vote with the connivance of common consent'. McFadden ('Edition', 75, 299n) considers that in these words Jocelin was confusingly alluding to more than one kind of canonical election; Bower may well have omitted them because he was not sure what they meant.

8. *abbot of Rievaulx*: i.e. St Ailred, abbot 1147-67 (Knowles and others, *Heads*, 140). Since Melrose was a daughter-house of Rievaulx (see below c.30, l.31), its abbot under the Cistercian constitution owed obedience to the abbot of the mother-house as to a father (see below l.15).

16-18. ... *care*: cf. Song of Songs 5:3.

20. *outside ... Melrose*: added by Bower to Jocelin's text; Bower presumably had personal knowledge of the site of Waltheof's tomb at Melrose, which was at the entrance to the chapter-house (*Melrose*, 87).

22. *since ... it*: added by Bower to Jocelin's text.

26-27. *namely ... later*: added by Bower to Jocelin's text; this was Abbot Arnold (see below c.35, l.1).

27. *was buried*: Waltheof died on 3 Aug. 1159 (*Melrose*, 35); see below c.34, l.22; for some remaining fragments of his tomb at Melrose see *RCAHM* (*Roxburgh*), ii, 289; cf.283.

Chapter 26
pp.349-51

Bower here interrupts his extracts from the *Life* of Waltheof to offer exempla and reflections on the implications of churchmen refusing office when elected.

1-8. *Nothing ... directs*: Augustine, *Epistles*, bk.I, no.21 (PL, 33, col.88).

8. *our general*: i.e. Christ.

14-33. *at St Victor ...light*: Cantimpré, *De Apibus*, I, c.xx, para.4.

14. *St Victor*: an Augustinian abbey in the university quarter of Paris.

34-49. ... *damned*: Bower's source for this exemplum has not been identified; but the same story (with extensive verbal similarity, but in shorter form) is included in *Anecdotes historiques ... d'Étienne de Bourbon*, ed. A.Lecoy de la Marche (SHF, 185 [1877]), 249.

34. *Clairvaux*: the Cistercian abbey, dép. Aube, France, of which St Bernard was founder and first abbot 1115-53 (*ODCC*, 162, 296). Peter of Blois is cited (*Anecdotes*, ut cit., 249, n.2) as mentioning (PL, 207, col.325) that the prior in question was Geoffrey de Péronne, so that the vacancy at Tournai occurred 1166 × 1171; but the story is placed during the pontificate of Eugenius III i.e. 1145-53 (*ODP*, 172-3), and so perhaps it relates to the monk of Clairvaux called Geoffrey who was St Bernard's secretary and biographer and is said to have been elected to an unnamed bishopric, but declined office (W.Williams, *St Bernard of Clairvaux* [Manchester, 1935], 378).

35. *see of Tournai*: in Flanders, then on the border of France and the Empire, now in Belgium; the see was vacant in 1149 (Mas Latrie, *Trésor*, col.1500).

49-54. *This is ... profoundly*: the two lines of verse are apparently introduced here by Bower as a comment on the preceding exemplum; they are frequently quoted in a slightly different form (Walther, *Proverbia*, no.21,633), and come originally from a poem of Hildebert of Lavardin (*Hildeberti Cenomannensis Episcopi Carmina Minora*, ed. A.Brian Scott [Teubner edn, 1969], 40).

56-61. *Great ... beaten*: 4c St Ambrose (*ODCC*, 42-43) is not known to have written a *Pastoral Care*; in MS CA Bower attributes this quotation to 'G.', which suggests 6c Gregory the Great (ibid., 594-5), who did write such a work; but this quotation cannot be traced through the modern concordance to Gregory's works; it remains unidentified.

61-64. *From this ... office*: this reflective passage probably presents Bower's view, but it could still be part of the preceding quotation.

66-70. *at one time ... success*: this is the start of a long exemplum from Cantimpré, *De Apibus*, I, c.1, para.4, which ends here in mid-sentence, and continues for the whole of c.27 below.

66. *Le Mans*, dép. Sarthe, France.

Chapter 27
pp.351-5

This whole chapter continues the exemplum from Cantimpré, *De Apibus* begun above c.26, l.66.

11. *Maurice*: a man of this name served as bishop of Le Mans 1216-31 (Eubel, *Hierarchia*, i, 180).

Troyes, dép. Aube, France.

17. *as a preacher*: 'officio' (text l.14) comes from the Cantimpré text.

34. *postulating*: 'postulation' is the technical term under canon law for a request to legitimate ecclesiastical authority to admit a nominee by dispensation when a canonical impediment is supposed to exist (*OED*); cf. below c.41, l.12.

38. *divine*: 'divine' (text l.28) comes from the Cantimpré text.

Chapter 28
pp.355-7

After seven lines of reflective introduction, Bower returns for ll.7-24 to an early part of the *Life* of Waltheof, c.II, para.29, and for ll.25-44 to para.30, picking up the story of Waltheof's early life when he was prior of Kirkham (see above cc.7-8); this story is then continued through cc.29-34 below; these chapters were omitted from MS CA, where (p.434) in a brief summary passage it is wrongly stated that Waltheof secretly entered the Cistercian Order at Melrose so as to avoid being elected archbishop of York.

10-11. *wafting ... fragrance*: cf. Ecclesiasticus 24:20 (*Vulgate*); 24:15 (*NEB*).

12-21.   *the clergy ... place*: for the disputed succession to the see of York after the death of Archbishop Thurstan in Feb. 1140, see D.Knowles, 'The case of St William of York', in *The Historian and Character and Other Essays* (Cambridge, 1963), 76-99, especially 78, 80-81.

12.   *the magnates*: McFadden translates 'magnates' (text 1.11) as 'officials', so implying clerics rather than laymen; but at least the count of Aumale was present at the archiepiscopal election (McFadden, 'Edition', 81), so that probably the word is intended to suggest lay influence.

15.   *King Stephen*: reigned 1135-54.

19.   *adversary Henry*: in 1140 the later King Henry II was only seven years old; Stephen's adversary then was Henry's mother the Empress Matilda.

25.   *count of Aumale*: William le Gros 1138-79 (*CP*, i, 353); he was Waltheof's second cousin once removed, his grandmother being a sister of William the Conqueror and Waltheof's grandmother a niece.

34.   *township of Sherburn*: perhaps Sherburn in Elmet YOW near Selby, or Sherburn YOE between Malton and Filey.

36.   *then hinted ... heresy*: added by Bower to Jocelin's text; Bower is typically quick to detect simony in stories which he includes.

41.   *throne*: after 'presidentem' (text 1.34) Bower omits 'nec te villam prenominatam possidentem' (AS; 'possessurum', DMS) from Jocelin's text, thus making Waltheof's attitude more pointed.

Chapter 29
pp.357-9

Bower devotes most of this chapter (ll.4-36) to a story from Cantimpré, *De Apibus*, I, xx, paras 5-6, fo.13; then he returns to his account of Waltheof's life, following in ll.40-43 the *Life* by Jocelin, c.III, start of para.31.

4.   *Cambrai*: a see in dép. Nord, France.

8.   *Vaucelles*: an abbey a few miles from Cambrai.

19-20.   *perfect in their behaviour*: this phrase ('in moribus ... perfectis'[text ll.16-17]) was substituted by Bower for 'junioribus dispensative' in the printed text of *De Apibus*.

32-36.   *... sinners*: Bower has much elaborated the sentence in Cantimpré's text: 'Hic ut dignum erat maluit sub regula latere sub habitu monachali quam pontificali infula decorari' (cf. text ll.26-29).

38.   *assumed it*: i.e. the office of abbot of Melrose (see below c.31, ll.32-34).

Chapter 30
pp.359-61

The text here (ll.1-18 ['idea']) continues to follow the *Life* of Waltheof c.III, para.31 without a break; then after one sentence inserted by Bower it follows para.33 (with omissions) for ll.20-33, and para.34 for ll.34-48.

1. *wanted*: for 'Velle sibi adjacebat' (text l.1) see Romans 7:18.

2. *proclaim ... steps*: cf. Job 31:37.

6. *as he used to say*: McFadden ('Edition', 236n) suggests that in this section Jocelin was evidently following Everard's account of Waltheof's own statements (cf. above c.8, ll.29-30).

8-9. *Angel of Great Counsel*: i.e. the Holy Spirit (McFadden, 'Edition', 237).

9-10. *spirit ...fortitude*: Isaiah 11:2.

12. *Satan ... light*: 2 Corinthians 11:14.

13-15. *and conceal ... things*: Professor Brian Scott suggests that this means that he [Waltheof] was on the lookout for this, and saw many examples in other men's careers. McFadden (p.237) has a very different translation (based on a slightly different text): 'or lead him up to what seemed a lofty and commanding height only to plunge him over a hidden precipice' (i.e. spiritual pride, says McFadden in a note). Professor R.J.Bartlett suggests that 'he' may be Satan rather than Waltheof.

18-19. *And just ... spring*: cf. Psalm 41:2 (*Vulgate*); 42:1 (*NEB*); this passage was added by Bower to Jocelin's text in place of a paragraph about Ailred abbot of Rievaulx whom Waltheof is said to have consulted at this stage; the two are presumed to have been companions during the years before ca 1134 (when Ailred became a monk) at the court of King David (*Life of Ailred*, p.xxxix). If Ailred was in fact abbot (rather than just a monk) at Rievaulx at this date, this would mean that Waltheof became a Cistercian in late 1147 at the earliest (see above c.25, l.8); but since his brother Earl Simon (see below l.22) was in 1147 friendly enough with the abbey of Warden to found a daughter-house for them at Sawtry (see below c.31, ll.45-47), it is unlikely that he and that abbey were in violent dispute just at that date, so that Waltheof's move was probably earlier than 1147. Furthermore he served for at least a full year as a Cistercian novice before being promoted as abbot of Melrose in 1148 (see below c.31, ll.26, 34). It has indeed been argued that he moved to his new order Aug.1143 × Aug.1145 (Baker, 'Legend', 76), and this is probably right, though at this time Ailred was absent from Rievaulx as abbot of a daughter-house at Revesby LIN (*Life of Ailred*, xci).

20. *Warden*: a Cistercian house near Biggleswade BDF founded in 1136 (*MRHEW*, 117; *VCH Bedfordshire*, i, 361).

22. *Earl Simon*: see above c.7, ll.8-11, and below c.31, ll.37-39.

26. *longer*: Bower here omits a sentence in the *Life* about the efforts of the Kirkham canons with threats of ecclesiastical censure to recall Waltheof to his duties as their prior.

27. *as the roaring of a lion*: cf. Proverbs 19:12.

31. *Rievaulx*: the famous Cistercian house near Helmsley YON founded in 1132 (*MRHEW*, 114; *VCH Yorkshire*, iii, 149).

31-32. *until ... over*: Psalm 56:2 (*Vulgate*); 57:1 (*NEB*).

33. *interfering*: Bower again omits two sentences in the *Life* about the continuing efforts of the Kirkham canons to get him to return.

48. *blushed in confusion*: cf. Jeremiah 31:19.
judged ... face: cf. Psalm 49:21 (*Vulgate*); 50:21 (*NEB*).

Chapter 31
pp.361-3

All of this chapter is selected from the *Life* of Waltheof; ll.1-8 ('soul') run on from the end of c.30 above in c.III, para.34; ll.9-29 come from para.35; ll.30-34 ('charge') from start of para.36; ll.34-37 ('reality') from para.37; and ll.37-52 from c.IV, para.48.

1-21. *... teach him*: McFadden ('Edition', 242n) suggests that this story was appropriated by Jocelin from some other saint's Life to demonstrate how Waltheof overcame the temptation of inconstancy.

1. *for a service*: 'ad horam canonicam' (text l.1), i.e. one of the times of daily prayer laid down in the Breviary (*ODCC*, 670).

15. *yoke ... light*: Matthew 11:30.

17. *Christ*: added by Bower to Jocelin's text, so changing the meaning; for Jocelin Waltheof was the modern Elisha.

17-18. *Elisha ... grace*:: cf. 4 Kings 4:38-41 (*Vulgate*); 2 Kings 4:38-41 (*NEB*).

22. *for the ... afflicted*: added by Bower to Jocelin's text.

25-26. *Bridegroom ... perfumes*: cf. Song of Songs 1:3; for Christian writers the Bridegroom here was taken allegorically to be Christ (cf. *ODCC*, 1289).

28. *rule ... Benedict*: i.e. in its reformed Cistercian version (*ODCC*, 295).

30-34. *... charge*: Bower here briefly summarizes a paragraph in which Jocelin discusses the discreditable reasons for Abbot Richard's deposition (not resignation as here). Richard had been abbot since the foundation of the abbey in 1136, and Jocelin says that King David was much angered by his deposition, since Richard was his much loved confessor.

33. *compelled by the father-abbot*: i.e. by Ailred abbot of Rievaulx (see above c.25, ll.7-10).

34. *in 1148*: added by Bower in the margin of MS C to Jocelin's text; this date is confirmed in the Melrose chronicle (*Melrose*, 34).

36. *name in fact*: for 'nomen re et' (text l.30) 'nomine et re' is probably intended.

37. *shadow ... name*: Lucan, *De Bello Civili*, I, l.135 (Loeb edn, 12).

37-38. *His brother*: Bower now jumps forward in the *Life* to include passages on the pious acts of Waltheof's brother; Jocelin's chronology is confused here.

Earl Simon: see above c.7, l.10; c.30, l.22.

41. *on the advice ... brother*: added by Bower to Jocelin's text.

41-42. *founded ... Northampton*: the Cluniac priory of St Andrew's Northampton was in fact founded by this Earl Simon's father, Earl Simon de Senlis I 1093 × 1100 (*MRHEW*, 99; *VCH Northampton*, ii, 102).

43. *monastery for nuns*: a house for Cluniac nuns called St Mary Delapré near Northampton was founded ca 1145 (*MRHEW*, 222; *VCH Northampton*, ii, 114).

46. *Sawtry*: a Cistercian abbey north of Huntingdon HNT founded in 1147 as a daughter-house of Warden (*MRHEW*; 114; *VCH Huntingdon*, i, 391); Earl Simon's reported wrath against Warden (see above c.30 ll.21-26) must have abated by this time; see below IX c.27, ll.29-32.

47. *Abbot Simon*: first abbot of Warden, in office × 1143 – 1151 × (Knowles and others, *Heads*, 146).

48. *buried*: Earl Simon died Aug.1153 (*ES*, ii, 153).

Chapter 32
pp.363-5

This chapter comprises two whole paragraphs from the *Life* of Waltheof, following directly from the text at the end of c.31 above, taken from c.IV – ll.1-22 from para.49, and ll.27-53 from para.50; in between Bower has added ll.23-26 himself.

1. *Henry earl of Huntingdon*: 'of Huntingdon' added by Bower to Jocelin's text; this son of King David I had a claim to the earldom of Huntingdon from 1136 until his death on 12 June 1152 (*HBC*, 466; *CP*, vi, 642).

3. *Holm Cultram*: Cistercian abbey at Abbey Town CMB, founded by King David as a daughter-house of Melrose abbey in 1150 (*MRHEW*, 109; cf. *VCH Cumberland*, ii, 162); here Bower had added 'quam pater eius' (text l.3) to Jocelin's text, so correcting Jocelin's error that Henry was the founder; but other sources are contradictory on this point.

4-5. *he sent ... he appointed*: 'he' in each case here is ambiguous; the first may mean King David or Earl Henry; the second probably means Abbot Waltheof.

6. *Everard*: see above c.8, l.30n.; c.30, l.6n.; Everard had been an Augustinian canon of Kirkham before becoming a Cistercian monk at Melrose; he served as abbot of Holm Cultram 1150-92 (Knowles and others, *Heads*, 135).

elected by them: presumably by the new community at Holm Cultram; but the abbot of the mother-house would have had a leading say on who was to direct the new foundation.

8. *man of God*: i.e. Waltheof.

14-15. *full of days ... great age*: cf. Genesis 25:8.

19. *Kinloss*: a Cistercian house near Forres MOR, founded by King David in 1150 (*MRHS*, 76; *Melrose*, 35).

20-21. *could raise ... level*: seems to refer to the progress of the building rather than of the community there.

23-26. *... Order*: an extra item of information added by Bower; his source is not the Melrose chronicle; see also below VIII c.25, 71-72.

23. *Countess Ada*: daughter of William de Warenne, second earl of Surrey, married to Earl Henry in 1139, widowed 1152, died 1178 (*SP*, i, 4; *CP*, vi, 642; *ESC*, 378; *RRS*, i and ii ad indices).

25. *Haddington*: this Cistercian nunnery in Haddington ELO was founded before 1159 (*MRHS*, 147).

27. *King Malcolm*: i.e. Malcolm IV 1153-65.

34-35. *he did not ... nothing*: cf. Romans 13:4.

38. *his uncle*: Bower adds 'patrui sui' (text 1.32) to Jocelin's text.

40. *Coupar*: various stages in the establishing of a Cistercian monastery at Coupar Angus PER as a daughter-house of Melrose can be traced 1159-64; 'on 12 July 1164 the full convent arrived from Melrose and an abbot was appointed' (*MRHS*, 73).

45. *This ... 1164*: added by Bower to Jocelin's text.

48-49. *these ... undertakings*: cf. 'hii preclari principes ... inducebantur' (text ll.39-40) with 'rex optimus ad opus tam preclarum perficiendum efficaciter inducebatur' in Jocelin's text (AS and DMS).

49-50. *Fountain of Life*: Psalm 35:10 (*Vulgate*); 36:9 (*NEB*).

52. *four rivers of Paradise*: Genesis 2:10-14.

Chapter 33
pp.367-9

Bower here continues without a break his extracts from the *Life* of Waltheof, now from c IV – ll.1-22 from para 51; ll.23-44 ('servants') from para.52; and ll.44-46 from start of para.53.

6-7. *... womb*: Job 31:18 (*Vulgate* only).

10. *sons*: presumably monks of Melrose to whom as abbot he was father.

13. *what they lacked*: exceptionally Bower here includes two words ('quo indigerent' [text l.11) which are in AS, but which cannot be found in DMS; see also below text l.40 ('illi').

15. *when ... famine*: cf. Genesis 12:10.

17. *necessary for life*: 'vite necessaria sive' (text ll.14-15) added by Bower to Jocelin's text.

20. *Fountain of Mercy*: cf. 'Fountain of Life' above c.32, ll.49-50.

28. *Thomas*: this is the name in AS.

29-30. *joyfully .. is this*: 'letabundus' and 'Quam terribilis est locus iste' (text l.26) added by Bower to Jocelin's text.

30. *Truly ... Lord*: cf. Genesis 32:2.

31. *My heart ... people*: cf. Mark 8:2.

42. *Eildon*: an estate south-east of Melrose ROX (J.S.Richardson and M.Wood, *The Abbey of Melrose*, official guide [Edinburgh, 1949], 25).

43. *Gattonside*: an estate across the river Tweed from Melrose ROX (ibid.).

Chapter 34
pp.369-71

Most of this chapter is selected from four different parts of the *Life* of Waltheof; ll.1-19 continue directly from the end of c.33 above, taken from c.IV, para.53; ll.22-27 are selected from c.VI, para.90; ll.28-44 ('bodies') are selected from c.IX, para.135; and ll.44-52 are selected from c.IX, para.136.

3. *genuflected*: after 'flexit' (text l.3) AS adds: 'orationem cum lacrymis fudit. Post modicam horam ab oratione surgens, baculum extraxit'; this passage is not in DMS; C follows DMS

7. *God ... grow*: cf. 1 Corinthians 3:6. and 2 Corinthians 9:10.

12-13. *in imitation ... flour*: 3 Kings 17 (*Vulgate*); 1 Kings 17 (*NEB*).

16. *became apparent*: i.e. the miracle of the corn that never became less stopped.

17. *sustained ... desert*: cf. Nehemiah 9:21.

20-21. *... death*: a bridge passage supplied by Bower.

23. *1160*: this year-date added by Bower to Jocelin's text. In fact Waltheof died 3 Aug. 1159 (*Melrose*, 35).

24. *from faith ... sight*: cf. 2 Corinthians 5:7.

25. *from the contest ... prize*: 1 Corinthians 9:24.

28. *Scottish*: added by Bower to Jocelin's text.

31-32. *insane ... body*: Jocelin is here probably referring to the Albigensian heretics of his own day, who rejected the doctrine of the resurrection of the body (*ODCC*, 31; see below vol.5, ad indicem).

32. *body*: Bower here omits Jocelin's account of five English saints, to whom he added Cuthbert and Waltheof (as below) to make a total of seven saints who should be a cause of rejoicing to the *English*. Bower apparently does not want Waltheof to be counted as an *English* saint.

33-35. *which ... faith*: Bower adds 'eiusdem ... ditata' (text ll.28-29) to Jocelin's text in place of 'cum tota dyocesi et vicinia'. For gifts to the church of Durham by Kings Duncan II, Edgar and David I see Barrow, *Kingdom*, 167-9.

35. *Cuthbert*: see above III c.51, and *ODS*, 104-6.

38. *associate ... bishop*: both Waltheof and Cuthbert served as monks at Melrose, but in fact in different monastic foundations on different sites and five hundred years apart.

39-40. *it was ... customs*: added by Bower to Jocelin's text.
　St Boisil: see above III c.51, l.7.

45. *kinsman*: 'cognatum' (text l.39) added by Bower to Jocelin's text.

46. *protector*: Bower here omits from Jocelin's text a sentence on how the whole Cistercian Order should rejoice, perhaps displaying his essentially Augustinian interests in devoting so much space to Waltheof.

47. *honey and heavenly dew*: McFadden ('Edition', 356n.) notes that this is a pun on *mel* ('honey') and *ros* ('dew') for *Melrose*.

49. *Again ... Rejoice*: Philippians 4:4.

50. *your father ... ours*: 'pater vester (ymmo et noster)' (text l.43) added by Bower to Jocelin's text; 'ours' shows Bower claiming Waltheof for Scotland.

50-51. *in the ... saints*: cf. Psalm 109:3 (*Vulgate*); 110:3 (*NEB*).

51. *made equal ... glory*: cf. Ecclesiasticus 45:2.

54-55. *... father*: a couplet added by Bower.

Chapter 35
pp.371-3

Bower resumes here his general account of the bishops of St Andrews.

1. *abbot of Kelso*: Arnold had served as abbot of Kelso ROX, O.Tiron., since 1147 (*Melrose*, 34); for his biography see *Series Episcoporum*, VI, i, 85-86.

3. *old church of St Andrew*: i.e. St Rule's church (see above c.24, l.57).

4. *William ... see*: William bishop of Moray had been appointed legate on 27 November 1159 during the St Andrews vacancy (*Series Episcoporum*, VI, i, 66-67).

6. *John*: served as abbot of Kelso until 1180 (*ES*, ii, 302; see below VIII c.29, l.4).

7. *Herbert*: bishop of Glasgow 1147-64 (*Series Episcoporum*, VI, i, 58-59).

8. *made legate*: Arnold held this office for a time during 1161, and then his appointment was rescinded (ibid., 85).

9. *founded the great church*: i.e. the main cathedral, whose ruins are still to be seen at St Andrews; see also *Wyntoun*, iv, 426-7.

11. *died*: Wyntoun (iv, 430-1) adds that he was buried in the old church (as above l.3).

13. *1165*: in fact Richard was probably elected early in 1163, for he had to wait two years for his consecration (as stated below l.15); the delay was caused by efforts made by the archbishop of York to make him come to York for the ceremony (*Series Episcoporum*, VI, i, 86).

13-14. *by the bishops of the kingdom*: they acted under a special papal commission, as noted in one version of *Wyntoun* (iv, 431; but cf. ibid., iv, 430 for a different story).

16. *5 May*: Wyntoun (v, 20-21) gives 3 May as the date (probably an error from the form '3 non. maii' [as here] in his source), without mentioning the place where he died; a Durham record gives 13 May (i.e. 3 id. maii) as the date of death (see *Chron.Holyrood*, 164, note 2); 5 May may well be the correct date, but Bower is wrong to give the year as 1177 (see below l.25); Wyntoun has the correct year 1178, as Bower himself has below VIII c.25, ll.70-71.

20-23. *... Heaven*: cf. *Wyntoun*, v, 58-59, where these lines (suitably adapted) are attached to the note on the death of Bishop Roger in 1202 rather than to that of Bishop Richard.

24. *John called Scot was elected*: Bower devotes the rest of the chapter and all of cc.36-40 below to the disputed tenure of this see by John and Hugh over the period 1178-88; the many sources apart from this account are assembled in *AMW*, 224-78 and *Scot.Pont.*, 88-139, and discussed in *Chron.Holyrood*, 164-8 and *Series Episcoporum*, VI, i, 46-47 and 87-89. For a biography of John Scot see Watt, *Graduates*, 485-8; cf. 426-7. Bower here based his account on a *Life* of John Scot (now lost) written by the mid-13c Cistercian monk William Bening, which he had seen at Newbattle Abbey MLO (see below c.40, ll.51-54). There are errors of fact and some wholly imagined details in Bower's account. Comments are offered here on selected points only. The Bening *Life* was clearly not known to Wyntoun, who (v, 20-27) limits his account of the dispute to the early years 1178-80, ending with the legatine council at Holyrood, and a brief statement that John received the see of Dunkeld in compensation for losing St Andrews, while Hugh retained the latter. He writes in the tradition of sympathy for John as the choice of the St Andrews chapter. Bower can see both sides of the question.

This case is outstanding as the only major dispute over episcopal appointments involving opposition to crown influence and resort to papal jurisdiction in medieval Scotland. It is all the more interesting that King William persisted in pressing his rights just at the time when he was cheekily celebrating the canonisation of St Thomas Becket (the martyr for church liberty against English crown influence) by founding Arbroath Abbey ANG in 1178 in his honour (*MRHS*, 66). Bower is aware of some parallels in the two situations (c.36, l.16n.; c.37, l.54n.), but does not develop a discussion of them.

was elected: probably in May 1178 or very soon afterwards.

26. *Hugh ... consecrated*: this took place before the end of 1178 (*Series Episcoporum*, VI, i, 88, n.162); Hugh is described by Wyntoun (v, 20-21) as King William's confessor as well as chaplain.

31. *Budworth*: for identification of this place see Watt, *Graduates*, 485.

31-34. *He had spent ... master*: the details here may well be just his biographer's guess about how he earned the title of 'Master' at this time; Wyntoun (v, 20-21) describes him simply as 'a great clerk and a famous man'.

38. *by the bishop*: apparently Bishop Richard (see above).

40. *obtained the archdeaconry*: this is an error; there is no room for him in the known series of archdeacons of either St Andrews or Lothian, the two such offices in the diocese of St Andrews (Watt, *Fasti*, 304, 309); but his uncle Matthew, bishop of Aberdeen 1172-99, did hold the archdeaconry of St Andrews before his appointment as bishop (*Series Episcoporum*, VI, i, 7).

43: *John de Monte Celio*: this appears to be a false reference to John of Salerno, cardinal of S. Stefano in Monte Celio, who visited Scotland as a papal legate in 1201-2 (see below VI c.41, 1.9; VIII c.62, ll.24-26; cf. *Scot.Pont.*, 154); but he was not in Scotland in 1178 when John Scot was elected.

Chapter 36
pp.375-7

Bower is probably continuing to base his story on Bening's *Life* of John Scot.

10   *condemned to exile*: it was only after the legatine council at Holyrood MLO in June 1180 that John and his relatives (including Matthew bishop of Aberdeen) were forced by King William to flee from Scotland (Watt, *Graduates*, 486); see below ll.45-48.

16.   *exile ... Canterbury*: a parallel is suggested here between the sufferings of John Scot and those of Thomas Becket; but the latter had gone into exile in 1164, not just four years earlier (see below VIII c.17, ll.64-65).

17.   *visit the apostolic see*: John probably went to the Roman court in 1179 and returned with the legate Alexis in 1180 (see below ll.31-32).

19.   *Alexander*: Pope Alexander III 1159-81.

29.   *Alexis*: then a subdeacon of the Roman court, later a cardinal (*AMW*, 228).

32.   *confirmed by the pope*: the pope annulled Hugh's election by early 1180, but did not himself confirm John; this was done in his name by the legate Alexis at the council of Holyrood (*Scot.Pont.*, 88, no.90; 96, no.100).

34.   *secured agreement*: in fact Alexis was empowered to investigate matters in Scotland and have John consecrated only if everything was in order (ibid.).

37-39.   *with even ... besides*: the excommunications and interdict are mentioned also in *Melrose*, 43.

43-44.   *8 June*: both *Melrose* and Bower give the date 8 June, whilst wrongly equating this with Trinity Sunday, which in 1180 fell on 15 June.

44.   *Matthew bishop of Aberdeen*: see above c.35, l.39n.

Chapter 37
pp.377-9

Bower is probably continuing to base his story on Bening's *Life* of John Scot.

1.   *stayed at the Roman court*: there is no confirmation that John visited the

Roman court in person between the council of Holyrood in 1180 and the settlement of 1183 (see below c.39, ll.11-23); cf. Watt, *Graduates*, 486-7.

15. *pope sent a letter*: probably a reference to the letter of Pope Alexander to King William dated summer 1180 × 30 August 1181, in which the pope threatened to place Scotland under interdict and to excommunicate William (*Scot.Pont.*, 97-99, no.101).

19-27. *For the pope ... protecting*: an interesting analysis (whether by Bening or Bower) of papal motivation in seeking to avoid another Becket crisis.

22. *four years earlier*: cf. above c.36, l.15; this is again a misleading statement.

27-32. *Therefore ... suppliant*: a similar analysis of William's attitude.

36-53. *When ... made*: probably a wholly imagined scenario, which, with its emphasis on the danger to souls in Purgatory if masses for the dead were suspended, perhaps owes more to the 15c thinking of Bower than that of 13c Bening (cf. *ODCC*, 1144-6).

52-53. *and he ... made*: the omission of this passage in MS CA (see textual note h) is probably a scribal error.

54. *exile for seven years*: a false parallel with Becket; John is likely to have been back in Scotland by late 1183 (Watt, *Graduates*, 487).

Chapter 37a
pp.379-83

Since in MS C this chapter is accidentally given the same number as the previous one by the scribe, it is convenient here to number it 37a, and so keep to the numbering of the subsequent chapters as in MSS C and D. Bower starts probably by continuing to base his story on Bening's *Life* of John Scot, but adds reflective passages that are likely to be his own.

1-8. *... suffer*: probably contributed by Bower.

2. *... cause of right*: Matthew 5:10.

5-8. *... suffer*: these lines are listed from here in Walther, *Proverbia*, no.14,513; where they are wrongly said to come from Prudentius; Professor Harry Hine advises that they are not known in the corpus of classical Latin.

9. *see of Dunkeld*: this see had in fact been vacant since late in 1178 (*Series Episcoporum*, VI, i, 46), and discussions regarding a possible move for John from St Andrews to Dunkeld had been under way since April × July 1181 (ibid.).

18-20. *Once ... Lord*: the arrangement that Hugh should stay at St Andrews and John move to Dunkeld was reached when both men attended the papal court at Velletri, Italy, in 1183, before June (Watt, *Graduates*, 487).

20-22. *who ... sustain it*: probably a comment by Bower.

26-42. *All and sundry ... way*: this passage ties in with c.37, ll.36-53 above;

Bower probably composed it, taking trouble to offer some justification for the king's attitude; for the oath in question see above c.36, ll.4-7.

43-77. *...for him*: a characteristic contribution by Bower on the implications of oaths, which displays his university training in canon law.

43. *oath of Herod*: Matthew 14:7-10; see also C.22 q.4 c.2, i.e. *Decretum*, part II, case 22, question 4, chapter 2 (Friedberg, i, col.875).

46. *as stated*: see C.22 q.4, i.e. *Decretum*, part II, case 22, question 4; the main heading of the whole question there is: 'Quod autem juramenta servari non debeant' (Friedberg, i, col.875).

47-48. *any oath ...justice*: these three characteristics are suggested in a comment by Gratian in C.22 q.4 c.23, i.e. *Decretum*, part II, case 22, question 4, chapter 23 (Friedberg, i, col.882), but the elaboration that follows is not by Gratian, and is probably Bower's own work.

54. *as stated*: C.22 q.4 c.8, i.e. *Decretum*, part II, case 22, question 4, chapter 8, 'Unusquisque' (Friedberg, i, col.877); Bower will have found in this chapter the references to Herod and Jephthah which he uses in this paragraph.

57-58. *in the same place*: the first reference that follows is probably to C.22 q.4 c.4, i.e. *Decretum*, part II, case 22, question 4, chapter 4, 'Juravit David'; the second has not been identified.

60. *as in ... 'Duo'*: see D.13 c.1, i.e. *Decretum*, part I, distinction 13, chapter 1, 'Duo', on 'Minus malum de duobus est eligendum'; but perhaps this reference has been miscopied in MS C, for it appears to be a reference to C.22 q.4 c.18, i.e. *Decretum*, part II, case 22, question 4, chapter 18 (Friedberg, i, col.879), where the text says: 'Illicitum juramentum non est servandum.'

69. *example of Jephthah*: Judges 11:30-31, 34-39.

76-77. *... for him*: listed in Walther, *Initia*, no.13,896 from here and elsewhere; Bower's source is unknown.

Chapter 38
pp.383-7

This chapter is entirely the work of Bower as a comment on the Scotland of his own day.

15-16. *... name*: Deuteronomy 6:13.

17-18. *... dispute*: Hebrews 6:16.

25-26. *... strength*: Proverbs 18:10.

41-42. *... perjurers*: Malachi 3:5.

68-70. *... house*: Ecclesiasticus 23:12 (*Vulgate*); 23:11 (*NEB*).

Chapter 39
pp.387-9

Some of this chapter is still devoted to general reflections by Bower; but ll.11-23 and some or all of ll.38-52 ('Considering ... shortage') may be based on Bening's *Life* of John Scot.

2-3. *vow ... oath*: see above c.36, ll.4-7.

4-6. *Annul ... guard*: both passages come from C.22 q.4 c.5, i.e. *Decretum*, part II, case 22, question 4, chapter 5 (Friedberg, i, col.876); the first is listed in Walther, *Proverbia*, no. 37,424h; cf. no. 37,425g.

9. *as in the chapter* etc.: see X 3.34.7, i.e. *Decretals*, book III, title 34, 'De voto et voti redempcione', chapter 7, 'Magne' (Friedberg, ii, col.591).

11-23. *At length ... authority*: the arrangements for John's move to see of Dunkeld were in fact agreed at the papal court in Italy × June 1183 (see above c.37a, ll.18-20); a parallel agreement made back in Scotland may lie behind this version of events, though it has too many inaccuracies to be based directly on some lost document – John's exile had not been as long as seven years (see above c.37, l.54), and he had never held an archdeaconry in St Andrews diocese (see above c.35, l.39); but it is likely enough that he did retain some revenues from St Andrews diocese as compensation for moving to the see of Dunkeld 1183-1203, for this possibility had been mentioned in various negotiations 1180-83 (Watt, *Graduates*, 486-7).

17 *decreed in common council*: probably a 12c term indicating the king's customary assembly of clerical and lay advisers (cf. Duncan, *Kingdom*, 609).

23. *consecrated*: John had already been consecrated to the see of St Andrews by authority of Alexis the papal legate in June 1180 (see above c.36, ll.42-43).

24-52. *... shortage*: perhaps the core (say ll.38-52) of this account of the setting up of a separate diocese of Argyll was included in Bening's *Life*; but the general tone seems pretty detached from the various stages of what happened in the 12c and from the motives of the parties involved, and probably owes much to Bower's own ideas of how and why such a development could have taken place; see *Series Episcoporum*, VI, i, 11-12 for a modern account.

24-25. *whole of Argyll ... long before*: episcopal authority over the Scottish DálRiata may well have been established in Dunkeld in connection with the 9c unification of the Scottish and Pictish kingdoms, when the centre of government was in the area (see above IV c.12, l.74); though there may have been bishops based on Iona in the mid-10c, the islands were taken over by the Norwegians from 1098 and a single diocese of the Isles emerged in the early 12c (D.E.R.Watt, 'Bishops in the Isles before 1203: bibliography and biographical lists', *Innes Review*, xlv [1994], 104-5, 111); this left mainland Argyll still under the bishops based on Dunkeld; the area was now to become a separate diocese in its own right.

25-28. *Argyll ... time*: this sentence expresses Bower's own view of Argyll in the mid 15c.

31-32. *who did not know this language*: this may well have been the case with Bishop John himself, but there must have been many even around Dunkeld itself who, like the men of Argyll, spoke Gaelic in his day and for centuries to come. Bower's argument for splitting the diocese which follows is therefore constructed on a false basis.

39-41. *the bishop ... people*: this suggests that Bishop John took the initiative; for an alternative argument that King William took the initiative against John's wishes 1186 × 1188 see *Series Episcoporum*, VI, i, 11.

44. *Harold*: a man of this name is the first known bishop of Argyll, but there is no surviving evidence of his tenure of the see until the late 1220s (ibid., 12-13).

52-67. *provided ... cold*: here Bower as a member of the regular clergy sermonizes about how leaders of the secular clergy of his day should behave.

57-58. *... place*: Horace, *Satires*, I, i, 105-6 (Loeb edn, 12); listed in Walther, *Proverbia*, no.7689.

60-61. *in commend*: the term in canon law for the practice of entrusting the duties and emoluments of an ecclesiastical benefice or office to someone to act as caretaker rather than to a rightful possessor e.g. a bishop might hold an abbacy in addition to his office as bishop; Bower disapproved of the practice, which in his day was just beginning to be followed in Scotland (see above III c.37, 1.9n., and below c.47, 1.6).

63-64. *... way*: cf. Horace, *Epistles*, bk.I, ep.1, 1.66 (Loeb edn, 256).

66. *blessed Martin*: St Martin, the monk who became bishop of Tours, France, 372-97; 'in art the most popular scene was that of dividing his cloak to clothe a beggar' (*ODS*, 287-8).

Chapter 40
pp.391-3

Here ll.1-28 continue Bower's imagined story about Bishop John's part in splitting the diocese of Dunkeld; then ll.29-53 may well come from the *Life* composed by William Bening specifically mentioned at ll.50-53; ll.54-59 end the story of the rivalry of John and Hugh for the see of St Andrews.

1. *reading the letter*: there is no proof that any such letter was ever sent; and it is not stated here which of the various popes in the 1180s is meant; the story which follows has the air of a literary conceit.

6-7. *... found*: the first line here comes from Juvenal, *Satires*, no.6, 1.165 (Loeb edn, 96-97); it is listed in Walther, *Proverbia*, no.26,260 with many references, one of which is to John of Salisbury, *Policraticus* (ed. C.C.J.Webb [Oxford, 1909], ii, 301), which could have been familiar to Bower. But the second line comes from some other untraced source, which is perhaps rather where Bower found both lines.

16. *Harold*: see above c.39, 1.44; though the see of Argyll was in existence by 1192 × 1193 (*Series Episcoporum*, VI, i, 11), it is not certain that Harold was in office as bishop during John's lifetime.

25. *very many bishops today*: again a comment by Bower on the 15c bishops of Scotland.

30. *death at Newbattle*: in 1203 (*Melrose*, 51); he chose to end his days outside his diocese at the Cistercian abbey of Newbattle MLO; his biographer (see below) is unlikely to have been already a monk there at this date, but he could have had at his disposal reports from older monks who had then been around.

50. *a book on his life*: no longer in existence.

51. *William Bening*: abbot of Coupar Angus PER 1243-58 (*ES*, ii, 535, 593).

54-59. *... 1188*: Bower in MS C started with a simple statement about the date of Bishop Hugh's death; then after finding additional material when composing VIII c.44, ll.19-26 below, he used some of it for a marginal addition here with the extra information that Hugh went to Rome, received absolution, and died near that city presumably on his way home; for details of John's last challenge to Hugh's tenure of the see of St Andrews, which had necessitated this visit to Rome, see *Series Episcoporum*, VI, i, 89.

Chapter 41
pp.393-5

1. *Roger*: the third son of Robert ès Blanchemains, the third earl of Leicester in England, and so a distant relative of King William, whose mother Ada had been a half-sister of Roger's grandfather the second earl of Leicester (*CP*, vii, 526, 533; xii, pt.i, 496); he had been chancellor only briefly (see below VIII c.44, ll.18-19; see also VIII c.46, ll.41-42).

3. *elected*: *Melrose* (47) agrees on the date, and adds that the election took place at Perth, presumably while the king and his court were there.

4. *consecrated*: *Melrose* (50) has the same date, but omits the name of the consecrating bishop; it was probably only in 1198 that he reached his thirtieth year, which was the required age for episcopal consecration under canon law (cf. *Series Episcoporum*, VI, i, 89).

5. *Richard*: bishop of Moray 1187-1203 (ibid., 68-69).

6-7. *ten years ... a half*: here as elsewhere not an exact calculation.

7. *died*: *Melrose* (51) gives only the year-date.
   Cambuskenneth: Augustinian abbey near Stirling STL.

8. *old church of St Andrew*: i.e. St Rule's church at St Andrews (see above c.35, l.3). *Wyntoun* (v, 42-43) notes that Bishop Roger founded and built the castle at St Andrews; see ibid. (v, 58-59) for his burial under a wrong date.

9. *legate called John*: John de Salerno, cardinal priest of S. Stefano in Monte Celio 1191-1208 (Eubel, *Hierarchia*, i, 47) held a formal legatine council at Perth, December 1201 (see below VIII c.62, ll.24-26); after a visit to Ireland (ibid.), he moved Malveisin from one see to another by legatine authority.

11. *William*: William Malveisin, bishop of Glasgow since his election in October 1199, and subsequent consecration at Lyons, France, on 24 September 1200 (see below VIII c.61, ll.21-22); for his biography see Watt, *Graduates*, 374-9).

12. *postulation and translation*: a bishop was said to be postulated to his office when he was not immediately eligible to hold it under the rules of the canon law, so that a papal dispensation was needed before he could be confirmed; cf. above c.27, l.34; he was said to be translated rather than appointed when moved by papal authority from one see to another, a practice which was formally forbidden under canon law (cf. *ODCC*, 1390).

20 September: in 1217 it was to be asserted that he had been postulated on 18 rather than 20 September (Theiner, *Monumenta*, 3, no.6); neither *Wyntoun* (v, 60-61) nor *Melrose* (51) gives a precise date.

20-27. *Yet ... expected*: a story which must have been handed down traditionally in Dunfermline Abbey FIF, where Bower is likely to have heard it; it is repeated below VIII c.62, ll.36-51 where Bower adds a critical comment of his own.

22. *Kinglassie* FIF: see Cowan, *Parishes*, 112.

Hailes MLO: now known as Colinton; see ibid., 79-80.

27. *Inchmurdo*: an episcopal residence (not on modern maps) near Boarhills FIF, between St Andrews and Crail (see below X c.28, l.36n.).

28. *new church of St Andrew*: i.e. the main cathedral (see above c.35,ll.9-10); see also *Wyntoun* (v, 92-95); for position of his tomb see McRoberts, *St Andrews*, 85.

30-33. *Geoffrey ... quashed*: Geoffrey de Liberatione, a king's clerk, was bishop of Dunkeld 1236-49; the pope (apparently at the king's urging) ordered the canons of St Andrews to hold a new election, 12 February 1239 (Theiner, *Monumenta*, 38, no.98), and this was done with the assistance (apparently at the king's urging) of certain additional clergy who were not members of the cathedral community and who had not participated in Geoffrey's election (cf. Barrow, *Kingdom*, 226); for Geoffrey see Dowden, *Bishops*, 54-57.

35. *David de Bernham*: had served as chamberlain probably from early 1235; see his biography in Watt, *Graduates*, 41-44.

36. *compromise procedure*: election by one or more *compromissarii* i.e. one or more persons to whom the electors delegated their powers to decide (*DDC*, v, col.243; J.Dowden, *The Medieval Church in Scotland* [Glasgow, 1910], 32-33).

36-39. *consecrated ... letters*: *Wyntoun* (v, 94-95) has the same information; William de Bondington, bishop of Glasgow 1233-48; Gilbert de Moravia, bishop of Caithness 1222/3-1245; Gregory bishop of Brechin 1218 - 1242 × 1246 (Watt, *Fasti*, 146, 58, 39).

39. *apostolic letters*: dated 1 October 1239 (Theiner, *Monumenta*, 39, no.100).

39-45. *This man ... disease*: Bower is here following a traditional view of Bernham as he was regarded by the canons of St Andrews cathedral priory, on whom he had been imposed as bishop, and with whom he had differences along party lines in the national politics of the minority of the young king Alexander III (Watt, *Graduates*, 43-44); Bower is more complimentary to Bernham below X c.8, ll.36-37.

42. *Inchture* PER: cf. Cowan, *Parishes*, 86; the circumstances of the bishop's interest in this church are not clear.

47. *Nenthorn* BWK: near Kelso Abbey.

47-48. *buried ... St Andrews*: Wyntoun (v, 118-19) explains (under the wrong date 1252) that he was buried away from St Andrews by his own choice; this is not surprising if he was at loggerheads with the canons of the cathedral priory at the time of his death.

Chapter 42
pp.395-9

1-2. *Robert de Stuteville*: dean of Dunkeld from 1245 × July 1250; already associated with St Andrews cathedral priory in some of their disputes; see biography in Watt, *Graduates*, 527-9. For this disputed election see below X c.8, ll.38-45, where it is stated that Stuteville's election was carried through with disregard for the specific recommendation of Gamelin (see below) by the Comynite government ruling in the young king's name.

3. *compromise procedure*: see above c.41, l.36.

4. *archdeacon of St Andrews*: Abel de Golin had been archdeacon of St Andrews since June 1248 × May 1250 (see biography in Watt, *Graduates*, 225-7); he had not been present at Stuteville's election, though he claimed as archdeacon the right to take part (ibid.).

6. *by the lord King*: i.e. by the Comynite minority government; Stuteville was an associate of the Durwardite party who were then out of office.

9-10. *truth yielded ... falsehood prevailed*: these phrases indicate that Bower was following a source preserved in the cathedral priory.

11. *elect ... favour*: Stuteville's election was quashed by the pope, and Golin provided instead, 20 February 1254 (Theiner, *Monumenta*, 59-60, no.162).

12. *vested in episcopal insignia*: Golin was consecrated at Rome on 1 March 1254 (*Lanercost*, 58); cf. *Wyntoun*, v, 118-19.

23. *... controlled*: this quotation from Bede has not been identified.

30. *died*: the date here, 1 December 1254, would normally be accepted as accurate, since it was presumably taken from a St Andrews source; but in this case the date 31 August 1254 (*Lanercost*, 60) is preferable (cf.Watt, *Graduates*, 227).

31. *buried*: for the site of his tomb in the great cathedral see McRoberts, *St Andrews*, 85.

31-32. *For him ... Chapter 8*: the first of three cross-references provided in this chapter in margin of MS C once Book X had been composed.

33. *Gamelin*: see his biography in Watt, *Graduates*, 209-14; as chancellor in the Comynite government he had been supported by it for election after Bishop Bernham's death; he was now elected by the compromise procedure (ibid., 210).

34. *postulated*: see above c.41, l.12n.; in this case the impediment under the canon law was perhaps Gamelin's possible illegitimate birth (cf. ibid., 209).

36. *bishop of Glasgow*: William de Bondington (see above c.41, ll.36-39).

36-39. *This was ... envoys*: the Comynite government had supported his confirmation by the pope on 1 July 1255 (Theiner, *Monumenta*, 66-67, no.176); but when a Durwardite council came into power in September 1255, Gamelin lost his position as chancellor, and it was in the teeth of hostility from the new council that he was consecrated; see below X c.9, ll.49-56 for another account by Bower which is not consistent with this passage; the obstructive action mentioned here was presumably taken by the earlier council to secure the smooth confirmation of his election; the later council, however, did try without success to have this papal decision reversed.

39. *quite wisely*: Bower is giving faint praise here; but in MS CA he adds after 'ecclesiam' (text l.34):

> sed levi occasione mota est dolorosa contencio inter regem et novum episcopum, pro eo quod episcopus denunciavit quemdam militem Johannem Dwnmore nomine rapientem injuste decimas canonicorum Sanctiandree excommunicatum, et dominus rex scripsit sibi ut absolveret suum militem, nulla satisfaccione preambula. Quod omnino episcopus facere recusavit, sciens quod venia non datur nisi correcto. Unde rex nimium commotus resaisivit omnia maneria episcopi et temporalitates sibi recognovit, putans per hoc episcopum flectere ut a censure fulminacione desisteret. Sed episcopus, sciens se esse positum tanquam murum pro domo Domini, exhibuit se antemurale. Accedens quod qui uni parcit, universe ecclesie parat interitum, sciens quod illa est falsa misericordia uni parcere et multos in discrimine adducere. Unde in ipsum dominum Johannem processus aggravavit, et in omnes illos qui'

leading into text as below X c.22, text l.29 ('qui') to text there l.35 ('satisfecit'). Thus in MS CA Bower provides here a variant version of the story in Book X (MS CA as well as MS C) regarding John Dunmore; and this is followed by material similar to X c.28, ll.36-40 below.

41. *Inchmurdo*: see above c.41, l.27; cf. *Wyntoun*, v, 125-7.
buried: for position of his tomb see McRoberts, *St Andrews*, 87-88.

44. *William Wischard*: see his biography in Watt, *Graduates*, 590-4; he had been elected to see of Glasgow sometime in 1270 (see below X c.27, ll.45-50; c.28, ll.40-54; c.31, ll.1-10; c.33, ll.26-34). In MS CA these last three passages are brought together here.

45. *postulated*: because he had already been elected to another see; the long delay over his consecration to either see was partly caused by a long vacancy in the papacy Nov.1268 – Mar.1272 (see below X c.28, ll.29-35).

46-47. *The Culdees ... election*: the clergy of the church of St Mary on the Rock at St Andrews as successors to the older community of Culdees had through their provost shared in some of the recent episcopal elections with the Augustinian canons of the cathedral priory (Barrow, *Kingdom*, 225-32); cf. below X c.33, ll.54-55.

48-50. *when ... expense*: for more details of his building work on the cathedral see *Wyntoun*, v, 127.

51. *escheats*: income arising from the temporal estates of the bishopric.

51-53. *In his day ... dispute with him*: cf. the case in the previous episcopate (below X c.22, ll.27-45); see also the summing up in *Wyntoun*, v, 128-9.

53. *Morebattle* ROX.

56-59. *He served ... nine days*: as usual these calculations are inaccurate.

Chapter 43
pp.399-401

1. *William Fraser*: for his biography see Watt, *Graduates*, 203-6.

2. *Culdees again excluded*: see above c.42, ll.46-47.

3. *Nicholas*: Nicholas III, pope 1277-80.

7. *Edward Longshanks*: King Edward I of England 1272-1307.

8. *withdrew to France*: he was one of a diplomatic mission on behalf of the Scottish magnates to secure the Franco-Scottish alliance of October 1295 (see below XI c.15, ll.59-66, and cc.16-17), and is not certainly known to have ever returned.

Auteuil: now in central Paris near the Bois de Boulogne.

11. *buried*: for the site where his heart was buried see McRoberts, *St Andrews*, 88; Wyntoun (v, 310-13) elaborates on the same facts.

11. *William de Lamberton*; see below.

13-21. *... plotting*: this is a duplicate entry of the account taken by Bower from *Fordun* (rather than from his St Andrews source) under the date 21 April 1296 below XI c.21, ll.1-9 (see discussion in notes there).

21-22. *William ... effect*: this marginal addition to MS C summarizes another passage taken by Bower from *Fordun* under the date 1297 (see below XI c.21, ll.50-54).

23. *William de Lamberton*: for his biography see Watt, *Graduates*, 318-25.

25-30. *with the Culdees ... no effect*: see above l.2; the revival of the claims of the successors to the Culdees to a share in the election of the bishop was apparently based on procedural arguments; but in the circumstances of the aftermath of the defeat of the English at Stirling Bridge on 11 September 1297 the real dispute may well have been political and personal.

26. *William Comyn*: for his biography see Watt, *Graduates*, 109-11; a younger son of Alexander earl of Buchan, he had been appointed provost of the church of St Mary on the Rock at St Andrews (which was probably in crown patronage) in 1287, when his father was one the guardians of Scotland following the death of King Alexander III (ibid., 109).

28. *Boniface VIII*: pope 1294-1303.

28-29. *challenged ... elected*: as a member of the greatest noble family in Scotland at that time, he was opposing in Lamberton a man of lesser social status who most surely had the support of Andrew de Moray and William Wallace, the leaders of the fight against the English (ibid., 319).

31. *confirmed the bishop-elect*: the official bull of confirmation was issued on 17 June 1298, some days after his consecration (Theiner, *Monumenta*, 165-6, no.362).

33-38. *... law*: Bower is here describing the normal procedure under canon law for the exercise of episcopal authority while a see was vacant.

35. *Nicholas de Balmyle*: see his biography in Watt, *Graduates*, 23-25; he was an experienced practitioner of the canon law in St Andrews diocese; later bishop of Dunblane 1307-19.

39-57. *... books*: into his original brief account in MS C of Lamberton's benefactions to the cathedral of St Andrews Bower intrudes (presumably from a different source) in the margin (1.41 ['while'] to 1.53 ['Wedale']) an anecdotal account of his building works on his temporal estates.

50. *fortress palace*: the castle of St Andrews – apparently an addition by Bower to the source he was following. Lamberton's work on this castle was all destroyed in the 1330s (see below XIII c.38; cf. *St Andrews Castle*, official guide, ed. C.Tabraham [Edinburgh, 1992], 2).

51-52. *Inchmurdo ... Wedale*: a list of some of the episcopal estates: Inchmurdo, Monimail, Dairsie and Torry FIF; Muckhart CLA; Kettins ANG; Monymusk ABD; [Kirk-]lliston ('Lynton' in the MSS is surely an error [cf. *CPL*, i, 61]), Lasswade and Stow in Wedale MLO; for details of these episcopal estates see *Rentale Sancti Andree*, ed. R.K.Hannay (SHS, 1913), ad indicem.

53. *chapter-house*: attached as an extension to the old one.

64-65. *in the room of the lord prior*: it is highly unusual for the bishop to be resident in the cathedral community (of which he was only titular abbot) rather than in his castle or in one of his manor-houses.

65. *buried*: for the site of his tomb see McRoberts, *St Andrews*, 88; cf. *Wyntoun*, v, 380-1.

Chapter 44
pp.403-5

2. *Culdees entirely excluded*: cf. above c.43, ll.26-31.

3. *method of a general vote*: cf. above c.41, l.36; election *per viam scrutinii* involved a vote by all the relevant electors (*DDC*, v, col.243).

4. *James Ben*: see his biography in Watt, *Graduates*, 36-38; cf. *Wyntoun*, v, 380-1, where an unspecified chronicle is cited.

5. *Alexander de Kininmund*: see his biography in Watt, *Graduates*, 299-301).
archdeacon of Lothian: the diocese of St Andrews was divided into two archdeaconries, St Andrews and Lothian, separated by the Firth of Forth.

6-7. *at the Roman court*: i.e. at Avignon.

8-9. *appointment of the lord pope*: Ben's bull of provision is dated 1 August 1328 (Theiner, *Monumenta*, 239-40, no.472).
John XXII: pope 1316-34.

9-10. *reserved ... world*: by extending the papal powers of reservation and provision John 'virtually removed the election of bishops from chapters' (*ODP*, 214).

11. *made bishop of Aberdeen*: Kininmund's bull of provision as bishop of Aberdeen is dated 21 August 1329 (Theiner, *Monumenta*, 245-6, no.482).

12. *William Comyn*: see above c.43, l.27.

12-13. *provost of the Chapel Royal*: this was the same office which he had held since the late 1280s; the collegiate church of St Mary on the Rock at St Andrews had probably by this time been given the status of a chapel royal (*MRHS*, 225; Watt, *Fasti*, 371).

15. *promoted ... Lothian*: by papal bull of provision 11 November 1329 (*CPL*, ii, 301).

18. *battle of Dupplin*: 11 August 1332 (see below XIII c.22).

19. *boy David ... crowned by him*: 24 November 1331 (see below XIII c.20).

20. *Loch Leven* KNR.

24. *Eeckhout*: an Augustinian monastery in Bruges, Belgium (*DHGE*, xiv, cols. 1456-9).

27. *William Bell*: see his biography in Watt, *Graduates*, 35-36; if the date here is correct, Ben must have previously resigned his see on leaving the country a day or two before; but in later papal letters (e.g. Theiner, *Monumenta*, 277, no.550) Bell's election is said to have followed Ben's death; cf. *Wyntoun*, vi, 156-7.

28. *compromise procedure*: see above c.41, l.36.

28-30. *Culdees ... no objection*: cf. above l.2, and c.43, ll.26-31.

32-33. *promotion ... Laundels*: see below ll.40-42.

38. *breathed his last*: for discussion of his possible tombstone see McRoberts, *St Andrews*, 86.

40. *18 February of the previous year*: there is no doubt that Laundels was provided to the see of St Andrews on this date (Theiner, *Monumenta*, 277, no.550); Bower's correction in MS CA (text note j) is therefore wrong.

40. *William de Laundels*: see Watt, *Fasti*, 294; Dowden, *Bishops*, 25-27; cf. Watt, *Graduates*, 328.

41. *church of Kinkell* ABD: a wealthy parish benefice in the patronage of the bishop of St Andrews (*CPP*, i, 113).

42. *consecrated*: he received a papal mandate to proceed from Avignon to his see after consecration, 18 March 1342 (*CPL*, ii, 557).

43-55. *The support ... same church*: this discussion of the influences which lay behind the papal appointment of Laundels to the see of St Andrews does not exactly conform to what is said in the papal bulls (see above l.40n.), where the pope refers to Bell's resignation at the Roman court and his reservation for papal provision of appointments to bishoprics resigned in this way; the pope had received evidence of Laundels's suitability from trustworthy persons (unspecified), and Laundels had also been recommended (not elected) by the prior and chapter of St Andrews; there is no suggestion that the pope demanded evidence of canonical election as a *sine qua non*. Bower must have been drawing here on a record at St Andrews which in reaction against the terms of the papal letter was concerned to assert more traditional capitular rights. A similar record touching on the same points lies behind Wyntoun's account (vi, 156-9; cf. i, 122).

42. *Benedict XII*: pope 1334-42.

44-45. *kings of France and Scotland*: Wyntoun (ibid.) too mentions their efforts on Laundels's behalf, explaining that when he was a young cleric in France, his friends had got King Philip VI there to write to the pope in his support for the see of St Andrews, and that young King David (who lived in France until June 1341) had also written on his behalf; he explains that the chapter of St Andrews did request the pope to appoint Laundels as their bishop, but they specifically avoided holding a second election (Bell still being their first choice), since that would be against canon law. It is clear that Bower's handling of the same source puts an emphasis on the over-riding importance of election in episcopal appointments that is an intrusion of his own views.

Chapter 45
pp.405-9

For this chapter Bower made a large number of changes when composing MS CA, including the insertion of two extra whole paragraphs (see below l.75); he was no longer copying earlier sources, but beginning to compile his own account; this applies especially to his remarks on Walter Trayl, who was bishop in the late 1390s when presumably Bower first became a canon in the Augustinian community who served St Andrews cathedral; he certainly writes about Bishop Trayl from personal knowledge.

2. *lord and heir .. Laundels*: he was heir to his brother John, a knight, who held estates in ROX (*RRS*, vi, 410-11, no.378; see also Barrow, *Kingdom*, 326-7).

3-4. *witty ... sons*: Bower is not writing here with personal knowledge, but he must as a young canon at St Andrews have spoken with older canons who had known Laundels.

5. *met his end*: cf. Wyntoun (vi, 306-7) for his death in the cathedral priory at St Andrews and his funeral.

6-7. *feast ... Adomnan*: 23 September was the feast day of both saints mentioned here.

7-8. *burning ... St Andrew*: see below c.53, ll.35-41, and XIV c.40 for details of the repair work achieved during the last seven years of his episcopate see *Wyntoun*, vi, 309-11.

8. *buried*: for the site of his tomb see McRoberts, *St Andrews*, 86-87.

11. *Walter Trayl*: for his biography see Watt, *Graduates*, 539-42. Bower here is writing from personal knowledge.

12-13. *knight ... arts*: Trayl had studied arts at the university of Paris, and then earned the degree of doctor of both laws (i.e. civil and canon) after further study there and at Orleans (ibid., 539); the informal phrase 'miles legum' (text l.10) is a literary flourish on Bower's part.

14.   *provision*: his papal bull of appointment as bishop is dated 29 November 1385 (ibid., 540).

Clement VII: pope 1378-94, later categorized an anti-pope; elected as a rival to Urban VI, and continued the schism thus created by setting up his own court at Avignon, while Urban remained at Rome (*ODP*, 228-30). As Bower's marginal addition in MS C notes he had a distant family connection with the Scottish kings – his father Amadeus III count of Geneva had married Mary (or Matilda) of Boulogne, who was descended (albeit through many changes of family in the female line) from Mary, the daughter of King Malcolm and Queen Margaret, who had married Eustace count of Boulogne in 1102 (see above V c.35, ll.16-17; Mas Latrie, *Trésor*, cols. 1564-5, 1547). Bishop Trayl knew Pope Clement personally, and would have spoken in Scotland about this link.

17.   *referendary*: he had joined Pope Clement's administration in a judicial capacity as an auditor of cases in 1378; then he moved in 1383 to the papal chancery as one of the senior officials called referendaries, who were responsible for preparing answers to petitions sent to the pope from all parts of the church who recognized his authority (cf. *DDC*, vii, cols. 492-3).

26.   *Stephen Pay*: see below c.53, ll.28-43; cf. *Wyntoun*, vi, 308-9.

34.   *unfortunate fire*: see above ll.7-8.

38.   *Alnwick* NTB.

42-43.   *family of middling status*: for his family connections see Watt, *Graduates*, 539.

46.   *hurried to his native land*: his first known episcopal act is dated 31 August 1386 (ibid., 541).

66-75.   *He reproached ... separation*: a collection of statutes (which includes the topic of concubinage), issued sometime in the 14c in the St Andrews diocesan synod, was probably enacted during Trayl's episcopate (cf. Robertson, *Concilia*, ii, 64-72, nos. 140-63).

75.   *separation*: after 'celebraret' (text ll.55-56) MS CA has the two following long additions before continuing with the text of this chapter at 'censor morum':

De eodem adhuc

Clericorum et religiosorum mores studuit sagaciter in melius reformare. Nam si quempiam videret vestibus dissolutum, statim increpavit. Unde in sermonibus suis quos communiter ipsemet in sinodis facere consueverat, multum instetit ut in omnibus humilitatis preberet secularibus exemplum, monens eosdem ut vel hanc aut hanc incomposicionem sic et sic reformarent, quod si post huiusmodi admoniciones quemquam reum inveniret, penam provide luit transgressor. Nam et hoc ego qui hec collegi scivi et bene novi honorabilem virum, generosum satis clericum, utpote fratrem magnatis militis in scolis summe graduatum, prepinguiter beneficiatum, in sinodo ab episcopo ipso exploratum, pluscula habere argentea clare deaurata sotularibus suis insuta, quod in facie illius congregacionis accito eo episcopus extracto cultellulo ipsa pluscula propriis manibus succidebat, et tam acriter eum arguebatur ut hoc videntes et audientes verecundia precellerentur. Aliis manicas profusas, aliis collares protensas et altas, aliis corniculas incompositas similiter abscideret, invicta eiis ultra hoc penitencia pro commissis. In causis eciam religiosorum dum fratres visitaret multa et edificativa solitus est proponere hortamenta, maxime ut nunquam munitissima necligerent cerimonialia, exemplicans ipsam religionem ad dolium continens optimum vinum quod colligatur tribus magnis ligneis ligaturis, per quas intellexit tria ordinis sabbatalia, et ille tres ligature vinciuntur cum multis munitis viminibus sive virgulis, per que cerimonialia intellexit. Unde deducendo ad propositum conclusit quod quando munite virgule deficiunt, statim grandes ligature solvuntur.Quibus solutis, tabule dissiliunt et totum vinum effunditur. Applica.

De eodem

De more eciam habuit diocesis sue quasi omni anno singulas ecclesias in propria visitare persona pueros confirmare et strictissimam inquisicionem de observata fide facere, maleficos et sortilegas stalare et punire, contra vetularum et vulgi prophanos ritus efficacissimos sermones protrahere, detractores et scandalizatores ultra creditum perseque [sic] hereticos et Lolardos procul a finibus propellere, vel diris carceribus usque ad emendam mancipare. Quamplurime dilexit sacerdotes sacerdotaliter viventes, et predicatoribus verbi Dei favorem maximum impendebat. Quid plura? Perversis erat rigidus et bonis dulcifluus, virtutes collaudans et contra vicia indesinenter tanquam canis latrans, predicator egregius, Latinista disertissimus, in habitu religiosus incedens, in monasterio Sanctiandr' humiliter in alba tunica et rocheta existens inter fratres tanquam unus ex eis, perlustrans in claustro canonicorum cellei cellas, et ab unoquoque inquirens in quo libro vel sciencia studebat, conferens cum eis et instruens eos ac si magister eis fuisset specialiter commissus, scriptores multum collaudans et operosos dissolutos objurgans et ociosos, interdum tanquam novicius et cum noviciis addiscens cerimonias circa altare in missa fiendas, tam in stacionibus, inclinacionibus quam in jactu thuribili, quia in huiusmodi voluit fratribus per omnia assimilari. Erat enim canus capite, brevis stature, gracilis corpore, anilis et rugatus facie, virilis voce. austerus et quasi efferus apparens vultu, sed secus sermone et loquele cultu. Erat enim censor ...

83.   *which ... foundation*: cf. above c.43, l.51n..

84.   *1401*: all the MSS leave blanks for the day and month of Trayl's death; it was apparently after 25 March and before 1 July 1401, when a successor was elected (see below c.46, l.1); see *Wyntoun*, vi, 394-5 for an encomium on Trayl's virtues; cf. below c.46, ll.15-16.

85.   *buried*: for the site of his tomb see McRoberts, *St Andrews*, 87-88); for details of the hangings, vestments and sacred vessels which he bequeathed to St Andrews cathedral see *Wyntoun*, vi, 311-13.

Chapter 46
pp.409-13

1. *Thomas Stewart*: see his biography in Watt, *Graduates*, 513-15.

elected: Wyntoun gives the date of this election as 1 July 1401, as part of a fuller account of the three elections to this see after Trayl's death before it was finally given by the pope to Henry de Wardlaw (*Wyntoun*, vi, 395-6, 398-401).

2. *elder King Robert*: i.e. Robert II 1371-90.

3. *archdeacon of St Andrews*: Thomas had held this office since 1380, and was to keep it for a total of fifty years until his death in 1430 (Watt, *Fasti*, 306).

5-6. *about to be transmitted*: Wyntoun states that the sub-prior of St Andrews did in fact go to Avignon to seek confirmation of Stewart's election, but could not obtain papal approval because (as was certainly the case) the pope was besieged in his palace and unable to deal with business. This contradiction in the accounts of two men who were canons of St Andrews and who must have known the facts is striking.

6. *renounced his election*: Wyntoun explains that he did this after persuasion by his brother the duke of Albany, who was the dominant figure in the government of Scotland at the time.

7. *Walter Danielston*: see his biography in Watt, *Graduates*, 142-3; his election was conducted by compromise (see above c.41, l.36) under pressure from Albany, and took place ca June 1402 i.e. 'little more than half a year' before his death the following Christmas (*Wyntoun*, vi, 399).

postulated: cf. above c.41, l.12; the legal impediment in his eligibility for election as bishop is not known; he died without consecration.

9-13. *... castle*: Danielston had been holding the royal castle of Dumbarton DNB since 1398 in open rebellion; it was his suggestion that if he was made bishop of St Andrews, he would surrender that castle; the deal had not been completed at the time of his death (cf. Watt, *Graduates*, ut cit).

13. *Someone has written*: not identified.

20-23. *An etymology ...lash*: Bower apparently develops his own thoughts here as part of a marginal addition to MS C; 'etymology' here may mean 'the true exposition or interpretation of a thing' (*OED*).

25. *Gilbert Grenlaw*: see his biography in Watt, *Graduates*, 237-9; he was bishop of Aberdeen 1390-1421, and chancellor of Scotland for an extraordinarily long time from 1397 until his death; Wyntoun (vi, 399-400) states that the prior of St Andrews again went to Avignon to obtain papal confirmation of Grenlaw's translation from one see to another (which was why he was postulated), but in vain.

29. *Benedict XIII*: pope 1394-1417, later categorized as an anti-pope.

30. *Henry de Wardlaw*: provided to see of St Andrews when residing at the papal court at Avignon, 10 September 1403; see his biography in Watt, *Graduates*, 564-9, especially 566; cf. *Wyntoun*, vi, 400-1.

31. *precentor of Glasgow*: since 1387 (Watt, *Fasti*, 157); this benefice had given him financial support for years of study abroad.

doctor of civil law: an error; he had studied some civil law, but his final degree was doctor of canon law (Watt, *Graduates*, 564).

31-32. *Walter de Wardlaw*: bishop of Glasgow 1367-87, cardinal in addition from 1384 (see his biography, ibid., 569-75).

37-38. *brought the university ... St Andrews*: see below XV, c.22.

38. *Guardbridge* FIF: Wardlaw obtained a papal indulgence on 21 August 1419 to assist the fund-raising for building this bridge across the river Eden three miles from St Andrews, after a tragic accident when fifteen priests had been drowned when fording this muddy tidal river (*CSSR*, i, 109).

39-41. *obtained ... one-third*: in fact this king in 1405 granted the whole of the St Andrews customs to Wardlaw and his successors (Watt, *Graduates*, 567-8).

45. *buried*: for the site of his tomb see McRoberts, *St Andrews*, 89-90.

49-81. *... initial letters*: in the Latin text ll.39-58 this epitaph is seen to have been composed in the form of an acrostic; we are indebted to Professor Brian Scott for help with the translation.

62. *salvation*: probably spiritual rather than bodily healing is meant.

72. *God's decrees*: more literally 'the holy decrees'.

74. *Rymont stream*: a reference to Kilrymont, the place which by this date was more usually called St Andrews (cf. above IV c.11, l.21); the small river that enters the sea at St Andrews is now called the Kinness Burn.

Chapter 47
pp.413-15

1. *James Kennedy*: see A.I.Dunlop, *The Life and times of James Kennedy, Bishop of St Andrews* (Edinburgh and London, 1950).

2. *countess of Angus*: Kennedy's mother was indeed Mary, sister of King James I; but it was only after the death of her first husband, George Douglas earl of Angus, that she was in 1405 married to Sir James Kennedy of Dunure AYR; James Kennedy here was the third son of Mary's second marriage (ibid., 2-3; *SP*, i, 18, 173; ii, 448-50; ix, 2).

3. *bishop of Dunkeld*: since 1437 (Watt, *Fasti*, 97-98).

postulated: because he was already bishop of another see, so that special papal dispensation was required (cf. above c.41, l.12).

4. *guidance of the Holy Spirit*: election *per viam Sancti Spiritus* implied acclamation wihout a ballot (*DDC*, v, col.243).

Florence, Italy.

5. *Eugenius*: pope Eugenius IV 1431-47.

6. *monastery of Scone in commend*: by papal grant dated 23 September 1439 he was authorised to hold the abbacy of the Augustinian monastery of Scone near Perth along with his see of Dunkeld; in practice this was probably ineffective, as a locally-elected abbot was in possession (Dunlop, *Kennedy*,

38-39); this example of the growing practice of 'commending' or 'entrusting' the duties and emoluments of an abbacy to a person who was not the legal holder of the office (which in such a case did not require him to make a monastic profession) is the first known case in Scotland (M.Dilworth, 'The commendator system in Scotland', *Innes Review*, xxxvii [1986], 51-72, especially 54 and note 37); the practice was one of which Bower as a religious superior (and an Augustinian to boot) strongly disapproved (see above III c.37, ll.6-15, and VI c.39, ll.60-61).

8. *provided ... St Andrews*: by papal letters dated 1 June 1440 (Cameron, *Apostolic Camera*, 25).

8-10. *He celebrated ... 1442*: Kennedy was back in Scotland as early as 24 May 1441, but his appearance at St Andrews was delayed by the presence there of a rival bishop-elect, James Ogilvie, who had been provided on 26 July 1440 by Pope Felix V, the pope appointed by the Council of Basel (Watt, *Fasti*, 295; Dunlop, *Kennedy*, 40.

10. *1442*: the rest of fo.126 (nearly half the page) and all of fo.126v in MS C have been left blank (see also below c.52, l.34n.), presumably in the expectation of entering further information on Kennedy and future bishops of St Andrews later than this entry dated 1442; this presumption is confirmed by Bower's omission of no.48 in the numbering of the chapters that follow; in this the scribes of MSS R, D and E followed the example of MS C; but there is no sign of any attempt in these four MSS to bring this story up-to-date with additional entries (Bower was to die in 1449, while Kennedy lived until 1465). See also end of c.57 below.

But the two other MSS do have addenda here. MS B (written 1480-1) continues:

> Hic construxit alme sumptuosissimum collegium in civitate Sanctiandr' et illud ditavit quampluribus jocalibus multisque redditibus. Cuius ossa ibidem requiescunt in preclarissimo tumulo tocius orbis. Obiit xxiiii maii anno 1465.

MS H (written 1484; see Hearne, iii, 614) continues:

> Hic dominus Jacobus Kennedi innumera bona in toto regno operatus est. Construxit enim alme et preclarum collegium in civitate Sanctiandr' et illud ditavit quampluribus jocalibus multisque redditibus imperpetuum. Duraturum ibique fabricari fecit monumentum opere sumptuosissimo ex alabastro, in quo sua ossa requiescunt in Domino.

The reference in each case is to the College of St Salvator founded by Bishop Kennedy in the university of St Andrews in 1450, and to his tomb in the college church. Despite these additions MSS B and H follow the others in numbering the next chapter 49.

Chapter 49
pp.415-17

Bower turns now to the succession of the priors of the Augustinian cathedral monastery at St Andrews, which had been formally founded in 1144 (*MRHS*, 96); his source was presumably in the archives of this house, of which he had himself been a member; he did not follow the brief list of priors contained in the Great Register of St Andrews (cf. *St Andrews Liber*, p.xxx), nor that which was the basis of the list copied in the early 16c by John Law (McRoberts, *St Andrews*, 140-1); his own account is not free from errors and inconsistencies (see below); for the later 14c he would have tapped the reminiscences of older fellow-canons, and then he had his own memories of the priors from James Bisset onwards.

This first chapter provides an introduction to cc. 50-57 that follow; the whole chapter was exceptionally copied into the smaller cartulary belonging to the priory (*St Andrews Liber*, 23, where the rubric wrongly identifies it as coming from Scotichronicon, Book VI, Chapter 1); this suggests that King James's definition of the precedence due to the prior of St Andrews (see below ll.26-36) was known to the canons there only through Bower's undated account here, which may well have been based on personal knowledge.

In France quite a high proportion of Augustinian houses attained the rank of abbey rather than priory, whilst in Germany and England only a very small proportion were abbeys rather than priories (J.C.Dickinson, *The Origins of the Austin Canons and their Introduction into England* [London, 1950], 80-81, 156-7; cf. 245-51 for the cathedral priory at Carlisle); it was not therefore out of character for the cathedral priory at St Andrews to remain a priory while other Augustinian houses in Scotland such as Cambuskenneth, Holyrood, Jedburgh and Scone became abbeys (*MRHS*, 88-89). 'One should not be misled by the fact that the house was only a priory into under-estimating its importance. As with the cathedral priories in England, there was evidently a feeling that it was more fitting for the superior not to be an abbot, but this was apparently a matter of sentiment and tradition, a survival perhaps from the time when the bishop was the superior of such a religious community and held the office of abbot' (M.Dilworth, 'The Augustinian chapter of St Andrews', *Innes Review*, xxv [1974], 15). 'In the days when the bishop was elected by the monks as their abbot, he appointed the prior and other monastic officials. When the prior became in effect their religious superior it was natural that the monks should claim the right to elect him as in other monastic houses. The bishop had a considerable interest in the matter, for the prior was the head of his chapter, but in general the community's right was recognised' (ibid., 23). At St Andrews Bishop Robert appointed the first prior (see below c.50, ll.1-2); but he granted to the canons the right of free election of their prior 1147 × 1159 (*St Andrews Liber*, 126).

2. *as we have already mentioned*: see above c.24, l.8.

7-8. *special privilege ... Scotland*: no formal award of such a privilege is now known; it was in 1418 asserted to be customary (*CSSR*, i, 9); cf. below (l.19) mention of 'prescriptive custom'; but there are late 14c examples of the prior of St Andrews taking precedence in assemblies of a parliamentary type following any bishops and preceding any abbots who were present e.g. *APS*, i, 501 (1367), 545 (1371), and 574 (1399); cf. ibid., 506 where in 1369 the prior is listed after rather than before three abbots; see also *SHR*, xxxv (1956), 134 and 136, n.1 (1404). As it happens the abbot of Kelso was not present on any of these occasions. The custom was observed also in assemblies of the provincial council of the Scottish church e.g. in 1420 (Robertson, *Concilia*, ii, 77), when the precedence accorded the representative of the abbot of Kelso was only sixth in a list of twelve abbots.

11. *first to be called as an apostle*: this refers to the tradition in John 1:40-42, where Andrew is said to have been attracted to Jesus before Peter; but see different accounts in Matthew 4:18-20 and Mark 1:16-18, where Andrew is not given precedence over his brother. For the implications see U.Hall, *St Andrew and Scotland* (St Andrews, 1994), ad indicem.

20-36. *For when ... right*: no mention of the sederunts or of this judgment by King James occurs in the surviving records of the parliaments held 1424-37 (*APS*, ii, 3-24).

29. *marquis*: this title of nobility was not as yet current in Scotland; James would have known of it in England only by reference to the ill-fated promotion of his wife's father, John Beaufort, to the marquisate of Dorset and Somerset 1397-9 in the last years of Richard II (*HBC*, 460, 482); James was dead before the title was revived in England from 1443 onwards (ibid., 460, 484); James's reference here is therefore recondite and not particularly apt; and we have only Bower's word for it.

33-34. *St Andrews ... Kelso*: this would be true in temporal terms only if the Augustinian foundation of 1144 at St Andrews was regarded as successor to the earlier Culdee community there, for Kelso ROX could trace its date of foundation back to the Tironensian community established at Selkirk SLK ca 1113 and removed to Kelso ca 1128 (*MRHS*, 70, 68); 'more important' (l.33) suggests an immeasurable value judgment (cf. *Kelso Liber*, i, xli).

35-36. *... right*: a common saying; see Walther, *Proverbia*, no.24,543c.

36-39. *We have ... day*: in MS C there is a marginal cross-reference here to III c.45 (correctly 44) above, where at ll.31-38 the text does not exactly support the exaggerated and irrelevant statement here (composed presumably by Bower) about the powers of Columba in his day.

Chapter 50
pp.417-19

1-3. *... St Andrew*: Bishop Robert (see above c.24, ll.37-58) had himself been prior of the Augustinian house at Scone PER when appointed bishop in 1124; he was now acting with the help of Æthelwulf bishop of Carlisle (since 1133), at a time when Cumbria was temporarily ruled by the king of Scots; in addition to having an Augustinian community to serve his cathedral, Æthelwulf had retained his earlier office of prior of the Augustinian house at Nostell YOW (which had been Bishop Robert's own first monastery); and he sent to St Andrews another Augustinian canon called Robert direct from Nostell (not from Scone as stated here) to develop a community there as a priory like that at Carlisle (*Chron.Picts-Scots*, 191-3; Barrow, *Kingdom*, 171-2; *Series Episcoporum*, VI, i, 84); Wyntoun (iv, 386-91) gives some extra details, and states that it was a group of canons who moved from Scone to St Andrews, not the prior; Bower's date for Prior Robert's arrival is a possible one, but this man cannot be shown to have been in office until May 1144, by which time both bishop and pope were confirming the arrangements made for the new community (*St Andrews Liber*, 122-3, 47-48).

6.   *book of stories about him*: a lost source which Bower presumably saw at St Andrews, but on which he uncharacteristically did not draw for more details here.

8.   *1162*: the Melrose chronicler recorded Robert's death and Walter's succession in 1160 (*Melrose*, 36); this date is to be preferred to Bower's '1162', since Walter occurs as prior when a witness sometime in 1161 (*RRS*, i, 223, no.182).

10.   *twenty-four years*: since Walter held office at least until 1195 (*St Andrews Liber*, 323), this is probaby an error for 'thirty-four years', which by Bower's dating of the start of his priorate indicates ca 1196.

11.   *Gilbert* [I]: found in office 1195/6 × 15 February 1197/8 (*Coupar Angus Chrs.*, i, 6-7, no.3), and again 24 August 1198 × 17 March 1198/9 (*Arbroath Liber*, i, 103, no.148).

15.   *Clackmannan* CLA.

16-21.   *On Gilbert's death ... fathers*: Gilbert must have died by early 1199 at latest (as in McRoberts, *St Andrews*, 140), for following Walter's brief return to office and death, Thomas is found as prior by 6 June 1199 (Raine, *North Durham*, no.467).

28.   *1211*: Thomas is last found in office March 1210 × July 1211 (*Aberdeen Registrum*, ii, 264-6); he presumably resigned shortly before 8 December 1211 (see below l.32).

33.   *Coupar Angus*: the Cistercian monastery PER (*MRHS*, 73).

34.   *succeeded*: Simon is first found in office in 1212 i.e. 25 March 1212 × 24 March 1213 (*St Andrews Liber*, 315).

37.   *1225*: i.e. 25 March 1225 × 24 March 1226.

40.   *priory of Loch Leven*: the Augustinian priory based on an island in Loch Leven KNR, which was a subordinate cell of the priory of St Andrews (*MRHS*, 93).

42.   *Henry de Norham*: first found in office sometime 1227 × 1228 (*Dunfermline Registrum*, 136, no.219).

44.   *1236*: i.e.after 25 March and before 21 May 1236 (see c.51, ll.5-6 below).

Chapter 51
pp.419-21

In MS C the chapters originally numbered 'li' to 'liii' inclusive have each had its number altered by the deletion of the final numeral to 'l' to 'lii' inclusive;

this was presumably done after the erroneous correction of the number of the next chapter from 'liiii' to 'liii' (see below), though the original numbering from chapter 'lv' onwards was kept. In MS D a different error was made by repeating the chapter number 'xlix', and then numbering the chapters one short to the end of the book; this error has been corrected throughout by the rubricator, so that the chapter numbers no longer correspond with those in the list of rubrics at the start of the Book. Here the correct series of numbers used in MS R from the start is followed.

7. *building*: for modern accounts of the building works undertaken by this and later priors see *RCAHM* (*FIF*), 230-7; McRoberts, *St Andrews*, 11-32, 63-120; *St Andrews Cathedral*, official guidebook (Historic Scotland, 1993).

10. *terrar*: the obedientiary of the monastery mainly concerned with the administration of its landed estate.

25-28. *... peace*: in MS C the scribe adopts a double-column layout for these lines (text ll.22-25); the schematic arrangement for the second pair of lines is apparently deliberate, and is copied in MSS R and D (this part of the text is missing in MS CA); but by the time that MS E was written these lines are arranged according to their sense (as in the translation here).

30. *archdeacon of St Andrews*: this office was normally held by a secular clerk rather than by an Augustinian canon; Mauchan had held it at least since 31 January 1301 (Watt, *Fasti*, 305); the stage of his career when he made his religious profession is not known.

31-32. *feast of the Seven Sleepers*: this was celebrated on 27 July, which in 1304 fell on a Monday.

Chapter 52
pp.421-3

2. *Lathrisk*: a parish in central Fife, which was appropriated to the priory (Cowan, *Parishes*, 128); this is an example of the practice of Augustinian canons whereby members of the community who were priests sometimes served in person a parish which had been appropriated to them; but in this case where the vicar held the time-consuming post of chamberlain (i.e. supervisor of the administration of the bishop's temporal estates), he is not likely to have been a resident incumbent.

3. *William de Lamberton*: see above c.43, l.24.

4. *guidance of the Holy Spirit*: i.e. by acclamation rather than by ballot (see above c.47, l.4).

7. *William de Lothian*: see below ll.24-25.

11. *new chapter-house*: see above c.43, ll.53-54.

12. *terrar*: see above c.51, l.10.

20-23. *He was compelled ... Perth*: information added in the margin of MS C, presumably from some different source; see below XIII c.38.

26. *general vote*: see above c.44, l.3.

34. *choir*: the excised rubric at the top of fo.128 in MS C after 'chorum' (text 1.30, footnote *a*) had been placed there to allow for an extra leaf of the MS (fos. 127-127v) to be left blank for material on future bishops of St Andrews (cf. above c.47, 1.10n.); but it had then been decided that too much space was being left, and the rubric was written again one leaf earlier at top of fo.127.

40. *Rossie* PER: an appropriated church west of Dundee (Cowan, *Parishes*, 173).

Chapter 53
pp.423-5

2. *general vote*: see above c.44, 1.3.

4. *Sir Thomas Biset earl of Fife*: this man was lord of Upsettlington BWK, and in 1363 married as her third husband Isabella countess of Fife, and was made earl of Fife in consequence; he died 1366 × 1369 (*SP*, iv, 13; *HBC*, 508).

25. *William Laundels*: see above cc.44-45.
1363: i.e. 25 March × June 1363 (see below).

26. *by the said bishop*: it was a characteristic of the Augustinian rule that the local bishop was responsible for supervising the affairs of monasteries of that order in his diocese.

29. *said sir Sephen Pay*: see above c.45, ll.25-40.

31. *guidance of the Holy Spirit*: see above c.52, 1.4

36. *accidental fire*: on 23 Sept. 1378 (see below XIV c.40).

41. *altars ... St Laurence*: these are thought to have been in the south transept (McRoberts, *St Andrews*, 80).

Chapter 54
pp.425-9

The rubric for this chapter in MS C must have been written without appreciation of its scope, for the writer thought that James Biset would be included as well as Robert de Montrose; when the necessary deletion was made, the chapter was wrongly renumbered 'liii' instead of 'liiii' (see above c.51 introductory note).

2. *prior of Loch Leven*: see above c.50, 1.40; Bower had originally thought that Robert had held the vicarage of Leuchars FIF, one of the priory's appropriated churches (Cowan, *Parishes*, 131).

2-3. *official of St Andrews*: i.e. judge of the episcopal court (Watt, *Fasti*, 324); as such he is likely to have studied earlier for a university degree in canon law, but no evidence of this has been found.

18-24. *... Esau*: Augustine, *Epistulae*, ed. A.Goldbacher, i (CSEL, 1895), letter 78, pp.343-4.

19. *ark of Noah*: Genesis 7-8.

19-20. *where ... found*: apparently a reference to Ham son of Noah (Genesis 9:22-25).

21-22. *... son*: Genesis 21:10.

23-24. *... Esau*: Malachi 1:2-3.

24-27.... *monasteries*: abbreviated from a letter of St Augustine included in D.47 c.9, i.e. *Decretum*, part 1, distinction 47, chapter 9, 'Quantumlibet' (Friedberg, i, col.173).

38-43. *... transgressions*: a proverbial saying, source not identified.

48. *prelate*: an officer of the church having an independent jurisdiction i.e. here the prior in relation to one of the canons.

50-51. *fell asleep in the Lord*: for date see below c.55, ll.4-5.

54. *mitre*: a special use of this word to indicate headgear made of papyrus, on which were written the name and crimes of an accused person, and worn as a symbol of his disgrace (*Du Cange*, s.v. 'mitra papyracea').

55. *Walter Trayl*: see above c.45, l.11.

Chapter 55
pp.429-31

1. *his house*: probably means the cathedral church which was the prior's responsibility.

7. *James Biset*: for his biography see Watt, *Graduates*, 51-53.

8. *licentiate in decrees*: he had studied canon law at the university of Paris, and probably also at Avignon (ibid., 51).

11. *Thomas Biset*: see above c.53, ll.1-27.

29. *courtyard*: Dr Richard Fawcett advises that this may refer to the outer courtyard or to the whole monastic precinct.

32-33. *churches ... monastery*: i.e. churches appropriated to the priorship and to the monastic community as a whole.

36. *the conventual part with spiritual texts*: i.e. decorated with texts the walls of the choirs of the churches appropriated to the cathedral monastery (the naves being the responsibility of the parishoners).

61. *became ... brothers*: cf. 1 Corinthians 9:22.

Chapter 56
pp.431-5

20. *sons of God*: i.e the canons of the priory.

27. *bishop of Ross*: John Bullock, 1418 – 1439 × 1440 (Watt, *Fasti*, 268; Dowden, *Bishops*, 216-18).

27-28. *abbots at Scone and Inchcolm*: both were Augustinian abbeys; in 1418 Adam de Crannach or Aberdeen was appointed to Scone PER, and Walter Bower himself to Inchcolm FIF (see below XV c.30, ll.93-97).

28-29. *priors of Monymusk* ABD: a subordinate cell of St Andrews priory (*MRHS*, 93-94); the priorship was much in contention during the 1420s and 1430s, with at least four canons of St Andrews securing appointment for a time – Robert de Paisley, William de Cupar, William de Cowes, and Robert de Keth – with other candidates for the office coming from other Augustinian houses at Holyrood MLO, Inchcolm FIF and Scone PER (*CSSR*, ii, iii and iv ad indices).

30. *two ... masters of theology*: one was James de Haldenston (see below c.57); the other may have been Adam de Crannach or Aberdeen (as above), though he is known as a bachelor of theology only in 1419 (*CSSR*, i, 43).

31-32. *two ... decrees*: not all of this group can be identified, though Walter Bower himself was one of them; John Bullock (as above l.27) was another (*CPL Benedict XIII*, 355); William de Camera and John Litstar (see below c.57, ll.1, 11) were others.

37-38. *preoccupations of Martha*: the biblical character who typified the active (as opposed to the contemplative) Christian life (*ODCC*, 879).

38-40. *the scion ... knowledge*: Bower here adopts a highly coloured style.

48. *ended his life*: see also below XV c.24, ll.1-2.

57-58. *... hermit*: perhaps Biset's epitaph.

Chapter 57
pp.435-9

1. *William de Camera*: cf. Watt, *Graduates*, 77-78; see below ll.97-99.

3-4. *guidance of the Holy Spirit*: see above c.47, ll.3-4.

4. *Roman court*: i.e. the court of Pope Benedict XIII, who now lived in Spain (see below l.15), and was to be deposed by the Council of Constance in July 1417 (*ODP*, 233).

5. *Bruges*: then in the county of Flanders, now in Belgium.

5-6. *after confirmation*: Camera received only conditional confirmation from Pope Benedict on 5 June 1417 (*CPL Benedict XIII*, 355), for his apparently unanimous election had already been challenged by John Bullock (later bishop of Ross [see above c.56, l.27]) and James de Haldenston (see below ll.16-17).

8. *church of St Giles*: a church in Bruges which still retains its earlier medieval nave.

11. *John Litstar*: for his biography see Watt, *Graduates*, 357; cf. below XV c.22, ll.8-9.

13-14. *with the prior-elect*: Bower is misleading here; Litstar was abroad in the company of a different prior-elect, namely James de Haldenston (ibid.); Pope Benedict provided Litstar to the vacant priory on 10 March 1418 (*CPL Benedict XIII.* 369-70).

15. *Peñiscola*: on the east coast of Spain, north of Valencia, then in the kingdom of Aragon.

16-17. *James de Haldenston*: see biography in Watt, *Graduates*, 248-51. He left a unique selection of his correspondence copied into a letter-book (*Copiale Prioratus Sanctiandree*, ed. J.H.Baxter [Oxford, 1930]).

18. *elected*: he had challenged Camera's election on unspecified grounds before 5 June 1417 (see above), and was himself elected after Camera's death, probably in late 1417 (Watt, *Graduates*, 249).

19. *Martin V*: the pope elected at the Council of Constance on 11 November 1417 (*ODP*, 239); he still had his court at Constance in southern Germany at this date, not Rome.

confirmed: 17 February 1418 (*CPL*, vii, 63, 69).

19-20. *before the withdrawal*: i.e. the Scottish withdrawal of obedience from Pope Benedict decided in October 1418 (see below XV cc.24-25).

21-22. *litigation ... still pending*: Litstar obtained another bull in his favour from Pope Benedict as late as 9/13 December 1418 (*CPL Benedict XIII*, 377, 382-3).

22-34. *But because ... 1418*: though the decision in Scotland to abandon Benedict in favour of Martin was probably taken at Perth in October 1418, the embassy mentioned here sent in the name of Governor Albany and the Estates did not reach Martin until July-August 1419 (cf. below XV cc.24-25; Watt, *Graduates*, 250); all three members of this embassy were connected with St Andrews.

23-24. *William ... Dunblane*: William Stephenson became bishop of Dunblane only in October 1419, when he had stayed on at the papal court after the conclusion of this embassy (see biography in Watt, *Graduates*, 506-9, s.v. 'Stephani'; cf. below XV c.22, l.12, and XVI c.9, l.18).

24. *John Scheves*: see his biography in Watt, *Graduates*, 480-3; cf. below XV c.22, ll.11-12.

27. *bearing*: 'portan'' (text l.24) in MSS C and D is ungrammatical; the sense is improved by the substitution of 'contulit' in MS CA.

31-32. *everyone ...action*: a comment that reveals Bower's own point of view.

33-34. *in one and the same year, namely 1418*: not accurate (see above).

35. *This*: the rest of this chapter from 'Hic dominus' (text l.29) has been added by the same scribe using different ink, presumably at a different time. It appears that the text to this point was copied before Haldenston's death in 1443, and the rest added after that date.

62-74. *... chapels*: for the implications of these changes made in the cathedral during Haldenston's priorate see McRoberts, *St Andrews*, especially 64-77 and plans at end.

64-65. *the nave ... Biset*: see above c.55, l.20.

68. *glass lamps*: 'luminariis vitriis' (text ll.56-57) may alternatively mean 'windows to give light'.

69-70. *He built ... foundations*: this is a curious statement; the east gable of the cathedral was certainly altered at this time by the insertion of a large window in place of six smaller ones; but the older masonry is still there.

71. *vestry*: Dr Fawcett advises that this refers to the retrochoir area behind the high altar, where the vestry was frequently situated in major churches.

74. *flanking chapels*: Dr Fawcett advises that the chapels on either side of the retrochoir at the eastern extremities of the aisles are meant here rather than the chapels of the transepts.

75. *lower chapter-house*: the meaning of 'inferius' (text l.63) is uncertain; Dr Fawcett advises that probably the earlier building which by this date formed the entrance-hall to the main chapter-house is meant; it had a lower ceiling than the main chapter-house, because the dormitory on the floor above restricted its height.

79-80. *Balone ... Kinninmonth*: Balone FIF to the south-west of St Andrews; Pilmore PER near Longforgan in Gowrie; Seggie FIF near Guardbridge; Kinninmonth FIF near Pitscottie.

81-82. *... priors*: Haldenston secured this privilege from Martin V as early as April 1418 (*CSSR*, i, 9-10; *CPL*, vii, 78); cf. above c.49, ll.7-8.

84-86. *He directed .. theology*: 'During the first years of the university [the Faculty of Theology] was little more than an appendage of the Priory, with the Prior acting as Dean virtually *ex officio*' (R.G.Cant, *The University of St Andrews. A Short History*, 3rd edn [St Andrews, 1992], 14). Haldenston was serving as dean as late as 1439 (Watt, *Graduates*, 248-9).

86-88. *As inquisitor ... obstinate ones*: he filled the office of *inquisitor heretice pravitatis* only in the last years of his life 1440-3 (ibid., 251); for an earlier inquisitor, Laurence de Lindores, see below XV c.20, l.3, and XVI c.20, ll.16-18.

89. *collector ... apostolic see*: appointed papal collector by Martin V 25 July 1419; ceased to hold this office before May 1431 (Watt, *Graduates*, 250).

90. *honorary papal chaplain*: secured this status from Pope Benedict XIII in 1414 (ibid., 249).

92. *William Bower*: as a canon he served the parish church of St Andrews as vicar (see below XV c.23, ll.16-18); for this altar see discussion in McRoberts, *St Andrews*, 73.

94-95. *William de Balbuthy*: see *St Andrews Copiale* (as above ll.16-17), ad indicem.

97. *in the time of his predecessor*: i.e. Prior James Biset.

97-98. *William de Camera*: see above l.1.

100. *rest*: in MS C about one-quarter of fo.130 is left blank at the end of this chapter, and the list of chapter-titles for Book VII starts at top of fo.130v.

Index

Both parts of this index are limited to the translation and to additional material found in the editorial notes.

I. Authorities cited

The many references to Ailred of Rievaulx, *Genealogia Regum Anglorum*, Jocelin of Furness, *Life of Waltheof*, Turgot, *Life of Margaret* and William of Malmesbury, *Gesta Regum Anglorum* are fully described in the Notes, and so are not listed here. Quotation marks indicate that the supposed quotation has not been identified.

II. Persons and Places